CONTEMPORARY SOCIETY

An Introduction to Sociology

Second Edition

JACKSON TOBY

Rutgers University

JOHN WILEY & SONS, INC.

New York • London • Sydney • Toronto

CONTEMPORARY SOCIETY

To rational analysis—

May it help in the evolution of a better society

developed by Talcott Parsons. Systematic theory offers criteria of sociological relevance, which I have used to relate the chapters to one another. Parsons assumes that every society has a set of basic values at the core of its institutional structure helping to hold that society together. In contemporary urban industrial society, a basic value is individual achievement, which is incorporated not only in economic organization but in the organization of family life, education, government, and other salient activities. The chapters of the book are linked to another by an underlying assumption that achievement values are important to urban industrial life.

Although sociology has few terms that are not recognized by the reader of newspapers, sociologists use terms like "role" and "status" in somewhat unfamiliar ways. In order to avoid misunderstanding, words used in a technical sense are printed in boldface type when they first occur and are defined in the glossary at the end of the book. Annotated bibliographies are appended to every chapter to help the student select his reading judiciously from the vast literature of sociology. In the *American Sociological Review* alone, 50 major articles were published and 261 books were reviewed in the 1968–1969 academic year.[4] The professional keeps up with the field by *selective* attention to the current literature. He reads reviews of new books to help him decide which deserve further attention; he scans the major journals for articles in his specialties; he may read a journal of abstracts such as *Sociological Abstracts.* The significant books and articles selected for summary in the bibliography offer a sample of the sociological literature as well as ideas and data to supplement the text. The summaries are sufficiently detailed to give you a flavor of the source. Yet reading them will not require more effort than can reasonably be expected in one semester. Of course, if you happen to develop an irrational passion for sociology, they offer a start on your addiction.

I am grateful to the many colleagues who have made constructive suggestions for improving the manuscript and especially to Richard L. Simpson, whose editorial advice I found consistently helpful. Out of family loyalty, Marcia, Gail, and Steven Toby helped in many ways not the least of which was to react at dinner time to preliminary formulations of various topics. Harriet Zucker carried much of the clerical burden with characteristic efficiency and vivacity. In short, although I had fantasies of producing the book entirely by myself—not only writing it but choosing the illustrations, setting the type, pasting on the covers, and carrying each copy personally to any campus where it will be used—I recognize in more lucid moments a debt of gratitude to the many people who have made publication possible.

Jackson Toby

March, 1970
Highland Park, New Jersey

---

[4] *American Sociologist,* Vol. 4, November 1969, p. 348.

CONTENTS

Part II

SOCIALIZATION: THE TRANSMISSION AND INTERNALIZATION OF CULTURE/65

CHAPTER 3

4   **Culture and Subculture/67**

CHAPTER 4

Initial Socialization in the Family of Orientation/103

CHAPTER 5

Socialization after Childhood/139

Part III

THE SOCIAL STRUCTURE OF URBAN INDUSTRIAL SOCIETIES/183

CHAPTER 6

Economic Differentiation in Industrial Societies/185

CHAPTER 13

Deviance and Social Control/477

CHAPTER 14

Social Change/513

Part I

GOALS, METHODS, CONCEPTS

Sociologists seek to understand society by studying human interaction. The cultural traditions that guide interaction in a society, the sensitivity of people to one another's reactions, and the coordinated organization of roles are considered in Chapter 1. The methods sociologists use to study contemporary societies are discussed in Chapter 2.

THE SOCIAL GUIDANCE OF HUMAN INTERACTION

Chemical Engineering Magazine

WHAT IS SOCIOLOGY?

What is sociology? It is not a program of social reform: reformers describe the world as they want it to be; sociologists try to describe it as it is. Nor is it synonymous with social work: social work is the profession concerned with helping people solve their personal and community problems; sociology is concerned with understanding certain aspects of human behavior—whether they can be changed or not. These distinctions make sociologists sound hardhearted; sociologists prefer to call themselves hard-headed. However much they wish to change the world or help their fellow man, sociologists take as their professional responsibility the search for truth.

Sociology, anthropology, and psychology are all sciences that seek to understand human behavior through disciplined observation. In recent years, the term "behavioral science" has been used to refer to sociology, social anthropology, and psychology.[1] One way to distinguish sociology from the other two behavioral sciences is this: social anthropologists concern themselves with developing societies like Uganda or Lapland or with preliterate peoples like the Australian aborigines, the Eskimos and the Kwakiutl Indians, whereas sociologists study the functioning of more complicated societies, especially urban industrial societies. Psychologists usually deal with what goes on inside the individual, whereas sociologists study processes within the **group.**[2]

The distinction between psychology and sociology is subtle. It is only a half-truth to say that sociology is concerned with the group and psychology with the individual. The group is composed of individuals. Groups cannot think or feel or act—mental and physical behavior are produced only by individuals. Thus sociologists cannot surrender their curiosity about the individual while claiming to be interested in the group. This does not mean that sociology and psychology are different terms for the same discipline—although there is some overlap between the two. (The field of social psychology lies squarely between them.) But psychology emphasizes the individual's needs and abilities and their organization within the personality, whereas sociology emphasizes the way individuals *relate* to one another. Both deal with human behavior, but they search for the *motivation* of the behavior in different places. For the psychologist, it lies within the organism and includes such variables as intelligence and aggressiveness. For the sociologist, it lies within the group and includes the ideas and sentiments the individual learns from groups he belongs to. Thus sociologists look for the motivation of human behavior in the guidance of other people, whereas psychologists look for the motivation of

---

[1] Leading scholars in these fields occasionally spend a year in residence at the Center for Advanced Study in the Behavioral Sciences in Palo Alto, California, pursuing their separate intellectual problems. This Center, begun with a $5,000,000 grant from the Ford Foundation, is affectionately known as the "think tank."

[2] All words and phrases appearing in boldface type will be defined in the glossary at the end of the book.

behavior within the personality. Sociologists differ from psychologists also in the behavioral *outcomes* that interest them. Psychologists are concerned largely with individual behavior, sociologists with the interactions of more than one person.

The Study of Human Interaction. Interaction involves more than just the simultaneous behavior of two or more individuals. It is not merely the action of *A* and the subsequent action of *B*. A fistfight or a conversation is interaction because of the taking account on the part of each participant of the potential reactions of the other. But interaction can be more subtle. Suppose you are a weekend guest at the home of a classmate. His mother has just served you a plate of scrambled eggs for breakfast and is chatting with you as you eat. Suddenly you start chewing on a hard, crackly substance: eggshell. Your first impulse is to spit it out, but you do not wish to offend your hostess. You swallow the eggshell with your egg. No one watching you would know that you are reacting to the presence of your hostess. This is interaction, nevertheless. The fact that you did *not* spit out the eggshell is just as much a response as spitting it out would have been. Interaction depends on sensitivity to the approval and disapproval of others and to the anticipation of their approval or disapproval. This sensitivity makes a social order possible. Without it, society would be a jungle—a "war of all against all." [3]

THE STABILIZING FACTOR IN HUMAN INTERACTION: SOCIAL GUIDANCE

What keeps interactive systems stable? Why do they change in an orderly fashion? Why are conflict and chaos the exceptions rather than the rule? These basic questions preoccupy sociologists. In order to pursue these questions, albeit in a preliminary way, consider a two-person **interactive system,** a newlywed American couple. How can two people with different interests and backgrounds expect to live together harmoniously, developing no irreconcilable conflicts over such issues as where they should live, whether they should have children, and who should cook supper? They can do this because marriage is an *established pattern* of male-female interaction in American society. Many of the potential conflicts between newlyweds have been settled in advance by customs governing marital rights and responsibilities. An argument is unlikely to develop over who should cook supper because this is the *traditional* responsibility of the wife. The expectation is less clear about where a couple should live—in the central city or in suburbia—although ac-

---

[3] In the seventeenth century, Thomas Hobbes coined this phrase to describe the chaos that would exist without government. See his famous analysis of life "in a state of nature" in *Leviathan; or the Matter, Forme and Power of a Commonwealth, Ecclesiasticall and Civill,* Cambridge, England: Cambridge University Press, 1904.

cess to the husband's place of work is customarily considered. Other potential conflicts are similarly avoided by conforming to established patterns. In
short, sociologists explain marital harmony by calling attention to subtle societal guidance: established expectations blueprinting husband-wife relations.

Sociologists have names for different types of established customs. The
nineteenth-century Yale sociologist William Graham Sumner made famous the
terms "folkways" and "mores," the former referring to conventional practices,
the latter to social requirements.[4] These terms are falling into disuse among professional sociologists, perhaps because the line between them is difficult to
draw. The central sociological concept embodying the notion of societal guidance now is **role** expectation. A role consists of what a person is expected to
do in a prescribed interactive relationship. The expectation is directed not at
the person in his full concreteness but at that segment of his personality involved in the particular relationship. Thus a college student is expected to register for courses at certain times, to attend class meetings, to borrow books
from the library, and perhaps to live in a dormitory. The role expectation for
college students applies to every student—regardless of his unique personal
characteristics. The application of expectations to *roles* rather than to concrete
people promotes organizational efficiency; a single expectation is relevant to
the situations of hundreds or even thousands of individuals. Furthermore, the
expectation is not limited to persons in the immediate interactive situation. Not
only students currently enrolled, but future generations of students will be
guided by the expectation for "students." In Part II and succeeding chapters we
shall consider the process whereby role players are taught to conform to role
expectations (i.e., **socialization**) or to resist them. And, toward the end of the
present chapter, we shall consider the role as the basic organizational unit of
interactive systems. For the moment, however, we are interested in the role
concept only as a vehicle bringing the tradition of the group to bear on the current behavior of the individual. Role expectation is a narrower concept than
cultural norms, another concept of social guidance we shall turn to later.

Role Expectations. A newlywed couple may subscribe to the romantic notion that they are living for one another and do not care what anybody else says
or thinks.[5] Sociologists contend that only a tiny percentage of marriages could
endure if the partners were "free" to find original answers to the thousands of
issues potentially pulling them apart. Marital harmony is likely because each
partner knows—even before the wedding ceremony—what husbands and wives
can expect from one another. *Role expectations* are one form of social guidance that holds a group together.

The sociological perspective emphasizes that the married couple is a
group, although a small one. All groups must cope with the problem of
achieving **consensus,** but consensus is especially problematic in a two-person

[4] William Graham Sumner, *Folkways,* Boston: Ginn, 1906.
[5] Jackson Toby, "The Case Against Romance," in Harry C. Bredemeier and Jackson Toby,
Social Problems in America, New York: Wiley, 1960, pp. 462-468.

group. A married couple cannot deal with conflicts by using the majority-rule formula because no majority can exist short of unanimity. But majority-rule is only one formula for resolving group conflict. Most societies minimize the danger of marital conflict by giving one member of the marital pair, usually the man, a greater voice in decisions. Thus in a patriarchal society like Japan, both husband and wife expect the husband to dominate the relationship. To express this point in sociological terms, the *role expectations* for "husband" have dominance built in. If Japanese men and women have learned the roles each is expected to play, they need not hammer out agreements on particular issues after the marriage ceremony. Agreement has been programmed in advance. As long as the wife believes, as she has been taught to believe, that her subordinate status is legitimate, the marriage can proceed as happily and harmoniously as in an equalitarian society. In every society, agreement on a standard procedure for resolving marital disagreements is crucial to harmony unless the husband and wife come to the marriage with identical values. If the issue of family authority has not been settled by tradition, that is to say, if there is no consensus on the role expectations for husbands and wives, the couple must work out for themselves techniques of conflict resolution. This is what happens in some American marriages.

One sociologist showed by an ingenious experiment how different cultural traditions legitimize varying degrees of male or female dominance in the marital relationship.[6] Ten married couples were chosen from each of three ethnic groups — Navaho, Mormon, and Texan — living side by side in a New Mexico town. Among the Navaho, women occupy a position of some power and independence in contrast to the Mormons, who regard the husband as the undisputed head of the family. Texans fall somewhere in between, adhering to a patriarchal pattern, but one with less power for the male than in Mormon society. The experiment was designed to show, among other things, that these cultural differences in the power structure of the family are reflected in the process of reconciling disagreements between husband and wife. With this in mind, each couple was asked to select a number of families well known to both spouses. From this list, each husband and each wife was individually instructed to judge which family was "the most ambitious," which had "the happiest children," and so on. Husbands and wives were then brought together and left alone to iron out their differences. Table 1.1 shows the number of decisions won by husbands and the number won by wives in each of the three cultures. In the culture where husbands were clearly dominant, the Mormon, husbands won the largest proportion of the arguments. In the culture where women had a greater voice than their husbands in decision making, the Navaho, wives won a larger proportion of the arguments than their husbands. In the more nearly equalitarian society of Texan farmers, disagreements were resolved in favor of husbands or wives in almost equal proportions.

[6] Fred L. Strodtbeck, "Husband-Wife Interaction over Revealed Differences," *American Sociological Review*, Vol. 16, August 1951, pp. 468-473.

TABLE 1.1

The Outcomes of Interaction between Husbands and Wives in Three Cultures over Differences in Judgment

| | | Decisions Won by: | |
| | Number of | --- | --- |
Culture	Couples	Husband	Wife
Navaho	10	34	46
Texan	10	39	33
Mormon	10	42	29

Source: Fred L. Strodtbeck, "Husband-Wife Interaction over Revealed Differences," *American Sociological Review,* Vol. 16, August 1951, p. 472.

Consider the implications of this analysis for the incidence of marital disharmony in American society. Two psychologically normal people can fail to achieve consensus in marriage (1) because they bring to the marriage different expectations for marital roles arising from different family and community backgrounds and (2) because each feels equally justified in putting his expectations into practice. For example, using surveys of American voting preferences,[7] we can predict that a Chicago-raised Irish Catholic man who went no farther in school than the eighth grade is probably a Democratic voter, whereas an Anglo-Saxon Protestant woman raised in rural Indiana who graduated from college probably prefers the Republican party. Thus, if one or both believed in political unity within the family, a marriage between such a man and woman might result in quarrels over politics. Or one might convince the other to change his political preference.[8] Or they might learn to tolerate political disagreement. Republican wives might avoid the discussion of politics with Democratic husbands. Or one partner might talk politics and the other fail to listen. In a voting survey in Erie County, Ohio, ten times as many of the wives as of the husbands said that they discussed politics with their mates.[9] This means that the husbands were bad listeners—but the failure to listen may have prevented disagreements. Of course, some young couples, even in complex urban industrial societies, are from similar backgrounds. And others, from varied

[7] Surveys of American voting preferences consistently show Republican preferences on the part of rural voters, better-educated voters, and Protestants; Democratic preferences on the part of city voters, less well-educated voters, and Catholics. One of the first such studies was Paul F. Lazarsfeld, Bernard Berelson, and Hazel Gaudet, *The People's Choice,* New York: Duell, Sloane & Pearce, 1944.

[8] Voting studies reveal more husband-wife consistency in political preferences than could arise from chance assortments from an American population divided fairly equally between Democrats and Republicans. In the study cited in the previous footnote, for instance, only one couple in 22 differed in political preferences. Either young people from similar political backgrounds are more prone to marry one another than young people from dissimilar backgrounds— or else political conversions follow the marriage ceremony.

[9] Lazarsfeld, Berelson, and Gaudet, *The People's Choice,* p. 141.

backgrounds, arrive at consensus over basic values during long engagements. But there is danger in a heterogeneous society committed to approximate equality between the sexes that young people will not realize before marriage how deeply they differ in the values they learned previously. These unappreciated differences may generate marital conflict—and possibly divorce—between psychologically healthy personalities.

Value differences between marital partners arise from social change as well as from the heterogeneity of the society. In the United States, for example, there has been a change over the past half-century in the expectation that women, including mothers, will be gainfully employed. In 1890, only 18.2 per cent of women over the age of 14 worked outside of the home, whereas in 1960, 34.2 per cent did so.[10] Still, *some* men feel robbed of their masculinity by their wives' desire to supplement family income by outside employment. And some women, especially better-educated women, regard this traditional attitude—"a woman's place is in the home"—as a denial of their right to self-realization.[11]

In societies where social change is proceeding even faster than in the United States, old-fashioned and modern role conceptions can collide dramatically and conspicuously. In Japan, for example, the subordination of women in the older generation is giving way to equality among the young. A visitor to Tokyo can observe in public parks a middle-aged couple walking in traditional fashion, the man three feet ahead, his wife trotting behind in her colorful kimono; fifty feet away two teen-agers in Western clothes may be strolling with arms wrapped around one another like pretzels. Rapid social change makes for marital disharmony because change is not uniform throughout a society; one partner may be committed to traditional role conceptions and the other to modern ones.

Sociologists call attention to marital disharmony that arises because of value conflicts resulting from social change or societal heterogeneity. *Psychologists* point out that marital disharmony can arise from difficulties within the personality of the husband or the personality of the wife. Each case of marital conflict contains a unique mix of disagreements arising from personality problems and from conflicting values. National statistics on divorce reflect both psychological and sociological factors in marital disharmony. They also reflect the cultural acceptability of divorce as a solution to marital conflict; in some countries (Ireland, Argentina, Peru) there is no legal provision for divorce and in others it is a last resort. Complicated though the interpretation is of national variations in divorce rates, sociological factors seem most plausible. In 1963, the United States had 2.3 divorces per 1000 population; Sweden had 1.1;

[10] Bureau of the Census, *Historical Statistics of the United States, Colonial Times to 1957,* Washington, D.C.: Government Printing Office, 1960, p. 72; Bureau of the Census, *Statistical Abstract of the United States: 1962,* Washington, D.C.: Government Printing Office, 1962, p. 225.

[11] Matilda White Riley, Marilyn E. Johnson, and Sarane S. Boocock, "Woman's Changing Occupational Role—A Research Report," *American Behavioral Scientist,* Vol. 9, May 1963, pp. 33-37.

Switzerland had 0.8; Japan had 0.7; and the Netherlands had 0.5.[12] Why was there so much more divorce in the United States? Greater equality between the sexes? Probably not a major factor. Sweden has greater sexual equality than the United States. The most likely explanation is the greater heterogeneity of the United States, leading to a higher incidence of disharmony in these two-person groups than in more homogeneous societies.

A married couple constitutes a unique kind of group in one respect: each member of the marital pair enters the group simultaneously. As a consequence, neither can be the authoritative spokesman for an established tradition. Unlike the newlywed, the freshman arriving at college joins a group that is ongoing. When a senior tells him that freshmen are supposed to wear certain kinds of hats and ties, the senior speaks from three years of prior membership in the group. Furthermore, freshmen are an outnumbered minority. Two newlyweds are freer to establish their own traditions of group life—provided that they do not depart too radically from the expectations for married couples of the larger society. But this greater freedom is purchased at the price of greater instability. Marriages break up more frequently than colleges—even in this era of campus confrontations.

Cultural Norms. "Cultural norms," another form of social guidance, refer to prescriptions for behavior that include, in addition to interaction, person-thing transactions (like driving a car) and **expressive actions** (like crying). The individual receives no less guidance for driving a car or for crying than for playing a role. The sociologist, although more interested in role behavior, is concerned with all behavior resulting from social guidance. Furthermore, the social guidance involved in cultural norms reflects past interaction and influences future interaction. Thus cultural norms governing the expression of hunger or pain ordinarily are learned in the course of the role playing between the child and his socializers. Once learned, they channel physiological drives in a seemingly natural way. Figure 1.1 tries to make this point diagramatically; belching, kissing, and crying are not simple responses to biological pressures.

Biological drives are structured by cultural norms interposed between the drive and its ultimate expression in behavior. Take a steak dinner as a response to hunger. While there are certain nutritional requirements that no society can ignore, a tremendous range of substances are nutritionally adequate: whale blubber, beefsteak, horsemeat, human flesh, grubs and worms, mice, fruit, nuts, vegetables, berries, roots. Nutrition cannot explain why Eskimos like whale blubber and Navahos like rattlesnake meat. Every society makes a selection from the edible things available and defines some of these as "food." Thus Americans think of beefsteak as succulent and horsemeat as fit only for pets. The explanation of America's discrimination against horses is not nutritional. The faculty club at Harvard had horsemeat steak on the menu for years. What

---

[12] *United Nations Statistical Yearbook, 1965,* New York: Statistical Office of the United Nations, 1966, pp. 796-799.

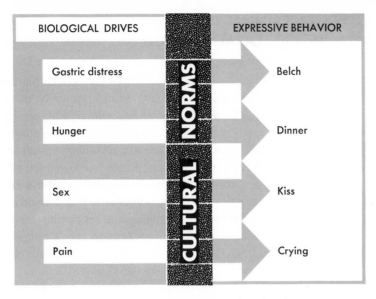

FIGURE 1.1 **The patterning of biological drives by cultural norms.**

it comes down to is this: Americans have sentimental attachments to horses, not to cattle, partly because of childhood memories of stories like *Black Beauty*. Even as adults, Americans look at television programs in which horses are given near-human qualities. As a result, Americans do not give horsemeat a fair chance to qualify as food on nutritional or taste grounds. Not recognizing how food preferences are selected by cultural norms, Americans consider Hindus unreasonable to regard cows as inedible and to become upset when a cow is killed. Yet the Hindu religion, affirming as it does the doctrine of reincarnation, provides a very good reason for the devout to dote on a cow. According to the cultural tradition of India, the cow might be a reincarnation of a close relative.

Reactions to pain are similarly selective. Although male infants cry just as much as female infants when they are hurt, American cultural norms teach older boys to respond to pain differently from girls. (The phrase, "American cultural norms teach . . .," is a shortcut way of summarizing dozens of interactions of a boy with parents and peers in which he learns that crying results in disapproval.) As a result of differential social experiences, the same level of physical suffering that causes American women to cry produce curses or silent heroism from American men. Other societies have cultural norms even more demanding of male fortitude. In the puberty rites of some American Indian tribes, the boy was required to undergo physical torture without flinching. Naive observers of these ceremonies were misled by the boy's pretense that the pain did not exist and came to the erroneous conclusion that the threshold of pain was higher for Indians than for whites.

A LABORATORY EXPERIMENT ILLUSTRATING THE COERCIVE POWER OF SOCIAL GUIDANCE

How sensitive is the individual to social guidance? This sounds like a meaningful question capable of being answered by research. Actually, many equally correct answers to the question exist depending on the type of social group and the individual's place in it. For example, a family is one kind of group; students specially recruited for an experiment in social psychology constitute another. If the students did not interact with one another before being recruited for the experiment, the group is a **contrived group** rather than a **natural group** like a family. Such an experimental group is not as anonymous as a group of strangers because the students attend the same college and recognize one another as fellow students. They care somewhat about one another's opinions. Still, a contrived experimental group lacks the **solidarity** of a group whose members have interacted for a long time. Therefore social guidance in an ephemeral group is at a minimum; an experimental group offers an opportunity to observe the individual's responsiveness to normative regulation under conditions of minimal sensitivity. Professor Solomon Asch, a social psychologist, explored the coercive power of group pressure under these conditions by rigging the situation so that the individual's eyes suggested one judgment and the other members of the experimental group suggested another.[13]

A group of seven to nine young men, all college students, are assembled in a classroom for a "psychological experiment" in visual judgment. The experimenter informs them that they will be comparing the lengths of lines. He shows two large white cards. On one is a single vertical black line—the standard whose length is to be matched. On the other card are three vertical lines of various lengths. The subjects are to choose the one that is of the same length as the line on the other card. One of the three actually is of the same length; the other two are substantially different, the difference ranging from three quarters of an inch to an inch and three quarters.

The experiment opens uneventfully. The subjects announce their answers in the order in which they have been seated in the room, and on the first round every person chooses the same matching line. Then a second set of cards is exposed; again the group is unanimous. The members appear ready to endure politely another boring experiment. On the third trial there is an unexpected disturbance. One person near the end of the group disagrees with all the others in his selection of the matching line. He looks surprised, indeed incredulous, about the disagreement. On the following trial he disagrees again, while the others remain unanimous in their choice. The dissenter becomes more and more worried and hesitant as the disagreement continues in succeeding trials; he may pause before announcing his answer and speak in a low voice, or he may smile in an embarrassed way.

What the dissenter does not know is that all the other members of the group

---

[13] Reprinted by permission. From Solomon E. Asch, "Opinions and Social Pressure," *Scientific American*, Vol. 193, November 1955.

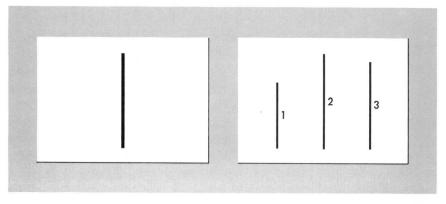

FIGURE 1.2 **Subjects were shown two cards. One bore a standard line. The other bore three lines, one of which was the same length as the standard. The subjects were asked to choose this line.**

were instructed by the experimenter beforehand to give incorrect answers in unanimity at certain points. The single individual who is not a party to this pre-arrangement is the focal subject of our experiment. He is placed in a position in which, while he is actually giving the correct answers, he finds himself unexpectedly in a minority of one, opposed by a unanimous and arbitrary majority with respect to a clear and simple fact. Upon him we have brought to bear two opposed forces: the evidence of his senses and the unanimous opinion of a group of his peers. Also, he must declare his judgments in public, before a majority which has also stated its position publicly.

The instructed majority occasionally reports correctly in order to reduce the possibility that the naive subject will suspect collusion against him. (In only a few cases did the subject actually show suspicion; when this happened, the experiment was stopped and the results were not counted.) There are 18 trials in each series, and on 12 of these the majority responds erroneously.

How do people respond to group pressure in this situation? I shall report first the statistical results of a series in which a total of 123 subjects from three institutions of higher learning (not including my own, Swarthmore College) were placed in the minority situation described above.

Two alternatives were open to the subject: he could act independently, repudiating the majority, or he could go along with the majority, repudiating the evidence of his senses. Of the 123 put to the test, a considerable percentage yielded to the majority. Whereas in ordinary circumstances individuals matching the lines will make mistakes less than 1 per cent of the time, under group pressure the minority subjects swung to acceptance of the misleading majority's wrong judgments in 36.8 per cent of the selections [see Fig. 1.3a].

Of course individuals differed in response. At one extreme, about one quarter of the subjects were completely independent and never agreed with the erroneous judgments of the majority. At the other extreme, some individuals went with the majority nearly all the time. The performances of individuals in this experiment tend to be highly consistent. Those who strike out on the path of independence do not, as a rule, succumb to the majority even over an extended series of trials, while those who choose the path of compliance are unable to free themselves as the ordeal is prolonged.

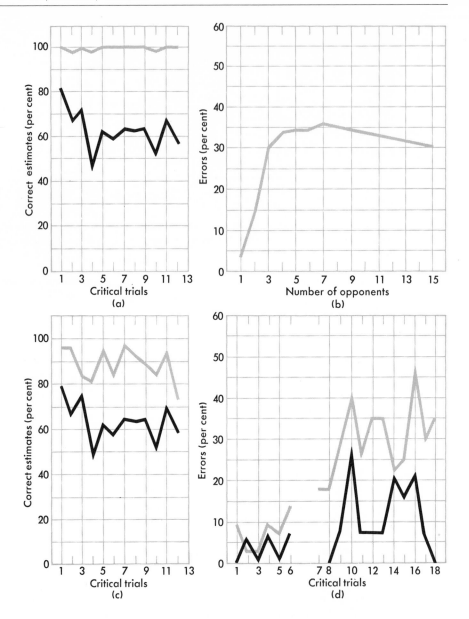

FIGURE 1.3

The effect of group pressure on individual errors in judgment. (*a*) **Error of 123 subjects, each of whom compared lines in the presence of six to eight opponents, is plotted in the broken curve. The accuracy of judgments not under pressure is indicated in the solid curve.** (*b*) **Size of majority which opposed them had an effect on the subjects. With a single opponent the subject erred only 3.6 per cent of the time; with two opponents he erred 13.6 per cent; three, 31.8 per cent; four, 35.1 per cent; six, 35.2 per cent; seven, 37.1 per cent; nine, 35.1 per cent; 15, 31.2 per cent.** (*c*) **Two subjects supporting each other against a majority made fewer errors (broken curve) than one subject did against a majority (solid curve).** (*d*) **Partner left subject after six trials in a single experiment. The broken curve shows the error of the subject when the partner "deserted" to the majority. The solid curve shows error when partner merely left the room.**

The reasons for the startling individual differences have not yet been investigated in detail. At this point we can only report some tentative generalizations from talks with the subjects, each of whom was interviewed at the end of the experiment. Among the independent individuals were many who held fast because of staunch confidence in their own judgment. The most significant fact about them was not absence of responsiveness to the majority but a capacity to recover from doubt and to reestablish their equilibrium. Others who acted independently came to believe that the majority was correct in its answers, but they continued their dissent on the simple ground that it was their obligation to call the play as they saw it.

Among the extremely yielding persons we found a group who quickly reached the conclusion: "I am wrong, they are right." Others yielded in order "not to spoil your results." Many of the individuals who went along suspected that the majority were "sheep" following the first responder, or that the majority were victims of an optical illusion; nevertheless, these suspicions failed to free them at the moment of decision. More disquieting were the reactions of subjects who construed their difference from the majority as a sign of some general deficiency in themselves, which at all costs they must hide. On this basis they desperately tried to merge with the majority, not realizing the longer-range consequences to themselves. All the yielding subjects underestimated the frequency with which they conformed.

Which aspect of the influence of a majority is more important—the size of the majority or its unanimity? The experiment was modified to examine this question. In one series the size of the opposition was varied from one to 15 persons. The results showed a clear trend. When a subject was confronted with only a single individual who contradicted his answers, he was swayed little: he continued to answer independently and correctly in nearly all trials. When the opposition was increased to two, the pressure became substantial: minority subjects now accepted the wrong answer 13.6 per cent of the time. Under the pressure of a majority of three, the subjects' errors jumped to 31.8 per cent. But further increases in the size of the majority apparently did not increase the weight of the pressure substantially. Clearly the size of the opposition is important only up to a point [see Fig. 1.3b].

Disturbance of the majority's unanimity had a striking effect. In this experiment the subject was given the support of a truthful partner—either another individual who did not know of the prearranged agreement among the rest of the group, or a person who was instructed to give correct answers throughout.

The presence of a supporting partner depleted the majority of much of its power. Its pressure on the dissenting individual was reduced to one fourth: that is, subjects answered incorrectly only one fourth as often as under the pressure of a unanimous majority [see Fig. 1.3c]. The weakest persons did not yield as readily. Most interesting were the reactions to the partner. Generally the feeling toward him was one of warmth and closeness; he was credited with inspiring confidence. However, the subjects repudiated the suggestion that the partner influenced them to be independent.

Was the partner's effect a consequence of his dissent, or was it related to his accuracy? We now introduced into the experimental group a person who was instructed to dissent from the majority but also to disagree with the subject. In some experiments the majority was always to choose the worst of the comparison lines and the instructed dissenter to pick the line that was closer to the length of the standard one; in others the majority was consistently intermediate and the dissenter most in error. In this manner we were able to study the relative influence of "compromising" and "extremist" dissenters.

Again the results are clear. When a moderate dissenter is present, the effect of the majority on the subject decreases by approximately one third, and extremes of yielding disappear. Moreover, most of the errors the subjects do make are moderate, rather than flagrant. In short, the dissenter largely controls the choice of errors. To this extent the subjects broke away from the majority even while bending to it.

On the other hand, when the dissenter always chose the line that was more flagrantly different from the standard, the results were of quite a different kind. The extremist dissenter produced a remarkable freeing of the subjects; their errors dropped to only 9 per cent. Furthermore, all the errors were of the moderate variety. We were able to conclude that dissent *per se* increased independence and moderated the errors that occurred, and that the direction of dissent exerted consistent effects.

In all the foregoing experiments each subject was observed only in a single setting. We now turned to studying the effects upon a given individual of a change in the situation to which he was exposed. The first experiment examined the consequences of losing or gaining a partner. The instructed partner began by answering correctly on the first six trials. With his support the subject usually resisted pressure from the majority: 18 of 27 subjects were completely independent. But after six trials the partner joined the majority. As soon as he did so, there was an abrupt rise in the subjects' errors. Their submission to the majority was just about as frequent as when the minority subject was opposed by a unanimous majority throughout [see Fig. 1.3*d*].

It was surprising to find that the experience of having had a partner and of having braved the majority opposition with him had failed to strengthen the individuals' independence. Questioning at the conclusion of the experiment suggested that we had overlooked an important circumstance; namely, the strong specific effect of "desertion" by the partner to the other side. We therefore changed the conditions so that the partner would simply leave the group at the proper point. (To allay suspicion it was announced in advance that he had an appointment with the dean.) In this form of the experiment, the partner's effect outlasted his presence. The errors increased after his departure, but less markedly than after a partner switched to the majority.

In a variant of this procedure the trials began with the majority unanimously giving correct answers. Then they gradually broke away until on the sixth trial the naive subject was alone and the group unanimously against him. As long as the subject had anyone on his side, he was almost invariably independent, but as soon as he found himself alone, the tendency to conform to the majority rose abruptly.

As might be expected, an individual's resistance to group pressure in these experiments depends to a considerable degree on how wrong the majority is. We varied the discrepancy between the standard line and the other lines systematically, with the hope of reaching a point where the error of the majority would be so glaring that every subject would repudiate it and choose independently. In this we regretfully did not succeed. Even when the difference between the lines was seven inches, there were still some who yielded to the error of the majority.

The foregoing experiment revealed the ability of the group to influence the individual even though the group made a scientifically incorrect judgment. This same sensitivity to group guidance can lead to riots and other forms of socially undesirable behavior.[14] Socially undesirable behavior can and does result from the desire of the individual to conform to the expectations of the people with whom he is interacting. Most of the time, however, social pressure is mobilized not to arouse the worst impulses of the individual but to provide ground rules establishing some measure of social harmony. Thus students rarely assault professors—even when they receive poor grades. Why not? Because all interactive systems, including universities, have norms limiting the mutual aggressiveness of role players. Apart from the danger of arrest, a student punching a professor who failed him in a course would be strongly disapproved by virtually everybody in the university community. The failing student knows this, and such knowledge serves to prevent aggressive fantasies from becoming father to the act. Organized society is possible because people behave predictably, and people behave predictably largely because they abide by role expectations and cultural norms. They want to do what they are expected to do. Ultimately, it is the motorist's sensitivity to social guidance that allows pedestrians to cross streets with some confidence. The pedestrian is aware that he may be run over, but he is reasonably confident that a motorist will not *aim* for him.

Sensitivity to social guidance varies from individual to individual and from situation to situation. The variation from individual to individual is of greater psychological than sociological interest, depending as it does on the early experience of the child in his family as well as on his biological endowments. But the variation in sensitivity to social guidance depending on the situation is a sociological problem. The sociologist predicts a greater tendency to yield to the (supposed) majority opinion in self-selected groups like football teams or families than in the experimental groups contrived by Asch because the members of a natural group care more about one another's reactions than they do about the reactions of strangers. Of course, some strangers are more psychologically important than others. American college students would probably be more sensitive to the reactions of *American* strangers than of *Chinese* strangers and to unknown American *college students* than to unknown American *truck drivers.* Sociologists identify this variation in the sensitivity to the reactions of other people in the concept of the **significant other.** A significant other is a person with whom the individual has a psychologically important relationship. Obviously, the more important the relationship, the more sensitive is the individual to a contingency that might jeopardize it. For the fraternity pledge, a "brother" may be a significant other but not necessarily vice

[14] Ralph H. Turner and Lewis M. Killian, *Collective Behavior,* Englewood Cliffs, N.J.: Prentice-Hall, 1957; Neil J. Smelser, *Theory of Collective Behavior,* New York: Free Press of Glencoe, 1963.

Francis Laping – D.P.I.

versa. Therefore, if the naive subjects were pledges and the instructed majority were brothers from their fraternities, yielding might occur more often than if the naive subjects were brothers and the instructed majority were pledges. This possibility could be tested by an experiment.

The sociological literature contains endless demonstrations of sensitivity to role expectations. The willingness of German soldiers to continue fighting at the end of the Second World War after all hope for victory had evaporated was not due to ideological commitment; social scientists found that their *esprit de corps* was primarily a result of the policy of the German army to keep small units intact.[15] Their friendship with and loyalty to "buddies" prevented them from deserting even after defeat was certain. American commanders were impressed with this finding. After the war the United States Department of Defense developed a new system of small-group enlistments based on the same principle. A group of friends was permitted to enlist together and remain together throughout a tour of duty.

In a quite different area of life, fund raising, studies have demonstrated that *personal* appeals for charitable contributions are more successful than written solicitations or mass media appeals.[16] People find it difficult to say "no" to a solicitor when that solicitor is a friend, neighbor, or co-worker. An applica-

[15] Edward A. Shils and Morris Janowitz, "Cohesion and Disintegration in the Wehrmacht in World War II," *Public Opinion Quarterly,* Vol. 12, Summer 1948, pp. 280-315.

[16] Aileen D. Ross, "The Social Control of Philanthropy," *American Journal of Sociology,* Vol. 48, March 1953, pp. 451-460.

tion of this principle helped to control inflation in the United States during the Second World War. Analysis of the second war bond drive revealed that only 25 per cent of all gainfully employed persons had been *personally* urged to buy bonds but that 47 per cent of such persons increased their bond purchases. On the other hand, 12 per cent of gainfully employed persons *not* personally solicited increased their bond purchases. This finding led to efforts to increase personal solicitation in the next bond drive. As Table 1.2 shows, the amount of personal solicitation increased to 50 per cent of gainfully employed persons in the third bond drive, and personal solicitations continued to influence bond sales. A billion dollars more bonds were sold in the third bond drive than in the second.

TABLE 1.2

The Effect of Personal Solicitation on the Sale of War Bonds in the United States during the Second World War

Bond Purchases of Gainfully Employed Persons	Second Bond Drive		Third Bond Drive	
	Personal Solicitation (25%)	No Personal Solicitation (75%)	Personal Solicitation (50%)	No Personal Solicitation (50%)
Increased	47%	12%	59%	17%
Did not increase	53	88	41	83
Total value of bonds purchased	$1,500,000,000		$2,500,000,000	

Source: Rensis Likert, "The Sample Interview as a Tool of Research and Policy Formation," in Daniel Lerner and Harold Lasswell, *The Policy Sciences,* Stanford, Calif.: Stanford University Press, 1951, pp. 244-245.

ROLES: THE INTERNAL STRUCTURE OF INTERACTIVE SYSTEMS

Sociologists are interested in the ability of a complex system of interaction like American **society** or a university to persist through time or to change in predictable ways. To some people, this interest is incomprehensible because they think it implies that the whole is more than the sum of its parts. In the following passage, a distinguished psychologist pokes fun at the notion that a university constitutes an entity with needs of its own:[17]

[17] Floyd Allport, *Institutional Behavior,* Chapel Hill: University of North Carolina Press, 1933, p. 3.

At a meeting of the faculty of a certain large university a proposal for a new administrative policy was being discussed. The debate was long and intense before a final vote of adoption was taken. As the professors filed out of the room an instructor continued the discussion with one of the older deans.

"Well," observed the latter official, "it may be a little hard on some people; but I feel sure that, in the long run, the new plan will be for the best interests of the institution."

"Do you mean that it will be for the good of the students?" inquired the younger man.

"No," the dean replied, "I mean it will be for the good of the whole institution."

"Oh, you mean that it will benefit the faculty as well as the students."

"No," said the dean, a little annoyed, "I don't mean *that;* I mean it will be a good thing for the institution itself."

"Perhaps you mean the trustees then — or the Chancellor?"

"No, I mean the institution, the *institution!* Young man, don't you know what an institution is?"

Sociologists think it makes sense to talk about "the best interests" of a university on the assumption that a complex system of interaction called a university has organizational requirements apart from the needs and wants of students, faculty, and trustees. This point of view has implications for the basic unit of analysis. For the sociologist, a university, or any interactive system, is composed of an organized system of meshing *roles,* not an aggregation of concrete *individuals.* Recall that a role consists of what a person is expected to do in a prescribed interactive relationship. The role concept is a way of looking at human behavior that emphasizes the requirements of the interactive system. Corresponding to each role is a **status.** How a person in a prescribed relationship is responded to by those with whom he interacts is the status associated with that role.

To be specific, a professor participates in the interactive system known as a university by giving lectures and grading papers. Students respond to his status as a professor by seeming to take notes while he lectures and by acting deferential while haggling over grades. The professor plays other roles (and consequently occupies other statuses) in other interactive systems. He is also a husband, a father, a son, a neighbor, a member of the Parent-Teachers Association of his community, a consultant to a private foundation, and a member of the American Civil Liberties Union. His students know only a small part of him as a concrete person because most of their knowledge of him is confined to interactions in which he participates as a professor and in which they participate as students. He is similarly ignorant about them; he does not know them as a parent, a neighbor, a chum, or a girl friend might know them. Sociologists assume that it makes sense to ignore all the other roles that the professor and his students play outside of the university, while concentrating on fitting together (intellectually) his activities as professor, the activities of deans and department heads, and so on, such that the functioning of the university as an interactive system is comprehensible. From the sociological point

Rene Burri — Magnum

of view, the problems of a university are *not* the problems of its constituent individuals added together. Thus the difficulty the professor has in meeting the mortgage payments on his house is not a problem of his university — except indirectly if it makes him an inadequate teacher.

The Organizational Requirements of Interactive Systems. The problems of the university are problems of organizing a role structure capable of getting teaching and research accomplished. Such problems fall into four categories of requirements basic to *all* interactive systems. For illustration, we shall discuss the form these requirements take in a university. But a three-member family and American society have the same four "system problems."[18]

1. **Adaptive requirements.** All interactive systems must come to terms with their environment. The central tasks of a university are the production of new knowledge and the stuffing of existing knowledge into the heads of students. Nevertheless, a university, like a business firm or a family, must obtain resources from its environment. It needs buildings in which to conduct classes and to house research projects; it needs money to pay salaries of faculty and staff; it needs equipment for its laboratories. These sound like economic needs, and indeed they are. The treasurer of a university

[18] Talcott Parsons calls these four prerequisites for a functioning interactive system "system problems" and he uses a slightly different terminology. See Talcott Parsons, Edward A. Shils, Kaspar D. Naegele, and Jesse R. Pitts, *Theories of Society: Foundations of Modern Sociological Theory,* Vol. 1, New York: Free Press of Glencoe, 1961, pp. 38-41.

must collect fees from students, research grants from government agencies and private foundations, gifts from alumni, and appropriations from a state legislature. But a university's dependence on its environment is not only economic. The university depends on favorable attitudes—or at least limited sullenness from the citizens of the town in which it is located. It depends also on many thousands of families being willing to send their children to it for an education and on the recommendations of guidance counselors from hundreds of high schools. In short, the environment of a university is not only physical but social; its relations with other inter-active systems—communities, families, schools—are crucial to its continued functioning. The concept of "adaptation" is broad enough to include obtaining favorable attitudes as well as hard cash. The Director of Public Relations as well as the Treasurer seek to facilitate the university's adaptation to its environment.

2. **Socializing requirements.** All interactive systems need to recruit and train people to play the roles of which they are composed. Even the society, whose inflow of babies seems too automatic to deserve the term "recruitment," must teach newcomers to the system how to fulfill the requirements of existing roles. In a university, the admissions office recruits students; deans and department chairmen stalk brilliant scholars and teachers; and personnel offices exist to process applications for secretarial and other non-academic jobs. Recruitment is only the first step. The new faculty member learns his role informally by observing and conversing with older colleagues, by attending faculty meetings, by serving on committees, and by interacting with students.[19] Although the new Ph.D. may be shaking in his shoes when he lectures to his first class, he gets an infusion of confidence from watching students take notes on his lecture. The new *student* may receive a more formal tutelage; the freshman attends orientation lectures during Freshman Week as well as receiving informal guidance from upper-classmen, professors, dormitory preceptors, and fraternity rushing committees. Socializing needs of interactive systems shade off into **social control** needs, which include extruding from the system those who cannot or will not learn to play their roles adequately. Even at a university, where faculty members are ultimately given permanent tenure, some are evaluated as unsuitable and fired; some students are expelled ("asked to withdraw").

3. **Policy-making requirements.** All interactive systems must resolve conflicts among role players, partly about goals and partly about the allocation of scarce resources. In a university, policy making goes on at many levels. At the level of academic deans, authoritative decisions prevent disruptive conflicts among departments. Without the coordinating decisions of a dean, department chairmen might come to blows about the most favorable schedules for their courses and the largest share of the college budget. But there must be an ultimate source of authority in a complex interactive system—a

[19] Logan Wilson, *The Academic Man,* New York: Oxford University Press, 1942.

court of last resort. At a university, it is the president and the board of trustees.

4. **Integrative requirements.** All interactive systems must resist the centrifugal forces threatening to disrupt them. Put more positively, interactive systems cannot continue to function without some minimum level of loyalty from the persons playing roles in them. Thus a university must promote a feeling of belonging together (solidarity) just as a family must. Students recognize this need when they refer to "school spirit," but the necessity for solidarity in a university goes beyond student enthusiasm displayed at rallies and extracurricular events. Solidarity implies the inclusion of most members of the interactive system in the web of community. In a university this means that persons playing *different* roles — faculty members, custodians, students, administrators — recognize the bond of common membership in the system as valuable, as something worth devoting effort to maintaining. If, for example, undergraduates became disinterested in reading their assignments and coming to classes, faculty morale would fall and the integration of the university would suffer — even though football games were well attended. Similarly, if faculty members refused to give graduate students as much research direction as they wanted, perhaps because of consulting activities outside of the university, graduate student morale would fall and the integration of the university would suffer. There must be mutual facilitation by different role players of one another's contributions. Mutual facilitation is accomplished in part by specialized subdivisions. Transportation and parking officials allocate privately owned vehicles to parking places and schedule a campus bus service for those without vehicles. The telephone exchange enables faculty and staff to communicate with one another despite physical separation. The scheduling staff make sure that one class (and only one) is scheduled for a particular classroom at a particular time. Unlike the other needs of the university, there is no one role or cluster of roles charged with the task of overall integration. Policy decisions by officials, routine coordination by transportation, communication, and scheduling personnel, ceremonial occasions like a commencement, and victories of the football team all contribute to this end.

The adaptive, socializing, policy-making, and integrative requirements of a university are obviously not the problems of teaching courses or doing research. Nor are they reducible to the problems of the human components of the university's role structure. The university has needs, not in a mystical sense, but as a consequence of the fact that roles must mesh in order to maintain a pattern of interaction, any pattern of interaction. From the sociologist's point of view, the courses being taught and the discoveries being made in the various laboratories of the university become relevant to his interests only when they have significance for the maintenance or the change of the complicated system of interaction called a university. That is, the sociologist ignores a great deal of the concrete activities, not to mention thought processes, within the university.

He abstracts only a small part of human behavior—the actions and reactions that link individual to group—and he tries to understand how some interactive systems persist and why others disintegrate.

One might argue that it makes no sense to study an interactive system as though it were self-contained, for example, to abstract the roles that people play in the university while disregarding the much larger number of roles they play in other interactive systems. Sociologists disagree; they assume that the first place to look if you want to understand the academic behavior of the teachers, students, deans, and administrative personnel of a university is at its **role structure**. They assume that the policy set by the director of admissions is primarily determined by the classroom and dormitory space available and only secondarily by the quarrels he might be having with his wife or by a possible sadistic streak in his character. True, there are occasions when commitments to interactive systems other than the university—for example, to his family—may interfere with the adequate discharging of obligations to the university. This situation, called **role conflict,** shows that an interactive system is only partially self-contained; sharing role players with other interactive systems forces an interactive system to modify its standards for the fulfillment of role obligations.

The nature of roles—and the possibility of role conflict—can be clarified by Fig. 1.4. The circles in the figure represent concrete people: Professor X, Henry, John, Jane. The triangles and quadrilaterals represent interactive systems. Only one role of Professor X, his role as a teacher in the introductory sociology course, is explicit; that role meshes with the student role of Henry and the student role of John in an interactive system called "introductory sociology." The role participations of Henry are shown more fully. Henry plays the boyfriend role in an interactive system that includes Jane (but only in her role as girlfriend). Henry also plays the role of son in an interactive system that includes his mother and father (not in their full concreteness, of course, but in family roles). The concrete Henry includes all of the roles he plays in all of the interactive systems in which he participates. Figure 1.4 explicitly shows four of Henry's roles, but this oversimplifies greatly the role involvements of an American college student. Just as the interactive system known as Rutgers University and the interactive system known as Henry's family require a certain amount of coordination if they are to persist, so too the role commitments of Henry to various interactive systems must be reasonably compatible. For example, Henry's role in his fraternity (pledge chairman) might be compatible with his boyfriend role and his son role but might not allow him enough time to study his sociology course. He is caught in the crossfire of competing obligations to two interactive systems, each of which claims him as a member. This is a *role conflict:* two groups defining the obligations of the individual insist upon the legitimacy of their claims. An obvious solution to a role conflict is to withdraw from one of the interactive systems, but Henry may wish to remain in good standing with both his fraternity brothers and his sociology professor. Thus role conflicts pose a dilemma for the individual, and sociologists

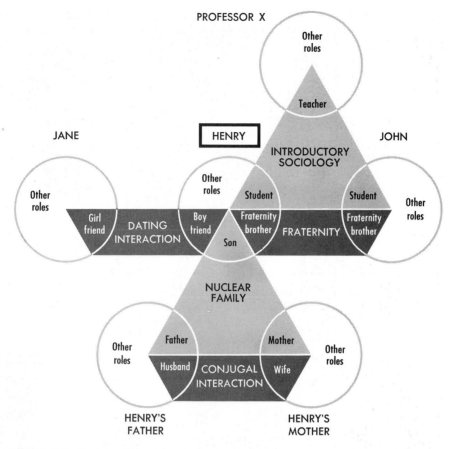

FIGURE 1.4 **Henry's roles.**

have studied the limited number of solutions people in role conflicts discover.

If role conflict were nothing more than a dilemma for the individual, a choice between two incompatible courses of action, it would be of interest to the psychologist alone. The sociologist is interested in role conflicts because they place individuals under **strain,** and strain is often the starting point of social change. Furthermore, in urban industrial societies role conflicts are chronic because the **social structure** is so highly differentiated that the individual is simultaneously a member of a number of independent interaction systems. He is a member of the family into which he was born (the **family of orientation**), the family he creates by marriage (the **family of procreation**), the corporation that he works for, his neighborhood, the educational institution in which he is taking courses, his circle of friends, and so on. Therefore, the probability of role conflict is much greater than in preliterate societies like that of the Australian Murngin where one social structure—kinship—predominates. When faced with a role conflict, the individual seeks to integrate his motivational commitments among interactive systems. This is not the same thing as *societal* integration or, on a less inclusive level, *group* integration. Henry's

Camera Press—PIX

problem—depicted in Fig. 1.4—is to balance his commitments among his various roles. The integrative problem of his fraternity is to coordinate the contributions of Henry, John, and other members so that the fraternity continues to be a viable interactive system.

The integrative problems of American society are more complicated than the integrative problems of Henry's fraternity. What must be coordinated are not only individual role players but complex organizations of role players called **institutions.** The term "institution" expresses the notion that certain prescribed activities in a society are more crucial than others to its continued functioning. Thus economic institutions are social structures that cope with adaptive problems. Political institutions are social structures that cope with policy-making problems. Families, schools, mental hospitals, and prisons cope with socialization and social control problems. Sociologists look for institutions or some equivalent of them in every society—on the assumption that complex role structures necessarily develop to cope with crucial functions.

However, there is no neat correspondence between the four basic requirements of interactive systems and the role structures that have developed to cope with them on the societal level. For instance, some adaptive problems of societies—in particular, relations with other societies—are dealt with by military and governmental organizations rather than by economic organizations. Similarly, integrative problems are dealt with by a variety of role complexes from the legal system to the communications industry. Recall that the integrative needs of a *university* are handled by a variety of people rather than by a few specialized role players (as financial needs are); the integrative needs of a *society* are also dispersed instead of concentrated in one main institution. Chapter 15 will return to the problem of societal integration.

A basic assumption of the sociologist is that interactive systems are self-contained enough to have four identifiable requirements. Role conflicts draw attention to one limitation on this assumption. Role conflicts are centrifugal forces, chronically threatening to pull the role players physically or emotionally out of poorly integrated interactive systems and thus destroy their integrity as systems. This sometimes happens. Marriages are dissolved. Corporations go into bankruptcy. The assumption that an interactive system is self-contained applies more forcefully to *societies* than to less inclusive interactive systems. For one thing, societies typically recruit members by biological reproduction and lose them through death; except for families, less inclusive interactive systems attract voluntary recruits and suffer defections. A society, though an interactive system, has a special feature: it includes all or nearly all of the interactive systems in which any of its members participate. In Fig. 1.4, for example, we observe Henry playing roles in four separate interactive systems, none of which includes the totality of roles that Henry plays. But American society includes Henry's university, Henry's fraternity, Henry's family, and Henry's dates—indeed all of the concrete Henry. Thus Henry's membership in American society is different from his membership in these microscopic interactive systems. Henry cannot be pulled out of American society by role conflict as easily as he can out of his fraternity. This gives societies a stability that less inclusive interactive systems do not enjoy.

CONCLUSION

Sociologists study the forms of dependence of the human individual on the human group. The human individual is partially created by his society: the very language that he speaks is a group legacy, enabling him to communicate with others, to express his emotions, to think, to remember, to anticipate. Advantageous though it is to walk erect and to have a thumb opposed to the other fingers, these characteristics do not account for the dominance of the human species on this planet. The interactive rather than the biological potentialities of human beings make us distinctive. Foremost among these potentialities is sensitivity to normative guidance. Social psychological experiments document this sensitivity; some people deny the plain evidence of their eyes in the face of the presumed expectations of significant others. True, this type of experiment reveals a danger of normative regulation: the individual may be led into errors he would not otherwise make—not only cognitive errors like misjudging the length of lines but political errors like voting for a demagogue. This danger is outweighed by the enormous benefit of social guidance: it provides a means of preventing chaos. Without role expectations and cultural norms, social order would be impossible. Individual life would not be free but rather, in the words of Thomas Hobbes, "solitary, poor, nasty, brutish, and short." [20]

Sociologists are also fascinated by the tendency of interaction to be organized in *systems*. Just as the physicist sees parallels between the solar system and the atom, so the sociologist sees similarities between the small family as a unity of interacting roles and giant industrial societies differentiated into complex institutions. Every interactive system has four basic needs: *adaptation* to its physical and social environment, *socialization* of new recruits, *policy making* about the allocation of scarce resources among role players and among alternative goals, and *integration* of most members in the web of solidarity. These basic requirements of interactive systems take different forms in small groups like families or mobs, in formal organizations like schools and labor unions, and in self-contained societies.

With complicated interactive systems, and especially for entire societies, it is convenient to have this systematic checklist to use in analyzing what is going on. Taking the four basic requirements as the point of departure for an examination of social structure guarantees that crucial roles will not be overlooked. There is a second value in using a systematic checklist. It facilitates comparison between interactive systems of different kinds and sizes. The rest of this book will examine the functioning of industrial societies using these four basic requirements as a checklist. In considering urban industrial societies, we will discuss social structures and social processes that contribute to societal functioning. Thus the modern family will be considered in Chapter 4 as a solution to some of the socialization problems of urban industrial societies. Economic institutions will be considered in Chapter 6 as more or less successful solutions to some of their adaptive problems. Social change will be taken up in Chapter 14. But before discussing how contemporary societies function, we must know how sociologists gather data for their analyses: Chapter 2 attempts to do this by explaining some empirical methods of sociological researchers.

SOME SIGNIFICANT PERIODICALS

Dozens of sociological journals exist including those published in France, England, Denmark, the Netherlands, India, and Japan. The following list is a selection of journals in the English lan-

[20] Hobbes, *Leviathan*.

guage where articles of sociological interest may be found. All of them are readily available in American universities.

American Journal of Sociology. Founded in 1894, this journal is published bimonthly at the University of Chicago, which long has been a major center of sociological teaching and research.

American Sociological Review. Founded in 1936, this is the official journal of the American Sociological Association, largest organization of professional sociologists in the world. The prestige of the *Review* is such that, although six issues appear each year, more than 85 per cent of the manuscripts submitted for publication must be rejected. As in other professional journals, authors of articles receive no payment except for a small number of free reprints. The editor of the *Review* is elected for a three-year term by the Council of the American Sociological Association from among distinguished members of the Association, and the editorial office moves to the university (or other institution) with which the editor is associated.

The American Sociologist. This quarterly journal was established in 1965 to communicate to members of the American Sociological Association professional news: employment opportunities, reports of officers, editors, and committees of the Association, obituaries, a calendar of professional meetings, and expressions of professional opinion on such subjects as the nature of sociology, its future direction, and the best ways of teaching it to students. Expressions of professional opinion are communicated either in the form of letters to the editor or in brief articles.

British Journal of Sociology. Founded in 1949, this quarterly journal is closely associated with the London School of Economics where sociology has developed more strongly than at Oxford or Cambridge. An interesting feature of this journal is long review articles of important books — in addition to shorter reviews such as are published in most professional journals.

Human Organization. Founded in 1941, this quarterly journal is the official organ of the Society for Applied Anthropology. Since it is concerned with the application of social science to practical problems, a wide range of topics is covered — from mental illness to technical assistance to underdeveloped countries. However, industrial sociology is a special emphasis, perhaps because the journal is published by the New York School of Industrial and Labor Relations of Cornell University.

Psychiatry. Founded in 1938, this quarterly journal is published by the William Alanson White Psychiatric Foundation in Washington, D.C. Until his death Harry Stack Sullivan was an influential figure in this psychoanalytic group and his theories of the interpersonal basis of mental illness make the journal receptive to sociological contributions.

Public Opinion Quarterly. Founded in 1936, this quarterly journal is devoted to survey research concerned with the mass media and with political behavior. It is the official organ of the American Association for Public Opinion Research, an organization made up of academic sociologists, psychologists, and political scientists, on the one hand, and market research professionals, on the other.

Rural Sociology. Founded in 1935, this quarterly journal is the official organ of the Rural Sociological Society, which is entirely independent of the American Sociological Association. Although the journal is an excellent one, explanation of its separate existence apart from the rest of sociology is historical rather than intellectual. The field of urban sociology is not similarly represented by a society and a journal.

Social Problems. This quarterly journal, founded in 1953, is the official journal of the Society for the Study of Social Problems. Articles are usually research reports on topics considered social problems: crime, delinquency, prostitution, natural disasters, war, race relations, mental health, alcoholism, drug use, imprisonment.

Sociological Abstracts. Founded in 1952, this bimonthly publication makes available summaries of sociological articles published in hundreds of periodicals from many countries. Thus it is an invaluable help to the sociologist who wishes to learn about recent developments on a particular topic and cannot himself consult all of the original sources. The articles are indexed under such headings as methodology, research technology, statistical methods, history and present state of sociology, sociological theories and ideas, interaction within (small) group structure, interaction between (large) groups, culture, social change and economic development, rural sociology (village), urban sociology (metropolis), social stratification, sociology of occupations and professions, industrial sociology, leadership studies, military sociology, bureaucratic structures, political sociology, social movements (and revolutions), communication (mass and otherwise), collective behavior, sociology of language and literature, sociology of education, sociology of knowledge (and ideology), sociology of religion, sociology of law, demography and ecology, sociology of the child (and socialization), sociology of the family, sociology of leisure, sociology of medicine, social psychiatry (mental health), and social disorganization (criminology, alcoholism, etc.).

Sociological Inquiry. Founded in 1929, this semiannual journal is the official publication of Alpha Kappa Delta, the sociology honor society. Like other sociological journals it contains research reports and theoretical analyses, often by leading sociologists.

Sociology of Education. Founded in 1927 as the *Journal of Educational Sociology,* this journal was published by the Payne Educational Sociology Foundation at New York University until 1963 when editorial responsibility was taken over by the American Sociological Association. It is now published quarterly by the Association as a specialized journal, parallel to *Sociometry,* which is devoted to social psychology, and to the *Journal of Health and Social Behavior,* which is concerned with the sociology of health.

EMPIRICAL RESEARCH IN CONTEMPORARY SOCIETY

Robert Beckhard – D.P.I.

THE SCIENTIFIC ASPIRATIONS OF SOCIOLOGY

"Is sociology objective?"

Most contemporary sociologists believe that it is. This was not always so. One hundred years ago, when sociology was just beginning, sociologists were like social reformers, eager to change the society in which they lived, not detached scientific observers trying primarily to describe how their society worked. Even a generation or two ago sociologists tended to be ministers or former ministers. Most contemporary sociologists find this historical association burdensome. They explain that they are not social workers or social reformers but scientists. They point out that the aim of sociology is to increase knowledge about human societies just as the aim of chemistry is to increase knowledge about elements and compounds. And again like chemists, sociologists conduct most **basic research** at the university.[1] Although sociologists may teach courses on "social problems," their main professional responsibility is gathering **empirical** knowledge, not applying it.

Thus some sociologists try to understand why people violate the criminal laws. This does not necessarily mean that they wish to prevent crime. Conceivably, they might wish to devote their knowledge to increasing delinquency and crime. Such bad citizenship would risk the disapproval of officials at the universities in which they are employed, but, as scientists, their behavior could not be criticized. Sociologists are usually respectable citizens, and, indeed, they frequently are consultants to or employees of government agencies or private foundations concerned with the alleviation of social problems. But the question of how knowledge is applied is not, strictly speaking, a scientific one. Atomic physicists may not be happy that their discoveries are being used for the construction of bombs, but their scientific task was finding out whether atomic energy could be released, not deciding the use to which atomic energy should be put.

Some sociologists regard this emphasis on descriptive accuracy as a blind alley. For them, knowledge in itself is pointless; sociological knowledge becomes worthwhile when it helps to improve the quality of social life. They are not interested in studying poverty unless such a study can help to eliminate poverty; they do research in the field of race relations because they hope that prejudice and discrimination can be reduced. For American sociologists, this is a minority view (although distinguished members of the profession belong to this humanistic minority). The majority view was set forth a half century ago by the German sociologist Max Weber. Weber pointed out that the selection of research problems is influenced by the values of the researcher. He insisted,

---

[1] About three-quarters of the members of the American Sociological Association teach in colleges and universities. Matilda White Riley, "Membership of the American Sociological Association, 1950–1959," *American Sociological Review,* Vol. 25, December 1960, pp. 914-926; Raymond W. Mack, "A Career in Sociology," Washington: American Sociological Association, no date.

however, that the canons of evidence are independent of the researcher's values.[2] This view is sometimes called "value free" sociology.

Objectivity in Sociology. Contemporary sociologists try to be objective in their evaluation of evidence. They do not always succeed, but in principle **objectivity** is possible in sociology just as it is in any descriptive discipline. Objectivity means simply that an observation does not depend on the peculiarities of the observer. When a physicist says that water freezes at 32° Fahrenheit, he means that a dozen trained observers will read the thermometer at about 32° when water starts to freeze. If one observer read the thermometer at 27° and another at 36°, the physicist could no longer talk about the freezing point of water as an objective fact. *Objectivity implies that trained observers agree.* Consider the implications of this statement not only for sociology but for any field with scientific aspirations. *The greater the precision of the measuring instruments, the greater the likelihood of consensus among trained observers.* The measurement of temperature is objective because the contemporary physicist has available standardized, precisely calibrated thermometers. If the contemporary physicist had the technical equipment of the ancient Greeks, temperature would move toward the realm of the subjective.

There are many technical difficulties that sociologists must overcome if they are to be rigorously objective. They must develop better tools for interviewing, for questionnaire construction, for observing interaction in groups. The technical difficulties of social research, however, are less responsible than the subject matter for the popular conception of sociology as inherently "subjective." For example, laymen may think that prejudice against minorities cannot be studied scientifically because prejudice is itself subjective. This kind of reasoning can be proved fallacious. Suppose a sociologist interviews an individual in connection with a survey of attitudes toward ethnic minorities. During the course of the interview, the respondent makes the statement, "I hate Negroes. I'd be happy if all of them were lined up against a wall and shot." (However much the sociologist disagrees with the statement, he is careful to record it because that statement is his datum about the respondent's feelings toward Negroes, just as the thermometer reading is the physicist's datum about temperature.) Later, when the researcher analyzes interviews from various respondents, he categorizes the one who wanted to see Negroes shot as the most prejudiced in the survey. The test of whether his research has been objective is: Would other sociologists having access to the transcript of the interview agree that this respondent was the most prejudiced? If rather good consensus occurs among trained observers on ratings of various degrees of prejudice, the ratings are objective *in precisely the same sense that temperature measurements are objective in physics.* (Scientists describe a measure as "reliable" when trained observers can agree as to how it should be applied. **Reliability**

[2] Edward A. Shils and Henry A. Finch (trans.), *Max Weber on the Methodology of the Social Sciences,* Glencoe, Ill.: Free Press, 1949; Talcott Parsons, *The Structure of Social Action,* New York: McGraw-Hill, 1937, p. 592.

can be measured quantitatively — and often is. For practical purposes, "objective" and "reliable" are synonymous.)

Though it is *possible* to study with scientific detachment even controversial phenomena like prejudice and juvenile delinquency, such detachment is not easily attained. If a sociologist believes that prejudice is morally wrong, can he faithfully interview an individual who tells him that Negroes should be lined up against the wall and shot? If a certain type of sex offense shocks his sensibilities, can he avoid communicating this repugnance to the prison inmate whose life history he wishes to record? Either is possible, but it requires training and self-discipline. Social scientists are fully aware of the tendency for the observer to be more than an observer — for example, to give the respondent subtle (or not so subtle) cues as to what answers the interviewer will approve.[3] A tremendous literature exists on interviewer bias and how to avoid it — including the report of a tendency in voting surveys for Republican pollsters to get more Republican political preferences than Democratic pollsters.[4]

The Regularities of Interaction. Training and self-discipline on the part of the social scientist would not suffice to make sociology scientific if social interaction were capricious and unpredictable. Science assumes that there are regularities in nature which become laws of the particular subject under study and that these can be discovered by controlled observation. If there were no regularities in social interaction, if human behavior were completely unpredictable, objectivity would be pointless — just as objectivity would be pointless if the freezing point of water and the acceleration of gravity varied chaotically from day to day. Human behavior is unpredictable only in the sense that perfect predictions about an *individual* are impossible. In the sense of statistical predictions about kinds of interaction, human behavior is highly predictable and therefore susceptible to objective study.

Thus when he comes to the assigned room at the beginning of the semester to give his first lecture, the professor is not surprised to find that students are waiting for him. He predicted that they would be there by consulting the schedule of classes. The students also made predictions: not only that the professor would come but how he would be dressed and what he would do when he got there. Students are accustomed to making correct predictions about role behavior, for example, that professors will talk about the subject promised in the course catalog. Although they are not aware of being prophets, they would feel bewildered and perhaps outraged if their professor arrived dressed in a toga and sang an aria instead of confirming pessimistic expectations of a dull lecture.

A student might say, "It is true that we make correct predictions in a sta-

[3] Curiously enough, this principle is equally applicable to physics. Nobel Prize winner Werner Heisenberg pointed out in 1927 that some subatomic particles defy accurate measurement because the light beam necessary for observation affects their velocity. See Lincoln Barnett, *The Universe and Dr. Einstein,* rev. ed., New York: New American Library, 1952, pp. 35-37.

[4] Herbert H. Hyman et al., *Interviewing in Social Research,* Chicago: University of Chicago Press, 1954.

tistical sense—such as that a professor will come to class dressed in a business suit and talk about his subject. But this isn't a very interesting prediction. What we mean when we say that human behavior is unpredictable is that we cannot tell in advance the *color* of the suit he will wear." In arguing for a predominant concern with the idiosyncratic, the student misunderstands science. As a scientist, the sociologist is concerned with continuing patterns—here he is concerned with uniformity of dress and behavior among college professors and rightly regards the differences in color and texture of fabrics as unimportant. Science is concerned with generalizations about classes of phenomena, not with unique cases. But a student frequently asks more of the sociologist than is expected of, for example, the zoologist. If a zoologist described to his class the feeding and swimming habits of whales, the student would not insist that he explain why Moby Dick drowned Captain Ahab. Students are not as interested in individual whales or in individual electrons as they are in individual human beings, and therefore they are more satisfied with statistical statements in the physical and biological sciences than in the social sciences.

TYPES OF EMPIRICAL RESEARCH IN SOCIOLOGY

Because contemporary sociology seeks to describe what *is* rather than to suggest what *should be*, a great deal of the professional literature consists of the recording of data about interaction (or about factors related to interaction) in face-to-face groups, in formal organizations, in communities of varying size and complexity, and in societies. The topics covered by these studies and the techniques of data collection and analysis vary widely—from elaborate questionnaire surveys analyzed by means of computers to qualitative accounts by participant-observers, such as the description of the training (socialization) of cadets in a military academy.[5] A **content analysis** of a popular comic strip, an investigation of trends in mental disease, the autobiographical account of a delinquent career, and studies of differential voting behavior of various population segments all can be found in sociological journals and monographs.[6] Many examples of sociological research will be found in this book, but they are incidental to developing basic sociological concepts or to stating substantive conclusions about the functioning of human societies. Therefore, the

[5] Leon Festinger and Daniel Katz, Eds., *Research Methods in the Behavioral Sciences,* New York: Dryden, 1953; Sanford M. Dornbush, "The Military Academy as an Assimilating Institution," *Social Forces,* Vol. 33, May 1955, pp. 316-321.

[6] Donald Auster, "A Content Analysis of 'Little Orphan Annie,'" *Social Problems,* Vol. 2, July 1954, pp. 26-33; Herbert Goldhamer and Andrew Marshall, *Psychosis and Civilization,* Glencoe, Ill.: Free Press, 1953; Clifford R. Shaw, *The Natural History of a Delinquent Career,* Chicago: University of Chicago Press, 1931; Paul F. Lazarsfeld, Bernard Berelson, and Hazel Gaudet, *The People's Choice,* 2nd ed., New York: Columbia University Press, 1948.

more common types of empirical research undertaken by contemporary sociologists will be reviewed here to provide better understanding of the examples in later chapters.

The Study of Interaction. Human interaction, which lies at the center of the sociologist's interests, is a complex process. It does not lend itself easily to systematic observation. And unless observation is systematic, the results will be illustrations rather than evidence. A major problem in interaction studies is recording the actions and reactions in the proper sequence when the group under study is large. In such studies it is necessary to identify not only the initiator of the action but its object. Sometimes its object may be one individual, sometimes a clique, sometimes the group as a whole. Experimentally minded small-group researchers have dealt with these problems by placing groups in specially constructed rooms. Members of the groups usually are aware that their conversations are being listened to through concealed microphones and their actions observed from behind what appears to be a mirror. Behind the one-way screen are not only observers but machines through which paper slowly moves, giving the observers an opportunity to record events in a prearranged detailed code.[7] A further problem in the direct observation of group interaction is the *analysis* of the mountains of data that quickly accumulate. Mathematical models cope with this problem by helping to select and organize what is relevant. The recent development of high-speed computers facilitates such analysis by distinguishing data that fit the model from data that do not.

Systematic observation of interaction is time-consuming and expensive. Recall the experiment reported in Chapter 1 where ten Navaho, ten Mormon, and ten white Texan couples interacted over disagreements in judgment revealed to them by the researcher. Though these were only two-person interactive systems, the researcher had to work hard to arrive at the results presented in Table 1.1. He probably spent hundreds of hours arranging the field operations and subsequently listening to the tapes of the husband-wife discussions. He had to count the number of wins and losses for each husband-wife pair before he could tabulate the data in final form (Table 1.1).

Direct systematic observation of interaction is difficult, so sociologists often use *reports* of participants to gather data about previous interaction.[8] The disadvantages of reports are obvious:

1. They may be incorrect because of honest errors of recall.
2. They may be incorrect because the participant wishes to reveal to the researcher only creditable information about himself.
3. They may be useless because the researchers asks the wrong question or misinterprets the answers.

---

[7] Robert F. Bales, *Personality and Interpersonal Behavior,* New York: Holt, Rinehart, & Winston, 1970. See also A. Paul Hare, Edgar F. Borgatta, and Robert F. Bales, Eds., *Small Groups: Studies in Social Interaction,* New York: Knopf, 1955.

[8] This discussion of the relative merits of direct observation of interaction versus reports about interaction leans on the formulations of Frank A. Fasick.

Authenticated News International

These disadvantages are partially overcome by methodological precautions: by skill in constructing questions and by setting up the interview or questionnaire situation so that respondents are motivated to cooperate. They are also out-weighed by the enormous *advantages* of reports:

1. They are economical for transmitting quickly and cheaply large amounts of information about previous interaction.
2. They can elicit attitudes from participants which would be difficult or im-possible to infer from direct observation of interaction.

The second feature is especially important, as the author of a leading text on sociological research points out in the following passage:[9]

> Answers to questions, although they do not always report interaction as the observer might perceive it, have the peculiar merit of reflecting directly the sub-jective states of the actors, the underlying dispositions to act. When skillfully used . . ., questioning frequently reveals dormant aspects of the system which are not acted out while the observer watches, and which may also be concealed from the other group members.

A study showing how husbands' and wives' attitudes toward the marital re-lationship affects the probability of divorce illustrates this point.

[9] Matilda White Riley, *Sociological Research: A Case Approach,* Vol. 1, New York: Harcourt, Brace & World, 1963, p. 167.

Alver Jacobson interviewed 100 married couples and 100 divorced couples living in and around Chillicothe, Ohio, between July 1, 1949, and April 30, 1950.[10] The sample of 100 divorced couples was obtained from among the 393 divorces recorded in Chillicothe between January 1, 1947 and July 1, 1949. The sample of 100 married couples was obtained from the marriage records of Chillicothe; each married couple was selected so that its marriage date coincided fairly closely with the marriage date of one divorced couple. Interviews were conducted with each husband and wife separately (400 interviews in all) either at the place of work or at the home of the respondent. Twenty-eight questions were asked, each question designed to give the respondent an opportunity to express a traditional male-dominant conception of the marital relationship or a more equalitarian conception of marriage. The questions were actually statements to which respondents could react in one of five categories ranging from Strongly Agree to Strongly Disagree. The following are some of the statements used: "The husband should help with the housework." "If the husband insists, the wife should quit a needed job." "If the husband runs around, so can his wife."

Table 2.1 presents Jacobson's analysis of his data. Notice that he used the interactive system rather than the individual as the unit of analysis. He was concerned not so much with whether a man had a male-dominant conception of the marital relationship as whether the man and his wife shared the *same* conception, male dominant or equalitarian. Therefore, he subtracted the score of the husband from the score of his wife and tabulated the resulting data for *couples*. Since the highest individual score, 140, reflected an extremely equalitarian conception and the lowest score, 28, reflected an extremely male-dominant conception, the two married couples in the topmost category and three divorced couples in the bottom category were furthest apart in their conceptions of the husband-wife relationship. The couples with negative joint scores were those in which the husband believed *more* in an equalitarian marriage than the wife, whereas the couples with positive joint scores were those in which the husband believed *less* than the wife in an equalitarian marriage.

Several inferences can be drawn from Table 2.1. First, men are more likely than women to subscribe to a male-dominant conception of the marital relation. What is the evidence for this inference? Observe that only 49 couples out of the 200 in the combined samples are in full agreement about the marital relationship (as reflected in differences between their scores of -9 to $+9$). Disagreements are not, however, equally likely to occur in both directions. Among only 7 couples is the husband more likely to believe in equality than the wife; among 144 couples the wife is more likely to believe in equality than the husband (as reflected in differences between their scores of 10 to 60). This may not seem like a startling discovery, but there is a world of difference between a plausible conjecture and hard evidence.

[10] Alver Hilding Jacobson, "Conflict of Attitudes toward the Roles of the Husband and the Wife in Marriage," *American Sociological Review,* Vol. 17, April 1952, pp. 146-150.

TABLE 2.1

The Effect of Different Conceptions on the Marital Relationship on the Probability of Divorce

Attitude	Differences in Scores	Married Couples	Divorced Couples	All Couples	Percentage Divorced
Husband believed in equality more than mate	−39 to −20	2	0	2	0
	−19 to −10	5	0	5	0
↑	− 9 to 0	18	0	18	0
	0 to 9	30	1	31	3.3
	10 to 19	36	16	52	30.8
↓	20 to 29	5	48	53	90.6
Wife believed in equality more than husband	30 to 39	4	23	27	85.2
	40 to 49	0	9	9	100
	50 to 60	0	3	3	100
Total		100	100	200	

Source: Alver Hilding Jacobson, "Conflict of Attitudes toward the Roles of the Husband and the Wife in Marriage," *American Sociological Review*, Vol. 17, April 1952, pp. 146-150.

Second, married couples are more likely than divorced couples to share the *same* conception of the marital relationship. What is the evidence? Compare the joint scores of married couples with those of divorced couples. Notice that the majority of the *married* couples (89) have less than 20 points of difference in their scores (−19 to −10, −9 to 0, 0 to 9, 10 to 19). Only 17 of the *divorced* couples fall in these three categories.

Third, differences in conceptions are more likely to destroy the marital relationship if they occur in one direction than in the other. This inference is the major finding of the study. Notice the percentages on the right-hand side of the table, ranging from 0 at the top to 100 per cent at the bottom. None of the 25 couples where the husband believed in marital equality more than the wife got a divorce. All of the 12 couples where the wife believed in equality *much more* than the husband got divorced. This is easy to explain. Husbands who believe more in marital equality than their wives are likely to be perceived by their wives as "nice guys" or as helpful companions. Their wives may not even be aware that they favor greater equality in the relationship. Such husbands may not be aware of the difference in viewpoint either. For example, they may not realize that their wives would quit jobs they liked if the husbands requested it. On the other hand, much more conflict is to be expected in situations where the husbands do not share the wives' conception of the marital relationship as equalitarian. An equalitarian-oriented wife perceives a husband who believes in male dominance as a tyrant, and he is likely to perceive *her* as a nag. Thus inconsistent ideas about the role of spouse help explain why the divorce rate increased in the United States from 0.9 divorces per 1000 population in 1910 to 2.5 per 1000 in 1965.[11]

In some ways this study resembles the study of the Navaho, Mormon, and Texan couples reported in Chapter 1. Consider the differences, however. The New Mexico study involved direct observation of interaction, whereas the Chillicothe study involved inferences about interaction from attitude data. Perhaps because collecting attitude data is easier than direct observations, the Chillicothe study included 200 couples, whereas the New Mexico study had only 30. This difference in the size of the sample had implications for analysis of the data and therefore for the inferences that could be drawn from them. Recall that in the New Mexico study the data for the ten Navaho couples, the ten Mormon couples, and the ten Texan couples were treated collectively instead of being reported couple by couple. The reason for this was partly the thrust of the study: the researcher was more interested in calling attention to differences *between* cultures than differences *within* cultures. Nevertheless, he lost an opportunity to find out how marital interactions work out *within* cultures because he had so few couples in each culture (ten) that he may not have thought that a finding based on them would be worth reporting.

The Study of Roles. Since "role" is the fundamental unit of social structure, it is not surprising that sociologists have described the ways of life involved in a wide variety of roles: medical students, prizefighters, union organizers, jazz musicians, clerks, business executives.[12] Many of these are *occupational* roles and, as such, are found only in industrial societies. But other roles have been studied also: the artist, the criminal, the military commander, the political leader, and the religious specialist.[13] In addition to learning the requirements of

[11] Bureau of the Census, *Historical Statistics of the United States, Colonial Times to 1957,* Washington, D.C.: Government Printing Office, 1960, p. 30; Bureau of the Census, *Statistical Abstract of the United States: 1967,* Washington, D.C.: Government Printing Office, 1968, p. 47.

[12] Robert K. Merton, George G. Reader, and Patricia Kendall, *The Student-Physician,* Cambridge, Mass.: Harvard University Press, 1957; S. Kirson Weinberg and Henry Arond, "The Occupational Culture of the Boxer," *American Journal of Sociology,* Vol. 57, March 1952, pp. 460-469; Bernard Karsh, Joel Seidman, and Daisy M. Lilienthal, "The Union Organizer and His Tactics: A Case Study," *American Journal of Sociology,* Vol. 59, September 1953, pp. 113-122; Howard S. Becker, "The Professional Dance Musician and His Audience," *American Journal of Sociology,* Vol. 57, September 1951, pp. 136-144; Peter M. Blau, *The Dynamics of Bureaucracy,* Chicago: University of Chicago Press, 1955; William H. Whyte, Jr., *The Organization Man,* New York: Simon and Schuster, 1956.

[13] Clifford R. Shaw, *The Natural History of a Delinquent Career,* Chicago: University of Chicago Press, 1931; Robert L. Hall, "Social Influence on the Aircraft Commander's Role," *American Sociological Review,* Vol. 20, June 1955, pp. 292-299; David E. Apter, *The Gold Coast in Transition,* Princeton, N.J.: Princeton University Press, 1955; Robert K. Merton, *Social Theory and Social Structure,* rev. ed., Glencoe, Ill.: Free Press, 1957, Chap. 10, "Patterns of Influence: Local and Cosmopolitan Influentials," pp. 387-420; Waldo W. Burchard, "Role Conflicts of Military Chaplains," *American Sociological Review,* Vol. 19, October 1954, pp. 528-535.

the role under scrutiny, often by systematic interviews with persons playing that role and sometimes by observing the role players directly, the sociologist tries to understand the process of recruitment into the role, the stresses on incumbents of the role, and the various ways in which incumbents of the role leave it. Role studies, it should be noted, are not studies of people in their full concreteness. Thus in an investigation of the role of the teacher in a big-city school system, the researcher ignored all aspects of the lives of the 60 teachers he interviewed except those directly relevant to their careers in the Chicago school system.[14] Howard Becker found that the beginning teacher typically entered the school system by being assigned to a slum school. This assignment was regarded as undesirable because students in such schools presented discipline and learning problems to a greater degree than students in more prosperous neighborhoods. The teachers also complained about traits of slum children Becker categorized as "morally unacceptable" — such as being physically dirty, sexually precocious, or unambitious. As a result of these evaluations, the majority of teachers sought to transfer to "better" schools in "better" neighborhoods as soon as they could. When openings occurred in these more desirable schools (because teachers retired or left the school system), younger teachers from the slum schools were waiting to take their places. One objective of Becker's study was to describe this unidirectional career movement of Chicago school teachers through the school system.

It may seem somewhat arbitrary to point to role studies as one research interest of sociologists and interaction studies as another. Are not interaction studies necessarily studies of the interactions of role players? Conversely, can roles be studied apart from their involvement with other role players in systems of interaction? These points are well taken. Classifying research as interaction studies and role studies emphasizes connections between the basic concepts of sociologists and their research activities. But this type of classification is somewhat arbitrary; the dividing line between role studies and interaction studies is difficult to draw. And it does not correspond to the more concrete categories sociologists use to describe their own research. Thus Professor Becker would be more likely to describe his investigation of the careers of Chicago public school teachers as in the field of the sociology of education than as a role study. And Dr. Jacobson would be more likely to classify his investigation of the effect of different conceptions of the marital relationship on the probability of divorce in the field of family sociology than as a role study.

The Community Study. Unlike studies of interaction or of roles, which are of general sociological interest, community studies are more clearly the work of specialists, of urban sociologists, of rural sociologists, or of **human ecologists.** The community study focuses on the locality, the tacit assumption being that group solidarity has a geographic or neighborhood locus. The locality sets a frame within which roles and the interactions of role players can be studied.

---

[14] Howard S. Becker, "The Career of the Chicago Public Schoolteacher," *American Journal of Sociology,* Vol. 57, March 1952, pp. 470-477.

Actually, the concepts of "role" and of "interaction" have moved to a central place in sociological thinking only within the past 35 years, whereas the concept of "community" is an ancient one. In 1892 Charles Booth published the first volume of his 17-volume survey of living conditions in the slums of London, *The Life and Labor of the People in London.* Perhaps inspired by this monumental work, sociologists on both sides of the Atlantic attempted to describe the social life of communities of varying sizes and types.

In the United States Robert Park and his colleagues and students at the University of Chicago in the 1920s started making detailed ecological studies of Chicago and its constituent communities.[15] In 1929 Robert S. Lynd and Helen Merrill Lynd published *Middletown,* a study of Muncie, Indiana, and in 1937 brought their account up to date by reporting the changes that the Great Depression helped to effect since their first visit.[16] In 1934 a three-volume study of the city of Liverpool was published.[17] In 1941 W. Lloyd Warner, already well-known for his study of the preliterate people of the Australian desert, published the first volume of what was destined to be a six-volume report on the way of life in Newburyport, Massachusetts.[18] Within the next decade the patterns of interaction in several other American communities came to be described.[19]

Most of these community surveys were carried out by research teams rather than by lone scholars. The number of man-hours involved in preparing questionnaires, interviewing hundreds of respondents, coding their responses to facilitate mechanical tabulation, analyzing quantitative as well as qualitative data, and pulling the entire operation together in a final report became too great an enterprise for the lone scholar working without research assistance. That is to say, community surveys are costly. Without financial support from

[15] Robert E. Park, *Human Communities,* Glencoe, Ill.: Free Press, 1952; Louis Wirth, *The Ghetto,* Chicago: University of Chicago Press, 1928; Harvey Zorbaugh, *The Gold Coast and the Slum,* Chicago: University of Chicago Press, 1929; Roderick D. McKenzie, *The Metropolitan Community,* New York: McGraw-Hill, 1933; Robert E. Park, Ernest W. Burgess, and Roderick D. McKenzie, *The City,* Chicago: University of Chicago Press, 1925; Clifford R. Shaw et al., *Delinquency Areas,* Chicago: University of Chicago Press, 1929; Ernest R. Mowrer, *Family Disorganization,* Chicago: University of Chicago Press, 1927; Robert E. L. Faris and H. Warren Dunham, *Mental Disorders in Urban Areas,* Chicago: University of Chicago Press, 1939.

[16] Robert S. Lynd and Helen M. Lynd, *Middletown,* New York: Harcourt, Brace, 1929; Robert S. Lynd and Helen M. Lynd, *Middletown in Transition,* New York: Harcourt, Brace, 1937.

[17] D. Caradog Jones, *The Social Survey of Merseyside,* 3 vols., Liverpool, England: University Press of Liverpool, 1934.

[18] W. Lloyd Warner, *A Black Civilization: A Social Study of an Australian Tribe,* rev. ed., New York: Harper, 1958; W. Lloyd Warner and Paul S. Lunt, *The Social Life of a Modern Community,* New Haven, Conn.: Yale University Press, 1941.

[19] Allison Davis, Burleigh B. Gardner, and Mary R. Gardner, *Deep South,* Chicago: University of Chicago Press, 1941; John Useem, Pierre Tangent, and Ruth Useem, "Stratification in a Prairie Town," *American Sociological Review,* Vol. 7, June 1942, pp. 331-342; James West, *Plainville, U.S.A.,* New York: Columbia University Press, 1945; August B. Hollingshead, *Elmtown's Youth,* New York: Wiley, 1949.

governments, private foundations, or university research funds, sociologists ordinarily are not able to undertake such studies. Even organized research teams, however, cannot describe *all* the patterns of interaction in Newburyport, Massachusetts, much less in London. This means that every community study is highly selective. Within the limits of a particular interpretive framework, a community study may be a model of objectivity. But the reader must bear in mind that an interpretive framework exists: Booth was interested in the effects of poverty, Hollingshead in "the impact of social classes on adolescents."

If so much interpretive discretion is permitted the sociological researcher, is his report more scientific than the observations of an intelligent resident of the community? Sociologists think so. One difference between living in a community and conducting a community survey is that a survey will involve many *more* observations than would be made in the course of mere residence. Even more important than the *number* of observations, however, is the *perspective* from which the observations are made. The ordinary resident observes the community from the vantage point of his roles in it. A 27-year-old garage attendant who left high school at the age of 16 and is not yet married sees a different community from that seen by the middle-aged wife of the town's leading industrialist. The researcher, aware that the community presents a different face to persons differently situated in the social structure, attempts to collect observations from many perspectives. To the extent that he succeeds, his description of the community is more objective than that of any of his informants. The same principle applies to other types of sociological research. The criminologist who studies a few dozen adolescent delinquents in their neighborhood milieu may learn more about delinquency than the policeman who has known thousands of delinquents. The policeman has extensive experience with delinquents, but it is obtained in the course of trying to arrest them. Thus he is not aware of the perspectives of their mothers, of their girlfriends, and of their street-corner associates. The criminologist, although his experience may be limited numerically, is more likely to achieve objectivity. This objectivity of the social researcher results partly from his special role in the community under study—detached observer—and partly from his sampling of data sources. He usually goes to considerable trouble to obtain a **random** (unbiased) **sample** of informants in the population he is studying.

In recent years, study of entire communities has become less popular among sociologists. Community research now tends to be more circumscribed—limited, for example, to a residential suburb or to a slum neighborhood being redeveloped.[20] Why the shift of emphasis? Probably because the traditional assumption that the ecological unit (the neighborhood) can de-

---

[20] Bennett M. Berger, *Working-Class Suburb: A Study of Auto Workers in Suburbia,* Berkeley: University of California Press, 1960: Herbert J. Gans, *The Urban Villagers: Group and Class in the Life of Italian-Americans,* New York: Free Press of Glencoe, 1962. Alexander H. Leighton, *The Governing of Men,* Princeton, N.J.: Princeton University Press, 1945, is an engrossing account of life in a relocation center of Japanese-Americans during the Second World War.

marcate an interactive system seems less valid in contemporary society, especially in urban communities. As Professor Richard Simpson put it:[21]

> The social relationships even of villagers extend far beyond the immediate localities where they live. More fundamentally, the forces which integrate modern communities are likely to lie in organizations, both private and governmental, centered outside of the community, and any analysis which fails to take account of this has not really analyzed the community social system as a whole. . . . But if the integration of a community's activities is accomplished from the outside, and if the community is divided into subcultural groups and special-interest groups which have relations, separately, to outside organizations but not to each other, it may be questionable whether a modern community *is* a unified whole in any real sense except that of geography.

In the small, isolated, homogeneous preliterate societies studied by cultural anthropologists, the role structure is less differentiated and more closely tied to location.[22] In urban industrial societies, the technology of modern communications and transportation frees interactive systems from close dependence on geography. Scattered on many campuses in 50 states, the membership of the American Sociological Association nevertheless is an integrated interactive system. In short, in modern societies geographic areas are less likely to be interactive unities, and interactive systems are less likely to be bounded geographically. One way to avoid sociological irrelevance is to restrict the community study to a small community that is likely to be a unified interactive system. The other is to make community-like studies in psychiatric hospitals, in prisons, and in factories, an increasingly popular approach.[23]

TECHNIQUES OF DATA GATHERING

Substance and methods cannot be separated in any concrete sociological investigation because a substantive research problem usually requires one of a limited number of data-gathering techniques. Not every data-gathering technique is appropriate to every type of empirical study. Similarly, methods and theory should not be radically separated because data gathering and analysis have implicit in them concepts of what is going on, which is the explicit concern of theory. Nevertheless, it is useful to separate for the sake of classifica-

---

[21] Richard L. Simpson, "Sociology of the Community: Current Status and Prospects," *Rural Sociology,* Vol. 30, June 1965, p. 130.

[22] Robert Redfield, "The Folk Society," *American Journal of Sociology,* Vol. 52, January 1947, pp. 293–308.

[23] William A. Caudill, *The Psychiatric Hospital as a Small Society,* Cambridge, Mass.: Harvard University Press, 1958; Gresham M. Sykes, *Society of Captives,* Princeton, N. J.: Princeton University Press, 1958; Fritz R. Roethlisberger and William J. Dickson, *Management and the Worker,* Cambridge, Mass.: Harvard University Press, 1939.

tion what should not be separated in practice. Therefore we now consider two data-gathering techniques: participant observation and surveys. We shall then discuss the place of the experiment in sociological research and the mutual dependence of theory and research.

Participant Observation. The **participant observer** has a role in the community or organization he studies; it is from this vantage point he observes other role players facing everyday situations. He talks with them and obtains their interpretation of events. [24] Thus he gains intimate "knowledge of acquaintance" concerning the interactive system under study. A classic illustration of participant observation was a report on an Italian slum community in the years from 1936 to 1940.[25] The author, William Foote Whyte, was then a Junior Fellow at Harvard University. He lived in the North End of Boston for three and a half years, "hung" on street corners with a group of unemployed young men in their twenties, and learned Italian, to communicate better with the older generation. In short, he became a member of the community in order to describe it firsthand. The result is a marvelously perceptive account of corner boys and, to a lesser extent, college boys, as well as of racketeers and politicians, all observed at close range over a period of several years. Since Whyte was a one-man research staff, what is missing from the book is whatever a 23-year-old graduate student was not in a good position to observe, such as family life. Participant-observation at its best provides deep insights, but it cannot deal systematically with all aspects of community life or with all levels of a large organization. The weakness of participant-observation is that the researcher must participate and observe in the role he has defined for himself in the interactive system. Sometimes this is a serious handicap.

Surveys of Population Characteristics. In order to understand how a society works, the sociologist should know something about the characteristics of the population and about recurring events that affect the population. Fortunately for him, births, deaths, marriages, accidents, immigration, emigration, and other such events are subject to official registration. Hence the sociologist can discover, relatively easily and cheaply, the level of birth and death rates in a particular society, the trends in marriage and divorce, and so forth. Fortunately also, every industrial nation, in the course of enumerating the population, collects statistical data of great interest to the sociologist. Thus the United States Bureau of the Census makes a decennial count of the American people as required by the Constitution for determining the representation of each state in the House of Representatives. But the information gathered in the 1960 census, for example, went far beyond the simple enumeration contemplated in the Constitution. The age, sex, and marital composition of the population, its relative distribution between rural and urban areas, its educational attainment and occupational characteristics, its income, its household arrangements, its na-

[24] Howard S. Becker, "Problems of Inference and Proof in Participant Observation," *American Sociological Review,* Vol. 23, December 1958, p. 652.

[25] William Foote Whyte, *Street Corner Society: The Social Structure of an Italian Slum,* 2nd ed., Chicago: University of Chicago Press, 1955.

tional and racial origins, all these data and more were carefully collected in April 1960 by thousands of specially trained enumerators. Tables 2.2, 2.3, and 2.4 come from the wealth of information tabulated from the 1960 **census** by means of high-speed computers and published by the Bureau of the Census.

Table 2.2 shows the age distribution of the American population in 1960 (for each sex separately). Taken by itself, Table 2.2 is not too enlightening — although it does reflect the higher mortality rates of males as compared with females. The ratio of males under 15 to females under 15 is 103.4, whereas the ratio of males 65 and over to females of the same age is 82.8. But Table 2.2 can be compared with other data. Thus a backward look at statistics from previous censuses shows that the **median** age of the American population has almost doubled in a century and a half.

Table 2.3, like Table 2.2, is of most interest when viewed in comparative perspective. That nearly 70 per cent of the American population lived in **urban places** in 1960 becomes more significant when one recalls that only 5.1 per cent of the population was classified as urban in the census of 1790. Or, to

TABLE 2.2

Male and Female Population of the United States, by Age, 1960

Ages	Males		Females	
	Number	Percentage	Number	Percentage
Under 5 years	10,339,475	11.7	9,982,389	11.0
5 to 9 years	9,448,557	10.7	9,170,588	10.1
10 to 14 years	8,562,507	9.7	8,253,463	9.1
15 to 19 years	6,698,833	7.6	6,588,606	7.2
20 to 24 years	5,283,228	6.0	5,519,941	6.1
25 to 29 years	5,333,271	6.0	5,537,115	6.1
30 to 34 years	5,840,287	6.6	6,111,422	6.7
35 to 39 years	6,089,776	6.9	6,418,540	7.1
40 to 44 years	5,649,404	6.4	5,917,812	6.5
45 to 49 years	5,374,935	6.1	5,553,943	6.1
50 to 54 years	4,764,728	5.4	4,931,770	5.4
55 to 59 years	4,184,653	4.7	4,411,294	4.8
60 to 64 years	3,384,493	3.8	3,727,404	4.1
65 to 69 years	2,883,429	3.3	3,303,334	3.6
70 to 74 years	2,138,977	2.4	2,522,159	2.8
75 years and over	2,286,560	2.6	3,072,778	3.4
Total, all ages	88,303,113	100.0	91,022,558	100.0
Median age[a]	28.5		30.4	

[a] The median is the value that divides the distribution into two equal parts — one-half of the cases falling below this value and one-half exceeding this value.

Source: Bureau of the Census, *U.S. Census of Population: 1960, United States Summary, General Social and Economic Characteristics,* Final Report PC(1)-1C, Washington, D.C.: Government Printing Office, 1962, pp. 199-200.

TABLE 2.3

Urban and Rural Population of the United States, by Size of Place, 1960

Size of Urban and Rural Places	Population	
	Number (in thousands)	Percentage
Urban total	125,269	69.9
Places of 1,000,000 or more	17,484	9.8
Places of 500,000 to 1,000,000	11,111	6.2
Places of 250,000 to 500,000	10,766	6.0
Places of 100,000 to 250,000	11,652	6.5
Places of 50,000 to 100,000	13,836	7.7
Places of 25,000 to 50,000	14,951	8.3
Places of 10,000 to 25,000	17,568	9.8
Places of 5,000 to 10,000	9,780	5.5
Places of 2,500 to 5,000	7,580	4.2
Places under 2,500	690	0.4
Unincorporated parts of urbanized places	9,851	5.5
Rural total	54,054	30.1
Places of 1,000 to 2,500	6,497	3.6
Places under 1,000	3,894	2.6
Other rural	43,664	24.3
United States total	179,323	100.0

Source: U.S. Bureau of the Census, *Statistical Abstract of the United States: 1962,* Washington, D.C.: Government Printing Office, 1962, p. 21.

make a contemporary comparison, only 17 per cent of the population of India was classified as urban in the census of 1951.[26]

Table 2.4 is more complicated than either Table 2.2 or Table 2.3. Table 2.4 does not refer to the entire American population, only to persons 25 years old or older. The explanation for this lies in the type of data being presented. The data in Table 2.4 are being used to show the comparative educational attainment of whites and nonwhites. It would confuse the issue to include persons whose educations are not yet completed (children). The selection of 25 years was made in order to separate those persons whose educations are presumably complete from those whose educations are still in process. Why 25 years? Some people continue their educations beyond the age of 25. If data are to be presented bearing on the educational attainment of Americans, however, *some definite* age must be chosen or else the issue will be hopelessly confused. The object is to select an age by which most people have completed their educations but that is still young enough to catch those whose educations have been

[26] *Demographic Yearbook of the United Nations, 1952,* New York: Statistical Office of the United Nations, 1952, p. 11.

TABLE 2.4

Years of School Completed by Persons Age 25 and Over, by Color, 1960

Years of School Completed	Whites		Nonwhites[a]	
	Number (in thousands)	Percentage	Number (in thousands)	Percentage
Less than 5 years	5,989	6.7	2,314	23.4
5 to 7 years	11,451	12.8	2,303	23.4
8 years	16,179	18.1	1,264	12.8
9 to 11 years	17,274	19.3	1,842	18.7
12 years	23,100	25.7	1,356	13.8
13 to 15 years	8,311	9.3	431	4.4
16 years or more	7,278	8.1	347	3.5
Total, all educational levels	89,581	100.0	9,857	100.0
Median school years completed	10.9		8.2	

[a] In 1960 the decennial census counted 18,871,831 Negroes and 1,619,612 nonwhites other than Negroes. Thus the comparison between whites and nonwhites is, for practical purposes, a Negro-white comparison.

Source: Bureau of the Census, *Statistical Abstract of the United States: 1962,* Washington, D.C.: Government Printing Office, 1962, p. 117.

completed quite recently. No doubt Census Bureau experts spent many hundreds of hours on this decision when questions on educational attainment were added to the census schedule in 1940.

Table 2.4 clearly demonstrates that *white* Americans receive, on the average, more years of formal education than *nonwhite* Americans. The median years of school completed by whites were 10.9 years in 1960 as compared with 8.2 years completed by nonwhites. Or, to express the same point another way, a majority of the nonwhites (59.6 per cent) got no further than grade school as contrasted with a minority of whites (37.6 per cent). This does not mean, of course, that *all* whites were better educated in 1960 than nonwhites. The two **frequency distributions** of educational attainment overlapped considerably. Thus the 7.9 per cent of the nonwhites with some college had *more* education than all but 17.4 per cent of the whites. Table 2.4 gives no hint as to the reasons for the differences between the races in educational attainment.

Important as the decennial census is as a source of basic population data, the ten-year intervals between censuses is a serious disadvantage not only to sociologists but also to government agencies and private businesses needing up-to-date population information. For instance, the President's Council of Economic Advisers and the Department of Labor require *monthly* estimates of unemployment. But it is impractical to conduct a complete population census every month. Not only is a census expensive; equally important, it takes many months to tabulate the results of millions of separate schedules. In 1940 the

Bureau of the Census solved this problem by establishing the Current Population Survey.

The Current Population Survey is a monthly **survey** of about 35,000 American households (containing about 80,000 persons 14 years old and over.[27] The strategy of the Survey is to use this tiny sample to give accurate estimates of hours worked during a given calendar week by the American labor force, the length of time the unemployed have been looking for work, and other aspects of American occupational activity. How can such a small sample represent the entire American labor force? The sample is so shrewdly drawn from the universe of American households that the discrepancy between its values and the values of the larger universe (the sample error) is negligible. Statisticians explain that a *random* sample has a known probability of error — just as an evenly balanced coin has a known probability of coming up "heads." Since we assume that extremely improbable events do not happen, some question would be raised about the balance of the coins (or the honesty of the tosser) if 50 coins in sequence turned up "heads." In the same way, it is extremely unlikely for the estimate of unemployment based on the Current Population Survey to differ by more than 1 per cent from the true percentage of unemployment in the United States.

The mathematical basis of random sampling is well established. Agricultural research, quality control in industry, and various branches of the physical and biological sciences use statistical theory for the design of experiments. But the application of random sampling to survey research on human populations presents special problems. A sample of people has the option of refusing to cooperate. Yet the basic requirement of random sampling is that each member of the population under investigation *has an equal chance of appearing in the sample.*

If suspicious, uncooperative individuals have less chance of appearing in the sample than friendly members of the population, it is no longer a random sample. Similarly, if people who are not at home when the field researcher calls are eliminated from the sample, the sample is biased in favor of those who spend more time at home. These considerations make clear that a random sample, far from being a *casual* collection of representatives of a larger universe, must be drawn from the universe in a rigorous fashion. It is not easy to obtain a random sample. A **quota-control sample** — in which interviewers stand on street corners or knock on convenient doors until they get so many men and so many women of certain ages, educational levels, and incomes — is not a random sample. If the quotas are filled in Newark, New Jersey, at 3 P.M., persons who happen to live in rural Kentucky at the time do not have much opportunity to be included in the sample. Quotas guarantee that the sample contains persons representative of the parent universe with respect to characteristics controlled by quotas, such as age, sex, educational attainment, income. Whether

[27] Daniel B. Levine and Charles B. Nam, "The Current Population Survey: Methods, Content, and Sociological Uses," *American Sociological Review,* Vol. 27, August 1962, pp. 585-590.

the sample is representative of the parent universe with respect to character-istics *not* controlled by quotas is another matter. The laws of probability are no help unless the sample is a random one.

Even if the sample is a random one, statistical readings derived from any sample—for instance, the median—are likely to differ slightly from the true values of the population. These differences are called **sampling errors.** It would be a mistake to infer from the existence of sampling errors that the results of the Current Population Survey are less trustworthy than the results of the decennial census. The accuracy of the Current Population Survey may be *greater* than the accuracy of the decennial census because other errors in the decennial census, errors resulting from field operations, are probably larger than the sampling error of the Survey. Consider the errors attributable to over-looked persons and to faulty communication between the enumerator and the respondent:

1. **Underenumeration.** In the hectic couple of weeks in April of a census year, every man, woman, and child is supposed to be enumerated. However, the population of an industrial society moves about; it does not stand still wait-ing for the census taker. As a result, some people are enumerated twice and others are not counted at all. The Census Bureau estimated that 1,309,000 people were overenumerated in 1950 and 3,400,000 people were under-enumerated out of a total population of 152,788,000—a net underenumera-tion of 2,091,000 people. Underenumeration does not occur uniformly throughout the population. Certain categories of persons are more likely to be missed than others. For example, newborn infants sometimes are missed, apparently because they are not yet thought of as residents of the household. Thus the 1950 census reported 3,146,948 children under 1 year; 10 years later the 1960 census reported 3,481,131 children between 10 and 11. Since these were essentially the same children enumerated at different ages, underenumeration of infants had occured.

2. **Response error.** Communication between the enumerator and the re-spondent may be faulty. The respondent may misunderstand the enumera-tor's question or the enumerator may misunderstand the respondent's answer. The enumerator may forget to ask a question he was supposed to ask. Or he may record an answer incorrectly. Although it is difficult to esti-mate the magnitude of these various response errors on the decennial census, it is certain that they are greater than response errors on the Current Population Survey. The research workers conducting field work for the Current Population Survey are full-time, permanent employees of the Census Bureau with extensive training and experience, whereas the census enu-merators are temporary workers, sometimes recruited through political con-nections. The short training course the enumerators receive prevents the most serious blunders, but it is no substitute for professional commitment to the survey task.

Strictly speaking, it is not correct to say that the Current Population Survey is a random sample of the American population. Random samples of human populations are almost impossible to obtain: refusal to cooperate on the part of some members of the sample destroys the randomness of the sample, as does the inability of interviewers to locate designated members of the sample. Leaving some people out of the sample or substituting others who are easier to locate violates the mathematical assumptions of random sampling. And unless the sample is random, the characteristics of the universe from which it is drawn cannot be estimated with a known probability of error. The Current Population Survey, like surveys conducted by the National Opinion Research Center of the University of Chicago and the Survey Research Center of the University of Michigan, uses an approximation of random sampling called **area sampling.** Area sampling substitutes a random sample of dwelling units for a random sample of Americans. This assumption is only approximately correct; some Americans have several dwellings, and some luckless ones have none. It is correct enough for practical purposes.

Area sampling on a national scale is very expensive. Recall that the Current Population Survey obtains interviews from 35,000 households every month. The more widely scattered these households are among the 3000 counties of the United States, the more traveling the interviewers must do for each interview, and the more expensive the survey becomes. In order to economize on time and money, the Census Bureau *stratifies* the sample of the Current Population Survey. This means that instead of visiting all 3000 counties, interviewers go to only 638 counties and independent cities for their sample. For instance, instead of sending interviewers to all of the cities with over 100,000 population in 1960, the Current Population Survey might select by a strictly random procedure 25 cities to represent all of the 132 cities of that size. Within each city selected, some neighborhoods might be selected by a similar random process so that interviewers would not have to go to all neighborhoods in each of the 25 cities. Finally, households would be randomly selected from neighborhoods. A weighting procedure is necessary at the end of a survey employing stratified sampling because stratification allows some cases to represent others not given an opportunity to appear in the sample. Thus data from the 25 cities would have to be weighted by the proportion of the American population not just in those 25 cities but in all 132 cities with over 100,000 population.

This ability of a **stratified sample** to give different weight to different portions of the universe sometimes achieves a more important economy than the saving of travel for interviewers. Bear in mind that the researcher can select the strata on bases other than geography. If he knows enough about subgroups within a heterogeneous population, he may choose to divide the universe into relatively homogeneous strata. Just as in the geographic type of stratified sampling, he selects random samples from each of the subpopulations and weights the data from each stratum in proportion to its size. But this type of stratified sampling obtains the same level of accuracy in estimating the true characteristics of the universe *with a much smaller sample* than would be necessary with simple random sampling. How this important economy is possible can be made clearer by a specific example.

Suppose the Health Department of a university needed to know the average height of its students. There are 4000 students attending the university. If an alphabetical list of all the students were available, a researcher could select every *twentieth* name, find out the heights of each of these students from health records, and compute the average height of students in the 5 per cent sample. Since the sample is a random one, the sample average would be a good estimate of the average for the total university population, which is 20 times as large. The sampling procedure, however, disregards at least two known facts: (1) the university contains female students as well as males, and (2) the average height of females is several inches less than the average height of males. Consider how these facts might be utilized to reduce the size of the sample *without sacrificing the accuracy of the sample estimate*. The researcher selects every *fiftieth* name and obtains the heights from health records as before. This time, however, the girls are separated from the boys and the average height is computed for each sex separately.

Even though a 2.5 per cent sample is smaller than a 5 per cent sample, it may be just as good. The smaller sample attempts two relatively easy tasks, estimating the average heights of boys and estimating the average heights of girls, whereas the larger sample attempts a more difficult task, estimating the heights of all students taken together. The latter task is more difficult, as Fig. 2.1 shows, because the variation of heights around the average height for all students is far greater than the variation around the average height for boys or the variation around the average height for girls. From the estimates of the average height for boys and the average height for girls, it is a simple matter to compute the average height for all students at the university. The girls' average is multi-

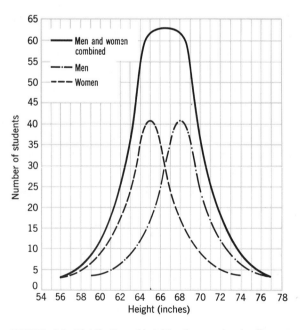

FIGURE 2.1 **Distribution of heights of a sample of college-age men and women.**

plied by the female enrollment at the university, the boys' average by the male enrollment at the university. Both are added and the sum is divided by the total enrollment.

This explanation of stratified sampling illustrates the underlying principle — even though the content is unrealistic. It simplifies the exposition to discuss the heights of males and females rather than the employment status of persons in rural and urban counties. A second inadequacy of this explanation is its avoidance of precise statistical concepts (like **variance**). Students with sufficient mathematical or statistical training will find a more rigorous treatment of stratified sampling in Leslie Kish, "Selection of the Sample" (in Leon Festinger and Daniel Katz, eds., *Research Methods in the Behavioral Sciences,* New York: Dryden, 1953).

RESEARCH DESIGN: THE EXPERIMENT AND ITS APPROXIMATIONS

The research ideal of science is experimentation. An experiment enables the researcher to investigate the effect of Factor *A* on Factor *B* while excluding the effects of all other potentially confounding factors. Insofar as sociologists have scientific aspirations, they yearn to use controlled experiments in their investigations.[28] Often, however, it is not feasible to set up artificially the conditions required to test a hypothesis. For example, consider the hypothesis that broken homes are more likely than intact homes to produce juvenile delinquents. In order to test this hypothesis in the classical experimental manner, it would be necessary to select (by some random procedure) two populations of infants, to break up the homes of infants in the experimental group, to let alone the homes of infants in the **control group,** and, after some years pass, to observe carefully the comparative incidence of delinquency in the two groups. From a technical point of view, this would be a rigorous experiment, but neither the sociologist nor the general public wants to pay the price (in human suffering) of manufacturing broken homes.

Does this mean that the relationship between broken homes and delinquency cannot be investigated? Instead of contriving an experiment to test the connection between broken homes and delinquency, the sociologist can let the experiment conduct itself. Some homes break up naturally; others do not. Some children become delinquent; others do not. The researcher can observe how many delinquents come from broken homes and how many from intact homes even though he had nothing to do with producing the broken homes. This is called a **natural experiment.** Natural experiments are often used to test

[28] Samuel A. Stouffer, "Some Observations on Study Design," *American Journal of Sociology,* Vol. 55, January 1950, pp. 355-361.

hypotheses relating one social variable to another. Sociologists are not alone in using natural experiments. Astronomers cannot manipulate the orbits of planets or stars; hence they also depend on natural experiments. There is no use pretending that the natural experiment is fully equivalent to the **contrived experiment;** it is not. But the natural experiment is often the sociologist's best approximation to controlled observation.

Table 2.5 illustrates the strengths and weaknesses of natural experiments. It presents a tabulation of responses from undergraduates from 11 universities to a question about cheating on examinations. This tabulation was made to explore the possibility that fraternity membership may be conducive to cheating. The percentage of admitted cheaters among *fraternity* members is greater than the percentage of admitted cheaters among *independent* students in all five years. Does this mean that fraternities somehow encourage cheating? Perhaps boys more likely to cheat are also more likely to join fraternities. Or perhaps boys more likely to tell the truth on anonymous questionnaires are more likely to join fraternities. In either case, it is a weakness of the study that the experimental group (fraternity members) and the control group (independents) *selected themselves.* The researcher cannot say with assurance that these groups were precisely the same before joining fraternities. Moreover, if the groups were different with respect to financial resources, religious affiliations, or values, perhaps these differences account for the greater tendency of fraternity members to confess to cheating. A *contrived* experiment would not be open to such questions. If, for the purposes of the experiment, entering freshmen at these 11 universities had been randomly allocated to fraternities or to the independent group, probability theory would guarantee that initial differences were minimal.

Actually, statistical techniques exist for coping with the **self-selection** problem in natural experiments. If it turns out that fraternity members come from higher socioeconomic levels, on the average, than independents, the researcher can separate both fraternity members and independents by socioeconomic level and make the fraternity-independent comparison separately for two (or more) socioeconomic levels. Thus it is possible to accomplish by statistical manipulation what has not been done in the real world: to make the experimental and control groups initially comparable.

Helpful though statistical procedures are, they do not solve the problem completely. **Statistical control** is only possible if the researcher is aware of a potentially confounding characteristic and sets out to control it. If a confounding characteristic exists and he does not happen to consider it, its uncontrolled variation is free to mislead him. When individuals have been randomly allocated to experimental and control groups, **probability theory** guarantees that the two groups are initially alike with respect to all characteristics, whether the researcher is aware of them or not. This problem does not exist for the contrived experiment.

Table 2.5 does not directly address this problem of the initial comparability of fraternity members and independent students. Instead it tabulates the

TABLE 2.5

The Percentage of Fraternity and of Independent Students Who Admit Having Cheated on Examinations, by Year in College

Year in College	Students Who Admit Having Cheated More Than Once (Percentage)	
	Fraternity Members	Independent Students
First	15 (178)[a]	12 (498)
Second	24 (255)	16 (375)
Third	30 (320)	22 (437)
Fourth	32 (306)	23 (440)
Fifth	42 (49)	31 (48)

[a] The figures in parentheses are the bases on which each percentage was computed. Excluded from these bases are 6 fraternity members and 11 independent students who could not be classified as to year in college, as well as 52 students who could not be classified according to fraternity membership.

Source: Rose K. Goldsen et al., *What College Students Think*, Princeton, N.J.: Van Nostrand, 1960, p. 79. The data were derived from questionnaires administered anonymously to students at 11 universities.

data by class in college. The small difference in the percentages of freshman fraternity members and of freshman independent students who admit to having cheated suggests that whatever *initial* differences existed between the two groups have little effect on the propensity to cheat. The fact that the differences between fraternity men and independents are *greater* in the sophomore and later years suggests that fraternity membership somehow makes for cheating. The data could, however, have supported the hypothesis much more strongly. There could have been *no* difference between fraternity men and independents in the freshman year and a progressive increase in the difference from the second to the fifth year. Knowledge of statistics and specifically the ability to use **tests of significance** helps the researcher to decide what data like those in Table 2.5 prove.

What the Experiment Proves: The Use of Tests of Significance. The purpose of a test of significance is to give the researcher some perspective on differences he discovers in various samples. In this case, the researcher wants to know whether fraternity membership makes for cheating. Table 2.5 reveals that 15 per cent of freshmen who were fraternity members and 12 per cent of independent freshmen admitted having cheated more than once on examinations. Should the researcher get excited about this 3 per cent difference, or should he dismiss it as a chance variation? Tests of significance enable the researcher to compute the precise probability that differences of specified size arise by chance. In Table 2.5, for instance, the question at issue is: Are fraternity members and independent students essentially similar in their disposition to cheat or are they essentially different? Or, as the statistician would put it, are they from the same universe or from different universes? For the freshman year, there are two samples, one of 178 fraternity members, one of 498 independents. A test of significance can tell the researcher whether, with samples of those sizes, the 3 per cent difference could have arisen by chance from a population in which fraternity members and independents were indistinguishable regarding cheating behavior. If the test of significance reveals a probability of less than five chances in a hundred that random samples from a single population would have differed by as much as 3 per cent, the researcher may reject the hypothesis of no difference between fraternity men and independents. (That is to say, he *disproves* the hypothesis of their similarity rather than *proving* their dissimilarity.) Or he may insist on a one in a hundred probability before he is willing to reject what statisticians call the **null hypothesis.** The null hypothesis is the hypothesis that no difference exists between the two (or more) groups under consideration. Once the null hypothesis has been rejected (disproved), the researcher has some confidence, although not certainty, that he is talking about a real difference rather than an illusory one. The next — and more difficult — step is to explain it.

It is, of course, an arbitrary decision as to how small the probability must be before the researcher assumes that the difference could not have arisen by chance. Most commonly, statisticians use the 5 per cent and the 1 per cent levels. To say that a difference is "significant at the .01 level" is a short way to say, "The chances are only one in a hundred that such a difference could have arisen as a result of random sampling from a single population."

Even if the 3 per cent difference were significant at the .05 level or less, which it is not, the researcher could not yet say that freshmen with fraternity affiliations differed from independent freshmen in cheating tendencies. Bear in mind that the statistical basis for tests of significance is random sampling. Suppose that the chances of a fraternity member filling out a questionnaire were not the same as the chances of an independent filling out a questionnaire. If a smaller proportion of fraternity members than of independents filled out questionnaires, this would violate the conditions of random sampling and would therefore invalidate the inference from the test of significance. Possibly the fraternity members less prone to cheat failed for some reason to fill out questionnaires, thus accounting for the observed difference.

This discussion of natural experiments should not be taken to mean that contrived experiments are unknown in sociology. Efforts are frequently made to reduce prejudice, to prevent delinquency, to improve morale, and so on. On the rare occasions that these efforts are systematically evaluated, a contrived experiment adds to the sociological literature. Needless to say, the value of such experiments does not depend on a demonstration that the goal of the action program was fulfilled. Sometimes the failure of the experimental group to differ from the control group has important implications. For instance, between 1924 and 1927 researchers from Harvard University and the Western Electric Company conducted at the Hawthorne works of the Company a variety of controlled experiments in order to discover whether higher levels of illumination would result in higher productivity.[29] At first the researchers were jubilant because productivity rose in the experimental groups. But it rose in the control groups also. Furthermore, *decreases* in illumination to a point considerably below ordinary levels in the main shop did not bring productivity down. The experiments had failed to show that level of illumination was an important variable in productivity. But the by-product of this failure was the discovery that *human relations* within the work group could enormously affect morale and, indirectly, productivity.

This discovery was not made quickly, although it may seem obvious in retrospect. A world-famous physiologist, Lawrence J. Henderson, was part of the research team, and his initial interest was in such variables as monotony and fatigue. But he and his colleagues, Elton Mayo and Thomas Whitehead, had the intellectual integrity to recognize a variable that had not been built into the experiment. The six girls who had been selected to work in the specially organized relay-assembly room:[30]

> . . . knew that they were taking part in what was considered an important and interesting experiment. They knew that their work was expected to produce results—they were not sure what results—which would lead to the improvement of the working conditions of their fellow employees. They knew that the eyes of the company were upon them. . . . In the regular department, the girls, like the other employees, were in the position of responding to changes the source and purpose of which were beyond their knowledge. In the test room, they had frequent interviews with the superintendent, a high officer of the company. The reasons for the contemplated experimental changes were explained to them. Their views were consulted and in some instances they were allowed to veto what had been proposed.

The improved morale resulted from the employees' feeling of participation in an important experiment, not from the specific changes made. Not only were high officials of the company concerned about their reactions; so were important Harvard professors. When their morale improved, the rate at which they assembled relays increased. Improvement of the morale of a group as a result of participating in an exciting experiment has occurred many times since the experiments at the Hawthorne works of the Western Electric Company. Many researchers take pains to design their experiments so as to distinguish between the effects of the variable being tested and an unintended "Hawthorne effect"—much as medical researchers include placebo doses in testing the curative properties of a new drug.

The failure of physiologically oriented experiments on worker productivity opened the eyes of the Harvard Business School researchers to social factors. This new turn which their investigations took proved rewarding. As a result, descriptions of the Western Electric researchers are usually eulogies, and it is

[29] Roethlisberger and Dickson, *Management and the Worker,* pp. 14-18.

[30] George C. Homans, "The Western Electric Researches," in *Fatigue of Workers: Its Relations to Industrial Production,* New York: Reinhold, 1941, Chap. 4.

not always remembered how the later achievements were built on initial failures. The word **serendipity** is used to describe "the fairly common experience of observing an unanticipated, anomalous and strategic datum which becomes the occasion for developing a new theory or for extending an existing theory."[31] Many important discoveries, including that of the drug penicillin, were serendipitous. Unfortunately, not every researcher has the flexibility to recognize the importance of unanticipated results, to distinguish between an experimental failure that is a dead-end and one that opens new vistas.

THE MUTUAL DEPENDENCE OF SOCIOLOGICAL THEORY AND SOCIOLOGICAL RESEARCH

Some people think of science as preoccupied with the collection of facts. If this conception were correct, the Chicago telephone directory would be the greatest scientific achievement of the twentieth century—2347 pages of names, addresses, and telephone numbers, alphabetically organized, four columns to the page. Despite the fabulous amount of time and painstaking effort that goes into the Chicago telephone directory, it is *not* regarded as monumental research. It has no relevance for a body of theory.

Scientifically important research is research that helps to define the fundamental units of the subject or the relationship among them. In other words, it contributes to the development of improved theories of what is going on. Therefore, sociology, for the very reason that it has scientific aspirations, cannot allow facts about interaction to pile up without attempting to set them in a theoretical framework. Human interaction is such an inclusive subject that almost any inquiry about human relations could be called sociological research. But sociological *theory* provides criteria for judging the value of sociological *research*. Do the facts discovered by the research suggest a *new* way of conceptualizing the processes of interaction that will be more fruitful? Although much research falls short of this ideal, a theoretical implication is, nevertheless, the criterion of important research.

Sometimes all of the theoretical implications of a piece of research are not grasped by the person who carries it out. More often, the theoretical implication can be grasped only when the results of two or more researchers are juxtaposed. Since research is customarily reported in the professional journals and in monographs, other members of the profession are in as good a position to perceive the theoretical implication of several independent research projects as are the researchers themselves. That is to say, it is possible to make signifi-

[31] Robert K. Merton, *Social Theory and Social Structure*, rev. ed., Glencoe, Ill.: Free Press, 1957, p. 104.

cant theoretical contributions, which is the ultimate goal of research, without engaging in direct research at all.

Thus sociological research gains its significance by helping to clarify sociological theory. On the other hand, sociological theory is crucial to the formulation of worthwhile research designs. The Chillicothe study of the effect of different conceptions of the marital relationships on the probability of divorce illustrates this point. The researcher needed more than an interest in divorce to organize his research. He needed a conception of marriage as a small interactive system consisting of complementary roles. Such a conception must have suggested to him the possibility that husbands and wives might fail to define these roles in the same way. Lack of attitude consensus might be reflected in overt disagreements, possibly leading to divorce. He also needed a conception of sampling to guide him in the selection of married and divorced couples. Finally, he probably needed a conception of social causation in terms of which he would assess the effect of an **independent variable (dissensus** about role conceptions) on an **intervening variable** (marital disharmony) and ultimately on a **dependent variable** (divorce). Once the researcher formulated the problem in this way, the development of questions to ask the husbands and wives was merely a chore to be completed through hard work. Locating the husbands and wives, getting them to agree to cooperate, and conducting the actual interviews similarly became a matter of putting in the time and effort. In short, the researcher's familiarity with sociological theory sensitized him to aspects of the problem he would otherwise have missed — or would not have known how to build into his scheme for data collection and analysis.

Theory and research are mutually dependent. Each helps the other. The rest of this book, like most introductory textbooks in sociology, is concerned mainly with theory. Research will be reported when it is necessary to explicate the concepts and the substantive propositions held by contemporary sociologists. In his respect, an introductory textbook has quite a different flavor from *The American Sociological Review, The British Journal of Sociology,* or *Acta Sociologica* (the journal published by Scandinavian sociologists); the professional journals assume that readers are acquainted with sociological theory and emphasize research reports.

CONCLUSION

The origins of sociology are diverse; intellectual debts are owed to history, philosophy, political theory, and economics as well as to religiously inspired humanitarianism and secular reform movements. Nevertheless, the direction of contemporary sociology is away from the traditions out of which the field emerged. Theorists like Talcott Parsons and organizers of huge research projects like Samuel A. Stouffer share this scientific approach to sociology. Such an approach is anathema to many intellectuals who vacillate between denying that science is applicable to human behavior and protesting that social science leads directly to the evil society depicted by George Orwell in his novel *1984*.[32] Sociological studies are increasingly concerned with both methodological sophistication and implications for systematic theory. The objective is to work back and forth between empirical data and descriptive concepts until a system of variables is developed capable of analyzing the complexities of even the most intricate interactive systems.

The guiding norm of research studies is objectivity. Thus the speculations of social philosophers, though often insightful, arouse little enthusiasm in a scientifically oriented sociologist. He is more attracted by the testability of a hypothesis than by its plausibility. He is less interested in the history of sociology than in keeping up with current journals. He is more likely to want to improve his ability in mathematics and statistics than to master a new foreign language. Some of the main types of empirical research currently being done by scientifically oriented sociologists are interaction studies, role studies, and community studies. Also described in this chapter were techniques of data gathering (participant observation and surveys) and of research design (the experiment). Perhaps more important than the details of how sociological research is conducted is the scientific spirit in which it is carried out, a spirit in which research is not an end in itself but a means of improving theories of what is going on in the interactive world.

SOME SIGNIFICANT LITERATURE ON SOCIOLOGICAL RESEARCH

Allen H. Barton and Paul F. Lazarsfeld, "Some Functions of Qualitative Analysis in Social Research," *Frankfurter Beitrage zur Sociologie,* Vol. 1, 1955, pp. 321-361, reprinted in Seymour Martin Lipset and Neil J. Smelser, *Sociology: The Progress of a Decade,* Englewood Cliffs, N.J.: Prentice-Hall, 1961, pp. 95-122. These two distinguished social researchers examined 100 studies in which investigators analyzed *qualitative* rather than *quantitative* data. They sought to contribute, on the basis of current research practice, a tentative answer to the following question: "What can a researcher do when confronted by a body of qualitative data—detailed, concrete, nonmetric descriptions of people and events, drawn from direct observation, interviews, case studies, historical writings, the writings of participants?" They found that qualitative data can, in the early stages of the investigation of a problem, contribute to the formulation of the problem, to classification of variables, and to hypotheses relating one variable to another. Qualitative observation can also provide support for large-scale, wide-ranging theories not amenable to quantitative testing, for example, theories of social change. Here qualitative data are " . . . more than simply illustration, but less than definitive proof."

[32] Bennett M. Berger, "Sociology and the Intellectuals: An Analysis of Stereotype," *Antioch Review,* Vol. 17, September 1957, pp. 275-290.

Harold Garfinkel, *Studies in Ethnomethodology,* Englewood Cliffs, N.J.: Prentice-Hall, 1967. The author of this book and his colleagues in the ethnomethodology tradition seek to make explicit the implicit understandings that underlie a social order. Garfinkel does this by studies that call these understandings into question. For example, he instructed his students to question remarks that are not usually questioned. The following is what happened in one case (page 44):

> The victim waved his hand cheerily.
> (Subject) How are you?
> (Experimenter) How am I in regard to what? My health, my finances, my school work, my peace of mind, my. . . ?
> (Subject) (Red in the face and suddenly out of control.) Look! I was just trying to be polite. Frankly, I don't give a damn how you are.

In another study students were instructed to spend fifteen minutes to an hour in their homes as though they were strangers to the household, thus making explicit (through contrast with more usual interaction) their personal understandings with parents and siblings and their accustomed handling of furniture and silverware. In still another study the student was instructed to violate the expectations of a person with whom he was having an ordinary conversation by bringing his nose so close it almost touched that of the unwitting subject. Ethnomethodological studies raise questions about what nearly everybody, including sociologists, take for granted and, by questioning, enable us to perceive the world from a fresh perspective. Thus Garfinkel reports in detail the perspective on the female role of an individual raised as a male until the age of nineteen who underwent a series of operations to change him into a biological female. What other females learned imperceptibly over two decades, Agnes had to learn quickly and consciously.

Travis Hirschi and Hanan C. Selvin, *Delinquency Research: An Appraisal of Analytic Methods,* New York: Free Press, 1967. This book is initially concerned with the methodological virtues and defects of sociological studies of delinquency published in the 1960s. But its relevance is by no means limited to delinquency research. It is a guide to the analysis of quantitative sociological data — and incidentally a set of essays on methodological topics. For example, Chapter 3, "Principles of Causal Analysis," illustrates through a reanalysis of published studies of delinquency the three points that must be proven in order to maintain that A is the cause of B:

1. A and B are statistically associated.
2. A is causally *prior* to B.
3. The association between A and B does not disappear when the effect of other variables causally prior to both of the original variables are removed.

In short, Hirschi and Selvin utilize actual studies in a narrowly delimited field of sociology (delinquency research) to teach students to be better analysts of quantitative data. For a discussion of methodological training in sociology, see Hanan C. Selvin, "The Teaching of Sociological Methodology in the United States of America," *International Social Science Journal,* Vol. 15, No. 4, 1963, pp. 597-615.

Herbert Hyman, *Survey Design and Analysis: Principles, Cases and Procedures,* Glencoe, Ill.: Free Press, 1955. This volume is a product of the Columbia University Planning Project for Advanced Training in Social Research. Since Columbia is a major center of graduate instruction in sociology that includes a quasicommercial social research organization, the Bureau of Applied Social Research, the book offers a bird's-eye view of what the professional sociologist ought to know about survey research. One axis on which the book turns is the distinction between descriptive and explanatory surveys. Whereas the objective of descriptive surveys is to categorize a population as precisely as possible, the objective of explanatory surveys is to relate one variable to another and, in particular, to find out whether factor *A* is a cause of factor *B*. This summary is based on a review by Edward A. Suchman, *American Sociological Review,* Vol. 21, April 1956, pp. 232-233.

Herbert H. Hyman, William J. Cobb, Jacob J. Feldman, Clyde W. Hart, and Charles H. Stember, *Interviewing in Social Research,* Chicago: University of Chicago Press, 1954. This book is concerned with an important source of error in survey research: communication failure between the interviewer and the respondent. A leading survey organization, the National Opinion Research Center, brought data from its own files to bear on this problem as well as examining the survey research literature. Communication failure results from a variety of sources: (1) The interviewer expects certain responses because he assumes consistency within a particular frame of reference. (2) The interviewer expects certain responses because he assumes people in a certain category will give them. (3) The interviewer interacts with the respondent in the interview situation in such a way as to influence the response. (4) Lack of structure in the interviewing situation permits responses irrelevant to the purposes of the study. These and other sources of interviewer bias may be offset partially, although probably not completely, by better methods of selection, training, and supervision of interviewers. This summary is based on a review by Charles E. Bowerman, *American Sociological Review,* Vol. 20, June 1955, pp. 356-357.

Robert L. Kahn and Charles F. Cannell, *The Dynamics of Interviewing: Theory, Techniques and Cases,* New York: Wiley, 1957. This book is described by the director of the Survey Research Center at the University of California at Berkeley as "... without question the most thorough and painstaking examination of the interviewing process in print." It discusses the practical questions of how to motivate the respondent, how to design questionnaires, and how to probe to obtain answers required by the research project. But it is also concerned with the psychology of the interview and in particular with the theory of nondirective interviewing (Carl Rogers) and field theory (Kurt Lewin). This summary is based on a review by Charles Y. Glock, *American Sociological Review,* Vol. 22, December 1957, pp. 761-762.

Matilda White Riley, *Sociological Research: A Case Approach,* New York: Harcourt, Brace and World, 1963. The distinctive feature of this standard textbook on the methods of sociological research is a close interweaving of theory and research. That is, the author stresses the *logic of inquiry* rather than disembodied methods that the student will only appreciate much later. In the implementation of this approach, examples of studies from the sociological literature are judiciously selected and analyzed to show alternative research strategies. In the preface Robert Merton described the approach as follows:

> A repertoire of methods is supplied for each stage of inquiry. The advantage of serially programming these stages is that the student becomes adept at using each of the alternatives from which he will select, in any given investigation, those methods best suited to the problem in hand. By providing a practiced versatility in the use of various research methods, qualitative as well as quantitative, this program helps the student to choose those methods most appropriate for dealing with the theoretical problem, thus helping him to avoid that familiar kind of "trained incapacity" which tempts researchers who are drilled in a limited range of methods to adapt the problem to the methods they happen to know best.

Matilda White Riley and Anne Foner, *Aging and Society;* Vol. 1: *An Inventory of Research Findings,* New York: Russell Sage Foundation, 1968. Empirical research in sociology has come to mean data-gathering operations in the field (through questionnaires or interviews) or data-processing in the laboratory (often with the help of computer technology). This book represents a different kind of research: a reference work that sifts the results of about 3000 studies in te field of aging and presents the results so that the reader gets an orderly picture of what is known and unknown. This is an inventory of research findings similar to a term paper done in the library by a student for his sociology course but on a more sophisticated level because (1) it examines far more studies than the most conscientious student can possibly read and (2) it evaluates the studies that are examined by criteria of research adequacy beyond all but highly professional sociological researchers. Research inventories have been relatively infrequent in sociology, but they are now becoming increasingly popular. The accumulation of studies in data banks will make possible not only the sifting of publications but more frequent reanalysis of data from such publications.

Samuel A. Stouffer et al., *The American Soldier,* 2 vols., Princeton, N.J.: Princeton University Press, 1949. These volumes represent a reanalysis of data collected during the Second World War by the Research Branch of the Information and Education Division of the United States Army. "The Research Branch existed to do a practical engineering job, not a scientific one. Its purpose was to provide the Army Command quickly and accurately with facts about the attitudes of soldiers which . . . might be helpful in policy formation." For instance, it found out through anonymous questionnaire surveys how enlisted men felt about officers and reported the findings to those responsible for officer training and soldier morale. Thus the Research Branch functioned for the Army much the way a market research firm functions for a manufacturer. The reanalysis was undertaken to utilize the Army data to answer questions raised by sociological and social psychological theories. This summary is based on a review by John W. Riley, Jr., *American Sociological Review,* Vol. 14, August 1949, pp. 557-559.

Theodore D. Woolsey, "Sampling Methods for a Small Household Survey," Public Health Monograph No. 40, Washington, D.C.: Government Printing Office, 1956. The survey reported in this monograph furnished estimates of the amount of illness and the number of persons available for work in the age group 45 years and over in Hagerstown, Maryland, in the summer of 1953. It is included in this bibliography because it serves as a model of a household survey based on a probability sample. The city directory provided a list of street addresses. Every seventh residential listing was marked for inclusion in the sample. (In the case of addresses of apartment houses or other multiple dwellings, the ratio of one in seven was preserved by listing the separate dwelling units and by designating households in a random way from the list.) Interviewers were then instructed to go to the designated households and ask whether a person in them had passed the forty-fifth birthday. If not, the interview was concluded. If so, the interviewer was instructed to list *all* of the persons in the household. This listing was necessary so that, if there were several persons past 45 in the household, the interviewer would know, in accordance with previously prepared instructions, which one to interview. For example, in households containing *two* persons over 45, *half* the interviewers were instructed to interview the older and *half* the younger. Households in which no one was available on repeated calls (including calls on Saturdays and Sundays and sometimes calls at the place of work) were dropped from the study. A table was compiled at the end of the survey showing how far the sample had departed from the ideal design. Thus, there were 19 refusals to be interviewed, 11 households in which no one could ever be found at home, and 600 completed interviews.

Part II

SOCIALIZATION: THE TRANSMISSION AND INTERNALIZATION OF CULTURE

The cultural dimension of a society consists of that society's distinctive symbols for communicating shared meanings. It is the stock of intellectual, expressive, and evaluative symbols understood by the bulk of the population. Thus the notion that culture is the art, music, and literature of a society is only partly true; culture does include these things, but it also includes language, eating habits, clothing styles—in short, the symbols that the people of a society share.

For a society to persist through time, its culture must be passed on from one generation to the next. This is accomplished through socialization. Socialization is the process whereby the individual is taught to fill certain role expectations and to internalize cultural norms. It begins with an infant in his family of orientation (Chapter 4) and continues as the child goes on in school. But socialization does not end with the end of formal education. For each time an individual accepts a new job or moves to a new community there are new roles he must fill. Socialization for adult roles will be considered in Chapter 5.

Socialization is only one of the four organizational requirements of society. But for adaptation, integration, and policy making to occur, there must be the socialized individual to fill the necessary roles in his society.

CULTURE AND
SUBCULTURE

CULTURAL MEANINGS IN HUMAN INTERACTION: SYMBOLIC COMMUNICATION

Interaction can occur on subhuman levels. When two dogs fight, growls, lunges, bites, and strategic retreats fit a pattern of action and reaction. One dog interprets the other's growl as a sign of hostility, and the battle is on. The dogs understand one another because here is an inherent connection between growling and hostility in the animal world; wherever they are, animals express themselves in much the same way.

Human interaction has the benefit of language. Take as an example a policeman who arrested a drunk on the streets of New Brunswick, New Jersey. The drunk, resentful, muttered a curse in Hungarian, his native tongue. The policeman happened to be of Hungarian extraction himself, understood the curse, and filed an additional charge against his prisoner: abusing an officer. Note that the drunk expressed his hostility not by growling but by using a linguistic code. In order to decode the message contained in the curse, the policeman had to know Hungarian. There are two differences between a curse and a growl. First, the drunk had to *learn* to curse. He did not invent for the occasion the sound he uttered. Nor was the curse linked directly to his feeling of hostility, as is a dog's growl. He drew it from the Hungarian cultural tradition — in much the same way as cooks draw upon the Hungarian cultural tradition for goulash. Second, the policeman had to *share* knowledge of the cultural tradition with the drunk for communication to occur. The policeman could not have inferred from the sound the drunk made or the expression on his face that he was "abusing an officer."

Learning of meanings is crucial to human communication — and therefore to human interaction — because the messages are usually in a cultural code. Language is the most obvious example of a cultural code, but virtually all human behavior has a *cultural dimension,* including behavior usually thought of as physiological. An American adult, for example, does not belch in public, no matter how acute his gastric distress, because American culture disapproves. In the Far East, on the other hand, belching may be considered an appropriate way to indicate to one's host that the meal was good. As a result, adults in one Oriental society *produce* belches for the same reason that American adults *suppress* them: to be polite.

Similarly, **cultures** define the meaning of masculinity and femininity.[1] All cultures begin with an initial biological difference between males and females, but each culture elaborates this initial difference in a distinctive way. In the United States, boys and girls receive different toys to play with, different clothing to wear, and, to some extent, different words to use when expressing themselves. Girls may or may not know the meanings of "bad words"; they are

[1] Margaret Mead, *Male and Female: A Study of the Sexes in a Changing World,* New York: William Morrow, 1949.

tempted to pretend not to know them whether they do or not, as an indication of their femininity. Boys, however, are expected to know the appropriate words and, on occasion, to use them as an expression of virility. Consider the situation in which two boys fight and one gets considerably the worse of it. If the loser cries because of his frustration at defeat and injury, he identifies himself as a "sissy" (according to American culture). On the other hand, if he lets loose with a stream of four-letter Anglo-Saxon profanity, he reassures himself and everyone around him that he is "tough" and will not resort to the female pattern of crying.[2] Careful study of the occasions when profanity is used shows that, far from being an irrational phenomenon, profanity is skillfully selected by males to express hostility, virility, or both simultaneously.[3]

The meaning of masculinity and femininity, the meaning of sexual intimacy, and the meaning of adolescence differ from one culture to another. These differences of meaning have implications for interaction. In a society that regards sexual intercourse as expressing the emotional intimacy of a *married* couple, courtship behavior may exclude coitus. In a society in which sexual intercourse is the tangible evidence of male success in a game of seduction, promiscuity may be a feature of adolescent life. Thus cultural definitions of the situation do not merely add a dimension of interpretation to factual events. Culture helps to complete a world that nature has left indeterminate. Sexual intimacy *can* symbolize love, but it can also symbolize conquest. For animals, sex is uninterpreted; it simply *is*. For human beings, the meaning dimension is always part of the situation. *Some* meaning is supplied by the cultural tradition and is shared, to varying degrees, by all members of the society. The degree of sharing varies because these meanings are not inborn but must be learned — and it is too much to expect that everyone will learn precisely the same interpretation of the cultural definition. *Some* meaning is contributed by the idiosyncratic values of the individual. When and if the idiosyncratic values of a particular individual spread to the rest of his society, they stop being idiosyncratic and become part of the culture; to this extent the culture has changed. But in either case the meaning dimension is part of the situation confronting human beings just as the time dimension is part of the situation.

Culture not only defines *physiological processes* and the role structure of interactive systems, it also defines the *physical environment*. Snow does not mean the same thing to Americans as it does to Eskimos. Nor is space understood in the same way by contemporary man as it was before the invention of airplanes, rockets, and missiles. Human beings do not perceive the world as mere events in space and time except in infancy. Adults see clearly what their culture calls attention to and disregard what their culture ignores. As linguists

---

[2] Ashley Montagu, "Should Strong Men Cry?" *The New York Times Magazine,* May 26, 1957, pp. 17-18.

[3] Henry Elkin, "Aggressive and Erotic Tendencies in Army Life," *American Journal of Sociology* Vol. 51, March 1946, pp. 408-413.

have pointed out, these cultural emphases are imbedded in the language we speak and thus, indirectly, in the thoughts we think:[4]

> Natural logic says that talking is merely an incidental process concerned strictly with communication, not with formulation of ideas. Talking, or the use of language, is supposed only to "express" what is essentially already formulated nonlinguistically. Formulation is an independent process, called thought or thinking, and is supposed to be largely indifferent to the nature of particular languages. . . .
>
> When linguists became able to examine critically and scientifically a large number of languages of widely different patterns, their base of reference was expanded; they experienced an interruption of phenomena hitherto held universal, and a whole new order of significances came into their ken. It was found that the background linguistic system (in other words, the grammar) of each language is not merely a reproducing instrument for voicing ideas but rather is itself the shaper of ideas, the program and guide for the individual's mental activity, for his analysis of impressions, for his synthesis of his mental stock in trade. Formulation of ideas is not an independent process, strictly rational in the old sense, but is part of a particular grammar and differs, from slightly to greatly, as between different grammars. We dissect nature along lines laid down by our native languages. The categories and types that we isolate from the world of phenomena we do not find there because they stare every observer in the face; on the contrary, the world is presented in a kaleidoscopic flux of impressions which has to be organized by our minds—and this means largely by the linguistic systems in our minds. We cut nature up, organize it into concepts, and ascribe significances as we do, largely because we are parties to an agreement to organize it in this way—an agreement that holds throughout our speech community and is codified in the patterns of our language. The agreement is, of course, an implicit and unstated one, *but its terms are absolutely obligatory;* we cannot talk at all except by subscribing to the organization and classification of data which the agreement decrees. . . . In English we divide most of our words into two classes, which have different grammatical and logical properties. Class 1 we call nouns, e.g., "house," "man"; Class 2, verbs, e.g., "hit," "run." Many words of one class can act secondarily as of the other class, e.g., "a hit," "a run," or "to man" the boat, but on the primary level the division between the classes is absolute. Our language thus gives us a bipolar division of nature. But nature herself is not thus polarized. If it be said that strike, turn, run, are verbs because they denote temporary or short-lasting events, i.e., actions, why then is fist a noun? It also is a temporary event. Why are lightning, spark, wave, eddy, pulsation, flame, storm, phase, cycle, spasm, noise, emotion, nouns? They are temporary events. If man and house are nouns because they are long-lasting and stable events, i.e., things, what then are keep, adhere, extend, project, continue, persist, grow, dwell, and so on, doing among the verbs? If it be objected that possess, adhere, are verbs because they are stable relationships rather than stable percepts, why then should equilibrium, pressure, current, peace, group, nation, society, tribe, sister, or any kinship term, be among the

[4] Reprinted by permission. From Benjamin Lee Whorf, "Science and Linguistics," in John B. Carroll, Ed., *Language, Thought, and Reality: Selected Writings of Benjamin Lee Whorf,* Cambridge, Mass.: M.I.T. Press, 1956, Chap. 15.

nouns? It will be found that an "event" to *us* means "what our language classes as a verb" or something analogized therefrom. And it will be found that it is not possible to define event, thing, object, relationship, and so on, from nature, but that to define them always involves a circuitous return to the grammatical categories of the definer's language.

In the Hopi language, lightning, wave, flame, meteor, puff of smoke, pulsation, are verbs—events of necessarily brief duration cannot be anything but verbs. Cloud and storm are at about the lower limit of duration for nouns. Hopi, you see, actually has a classification of events (or linguistic isolates) by duration type, something strange to our modes of thought.

Culture not only provides the lens through which human beings perceive the world, including the role structure of interactive systems. Culture also guides human beings in *responding* to what they perceive. The favorable evaluation of bodily cleanliness, so natural to Americans, is a cultural response. The early Christians were deeply suspicious of bathing, associating it as they did with Roman orgies and preoccupation with the body instead of the soul. Vestiges of this negative evaluation underlay the public criticism of President Fillmore in 1851 for installing the first bathtub in the White House.[5] Today cleanliness is considered virtuous and Body Odor sinful. In one study, college freshmen disapproved more strongly of a fellow student who did not take baths than of one who stole or cheated on examinations.[6]

In short, human beings live in a world one constituent of which is their cul-

[5] Anthropologist Edward Wellin traced the changing cultural definition of bodily cleanliness in an unpublished lecture at Rutgers University, 1963.

[6] Clarice Stasz Stoll, Thieves, Cheats, and Slovens: The Social Psychology of Social Control, Unpublished Ph.D. Dissertation, Rutgers University, 1967.

tural tradition. Language is perhaps the clearest illustration of this point, but nonverbal behavior and cultural artifacts also communicate shared meanings. If New York City were destroyed in a nuclear war, archeologists five centuries hence might learn a little about American life from the material objects found in the ruins: houses, clothes, toothbrushes, typewriters, boxes of cigars, diamond rings, automobiles, and fluorescent lights. They would infer from typewriters, for example, that written communications were common. If the streets were sufficiently intact for the distribution of mailboxes to be observed, further inferences could be made about the communications habits of New Yorkers. Thus cultural meanings are to some extent encapsulated in physical objects — but never completely.

Knowing that New Yorkers clean their teeth with toothbrushes would not make clear the full meaning of the morning and evening ritual. Brushing teeth is more than dental hygiene just as eating caviar is more than reducing hunger pangs; both are also **symbolic acts.** The physical artifact is a good clue to one level of meaning, especially when the main significance is utilitarian, as is the case with a chair or a pot. But there is often a second level of meaning: the significance of the use of a physical object for defining the person using it. Thus a Harley-Davidson is not only a means of transport; it is also a way for its driver to communicate to others his youthful, adventurous image of himself. Some material objects are better understood on this second level of meaning than on the first. Consider the cigarette from this point of view. What is the 13-year-old boy communicating to the world by puffing on a cigarette? That he is an adult? That he is rough and tough? That he is sophisticated? True, each 13-year-old boy communicates a somewhat different message, but the range of meanings is limited by the significance of the cigarette in American culture.

Advertising agencies are well aware that cigarettes, liquor, automobiles, soft drinks, perfume, and virtually every other commodity have characteristic meanings to potential buyers: Coca-Cola evokes one **product image** and Ford Thunderbirds another. One of the main objectives of the advertising industry is to develop favorable "product images" for its clients.[7] If an unfavorable image develops inadvertently, the advertising agency handling the account seeks to change it. For example, when scientific studies demonstrated a relationship between cigarette smoking and lung cancer, new brands of cigarettes were developed with filter tips. Sales were poor, however, because a filter-tipped cigarette had a *female* product image, and men would not buy them. When one tobacco company launched a massive advertising campaign featuring a tattooed Marlboro Man smoking filter-tipped cigarettes, the meaning of smoking filter-tipped cigarettes changed. A virile image of the Marlboro smoker developed in American culture. At any rate, sales boomed.

The cigar industry also has a history of cultural ups and downs. Cigars were popular in America from colonial times (when they were smoked by women as well as men), but they lost out to cigarettes during the First World War. The

[7] Martin Mayer, *Madison Avenue, U.S.A.*, New York: Harper, 1958.

ruin of the cigar industry was completed by a movie stereotype that developed in the 1920s and the 1930s: the association with villains and gangsters. In 1940 the cigar industry counterattacked, founding the Cigar Institute of America and hiring a top-flight advertising man. The Cigar Institute of America let news photographers know that monthly cash prizes would be given for the best *published* photographs of people smoking cigars. As a result, celebrities were increasingly photographed smoking cigars. The Cigar Institute also promised Hollywood producers to spread posters across the nation advertising movies with "good cigar scenes." Since there were 25,000 cigar counters and about 27 million people passed them each week, this free publicity was tempting. Heroes started smoking cigars, and cigar sales boomed.[8]

The Cigar Institute of America probably wanted to know whether it was getting its money's worth. To what extent did the motion picture industry stop portraying villains with cigars between their teeth? Were heroes more frequently seen smoking cigars? The answers to questions like these are obtained by the research technique called *content analysis*. Content analysis is the *quantitative analysis of symbolic communications*. In principle, content analysis can be applied to conversations between individuals, to personal documents like letters or diaries, or to symbolic gestures, but the most extensive use of content analysis is in the study of meanings in the mass media: in newspapers, magazine articles, radio or television broadcasts, or films. Thus the Cigar Institute of America might have selected a random sample of American films in 1940, 1941, and 1942, established careful criteria of favorable and unfavorable cigar scenes in advance, and proceeded to count the number of such scenes for those years. If the ratio of favorable to unfavorable scenes increased from 1940 to 1942, the public relations campaign probably had paid off. Commercial use of content analysis is extensive; advertising agencies are under pressure to demonstrate to clients the effectiveness of their efforts. But the technique is equally applicable to noncommercial research. During the Second World War, the United States carefully monitored German, Italian, and Japanese broadcasts; military intelligence units as well as staff members of the Office of War Information counted the recurrence of certain themes in enemy broadcasts to their own populations as well as in those intended for Allied consumption. Since the mass media in Axis countries were controlled directly by their governments, shifts in content sometimes antedated by precious days forthcoming military moves. In preparing their own populations for what lay ahead, Axis broadcasters also tipped off American analysts. Commercial and military uses of content analysis employ exactly the same techniques as purely scientific uses. In scientific uses of content analysis, the objective is better understanding of human behavior, of which communication is an important part. Precise **coding** of units of meaning and their counting become a means to sociological or psychological knowledge.

---

[8] Material on the cigar industry comes from Keith Monroe, "They Made the Cigar Respectable," *Harper's Magazine,* Vol. 210, February 1955, pp. 37-41.

THE ARBITRARY CONNECTION BETWEEN CULTURAL SYMBOL AND COMMUNICATED MEANING

In Chapter 2 we saw that sociologists use reports about interaction to determine attitudes of participants that could not be determined by direct observations. Reports allow the individual to employ verbal symbols to describe past events or to anticipate future experiences. Symbols make expansion into the past and future possible because the connection of a symbol with the reported event is arbitrary. Unlike the connection between the growl of a dog and his feeling of hostility, the curse of the Hungarian drunk had no *intrinsic* connection between symbol and meaning; this frees human communication from the particularities of the immediate situation. When a young executive refers to "dinner" he may be thinking of a family ritual that includes candlelight, a clean tablecloth, and polite conversation. But if he is busy working overtime, "dinner" may mean a sandwich sent to his office from a delicatessen. The same word is used for both meals. The noise "dinner" abstracts from the millions of interactive situations in which food is consumed near the end of the day; the reference is necessarily imprecise. The imprecision of symbolic communication implies that a given symbol may convey different meanings to the speaker and to the listener—one symbol may refer to a wide range of events, real and imaginary, past and present.[9] Thus using the symbol "dinner" enables human beings to think about actual and potential meals just as the use of the symbol "Negro" enables human beings to think about known and unknown persons with dark pigmentation.

But the arbitrary connection between cultural symbol and communicated meaning also makes possible communication failure, accidental or deliberate. A man removes his hat on entering a church as a symbolic act of respect in a sacred place. However, an Orthodox Jew entering a synagogue would keep his hat *on* for precisely the same reason. A Christian, unaware that Jewish men cover their heads out of deference, might be shocked to see men with their hats on in a synagogue. This is a communication failure resulting from the circumstance that the same symbol (uncovering the head) has opposite meanings in the Christian and the Jewish cultural traditions.

Human communication is precarious because it relies on symbols, which by definition have no intrinsic connection with their meanings. Moreover, the **subcultures** of modern societies may interpret the same symbol differently. Modern societies are so large that many subcultures coexist within them. Persons reared in the South interpret skin pigmentation differently from persons reared in the North and West. Beethoven symphonies are considered masterpieces of artistic achievement by some and regarded contemptuously by devotees of Bach. Difficulties in communication can even occur within the same

---

[9] Susanne K. Langer, *Philosophy in a New Key*, New York: New American Library, 1948, Chap. 3.

family when the same symbol is interpreted differently by different members of the family. A 14-year-old girl arrives home from school wearing makeup; all of her friends do, so wearing makeup is a symbol of her membership in her clique. Her parents, coming from a fundamentalist Lutheran background, are horrified. To them, makeup means sex and sin. Such a failure of communication can have tragic consequences. Studies of the early lives of prostitutes have shown that some started to define themselves as "bad" because of this type of experience with excessively strict parents.[10] Although communication breakdowns occur even in a family, they are more likely in a society with a multiplicity of subcultures.

Communication failures can occur accidentally, despite the best efforts of human beings to understand one another, when different subcultures attach different meanings to the same symbol. On the other hand, communication failures can be engineered for self-seeking reasons, as when one person lies to another. A boy tells a girl that he loves her and in other ways implies that he is interested in an evolving commitment; in point of fact the boy may be interested only in sexual intimacies.[11] The advertiser or the salesman tries to communicate messages that will induce people to buy a product; often these messages are misleading if not outright fabrications. In short, symbolic communication is a tremendous achievement of the human species, but the looseness of the connection between the cultural symbol and its meaning makes possible not only accidental communication failures but also deliberate deception.

The extent to which advertising agencies are successful in changing the meaning of commodities for consumers is not clear. Maybe cigars would have come back into popular favor without the efforts of the Cigar Institute of America. Maybe filter-tipped cigarettes would have been adopted by American men without the Marlboro Man. That such efforts are made at all is an indication that meanings *do* change with the passage of time; the advertising industry simply tries to guide cultural change in the interests of its clients.

The Cultural Elaboration of Expressive Meanings. The connection between cultural symbol and communicated meaning is arbitrary even with purely cognitive symbols. But culture not only defines the world intellectually. Culture arouses feelings and provides vehicles for their expression. The strength of these feelings—and even their direction—is more related to arbitrary associations within the symbol system than to events in the physical world to which they refer. For instance, "ice cream sodas" and "rides on roller coasters" arouse pleasant feelings, although in the physical world they may make their consumer ill. Similarly, the symbol "junkie" triggers hostility among people who may have no personal experience with drug addicts. Culture also provides prescribed ways to *express* feelings. Hostility may be expressed by using words

[10] Edwin M. Lemert, *Social Pathology,* New York: McGraw-Hill, 1951, pp. 236-280.

[11] Willard Waller, "The Rating and Dating Complex," *American Sociological Review,* Vol. 2, December 1937, pp. 727-734.

normally barred from polite conversation. Affection may be expressed by a kiss. The elaboration of expressive meanings, so necessary to social interaction, depends on the arbitrary connection between cultural symbol and its referent.

Experiencing another culture dramatizes the arbitrariness of the expressive meanings of a particular society; the individual can observe uniformly different responses to familiar symbols. In the Arab culture of North Africa, for instance, angry men fight with knives but not with fists. During the Second World War, American soldiers in the North African theater were cautioned not to start fist-fights—partly for the good reputation of Americans, partly to avoid getting stabbed. This capacity of cultural symbols to stimulate and channel the expression of strong emotions has potentialities both for building group solidarity and for arousing divisive conflicts. Sometimes a cultural symbol (like a flag or a cross) calls forth in an individual sacrificial devotion to country, to God, or to humanity. Sometimes cultural symbols trigger off persecution and bloodshed. Recall that the First World War began following the assassination of an Austrian archduke by Yugoslavian nationalists and that the Second World War might never have occurred had the Nazis not invented the cultural symbol, "pure Aryan race." Within American society, homicide by lynch mob was fairly common until about 1950. Between 1882 and 1951, 1293 whites and 3437 Negroes were lynched, mostly in the South.[12] The following account of a Southern lynching dates from an era of white supremacy and Negro intimidation which is passing, if not wholly gone. It shows the illegal but culturally approved response to the alleged rape of a white woman by a Negro man.[13]

> One Saturday morning in the spring of the early 1930's the Negro laborer on a white man's farm, near Leeville, Texas, came to his employer's house to collect his wages. On being told by the farmer's wife that her husband had gone to town and had not left the wages, the Negro, disappointed, left the house, but returned shortly with a shotgun, forced the woman into her bedroom, and assaulted her several times. Fearing that the woman's five-year-old son in the back yard might give an alarm, the Negro went to look for him, but first tied his victim to the bed, telling her he would return soon. She broke loose and fled across a field to a neighbor's house where the sheriff was telephoned. Meanwhile, some men came walking along the road, and the Negro fled toward a creek bottom.
>
> Although the above is the commonly accepted story of the crime, there are other versions, as is frequently the case in charges of this nature. Most of the Leeville Negroes and some whites believe that no assault occurred. Medical records show that the illicit relationship did occur.

THE ARREST AND BEGINNINGS OF MOB ACTION

> One deputy sheriff came to the scene and arrested the Negro, who, it is claimed, fired at him. The Negro confessed, agreed to plead guilty, waived all

---

[12] Marvin E. Wolfgang, "Lynching," *The World Book Encyclopedia,* Vol. 12, Chicago: Field Enterprises, 1965.

[13] Reprinted by permission. From Durward Pruden, "A Sociological Study of a Texas Lynching," *Studies in Sociology,* Vol. 1, Summer 1935, pp. 3-9.

rights, and was secreted in a jail in a town some miles distant from Leeville. The next Monday night a small group of men and boys loitered near the Leeville jail. By Tuesday many exaggerated versions of the details of the assault were being repeated on the street. Tuesday night a large group of boys and men appeared at the jail and demanded the Negro. They refused to leave until the sheriff allowed some of their leaders to go through the jail and see that the Negro was not there. There were no more attempts at mob action until the next Friday, the date set for the trial.

THE ATTEMPT AT TRIAL

On the morning of the trial many people came to the Leeville business center, both local residents and others from farms and small communities of the adjacent trading area. The judge refused to change venue, but had four Texas Rangers present to guard the court. The Rangers took the Negro into the courthouse early in the morning before the crowd gathered. All morning, as the jury was being selected, the crowd around the courtyard and in the courthouse halls grew larger and more belligerent. Just as the situation was hanging in the balance between an orderly trial and a riot, a rumor was circulated that the governor of the state had telegraphed the Rangers not to shoot anyone in trying to protect the Negro. Although the rumor was untrue, yet it was accepted by the mob and so encouraged its members as to make the Rangers practically helpless without extensive bloodshed. The precipitating event which changed the huge, curious crowd into a vicious and active mob, was the bringing of the woman from the hospital to the courthouse in an ambulance, and carrying her on a stretcher through the crowd into the courtroom. This was about 1 o'clock. After that the mob went wild. It broke in the courtroom, and was repeatedly driven back by the Rangers, with drawn guns and tear gas. Several shots were fired. The judge at last decided to change venue, and the Negro was hurried into the second-floor, fireproof vault room of the district clerk's office.

BURNING THE COURTHOUSE

When the mob saw that the Rangers were determined to hold the courthouse, they determined to burn it. A group of teen-age boys, led by an excited and vociferous woman dressed in red, broke out the courthouse windows with rocks, threw gasoline in, and fired the building about 2:30 in the afternoon. The fire department used its ladders to carry the people from the second-floor courtroom. There was some objection to the rescuing of the judge, county attorney, sheriffs, and Rangers; but, finally, all were removed except the Negro in the district clerk's vault. As the firemen tried to fight the blaze during the afternoon, the mob cut the fire hose and sometimes attacked the firemen.

THE BATTLE WITH THE SOLDIERS

The Rangers, who had left the courthouse, telephoned the governor for assistance, and about 4 P.M. a small detachment of National Guards arrived from a neighboring town. They marched around the falling ruins of the courthouse, saw that they were too far outnumbered to restore order, and returned home. About 6 P.M. a larger unit of 52 soldiers from a large city to the south arrived.

Leaving a detachment to garrison their headquarters at the county jail three blocks west of the courthouse, the remainder deployed around the smoldering courthouse ruins to push the crowd back from the hanging walls. As darkness fell, the spirit of the mob became uglier. They reasoned that if the governor would not let the Rangers shoot at them, he surely would not let soldiers shoot either. They began to abuse the soldiers, and soon a pitched battle ensued in which the troops were forced to retreat the three blocks back to the jail, followed by the angry mob throwing bricks, rocks, pieces of timber, chunks of concrete, broken bottles, sticks of dynamite, etc. Several soldiers were badly cut and beaten, others had their rifles taken from them, and some of the mobsters received minor bullet wounds. Reinforced by their comrades at the jail the troops made a determined stand there and started shooting into the air. The mob then withdrew and returned to the courthouse square to open the vault and get the Negro, about whose condition there was much speculation.

From around 8 P.M. to midnight various efforts were made to open the upper room of the great two story steel and cement vault. A gigantic crowd packed the entire square and side streets. Finally, the mob leaders confiscated an acetylene torch; and, working from the top of a ladder, were able to open a hole large enough to insert dynamite and blow out a hole which the mob leader entered and threw out the dead body of the Negro.

The corpse was dragged behind a Ford roadster containing two young men and two girls to the Negro business section, a distance of seven blocks. Thousands of people followed in a frenzied midnight parade, yelling, singing, tooting horns of automobiles. At an important corner in the Negro section the body was drawn up to the limb of a cottonwood tree in front of a Negro drug store. The store was forcibly entered and ransacked, the money and valuables pocketed, confections passed out to the crowd, and the furniture and furnishings piled under the Negro's body for fuel. Some versions have it that the leader unsexed the Negro in the presence of the crowd of men, women, and children before lighting the fire. The crowd gave a mighty cheer as flames enveloped the Negro's body. After the burning of the body some of the crowd—the onlookers—went home, but the more vicious elements continued ransacking and burning with gasoline the Negro business places including a hotel, drug store, two cafes, two barber shops, two dentists' offices, a doctor's office, two undertaking establishments, an Odd Fellows' Hall, a Knights of Pythias building, a theater, a lawyer's office, a life insurance office, a cleaning and pressing shop, and several residences. They swore that they would "run all the damn niggers out of Leeville." Many of the remaining mob were very drunk. The fire department was not permitted to put any water on the fires except on nearby property owned by whites.

EXODUS OF THE NEGROES

Meanwhile all of Leeville's 2,000 Negro inhabitants were under cover. Some were given refuge by white friends and employers in Leeville; the others, with their old people, their sick, their babies and children, hurried away in old automobiles, wagons, buggies, on mules, and by foot. Some reached Negro friends in adjacent cities; less fortunate individuals spent a harrowing night in ditches, ravines, clumps of bushes, under houses or bridges, etc.

MARTIAL LAW

About 1 o'clock Saturday morning 150 more National Guards arrived with machine guns, rifiles, side arms, and tear gas. They, together with the previously mentioned soldiers at the jail, were at last able to break up the mob and disperse it. At 3 A.M. more troops arrived. At dawn the soldiers had the town under control with machine guns mounted at strategic points. Martial law was declared and arrests began. During the next few days there were continual rumors that the mob would reassemble on the outskirts of town at dark, make a new march against the soldiers, and complete their avowed job of burning all Negro dwellings and driving their occupants out of town permanently. The armed force was increased to 419 men and more arms were brought in, but nothing more of importance occurred. A notice was found tacked on a white employer's office door warning him to fire his Negro workers and engage whites. Warnings to leave town were discovered on some Negro dwellings. A military court of investigation turned over 29 persons and 600 typewritten pages of confidential evidence to the civil authorities, who indicted 14 men and boys. They were removed to jail in the large metropolitan city to the south; a citizens' committee to maintain order was organized, and the troops left Leeville after being there nine days.

LEGAL DISPOSITIONS

After many seemingly unnecessary delays on the part of the Leeville county attorney, the rioters were brought to trial in the aforementioned metropolitan city, where, to the surprise and chagrin of the judge, a jury of urban men could not be found who would agree to convict even if the defendants were proved guilty. On another change of venue to the state capital city, one young man was finally given a two-year term for arson. This was more than a year after the lynching. The defendant was already at odds with the law on other charges. Before ending his sentence he was released by the governor on petition of Leeville citizens on account of the illness of his mother. The other 13 men were never tried.

THE ACTIVE MOB

A compilation of data on the men and boys charged or suspected by the military authorities, and some others revealed by private investigation, gives a fairly accurate sample of the active mob. Table 3.1 classifies 58 of these individuals by occupational status.

At least 11 of the active participants in the riot were known to have had previous police records. Nine had been in the hands of the law for stealing, fighting, or bootlegging (this was before repeal). Two were under suspended stentence for stealing; and one, a hobo, had spent 12 years as an inmate of an insane asylum.

PERTINENT FACTS ABOUT THE MOST ACTIVE LYNCHERS

The acknowledged leader of the mob was a man 40 years old who could neither read nor write, and had no particular profession, but occasionally did a little cattle trading and "bronc bustin" in rodeos. He drank a great deal, and was

TABLE 3.1

Active Mob Members Classified by Occupational Status

Do not work, or do odd jobs	8
Unemployed teen age boys	6
High School boys	5
Total unemployed	19
Mill and factory workers	7
Road workers	4
Truck driver	1
Shrubbery worker at nursery	1
Total common laborers	13
Farmers and farm-hands	8
Total farmers	8
Mechanics	4
Welder-plumber	1
Cement worker	1
Bricklayer	1
Railroad switchman	1
Total skilled laborers	8
Grocery store operator	2
Filling station operator	1
Dry goods store operator	1
Total owners of small businesses	4
Gin operator	1
Advertising manager of a department store	1
Bank clerk (a youth)	1
Total salaried people	3
Fruit peddler	1
Banjo player and singer	1
Insurance agent	1
Total miscellaneous	3

described by officers as "a rough and ready bully." He had been before the courts several times as a bootlegger. With his wife and little daughter he lived in a shabby part of town near some Negro shanties. He owned no property, and belonged to no church. The wife provided most of the family's support by taking in washing. His attitude at the opening of the vault was described as that of a great benefactor—a protector of womanhood—doing his duty in a brave and dramatic manner. A few years after the lynching he was killed in a drunken brawl on a South Texas sheep ranch.

The boy who was given the two-year prison term was 17 years old, his father was dead, and his mother was a low paid worker at a shirt factory. At an early age he began truanting from school, stealing chickens, coming into the hands of the police, and was eventually brought before the courts for cattle stealing. At this time he had returned from prison and had again been before the courts for stealing.

One of the men who helped open the vault later had trouble with a farmer because he raped the farmer's wife. . . . Still another mob member was an inebriate; and the hobo member, at the time of the lynching, was sleeping in a city park and confessed that his breakfasts consisted of bread and milk stolen early in the morning from various grocery stores. He had often been picked up for vagrancy in other cities following his release from the insane asylum. An 18-year-old boy who fought the firemen was described by those who knew him as "a sort of a half-wit." Only one of the 14 indicted owned a home.

The five high school participants are all described by school officials as problem boys, "overgrown and hungry for notoriety." The mother of one was a prostitute, and the father of one (a city fireman) committed suicide recently. Two boys from fairly well fixed homes were involved.

A summation of the evidence about the personnel of the mob indicates that the active leaders and participants—mostly from the lowest economic group—included:

1. Some vicious criminals.
2. Many teen age, excitable youths, impatient at restraints of the law.
3. Many propertyless, uneducated, unattached men of the domino parlor clientele type.

Why did the lynching occur? Clearly, the lynch mob felt outraged over what the Negro laborer was alleged to have done. But why? Because they considered rape a horrifying act? This could not be the explanation because *Negro* men who raped *Negro* women did not arouse comparable hostility—the customary penalty in Leeville when a Negro man assaulted a Negro woman was a fine of $12.50. Nor did *white* men who raped *white* women (or Negro women) get lynched. Recall that one of the leaders of the mob "later had trouble with a farmer because he raped the farmer's wife." Why was it that the rape of a *white* woman by a *Negro* man tapped a special reservoir of indignation? In order to answer this question satisfactorily, one must understand how white supremacy was traditionally symbolized in the South. The following rules of race etiquette were observed by those who subscribed to the implicit assumption of Negro inferiority:

1. Whites should never shake hands with Negroes on being introduced. No matter how well educated the Negro, no matter what his professional attainments, white persons should always address him by his first name. Negroes, on the other hand, must address whites as "Mr.," "Mrs.," or "Miss."
2. Whites should never eat a meal with Negroes.
3. Negroes should sit in the *back* of a bus, train, or street car, whites in the *front*.
4. A white person must not marry a Negro.

These rules of etiquette used to be strictly enforced. Negroes who violated them were suspected of getting "uppity," that is, of resenting the inferior place assigned to them by whites. The penalties for not knowing "their place" was often harassment and sometimes violence. In the context of these rules for symbolizing social inferiority, the rape of a white woman by a Negro man is not so much a sexual act as an attack on the system of white supremacy. For a white supremacist, it is presumptuous for a Negro man to stare at a white woman; impertinent for him to speak to her on a first-name basis; and unthinkable to ask her for a date, much less to propose to have sexual relations with her. The degree of coercion exerted on the alleged victim was not examined too closely in Leeville, as it would have been in a Northern court, because the mere existence of a sexual act between a Negro man and a white woman was defined as an attack on white supremacy. The *men* felt violated; the woman became a secondary issue.

The Leeville lynching is generally forgotten, and it did not attract national attention when it occurred. Lynching was far more common 35 years ago than it is now. Between 1951 and 1960 only five lynchings were recorded in the United States. But on June 21, 1964, Deputy Sheriff Cecil R. Price of Neshoba County, Mississippi, handed three young civil-rights workers to a Ku Klux Klan lynch mob, thereby dramatizing their cause in the glare of international publicity. The three young men were taken to a lonely road under cover of darkness and killed. Newspapers, magazines, and television stations on every continent carried stories about the disappearance of two white civil-rights workers from the North and one 21-year-old Negro worker from Meridian, Mississippi. State and local law enforcement officers did not take action. But the Federal Bureau of Investigation, under explicit orders from the President, poured agents into Neshoba County. Forty-four days after the deaths, agents of the F.B.I. discovered the three bodies buried in an earthen dam at a farm pond five miles southwest of Philadelphia, Mississippi. On February 28, 1967, 19 men were indicted under the felony provision of an 1870 civil rights statute providing a maximum penalty of 10 years in prison and a $5000 fine.[14] Superficially, the two lynchings were different. The first was a race riot and public spectacle resulting from an alleged sexual crime, while the second, a clandestine murder, resulted from no crime at all. The first went largely unpunished; the second led to indictments that produced convictions and prison sentences. The similarities lie in the meaning of the victims' behavior to their murderers. In Neshoba County no less than in Leeville, the lynch mob consisted mainly of poorly educated, working-class men who might well have entertained secret doubts of their superiority to Negroes. And in both lynchings the mob was incensed because of a failure of the victims to observe the etiquette of white supremacy. In the Leeville case, the failure was incidental to sexual activities; in Neshoba County it was a deliberate, principled attack on white supremacy as a way of life. White supremacists probably regarded the second failure as worse than the first. "They asked for it" was one response to news reports of the murder.

How is it possible for a lynching to result from a mere breach of etiquette? If etiquette is thought of as the symbolic expression of cultural judgments of what is good and bad, of who is important and who unimportant, then a breach of etiquette can be a very serious matter.

---

[14] *The New York Times*, March 1, 1967, p. 1. Seven of the accused, including Deputy Sheriff Price, were later convicted and sentenced to prison terms.

The Self-Fulfilling Prophecy: A Force for the Maintenance of Old Meanings. That lynchings are now rare indicates that the meaning of a darkly pigmented skin is changing in the United States. A cynic might say that this change, long overdue, became a political necessity as American contact increased with the new nations of Asia and Africa.[15] A rationalist might argue that this change became inevitable when science undermined the intellectual respectability of race prejudice.[16] That the change is so slow[17] is accounted for by the principle of the **self-fulfilling prophecy** outlined by sociologist Robert K. Merton.[18] A self-fulfilling prophecy is a cultural definition, initially untrue, which affects interaction in such a way as to generate its own confirming evidence. Thus in a culture that interprets a darkly pigmented skin to mean intellectual inferiority, teachers of black children feel they are working at a hopeless task and Negro students develop low educational aspirations. Like the college students in the perception experiments of Professor Asch described in Chapter 1, they are sensitive to the expectations of significant others. The result will be educational failure, early school leaving, and disproportionately infrequent college attendance. It is sociologically naive to infer from the poorer scholastic accomplishments of black students under these circumstances that the initial belief in their intellectual inferiority was justified. Belief in the intellectual inferiority of Negroes leads to Negroes being given fewer educational opportunities than whites of equal intelligence, and the prophecy is fulfilled.

The seeming fulfillment of the prophecy reinforces the original meaning of the symbol, not only with regard to racial stereotypes but in any circumstances where a widely shared belief generates its own supporting evidence. A folk notion maintains, for example, that redheaded persons have fiery tempers. If this interpretation of red hair results in a general expectation that redheaded persons cannot control themselves as well as other people, redheads are encouraged to live up to their reputations. It then becomes difficult to persuade the public that there is no biological connection between the gene controlling hair color and the complex emotional reactions involved in a temper tantrum. Experience appears to confirm the folk-belief. Self-fulfilling prophecies are ubiquitous because cultural definitions, correct or incorrect, influence the course of interaction. Or, as W. I. Thomas put it, "If men define situations as real, they are real in their consequences." Japanese culture takes a dim view of a boy raised without a father in the home. How can he receive the proper moral and disciplinary training? As a result of this assumption, Japanese business firms

---

[15] Rupert Emerson and Martin Kilson, "The American Dilemma in a Changing World: The Rise of Africa and the Negro American," *Daedalus,* Vol. 94, Fall 1964, pp. 1055-1084.

[16] Franz Boas, *The Mind of Primitive Man,* rev. ed., New York: Macmillan, 1938; Ruth Benedict, *Race: Science and Politics,* New York: Modern Age Books, 1940; Otto Klineberg, *Negro Intelligence and Selective Migration,* New York: Columbia University Press, 1935.

[17] Martin Luther King, Jr., *Why We Can't Wait,* New York: Harper & Row, 1964.

[18] Robert K. Merton, "The Self-Fulfilling Prophecy," *Antioch Review,* Vol. 8, June 1948, pp. 193-210.

Lynn McLaren—Rapho Guillumette

discriminate against orphans (and sons of divorced parents) in their hiring policies. One consequence of this cultural interpretation of orphanhood is that orphans have less chance than young men from intact homes of achieving successful careers in business.[19]

The concept of the self-fulfilling prophecy calls attention to the built-in inertia of cultural systems. Despite the arbitrariness of the connection between cultural symbol and communicated meaning—a darkly pigmented skin can be

[19] Ezra F. Vogel, *Japan's New Middle Classes,* Berkeley: University of California Press, 1963, p. 18.

interpreted "biologically superior person" as well as "biologically inferior person—once either connection has been made, the social psychological mechanisms described by Professor Merton tend to perpetuate it: for example, relatively unprejudiced whites can observe "evidence" of Negro inferiority without realizing that cultural expectations produced it. The more people understand the self-fulfilling potentialities of cultural definitions, the less likely they are to accept self-confirming prophecies. And the greater the sociological sophistication in a population, the less likely people are to infer permanent connections between cultural symbols and traditional meanings. To put it another way, cultural imputations can be self-destroying as well as self-fulfilling. Suppose that Americans were profoundly shocked by the existing relationship between low family income and high infant mortality. Special governmentally supported health programs might be established to make the chances of a child's surviving the first year of life independent of his parents' economic resources. If they succeeded, a cultural definition, initially true, would have affected interaction so as to result in that definition's refutation.

THE CULTURAL CONSISTENCY OF A SOCIETY

From one point of view, a culture consists of individual bits of meaning and the symbols that evoke them—much as a dictionary can be thought of as a list of individual words and their definitions. On the other hand, not all culture traits are mutually compatible. Belief in witchcraft and belief in science are difficult to reconcile. If Americans regard illness as due to the machinations of witches (as Navaho Indians traditionally did) but regard the weather as understandable in terms of scientific meteorology, American culture would be straddling the issue of science versus superstition.[20] In fact, there is a strain to consistency in a culture. Culture traits are not wholly independent of one another; they tend to blend, to form *patterns* of meaning. Insofar as a culture changes (a topic that will be discussed further in Chapter 14), it tends to become more consistent. This occurs by a process of *discarding* meanings inconsistent with its pervasive themes as well as by *adding* traits that fit in congenially.

A good illustration of the strain to consistency in a culture is the changing meaning of skin pigmentation in American society. American culture faced a dilemma with respect to Negroes.[21] The dominant cultural value of equality collided with the traditional subordination of the Negro deriving from slavery. Another aspect of the dilemma was the inconsistency of American admiration for science and American disregard of scientific evidence bearing on the trivi-

---

[20] Clyde Kluckhohn, *Navaho Witchcraft,* Cambridge, Mass.: Harvard University Press, 1944.

[21] Gunnar Myrdal, *An American Dilemma: The Negro Problem and Modern Democracy,* New York: Harper, 1944.

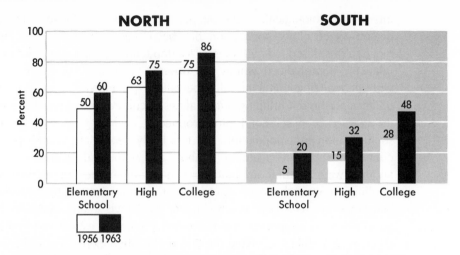

FIGURE 3.1 **The differential acceptance of school integration by northern and southern whites as a function of educational level, 1956–1963. Degree of education and attitudes toward integration of schools are compared. Each bar shows the percentage of whites in that category supporting integration of public schools. Although support for integration rises with degree of education and has gone up in all categories, even college-educated Southerners have yet to attain the level of support for integration of public schools shown in 1956 by Northerners of grammar schools education.** Source: National Opinion Research Center surveys reported in Herbert H. Hyman and Paul B. Sheatsley, "Attitudes toward Desegregation," *Scientific American,* Vol. 211, July 1964, p. 22.

ality of race differences. Increased concern over the civil rights of blacks is helping to resolve this cultural dilemma. The belief in equality of opportunity has become more consistently established in American society, and rationalizations by the misinformed are more firmly rejected by a scientifically oriented citizenry. The rising levels of education in American society exposed greater proportions of the population to the scientific point of view, thus making it more difficult for folk notions of Negro inferiority to survive. To say, "I may be prejudiced, but . . .," became equivalent to saying, "I may be an ignorant clod, but. . . ." Figure 3.1 documents the relationship between the educational level of whites and their willingness to grant equality to Negroes. Figure 3.1 shows the results of a cross-sectional survey — that is, a survey taken at one point in time; but surveys taken between 1942 and 1963 show dramatic shifts in the proportions of whites favoring equal access by Negroes to housing and non-discriminatory seating in public transportation.[22] In short, the respectability of race prejudice is declining in the United States, and a factor in its decline is its incompatibility with other, more highly valued, American culture traits.

[22] The following questions were asked in national surveys: "If a Negro with the same income and education as you have moved into your block, would it make any difference to you?" and "Generally speaking, do you think there should be separate sections for Negroes on streetcars and buses?" Paul B. Sheatsley, "White Attitudes toward the Negro," *Daedalus,* Vol. 95, Winter 1966, p. 222.

Every culture tends toward internal consistency. In the enormously complex cultures of modern societies, however, inconsistencies are less likely to confront one another. Hence the unity of a culture, the internal consistency of its themes, is clearer in the preliterate societies studied by cultural anthropologists. Ruth Benedict, in her classic study, *Patterns of Culture,* described three such cultures.[23] First, she showed how a variety of culture traits of the Pueblo Indians of the Southwest (the Zuñi) reveal a ceremonious people who pursue moderation in all things:[24]

> The ideal man in Zuñi is a person of dignity and affability who has never tried to lead, and who has never called forth comment from his neighbors. Any conflict, even though all right is on his side, is held against him. Even in contests of skill like their foot races, if a man wins habitually he is debarred from running. They are interested in a game that a number can play with even chances, and an outstanding runner spoils the game: they will have none of him.

Marriage among the Zuñi is not the result of violent passions but a rather casual matter. When girls carry water jars to the spring for water, a boy may ask one for a drink. She gives it to him if she likes him, and he may give her a present of rabbits he killed in a rabbit hunt. Traditionally they are not supposed to have any further meetings after this:[25]

> When a boy decides to ask her father for the girl, he goes to her house. As in every Zuñi visit, he first tastes the food that is set before him, and the father says to him as he must say to every visitor, "Perhaps you came for something." The boy answers, "Yes, I came thinking of your daughter." The father calls his daughter, saying, "I cannot speak for her. Let her say." If she is willing, the mother goes into the next room and makes up the pallet and they retire together. Next day she washes his hair. After four days she dresses in her best clothes and carries a large basket of fine corn flour to his mother's house as a present. There are no further formalities and little social interest is aroused in the affair.

If the core value of Zuñi culture is moderation, the core value of the second society described by Dr. Benedict is hostility. Dobu is an island off the southern shore of eastern New Guinea. Up to a few generations ago, the inhabitants were cannibals. The Dobuans are suspicious of and treacherous toward outsiders, but they also lavish these qualities on one another. They rarely laugh. Sullenness is regarded as a virtue and laughter as foolishness. Their marital customs reflect their paranoid conception of human life. All marriages begin as "shotgun weddings." From the time of puberty, a boy sleeps each night in the house of one or another unmarried girl, leaving her side well before daybreak. When he tires of roaming, he deliberately oversleeps, thus permitting the mother of his girlfriend to trap him in the house. There is no other way to be-

[23] Ruth Benedict, *Patterns of Culture,* Boston: Houghton Mifflin, 1934.
[24] Benedict, *Patterns of Culture,* p. 99.
[25] Benedict, *Patterns of Culture,* pp. 73-74.

come engaged. His future mother-in-law blocks the doorway, thereby attracting the attention of the villagers, who come to stare at the humiliated couple.
This is betrothal. Marriage is equally painful. The couple lives in alternate years
in the village of the bride and of the groom.[26]

> Each alternate year one spouse has the backing of his own group and com-
> mands the situation. The alternate year the same spouse is a tolerated alien who
> must efface himself before the owners of his spouse's village. . . . By all the tradi-
> tional means at its command Dobuan society demands that during the year in the
> spouse's village the spouse who is on alien territory play a role of humiliation. All
> the owners of the village may call him by his name. He may never use the name
> of any one of them. . . .
>
> Tension of an even more intimate kind is also present. Faithfulness is not ex-
> pected between husband and wife, and no Dobuan will admit that a man and
> woman are ever together even for the shortest interval except for sexual pur-
> poses. The outsider spouse of the year is quick to suspect unfaithfulness. Usually
> he has grounds. In the suspicion-ridden atmosphere of Dobu the safest liaison is
> with a village "brother" or a village "sister." During the year when one is in
> one's own village circumstances are propitious and supernatural dangers at a
> minimum. Public opinion strongly disapproves of marriage between such classi-
> ficatory "brothers" and "sisters." It would disrupt the village to have obligatory
> marital exchanges between two parts of the settlement. But adultery within this
> group is a favourite pastime. It is celebrated constantly in mythology, and its oc-
> currence in every village is known to everyone from early childhood. It is a matter
> of profoundest concern to the outraged spouse. He (it is as likely to be she) bribes
> the children for information, his own or any in the village. If it is the husband, he
> breaks his wife's cooking-pots. If it is the wife, she maltreats her husband's dog.
> He quarrels with her violently, and no quarrel can go unheard in the close set,
> leaf-thatched houses of Dobu. He throws himself out of the village in a fury. As a
> last resort of impotent rage he attempts suicide by one of several traditional
> methods, no one of which is surely fatal. He is usually saved and by this means he
> enlists his wife's susu [relatives]; in fear of what his relatives might do if the out-
> raged spouse succeeded in his attempts at suicide, they are moved to a more con-
> ciliatory behavior. They may even refuse to take any further steps in the matter,
> and the partners to the marriage may remain sullenly and angrily together. The
> next year the wife can retaliate similarly in her own village.

Thus, in their marital practices as in other traits of Dobuan culture, the theme of
mutual hostility is consistently reinforced.

The central theme of the third preliterate society reported on by Dr. Benedict, the Kwakiutl Indians of the Pacific Northwest, is competitiveness. Even
hospitality becomes an occasion for outdoing one's rivals. The Kwakiutl *potlatch* is a feast so wasteful that the guests will be unable to reciprocate. Wealth
is sought in order to be given away or consumed at potlatches, thereby giving
prestige to its possessor. As the Kwakiutl put it, "We do not fight with weapons.

---

[26] Reprinted by permission. From Benedict, *Patterns of Culture,* pp. 136-139.

We fight with property." An important form of property consists of etched sheets of copper of little intrinsic worth but great symbolic value. The value of coppers—sometimes as much as 10,000 blankets—derives from their history, that is, from the great potlatch feasts in the course of which they were given away. Guests at the potlatch are challenged to reciprocate with an even bigger display of aggressive hospitality. Of course, guests try not to reveal by their demeanor at the potlatch that they have been outdone. They feign indifference to the conspicuous consumption they are witnessing. The host pours vast amounts of candlefish oil on the fire. The more he pours, the more the guests suffer from the intense heat, for they are seated close to the flames. It would be shameful to them to draw back or to acknowledge the heat in any way. This is, after all, a contest. The host's party prepared mocking life-size carvings of the chief guest, his poverty symbolized by protruding ribs, his lack of status by an undignified position.

The point of Dr. Benedict's comparative descriptions of Zuñi, Dobu, and Kwakiutl cultures is that each society has *distinctive* cultural themes. Once these themes are identified, the scientific observer can better understand individual culture traits as expressions of underlying values. For example, without knowing about funeral observances among the Zuñi, the anthropologist would expect restrained ceremonials rather than emotional binges because of the Zuñi idea of moderation in all things. Knowing the paranoid quality of Dobu culture, he would expect death to be associated with recriminations, and indeed it is. The Dobuans have no concept of natural death; they believe that deaths occur because an enemy has mobilized black magic. Hence the initial consideration is to locate the culprit on whom the murder can be blamed. Not surprisingly, considering the hostility between man and wife, the murderer is usually identified as the spouse. Dr. Benedict's assumption of the consistency of the traits of a culture—their organization into a limited number of value configurations or patterns—describes small preliterate societies rather well. The assumption of value consistency holds less well in urban industrial societies. Urban industrial societies are not only larger; they are internally much more differentiated. These differentiations make it likely that the interactional subsystems (and their distinctive symbols) confront one another infrequently. Thus the complex society can be thought of as possessing a mosaic of overlapping subcultures rather than a single culture. Obviously, the possibility of cultural inconsistency is greater under such circumstances.

SUBCULTURAL DIFFERENTIATION IN COMPLEX SOCIETIES

Culture facilitates human communication, but its mode of transmission, *learning,* imposes a limitation, especially in a complex society. How can the indi-

Marc & Evelyn Bernheim—Rapho Guillumette

vidual American learn all the meanings developed by his society? How much is he likely to learn of the specialized symbols used by pig farmers, physicists, ballet dancers, and archbishops? Modern societies have remarkable technologies for helping the individual to understand their cultures: dictionaries, encyclopedias, libraries, museums, electronic data-retrieval systems. Nevertheless, there are limits to the storage capacity of the human brain and the time an individual can spend in trying to learn the meanings of the vast number of culture traits that exist. Given these limits, a complex society cannot have a culture in the same sense that smaller interactive systems like families possess cultures. All Americans cannot share common symbols to which they attach precisely the same meanings. Instead, a complex society consists of a mosaic of cultures, partly overlapping, but so large in the aggregate that the sharing of meanings between individual members is necessarily partial. *Subculture* is the term used by sociologists to identify distinct patterns of the mosaic: clusters of culture traits shared fairly completely by subgroups within the larger society.

Subcultural **differentiation** results partly from unevenness in communication. The communication of physicist with physicist—through reading one another's articles as well as in face-to-face conversations—sustains the subculture of physics. Similarly, the communications of Navaho Indians with other Navahos on the same New Mexico reservation sustain the subculture of that tribe. But this intensity of communication within a subculture is more a defining characteristic than a causal explanation. Why do subcultures develop in the particular forms that they do? A full answer to this question requires an exhaustive analysis of modern societies since the cultural is but one dimension of human interaction. The interactional *subsystems* of the society should be examined in order to understand its subcultures thoroughly. The partial treatment of subcultures given here will be expanded in the institutional analyses of later chapters.

Subcultures arise from three main sources:

1. Some arise because of the isolation of groups from contact with the larger society. This isolation may be geographic in origin as in the subculture of Ozark Mountain whites.[27] Or the isolation may be the result of common ancestry or history, self-imposed among Daughters of the American Revolution, imposed largely by others in the case of Mexican-Americans.

2. Some arise because of institutional differentiation. Instead of having one paramount institution, the family, as in most preliterate societies, modern societies have a variety of differentiated activities — economic, educational, recreational, scientific, artistic. Associated with each are specialized symbols.

3. Some subcultures are constituted in *opposition* to values of the dominant culture, not totally but to an important degree. Delinquent youth cultures have a distinctly negativistic character. To the degree that a subculture is oppositional and is sustained by the personality needs of the participants, it may be called a **contraculture**.[28]

These three types of subcultures will now be discussed in greater detail.

Ethnic and Ecological Subcultures. Presumed biological relatedness is the core of ethnic identity. Thus Negro Americans may not actually have common ancestry, but they are regarded by whites (and sometimes by one another) as having a similar heredity. In addition, they share a collective history and collective memories of their American experiences. In an analogous way, Irish-Americans, Italian-Americans, Jews, Chinese, Japanese, and American Indians constitute **ethnic groups.** There is a social psychological test of ethnic identity: Do members of a racial, religious, or national group consider themselves one people and are they so considered by others? **Assimilation** of an ethnic group occurs when the members no longer feel bound to one another by ties of blood and history and when the rest of the society does not remind them of their supposedly distinct identity. This means that assimilation can occur more quickly than biological mixture. From this point of view, Negroes could cease to constitute an ethnic group in America even though persons of dark pigmen-

---

[27] Walter O. Cralle, "Social Change and Isolation in the Ozark Mountain Region of Missouri," *American Journal of Sociology,* Vol. 41, January 1963, pp. 435-446.

[28] J. Milton Yinger, "Contraculture and Subculture," *American Sociological Review,* Vol. 25, October 1960, pp. 625-635.

tation and Negroid features remained within the population. These biological variations would no longer be socially important. Whites would disregard them in day-to-day interactions as differences in eye color are now disregarded. In addition, blacks would have to forgo any special pride in black achievements; they would have to think of Crispus Attucks, one of the patriots killed in the Boston Massacre, primarily as a patriot rather than primarily as a Negro.

A half century ago the United States was thought of as a melting pot in which distinct ethnic identities were becoming fused and out of which a homogeneous population would emerge. This may have been an unrealistic expectation. True, *external* obstacles to assimilation are crumbling; prejudice and discrimination against ethnic minorities are decreasing. No one sees signs, such as those posted on nineteenth-century neighborhood taverns, "Irish and dogs — keep out." But *internal* obstacles to assimilation remain. Ethnic groups frequently possess subcultural traits that bind members to one another. Sometimes the subculture includes little more than dietary preferences; the family likes to patronize a Greek restaurant rather than a Chinese or an Italian one. Sometimes the subcultural commitment includes a second language, songs and other recreational interests, religious beliefs, national loyalties. In short, membership in ethnic groups may result partly from exclusion from full participation in the larger society but also from voluntary commitment to subcultural values. Such voluntary commitment may decrease as generations pass but not at a linear rate. As one student of immigrant adjustment to America observed, "What the son wishes to forget, the grandson wishes to remember."[29] And to the extent that ethnic groups remember their subcultures, **cultural pluralism** is more characteristic than assimilation. Cultural pluralism refers to the peaceful coexistence of ethnic subcultures within modern societies.

Ethnic subcultures are conspicuous in ethnic communities: in Chinatowns, Little Italies, Harlems. When people sharing an ethnic subculture live close together, they can communicate easily with one another in ethnic symbols, and they teach these symbols to the next generation. Thus in Puerto Rican neighborhoods in New York City are found some persons who speak Spanish rather than English.[30] But neighborhoods need not be ethnically homogeneous to maintain a subculture. To the extent that a locality creates distinctive symbols to communicate shared meanings, it constitutes a subculture regardless of its ethnic composition. Hence the Lower East Side of Manhattan may constitute an ecological subculture different from the ethnic subcultures (Jewish, Italian, Puerto Rican) present in that area.

Spatial adjacency gives rise to ecologically based subcultures. Propinquity

[29] Marcus L. Hansen, *The Problem of the Third Generation Immigrant,* Rock Island, Ill.: Augustana Historical Society, 1938; see also Oscar Handlin, *The Uprooted: The Epic Story of the Great Migrations That Made the American People,* Boston: Little, Brown, 1952.

[30] For a discussion of the Puerto Rican communities of New York City, see Nathan Glazer and Daniel Patrick Moynihan, *Beyond the Melting Pot: The Negroes, Puerto Ricans, Jews, Italians, and Irish of New York City,* Cambridge, Mass.: M.I.T. Press, 1963, Chap. 2.

Ken Heyman

increases the probability of interaction; distance is an obstacle to communication. In modern societies, with their telephones, radios, television sets, and high-speed methods of transportation, distance is not as important a barrier to interaction as it was 100 years ago. Nevertheless, distance imposes costs, as the students of human ecology say. As long as it remains more difficult to interact with persons spatially distant from us, subcultural differentiation will occur on ecological bases. The ethnic mix in a given locality will affect the ecological subculture—for instance, the Boston accent owes much to the nineteenth-century tide of Irish immigration. Historical experiences act in the same way: the regional subculture of the American South cannot be understood without reference to the Civil War. Ecological subcultures are nonetheless realities apart from the factors that influenced their development in a particular form.

Subcultures of Specialized Institutions: Art, Science, Religion. In every society people invent stories, songs, and dances for the enjoyment of themselves and others; they paint, carve, and sculpt. But such persons are not "artists" unless their artistic efforts help to define their identities and become a social expectation—that is, are performed in the context of a specialized role. There is, in short, a difference between the exuberant paintings of prehistoric hunters on the walls of their caves and the daily quota of work in his studio by Pablo Picasso. One aspect of the differentiation of the role of the artist is that those who spend their lives producing art develop a specialized artistic subculture that the casual consumer of their work may neither understand nor appreciate. This cultural gap between the artist and his audience is an inevitable

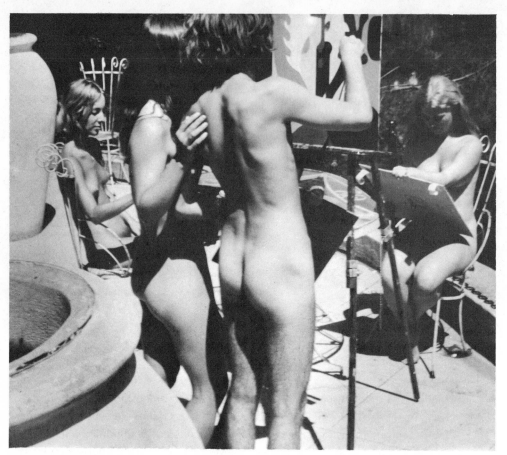

Blau – PIX

consequence of specialization: some members of a society devote their lives to producing art that is to be accepted or rejected by an anonymous cross section of the society (the mass audiences characteristic of urban industrial societies).[31] Artists develop symbols that communicate meanings more clearly to other artists than to members of the society at large. When cubism and other forms of nonrepresentational painting developed in Europe half a century ago, the general public was bewildered. The innovators depended on other artists for recognition that they were pioneering.

Just as every society produces art but not necessarily artists (socially recognized specialists), so every society utilizes technical know-how, but only modern societies possess scientists. Scientists have the right and the obligation to be skeptical of what everyone knows to be true because they occupy specialized roles that require them to search for knowledge. Columbus was skeptical about the flat-world theory, and he undertook a voyage that disproved it.

[31] Joseph Bensman and Israel Gerver, "Art and the Mass Society," *Social Problems*, Vol. 6, Summer 1958, pp. 4-10.

But Columbus was not a scientist. His society did not place him in a role requiring him to be curious and expecting him to produce new knowledge with some regularity. The circumstances giving rise to an atmosphere hospitable to science constitute a fascinating problem in intellectual history.[32] Sociologists have shown that these circumstances are not only intellectual but religious, economic, and political; science can develop and flourish only in a certain type of society.[33] The economic growth of Europe in the eighteenth and nineteenth centuries was a circumstance favorable to scientific development because science obviously had technological applications. But it should be kept in mind that James Watt, the inventor of the steam engine, was no more a scientist than Columbus was. He was a gadgeteer, an inventor, a practical man who was looking for a better way to accomplish a practical objective.

However much science depends on an encouraging attitude from society in its early stages of development, the subculture of science cannot flourish without some autonomy. Although the university originated in Western society long before the emergence of science, the university was an ideal climate for the growth of the scientific subculture. The university provides autonomy; it removes the pressure for immediate results and practical applications. Some would argue that in the long run ,his is the best way to stimulate inventions: to give impractical scientists the freedom to pursue their idle curiosity and let society cash in on the unintended technological applications. But the subculture of science does not justify itself in these terms. Professor Merton calls attention to a toast at a dinner for scientists at Cambridge University: "To pure mathematics, and may it never be of any use to anybody!" This toast sounds a trifle outdated. Clearly, mathematics is crucial to modern technology. But the spirit of the toast reflects the contemporary scientific subculture. Scientists seek truth for its own sake. The utilization of the truths they discover—for example, the power locked in the atomic nucleus of hydrogen—is not their special obligation.

Veracity is the paramount value of the scientific subculture; in this subculture the forging of data is the cardinal sin. Originality is another value of the subculture of science. The desire to show evidence of originality accounts for the bitter controversies over who discovered what first.[34] Newton and Leibniz each claimed to have invented calculus; Galileo attacked Father Horatio Grassi for trying "to diminish whatever praise there may be in this [invention of the telescope] which belongs to me"; and Saint-Simon and Comte quarreled over which was the father of sociology. Professor Merton points out that these seemingly petty squabbles over priorities arise not because scientists are more hungry for fame than are persons in other occupations but because the

[32] Alfred North Whitehead, *Science and the Modern World,* New York: Macmillan, 1947.

[33] Robert K. Merton, *Social Theory and Social Structure,* Glencoe, Ill.: Free Press, 1957, Chap. 15-19.

[34] Robert K. Merton, "Priorities in Scientific Discovery: A Chapter in the Sociology of Science," *American Sociological Review,* Vol. 22, December 1957, pp. 635-659.

subculture of science uses originality as the major criterion of successful performance in the role of scientist:[35]

> It is not necessary that individual scientists begin with a lust for fame; it is enough that science, with its abiding and often functional emphasis on originality and its assigning of large rewards for originality, makes recognition of priority uppermost. Recognition and fame then become symbol and reward for having done one's job well.

Religious activities, like artistic and scientific activities, generate distinct subcultures in modern societies. There are religious specialists (ministers, priests, rabbis) just as there are artistic and scientific specialists. Unlike artistic and scientific subcultures, however, religious subcultures are understood by nonspecialists to a much greater extent. Catholic liturgy and dogma are not as fully understood by Catholic laymen as by priests, but except for the subculture's monastic orders the religious symbolism is freely shared. The clergy are delighted to teach communicants as much ritual and dogma as they are willing to learn. One reason for this is that a religious denomination in a pluralistic society constitutes an interactive group as well as a subculture. The artist and his anonymous mass audience do not constitute an interactive group in the same sense. Religious subcultures resemble in their interactive aspect ethnic and ecological subcultures, and indeed ethnic and ecological factors can reinforce a religious subculture. For instance, Hasidic Jewish communities are ecologically segregated as well as ethnically and religiously homogeneous.[36] And the Catholic Church in the United States used to be organized informally along ethnic lines.[37]

Just as ethnic and ecological subcultures differentiate a society, posing problems of overall cultural integration, so too can religious subcultures be incompatible.[38] In India the Moslem subculture and the Hindu subculture interpret the universe in such different terms as to jeopardize political stability. In the United States, on the other hand, the major religious groups, despite important disagreements about theology and ritual, tacitly agree on the legitimacy of other religious subcultures. This consensus on denominational pluralism is incomplete. Sects like Christian Science, Jehovah's Witnesses, and the Church of the Latter-Day Saints (the Mormons) deny, in theory if not in practice, that traditional Catholic, Protestant, and Jewish groups have legitimate paths to salvation. But they are not sufficiently numerous or determined that they jeopardize the framework of **denominational pluralism.** Perhaps because the overwhelming majority of American denominations derive

---

[35] Merton, "Priorities in Scientific Discovery," p. 640.

[36] Solomon Poll, *The Hasidic Community of Williamsburg,* New York: Free Press of Glencoe, 1962.

[37] Will Herberg, *Protestant-Catholic-Jew: An Essay in American Religious Sociology,* Garden City, N.Y.: Doubleday, 1955, Chap. 7.

[38] Allan W. Eister, "Religious Institutions in Complex Societies: Difficulties in the Theoretic Specification of Function," *American Sociological Review,* Vol. 22, August 1957, pp. 387–391.

from the Judeo-Christian tradition, mutual understanding among religious subcultures is easier to attain than between the Hindu and Moslem subcultures
on the Indian subcontinent.

Oppositional Subcultures. In complex societies some groups establish
identities in the course of unfriendly interaction with the rest of society. To
some extent this can be said about many subgroups including the religious
sects mentioned in the previous section: Christian Scientists, Jehovah's Witnesses, Mormons. But the subcultures of these sects developed independently
of their conflicts with American society; presumably their distinct symbols were
not responses to social condemnation. On the other hand, the subculture of
homosexuals appears derived as much from the need to fend off condemnation
and discovery from the larger society as from the peculiarities of homosexual
preoccupations.[39] The concept of *oppositional subcultures* refers to subcultures that have many traits which can be explained in terms of social stigma
and the defensive reactions of interacting victims of this disapproval. For
example, a leading theory of adolescent delinquency explains the delinquent
subculture as a collective response of working-class boys to middle-class
competition in which they feel disadvantaged.[40] According to this theory,
delinquents steal and deface property less to obtain money and fun than to
express frustration at the drubbing their egos sustain in the educational and
occupational systems. As time goes on, they gradually learn of the existence of
others who are also treated with contempt by teachers and suspicion by the
police. They encourage one another to disregard the opinions of these conventional persons. They mutually reinforce one another's self-respect by creating
a different type of competition—in which the goals are stealing, fighting, and
community hell-raising—because this is a contest they can win. Criminologists
describe the interactive system they have created as a "delinquent gang" and
its distinctive symbols as a "delinquent subculture."

A similar explanation has been developed for rebellious behavior in American high schools.[41] Since teachers are present in the classroom, school
rebellion is more than the violation of school regulations; it is simultaneously
the flouting of adult authority. Stinchcombe believes the motivation for this
deliberate defiance is resentment, and those students who cannot see the
relevance of schoolwork for their adult lives are the most rebellious. They develop a subculture of rebellion in terms of which they demand symbols of
precocious adulthood: the right to smoke, to drive a car, to marry young. In
terms of this subculture the boy who lights a cigarette in front of a teacher is
not merely being personally provocative. He is communicating by a subcultural gesture his rejection of adolescent subordination to rules made by
adults. The less successful the student is in school, the less relevant school-

[39] Maurice Leznoff and William A. Westley, "The Homosexual Community," *Social Problems,*
Vol. 4, April 1956, pp. 257–263.

[40] Albert K. Cohen, *Delinquent Boys: The Culture of the Gang,* Glencoe, Ill.: Free Press, 1953.

[41] Arthur L. Stinchcombe, *Rebellion in a High School,* Chicago: Quadrangle Books, 1964.

work is to his future, and the more attractive becomes the subculture of rebel-lion. "Adolescence comes to be undesirable to students whose future is not attractive enough to justify current subordination."[42]

Bear in mind that no subculture is completely oppositional. The opposi-tional component of a subculture is a matter of degree — to be assessed on the basis of empirical investigation. The concept of an oppositional subculture (or contraculture) is nevertheless useful because it sensitizes the sociologist to one basis for subcultural differentiation. Professor Howard Becker, in his study of jazz musicians, found that the rejection of "square" values — for example, a clear melody and a regular beat — was important in this artistic subculture.[43] Other artistic and scientific subcultures are probably less embattled than that of jazz musicians. The concept of contraculture may not be relevant to physics or to opera.

CONCLUSION

Reality has for human beings a cultural dimension. Words, acts, and even the physical environment are examined for *meaning* before they are reacted to. Culture, in providing a shared vocabulary of meanings for the members of a society, makes possible common interpretations of the world and of human behavior in it. Thus culture is a prerequisite for sustained systems of interaction.

In common speech "culture" is used to refer to the esteemed traditions of a society, such as painting, poetry, music, and literature. As this chapter has made clear, sociologists and anthropologists do not use the term in this way. For the social scientist, the cultural tradition of a society consists of its distinc-tive symbols for communicating shared meanings; thus culture is a social heritage that each generation must relearn as well as augment. The culture of the United States includes the English language, obscene gestures, safe crack-ing, profanity, cooking, and furniture making as well as artistic achievements. Every society, from the most advanced industrial countries to technologically primitive tribes, has certain symbols that are understood by that society's population. *This is its culture.* Culture is the cement that holds systems of inter-action together. Without culture human communication would necessarily remain at the level of the snarls and barks by means of which dogs express themselves.

The advantages of symbolic communication are obvious. The disadvan-tages should be noted also. The doctrine of white supremacy is a cultural

---

[42] Stinchcombe, *Rebellion in a High School,* p. 132.

[43] Howard S. Becker, "The Professional Dance Musician and His Audience," *American Journal of Sociology,* Vol. 57, September 1951, pp. 136-144.

phenomenon. A Southern lynching, far from being a reversion to subhuman brutality, is comprehensible only when the cultural definition of pigmentation is understood, when, for example, the rape of a white woman by a black male is interpreted in the context of the etiquette of race relations defined by white supremacy. Tigers kill, but human beings hate. In short, some of the least attractive features of human society—cruelty, greed, lust, envy—depend on culture. A second disadvantage of symbolic communication is a consequence of the fact that the meanings of symbols are arbitrary. Since the meanings must be *learned* from other people, the possibility always exists that misunderstandings will arise because different persons learn different meanings for the same symbol. And even when the meaning of a symbol is shared, there is no guarantee that communication failure will not occur. Symbols facilitate deception as well as honest communications.

Although the possibility of communication failure, deliberately engineered or accidental, is inherent in the nature of cultural symbols, the subcultural differentiation of complex societies makes communication failure more likely. One reason for this is that ethnic groups develop subcultural meanings not shared by others. Second, ecological segregation produces subcultures in local communities that are to some degree unique. Third, the differentiation of institutional activities into specialized interactive subsystems—art, science, religion—stimulates subcultural differentiation. Furthermore, these institutionally generated subcultures sometimes develop an oppositional character that further differentiates them from the larger society. The individual living in an urban industrial society cannot comprehend the meanings of all the traits he encounters in what is a mosaic of subcultures. Nonetheless, there exist strains to consistency among culture traits and even among subcultures. Communication failure occurs, but it is not inevitable. Handsomely compensating for the risks of communication failure in a heterogeneous society is the richness of meanings available in a cultural mosaic.

SOME SIGNIFICANT LITERATURE ON CULTURE

Bernard Barber, *Science and the Social Order,* Glencoe, Ill.: Free Press, 1952. The possession of a method for adding systematically to knowledge is one of the distinguishing features of the cultures of urban industrial societies. In his book Professor Barber analyzes the place of science in democratic and despotic societies, the social control of science, and the social organization of science. Concentrating particularly on American society, he discusses the scientist in the university, in industry, and in government. The book concludes with a chapter on the social sciences. This summary is based on a review by Robert Bierstedt, *American Sociological Review,* Vol. 18, December 1953, pp. 721-722.

James H. Barnett, *The American Christmas: A Study in National Culture,* New York: Macmillan, 1954. If a sociologist from Mars came to the United States, he would be interested in national festivals and their significance in American life. Barnett subjects Christmas to this kind of analysis. This summary is based on a review by Frederick Elkin, *American Sociological Review,* Vol. 20, June 1955, p. 366.

Ruth Benedict, *Patterns of Culture,* Boston: Houghton Mifflin, 1934. What Ruth Benedict attempts in this book is to show that it is possible to describe three preliterate cultures as *wholes* rather than to catalog hundreds of unrelated customs and practices. When the dominant theme of each culture is recognized (the *pattern* of its culture), the detached observer from a totally different society can understand how the culture organizes its social life meaningfully around this theme. Of course, the well-integrated preliterate society is more amenable to such configurational analysis than urban industrial societies, but Benedict also tries (in another book) to apply the configurational approach to contemporary Japan. See her book, *The Chrysanthemum and the Sword,* Boston: Houghton Mifflin, 1946.

Bernard Berelson, *Content Analysis in Communication Research,* Glencoe, Ill.: Free Press, 1952. The analysis of the symbolic content of newspapers, magazines, radio broadcasts, and motion pictures has been used for a number of purposes: (1) to trace trends, (2) to compare one medium of mass communication with another, (3) to audit the quality of the communication, (4) to measure readability, (5) to obtain military intelligence, and more. Berelson describes the technical problems involved in content analysis. What units of analysis should be used — small units like the word or larger units like the sentence or the theme? How should material be sampled so as to increase the reliability and validity of the quantitative analysis? He also addresses the criticisms of content analysis and especially the complaint of humanists that it is unrealistic to hope to reduce the subtlety of linguistic communication to rows of percentages. This summary is based on a review by Ithiel De Sola Pool, *American Sociological Review,* Vol. 17, August 1952, pp. 515-516.

Henry Elkin, "Aggressive and Erotic Tendencies in Army Life," *American Journal of Sociology,* Vol. 51, March 1946, pp. 408-413. The author of this article drew upon his observations of Army life while he served in the Armed Forces during the Second World War. Specifically, he was struck by the exaggerated emphasis on certain symbols of masculine virility among American troops: excessive drinking, preoccupation with sex, brawling, and constant use of profane language. "Apart from expressing a general rebelliousness, profanity most perfectly suggests that the user is capable of asserting his will, using his fists, drinking inordinate quantities of alcohol, taking women in contemptuous, domineering stride, and engaging in such other pursuits as are becoming to the virile American male."

Raymond Firth, *We, the Tikopia: A Sociological Study of Kinship in Primitive Polynesia,* New York: American Book Co., 1936. This account of the kinship system of a Polynesian community is typical of the anthropological method. The author immersed himself in the culture, living in a primitive village of 1200 individuals for one year. He learned to speak with the natives in their own language. The result is a work rich in detail. Firth showed that informal behavior toward relatives — much more than formal behavior — depended on the closeness of the kinship tie, the number of persons involved, and how far away they lived. This summary is based on a review by A. Irving Hallowell, *American Sociological Review,* Vol. 2, October 1938, pp. 558-560.

John Irwin and Donald R. Cressey, "Thieves, Convicts and the Inmate Culture," *Social Problems,* Vol. 10, Fall 1962, pp. 142-155. Criminologists have observed that the culture in prisons differs from the culture of the larger society. This article is a sophisticated attempt to analyze the components of the "inmate culture." One component of inmate culture is the *thief* subculture of the larger society: the traditions of those who steal for a living and who regard incarceration as one of the hazards of their profession. Another component is the system of utilitarian and manipulative values of those who compete for status and power within the prison—"convicts." Not all inmates of a prison are oriented to either of these components of inmate culture. Some inmates bring to the prison both antithief and anticonvict values. "They are people such as a man who, on a drunken Saturday night, ran over a pedestrian and was sent to the prison for manslaughter, a middle-class clerk who was caught embezzling his firm's money, and a young soldier who stole a car in order to get back from a leave."

Theodora Kroeber, *Ishi in Two Worlds: A Biography of the Last Wild Indian in North America,* Berkeley: University of California Press, 1967. On August 29, 1911, Ishi, the last survivor of the Yahi tribe of California, emerged from years of hiding. Three years before, his last companion had died, leaving him totally alone as he wandered half-starved and always fearful of death at the hands of the white man. Finally the loneliness and exhaustion were too much; indifferent to whether he lived or died, he emerged from hiding and permitted himself to be captured. Two anthropologists, T. T. Waterman and Alfred Kroeber, learned of the discovery of "the last wild Indian in North America" and hurried to the county jail in Oroville, California, where Ishi was being held. Slowly and painfully, Waterman established communication with him using a file of recorded vocabularies of tribes believed to be extinct. The author of this book, the wife of the other anthropologist who befriended Ishi, tells the story of his frightened wanderings and his subsequent cultural change to modern man. He became self-supporting, serving as an assistant janitor and general helper in the museum the anthropologists were affiliated with.

Edward Sapir, *Language: An Introduction to the Study of Speech,* New York: Harcourt, Brace, 1921. Sapir defines language as follows: "Language is a purely human and non-instinctive method of communicating ideas, emotions, and desires by means of a system of voluntarily produced symbols." He contrasts locomotion, which depends on biological maturation, with speech, which depends on learning the culture of one's society. He argues that speech makes thought possible and that in the evolution of man prerational speech antedated the intellectual uses of language. However, speech and thought are mutually stimulating; ". . . thought processes set in, as a kind of psychic overflow, almost at the beginning of linguistic expression . . . the concept, once defined, necessarily reacted on the life of its linguistic symbol, encouraging further linguistic growth." Some experts in the field of linguistics have criticized the Sapir-Whorf theory of language in recent years; other experts maintain that Sapir and Whorf are correct in their emphasis on the patterning of thought by language.

J. Milton Yinger, "Contraculture and Subculture," *American Sociological Review,* Vol. 25, October 1960, pp. 625-635. In societies as complicated as the contemporary United States, sociologists have felt a need to develop a concept capable of distinguishing *internal* variations in culture. The word "subculture" has been used for this purpose. Professor Yinger argues, on the basis of his review of 100 uses of the concept of subculture in the sociological literature, that it is an overworked concept. He suggests that some of the meanings attached to "subculture" should be allocated to *"contraculture,"* a word he coined to express these meanings. Subculture and contraculture are defined as follows: Subcultures are normative systems of groups smaller than a society, which, because of isolation or other inadequacies of communication, have a different tradition from the larger society of which they are a part—for example, the subculture of American Indians. Contracultures are the normative systems of groups caught in frustrating situations; they are understandable in terms of social and psychological reactions of subgroups hostile to the larger society— for example, delinquent gangs.

INITIAL SOCIALIZATION IN THE FAMILY OF ORIENTATION

We have said that culture is the cement that holds systems of interaction together. Thus culture must be passed on to new generations in order to maintain any interactive system. This is accomplished partly by the process of socialization.

Although all interactive systems must socialize new recruits, some interactive systems (armies, corporations, **voluntary associations**) receive for membership candidates who have already learned to play roles in other interactive systems. This is a different situation—and usually an easier problem—than societies face in starting role training with a newly born organism. Biological recruitment of role players superimposes the problem of teaching the infant to communicate on the problem of training. Only after the infant understands what his society wants can he conform to or rebel against its demands. In all known societies the main responsibility for initial socialization of the child has been assigned to adults considered biologically related to him. The family of orientation, different though its responsibilities are in preliterate and industrial societies, is universally given *this* responsibility.

In all societies, industrial and preliterate, infants constitute a barbarian invasion. They want what they want when they want it. Such amorality is intolerable. Hence all societies try to civilize the barbarians: to teach children to play roles that adults define for them. "Socialization" is the name for the process whereby the individual is taught to fill existing roles and to internalize cultural norms. Usually the infant is exposed to the social and cultural rules through his family, which acts as the agent of society in his humanization.

The importance of society's contribution is easy to overlook because nearly everybody is routinely exposed to adult guidance. One might assume (incorrectly) that the infant is *born* human just as the squirrel is born a squirrel. However, a squirrel taken from its mother at birth and raised in total isolation from other squirrels grows up to be a recognizable member of the species: climbing trees, eating nuts, and so on. The essence of being a squirrel is to have squirrel heredity. Adult guidance is not crucial.[1] For the infant, on the other hand, heredity is only a beginning, a potentiality for human development. A normal infant can develop into a subhuman monster if he does not have sufficient contact with human beings to learn not only the culture of his society but also its role structure. Cases of children raised with minimal parental care provide an opportunity to see the effect of social impoverishment on child development. They are unintended experiments, illustrations of the sociological assertion that human beings are made and not born.

In a classic article Kingsley Davis put into the sociological record two con-

---

[1] Research has demonstrated that certain types of monkeys, like human beings, require training by other monkeys for normal development. See Leonard Engel, "The Troubled Monkeys of Madison," *The New York Times Magazine,* Jan. 29, 1961, pp. 62-64. As far as we know, however, members of most species of animals do not require group guidance—except to facilitate physical survival.

trasting cases of extreme infant neglect: Anna and Isabelle.[2] Anna was the illegitimate child of a feebleminded farm woman; she was kept until she was nearly six in an attic-like room on the second floor of her grandfather's farmhouse. Her mother did not take her downstairs because that would have aroused her grandfather's anger. Anna received only enough care to keep her alive; she was barely moved from one position to another. When found and removed from her grandfather's house at the age of six, she could not walk or talk, and she seemed feebleminded. Having been fed on little but cow's milk, she was emaciated. She was so apathetic that it was uncertain whether she could hear. After four years in a school for retarded children, Anna could walk and run, though clumsily. She talked in phrases rather than complete sentences but tried to carry on a conversation. She loved her doll and was helpful to other children. Unfortunately, she caught jaundice and died at the age of ten and a half. It was therefore impossible to tell whether she would eventually have reached the normal range of intelligence and social functioning—and, if not, whether early social deprivation or genetic deficiency was responsible. Isabelle was found at about the same age as Anna (six and a half) and like Anna had been hidden from the world because of her illegitimacy. Her mother was a deaf-mute, so she had had no opportunity to learn speech. When found, she made only croaking sounds and showed fear of and hostility toward people. Like Anna, Isabelle seemed feebleminded. Unlike Anna, however, Isabelle received intensive, expert training in speech and intellectual skills, and she lived to maturity. By the age of eight and a half, she tested within the normal range of intelligence for her age. At fourteen she passed the sixth grade and participated in all school activities with her younger classmates. The case of Isabelle demonstrates that the damaging effects of social isolation are at least partially reversible, but special compensatory efforts must be made to cram two or more years of intellectual progress into one.

Anna and Isabelle, when they were discovered, seemed feebleminded— even subhuman—and were clearly outside of society. They did not know how to communicate symbolically and they had not learned to care about other people's reactions to them. As a result, they failed to conform to expectations made of those in the role of "child." But socialization is not mere conformity. Socialization is learning to like doing what one has to do anyway. Thus their attitudes, as well as their behavior, had not yet become "civilized." Perhaps an example will point up the importance of attitude in socialization. In American society, as in most societies, toilet training is part of early socialization. Americans teach children about toilets and toilet paper, about closing the bathroom door, and about washing their hands afterwards. Once Americans learn these lessons though, they greatly prefer using bathrooms to a return to the free and easy ways of the infant.

[2] Kingsley Davis, "Final Note on a Case of Extreme Isolation," *American Journal of Sociology,* Vol. 52, March 1947, pp. 432-437.

Not all socialization is as successful as toilet training. Taught as children that they must not steal, some American adults are incapable of theft. They think of themselves as honest, and this self-conception prevents them from even considering opportunities to steal. However, in 1968 more than 1,800,-000 burglaries, 750,000 auto thefts, and 1,200,000 cases of larceny of property valued at $50 or more were known to the American police.[3] And it is likely that more stealing would have occurred had it not been for police forces. Apparently Americans are less deeply committed to the cultural prohibition against theft than they are to the use of modern plumbing.

The difference arises because American society is so organized that honesty does not *always* seem to be the best policy. Chapter 13 will show the process by which the temptation to commit crimes overcomes the individual's moral scruples. Since crimes occur with some regularity—crime is a "normal phenomenon," as the French sociologist Émile Durkheim put it—the thought of stealing may cross one's mind even though most people ultimately abandon the idea. On the other hand, no one defecates in the street; such an idea is *unthinkable*. Socialization is thus a matter of degree. Some cultural norms are *internalized* so completely that the individual does not perceive any conflict between social rules and his own inclinations. In other instances, the norms are imbedded deeply enough to prevent the individual from violating them, but he experiences some temptation. With regard to still other norms, the individual is socialized only to the extent that he is aware of the social disapproval which would result from public violations. He treats the rule pragmatically, violating it if the chances for his escaping social sanctions are good and conforming if he believes that he cannot get away with it.

Individuals differ in the extent to which norms of their society are internalized. These internal variations are small and unimportant compared with the enormous differences in roles, rules, and self-conceptions from one society to another. If the observer focuses on the *outcomes* of socialization, human beings seem very different—virtually of different species—depending on their society of origin. If he focuses instead on the *process* of socialization, the similarities seem more remarkable than the differences. In all societies the individual joins the human community in the same way: by identifying with previously socialized members of the society and by adopting *their* social roles and cultural norms.

THE SOCIALIZATION PROCESS

The end-product of socialization, a moral being, is so far removed from the original amoral barbarian that the transitional process is difficult to describe

---

[3] Federal Bureau of Investigation, Department of Justice, *Uniform Crime Reports for the United States,* Washington, D.C.: Government Printing Office, 1968, p. 59.

credibly. How is the egocentric infant transformed? Human infancy—a prolonged period of helplessness—lasts longer than the infancy of any other species. What for other species is an episode, for the human infant is a career. Without this prolonged dependence on the mother, the infant would not be so receptive to parental guidance. An infant perceives the world as a frightening and potentially frustrating place. Strange noises startle him because he does not yet share the cultural interpretation of the ringing of a doorbell or the honking of an automobile horn. There is a hard object called a "floor" that comes up and hits him every once in a while. And a shiny object that looks and sounds interesting turns out to be dangerously hot. Of course, there are pleasant things in the world, too: that warm white stuff that comes in bottles and those marbles and rattles that he can touch and take into his mouth. Best of all, there is a benevolent monster who brings good things to eat and is generally helpful at critical times, for example, when a diaper pin is sticking him. A loud cry brings her on the run. In short, his first interest in his mother is thoroughly egocentric. She is not a *person*, only a source of important gratifications. He does not care about *her*; he cares about what she does for him.

Gradually the infant learns that his mother is not merely "the monster" who feeds him and changes his diapers. She possesses a unique feature: reactions. He smiles; she smiles back. He cries, she cuddles. They begin to participate in an interactive relationship. He has developed an interest in her *attitudes* and moods because he dimly recognizes that they underlie the services she renders. Furthermore, he learns that what *he* does can please her or make her angry. For reasons beyond his comprehension, the monster is delighted when he performs the dangerous feat of getting about on two limbs the way she does. So, although crawling is a perfectly satisfactory way of getting about, he humors her and tries to walk. On the other hand, she gives him a sour look when he sends a pile of dishes crashing to the floor. Since her attitude is important to him, he tries to control the impulse to destroy the crockery. Note that he does not consider breaking dishes *wrong*; he considers it *dangerous* because, for inexplicable reasons, it antagonizes the monster. This is pragmatism, not morality.

A further stage of socialization is reached when the child **identifies** with his mother and looks at *his* behavior from the perspective of *her* values. Charles Horton Cooley compared the process by which the child **internalizes** parental values with the observation of one's reflection in a looking glass:[4]

> As we see our face, figure, and dress in the glass, and are interested in them because they are ours, and pleased or otherwise with them according as they do or do not answer to what we should like them to be; so in imagination we perceive in another's mind some thought of our appearance, manners, aims, deeds, character, friends, and so on, and are variously affected by it.
>
> A self-idea of this sort seems to have three principal elements: the imagination of our appearance to the other person; the imagination of his judgment of that appearance; and some sort of self-feeling, such as pride or mortification.

[4] Charles Horton Cooley, *Human Nature and the Social Order,* New York: Scribner's, 1922, pp. 184-185.

The comparison with a looking-glass hardly suggests the second element, the imagined judgment, which is quite essential. The thing that moves us to pride or shame is not the mere mechanical reflection of ourselves, but an imputed sentiment, the imagined effect of this reflection upon another's mind. This is evident from the fact that the character and weight of that other, in whose mind we see ourselves, makes all the difference with our feeling. We are ashamed to seem evasive in the presence of a straightforward man, cowardly in the presence of a brave one, gross in the eyes of a refined one, and so on. We always imagine, and in imagining share, the judgments of the other mind. A man will boast to one person of an action — say some sharp transaction in trade — which he would be ashamed to own to another.

In the context of the relationship with his mother, the child learns to transcend egocentricity. He not only cares about her judgments of his behavior; he also adopts the **values** implicit in them as his own. Furthermore, the lesson he learns is applied beyond the family. His sensitivity to disapproval is gradually extended to human beings generally. As George Herbert Mead put it, the individual develops the capacity to *treat himself as an object.*[5] And the perspective that he takes toward himself, although initially that of his parents, ultimately becomes that of society — or, as Mead put it, that of the **generalized other.** This adoption of societal standards makes it possible to civilize the barbarians. Once this internalization occurs, society has an ally within the psyche of the child. Parental vigilance can be reduced because, from then on, the child helps to police himself.

Many gaps exist in this explanation of socialization. Especially puzzling is the child's step from conforming pragmatically to the demands of an external authority to identifying with his mother and adopting her standards of right and wrong. Most students of socialization agree that the mother is crucial to moral development, not necessarily the biological mother, but some adult (1) who gives the child love and (2) who judges the child's behavior in terms of adult standards. These two conditions are to some extent contradictory. If maternal affection were unconditional, gushing forth regardless of the child's behavior, the child would have no incentive to judge his behavior from his mother's perspective. If, on the other hand, he were judged but not loved, his mother's disapproval would not be so threatening, and therefore he would once again lack the incentive to identify with her and, concomitantly, to internalize her moral standards.

Successful socialization steers a middle course between overindulgence and rejection. Maternal love convinces the child of a qualitative distinction between a frustration imposed by the physical environment (touching a hot radiator) and a frustration imposed by his mother in the name of discipline (a spanking). The two experiences may be equally painful. One has moral significance, however, and the other does not. The child has no reason to **empathize** with the radiator. It burned him because that is its nature. If he touches

---

[5] George Herbert Mead, *Mind, Self, and Society,* Chicago: University of Chicago Press, 1934.

it again, it will burn him again, regardless of whether he has been "good" or "bad." His action in touching it was foolish, careless, ill-advised, *but not wrong*. On the other hand, when his mother spanks him, a relationship is at stake. His mother punishes him, not because it is her nature to do so, but because she evaluated his behavior unfavorably. The spanking symbolizes her righteous indignation: "You have done something so wrong that I don't feel like loving you at this moment. You had better mend your ways." In these traumatic moments when maternal affection is in jeopardy, the child exerts the prodigious effort necessary to transcend infantile egocentricity: "What did I do to make her angry?" In order to win back his mother's approval, he must look at his behavior through her eyes. Conscience is built upon experiences in which the child transcends his egocentric perspective in order to forestall or cut short parental disapproval.

To say that successful socialization steers a middle course between overindulgence and rejection simplifies a complicated process. Sociologists have tried to be specific about the conditions for successful socialization. The following five conditions for successful socialization, gleaned from social psychological research, form the dynamics of the process, although experts differ on the number of conditions and the weight each has:[6]

1. *Clear definition of the appropriate* **norms**. Unless the child knows precisely what behavior his socializers expect of him, he will have difficulty modifying his previous behavior pattern. This condition is particularly important in modern societies where there is little consensus among socializers. Suppose, for example, that the father of a boy has a more aggressive conception of the male role than the mother. These inconsistent expectations of the parents make it difficult for the boy to discipline childish impulses in the interest of conforming to "the male role."

2. *Solidarity between the person being socialized and the socializing agent.* Unless the child feels accepted by his family, he will not value membership in the family and will have no great incentive to conform to the demands family members impose upon him.

3. *A permissive attitude on the part of socializing agents toward a limited amount of* **regressive behavior.** Unless the child is permitted some missteps (and some backward steps) as he moves toward mature behavior, he will be afraid to try out the new behavior expected by his parents. In Chapter 5 stuttering is explained in terms of this principle; the child who stutters is usually a child who was not permitted to speak unfluently in the course of speech training. Talcott Parsons has an intriguing hypothesis about parental permissiveness. He suggests that both parents, in tandem, are important to successful socialization: one tends to be permissive and the other demands

---

[6] Talcott Parsons, *The Social System,* Glencoe, Ill.: Free Press, 1951, Chap. 6; Harry C. Bredemeier and Richard M. Stephenson, *The Analysis of Social Systems,* New York: Holt, Rinehart & Winston, 1962, Chap. 3 and 4.

increasingly mature behavior. Parsons believes that this division of parental labor is more effective than one in which parents are equally responsible for pressure and permissiveness. The female parent is usually the permissive one in Western societies, but Parsons regards it as less important which parent is permissive than that there be role differentiation between the parents.

4. *An emotionally controlled reaction on the part of socializing agents toward rebellious behavior.* A common reaction of children toward parental demands is counterattack. The child challenges parental authority by a rebellious tantrum, by refusing to obey, or by conspicuous disregard of the request. It is tempting for the parent, especially an insecure parent, to meet the challenge by a temper tantrum of his own. However, socialization of the child will occur more quickly if the parent preserves his "cool" — pressing his demands firmly but refusing to reciprocate the child's hostility.

5. *Rewards for learning the role and an absence of reward for failing to learn it.* The child must feel that his efforts to learn what his parents expect him to learn have paid off. This does not mean he must receive candy or money or toys. The most important reward available to parents (or to any socializing agent) is a relational reward, that is, a favorable attitude. But parents in industrial societies do not control all the rewards available to children, even relational rewards. One reason parents are sometimes unsuccessful in teaching their children what they want to teach them is that the peer group may reward the *failure* to learn. In short, the efforts of socializing agents can be neutralized by significant others opposed to their goals.

If these five conditions are met, socialization proceeds successfully, not only in the family but in any situation where an interactive group is attempting to train a new member. (Chapter 5 turns to the conditions of successful socialization *after* childhood.) The outcome of a successful socialization process is twofold: (1) behavioral conformity to role requirements and (2) a **self-conception** compatible with such conformity.

OUTCOMES OF THE SOCIALIZATION PROCESS

The outcome of initial socialization is successful to the extent that it prepares the child for the roles he is expected to play. In a preliterate society the child is expected to play mainly kinship roles; hence the child who learns appropriate behavior and attitudes in his family of orientation is prepared for a lifetime of role playing. Learning the role of son prepares the boy for the role of father he will later assume. The content of the "son" role is learned mainly in the course of interacting with a mother and a father. In order to play the role of son symbolically as well as physically, the boy must take the points of view of both his father and his mother and regard his behavior through their eyes.

Owen Severin—Black Star

This means that he simultaneously internalizes three roles: that of son, father, and mother. He plays the role of son, and he stores in his memory the intellectual content and the attitudes appropriate for the father and mother roles. Years later, when he becomes a father, he retrieves from memory what he internalized about the role from interacting with his own father. What about the mother role? A man does not actively employ the mother role, but he does not forget it either. If his conception of the mother role is greatly different from the mother role learned by his wife from *her* mother, this can produce marital conflict.

In an industrial society, the child is prepared to play kinship and nonkinship roles by his family of orientation. But industrial societies are so much more complicated than preindustrial societies that initial socialization in the family cannot prepare the child for the many nonfamilial roles he will play. Later socialization is necessary to teach specific content of postchildhood roles. However, this content builds upon a *general willingness* to play roles, and such willingness depends on socialization experiences in the family of orientation. In other words, adequate child socialization in industrial societies prepares the child to play family roles, both as a child and as an adult, and it also establishes a general predisposition to accept further socialization into nonfamilial roles. Even if a child plays his role satisfactorily in his family of orientation, initial socialization has not proceeded successfully unless he is also receptive to roles at school, in voluntary associations, in the occupational system, and in the political system.

Inadequate Socialization. The most important failure of initial socialization occurs when a child does not acquire general receptivity to socialization. A common reason for this failure is that some children conclude from interaction with one or both parents that self-discipline is not worth it. When the parent does not offer *rewards* for abandoning infantile behavior, only *punishments* for failing to do so, much of the incentive for abandoning egocentricity is lost. The main reward parents have at their disposal is the expression of approval and love. Parents who dislike their children or who find them a burden are incapable of bestowing love and approval. Although their children may conform behaviorally, they feel subconsciously that they have given up the pleasures of irresponsible freedom for very little. The next time they face a socializing agent, they are inclined to resist his influence because they identify him with their rejecting mother or father. In short, initial socialization creates in some children a psychological need to ignore the expectations of socializing agents. Such children are described as rebellious toward authority figures, negativistic, unreliable.

Inadequate socialization is by no means the only cause of deviant behavior (see Chapter 13), but it is a predisposing factor because it reduces the individual's inclination to conform to the expectations of rule makers and enforcers: teachers, employers, policemen. Prisons and reformatories contain disproportionate numbers of inadequately socialized persons. Examination of case histories reveals bleak childhoods, sometimes because parents were neglectful or preoccupied, sometimes because children were shifted from one foster home to another during their formative years. Although rare even in prisons, the **psychopath** carries incapacity for socialization to its logical extreme. Some consideration of the characteristics of the psychopath may throw light, by contrast, on successful socialization outcomes.[7]

A psychopath does not appear mentally ill to the untrained observer. The psychopath does not have hallucinations or delusions; he is not plagued by guilt feelings; he is not unhappy. He merely has no sense of right or wrong. On superficial acquaintance, this may not seem such a serious defect. Lacking inhibitions, the psychopath is charming, gay, cheerful. He is also a chronic liar, extremely persuasive because he has no respect for truth. He feels no embarrassment when caught in a lie. With a bland smile, he invents a new tale to suit his immediate convenience. He can talk his way into almost any job because he is a supersalesman. But he gets bored easily; hence he rarely stays long in a job. He is fabulously successful with women, perhaps because of his devil-

---

[7] Hervey M. Cleckley, *The Mask of Sanity,* St. Louis, Mo.: Mosby, 1941.

may-care attitude, perhaps because they foolishly expect to reform him. Since he is incapable of identifying with anyone, he cannot love. He exploits women as long as they put up with his monumental irresponsibility and believe his solemn promises to change. He marries often, frequently without troubling to divorce the previous victim of his charm. Since he does not worry about consequences, including consequences to himself, he drinks heavily, philanders relentlessly, and generally does what he pleases. His crimes, like his other behavior, can be understood as impulses of the moment. He forges a check or sells Brooklyn Bridge because he happens to be short of cash; he sets fire to a house for kicks; he provokes a fight to relieve boredom. In short, the psychopath is a public menace because he behaves exactly as an infant behaves — except that he talks and dresses like other adults. Harrison Gough, a psychologist, summed up the egocentricity aspect of psychopathy when he remarked that the psychopath is deficient in role-playing ability.[8]

What causes psychopathy? At one time psychiatrists believed that some constitutional deficiency was responsible. Now psychiatrists emphasize parent-child interaction — although they do not rule out the possibility of constitutional predispositions. Both extremes, rejection and overindulgence, increase the probability of psychopathy.

The overprotective mother gives her children too much love and too little control.[9] A rejecting mother, in contrast, gives too little love, sometimes because of her own personality problems, sometimes because her situation poses obstacles to her playing the role of mother. The unwed mother, for example, faces an extremely hostile social reception in all of the industrial societies, except Sweden, if she elects to keep her baby. If she chooses to give up the child, that youngster may face a complicated world without the parental support most children need. This is particularly true if the child is black, since the larger proportionate number of black illegitimate births and the smaller proportionate numbers of childless couples with adequate financial resources gives such a child fewer chances for adoption.

Psychopaths are rare. But milder outcomes of inadequate socialization are common. Many adolescents and adults get involved in fights, sometimes with lethal weapons; they have not learned as a result of initial socialization how to control their tempers. Social psychological research helps explain why. In order to assess the effect of child-rearing practices on explosively aggressive behavior, psychologists Albert Bandura and Richard Walters selected for study (from the caseload of a probation department) 26 adolescent boys with histories of assaultive behavior.[10] These boys were not members of ethnic minorities; they came from intact homes located in neighborhoods at least average in socioeconomic status. Hence several factors that might confuse the

[8] Harrison G. Gough, "A Sociological Theory of Psychopathy," *American Journal of Sociology,* Vol. 53, March 1948, pp. 359-366.

[9] David M. Levy, "Maternal Overprotection," *Psychiatry,* Vol. 2, November 1939, pp. 563-567.

[10] Albert Bandura and Richard H. Walters, *Adolescent Aggression: A Study of the Influence of Child-Training Practices and Family Interrelations,* New York: Ronald, 1959.

Suzanne Szasz

relationship between child-training practices and aggressive behavior were eliminated in advance. Another group of 26 boys who did not manifest explosive aggressiveness were also interviewed as a comparison group. The parents of the aggressive boys differed from parents of boys in the control group in the following ways: they were harsher toward their sons, more disapproving of dependent behavior, less consistent in their demands, and less likely to make any demands at all. They relied more on physical coercion than on reasoning in attempting to enforce the demands they made. The aggressive boys developed less identification with their fathers, felt more hostile toward them, spent less time with them, and avoided seeking their help. Outside of the home the aggressive boys expressed more direct hostility toward teachers and peers and felt no guilt following aggressive episodes.

Inadequate socialization can and does result from deficiencies in the personalities of parents. It can also result from circumstances over which the parents have no control. For example, psychologists have long believed that a girl learns appropriate feminine traits by identifying with an adult female and a boy masculine traits from identification with an adult male. If in the small households of Western industrial countries one parent is missing, the child may have difficulty finding a substitute socializer of the same sex with whom to identify. Predispositions toward homosexuality may result. Of course, children learn how to play their sex roles not only from parents but from other adults and from **siblings.** Does a boy with an older brother or a girl with an older sister have a built-in advantage in sex-role learning? Orville Brim explored the possible contribution of brothers and sisters to sex-role identification through the analysis of data on 384 native white children from *two-child* unbroken families.[11] At the time the data were collected the children were five or six years old. Dr. Brim found (1) that children with siblings of the same sex tended to assimilate more traits of the same sex than did children with siblings of the opposite sex and (2) that this effect was especially pronounced if the child was younger than his sibling of the same sex.

CHILD SOCIALIZATION IN INDUSTRIAL SOCIETIES

In preindustrial societies, the family has important functions in addition to the socialization of children. In industrial societies, the family has lost many economic, political, religious, recreational, and welfare functions. Specialized institutions have assumed them, as Fig. 4.1 shows. No longer the dominant institution of society, the family is now one of many institutions, but it is still a major agency of initial socialization. Teachers, peers, and neighbors also contribute to the socialization of the child, but the family gets the child first. Child socialization presents different problems in the small, **conjugal families** of the United States, Sweden, Great Britain, or even Japan than in the **extended families** of preliterate societies. Families in industrial societies pass through a life cycle of establishment, development, and dissolution not characteristic of preliterate societies. From the point of view of the individual, *two* families exist rather than one: the family into which he is born, consisting of himself, his father, mother, sisters, and brothers, and the family he creates by marriage, consisting of himself, his wife, and their dependent children.

In industrial society, the individual leaves the household of his *family of orientation* and sometimes immediately, sometimes after an interval of living by himself or with strangers, establishes a new household for his *family of procreation*. The emphasis on the conjugal relationship in family organization in industrial societies (instead of on the parent-child relationship) guarantees the eventual destruction of every household. Very likely, this is unavoidable; an extended kinship unit would not be mobile enough for an industrial economy.

[11] Orville G. Brim, Jr., "Family Structure and Sex-Role Learning by Children," *Sociometry,* Vol. 21, March 1958, pp. 1-16.

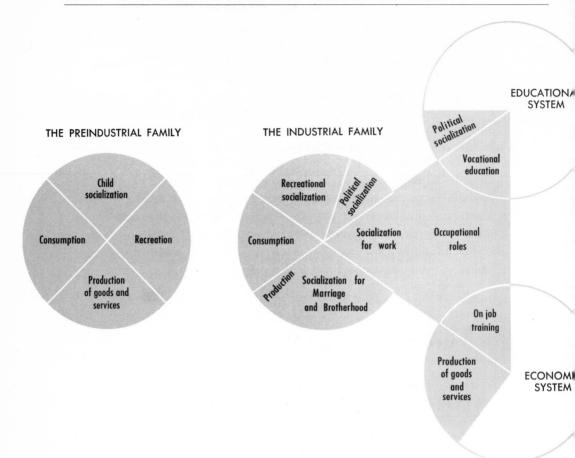

FIGURE 4.1   **The differentiated institutions of industrial societies.**

Nevertheless, socialization is less uniform in a conjugal family system than in one with continuity from one generation to the next. In a preindustrial society, such as those of the rural Ibo of Nigeria or the Murngin of Australia, the conjugal unit is far less important than the family line of grandparents, parents, and children. Among the Ibo, a husband and wife do not think of themselves as belonging to the same family. The wife lives with the husband among *his* relatives, but *her* family consists of her siblings, father, paternal grandfather, and paternal aunts and uncles. Since the Ibo are **patrilineal** rather than **matrilineal,** her mother does not belong to *her* family, and neither do her maternal grandparents, paternal grandmother, and maternal aunts and uncles.[12] This

---

[12] A patrilineal society is one in which descent is traced through *males,* the way names are inherited in Western countries. A matrilineal society is one in which descent is traced through *females;* that is, a woman, all of her children, and the children of her daughters (but not of her sons) belong to the same family. American society is neither matrilineal nor patrilineal; the child is related equally closely to his mother's and to his father's families. A patrilineal society is usually patrilocal; that is, the newly married couple lives in the household of the groom's family. This is logical because the offspring of the union belongs to the groom's family, not to the bride's. Matrilineal societies are usually matrilocal.

sounds confusing to Westerners, who do not discriminate between maternal and paternal lines in the designation of biological kin. Nor are Westerners sympathetic to the tacit assumption, made by all preliterate peoples, that the conjugal relationship is of lesser importance than lineal kinship. Once these premises are grasped, a Westerner can appreciate the strength of an extended family system. It is so much larger than the conjugal family that children need not depend for socialization on parents alone; other relatives are available as socializers if their parents default for any reason. The strength and resiliency of an extended family as an agency of child socialization is apparent when divorce occurs. As Kingsley Davis shows in the following passage, divorce does not have the deleterious effect on children in preliterate societies that it does in modern societies:[13]

In countless societies the immediate family is so interwoven with other institutional groups that, in case of divorce, the children do not constitute a social problem. The break-up of the immediate family is the same as in our society, and the anomaly of the child's position is potentially the same, but actually the parents' relation to other persons—often to clansmen and joint householders—is such that the child continues largely under their care.

The success of non-Western societies in solving the problem of the post-divorce child is explained by their wider use of kinship groups other than the immediate family. With them the immediate family is not the sole, nor even the most important kinship unit. Instead the clan, the extended family, and the joint household serve as important parts of social organization and perform functions which with us are left either to nonkinship groups or to the immediate family. Let us take as an example the Ibo society of Southern Nigeria, whose divorce customs have been ably reported.

The first thing to note is the nature of Ibo marriage. It is not an agreement between the two prospective mates, but rather a contract between the parents and more fundamentally the clans of the mates. Without the prior consent and agreement of the two parental families no marriage could take place. Secondly, the prospective groom or his family must pay a bride-price to the girl's relatives, without which the union would have no legal standing. Thirdly, in spite of the marriage, the husband and wife remain socially and religiously members of their respective clans. The wife joins her husband's family physically but not spiritually. She must participate in the economic activities of his household, and above all she must bear children for his clan. But her underlying allegiance remains with her own family, and she may at any time return to it. The bride-price is the compensation that her parents, having gone to the expense of rearing her, receive for the loss of her services. It is not the price of her person, as such, for she continues to belong to her clan, but the price of her services. In return she has obligations toward her husband and his family. He also has obligations toward her, and unless these are properly observed her services may be withdrawn. She does not share her husband's possessions, inherit any of them after his death, or hold any claim to the children borne by her. Her husband has the right to contract as many marriages as he or his family can afford, and since a man's prestige de-

[13] Reprinted by permission. From Kingsley Davis, "Children of Divorced Parents," *Law and Contemporary Problems,* Vol. 11, Summer 1944, pp. 700-720.

pends on his wealth, and his wealth is most effectively displayed by the number of wives, he will try to secure as many as possible.

Being a private contract between the two families, a marriage may be revoked at will by either side. If he is willing to forget the bride-price the husband may send his wife back for any cause whatsoever. On the other hand, the wife may not be able to leave her husband even for just cause if her family refuses to refund the bride-price. Only if she has good prospects of remarrying, which means that another man stands ready to pay her family the bride-price (which then is returned to the original husband), may she leave of her own free will.

One of the most frequent causes of the dismissal of Ibo wives is barrenness. If several years elapse without a child being born, the wife may be sent home and the bride-price recovered. If, on the other hand, the wife has fulfilled her duty by bearing at least two children, including one son, it is extremely difficult for the husband to return her to her parents and receive back the bride-price. The charge of barrenness often elicits the counter-charge of impotence. If the wife fails to conceive for some years after marriage, she or her family and possibly her husband may make arrangements for extra-marital relations. A child born under such circumstances is of course the property of the husband and bolsters the position of the wife.

Obviously in Ibo society there can be no question of the custody of the children when a marriage is dissolved. They belong to the husband's family. It was largely for them that the marriage was contracted and the bride-price paid in the first place. The question may be raised as to how they can be taken care of without their mother, but the truth is that the mother's care is not necessary. Since the household usually includes some of the husband's female relatives, perhaps other wives, there is little difficulty about rearing the children.

The case of the Ibo has been chosen because its handling of divorce is, in its major outlines, typical of that in many primitive societies. The marital relation is dominated by lineal kinsmen, and the custody and rearing of the children do not depend on the continuance of the immediate family. The fact that the Ibo are patrilineal in their clan organization means that the child is viewed primarily as a member of the father's clan. This is sometimes thought to be the most difficult case for post-divorce children in kinship societies, because of the young child's physical dependence on its mother. Actually in some patrilineal societies the children do remain with the mother while they are infants and are returned to the father at a later date.

This description of the kinship system of the rural Ibo was valid a generation ago. Since then, Nigeria left the British commonwealth and until the Biafran secession made considerable educational and economic strides. More than a quarter of a million people live in Lagos, its capital, and nearly a half million in Ibadan; the rural hinterland is affected by these modern, industrialized cities. The patrilineal kinship system — in the context of which a chief or a rich man could take many wives — is less dominant, and the emphasis on conjugal family relationships is stronger. Although most Ibo do not identify industrialization and urbanization as the major factors weakening the traditional patrilineal family, they have come to feel that marriage today is different from what it used to be and that one wife is enough. The same forces are at work in the other emerging nations of Africa. In a dispatch from Nairobi, the capital of Kenya, a *New York Times* correspondent reported his interview with a Kikuyu chief:[14]

> "Women are different now," said Chief Njiri Karanja, leaning forward on his stool to pull one stiff, sinewy leg over the other. "Women are getting clever. They are wearing expensive dresses instead of skins. They are painting their faces with cosmetics instead of mud. They are wearing high wigs that look like beehives. All these things cost money, and women didn't know about money before. Now there are school fees, too; it is very expensive to educate many children.
>
> "Let me tell you: I had 52 wives, and finally they were like 52 pots of poison. If I had to start over now, I think one at a time would be plenty."

The increasing cleverness of women noted by Chief Njiri is partly the result of education. Many women are now able to read newspapers, which give them ideas not only about clothes and cosmetics but about a more equalitarian relationship with their husbands. The letters columns of newspapers are filled with resentful remarks concerning polygamy and the bride-price. Urbanization and the spread of a money economy[15]

> . . . are having a much faster effect on the old customs than the whole chorus of angry female voices. The need for money has been made inevitable by the desire for education and by the growing demand for bicycles, radios, suits, motor scooters and all the other accoutrements of "civilization."
>
> Even a skilled and relatively well-paid worker in Nairobi, earning as much as $150 a month, will have to weigh his resources carefully before he thinks seriously about taking on a second wife; especially if her family is going to find out how much he is earning.

The detribalization process represents progress toward modernization. Women have greater freedom in the conjugal family than they enjoyed in the traditional extended family. But the emerging conjugal family system has drawbacks for child socialization. Rising delinquency rates from Nairobi to Johannesburg reflect the vulnerability of the conjugal family to the inevitable inadequacies of some parents.[16]

The Vulnerability of Children in Isolated Conjugal Families. If something goes wrong with a conjugal family, it goes very wrong. Consider, for example, the consequences of the death of a parent. In industrial societies, life expectancy is high; consequently orphanhood is a diminishing problem. But even in low-mortality industrial societies, *some* parents die prematurely. When this happens, no one is readily available to take over—as there would be in a

---

[14] Lawrence Fellows, "Kenya Report: Market in Brides," *The New York Times Magazine,* February 19, 1967, p. 12.

[15] Fellows, "Kenya Report," pp. 16-19.

[16] S. Kirson Weinberg, "Juvenile Delinquency in Ghana: A Comparative Analysis of Delinquents and Non-Delinquents," *Journal of Criminal Law, Criminology and Police Science,* Vol. 55, December 1964, pp. 471-481.

household consisting of an extended family and containing more than two adults. Orphanhood is rarer in industrial societies, but when it comes, it creates more serious socialization problems for children than in preindustrial societies. Similarly, divorce and separation have more pernicious consequences for children in industrial societies than they have in societies where socialization is the responsibility of the extended family.

Not only do *death, divorce,* or *separation* of parents interfere with child socialization in industrial societies. *Any* kind of parental failing has serious emotional consequences for children: alcoholism, mental illness, unemployability, rejection, neglect. In preindustrial societies, where children spread their dependence over a larger number of kin, the imperfections or misfortunes of parents are not translated as directly into difficulties for children.

When homes break up in industrial societies, as some inevitably do, even financial arrangements for children are precarious. Studies have shown that among those of lower socioeconomic status, fathers absent from the home because of divorce, separation, or desertion generally do not contribute to the support of their children.[17] An even smaller proportion of the fathers of *illegitimate* children make financial contributions.[18] These conclusions hold despite the efforts of law-enforcement agencies to *force* absent fathers to support their children—including the imprisonment of substantial numbers of them for desertion and nonsupport.

Faced with these financial problems, some mothers give up the hope of maintaining a home for their children. Some children are sent to live with other relatives, some to foster homes, some to institutions for dependent and neglected children.[19] Some mothers surrender newborn illegitimate children for adoption.[20] (This is not a viable option for black mothers of illegitimate children because the number of illegitimate black babies exceeds the number of childless black parents.) Some mothers struggle to maintain a home for their children despite the necessity of playing a double role: breadwinner and homemaker. Under urban industrial conditions, however, the mother who works full-time has difficulty arranging for the proper supervision of her young chil-

[17] A study was made of support by absent fathers to children receiving Aid to Dependent Children assistance in the summer of 1955. Only 18 per cent of fathers currently or previously married to the mothers of the children contributed *anything* to their support. See Saul Kaplan, *Support from Absent Fathers of Children Receiving ADC, 1955,* Public Assistance Report No. 41, Washington, D.C.: Government Printing Office, 1960, p. 17.

[18] In the same study reported on in footnote 17, it was found that only 10 per cent of the fathers of *illegitimate* children on A.D.C. contributed *anything* to their support. (Kaplan, *Support from Absent Fathers,* p. 35.)

[19] On November 30, 1958, more than 54,000 children were in institutions for dependent and neglected children in 45 states. See Helen R. Jeter, *Children Who Receive Services from Public Child Welfare Agencies,* Children's Bureau Publication No. 387, Washington, D.C.: Government Printing Office, 1960, p. 12.

[20] About 100,000 adoptions were authorized by American courts in 1960. See Bureau of the Census, *Statistical Abstract of the United States, 1962,* Washington, D.C.: Government Printing Office, 1962, p. 301.

TABLE 4.1

Child-Care Arrangements Made by Full-Time Working Mothers in Broken Homes, United States, 1958

Type of Child-Care Arrangement	Children under Twelve	
	Number	Percentage
Supervised by father	11,000	1.2
Supervised by relative under 18	123,000	13.9
Supervised by relative over 18	389,000	43.8
Supervised by neighbor	73,000	8.2
Supervised by other nonrelative	90,000	10.1
Group care	54,000	6.1
Self-care	91,000	10.3
Other arrangements	57,000	6.4
All arrangements	888,000	100.0

Source: Henry C. Lajewski, *Child-Care Arrangements of Full-Time Working Mothers,* Children's Bureau Publication No. 378, Washington, D.C.: Government Printing Office, 1959, p. 21.

dren. Table 4.1 shows the variety of child-care arrangements made in 1958 by American working mothers in broken homes.

Very little is known about the *quality* of these child-care arrangements although in 1958, 91,000 children under 12 took care of themselves while their mothers were at work, and this is unsatisfactory supervision by any standard. Even this need not be deliberate neglect. Mothers who do not have relatives or neighbors to put in charge of their children may have no alternative but to leave them unsupervised. The cost of group care or paid baby-sitters is usually beyond their resources. A generation ago the federal government recognized the seriousness of this problem and undertook to subsidize child care. The philosophy of the child support program is written into the originating legislation: "No child shall be deprived of care in his own home because of poverty alone."[21] By 1960 more than two million American children received benefits each year under the Aid to Families of Dependent Children program; more than a billion dollars were disbursed.[22] Some critics of this program are appalled at the large number of recipients and the high cost to the taxpayer;

[21] For a good discussion of the philosophy and the practicalities of government support of child welfare in the United States, see Eveline M. Burns, "The Government's Role in Child and Family Welfare," in Eli Ginzberg, Ed., *The Nation's Children,* Vol. 3, New York: Columbia University Press for the Golden Anniversary White House Conference on Children and Youth, 1960, pp. 148-179.

[22] *Health, Education, and Welfare Trends,* 1961, Washington, D.C.: Government Printing Office, 1961, pp. 81-82.

they fear that child-care benefits are being given to persons who do not need them. However, Table 4.2 shows that the bulk of children receiving child-care benefits come from fatherless homes or from homes where the father is unable to provide support because of a physical disability.

Given the system of isolated conjugal families in industrial societies and given the occurrence among them of broken homes (because of death, divorce, separation, desertion, or illegitimacy), the Aid to Families of Dependent Children may be the most economical way of dealing with society's responsibility for child socialization—but perhaps it is too economical. For nearly half of the A.F.D.C. families, total income from all sources (including earnings of family members) did not attain the modest monthly requirements as defined by state assistance standards.[23] Even if the child-care benefits were *doubled,* the cost of A.F.D.C. would be a fraction of the cost of placing the children in schools for dependent and neglected children. Moreover, payment of child-care benefits is

---

[23] "The average amount needed by all families was $143; the shortage for families with unmet needs was $39 per month." Bureau of Public Assistance, *Illegitimacy and Its Impact on the Aid to Dependent Children Program,* Washington, D.C.: Government Printing Office, 1960, p. 45.

TABLE 4.2

The Status of the Fathers of Children Assisted by the Aid to Dependent Children Program, October-December 1958

	Children Assisted by A.D.C.	
Status of Fathers	*Number*	*Percentage*
Dead	219,970	10.3
Incapacitated	558,443	26.1
Absent	1,319,165	61.6
Divorced or legally separated	276,979	12.9
Separated without court decree	187,174	8.7
Deserted	397,094	18.5
Not married to mother	335,830	15.7
Imprisoned	101,618	4.7
Absent for other reason	20,470	1.0
Other status[a]	44,818	2.1
Total	2,142,396	100.0

[a]Includes father in home as caretaker because of death, incapacity, or absence of the *mother*.

Source: Bureau of Public Assistance, *Illegitimacy and Its Impact on the Aid to Dependent Children Program,* Washington, D.C.: Government Printing Office, 1960, p. 81.

the most practical way of aiding illegitimate children. Alternative child-care arrangements are very difficult to find; there is a chronic shortage of foster homes, even marginally satisfactory ones. If the sole criterion is a suitable home for the child, studies have shown that mothers whose sexual behavior shocks the community may nevertheless care for their *children* conscientiously.[24]

Broken families overlap the larger universe of *problem* families, that is, families unable to function adequately by community standards without help from voluntary or governmental agencies. The size of the problem-family universe is difficult to estimate because it is not clear how many health, educational, delinquency, psychological, and economic difficulties turn up in the *same* families — although the popularity of the term **multiproblem family** suggests a tendency for a sea of simultaneous troubles to flood the same family. Perhaps a quarter of American families have one or more problems necessitating outside help.

Frequently family problems are caused by economic disadvantage. Minority groups are most often the victims of discrimination leading to economic troubles. Black families can be understood in terms of the same underlying variables as can families of other ethnic backgrounds. However, Negroes came

[24] Bureau of Public Assistance, *Illegitimacy,* pp. 49-50, 54-57.

TABLE 4.3

Rate of Separation and Divorce among Ever-Married American White and Nonwhite Men in 1950, Cross-Tabulated by 1949 Income

White Men, 14 Years and Over

Income	Ever Married	Separated	Divorced	Separated per 1,000 of Ever Married	Divorced per 1,000 of Ever Married	Both Divorced and Separated per 1,000 of Ever Married
No income	1,794,750	46,950	64,800	26.16	36.10	62.26
$1-$999	4,242,940	119,940	188,580	28.27	44.44	72.71
$1000-$1999	5,211,410	98,130	167,190	18.82	32.08	50.90
$2000-$2999	8,334,000	131,220	255,150	15.74	30.62	46.36
$3000-$3999	7,320,240	70,740	167,610	9.66	22.90	32.56
$4000 and over	7,261,920	5,100	18,090	0.70	2.49	3.19
Total	34,165,260	472,080	861,420	13.82	25.21	39.03

Nonwhite Men, 14 Years and Over

Income	Ever Married	Separated	Divorced	Separated per 1,000 of Ever Married	Divorced per 1,000 of Ever Married	Both Divorced and Separated per 1,000 of Ever Married
No income	254,660	28,590	7,770	112.27	30.51	142.78
$1-$999	1,096,740	98,130	25,440	89.47	23.20	112.67
$1000-$1999	1,022,010	86,190	23,700	84.33	23.19	107.52
$2000-$2999	802,860	57,120	19,650	71.14	24.48	95.62
$3000-$3999	239,670	12,870	6,840	53.70	28.54	82.24
$4000 and over	63,390	210	210	3.31	3.31	6.62
Total	3,479,330	283,110	83,610	81.37	24.03	105.40

Source: Compiled from the 1950 census by Karen G. Hillman and published in Winch, Mc-Ginnis, and Barringer, Eds., *Selected Studies in Marriage and the Family,* rev. ed., New York: Holt, Rinehart and Winston, 1962, pp. 604-605.

to North America under peculiarly disadvantageous cricumstances. They were involuntary migrants, kidnapped from their communities in Africa by Arab slave traders and transported across the Atlantic under conditions that made survival almost miraculous. During slavery, Negro family life was precarious because many masters sold individual slaves without regard for their family ties. After emancipation the Negro family remained weak because the men found it difficult to support their wives and children. This was due partly to lack of marketable skills, partly to white prejudice. Negro women had a better chance of getting jobs as domestic servants than Negro men had of being employed in factories and offices. As a result, the women were more often the breadwinners in their families—and more often the authority figures. A man not crucial to the economic stability of his family was more likely to desert, and

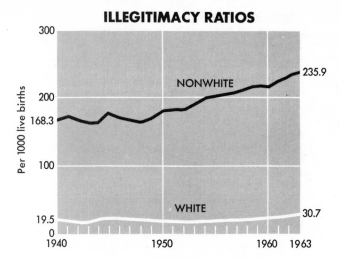

FIGURE 4.2 **Percentage of illegitimate births by color, 1940–1963.** Source: Anders S. Lunde, "White-Nonwhite Fertility Differentials in the United States," *Health, Education, and Welfare Indicators,* September 1965, Washington, D. C.: Government Printing Office, 1965.

his wife was more likely to ask him to leave the household. Thus the broken family has been more characteristic of black than of white Americans.[25]

The cumulative effect of these historical circumstances results in what Daniel Moynihan has called "the ordeal of the Negro family."[26] The United States unwittingly conducts a natural experiment testing the vulnerability of children in the isolated conjugal family system. Negro children grow up in much more disadvantaged family situations than white children, thus permitting inferences about the effect of such situations on child development. Consider the following comparisons between Negro and white children in the United States:

1. Negro children are about eight times as likely as white children to be born illegitimately (Fig. 4.2).

2. Negro children are twice as likely as white children to grow up in a family that lives in poverty.[27] One factor in this poverty is that their fathers are more likely than white fathers to be unemployed (Fig. 4.3). (To compensate for the underemployment of Negro men, Negro women, probably out of financial necessity, are more likely than white women to be in the labor force.[28]) Another reason for the poverty of black children is that their parents, if employed, are more likely than white parents to work at poorly

[25] E. Franklin Frazier, *The Negro Family in the United States,* Chicago: University of Chicago Press, 1939.

[26] Daniel Patrick Moynihan, "Employment, Income, and the Ordeal of the Negro Family," *Daedalus,* Vol. 94, Fall 1965, pp. 745-770.

[27] Conference on Economic Progress, *Poverty and Deprivation in the United States: The Plight of Two-Fifths of a Nation,* Washington, D.C.: Conference on Economic Progress, 1962, p. 55.

[28] Moynihan, "Employment, Income, and the Ordeal of the Negro Family," p. 761.

UNEMPLOYMENT RATES

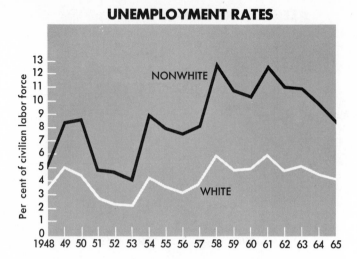

FIGURE 4.3 **Percentage of civilian labor force unemployed, by color, 1948–1965.** Source: U.S. Bureau of Labor Statistics, *The Negroes in the United States: Their Economic and Social Situation,* Bulletin No. 1511, Washington, D. C.: Government Printing Office, 1966, p. 20.

paid blue-collar occupations. Figure 4.4 shows the proportions of whites and nonwhites in five occupational categories. One consequence of nonwhite poverty is that black children are more likely than white children to live in overcrowded, deteriorating, or dilapidated housing lacking a private toilet and hot and cold running water. Figure 4.5 documents this bleak fact.

3. Black children born to married parents are less likely than white children

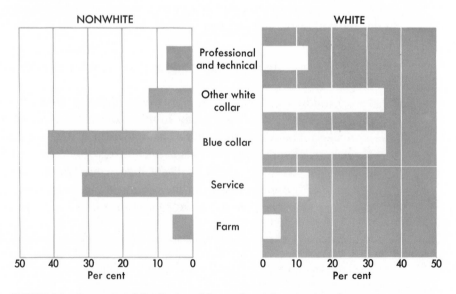

FIGURE 4.4 **Occupational distribution of the employed, by color, March 1965.** Source: Bureau of the Census, *Americans at Mid-Decade,* Washington, D. C.: Government Printing Office, 1966, p. 27.

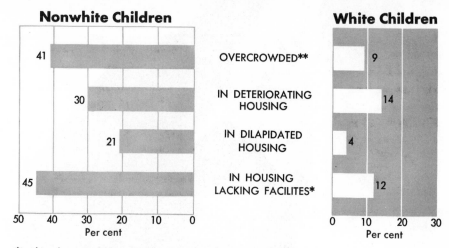

*Lacking hot or cold running water and exclusive use of toilet
and tub or shower inside the unit

**1.51 persons or more per room

FIGURE 4.5   **White and nonwhite children living in substandard housing in 1960.** Source: U. S. Bureau of Labor Statistics, *The Negroes in the United States: Their Economic and Social Situation,* Bulletin No. 1511, Washington, D. C.: Government Printing Office, 1966, p. 41.

born to married parents to grow up in an intact home. This is because low-income parents are more prone to separate, and more black than white families have low incomes; moreover, Negro families are more likely than white families of the same income level to break up. Table 4.3 shows both of these factors at work. As a result, between two and three times as large a proportion of Negro as white families are headed by women, sometimes a grandmother (Fig. 4.6).

The effects of the disadvantaged family situations of black children are large because so much depends on the conjugal family in an urban industrial society. Table 4.4 (p. 130) shows that black children are more likely than white children to be arrested for delinquency, and the difference holds both for broken and intact families. The effect of disadvantaged family situations is reflected also in the differential educational achievements of whites and non-whites (seen in Fig. 4.7, p. 131). The relative weakness of the Negro family compared with the white family increases the probability of school maladjustment for black youngsters, and poor educational preparation increases the probability of marginal participation in the economic system. This marginal participation in turn may lead to other adversities of Negro life including higher rates of hospitalization for mental breakdown.[29]

The conjugal family system is one factor contributing to the difficulty in

[29] Robert E. Clark, "Psychoses, Income, and Occupational Prestige," *American Journal of Sociology,* Vol. 54, March 1949, pp. 433-440; Bureau of the Census, *Special Report on Institutional Population,* Washington, D.C.: Government Printing Office, 1953.

Ken Heyman

achieving social and economic equality between blacks and whites. In the conjugal family system the tendency is to convert situational disadvantages in the parental generation (here resulting from historical injustices) into inadequate child socialization. The major liability of the small conjugal family as a child-rearing institution is its vulnerability to parental inadequacy or personal crisis: it lacks the resilience to cope with serious illness, death, parental incompatibility, and other catastrophes. However, in aspects not related to child socialization, the conjugal family system has advantages that make it particularly suitable to modern societies. Not only is it compatible with the population mobility of industrial societies, as extended families are not; it is also more adaptable to social change than are patrilineal or matrilineal families. The phenomenal sales in the United States of Dr. Benjamin Spock's book on baby and child care reflect the uncertainty of today's parents with a newborn infant and without the guidance of an older, more experienced woman *in the household*. They reflect also the uncertainty of living in a time of changing expectations. Today's parents buy Dr. Spock's book and others like it because they cannot draw so easily on an unchanging tradition of child care—as can parents in societies where children are socialized in households where other children have recently passed through the same developmental stage and where the same expectations prevail for each succeeding generation. The uncertainty of parents in industrial societies makes them more receptive to advice from pediatricians, child psychologists, and other transmitters of the latest research. Insofar as it can be assumed that folk traditions of child care are not perfect, this receptivity to change makes improved socialization techniques possible. Whether the changes in socialization practices in the United States

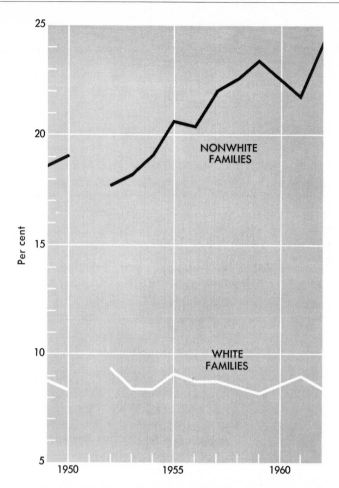

FIGURE 4.6 **White and nonwhite families headed by a woman, 1950–1962.** Source: U.S. Department of Health, Education and Welfare, *Social Development,* Publication No. 15, Washington, D.C.: Government Printing Office, p. 48.

in the past couple of generations have been improvements is not certain; there is no doubt, however, that changes have occurred.[30] If and when a scientific basis for child socialization is established, the introduction of improvements in child-rearing practices will not be so difficult.

The Increasing Participation of Children in Family Decisions. Modern families are increasingly democratic. Several mutually consistent studies indicate a trend toward increased participation of children in family decision making characterizes not only the United States but other industrialized and

[30] Daniel R. Miller and Guy E. Swanson, *The Changing American Parent,* New York: Wiley; 1958; John Sirjamaki, *The American Family in the Twentieth Century,* Cambridge, Mass.: Harvard University Press, 1953, Orville Brim, Jr., *Education for Child Rearing,* New York: Russell Sage Foundation, 1959; Urie Bronfenbrenner, "Socialization and Social Class Through Time and Space," in Maccoby, Newcomb, and Hartley, Eds., *Readings in Social Psychology,* 3rd ed., New York: Holt, 1958, pp. 400–425.

TABLE 4.4

The Relationship between Coming from a Broken Home and Appearing in Juvenile Court, by Color and Sex, Philadelphia, 1960

	Girls			
	Nonwhites		Whites	
	From Broken Homes	From Intact Homes	From Broken Homes	From Intact Homes
Juvenile Court appearance	669	317	196	278
No Juvenile Court appearance	26,925	64,367	16,880	182,904
Total population	27,594	64,684	17,076	183,182
Delinquency per 10,000 population	242	49	115	15

	Boys			
	Nonwhites		Whites	
	From Broken Homes	From Intact Homes	From Broken Homes	From Intact Homes
Juvenile Court appearance	2,081	1,660	732	1,730
No Juvenile Court appearance	24,859	61,490	16,482	182,892
Total population	26,940	63,150	17,214	184,622
Delinquency per 10,000 population	773	263	425	94

Sources: The data on juvenile court appearances in Philadelphia come from the *Forty-Seventh Annual Report of the County Court of Philadelphia (1960)*, pp. 122–123; the data on the family composition of the population of Philadelphia County come from Bureau of the Census, *U.S. Census of Population: 1960*, Vol. 1, Part 40 (Pennsylvania), p. 620; the rates computed are considerably lower than the true rates because the base population contains *all* children under 18, whereas the juvenile court statistics refer with minor exceptions to children under 18 but over 7.

industrializing countries. For instance, one investigation utilized survey data from five countries, analyzing by the age of respondents replies to the question, "In general, how much voice do you think children of 16 should have in family decisions?" Younger respondents were more likely to give the demo-

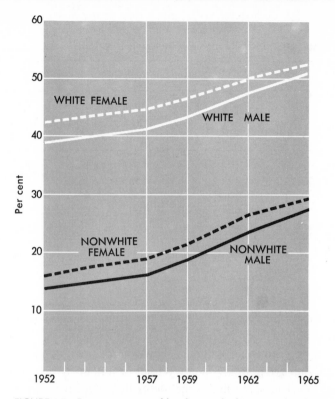

FIGURE 4.7   **Persons 25 years old and over who have completed 4 years of high school or more, 1952–1965.** Source: Bureau of the Census, *Americans at Mid-Decade,* Washington, D.C.: Government Printing Office, 1966, p. 19.

cratic responses, "a great deal" or "some."[31] Older respondents were inclined to reply "little" or "none," which the researcher interpreted as reflecting an autocratic family ideology. Table 4.5 presents the detailed data for the United States, Great Britain, West Germany, Italy, and Mexico. Note that in all five countries, respondents 18 to 25 were less likely to give the autocratic response than respondents 61 or older, but the effect is stronger in the more industrialized countries (United States, Great Britain, and West Germany). The data of Table 4.5 were collected at a single point of time. The trend is inferred through the analysis of responses in terms of ages of respondents. Such a cross-sectional study is not as conclusive as a prohibitively time-consuming study of successive cohorts of the population polled at the same age, say, 30, because some of the variation between older and younger people may result from a tendency for *older* people to be more authoritarian regardless of the era in which they were born. We have evidence, however, that Table 4.5 reflects more than life cycle changes since, at each stage of life, whether young or old, the more industrialized the society, the less authoritarian are its members.

[31] Glen H. Elder, Jr., "Role Relations, Sociocultural Environments, and Autocratic Family Ideology," *Sociometry,* Vol. 28, June 1965, pp. 173–196.

TABLE 4.5

Percentage Autocratic in Family Ideology by Age and Nation

	Age (and year of birth)						
	18–25 (1934–41)	26–30 (1929–34)	31–35 (1924–29)	36–40 (1919–24)	41–50 (1909–19)	51–60 (1900–09)	61+ (Before 1900)
United States	10	10	14	13	16	25	31
Great Britain	31	29	35	32	25	52	58
West Germany	24	40	45	39	44	44	58
Italy	58	69	70	64	71	83	74
Mexico	53	44	43	45	44	54	66

Source: Glen H. Elder, Jr., "Role Relations, Sociocultural Environments, and Autocratic Family Ideology," *Sociometry*, Vol. 28, June 1965, p. 182.

The *reasons* for the changing attitudes toward participation of adolescents in family decision making are not entirely clear. Certainly rising educational levels are partly responsible; the data show that democratic family ideology is associated with going to secondary school or further. Urbanization is also responsible; the data show that respondents living in urban areas are more likely than rural respondents to subscribe to a democratic family ideology. The social psychological mechanism by which superior levels of education and urban residence produce a democratic ideology may simply be greater exposure to democratic ideas in books and the mass media. Or it may have a more complicated explanation. Perhaps better educated, urban respondents are more aware of the speed with which new knowledge accumulates in modern societies. Knowing this, they concede that the younger generation is likely to possess useful ideas to which parents should pay attention.

Whatever the precise mechanism, families are becoming increasingly democratic. One reflection of this—admittedly in a highly educated American sample—is a shift in kinship terminology toward greater symmetry. An anthropologist and a sociologist asked students and colleagues to describe in detail the terms used in their families in referring to relatives.[32] Searching interviews were conducted to find out the reasons for variations from ordinary kinship usage—for example, why some uncles were addressed by their first names and others as Uncle _____. One variation was particularly interesting from the point of view of socialization: the reciprocal use of first names between children and parents. Since this terminology suggests social equality, the authors were not surprised to be told that parents in these situations had greater difficulty asserting their generational authority. "Parents always have the problem

[32] David M. Schneider and George C. Homans, "Kinship Terminology and the American Kinship System," *American Anthropologist*, Vol. 57, December 1955, pp. 1194–1208.

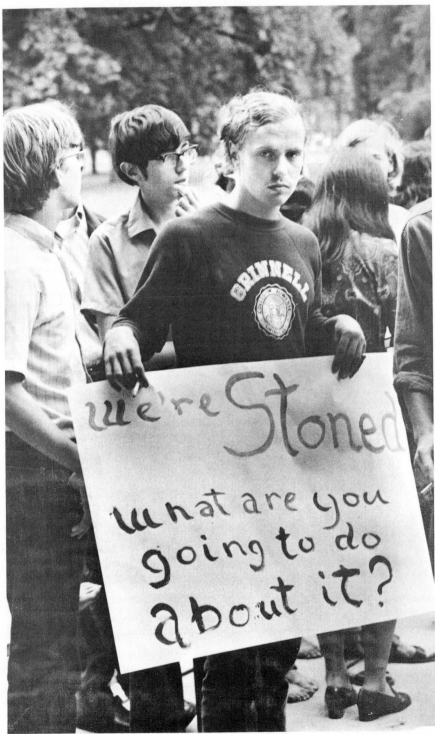

Henry Wilhelm — Bla

of dealing with children who, at certain ages, insist that, 'If you can do it, why can't I?' But where first names are used reciprocally, we find that this problem is especially acute and especially difficult to handle.''

Whether the trend to increasing participation of children in family decision making is as marked in dictatorial countries is not known. Recall that socialization in the family of orientation prepares the individual not only for life in the family of procreation but for participation in the various institutions of a differentiated society. If children participate in family decision making, they will be predisposed to speak up in the schools and colleges they attend, in the jobs they obtain as young adults, and in the political process. This may account for some of the rebellious behavior of students and intellectuals in Spain, the Soviet Union, Poland, and East Germany.

CONCLUSION

Faced with a barbarian invasion of egocentric infants, every society responds by setting up an informal teaching program, usually run by the family, in which the child learns to behave in accordance with the society's standards for human beings. "Socialization" is the name for this process of learning to play roles and abide by cultural norms, first in one's family and then in other groups. It consists not only of external conformity to social rules but also of learning to like doing what one would be compelled to do anyway, that is, of the development of a certain kind of self-conception. In all societies the individual joins the human community in the same way: by identifying with previously socialized members of the society, by intrapsychic incorporation of their cultural norms, and by learning to play the roles already being played.

Since socialization is a type of learning, failures are inevitable. No educational program is 100 per cent successful. Most mental illness is complicated by if not the direct result of the emotional scars of childhood socialization. An extreme form of socialization failure is the psychopathic personality, whose appearance is adult but whose morality is that of the egocentric infant.

Because industrial societies assign responsibility for child socialization to the conjugal family, industrial societies are especially vulnerable to socialization failure. When things go wrong in a conjugal family, they go *very* wrong. The conjugal family system lacks the resilience to absorb the personal catastrophes which past experience would suggest are inevitable. On the other hand, the conjugal family system has a built-in receptivity to change, and this opens the door to improvements in child-rearing techniques as scientific knowledge of socialization grows. It also opens the door to democratization as urbanization and educational upgrading challenge the received wisdom of the past. Better education means that children may have as much or more academic knowledge as their parents, thus making it difficult for parents to exclude them from participation in family decision making. And if they have grown up in democratic families, they will press for democratic procedures in the institutions they enter as adults. In autocratic societies this can be subversive. Even in democracies, it can be unsettling, as American college and university presidents have learned.

SOME SIGNIFICANT LITERATURE ON INITIAL SOCIALIZATION

Leonard S. Cottrell, Jr., "Interpersonal Interaction and the Development of the Self," in David A. Goslin, Ed., *Handbook of Socialization Theory and Research,* Chicago: Rand McNally, 1969, pp. 543-570. Drawing upon the symbolic interactionist tradition going back to George Herbert Mead, Cottrell explains the development of the self as a social process. As a result of interaction with significant others, the individual internalizes the conception of himself that others have of him. For example: "The incipient act to cheat on an examination present in the student evokes incipient mobilization of derogating and rejecting responses he has incorporated through taking the role of significant reference others in their responses to similar behavior, either his own or that of an observed other who has cheated" (page 549). Cottrell describes in some detail the case of Otto, who at 15 rebelled violently against an authoritarian German father. Some years later Otto's young wife went to a clinic for help because of her husband's harsh and strict treatment of their 2½-year-old son. Otto had learned from interacting with his own father not only the role of rebellious son but that of punitive father. In short, a learned self-other pattern of interaction tends to persist. It changes only when the defining responses of its reference others change. But these reference others need not be the objectively present others; internalized others may support a self-conception that is attacked by objectively present others.

Paul C. Glick, *American Families,* New York: Wiley, 1957. A wealth of data on family organization and living arrangements exist in the census reports of modern countries. This monograph, one of a series commissioned by the Social Science Research Council, undertakes to exploit data on American families drawn largely from the 1950 census of population. It covers such topics as (1) family living arrangements, (2) the life cycle of the family, (3) changes in family composition during the life cycle, (4) first marriages and remarriages, and (5) separation, divorce, and widowhood. As background for understanding American child socialization, a researcher may wish to know such things as the percentage of American families living with relatives or in rooming houses rather than in their own households or the percentage of families without two parents in the home. He has a good chance of finding answers in this monograph. This summary is based on a review by Sheldon Stryker, *American Sociological Review,* Vol. 22, October 1957, pp. 605-606.

Norman Goodman, Stephen A. Richardson, Sanford M. Dornbusch, and Albert H. Hastorf, "Variant Reactions to Physical Disabilities," *American Sociological Review,* Vol. 28, June 1963, pp. 429-435. Research has shown that American children and adults respond more favorably to drawings of a child without handicaps than to drawings of a child with crutches, with a missing left hand, or with a facial disfiguration. And, curiously enough, they respond even more negatively to a drawing of an obese child than to drawings of crippled or disfigured children. The research reported in this paper takes the rank order of reactions to disabilities as the result of normal—albeit subtle—socialization, and goes on to predict that certain categories of children will react differently. Mentally retarded and psychiatrically disturbed children will rank the drawings differently because their intellectual and emotional problems interfere with learning in general and especially with learning values which are implicit rather than explicit. Children from particular ethnic traditions will rank the drawings differently because they have learned special subcultural values at variance with the point of view of the larger society. The research undertaken by the authors confirmed their predictions.

Talcott Parsons, "The Superego and the Theory of Social Systems," *Psychiatry,* Vol. 15, February 1952, pp. 15-25. Along with other insights, this theoretical article suggests an explanation of the child's development from being a pragmatist yielding to superior power to becoming a moral being. Parsons also points out here that mother-child interaction implicitly teaches the child expressive concepts describing the relationship between his mother's acts and her underlying feelings. This symbolic learning makes possible emotional communication between them. Only after the child has learned the expressive concepts of his culture, concepts already known to his mother and embodied in her responses to him, can he learn to love his mother or to care about her love for him.

Stephen A. Richardson, "The Effect of Physical Disability on the Socialization of a Child," in David A. Goslin, Ed., *Handbook of Socialization Theory and Research,* Chicago: Rand McNally, 1969, pp. 1047-1064. The author of this article brings together the findings of a large number of studies of handicapped children, some dealing with their reactions to their handicaps and others with the reactions to them of nonhandicapped children and adults. He concludes that a physical handicap "impoverishes the experiences necessary for a child's socialization." The loss is greater with some handicaps than with others, and it tends to be cumulative in both mandatory relationships (parents, teachers) and voluntary relationships (friendships).

Morris Rosenberg, "Parental Interest and Children's Self-Conceptions," *Sociometry,* Vol. 26, March 1963, pp. 35-49. Through a questionnaire survey of 1684 juniors and seniors in 10 high schools in New York State, the relationship between level of parental interest in their children and children's self-esteem is examined. Three indices of parental interest are used: (1) the parents' knowledge of the child's friends when he was 10 or 11 years of age; (2) the parents' response to his report card when he was in the fifth or sixth grade; and (3) the degree of current participation of the child in mealtime conversation. Dr. Rosenberg reports that children whose parents can be described as disinterested in them (by any of the three criteria) score lower on a test of self-esteem, on the average, than children whose parents are interested in them—lower in fact than children of parents whose interest is mainly punitive:

> Very likely such lack of interest in the child goes along with lack of love, a failure to treat the child with respect, a failure to give him encouragement, a tendency to consider the child something of a nuisance and to treat him with irritation, impatience and anger. . . . The feeling that one is important to a significant other is probably essential to the development of a feeling of self-worth.

Anselm Strauss and Karl Schuessler, "Socialization, Logical Reasoning, and Concept Development in the Child," *American Sociological Review,* Vol. 16, August 1951, pp. 514-523. A series of test items were administered to young children involving coin recognition, comparative value of different coins, and making change. The researchers concluded that because young children were inferior to adults in logical reasoning, they did not have the concepts necessary for learning adult motives and roles. Only when they have mastered these concepts, passing from simple to more complex symbols, can socialization proceed to levels expected by adult society.

Jackson Toby, "The Differential Impact of Family Disorganization," *American Sociological Review,* Vol. 22, October 1957, pp. 505-512. The family not only transmits socially acceptable values to the young child; it also tries to prevent him from being influenced by socially unacceptable values. By means of an examination of American delinquency data, this article explores the differential consequences to girls and boys, to younger and older children, of ineffective parental guidance. Since girls and preadolescents tend to be better supervised by the average urban industrial family than adolescent boys, a defective family situation makes a greater difference to girls and preadolescents than it does to adolescent boys.

Clark E. Vincent, "Unmarried Fathers and the Mores: 'Sexual Exploiter' As an Ex Post Facto Label," *American Sociological Review,* Vol. 25, February 1960, pp. 40-46. In view of the difficulties in providing for the socialization of illegitimate children in industrial societies, unmarried motherhood is relevant to the topic of child socialization. In 1954 Dr. Vincent studied 201 out-of-wedlock births to white women in Alameda County, California, where the identity of the father was known. He reported that the fathers did not conform to the popular stereotype of the exploiting male. By and large, the fathers resembled the mothers in age and education; he concluded that any exploitation present in the relationship when illicit sexual relations were occurring was likely to be reciprocal. This suggests that unmarried parenthood is not explainable in terms of naiveté of inexperienced girls and also that the social obstacles to the marriage of the father and the mother of the child are fewer than were supposed. For a more detailed discussion of the characteristics of the unmarried mothers, including the factors associated with their decision to keep their babies or surrender them for adoption, see Clark E. Vincent, *Unmarried Mothers,* New York: Free Press of Glencoe, 1961.

Leon J. Yarrow, "Separation from Parents during Early Childhood," in Martin L. Hoffman and Lois W. Hoffman, Eds., *Review of Child Development,* Vol. 1, New York: Russell Sage Foundation, 1964, pp. 89-136. This careful review of the research literature seeks to assess the damage, if any, to the personality of the child as a development of early separation from his parents, especially from his mother. For example, how traumatic is hospitalization or foster home placement in early childhood? The conclusion is that such separation is damaging to the extent that it disrupts an emotionally significant relationship—and especially when this disruption is followed by other traumatic experiences that reinforce the feeling of loss. "On the whole, the data do not differentiate clearly between the effects of the separation experience per se and the reinforcing conditions following separation. Several kinds of experiences following separation have been repeatedly implicated in the development of personality disorders: placement in a depriving institutional environment and placement in an unstable foster home, with recurrent changes in parental figures" (page 127).

SOCIALIZATION AFTER
CHILDHOOD

As long as an individual lives, he joins new groups and assumes new roles in groups to which he already belongs. These changes require him to learn new ways of relating to other people. This is accomplished by *continuing socialization*. Sociologists call attention to the similarity between early and later socialization by including them both within the single concept of "socialization." But they are not *identical* learning experiences. Infant socialization is the first contact with society. In a sense, all later socialization experiences are an anticlimax. Initial socialization is unique in two respects:

1. The infant does not understand language, and therefore he cannot (initially) communicate with the socializing agent. He is *ignorant* of many of the expectations of those with whom he interacts.
2. The infant is not (initially) concerned about his mother's reactions to him; he may not be aware that she is reacting. He is not *motivated* to fulfill even those expectations of which he is aware.

Subsequent socialization contrasts with infant socialization in both respects. The learning of language in early childhood means that later socialization experiences will involve symbolic communication between the socializing agent and the individual undergoing socialization. Second, the relationship between mother and child is transferred to all human beings—to some extent. The child's experience with his mother has made it impossible for him to adopt as an adult the devil-may-care attitude of the infant toward other people. In the course of worrying about her reactions, the child learned to care about the reactions of practically everybody. We do not care *as much* about the reactions of strangers as about the reactions of emotionally important people (significant others) like parents. But early socialization has made us "other-directed," as David Riesman termed it; socialized persons cannot help being sensitive even to the reactions of strangers.[1] Before his mother got to work on him, the infant was only slightly more sensitive to people than to trees or stones. In short, early socialization provides the intellectual and motivational basis for later socialization.[2] Later socialization assumes that the individual can understand what is expected of him and wishes to acquiesce. Thus adult socialization concentrates on teaching role *content*, not in inculcating motivation or building a vocabulary. The new employee is simply told the job requirements on the assumption that he will *want* to come to work on time when he is aware of the schedule.

There is another difference between child and adult socialization. Child socialization, occurring as it does early in the life cycle, is entangled with the mysterious emergence of personality from its organic base. The capacity for self-awareness that develops in childhood depends on the ego-defining interactions the child has with various significant others. The character of these in-

[1] David Riesman et al., *The Lonely Crowd,* New Haven, Conn.: Yale University Press, 1950.
[2] Orville G. Brim, Jr., and Stanton Wheeler, *Socialization after Childhood: Two Essays,* New York: Wiley, 1967, pp. 24-28.

teractions establishes his initial identity.[3] Identity changes as the early socializing agents (parents) become less salient, and new socializers become emotionally significant. Nevertheless, the emergence of the initial identity is a bigger step than subsequent changes in that identity—although anthropologist Ruth Benedict pointed out that postchildhood socialization experiences present varying learning problems for the individual depending on whether later roles are similar to or different from the early roles played in the family.[4] Thus Professor Benedict hypothesized that *the greater the number of familiar elements in the new role as compared with earlier roles, the easier it is to learn the new role.* This certainly seems plausible. The son of a farmer has a good chance to gain gradual experience in the role of farmer. Youths in urban areas—where the world of work is more likely to be separated from the place of residence—find occupational roles more disconnected from their childhood roles. In short, there is a possibility of later socialization building on earlier socialization, although this possibility is realized to varying degrees in the actual learning of adolescent and adult roles.

Professor Benedict perceived an additional problem. Early socialization can be misleading and may be an obstacle to the learning of adolescent or adult roles. For example, some parents attempt to control childhood sexuality by communicating to children that sex is a nasty, dirty thing. Effective though this may be at preventing premature interest in sex, such attitudes must be unlearned before these children marry. In this instance childhood socialization creates what Thorstein Veblen called "trained incapacity." *The less unlearning of elements in previous roles that the new role requires, the easier it is to learn the new role.*

SOCIALIZATION FOR INDEPENDENCE

Family socialization is only a beginning—the effectiveness of family socialization will determine the responsiveness of the individual to all later socialization experiences. How accessible the individual is to socialization in the **peer group,** at school, in marriage, and at work depends in part on the patterns of interaction established in the family. This explains the concern of psychoanalysis with childhood relationships.[5] Psychoanalytic theorists point out that the child who rebels against the authority of his first socializers will probably transfer his feelings of hostility toward **authority figures** generally— and express them in subsequent socializing experiences. Instead of wanting to live up to the expectations of others, the normal outcome of family socializa-

---

[3] Brim and Wheeler, *Socialization after Childhood,* p. 33.

[4] Ruth Benedict, "Continuities and Discontinuities in Cultural Conditioning," *Psychiatry,* Vol. 1, May 1939, pp. 161-167.

[5] Harry Stack Sullivan, *The Interpersonal Theory of Psychiatry,* New York: Norton, 1953; Eric H. Erikson, *Childhood and Society,* New York: Norton, 1950.

tion, this type of person needs to *violate* the expectations of others and incur their disapproval. More accurately, the balance within his personality between the need for approval and the need for disapproval is upset although socialization experiences cannot extinguish completely the need for approval. Even in homes where parents are vicious or stupid, children learn to appreciate some positive aspects of family relationships.

If the norms parents are trying to inculcate are clearly defined, if the child feels basically accepted by his parents, if the parents permit some missteps while the new pattern is being internalized, if the parents control their tendency to respond with hostility to rebelliousness, and if the child perceives that greater rewards are available for learning the new pattern than for clinging to the old—the child internalizes the role his parents are trying to teach him. He also learns to accept socialization experiences with minimal rebelliousness. This does not guarantee that the content of the patterns he internalizes are appropriate for the society in which he will live as an adult. Industrial societies require considerable independence on the part of adults. A child successfully socialized for dependence on loving but domineering parents is **inappropriately socialized** in terms of ultimate expectations for adult behavior.[6] A peculiar feature of family socialization in industrial societies is the shift from dependence training in early childhood to independence training in adolescence and young adulthood.[7]

In all urban societies, the family is an island of emotional intimacy in a sea of strangers. Because the American family is typically a conjugal unit, the child may have brothers and sisters in his household, but he usually does not have the cousins who would be living in his home in a preindustrial society.[8] This limits considerably his possible experiences with agemates. An older brother or sister, even one who is only a year or two older, is at a different stage of development. An older sibling tends to have an advantage in every game, a younger sibling a disadvantage. In order to learn how to compete on *equal* terms, most children must go *outside* the family and locate agemates in the neighborhood. Given the relative anonymity of urban neighborhoods, this is not easy for less venturesome children. Not only must the child "make friends" with strangers, that is, initiate interaction without the help of an established relationship; he must also relate to these new friends in quite different ways from the patterns established with his mother and father.[9]

[6] Socialization within a subsystem to patterns inappropriate to the larger society in which the individual will interact is a chronic problem in complex societies. See Harry C. Bredemeier and Richard M. Stephenson, *The Analysis of Social Systems,* New York: Holt, 1962, pp. 126-128.

[7] Failure to shift personality gears can lead to neurosis. See Arnold W. Green, "The Middle Class Male Child and Neurosis," *American Sociological Review,* Vol. 11, February 1946, pp. 31-41.

[8] See Paul C. Glick, *American Families,* New York: Wiley, 1957, for a comprehensive statistical report on family organization in the United States.

[9] John D. Campbell, "Peer Relations in Childhood," in Martin L. Hoffman and Lois W. Hoffman, Eds., *Review of Child Development Research,* Vol. 1, New York: Russell Sage, 1964, pp. 289-322.

In dealing with doting parents, a child learns techniques by which power-less persons get what they want from powerful persons: pleading, appealing for sympathy, cajoling. When he goes out into the neighborhood to interact with peers, his skills at crying, throwing himself on the ground and making a fuss, or smiling winsomely may be useless. He is no longer dealing with benevolent despots. He must therefore *unlearn* the techniques of manipulation which proved successful within the family circle. He must learn to fight for his rights, to bluff, to negotiate. (Presumably an ''only'' child is at a disadvantage in learning to relate to peers as compared with a child having siblings of about the same age.) Some children never learn how to interact with agemates. They need not necessarily have unhappy childhoods. The world of books or fantasy may provide compensations. Or they may become precociously skillful at in-teracting with adults, a talent which yields higher dividends as the years go by.

But there is evidence that children who do not develop viable peer relationships are more prone to mental illness.[10]

In all societies, children are taught to interact with peers. In industrial society, however, peer socialization presents special difficulties:

1. In the United States, as in other industrial societies, the isolation of the conjugal family and the anonymity of the urban community accentuate the qualitative differences between relationship *inside* and *outside* the family.
2. In the United States more than in other industrial societies of the contemporary world, ideological pressure for "adjusting" to peers is well nigh inescapable. A youngster who lives in a world of books or dreams is forced by the expectations of his parents and of other adults in the community to come to terms with his peers—sometimes at the cost of his individuality. Riesman argues persuasively that Americans are excessively preoccupied with peer group adjustment.[11] In France, on the other hand, the ideological pressure is quite different; children are expected to orient themselves to parents rather than to peers.[12]
3. In urban industrial societies, geographic and social mobility produces kaleidoscopic instability of interpersonal relations. Adjustment to peers is not settled at any particular age. Equalitarian interaction is a problem for the individual for two decades after the walking-and-talking stage.

The small conjugal family system characteristic of industrial societies tends to make children highly dependent on their parents. Other sources of emotional support are not readily available. Nonetheless, the expectation is that the family into which one is born will disintegrate. Children cannot remain dependent throughout life. They must leave the nest. The expectations surrounding occupational choice and the establishment of a family of one's own (family of procreation) create pressures to be more independent. During adolescence these two forces meet head-on: the structurally fostered *dependence* of an isolated family system and the *independence* required by a dynamic society. The turmoil of adolescence in industrial societies is largely due to the collision of these incompatible forces. Adolescents are rebellious not only because parents sometimes try to keep them children too long but also because they must struggle against their own inclinations to remain protected and dependent. In the following autobiographical anecdotes, contributed as a class assignment, college students report on adolescent conflicts with their parents and reveal their own ambivalence.

---

[10] Stuart D. Loomis and Arnold Green, "The Pattern of Mental Conflict in a Typical State University," *Journal of Abnormal and Social Psychology*, Vol. 42, July 1947, pp. 342-355; Nicholas J. Demerath, "Adolescent Status Demands and the Student Experiences of Twenty Schizophrenics," *American Sociological Review*, Vol. 8, October 1943, pp. 513-518.

[11] Riesman, *The Lonely Crowd*.

[12] Jesse Pitts, "The Family and Peer Groups," in Norman W. Bell and Ezra F. Vogel, *A Modern Introduction to the Family*, Glencoe, Ill.: Free Press, 1960, pp. 266-286.

CASE 1

One of the earliest and most notable clashes of expectations between me and my parents occurred when I was about 15 years old. The matter was precipitated by the wedding of an uncle. It was the type of an affair at which I was supposed to be present, but the thought of being there filled me with dread.

Why did I fear? At this particular age, my awkwardness was appalling. I was painfully aware of this but had never taken any steps toward self-improvement. I predicted my actions at the wedding reception weeks before it took place; I could not and would not dance. Not only that; but I would sit alone, shunning conversation with other people.

I believed my parents understood my shortcomings and consequently would not place me in a position in which those faults would be brought to public attention. My ultimate desire at this assemblage was to enter unseen, sit alone and unnoticed, and leave quietly.

At the reception my parents started prodding me to dance with this girl and that girl, which brought about a slow mounting of anger and some hasty "Leave me alone!" 's from me. The hushed exchange of words continued until suddenly there erupted a verbal argument that reached the ears of everyone. Distinctly mortified at my own behavior, I left the reception.

CASE 2

Mother and father had been separated for a long time and I lived with mother on a farm. Both of us were lonely in this environment. I had few friends and was closely attached to mother, who had practically built her entire life around me. Although not a disciplinarian, mother dominated the scene and I was obedient, having considerable respect for her. Then, when I was 13, we moved into town, and the situation was immediately changed for me. No longer did I desire to remain devoted to mother but rather to the numerous newly found friends that I had acquired. Of course, mother was not prepared for my "breaking away." She never consciously attempted to keep me to herself, for she knew that what was happening was natural. But, nevertheless, I remained to her the little boy, ever so helpless, submissive, and devoted. Meanwhile, I began considering myself a young man—at least as wise as his mother and certainly more up-to-date. I was only dependent on her for room, board, clothing, and a little spending money— just the material things. No longer was she my companion or my boss; in fact I could tell her a thing or two.

Now when she gave me a command, even in the gentlest tones, I flew into a rage. Furthermore, mere advice or the use of words which I associated with domination would bring violent resentment on my part. The fact that good intentions were behind all her behavior towards me meant little, for I was reacting solely against being dominated by mother. On the occasion of the first scenes we had, mother was indignant at my arrogance. How dare her child retaliate! The rebellion must be punished by a good whack across the face, so she thought. But how dare mother hit her son, a man! I increased the violence of my attack, and mother, shocked, recoiled in fear. Then she would cry hard and tell me how mean I was. Immediately I felt ashamed; my poor helpless mother was now drenched in tears. I had to justify my actions, somehow to demonstrate to mother and perhaps to myself that I wasn't a bad boy. "Well you deserved it," I blurted out, "I'm not to be dominated; I'm a man. This was the only way I could make you realize, mother dear." She continued to weep; I became frantic and occasionally broke into tears myself. It was best to leave the scene. Mother treated me coldly for a few days; she was hurt and thought me undeserving of her affection. I tried to make it up to her by being extra good, but not so as to permit her to feel that I was backing down on my demands. Soon the relationship was restored to normal only to be followed by future scenes.

CASE 3

When I was being discharged from the Army last year, I had already planned to attend Rutgers—it was all set. As usual, I didn't consult my parents because they left decisions like that entirely up to me.

But the situation had changed at home. My older brother and sister had recently been married, and my younger brother had just joined the Navy. Unknown to me, my mother was heavily counting on me to reenter Brooklyn College so she would have at least one of her children at home.

When I announced I was going to Rutgers, 35 miles away, I could see she was disappointed.

"Do you always want to be away from home?" I remember her bitterly asking me. "First, it was California, then the Army, and now New Jersey." (I had been away to California for a year.)

It took a lot of explaining of the many advantages Rutgers held for me over Brooklyn College, coupled with the faithful promise that I would be home every weekend, before my mother reluctantly gave approval.

At first all seemed to go well. My mother still wanted me home all the time but she seemed satisfied that I was coming home each weekend. When I would come home, my mom treated me like a king. She would cook my favorite dishes, wash all my clothes and, in general, dote on me in every way. For the first time I realized my mother got a big kick out of doing things for her kids and now that I was the only one around, lavish attention was heaped upon me.

And then, two things happened to further the split that was growing between myself and my home. I got a job working nights, and I met Marie.

The only time I was able to see Marie, who lives near the University, was during the weekend, and I began staying away from home, sometimes two and three weekends in a row. I didn't realize the effect this was having on my mother until a Saturday afternoon not long ago.

I had arrived home, opened the door and had just laid my laundry on the floor. I saw my mom and grabbed her in an affectionate greeting.

She shoved me away, saying, "That's all you come home for, for me to wash your clothes and for you to sleep and eat for two days!" She was crying. "Don't you love your home and mother any more?" she blurted out as she pushed past me.

What could I say? Of course, I loved my mother but how could I explain the way I felt—how could I reconcile my love for Marie and for my parents and home?

"I'm a grown-up man now," I told my mother. "I've got to make decisions and go my own way. I can't be your little son forever." I talked on in this way for a long time but, in the end, it was to no avail. My mother was convinced that she had forever lost my love and that I no longer needed her. I could see she was terribly hurt.

The 15-year-old boy who had a violent argument with his parents at his uncle's wedding was not merely reacting to nagging. He was also responding to his expectation for himself—he ought to have been able to dance. In this instance, parents were eager to see their child developing toward adulthood, but the child was not ready to move forward. In the second and third anecdotes, the mother was *not* fully prepared to see her son grow up. The boy faced a double problem: his own inadequacy feelings and his mother's emotional need for his continued dependency.

The term "adolescent revolt" suggests that independence is won by youngsters from reluctant parents. However, industrial societies are organized to promote adolescent independence; thus as parents prepare their children for society, they unintentionally pave the way for revolt. In encouraging high levels of performance at school and college attendance, parents undermine the intellectual basis of their authority. Especially if parents are themselves poorly educated, the school makes available to the child ideas his parents do not understand. But even college-educated parents find their children learning a more advanced body of knowledge than *they* were exposed to. In granting children freedom to select a congenial occupation, parents again foster independence. Some parents seek to control the occupational choice of their children, but they find it difficult for several reasons:

1. The culture of industrial societies defines occupational selection as an individual prerogative; thus parental pressure should not be a decisive factor in the choice of occupation.
2. The educational system plays such an important part in occupational preparation that it is not possible for parents to push for any but the most untechnical vocations without reference to the school performance of their children.
3. The changing structure of occupations necessarily undermines the basis for parental guidance, namely, parental expertise.

In short, parents encourage educational achievement and expect the child to select his own career. Since parents cannot easily promote independence in these realms and deny it within the family, the adolescent "revolt" can be regarded as programmed by the values of industrial societies.

Some sociologists maintain that the family of orientation helps the adolescent to become independent by providing emotional support and encouragement for sallies into the competitive world of school and work.[13] Parental encouragement fosters the child's initial motivation to do well in school. When

[13] Talcott Parsons and Winston White, "The Link between Character and Society," in Seymour Martin Lipset and Leo Lowenthal, Eds., *Culture and Social Character: The Work of David Riesman Reviewed,* New York: Free Press of Glencoe, 1961.

the child considers attending college, it matters less whether parents have themselves attended college than that they believe in college for their child (discussed further in Chapter 11). At the same time that parents are encouraging children to compete at school and later at work, the family provides emotional asylum. Parental expectations for independence outside the family are balanced by parental support of dependence within the family circle. Helpful though parental support is psychologically, it is self-limiting. The adolescent knows that the time will come when it is no longer appropriate to rush home to Mother with tales of unfair teachers or ruthless supervisors. Anticipation of becoming detached from the family into which he was born and nurtured creates a period of insecurity for the adolescent. Whether he wishes freedom or not, he is forced to seek it because it is a necessary condition for the transition to his family of procreation. But it is not easy to live in limbo. The adolescent peer group bridges the transition between the family of orientation and the family of procreation; peers provide *temporary* emotional security. The peer group enables the adolescent to have it both ways: to be as independent of his parents as his personality development permits, while slavishly conforming to the latest peer group fashions in clothing or popular music.

While some parents encourage the independence of their offspring, some develop vested interests in the parent role. The theme of the possessive mother is a familiar one in the theater and literature.[14] As clinical descriptions, these accounts are often excellent. As *explanations* of Momism, they leave much to be desired. Consider the relationship between the possessiveness of mothers and their role in society. In industrial societies, women typically live 20 to 30 years after their children are fully grown. Furthermore, they often outlive their husbands, who are usually older to begin with and who also have a higher mortality rate at every age (for reasons that are not well understood).[15] This results in a situation in which the developing maturity of children may precipitate a crisis for their mothers. Threatened with loss of her child-rearing function, anticipating long years of uselessness, a mother may consciously or unconsciously fight against retirement from active supervision of her children. She has a vested interest in the parent role—unless she has an occupation to return to. Since the moment when the son is able to fend for himself is a matter of judgment, his mother may consider herself crucial to his physical survival when he no longer needs her guidance and protection. By the time the son is 45, it seems clear that he will not starve to death even if deprived of "Mom's home cooking." But when he is 19 or 20, there is more room for argument, and some mothers are tempted to shade the doubts in favor of their own indispensability.

---

[14] See, for example, Sidney C. Howard, *The Silver Cord,* in *The Theatre Guild Anthology,* New York: Random House, 1936; Philip Wylie, *Generation of Vipers,* New York: Farrar and Rinehart, 1942.

[15] Bureau of the Census, *Statistical Abstract of the United States: 1968;* Washington, D.C.: Government Printing Office, 1968, p. 54.

Socialization into Occupational Roles. Conjugal families produce an output to the economy—young adults independent enough to compete for occupational roles. Family socialization also produces people who are kind to dogs and are passionate lovers—but less uniformly. The family in industrial societies *always* tries to propel able-bodied males and a majority of females into the occupational system. Exceptions are made in some European countries for the aristocracy, but since the United States lacks this heritage of a feudal past, even the rich are expected to have an occupation. The playboy may be envied, but he is not respected. The emotional investment in "work" in industrial societies can be assessed by considering the impact of unemployment. Far from being regarded as an opportunity to relax and enjoy life, unemployment usually is treated as a disaster.[16] This is the result of socialization rather than because employment is the economic basis for the family. In Great Britain, where National Assistance is readily available, unemployment is no less feared than in less welfare-minded societies.[17] The enormous numbers of employed persons and of persons frantically seeking employment are evidence of the success of socialization for occupational competition in industrial countries. Beside these huge totals, the professional criminals, the gamblers, the pimps, and the loafers sink into statistical insignificance.

Absenteeism and high rates of job turnover are regarded as pathological in industrial societies. Consider, however, that there is no timeclock-punching instinct to help men get up early, gulp their breakfasts, pack into cars, buses, or subways, and do their day's work. Still, as the rush-hour traffic jams prove, the delights of lounging in bed are forgone by the majority. **Anticipatory socialization** in the family of orientation develops a need on the part of most males (and many females) to play an occupational role. One's occupation is regarded as a major part of an adult identity: the person who fixes leaky faucets *is* a plumber; even when he is sunning himself on the beach during his summer vacation, people who know him think of him as a plumber, and he thinks of himself as a plumber. Since plumbers are not evaluated as favorably as lawyers, the choice of an occupation is not only a search for personally congenial work but for an **identity** that carries sufficient community prestige. What is "sufficient"? This depends a great deal on the values communicated in the course of socialization for work in the family of orientation.[18]

Most families develop enough **status consciousness** about the process of occupational selection that competition is keen for the more prestigeful occupations—even though considerable time, energy, and training are required in preparation for them. Long educational preparation has been characteristic

---

[16] E. Wight Bakke, *The Unemployed Worker,* New Haven, Conn.: Yale University Press, 1940; Mirra Komarovsky, *The Unemployed Man and His Family,* New York: Dryden, 1940.

[17] Barbara Wootton, *Social Science and Social Pathology,* New York: Macmillan, 1959, pp. 41-44.

[18] Theodore Caplow, *The Sociology of Work,* Minneapolis: University of Minnesota Press, 1954, Chap. 9, "Vocational Choice," pp. 214-229; Eli Ginzberg et al., *Occupational Choice,* New York: Columbia University Press, 1951.

of the professions: engineering, law, medicine, teaching. It is increasingly characteristic of business, especially in the United States. Most business executives today do not work their way up from blue-collar jobs. They go to college and often to graduate schools of business.[19] The lengthening educational preparation for business and professional careers is characteristic of industrial societies: the family begins the process of occupational socialization; the educational system adds to it; but it cannot be completed until job placement. For occupations requiring long training, placement comes years after initial commitment to the occupation. A college student cannot get a part-time executive position to find out how he likes business or an apprenticeship to a pediatrician to find out whether medicine is for him. Occupational reality sometimes has a shocking impact on the conceptions of the role developed in the course of educational preparation. The aeronautical engineer who entered the field because, as a boy, he was fascinated by model airplanes may not be happy with his work—although he may grow to like it as a result of further socialization. Job satisfaction, like marital happiness, may be due as much to successful socialization as to judicious selection.

Where the occupation has low prestige, such as that of psychiatric attendant in a mental hospital, socialization must overcome an initially unfavorable occupational self-image:[20]

> Members of occupational groups often develop occupational self-images: sets of beliefs, attitudes, and evaluations regarding their work. By stressing certain highly valued aspects of the work—the skill it requires, its social utility, the perquisites it affords—an occupational self-image can provide work motivation and work satisfaction. The person in a high-status occupation is aided in maintaining a flattering self-image by the social prestige of his occupation. Occupations such as those of the physician and the business executive are widely known to require skill and to carry high income and pleasant working conditions. Low-ranking occupations, however, do not command favorable society-wide evaluations; the public evaluates many jobs as unappealing or, oftentimes, distasteful.
>
> How then do people in low-status occupations maintain favorable self-images? A number of plausible answers may be suggested. One is that they do *not* maintain favorable self-images, but are dissatisfied with their work and would leave it if they could. Another is that they are dissatisfied with their work but project their aspirations onto their children. Still another is that they reject or fail to internalize the value of occupational success, perhaps seeking personal fulfillment in activities off the job. Probably all of these patterns are to be found; yet it also seems likely that many low-status workers are satisfied with their jobs and have favorable occupational self-images.

[19] Seymour M. Lipset and Reinhard Bendix, *Social Mobility in Industrial Society,* Berkeley and Los Angeles: University of California Press, 1960, Chap. 4.

[20] Richard L. Simpson and Ida Harper Simpson, "The Psychiatric Attendant: Development of an Occupational Self-Image in a Low-Status Occupation," *American Sociological Review,* Vol. 24, June 1959, pp. 389-392.

Research in mental hospitals in North Carolina shows that psychiatric attendants, in the course of socialization at work, learn to build their occupational self-image on a socially valued aspect of their work, patient care, even though housekeeping duties actually take up more of their work time. Psychiatric attendants get satisfaction out of an occupation regarded by their society as demeaning. From one point of view, these psychiatric attendants are socialized to live with occupational failure. Socialization to failure is necessary in a competitive society because competition is, by definition, a situation where a winner wins when losers lose. Socialization to failure occurs not only at work where people settle for jobs below their original aspirations, where prospective sales do not materialize and promotions are given to others, but in the family, at school, and among peers. Without learning to bear up under the experience of failure, an independent existence is not feasible in an urban industrial society.

The commitment that an occupational role requires in industrial societies makes occupational failure especially threatening to the individual's self-conception. Nevertheless, we learn how to fail occupationally—and be reasonably good sports about it. Studies of executive demotion in industry show that failure is generally borne well—helped by tact on the part of corporate employers and the human capacity for rationalization.[21] Retirement from an occupational role is often experienced as failure, partly because retirement is usually abrupt. One week an aging personnel man is so preoccupied with decisions that he feels there are not enough hours in the day, and the next he has more leisure time than he can handle. An even more important reason why retirement is experienced as akin to failure is that one's sense of identity is bound up with one's occupational role; retirement, over and above the problem of hobbies and killing time, may create a feeling of uselessness.

Socialization to failure begins in the family even though families are not inevitably divided into winners and losers. A mother can love all of her children; affection for one child is not necessarily at the expense of the rejection of another. Competitive achievement is, however, so pervasive a principle of social organization in industrial societies that it seeps into the family. Some parents prefer achievers to children who dash parental hopes for school and community success. And whether parents actually make such discriminations, children think they do; that is why sibling rivalry develops. In sum: the family begins the training for failure as well as for success. Erving Goffman points out that failure is as inevitable as death itself; in teaching children how to live with both failure and success, the family trains for social participation:[22]

> . . . [A] person who can no longer sustain one of his social roles and is about to be removed from it . . . is a person who is losing one of his social lives and is

[21] Fred H. Goldner, "Demotion in Industrial Management," *American Sociological Review,* Vol. 30, October 1965, pp. 714-724.

[22] Erving Goffman, "On Cooling the Mark Out," *Psychiatry,* Vol. 15, November 1952, pp. 462-463.

about to die one of the deaths that are possible for him. This leads one to consider the ways in which we can go or be sent to our death in each of our social capacities, the ways, in other words, of handling the passage from the role we had to a state of having it no longer. One might consider the social processes of firing and laying-off; of resigning and being asked to resign; of farewell and departure; of deportation, excommunication, and going to jail; of defeat at games, contests, and wars; of being dropped from a circle of friends or an intimate social relationship; of corporate dissolution; of retirement in old age; and lastly, of the deaths that heirs are interested in.

Political Socialization. Conjugal families produce an output to the polity, namely, young adults able and willing to participate in the forms of collective decision making of their society. In democratic societies children learn the responsibilities of voting as well as the desirability (or undesirability) of holding office. In despotic societies (e.g., the Soviet Union, Spain) children learn the virtues of the official state party and the reprehensibility of challenging its wisdom; they learn to think of utterances critical of political leadership as offensive, disloyal, and punishable by the state. Thus political socialization differs from one industrial society to another depending on the political structure.

Political socialization is not accomplished by the family of orientation alone. The school helps to inculcate values underlying the political process and to communicate information helpful for political participation. In democratic societies the educational system has especially important responsibility for political socialization because voting requires both knowledge and political sophistication. The premise that a democratic society draws strength rather than incurs weakness by encouraging a free market in ideas may be difficult to accept. The free-speech principle requires intellectual discipline on the part of citizens if it is to be applied to situations where *distasteful* ideas are being marketed. In the summer of 1954, a period of concern in the United States about supposed dangers to American security caused by Communist activities, a survey research project probed the effectiveness of political socialization in the area of civil liberties. The project asked a cross section of the American population 15 questions about civil liberties for *Communists*. Figure 5.1, based on these questions, relates tolerance of political nonconformists to respondents' ages and education. The greater the educational attainment of respondents, the higher the probability of a tolerant response. There was also a tendency in every educational category for *younger* respondents to be more tolerant of nonconformity than older respondents. For example, 77 per cent of the college graduates who were 21 to 29 years of age at the time of the survey were tolerant compared with only 31 per cent of college graduates 60 years of age and over. Note, however, from the numbers following the bars, that college graduates were rare among the 60-and-over respondents, whereas they were more common than respondents with a grade school education in the 21 to 29 age group. Maybe the reason for the relative intolerance of free speech for Communists in the older age cohorts is that higher education used to be more socially selective and therefore to start with youngsters from very con-

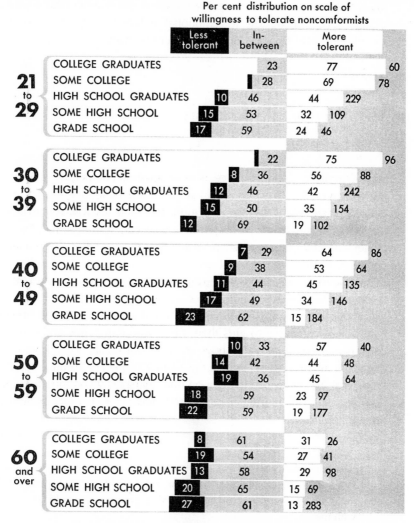

Per cent distribution on scale of
willingness to tolerate noncomformists

		Less tolerant	In-between	More tolerant	
21 to 29	COLLEGE GRADUATES		23	77	60
	SOME COLLEGE		28	69	78
	HIGH SCHOOL GRADUATES	10	46	44	229
	SOME HIGH SCHOOL	15	53	32	109
	GRADE SCHOOL	17	59	24	46
30 to 39	COLLEGE GRADUATES		22	75	96
	SOME COLLEGE	8	36	56	88
	HIGH SCHOOL GRADUATES	12	46	42	242
	SOME HIGH SCHOOL	15	50	35	154
	GRADE SCHOOL	12	69	19	102
40 to 49	COLLEGE GRADUATES	7	29	64	86
	SOME COLLEGE	9	38	53	64
	HIGH SCHOOL GRADUATES	11	44	45	135
	SOME HIGH SCHOOL	17	49	34	146
	GRADE SCHOOL	23	62	15	184
50 to 59	COLLEGE GRADUATES	10	33	57	40
	SOME COLLEGE	14	42	44	48
	HIGH SCHOOL GRADUATES	19	36	45	64
	SOME HIGH SCHOOL	18	59	23	97
	GRADE SCHOOL	22	59	19	177
60 and over	COLLEGE GRADUATES	8	61	31	26
	SOME COLLEGE	19	54	27	41
	HIGH SCHOOL GRADUATES	13	58	29	98
	SOME HIGH SCHOOL	20	65	15	69
	GRADE SCHOOL	27	61	13	283

FIGURE 5.1 **The older generation and the less educated are less tolerant of nonconformists.**
Source: Samuel A. Stouffer, *Communism, Conformity, and Civil Liberties: A Cross-Section of the Nation Speaks Its Mind,* Garden City, N.Y.: Doubleday, 1955, p. 93.

servative backgrounds. Such students were not receptive to this aspect of political socialization, and as leaders of society they consequently lowered the tolerance level in the society at large. An alternative hypothesis—equally compatible with the data—is that aging produces intolerance of nonconformity; these older respondents were as tolerant in their youth as the younger respondents at the time of the survey.

Political socialization in the family and in the school system is incidentally socialization for independence. In the course of preparing youngsters to participate in the political process, adults arouse in them expectations of responsibility that will eventually be theirs. Just as children anticipate occupational roles, they anticipate receiving the franchise. Such anticipations probably facilitate development toward emotional independence at adolescence, although empirical research on this problem is scant.

SOCIALIZATION FOR DATING AND MARRIAGE

Socialization for independence is conducive to competitive performance in the educational and occupational systems. Independence is also involved in **courtship** behavior, especially in industrial societies where marriage is contracted increasingly on the basis of mutual choice rather than by family arrangement, even in Japan where matchmaking is traditional.[23] Socializing experiences in the preadolescent peer group, which usually consists of one sex, do not facilitate initiative with the opposite sex. Boys and girls find that some of the skills which have made for success among peers in preadolescent years are less important now or even irrelevant. Thus a boy who excels in street fighting may be less attractive to girls than a boy who can dance and is a "smooth" conversationalist. Gradually, boys and girls learn what is expected of them on dates, but the process of learning the "dating" aspect of the adolescent role can be painful — or funny, depending on one's perspective on the miscommunications characteristic of the first date. The following are the recollections of male undergraduates:

> CASE 1
> I remember walking to Jane's house that night — my first date. I was excited. Jane was so pretty; all the guys said so. Yes, tonight I was to be suave and charming, I would sweep Jane off her feet and, of course, she would fall madly in love with me.
>
> But I felt a lump well in my throat as I neared her house. I felt sort of frightened at the thought of being with a girl all evening, just her and me. All my life had been with boys like myself, playing baseball and football together and talking the same vulgar and sometimes lewd sort of language. "What did *girls* talk mostly about?" I asked myself.
>
> These meditations were abruptly halted as I found myself ringing the doorbell of Jane's house.
>
> A bumbling "hello" later to Jane's parents and a promise to return her before midnight, and Jane and I left for our "big night." My original plan was to attend the neighborhood theater and then, afterwards, go for a coke and hamburger.
> It wasn't long before I realized that Jane knew nothing of my favorite topic —

[23] The family of procreation will typically have no residential or occupational ties with the kin of the bride and groom. This structural isolation reduces the interest of parents in influencing marriage choice. See Talcott Parsons, *Essays in Sociological Theory*, rev. ed., New York: Free Press of Glencoe, 1954, p. 187.

sports. And when she asked me if I knew what the "top 10" records were, I realized I knew nothing of her main interest either. This was the first time Jane and I were really alone. Always it had been with a group of mutual friends. Now I felt like a fool when I began talking of something she either didn't know anything about or else was completely disinterested in. When I began talking of something else, she neither encouraged nor discouraged me, most of the time not responding at all.

After a while I was convinced I was saying the wrong thing. This petite girl certainly was quite different from my usual associates.

About two blocks and five minutes of silence later, we arrived at the theater. I thought some of the mounting tension would ease once we were inside, but it only heightened somewhat as I wasn't quite sure just what was the proper thing for me to do. Should I hold her hand — would that be the proper thing? How would I suggest going for a hamburger later?

On the way home (she demurred at my suggestion of a coke) I again tried to strike up a conversation and wasn't very successful. The walk home seemed so long — I thought it would never end. I began to think of how to say "good-night" to her. Should I try to kiss her or should I just hold her hand? Maybe I should ask her for a kiss. But I couldn't bear it if I tried and was rejected by her — my ego wouldn't stand it.

When we reached her door I told her what a nice time I had with her (what a liar) and she thanked me for a "wonderful evening" (another liar).

We looked at each other for a moment and then, in an impulse born of desperation and desire, I clumsily threw my arms around Jane and attempted to kiss her.

She recoiled from me as if I were a monster, blurting out, "I don't think it's nice to kiss on the first date."

CASE 2

Recently, I had a blind date with a girl recommended to me by a friend. When I called her, I said we would probably go to the movies. I thought she knew how to dress for the occasion so I did not mention it. I called for her, and to my surprise she was wearing an off-the-shoulder cocktail dress. I did not want to press the movie issue, but saw in an instant she either did not want to go to the movies or did not know how to dress. When I noticed the quarter of an inch of powder packed on from her head to her chest, I assumed it was the latter. We said "good-night" to her parents, and she beat me to every door, including the car door. Ordinarily I would have opened it, but evidently she did not think it was necessary. I suggested that we go to a nightclub to dance, and she agreed. I was hoping then that none of my friends would see me "sporting" this girl, although they could probably smell her, with the amount of perfume she wore. I offered her a cigarette trying to be as polite as possible. What a mistake! I saw in a few moments that she probably had never smoked before. All she had to do was tell me that she didn't smoke. But no! She smoked until she became dizzy and then told me she was not used to that brand of cigarettes. We finally arrived at the nightclub and ordered a few drinks. I noticed that she gulped down liquor like it was fruit juice. I didn't mind her drinking, but she drank as if liquor were going out of style. I suggested that she stop drinking so fast, but that only made her increase her pace. Soon, she became very pale and loud. I decided it was time to take her home. We had just reached the car when she regurgitated all over the front seat. I was heartsick! Thoroughly disgusted, I did not say a word the entire trip home. When we arrived at her home, I offered to help her to the front door. She bluntly refused to move and said it was too early to go to bed. After much persuasion, I finally got her to the doorstep. She then asked me to kiss her goodbye. I was dumbfounded! I took two steps backward, patted her on the shoulder, and walked away. Needless to say, I never called her again.

CASE 3

My first date was about six years ago with the girl to whom I am now engaged.

The church I belonged to had chartered a bus to go to an amusement park and all members and their friends were invited to go. Since all the young people of the church were going in couples, I asked the minister's daughter, Alice, if she would go with me.

Alice's acceptance of my request was the first example of how our expectations for one another coincided. A few weeks before this event, we had been attracted to each other when we first met in church. From that time on we exchanged love notes and ogles. When it was announced that a trip to an amusement park was to take place, Alice was my choice as a date, and she naturally expected me to ask her—unless I had only been leading her on with my flirting.

On the day of the big affair, a peculiar thing happened when I called for Alice at her home. As she and I were about to leave for the bus, her father handed her a couple of dollars, saying she might need it. Although my experience in dating had been limited up to this time, I knew enough to realize that the guy footed the bill. Undoubtedly, Alice wasn't sure I knew this, so she wanted to be prepared to save me any financial embarrassment.

By the time the bus brought us to the park, we got fairly well acquainted, and I convinced her I was in a position to pay the expenses. (Since it was a church group, tickets were only half-price anyway.)

As we walked around the park, it seemed anything I wanted to do was agreeable to her. If I motioned to hold hands, she put her hand in mine; when I put my arm around her, she didn't resist. In fact, if I didn't take the initiative, she sometimes would. She would either take my hand or walk so close beside me that the only thing I could do with my arm was to put it around her, since I couldn't swing it.

The fifth time through the Tunnel of Love, Alice proved once more that she liked me as I did her. When we were half way through—in the darkest spot—she took hold of the guide rail and stopped the boat, thereby allowing us a few minutes more to smooch. The same thought had occurred to me but Alice acted first.

The entire day went along smoothly. On the return bus trip we sang with the rest of the group and also found time to display affection for each other. After spending so much time in the Tunnel of Love, that goodnight kiss on her front porch—though nice—wasn't completely novel.

Relating to the opposite sex in dating shades off into courtship—with expectations of a permanent relationship. Marriage is not merely more intimate dating, and therefore socialization into the dating subculture may have little carryover into marriage.[24] Additional socialization is necessary to make a successful marriage between a young man and a young woman who have dated one another steadily and consider themselves in love. The responsibilities of the marital role are far removed from the pleasure-seeking dalliance of dating. It is easier to be charming and witty when dancing to nightclub music than while changing a dirty diaper or washing dishes. Even physical appearance changes. A fiancée is more chic than a wife because she has more time to primp. Husbands who expect their wives to look the way they did before marriage are unrealistic. Elaborately manicured nails and an impeccable coiffure may be obtained at a cost the husband is unwilling to pay: a dirty house and inedible dinners.

Marriage forces the boy and the girl to look at one another in the context of family and friends. During courtship days they were essentially alone with one another. In industrial societies and especially in the United States, there is no legal or social requirement that the respective families know the future spouse—much less give their consent to the marriage. Romantic songs glamorize this absence of social context: "A sleepy lagoon, a tropical moon, and two on an island. . . ." But a *married* couple is no longer "two on an island." Each spouse has friends and relatives, and these emerge as important factors in the success or failure of many marriages. Marital incompatibility sometimes arises, not because the personalities of the bride and groom fail to mesh or even because their values are incompatible, but because one or the other is emotionally dependent on his family of orientation. In one case, reported in a general-circulation magazine for women, the husband expected his wife to wake him up every morning (several times); he took no responsibility for getting himself to work.[25] Ava could not accept the task of waking Chad as part of the morning housework because she interpreted his talent for sleeping as a recapitulation of childhood dependence on his mother. Furthermore, each time she shook him awake, she was reminded of his continuing reliance on his mother for occupational guidance, home-buying advice, and other decisions. In a traditional Chinese or Japanese family, a daughter-in-law was as concerned with getting along with her mother-in-law (in whose home she lived) as with her husband, and her husband was expected to continue deferring to parental guidance. In the family systems of industrial societies, on the other hand, the expectation is for the conjugal unit to be emotionally independent—although it may take several years of mutual socialization before husbands and wives look to each other for the security they used to receive elsewhere. Sometimes the previous source of this security is the peer group rather than the family of orientation. Marriages founder on occasion because the husband takes too

---

[24] Jackson Toby, "The Case Against Romance," in Harry C. Bredemeier and Jackson Toby, *Social Problems in America*, New York: Wiley 1960, pp. 461-468.

[25] Dorothy Cameron Disney, "Can This Marriage Be Saved?", *Ladies' Home Journal*, Vol. 73, March 1956, pp. 73, 199-205.

many nights out with "the boys" or the wife continues strong emotional involvements with "the girls."

Marriage involves socialization because the man and the woman must learn new roles in order to live harmoniously with one another. Marriage involves **mutual socialization** because unlike most other socialization experiences, marriage is not a situation in which an individual becomes incorporated into an established structure, that is, a situation in which he feels from the start that *he* is in the minority and it is up to *him* to make the adjustments. Each marriage is a new interactive system, and in industrial societies each partner tends to have an equal voice in the definition of the rules of that system. Consequently, the roles of "husband" and "wife" must be *mutually* defined and accepted in order for the marriage to work. Even in societies where husbands are expected to dominate the marital relationship, such as Japan, the urban industrial pattern of separate households for conjugal families permits a close relationship between husband and wife and increases mutual sensitivity. The following account of "husband-management" in a Tokyo suburb illustrates growing mutuality within a nominally authoritarian relationship:[26]

> Because the husband is accorded a superior position, he can be direct in stating his wishes. Wives can be direct in stating their children's needs and basic household requirements, but most are reluctant in stating their own personal desires. However, some modern young wives enjoy frank discourse with their husbands, and in some older families the woman runs the household either because she has higher social status or stronger temperament.
>
> Still, most [suburban] wives attain their wishes by subtle strategy rather than open request. The strategy is not always conscious, for in many ways a woman deals with her husband as she deals with anyone: by keeping a harmonious relationship and avoiding any show of unpleasantness. But this often requires such planning that it takes on the quality of an art—the art of husband management.
>
> The [suburban] wife's arts for managing the husband are similar to those of an experienced American secretary in dealing with her boss. She studies his character and knows his moods. She knows when he must be left alone, when he can be humored, when she can take advantage of his "good days." She knows what issues she can decide on her own, what issues she can discuss openly, what issues she can discuss providing she hides certain facts and exaggerates others. In face of his anger, she knows how to plead innocence or misunderstanding and how to lighten the anger by criticizing her own stupidity, ignorance, or inattentiveness, or by simply waiting until the anger has dissipated.
>
> But the [suburban] wife works much harder to please her husband than a secretary does to please her superior, and in some ways she treats her husband as her eldest child. As in dealing with her child, she tries to keep him continuously happy and satisfied, because then he will respond automatically to her wishes.
>
> A young bride searches out every little indication and listens carefully to every phrase to discover what things please her husband. She tries to avoid any direct criticism of his behavior and any assaults on his masculine ego. At most, within

---

[26] Reprinted by permission. From Ezra F. Vogel, *Japan's New Middle Class: The Salary Man and His Family in a Tokyo Suburb,* Berkeley: University of California Press, 1963, pp. 200-202.

the hearing of her own husband she might give him a hint indirectly by complimenting another wife on something that wife's husband had done. If the husband presents a view as fact, she will not offer contrary evidence even if she is convinced he is wrong. When she wants something, she makes vague suggestions that appeal to his desires rather than to logic or her own desires. If she wants an item for the home, she is not likely to talk about its use or cost, but about how beautiful it would look or how magnificent an important friend thought it was. These hints and vague suggestions do not require the disapproving husband to make a definite refusal, a refusal that might be embarrassing for him to change later.

Yet, many a wife who is reserved and self-effacing is amazingly persistent over time, continuing to find new examples, or new authorities, or new ways to point up the advantage of her plan. Some husbands yield not because they have been sold on the advantages or have been taken in by the cleverness of the wife's strategy but because they are not strongly enough convinced of the disadvantages to be able to withstand the wife's persistent efforts.

A persistent campaign may be illustrated by the woman who decided that it was time for their family to have a television set. One day she commented to her husband that a neighbor had just bought a nice-looking Hitachi television set through a dealer friend for only 48,000 yen [$133]. A few days later she incidentally told her husband that she had heard of another family who bought a television set at a different place for even less money, but that it did not look quite as nice as the first set. Since the husband still showed no interest, she dropped the topic. But a few nights later she called his attention to an article about a special educational television program being run and she openly wondered whether such programs really helped the children's studying. In the meantime, she and the children talked about how nice it would be if the father would buy a television set and the children began asking him for one. It was not long before the father announced that he had decided it was time to buy a television set.

It is usually difficult for the father to refuse his children directly, and it is not unusual for a mother to coach a child on how and when to make a request of the father or to stimulate the child's desire so much that he will ask the father for it without the mother's urging.

Not all husband management is positive, for there are times when the wife must cope with ill temper and anger. When a man is critical of his wife she suggests, but does not openly state, her self-sacrifice to the husband by working harder, paying more attention to the husband's desires than usual, heaving an extra sigh or two, or by looking haggard, tired, and harrassed. Other wives respond to anger or criticism with somber quiet, or great surprise and innocence at the husband's criticism, or with self-accusations of inadequacy. Rarely does a [suburban] wife stand up directly against her husband to defend herself.

Marriage involves mutual socialization also because self-selection—especially self-selection in accordance with an ideology of romantic love—results in diversity of origin among some married couples. Appreciable numbers of interfaith, interclass, and (to a lesser extent) interracial marriages occur. In the United States, for example, a Census Bureau survey showed that in 1957 12.1 per cent of married Roman Catholics, 4.5 per cent of married Protestants, and

3.7 per cent of married Jews were married to a person of another religion.[27] If there were no mutual socialization, a high proportion of marriages of persons from diverse backgrounds would be disharmonious and likely to end in divorce or separation. Judson Landis questioned students at Michigan State about their parents' marriages.[28] As Table 5.1 shows, the students reported that religious differences had *not* been a major handicap in their parents' marriages, although a higher proportion of students from mixed Protestant-Catholic marriages than from Catholic-Catholic or Protestant-Protestant marriages reported "great" or "very great" religious handicaps. Consistent with the data of Table 5.1 are other data collected by Professor Landis from the same students. The proportion of parental marriages ending in divorce or separation was 4.4 per cent of the homogeneously Catholic, 6.0 per cent of the homogeneously Protestant, 6.7 per cent when a Protestant father was married to a Catholic mother, and 20.6 per cent when a Catholic father was married to a Protestant mother. Apparently religious differences were successfully resolved in most marriages, including mixed-faith marriages, but mutual socialization was least successful in marriages involving Catholic men and Protestant women. We saw in Table 2.1 (a differently focused study of marital disharmony) that the divorce rate in marriages where the wife believed more than the husband in an equalitarian relationship was *higher* than in marriages where the husband believed in equality more than the wife. Perhaps Catholic men, because of religion and nationality, are prone to hold a patriarchal conception of the marital relationship, whereas Protestant women tend to believe in greater equality.

TABLE 5.1

Children's Statements of the Degree to Which Religious Differences Had Handicapped the Parents' Marriage in Religiously Mixed and Nonmixed Marriages (Per cent distribution)

Degree of Handicap	Both Protestant N=721	Both Catholics N=103	Father Protestant, Mother Catholic N=90	Father Catholic, Mother Protestant N=102
Not at all	85.7	87.4	59.2	45.2
Very little	11.4	8.8	21.0	20.5
Somewhat	2.7	2.8	13.2	23.3
Great	0.2	1.0	5.3	5.5
Very great	—	—	1.3	5.5

Source: Judson T. Landis, "Marriages of Mixed and Non-Mixed Religious Faith," *American Sociological Review*, Vol. 14, June 1949, p. 405.

[27] Bureau of the Census, "Religion Reported by the Civilian Population of the United States: March 1957," Current Population Report, P-20, No. 79, Washington, D.C.: Government Printing Office, 1958. Quoted in Hyman Rodman, Ed., *Marriage, Family, and Society: A Reader,* New York: Random House, 1965, p. 53.

[28] Judson T. Landis, "Marriages of Mixed and Non-Mixed Religious Faith," *American Sociological Review,* Vol. 14, June 1949, pp. 401-407.

Mutual socialization in marriage cannot bridge all background differences. Research on marital harmony shows that couples from similar backgrounds have a better chance for happy marriages than couples from dissimilar backgrounds.[29] Furthermore, persons of the same social class, racial and religious background, and educational experience are more likely to marry one another than are persons dissimilar in these and other characteristics; sociologists call this the principle of **homogamy.**[30] Homogamy is the empirical tendency, and homogamous marriages offer a better chance for husband-wife consensus than **heterogamous** marriages. Nonetheless, the requirement that young adults choose sexual and marital partners outside their families of orientation—the famous **incest taboo**—means that some of these choices will be from another social class, religion, or race. The incest taboo propels the young adult out of his family of orientation because it prohibits erotic interests within it.[31] The adjustment problems resulting from the emotional transition from family of orientation to family of procreation are obvious, but there are compensating social and individual gains.

Consider, for instance, the *social* benefits from interfaith marriages. Given a plurality of religious groups in a society, interfaith marriages break down the isolation of religious communities from one another. Cleavages among Catholics, Protestants, and Jews in the United States would be more divisive if intermarriages did not develop family ties and associations across religious lines. A similar argument applies to the effect of heterogamy on social class and ethnic differences. Marital ties cross-cut a variety of social groupings and help to cement a heterogeneous society. Moreover, the benefits of the incest taboo for the individual outweigh in most cases the strain of transferring emotional loyalties from the family of orientation to the family of procreation. The major benefit is a new context in which to complete emotional development. The security parents provide for their children is always coupled with conditions of dependence. The incest taboo means that the individual will marry outside of this original family and will be forced to develop emotional and erotic intimacy with an agemate of the opposite sex and, with parenthood, a nurturant relationship toward children. Thus marital socialization carries the emotional development of the individual further.

The incest taboo makes mutual socialization in marriage necessary. The public is aware that marital socialization sometimes fails. In the United States the divorce rate was 10.0 per 1000 married females in 1964, and the divorce rate is merely an index of a larger number of unhappy unions that are not formally dissolved.[32] Still, marital socialization generally succeeds. The conjugal

[29] Ernest W. Burgess and Paul Wallin, *Engagement and Marriage,* Philadelphia: Lippincott, 1953.

[30] Rodman, *Marriage, the Family, and Society,* pp. 50-52.

[31] Talcott Parsons, "The Incest Taboo in Relation to Social Structure and the Socialization of the Child," *British Journal of Sociology,* Vol. 5, June 1954, pp. 101-117.

[32] Bureau of the Census, *Statistical Abstract of the United States: 1968,* Washington, D.C.: Government Printing Office, 1968, p. 61.

family system is based on the assumption that harmony can be *achieved* between persons of different backgrounds, and the popularity of marriage suggests that the assumption is correct. As Fig. 5.2 shows, about 90 per cent of Americans over 25 are either married or formerly married. Either romance makes people incurably optimistic or marital socialization produces compatibility.

A humorous song of the 1940s illustrates the incest taboo and its consequences. The lyrics are a caricature of the confusion that would arise without a rule forcing the individual to seek sexual gratification and marriage *outside* of the family of orientation:[33]

> Many, many years ago, when I was 23
> I was married to a widow who was pretty as can be.
> This widow had a grown-up daughter who had hair of red,
> My father fell in love with her,
> And soon they too were wed.
> This made my dad my son-in-law and changed my very life,
> For my daughter is my mother because she is my father's wife.
> To complicate the matter, even though it brought me joy,
> I soon became the father of a bouncing baby boy.
> My little baby then became a brother-in-law to Dad
> And soon became my uncle though it made me very sad,
> For if he was my uncle, then that also made him brother of
>   the widow's grown-up daughter.
> Who of course was my step-mother.

SOCIALIZATION INTO ILLEGITIMATE ROLES

Consider the situation of an adolescent boy who wants to impress his girlfriend by taking her out in an expensive convertible. He tries to borrow such a car but fails. He feels desperate. This girl is important to him, and he believes that a car is essential to a successful date. So, although he never stole a car before, he "borrows" the red convertible parked half a block from his house with the keys in it. After his big date, he returns the car to the spot from which he had taken it. Since he does not think of himself as a "car thief"—only as a boy whom circumstances compelled to "borrow" a car—he may well ignore future opportunities to steal cars. On the other hand, a boy who has been caught by the police in a stolen car and branded a "car thief" by arrest and trial begins to think of himself not merely as a boy who "borrows" cars for joy rides but as

---

[33] Reprinted by permission. From "I'm My Own Grandpa," by Dwight Latham and Moe Jaffe, New York: General Music Publishing Company, 1947.

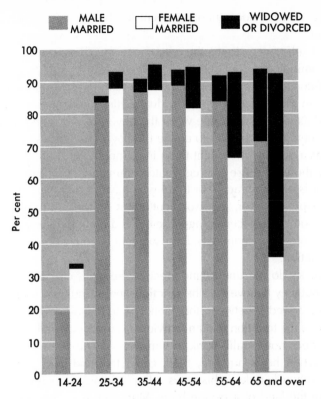

FIGURE 5.2 **Marital status by age and sex, 1965.** Source: Bureau of the Census, *Americans at Mid-Decade,* Washington, D.C.: Government Printing Office, 1966, p. 27.

a "car thief." As a car thief, he begins to *look* for opportunities to steal cars, and he may see them in circumstances the first boy would miss. He becomes proud of his skill at stealing cars. He learns from more sophisticated car thieves how to break into a locked car and how to start cars without keys. One 17-year-old car thief specialized in stealing Lincolns. He had stolen 80 Lincolns before he was sent to a reformatory. He would not demean himself by stealing smaller, less expensive cars even though he was aware that he was more likely to arouse suspicion in a Lincoln. "When the police see a young kid driving a $6000 Lincoln, they get suspicious. They stop you and ask to see the registration. That's how I got caught." Whereas the dedicated car thief is on the alert wherever he goes for chances to practice his craft, the occasional offender must rationalize the crime in order to make it acceptable to an essentially conventional self-conception. Granted that human powers of rationalization are great. Nevertheless, the necessity of rationalizing imposes a limitation that does not exist for the professional criminal.[34] Nothing in the self-conception of the self-defined car thief deters him from stealing cars; on the contrary,

[34] John Bartlow Martin, *My Life in Crime: The Autobiography of a Professional Criminal,* New York: Harper, 1952.

his self-conception provides encouragement for the further development of a deviant career.

A criminal self-conception is the outcome of socialization. Nearly all contemporary criminologists believe that criminals are made rather than born. Criminal self-conceptions develop in much the same way as noncriminal self-conceptions: in the course of the individual's interactions with other people. The outraged attitude of the judge when the boy who had stolen 80 Lincolns was brought before him helped to define the boy to himself as well as to the community as a person who ought to be imprisoned. Jail is not merely incarceration. For those who use the legitimate community as a **reference group,** imprisonment is also disgrace. For those who have shifted their allegiance to antisocial groups, however, imprisonment is not disgrace. It may even bring honor—as in some adolescent gangs where it is a mark of delinquent sophistication. For professional criminals, imprisonment is simply one of the hazards of their occupation.

Criminologists do not understand precisely how this change in allegiance takes place, but they believe that the **sanctions** mobilized by law-enforcement agencies drive a wedge between the offender and law-abiding groups.[35] Perhaps because of the tradition that an individual is innocent until proven guilty, the offender does not usually think of himself as a criminal until the law so labels him. When he is arrested, tried, convicted, and jailed, the resulting stigma simultaneously reduces his status in law-abiding groups and changes his conception of the kind of a person he is. Moreover, it is quite likely that he will find—in correctional institutions or in the free community—persons very much like himself. He and his new friends mutually reinforce one another's delinquent tendencies by turning the values of the law-abiding community upside-down. The boy who stole 80 cars is given credit by fellow reformatory inmates for his enterprise. But he is patronized for his lack of sophistication. He abandoned the cars after using all the gas in the tanks. Didn't he realize that he could make money by stripping the cars of radios, heaters, hub caps, and tires? If he had had "connections," he would have known how to sell the entire car to "fences" who make a specialty of transforming stolen cars and reselling them. His new friends make him feel welcome, but they prove to him that he has much to learn. Thus he reaches a point where the condemnations of the legitimate community are irrelevant to his self-respect. In the face of the rejecting definition of his behavior by the legitimate community, he gravitates toward other outcasts; he needs *their* approval.

Is it accident then that determines who becomes a criminal (in the role sense) and who does not? Do those who are caught and stigmatized become criminals? This does not seem to be a sufficient explanation. Very likely cir-

---

[35] Ernest W. Burgess, testimony in *Hearings before the Committee on Low-Income Family of the Joint Committee on the Economic Report,* 81st Congress, December 1949, Washington, D.C.: Government Printing Office, 1950, pp. 375-400.

cumstances do predispose some persons toward **deviant roles**.[36] Personality disturbances may incapacitate the individual for legitimate roles and, if
they do not also incapacitate him for criminal roles, may explain why some
offenders transfer allegiance so readily from the legitimate community. Social
and cultural factors also can pose obstacles to the playing of legitimate roles.
Consider the developmental history of the typical reformatory inmate. He
came from a low-income family—possibly of minority origin (Negro, Puerto
Rican, Mexican). His parents exercised ineffectual control over him, not necessarily because of indifference but because they were preoccupied with their
own problems: chronic warfare in the household; desertion by the father;
serious illness of the mother; alcoholism; too many children for an unskilled
father to support or a harried mother to supervise. When he started school, no
one at home made schoolwork seem meaningful to him, so he had little incentive to try to learn. Within a few years, he was retarded in such basic skills as
reading and arithmetic. The more successful students considered him "dumb"
and said so; the teachers showed that they thought so too by shunting him into
programs for "slow" learners. Being a failure at school increased his disinterest, and he began to truant and to rebel against the authority of the teachers.
He quit school "to go to work" as soon as he could legally do so.

He floundered in the labor market, shifting from one blind-alley job to another—with intervals of unemployment between. Employers were reluctant to
hire him because of his failure to complete high school, the competition of
older, more experienced workers, and the stipulations of the child labor laws.
But he was not a desirable worker on other grounds: he had a poor job attendance record; he transferred to supervisors the hostile attitude he had toward teachers; he quit jobs suddenly, usually without notice. In short, he found
employment no more interesting than school had been—and no more rewarding in terms of recognition. As a result, he withdrew from the labor market
whenever he had the money to do so; he did not regard a job as his normal
activity; a job was a chore he assumed when pressed for money. Psychologically uninvolved in school or job, he hung out on the street corner with other
unsuccessful youngsters. He became known as a hoodlum. When family and
neighbors added their condemnations to those of teachers and employers, all
bridges to respectability were burned.

This composite history of a reformatory inmate reveals a boy who was defeated in two of the major arenas of urban industrial life: school and work. Rejected by respectable people, he looked instead to a clique of street-corner
loafers for approval. Cultural, social, and (possibly) personality disabilities can
incapacitate an individual for legitimate roles and thus make more likely his
attraction to a group in which these disabilities do not count against him—or do
not count as much.

---

[36] Michael Argyle, "A New Approach to the Classification of Delinquents with Implications
for Treatment," Monograph No. 2, California State Board of Corrections, July 1961, pp. 15–26.

Some boys become accessible to socialization by adolescent gangs because they feel, rightly or wrongly, that "they have no future." The gang offers "pleasures of the moment" instead of the future that more fortunate youngsters look forward to. Presumably, the gang would have trouble recruiting new members if all the boys in the neighborhood stayed in high school until graduation and were confident about getting a good job, or going to college, afterwards. This explanation of the attractions of an illegitimate role assumes that it is adopted after a legitimate role is perceived as unavailable. In order to test this explanation further, let us examine a quite different illegitimate role: that of the stutterer. To be a stutterer is undesirable. A stutterer may receive more sympathy than a delinquent gang member, but neither role is an approved one. From one point of view, the role of stutterer is even more disadvantageous. At least the delinquent has the support of the other members of his gang; the stutterer is characteristically surrounded by fluent speakers. Can the development of stuttering be explained as another instance of the social psychology of defeat? Are stutterers people who encountered obstacles in their childhood which made normal speech seem unattainable? Wendell Johnson, a world-renowned authority on stuttering, states the case for this explanation in the following article:[37]

> The 4-year-old is breathless with excitement as he reports a drama he has just observed.
>
> "And then the dog, the dog," he says, "the dog chased the k-k-kitten right up that, that tree, the one, one by the corner. And J-Jack, Jack was so mad. He hollered and hollered at that old dog. Boy!"
>
> Mother and dad listen to the incident with interest. It's nothing new for an old dog to chase a kitten but they enjoy hearing their young man tell about it. The little fellow is lucky. In some homes his first flow of enthusiasm might have been dammed with a "Stop and start over" or "Take a deep breath" or even "Stop that stuttering." In others, though the parents keep their remarks to themselves, they may show their tension at all these repetitions and start wondering if their youngster is going to be a stutterer. Recent research indicates that stuttering gets its start in just this way—not in the child's mouth but in the parent's ear....
>
> Although the problem is as old as civilization—it is, indeed, probably a part of the price we pay for civilization—there was little scientific knowledge of stuttering before 1925. Since that date, however, a great deal of research has been carried out—at the University of Iowa and elsewhere—and while much remains to be done, the substantial research dividends to date are heartening.
>
> University of Iowa studies have involved nearly 1,000 mothers and fathers and 500 children. Half the children were regarded by their parents as stutterers, and for study purposes each of these was compared with a non-stuttering "control" child of like age, sex and socio-economic family status.
>
> It turned out that the original diagnoses of stuttering had been made by persons—usually the supposed stutterer's mother—who lacked essential informa-

---

[37] Reprinted by permission. From Wendell Johnson, "For the Stutterer, a Sympathetic Ear," *The New York Times Magazine,* Feb. 13, 1955, p. 42.

tion regarding normal speech development and the conditions affecting it. In general what was taken for stuttering was the normally hesitant and repetitive speech of early childhood.

A study of approximately 200 normal children, aged 2 to 5, has revealed that the average child repeats a sound or a word or a phrase forty-five times every 1,000 running words. Most parents either disregard or do not notice these repetitions. A few parents worry about them.

While most of the parents studied said they had "done nothing" about these repetitions and "tried not to let the child know" they had been noticed, it was quite clear that through facial expressions, vocal inflections, bodily tensions and other means they had unknowingly conveyed their concern and disapproval to the children. Some, of course, had quite openly and insistently tried to get their youngsters to "stop all that stumbling."

The general consequence appeared, in the usual case, to be a gradual loss of confidence on the part of the child. As a result he spoke somewhat more hesitantly and appeared, as time went on, first to build up a positive fear of speaking in certain situations and then to speak with more and more tension. All the while the parents became more concerned and expressed their anxiety more and more clearly. Thus, without meaning to, they bothered the youngster all the more in his attempts to talk clearly. Generally speaking that is how stuttering begins — as the child tries not to do something his parents find unacceptable. Full-blown stuttering turns out to be simply what the so-called stutterer does in his effort not to stutter again.

Another way of stating the foregoing explanation of joining a delinquent gang and of becoming a stutterer is this: People want to conform. They prefer legitimate roles. However, when legitimate roles are unattainable or are thought to be unattainable, people seek an illegitimate role (gang membership) or unconsciously accept a definition of self which makes an illegitimate role commitment unavoidable (stuttering).

Resocialization to Conventional Roles. Once obstacles to playing a *legitimate* role have led to acceptance of a deviant role, how can a person be induced to abandon this disapproved role he has been socialized into? One possibility is psychiatric therapy or other means to help the deviant individual cope with his initial problems and with the additional problem of stigma. In the Cambridge-Somerville Youth Study, counselors helped an experimental group of boys identified as "predelinquent" by teachers and police while a control group of comparable boys were left to their own resources. For about five years the counselors made friendly visits to the homes of boys in the experimental group, helped them with school work (tutoring them if necessary), took them on recreational outings, and assisted with various medical and welfare problems. Did the attempt at resocialization work? Table 5.2 shows *no significant difference* between the criminal records of the experimental and control groups; this lack of demonstrable effect holds true for boys *under* the age of 18 (when most of the boys were still being helped) and *over* the age of 18. The probable reason for the failure of the experiment was the relative weakness of the counselors' socializing influence on their clients compared with the social-

TABLE 5.2
Juvenile Court and Adult Criminal Court Convictions of Subjects in the Cambridge-Somerville Youth Study

		Boys Convicted		Convictions	
		Number	Percentage	Total	Per Boy
Experimental group	(253)	104	41	315	1.24
Control group	(253)	93	37	343	1.36

Source: Joan and William McCord, "A Follow-up Report on the Cambridge-Somerville Youth Study," *Annals of the American Academy of Political and Social Science,* Vol. 322, March 1959, pp. 89-96.

izing influences of the boys' families, their pals, and neighborhood associates. The counselors were not in contact with the boys often enough to be a major socializing force (one contact a week was above the average). Besides, the influence of the counselors may have suffered because they were middle-class adults seeking to influence working-class adolescents. For the counselors, the predelinquent behavior of the boys was a problem, but it was not a problem for the boys themselves.

Like the boys in the Cambridge-Somerville experiment, many incumbents of deviant roles do not feel that they have unusual problems. That is why they do not take kindly to the suggestion that they seek treatment from a "shrink." Bear in mind though that the desire to conform to social expectations cannot be extinguished completely. In some corner of his personality, even the delinquent gang member would prefer more widespread approval than he can obtain from his pals. Thus he "shows off" in public and is preoccupied with his reputation. Under these circumstances, socialization to conventional roles is possible, but it is more likely to succeed if the effort is intensive and if influential primary group members make it. For instance, the reintegration of delinquent gang members into the legitimate community often begins when they get interested in conventional girlfriends and continues when they eventually marry. Anticipation of family responsibilities makes them willing to take jobs where they are exposed to occupational socialization. Their wives constantly propagandize against the boys' delinquent associates: "Stop hanging out with those bums. They'll only get you into trouble. Stay home with me." Sometimes the marriage breaks up. More often, the gang breaks up as boy after boy gets absorbed in the problems of marriage and children. Marital socialization thereby compensates for deficiencies in parental and community socialization.

Effective though *some* girls may be at inducing *some* boys to abandon the delinquent role, society is not content to rely on the vagaries of romance for delinquency control. Systematic programs exist; some of these *contrive* peer groups and attempt to mobilize their coercive force in favor of rehabilitation.

The following account describes the Pinehills program conducted in Provo, Utah, with juvenile court probationers:[38]

Attempts to involve a boy with the peer group begin the moment he arrives. Instead of meeting with and receiving an orientation lecture from authorities, he receives no formal instructions. He is always full of such questions as, "What do I have to do to get out of this place?" or "How long do I have to stay?", but such questions as these are never answered. They are turned aside with, "I don't know," or "Why don't you find out?" Adults will not orient him in the ways that he has grown to expect, nor will they answer any of his questions. He is forced to turn to his peers. Usually, he knows someone in the program, either personally or by reputation. As he begins to associate with other boys he discovers that important informal norms do exist, the most important of which makes *inconsistency* rather than *consistency* the rule. That which is appropriate for one situation, boy, or group may not be appropriate for another. Each merits a decision as it arises.

Other norms center most heavily about the daily group discussion sessions. These sessions are patterned after the technique of "Guided Group Interaction" which was developed at Fort Knox during World War II and at Highfields. Guided Group Interaction emphasizes the idea that only through a group and its processes can a boy work out his problems. From a peer point of view it has three main goals: (1) to question the utility of a life devoted to delinquency; (2) to suggest alternative ways for behavior; and (3) to provide recognition for a boy's personal reformation and his willingness to reform others.

Guided Group Interaction grants to the peer group a great deal of power, including that of helping to decide when each boy is ready to be released. This involves "retroflexive reformation." If a delinquent is serious in his attempts to reform others he must automatically accept the common purpose of the reformation process, identify himself closely with others engaged in it, and grant prestige to those who succeed in it. In so doing, he becomes a genuine member of the reformation group and in the process may be alienated from his previous pro-delinquent groups. Such is an ideal and long term goal. Before it can be realized for any individual he must become heavily involved with the treatment system. Such involvement does not come easy and the system must include techniques which will impel him to involvement. Efforts to avoid the development of formal structure have already been described as one technique. Group processes constitute a second technique.

Before a group will help a boy "solve his problems" it demands that he review his total delinquent history. This produces anxiety because, while he is still relatively free, it is almost inevitable that he has much more to reveal than is already known by the police or the court. In an effort to avoid such involvement he may try subterfuge. But any reluctance on his part to be honest will not be taken lightly. Norms dictate that no one in the group can be released until everyone is honest and until every boy helps to solve problems. A refusal to come clean shows a lack of trust in the group and slows down the problem-solving process. Therefore, any recalcitrant boy is faced with a real dilemma. He can either

---

[38] Reprinted by permission. From Lamar T. Empey and Jerome Rabow, "The Provo Experiment in Delinquency Rehabilitation," *American Sociological Review*, Vol. 26, October 1961, pp. 679-695.

choose involvement or relentless attack by his peers. Once a boy does involve himself, however, he learns that some of his fears were unwarranted. What goes on in the group meeting is sacred and is not revealed elsewhere.

A second process for involvement lies in the use of the peer group to perpetuate the norms of the treatment system. One of the most important norms suggests that most boys in the program are candidates for a reformatory. This is shocking because even habitual delinquents do not ordinarily see themselves as serious offenders. Yet, the tradition is clear; most failures at Pinehills are sent to the Utah State Industrial School. Therefore, each boy has a major decision to make: either he makes serious attempts to change or he gets sent away.

The third process of involvement could only occur in a community program. Each boy has the tremendous problem of choosing between the demands of his delinquent peers outside the program and the demands of those within it. The usual reaction is to test the situation by continuing to identify with the former. Efforts to do this, however, and to keep out of serious trouble are usually unsuccessful. The group is a collective board on delinquency; it usually includes a member who knows the individual personally or by reputation; and it can rely on the meeting to discover many things. Thus, the group is able to use actual behavior in the community to judge the extent to which a boy is involved with the program and to judge his readiness for release. The crucial criterion for any treatment program is not what an individual does while in it, but what he does while he is *not* in it.

The fourth process involves a number of important sanctions which the group can impose if a boy refuses to become involved. It can employ familiar techniques such as ostracism or derision or it can deny him the status and recognition which come with change. Furthermore, it can use sanctions arising out of the treatment system. For example, while authorities may impose restrictions on boys in the form of extra work or incarceration in jail, the group is often permitted, and encouraged, to explore reasons for the action and to help decide what future actions should be taken. For example, a boy may be placed in jail over the week-end and told that he will be returned there each week-end thereafter until his group decides to release him. It is not uncommon for the group, after thorough discussion, to return him one or more week-ends despite his protestations. Such an occurrence would be less likely in an ordinary reformatory because of the need for inmates to maintain solidarity against the official system. However, in this setting it is possible because boys are granted the power to make important decisions affecting their entire lives. Rather than having other people do things to them, they are doing things to themselves.

The ultimate sanction possessed by the group is refusal to release a boy from the program. Such a sanction has great power because it is normative to expect that no individual will be tolerated in the program indefinitely. Pinehills is not a place where boys "do time."

When the illegitimate role receives *encouragement and support* from a **primary group,** the organization of a countering primary group pressing for abandonment of the role is an effective rehabilitative strategy. Even when the deviant role is not supported by a primary group, as with advanced alcoholism, it appears that primary group support can increase the likelihood that the individual will rejoin the legitimate community. The vitality of Alcoholics

Anonymous stems from its ability to make the struggle for sobriety a collective effort.[39]

The method of Alcoholics Anonymous is spreading beyond the problem of alcoholism. Synanon, Weight Watchers, and Divorcees Anonymous pattern their therapeutic programs after the more famous A.A. Not all illegitimate roles, however, are amenable to group-facilitated reintegration. In the case of stuttering, the major therapy is individual; no self-help organization of stutterers has developed. Nevertheless, the social factor cannot be ignored. Just as A.A. tells the alcoholic that he will always be an alcoholic, so the speech therapist tells the stutterer that he will always stutter. A.A. has learned from bitter experience with alcoholics that the hope of a miraculous cure turns the slightest slip into a disaster. Similarly, speech therapists have learned that the way to *reduce* stuttering is to enable the stutterer to stutter without feeling that he is a failure. Therefore he is not promised a cure. Quite the contrary: part of the early therapy is to practice *increased* stuttering, perhaps in a group situation. The paradoxical fact is that the more the stutterer *wants* to stutter, the less able he is to do so. When he reaches the point where he can accept his stuttering without anxiety, he stutters very little. What has this to do with group support? Just this: the stutterer is anxious about his nonfluency because he listens to his own speech from the viewpoint of a condemning group. What therapy does for him is to transform his conception of the group into a more tolerant one.

SOCIALIZATION FOR ROLE CHANGE

Socialization proceeds throughout the life cycle, much of it following the same sequence for everybody. Some adult socialization is experienced only by a segment of the population—for example, military service.[40] And some socialization is experienced at different stages of the life cycle by various members of the population—for example, moving from one community to another. Although change of residence always involves socialization, the ease of the transition depends partly on the *meaning* of the move to the mover, and this varies with the *reason* for the move. An elderly couple may sell a large house in the suburbs after the children have left home and rent a small apartment in

[39] Robert F. Bales, "The Therapeutic Role of Alcoholics Anonymous as Seen by a Sociologist," *Quarterly Journal of Studies on Alcohol,* Vol. 5, September 1944, pp. 267-278; Milton A. Maxwell, "Alcoholics Anonymous: An Interpretation," in David J. Pittman and Charles R. Snyder, Eds., *Society, Culture, and Drinking Patterns,* New York: Wiley, 1962; Irving P. Gellman, *The Sober Alcoholic: An Organizational Analysis of Alcoholics Anonymous,* New Haven, Conn.: College and University Press, 1964.

[40] For a discussion of socialization into military service, see Samuel A. Stouffer et al., *The American Soldier,* 2 vols., Princeton, N.J.: Princeton University Press, 1949, especially Vol. 1, Chaps. 3-5, and Vol. 2, Chap. 5.

the central city; a 30-year-old unmarried engineer may give up his furnished apartment because he is moving to another city to take a better job; a 9-year-old boy may change schools and peer groups because his parents have bought a larger house to accommodate a new addition to the family. In terms of Ruth Benedict's first proposition, some moves involve fewer discontinuities than others because the mover's role in the new community is much the same as his role in the old. In all of the industrial countries internal migration is appreciable. Furthermore, because of the increasing productivity per worker in agriculture, there tends to be a net rural-to-urban flow of population. Under the sponsorship of the Food and Agriculture Organization of the United Nations, the adjustment problems of rural migrants in urban settings have been studied in 12 European countries.[41] As might be expected, the wider the cultural gap between city and countryside, the more difficult is the adjustment of the migrant.

Perhaps because the United States is so fully industrialized, perhaps also because there is no peasant tradition of clinging to the land, internal migration in the United States is on a large scale. Between 1955 and 1960 about *half* of the American population changed places of residence.[42] A third of these movers remained within the same county, but the other two-thirds moved to a different county, some to a different state. As in most industrial societies, the American people move frequently and for a variety of reasons: to escape disadvantageous economic situations or to take advantage of occupational opportunities, to further educational goals, to enjoy a more favorable climate, and sometimes out of sheer restlessness. By the standards of peasant societies, where families who have lived in a community for only 200 years may not be fully accepted, Americans are incredibly rootless, a society of transients.[43]

American society works. The transients are absorbed into the communities into which they move, partly because the communities of origin are not so different from the communities of destination, partly because most Americans have adjusted themselves to the changes that moves involve. As one of the editors of *Fortune* observed, men in the middle echelons of the corporate hierarchy *expect* to be transferred from place to place.[44] Varied experiences further their careers. They are as ready to move across the country as are the players in a game of musical chairs to give up their seats when the music starts. Particularly for better-educated, higher-income families and individuals, a move is an adventure, not a disorganizing experience. For some Americans, however, migrations means uprooting themselves: abandoning a secure way of

---

[41] G. Beijer, *Rural Migrants in Urban Setting: An Analysis of the Literature on the Problem Consequent on the Internal Migration from Rural to Urban Areas in 12 European Countries (1945–1961)*, The Hague: Martinus Nijhoff, 1963.

[42] Bureau of the Census, *Statistical Abstract of the United States: 1962*, Washington, D.C.: Government Printing Office, 1962, p. 39.

[43] Theodore Caplow, "Transiency as a Cultural Pattern," *American Sociological Review*, Vol. 5, December 1940, pp. 731-739.

[44] William H. Whyte, Jr., *The Organization Man*, New York: Simon & Schuster, pp. 269–275.

Ken Heyman

life in exchange for bewildering problems. This is particularly true of poorly educated, unskilled rural people who move to large cities. These problems of community adjustment stem partly from the American tradition of self-reliance — in the sense that rural migrants to the city are not systematically retrained (socialized) for urban life; they are left to adjust or fail on their own (with the marginal help of relatives and friends). An exception to this generalization is the American Indian Relocation Program of the Bureau of Indian Affairs. This program seeks to persuade Indians on poverty-stricken reservations to choose relocation in cities, and it actively tries to solve their housing, employment, and other problems on arrival, as the following report on the program shows:[45]

> The man and his family present themselves at the Relocation Office. . . . A receptionist, usually Indian, is expecting them. The man is wearing his best pants, a pair of new blue jeans, cowboy boots and, possibly, a ten-gallon hat. His wife is wearing a cotton housedress, wrinkled from the long train ride. Two of her little children will be put in the office play-pen, one will cling to her knees, and she may be nursing the youngest — unless she does that later on the street. She will remain quiet while a Relocation Officer confers with her husband. The Relocation Officer, a woman in most cases where there is guidance work to be done, tells the man how to use the checking account in which his subsistence money

[45] Reprinted by permission. From La Verne Madigan, "The American Indian Relocation Program," New York: Association on American Indian Affairs, December 1956.

will be deposited, and how to operate a dial telephone. She gives him a map of the city and tells him how to use it, although he is tired now and will probably forget what she said. She looks over her check-list of things to be remembered, and asks him whether he owns an alarm clock, promises to see that one is bought if he does not, and slips in a word of advice about getting to work on time. She tells him to rest with his family for the remainder of the day, and to return to the office tomorrow in order that the Relocation Officer in charge of employment may refer him to a job. Then she takes the family to a cheap apartment house or hotel which is used to quarter large families until the man is working and permanent housing can be found near his place of employment. She drives the family to this temporary residence, advises them to eat in a cheap, clean nearby restaurant, and then goes on to pay a home visit to a couple who arrived the day before.

HOUSING

The temporary housing in which the family and all newcomers will be placed ... will have been chosen as the newcomers' first stopping place because it is near the Relocation Office which the man will have to visit frequently for the next week; because it is cheap enough not to exhaust the family's subsistence allowance too quickly; and because it has space for Indian families which seldom number less than four and occasionally number as high as thirteen. The rooms will be shabbily but not wretchedly furnished. In one city there will be cooking facilities in the temporary quarters. In another, the quarters will be in a hotel which has seen better days but does not yet qualify for the skid-row category; here there will be no stove, but there will be pay television. Single men and women are more easily and better housed in Y.M. and Y.W.C.A. residences, and all-male or all-female boarding houses. The temporary housing is used only until the man is employed.

The second quarters into which the family moves ... will be passable according to working-class, inadequate according to middle-class standards. . . .

Currently the Chicago Relocation Office is finding housing for Indians in those erstwhile luxury neighborhoods, familiar in all large industrial or commercial cities: neighborhoods where the streets are wide and tree-lined, the building fronts still elegant, the interiors shabby and in dismal contrast. The shabbiness is the peculiar shabbiness of old hall carpets which were once deeply piled, threadbare over-stuffed divans which were once opulent, a plastic shower curtain hanging at a window which once had a velours drape, an extra bed standing in the living room. That would be a furnished apartment.

The Relocation Offices in all cities are now, with the new $250 furniture allowance, trying to move families as quickly as possible into cheaper, roomier unfurnished flats. The furniture will still be second-hand, purchased from Goodwill Industries or the Salvation Army, but it will be refinished simple furniture, not decaying rococo. . . .

EMPLOYMENT

The day after a man's arrival, or the same afternoon if he is not too tired, and his family feels safe in its temporary quarters, he goes to the Relocation Office for referral to a job. He is interviewed by an employment specialist who discusses his aptitudes and desires. In many cases, the man has had only a few years of schooling, has worked solely as an agricultural stoop-laborer, and the city's lure for him was the possibility of year-round rather than soul-satisfying work. If he had—and a few Indians do have—a developed skill and a well-defined ambition, opportunity could readily be found for him. It is not difficult, in any event, to place him at the prevailing wage in a given industry, since city Relocation Offices are situated where employment is diversified and plentiful. The problem is that the prevailing wage in the industry may be inadequate for the support of his family. That is not to say that it would be inadequate for the support of a non-Indian family, which would not include five or six school and pre-school children and accept as both agreeable and inevitable the possibility that another child would be born each year. . . .

The city Relocation Offices are usually able to place a man after from one to three referrals; and they themselves cannot be held accountable for the lack of education, urban work experience and emotional serenity which may cause him to fail at this first job, and the third, and, if his troubles are unusually bad, [at] all he ever attempts. The man's ability to adapt himself to and improve his skill in urban employment cannot be predicted before he tries. Whether he should be discouraged from trying at all because he may fail, or whether all Indians should be encouraged to remain in their reservation areas for the years it will take to produce a skilled generation is a question. . . .

While a man is seeking employment, the Relocation staff is performing various services for his family. One member helps hunt the permanent housing referred to above. Another . . . visits the home at least three times to take the mother out to buy clothes with the family's clothing allowance, to help her select used furniture for the $250 permitted for that, to enroll her at the prenatal clinic, to see that the children are registered in school, to learn whether the family is in any kind of trouble it has kept to itself. On these visits Relocation Officers have been known to wash a man's shirt and give a long-braided woman a hair-cut.

Since the limit on home-visiting must be set somewhere, unless the staff is to be indefinitely extended, mail communications are used on some occasions to serve the same purpose. The files of the Chicago office, examined in privacy and at random, revealed that mimeographed notices were broadcast to relocated families telling the date of school opening and warning that all school-age children must be enrolled, and announcing the availability of Salk shots. . . .

Whether the Indian Relocation Program is succeeding is not clear. Unlike the larger migration of rural Negroes into urban areas, however, the Indian migration is sponsored and supported by the federal government. Organized efforts are made to facilitate the socialization of Indians at their urban destinations. This represents a break with American traditions. In the years from 1890 to 1914, when millions of European peasants crowded into the large cities of the East, the federal government did not take responsibility for their socialization—or for the welfare problems resulting from their initial maladjustment. And currently the federal government has no program to facilitate the exodus of Negroes from the rural South and their integration into cities. The unintended consequence of this *laissez faire* policy is that Negro, Puerto Rican, and Spanish-American migrants from rural areas, as well as Appalachian Mountain whites, flounder for months and sometimes years as they try to cope with the urban environment. Private health and welfare agencies and municipal services eventually offer assistance, but it is difficult to undo the demoralizing effects of initial experiences. The rising cost of health and welfare services in large American cities may tempt the federal government to extend the concept of planned relocation to rural communities not served by the specialized Indian Relocation Program. When that happens, one of the major types of adult socialization in industrial societies, socialization of migrants, will receive explicit recognition.

Change of residence, a role change in itself, is also incidental to some other role changes. Military service is not primarily a change of residence; institutionalization in a hospital or prison also is only incidentally a change of residence—many of the individual's roles are involved.[46] Conversely, returning home from the hospital or the prison requires reorganization of the personality. That is the reason halfway houses have become popular for former mental patients as well as former prison inmates. The term "re-entry crisis" is applied to the adjustment problems of Peace Corps alumni when they return to the United States, but it applies with even greater force to former mental patients and prison inmates because their absence is discreditable.

Socialization or resocialization is necessary to promote adequate functioning of the person taking up his new role. What seems impressive is not the personality strains that often accompany role changes but the large numbers of persons socialized to anticipate role changes in modern societies so that they take social relocations in stride. Industrial societies demand great adaptability of the individual. In this as in other respects, human beings generally fulfill social expectations.

CONCLUSION

Socialization continues throughout life as the individual learns new roles in new groups. Early socialization may facilitate later socialization, as happens when there are familiar elements in the new role. But sometimes early socialization interferes with later socialization, as happens when the new role requires the *unlearning* of elements in previous roles. In any case, socialization can never be regarded as finished. Learning of new roles continues until death.

The responsiveness of the individual to socialization in the peer group, at school, in the work situation, and in the family he forms by marriage depends partly on his experiences with socializing agents in the family of orientation. A

[46] Donald R. Cressey, Ed., *The Prison: Studies in Institutional Organization and Change,* New York: Holt, Rinehart & Winston, 1961, especially Part I.

rebellious or compliant attitude toward authority develops. In industrial societies successful socialization in the family of orientation requires learning
enough compliance to accept further socialization and enough rebelliousness
(independence) to leave the protective environment of the family and participate in nonfamilial institutions. Ideally the family of orientation *pushes* the
young out of the nest by encouraging independence, and later socialization
pulls the individual into roles in other social structures. Socialization into
neighborhood peer groups involves learning equalitarian relationships. Socialization at school involves learning to participate in an impersonal organization that rewards differential achievement. Socialization into the world of work
involves further experience with differential rewards and thereby with the
problem of maintaining self-respect in the face of failure.

Although the individual is taught to accept competitive defeat with reasonable sportsmanship, failure is defined by others and by the individual himself
as a sign of inadequacy. To escape such definitions from representatives of
legitimate groups, the competitively unsuccessful individual may expose himself to socialization in deviant subgroups, such as delinquent gangs. There the
ability to steal 80 Lincolns may more than compensate for an inability to get
good marks in school. Even after socialization into illegitimate roles occurs, the
individual retains somewhere within his personality a desire to live up to the

expectations of conventional people. This ambivalence between rebellion and conformity provides an entering wedge for resocialization into conventional roles, especially if the agent of resocialization is a significant other like a wife or a girlfriend.

Role change is such a frequent experience in industrial societies that individuals learn to expect to shift places of residence, schools, and jobs. These changes of role require additional socialization, but the anticipation of such changes makes the individual amenable to the necessary learning. Perhaps the most drastic role change is the shift from the emotional mooring of the personality in the family of orientation, first to disengagement from dependence on parents, and then to a security base in the family of procreation. This transition is facilitated by the incest taboo as well as by the training for independence in educational, political, and occupational contexts.

As the individual proceeds through the life cycle, he experiences socialization imposing varying degrees of personality strain. Socialization theory has not yet developed to the point where the comparative difficulty of, say, occupational and marital socialization can be assessed. The problem of the personality strains involved in socialization is one where interdisciplinary research can add to scientific knowledge as well as to policy recommendations as to how human development can be promoted most effectively.

SOME SIGNIFICANT LITERATURE ON SOCIALIZATION AFTER CHILDHOOD

Elaine Cumming and William E. Henry, *Growing Old: The Process of Disengagement,* New York: Basic Books, 1961. The authors of this research monograph, having interviewed a large sample of old people in metropolitan Kansas City, address the question, "What are healthy, economically secure old people like?" Aging is conceived of as disengagement, defined as "an inevitable process in which many of the relationships between a person and other members of society are severed and those remaining are altered in quality." This summary is based on a review by Gordon F. Streib, *American Sociological Review,* Vol. 27, August 1962, pp. 561-562.

S. N. Eisenstadt, *The Absorption of Immigrants: A Comparative Study Based Mainly on the Jewish Community in Palestine and the State of Israel,* Glencoe, Ill.: Free Press, 1955. During the nineteenth century the United States was called a "melting pot" because it absorbed a heavy influx of immigrants, largely of European origin. In the twentieth century the state of Israel has faced a proportionately heavier influx of immigrants from Europe, Africa, and the Middle East. Eisenstadt describes and analyzes the emergence of a pluralistic society in Israel which cushions the adult socialization process for immigrant groups and enables them to maintain some degree of separate identity. This summary is based on a review by Arthur Jordan Field, *American Sociological Review,* Vol. 20, August 1955, pp. 487-488. An interviewing survey of a sample of 1866 adult immigrants was conducted in 14 Israeli transit camps in 1949–1950. One interesting finding was that Jewish immigrants from Africa and the Middle East had a more favorable overall attitude toward Israel than immigrants from Europe. Higher expectations of the Europeans apparently accounted for their poorer morale: an example of what is called in the next chapter "relative deprivation." Judith T. Shuval, *Immigrants on the Threshold,* New York: Atherton, 1963.

Renée C. Fox, *Experiment Perilous: Physicians and Patients Facing the Unknown,* Glencoe, Ill.: Free Press, 1959. Dr. Fox reports on her participant-observer study of a 15-bed metabolic research ward in a large city hospital. The patients had a variety of chronic and, in some cases, fatal illnesses. Their futures were at best uncertain. Their physicians attempted to treat their illnesses with new drugs, but the prospects of successful treatment were slim. In describing the way patients and doctors handled the stresses of their situations, Fox provides examples of socialization to failure. This summary is based on a review by H. Warren Dunham, *American Sociological Review,* Vol. 25, February 1960, pp. 133–134. Two more explicit studies of dying as a social role are Barney G. Glaser and Anselm L. Strauss, *Awareness of Dying,* Chicago: Aldine, 1965, and David Sudnow, *Passing On: The Social Organization of Dying,* Englewood Cliffs, N.J.: Prentice-Hall, 1967.

Robert L. Hall and Ben Willerman, "The Educational Influence of Dormitory Roommates," *Sociometry,* Vol. 26, September 1963, pp. 294-318. The effect of college roommates on each other was studied under two conditions: (1) where roommates mutually chose one another and (2) where roommates were assigned to one another on the basis of their high school percentile ranks. (Research indicates that a student's percentile rank in his high school graduating class is the best single predictor of his academic performance in college.) The major hypothesis tested by the *experimental* assignments was that students living with high-ability roommates would get better grades than students living with low-ability roommates; no appreciable tendency for this to happen was observed. However,

> . . . roommates were more alike than chance expectancy in attendance at plays and in belonging to student organizations — and this was true for both experimentally assigned and mutually selected roommates. The mutual roommates were also alike in time spent studying . . . and academic achievement. The similarities that occur only between *mutual* roommates are presumably the result of their methods of selecting a roommate, rather than of mutual influence.

For another study of the process by which college students influence one another, see Theodore M. Newcomb, *The Acquaintance Process,* New York: Holt, Rinehart and Winston, 1961.

Maxwell Jones, *The Therapeutic Community: A New Treatment Method in Psychiatry,* New York: Basic Books, 1953. In April 1947 an Industrial Neurosis Unit opened at Belmont Hospital in England to deal with unemployable neurotics. Jones and his colleagues assumed that traditional mental hospitals generated a cultural climate which interfered with therapy; hence they attempted to create a therapeutically favorable culture by breaking down the usual cleavages between staff and patients. They established small discussion groups that included doctors and nurses as well as patients and abolished one-to-one contacts of doctors and patients in offices. These daily discussion groups talked about current events, the psychiatric problems of the patients that incapacitated them for a normal job, and patient behavior in the hospital. Patients stayed in the hospital no more than six months and, on discharge, obtained jobs with the help of a rehabilitation officer trained in job placement. (There was substantially full employment in Great Britain at the time, and this made the placement task easier.) Of the 103 patients whose job performance was followed for 6 months, 44 per cent made a satisfactory work adjustment. This result sounds impressive in view of the chronic nature of the presenting problems — even in the absence of a comparison group of untreated unemployables. This summary is based on a review by H. Warren Dunham, *American Sociological Review*, Vol. 19, June 1954, pp. 359-360.

Robert K. Merton, George G. Reader, and Patricia Kendall, Eds., *The Student-Physician: Introductory Studies in the Sociology of Medical Education*, Cambridge, Mass.: Harvard University Press, 1957. In urban industrial societies *occupational* socialization is of major importance to both the individual and the community. This study of medical students thus serves as an illustration of the lengthy process of occupational socialization entailed by some careers. Eight separate reports are included by various members of the research team. One thread running through the reports is the changes in values of medical students as they progress in their training. For example, students farther along in school are more likely to report that they think of themselves as doctors in contacts with patients than students less far along; they are also more capable of bearing the uncertainties inherent in medical treatment. Another thread is Merton's concept of anticipatory socialization: the adoption of the values of a group to which one does not yet belong but which one wishes to join. Medical students are not yet physicians, but their tendency to think of themselves as physicians helps them to learn the role. For a discussion of the sociology of occupations—of which occupational socialization is but one aspect—see Everett Cherrington Hughes, "The Study of Occupations," in Robert K. Merton, Leonard Broom, and Leonard S. Cottrell, Jr., Eds., *Sociology Today: Problems and Prospects*, New York: Basic Books, 1959, pp. 442-458.

C. Wright Mills, Clarence Senior, and Rose Kohn Goldsen, *The Puerto Rican Journey*, New York: Harper, 1950. In 1948 the Bureau of Applied Social Research at Columbia University undertook a survey of Puerto Ricans living in New York City. The characteristics of 5000 Puerto Rican immigrants were studied in an attempt to understand why they had been dissatisfied with Puerto Rico and attracted to New York. The migrants were likely to come from *urban* areas in Puerto Rico and to be otherwise better equipped to compete in a metropolis than the islanders they left behind. Nevertheless, their average educational level of six years, their lack of occupational skills, and their language handicap constituted obstacles to successful adjustment. One-third of the migrants were nonwhites, and this added to their difficulties. For a moving account of the socialization of *nineteenth-century* immigrants, based on their own and other contemporary accounts, see Oscar Handlin, *The Uprooted: The Epic Story of the Great Migrations That Made the American People*, Boston: Little, Brown, 1951.

Henry W. Riecken, *The Volunteer Work Camp: A Psychological Evaluation*, Cambridge, Mass.: Addison-Wesley, 1952. This study is an example of evaluative research: research aimed at finding out the *actual* impact of an action program as opposed to its *intended* impact. The action program studied was the summer work camps of the American Friends Service Committee. The college students who volunteered for community service during their summer vacations filled out questionnaires three times: (1) before working in the camps in 1948, (2) at the end of camp, and (3) ten months after the closing of the camps. Thus it was possible to distinguish superficial short-run changes in the participants from more lasting changes. Long-run changes were reported in the direction of less authoritarian, less ethnocentric, and more democratic attitudes. Short-run changes in a pacifist direction were noted immediately following the closing of the camps, but there was a reversion toward nonpacifist attitudes after ten months. Bear in mind, in considering the implications of summer camps for adult socialization, that the participants were self-selected to begin with and were therefore sympathetic to the "liberal" objectives of the program. This summary is based on a review by R. A. Schermerhorn, *American Sociological Review*, Vol. 18, August 1953, pp. 468-469.

Harold Sampson, Sheldon Messinger, and Robert D. Towne, "The Mental Hospital and Marital Family Ties," *Social Problems,* Vol. 9, Fall 1961, pp. 141-155. A strategic consideration for those who operate mental hospitals is ". . . to help preserve and reinforce those ties which link the deviant to the world beyond the walls." This article reports factors conducive to the maintenance of such ties among white, married women whose schizophrenic breakdown occurred in the course of prolonged marital conflict: "First, hospitalization tended to *interrupt* the divisive processes at work in the marital family, narrowing opportunities for conflict and delaying permanent withdrawal by or exclusion of an errant member." Second, hospitalization helped to define the bizarre behavior of the wife as involuntary and thus helped to prepare for the gradual resumption of marital relationships. Finally, absence often made the hearts of both husband and wife grow fonder, partly because each learned the disadvantages of life without the other, partly because the requirements that the hospital placed on the responsible party (the husband) tied him more closely to his wife. For an approach to marital socialization stressing the *interpersonal competence* of the individual spouses, see Nelson N. Foote and Leonard S. Cottrell, Jr., *Identity and Interpersonal Competence: A New Direction in Family Research,* Chicago: University of Chicago Press, 1955.

Stanton Wheeler, "Socialization in Correctional Communities," *American Sociological Review,* Vol. 26, October 1961, pp. 697-712. Criminologists have been interested for a long time in an unintended consequence of imprisonment: deepening the commitment of inmates to criminal values. ("Prisonization" is the term Donald Clemmer coined in *The Prison Community* to identify the process of assimilating the inmate culture.) It has been assumed that the longer an inmate remains in prison, the more "prisonized" he becomes. The research reported in this article — based on data from a reformatory in the state of Washington — shows that it is not only how long the inmate stays in prison but also how long he *expects* to stay in prison that affects his choice between inmate and conventional values. ". . . [I]nmates who recently have been in the broader community and inmates who are soon to return to that community are more frequently oriented in terms of conventional values. Inmates conform least to conventional standards during the middle phase of their institutional career." One implication of this research is that shorter sentences would redirect the interests of inmates in prisons and reformatories toward legitimate society. For a broader perspective on socialization in organizational settings, see Stanton Wheeler, "The Structure of Formally Organized Socialization Settings," in Orville G. Brim, Jr., and Stanton Wheeler, *Socialization after Childhood: Two Essays,* New York: Wiley, 1966, pp. 53-116.

Part III

THE SOCIAL STRUCTURE OF URBAN INDUSTRIAL SOCIETIES

The social structure is nothing more than the interlacing roles of a society. Since roles are relatively stable — typically they change their normative content slowly — it is useful to think of the organization of roles as a stable structure. Role players are socialized individuals who man the structure for a time and then depart, leaving the structure intact. The social structure can also be thought of as solutions to the universal problems of interactive systems described in Chapter 1: adaptive, socializing, policy-making, and integrative problems. For example, a crucial adaptive problem of every society is to transform the raw materials in its environment into products desired by its inhabitants. Feudal society no less than contemporary industrial societies addressed this problem. But the complex of roles that dealt with agriculture, trade, and manufacture under feudalism was different from the economic institutions of contemporary societies. Economic processes are universal; the role structures that channel them differ from one society to another.

To talk of social structures apart from interactive processes is an act of abstraction. In reality, the role structure of a society is a description of relatively stable patterns of interaction. The stability of these patterns in modern societies provides a normative framework within which particular kinds of interaction occur. Chapter 6 considers the differentiation of the economic structures of contemporary societies and the way of life they sustain. Chapter 7 treats the emergence of urban societies, in which a majority of the population lives in cities, as part of the way of life made possible by industrialism. Chapter 8 deals with the religious solution to the problem of the ultimate meaning of life as an aspect of socialization and social integration — and the special situation of religious organizations in industrial societies. Chapter 9 views governmental structures of contemporary societies as solutions to the basic political problems of interactive systems: resolving conflicts of interest, making decisions, and choosing leaders. Chapter 10 deals with large-scale formal organization of specialized tasks (bureaucracy). Although not unique to contemporary societies, bureaucracy is a pervasive feature of industrial societies, being found in economic, educational, military, welfare, and religious organizations. Finally, Chapter 11 considers the principal structure for culture transmission in industrial societies, the system of formal education.

The role structure of a society is part of its culture. Like the meanings of language or gestures, the meanings imbedded in the role structure are symbolic; they are shared; and the individual learns them from other members of his society. But the social structure is a very special part of the culture of a society. Recall the definition of role given in Chapter 1: what a person does in a prescribed interactive relationship. In regulating interpersonal relations, the social structure establishes the fundamental patterns of life in a society. These patterns change slowly, partly because role players resist changing the rules after they have learned them, but, more importantly, because the meshing of roles and the interrelationship among institutions create multiple vested interests supporting the existing structure. For example, the development of the factory system (to be discussed in Chapter 6) required the shift of economic activities from the home to premises controlled by the employer. It involved, therefore, not only the emergence of a new pattern of interaction between the worker and his employer but redefinition of the relationship between the worker and members of his family. Obviously, such a change was more fundamental than the adoption of a new style of clothes or the learning of current slang. Chapter 14 will return to a more systematic discussion of this difficult problem: social change.

ECONOMIC DIFFERENTIATION
IN INDUSTRIAL SOCIETIES

Adaptation to the environment is one of the four basic problems of interactive systems. But what *is* the environment of an interactive system?[1] For small interactive systems like families, the environment includes the physical world (buildings, streets, clothing, furniture, household appliances) and some things the nonsociologist would not think of as part of the environment, such as the bodies of family members. Another part of the environment of the family is interactive systems with which the family has relations: the electronics factory where the husband-father works, the schools that the children attend, other families living in the neighborhood, the stores where the family shops.

Certain roles within the interactive system have primary responsibility for wrestling with adaptive problems. Thus in the American family the father provides the food, clothing, and shelter by contributing his occupational earnings; the mother plays another adaptive role by acting as purchasing agent. The father and mother may be jointly concerned with the health of the organisms of family members, although they will probably call in an outside expert (a physician) or appeal to an outside organization (a hospital) when biological malfunctions appear serious.

Analyzing interactive systems in terms of the four basic needs facilitates comparison between different interactive systems. For example, the similarity between a mother visiting a local hospital to arrange for the admission of her son for a tonsillectomy and the American ambassador negotiating with the Foreign Minister of the Soviet Union on the nonproliferation of atomic weapons is not obvious. Yet both activities are directed toward solving the adaptive problems of their respective interactive systems.

THE INDUSTRIAL ECONOMY

Many of the adaptive roles of a society are concerned with the production and distribution of goods and services, that is, with what is usually thought of as economic activity. Even in primitive societies, a major portion of the effort of the population goes into agriculture, hunting, fishing, and transforming environmental materials into valued objects. But these societies lacked a distinct **economy**; economic activities are part of undifferentiated kinship-tribal roles. In modern societies the role structure is much more specialized, and it is possible to identify economic roles that are independent of kinship and political roles or of membership in a local community. This complex of economic roles is relatively autonomous in industrial societies, whereas in preindustrial

[1] Talcott Parsons, *Societies: Evolutionary and Comparative Perspectives,* Englewood Cliffs, N.J.: Prentice-Hall, 1966, pp. 10-16.

societies they are usually fused to the rest of the social structure. This is the sense in which industrial societies have distinct economic institutions, which can be thought of collectively as "the economy."

The Market for Goods and Services. Although goods and services are exchanged in all known societies, institutions regulating exchange and the meaning of transactions to participants vary from society to society. In preliterate societies, for example, barter is not a purely economic transaction but a social ritual. Raymond Firth, the anthropologist, illustrates this point with a story of his purchase of a fish in a Malayan village.[2] He went to the beach where fishermen gather with their catch, found a fish he wanted, asked its price from a fisherman, paid it without a word, and started off with his purchase. The flabbergasted fisherman pursued Firth, screaming his tale of frustrated expectations to all who would listen, "He didn't bargain! He took my first price!" The fisherman had quoted an initial price three times what he ultimately planned to receive for the fish; he expected Firth to respond with a lower offer than he intended to pay. A violent argument should have followed in the course of which the fisherman would have reduced his price and Firth would have raised his offer. After much dickering and sharp words, a price should have been agreed upon, and each party to the transaction should have stamped off, protesting loudly that he had been cheated while secretly believing that he had had the better of the bargain. When Firth paid the initial price, the fisherman was disappointed to the point of shock. True, he received three times what he expected to *get* for the fish, but he was deprived of participating in a haggling ritual. On balance, he felt cheated.

In contemporary industrial societies, exchange relationships are depersonalized and separated from the rest of social life. On the New York Stock Exchange, for example, buyers and sellers never meet; they execute orders through brokers—solely on the basis of price. If a customer instructed his broker to purchase 100 shares of American Can "provided that the seller had good morals," the broker would suspect the customer of having lost his mind. In a large department store in New York, London, Paris, Stockholm, or in any large city of an industrialized society, the buyer and the seller meet face to face, but the relationship is almost as impersonal and devoid of ritual. Customers of R. H. Macy & Company do not expect to haggle with the sales clerk, and the sales clerk is not trained (or permitted) to do so. The price is written on a tag; the customer decides to buy or not, and the transaction ends. Not only goods but *services* are impersonally bought and sold in contemporary industrial societies. In a hotel, for example, complete strangers can obtain food, drink, and a bed in which to stay one or more nights merely by paying money. Such an arrangement would shock an aboriginal Murngin from Australia because he lives in a society where sleeping accommodations are determined by kinship

---

[2] The story comes from an unpublished lecture delivered at Harvard University. For background, see Raymond Firth, *Malay Fishermen: Their Peasant Economy,* London: Kegan Paul, Trench, Trubner, 1946, Chap. 7.

and are therefore far too personal to sell.[3] A Murngin would be equally horrified to learn that Americans pay nurses to take care of them when they are sick and buy blood from blood donors.

In contemporary industrial societies, most valuable goods and services are transferred impersonally in what is called a "market." A market is not, of course, a physical location but a form of relationship between buyer and seller. In the pure market situation, the buyer and seller are connected only by their economic interests; their other human qualities are irrelevant.[4] What is remarkable about industrial societies, however, as contrasted with preindustrial societies, is *the extent to which exchange occurs in an impersonal market place where transactions are stripped of all except economic meaning.* Robert Heilbroner, the economic historian, describes industrial society as a "market society" and explains how it emerged out of feudalism through the increased use of monetary transactions:[5]

> One prerequisite of a market society should by now be clear: a market society must involve the process of exchange, of buying and selling, at every level of society. But for this to take place men must have the wherewithal to enter a market; that is, they must have cash. And, in turn, if society is to be permeated with cash, men must earn money for their labors. In other words, *for a market society to exist, nearly every task must have a monetary reward.*
>
> Even in our highly monetized society we do not pay for *every* service: most conspicuously not for the housekeeping services of a wife. But all through the pre-market era, the number of unpaid services—the amount of work performed by law without monetary compensation—was vastly larger than in our society. Slave labor was, of course, unpaid. So was most serf labor. Even the labor of apprentices was remunerated more in kind, in food and lodging, than in cash. Thus at least 60 or 70 per cent of the actual working population of an ancient or medieval economy labored without anything resembling full payment in money.

A *pure* market society perhaps existed in nineteenth-century England. It does not exist today, certainly not in the Soviet Union where centralized planning of production limits the sovereignty of consumers, nor in the United States

---

[3] W. Lloyd Warner, *A Black Civilization: A Social Study of an Australian Tribe,* rev. ed., New York: Harper, 1957. The Murngin tribes live in a tropical area marked by sharp seasonal cycles of rainy and dry periods and possess a Stone Age culture. The men spear kangaroos, wallabies, and emus and harpoon turtles and porpoises. According to Warner, Murngin society has an elaborate kinship system in accordance with which everyone is related to everyone else. Seven lines of descent are recognized with five generations in each line. The 35 different relatives are distinguished by sex, thus creating 70 categories of relationship; to this is added the distinction between an older and a younger brother, making 71 relationships possible for each member of the society.

[4] Even in contemporary industrial societies, not all goods and services are for sale in the market place. For instance, the unpaid volunteer performs crucial services in hospitals and social agencies. Because she does not sell her services, she is not regarded as part of "the labor force" for purposes of economic calculation.

[5] Robert L. Heilbroner, *The Making of Economic Society,* Englewood Cliffs, N.J.: Prentice-Hall, 1962, p. 42.

where tariffs, strikes, and the rigid price policies of great corporations interfere with the free market.[6] Nevertheless, all contemporary industrial societies involve a great deal of market behavior. This is because the industrial societies, both Communist and capitalist, have pushed the division of labor to the point where *everyone* must enter the market in order to consume, even farmers. In the United States, for example, subsistence farming is rare. Even small farmers produce one or more cash crops to be sold in the market. The income so obtained is used to buy much the same goods and services as city people: packaged foods, ready-made clothing, automobiles, television sets, magazines, admission to the latest Hollywood movie.

Because money is the means — and usually the only means — of consuming part of the production of an industrial society, Americans and Russians and Swedes worry about money. In preliterate societies, where very little consumption is organized through markets, lack of interest in money is understandable. Malinowski reported that the Trobriand islanders, though excellent divers, could not be induced to dive for pearls because the monetary rewards offered to them by traders had little meaning in their society.[7] A similar situation prevails in underdeveloped countries starting to industrialize. High factory wages are not as effective an incentive as in fully industrialized societies because the population does not depend much on money to satisfy its wants.[8] The good things of life are not for sale in the market place. This circumstance helps to explain the difference in the per capita incomes of industrialized and underdeveloped countries (Table 6.1). Part of the reason the average Pakistani can survive with an average income of $52, less than $1/50$ the average American's income, is that some of his consumption is not reflected in his money income; he is less dependent than an American on market consumption. Needless to add, the differential scope of the market is only part of the explanation; the rest of it is sheer poverty.

Citizens of the United States and of the Soviet Union are alike in a respect in which they differ from citizens of Pakistan: they are equally dependent on money incomes for an opportunity to consume. One important *difference* between the Soviet Union and the United States is in the extent to which *wealth* is marketable. In the United States, virtually every possession is transferable through the market place: buildings and real estate; automobiles and other consumer durables; home furnishings, clothing, jewelry; and, most important, fractional shares of ownership in huge corporations. That is, American society is unusual not only for its per capita wealth, but also for the latitude given the individual to hold his wealth in whatever form he wishes: bank balances, stocks and bonds, real estate, small business enterprises, precious stones and

[6] National Resources Committee, *The Structure of the American Economy*, Washington, D.C.: Government Printing Office, 1939, pp. 153-170, reprinted in Bendix and Lipset, Eds., *Class, Status and Power*, Glencoe, Ill.: Free Press, 1953.

[7] Dorothy Lee, *Freedom and Culture*, Englewood Cliffs, N.J.: Prentice-Hall, 1959, pp. 98-99.

[8] Wilbert E. Moore, "Primitives and Peasants in Industry," *Social Research*, Vol. 15, March 1948, pp. 44-81.

TABLE 6.1

Relationship between Per Capita Income and Per Capita Consumption of Energy, 60 Countries, 1957

Country	Per Capita Income (in U.S. dollars)	Per Capita Energy Consumption (in kilograms of coal or equivalent)	Country	Per Capita Income (in U.S. dollars)	Per Capita Energy Consumption (in kilograms of coal or equivalent)
United States	$2101	7771	Lebanon	$304	531
Canada	1458	5543	Colombia	153	464
United Kingdom	954	4775	Jamaica	257	436
Belgium	920	4225	Panama	254	392
Luxembourg	1066	4225	Greece	291	360
West Germany	741	3631	Iraq	135	351
Australia	1074	3522	Portugal	197	335
Iceland	1218	3458	Brazil	251	303
Sweden	1276	2974	Peru	123	297
Venezuela	806	2593	Turkey	365	257
Netherlands	690	2538	Egypt	112	248
France	847	2508	Costa Rica	274	240
Norway	914	2359	Malaya	355	237
Denmark	869	2346	Syria	153	223
South Africa	336	2311	South Korea	135	173
Austria	543	2044	Dominican		
New Zealand	1166	2028	Republic	239	163
Switzerland	1223	1752	Honduras	181	158
Ireland	451	1750	Bolivia	69	156
Finland	648	1463	Ecuador	151	150
Puerto Rico	473	1088	Guatemala	162	131
Argentina	475	1085	Philippines	194	129
Israel	722	1079	India	62	127
Japan	252	926	Ceylon	116	122
Italy	403	915	Ghana	161	99
Chile	360	840	Belgian Congo	74	86
Spain	310	829	Paraguay	115	62
Mexico	234	820	Pakistan	52	53
Cuba	362	735	Thailand	85	53
Southern			Burma	48	41
Rhodesia	122	565	Nigeria	69	38

Sources: Suphon Andic and Alan T. Peacock, "The International Distribution of Income, 1949 and 1957," *Journal of the Royal Statistical Society*, Series A (General), Vol. 124 (Part 2, 1961), pp. 214-215; United Nations, *Statistical Yearbook: 1961*, New York: United Nations, 1961, pp. 278-280.

metals. What is true for the individual is not true of American society as a whole. If everyone wanted to liquidate his real-estate holdings simultaneously, the market price of real estate would drop precipitously, but title would continue to be held by somebody. This freedom to liquidate one's holdings whenever one wants to receive their "market value" in cash encourages savings and investment. The high rate of capital formation (investment) in free-enterprise industrial societies reflects confidence in the continued liquidity of investments. In industrial societies like the Soviet Union, the rate of capital formation is as high as or higher than in free-enterprise industrial societies, but it does not depend on confidence in the continued liquidity of investments because investments are largely involuntary. They are made out of "forced" savings, such as taxes or artificially high prices.

In capitalist countries money functions not only as a medium of exchange and a storehouse of value, but also as a unit of account in terms of which wealth is constantly reevaluated. Especially in time of crisis, the monetary value of investments may rise sharply or fall precipitously. The prospect of capital gains or losses adds a speculative flavor to investment. The chance of loss is not sufficient, however, to dim the long-run confidence that one can invest wealth today with a good prospect of liquidating the investment tomorrow. In Communist countries, severe restrictions are placed on the transfer of wealth through the market place. Factories, mines, farms, utilities, and other productive organizations are owned by the government instead of privately as in the Western countries. No stock exchanges exist where shares of ownership in such enterprises may be transferred. However, Soviet citizens do have bank accounts and own clothing, jewelry, and home furnishings much as Americans do. Although the market is a more important exchange institution in the United States than in the Soviet Union, it plays a much greater role in both these industrial societies than in preliterate economies.

The Differentiation of Occupational Roles. People work in all societies. But the *organization* of work differs fundamentally in preindustrial and industrial societies. A Murngin hunter hunts because all Murngin men hunt—just as all Murngin women cook; neither hunting nor cooking is an "occupation." The Murngin would find it difficult to understand what an "occupation" is because he has no experience with a work role unrelated to his kinship and tribal roles. Nor could he comprehend the buying and selling of a specified number of hours of a worker's services for a given price, the main mechanism by which industrial societies place workers in jobs.

In industrial societies persons playing **occupational roles** do the bulk of the productive work. Since one of the features of occupational roles is that they yield money income, or perquisites of monetary value, occupations constitute the link between production and consumption. By virtue of his work, the worker receives title to a portion of what his society has available for consumption. As noted in Chapter 5, adult males are socialized to follow an occupation in industrial societies; many possessors of inherited wealth or social position are "gainfully employed" even though their incomes do not depend mainly upon working.[9]

The phrase "gainfully employed" refers to persons having an occupation in

---

[9] Privileged persons who need *not* work constitute only a tiny fraction of the adult male population in the United States, the "idle rich." In Western European countries with a titled aristocracy, especially those with constitutional monarchies (Great Britain, The Netherlands, Denmark, Sweden, and Norway), the landed gentry tradition of the Middle Ages persists and makes for a larger leisure class than in the United States. Soviet society, which is only 50 years old, has no leisure class at present. Although Soviet ideology strongly condemns "parasites," it is possible that high Communist officials will form the nucleus of a hereditary aristocracy.

which they earn money or a money equivalent. Some gainfully employed persons are self-employed—a physician in private practice, the owner of a restaurant, a farmer. Such persons are directly dependent on the market for income; they sell goods or services to the public. Most Americans are only *indirectly* dependent on the sale of the goods and services they help to produce. They work for an employer or, more usually, an employing organization, such as General Motors, the Pennsylvania Railroad, the Post Office Department of the Federal government. Table 6.2 documents the extent to which American workers are employees rather than self-employed entrepreneurs.[10] Only in agriculture are a majority of male workers self-employed. In manufacturing, the largest industry, less than 4 per cent of the male workers are self-employed. Table 6.2 shows that nearly 85 per cent of American male workers were employees in 1960. More than 90 per cent of *female* workers were employees in 1960.[11]

TABLE 6.2

Self-Employed Male Workers Age Fourteen and over in the Five Largest American Industries, 1960

Industry	Total Employed Workers	Self-Employed Workers	
		Number	Percentage
Manufacturing	13,111,965	331,579	2.5
Wholesale and retail trade	7,398,070	1,563,104	21.1
Agriculture	3,932,225	2,462,351	62.6
Transportation, communication, and other public utilities	3,687,448	177,553	4.8
Construction	3,662,393	722,136	19.7
All industries (including those not among the largest 5)	43,466,955	6,834,327	15.7

Source: Bureau of the Census, *United States Census of Population: 1960, United States Summary, Detailed Characteristics,* Washington, D. C.: Government Printing Office, 1963, p. 571.

The extent to which industrial societies are employee societies points up the fact that the market for *services* is at least as important as the market for *goods* in the contemporary world. Economists are not concerned with this development. To the economist, labor is a factor of production precisely as natural resources and capital are factors of production; labor markets, commodity

[10] Peter F. Drucker, "The Employee Society," *American Journal of Sociology,* Vol. 58, January 1953, pp. 358-363.

[11] Bureau of the Census, *United States Census of Population: 1960, United States Summary,* Washington, D.C.: Government Printing Office, 1963, p. 549.

markets, and capital markets fit the same framework of supply and demand. To the sociologist, the difference between services and commodities is more important than the similarity. Commodities lie wholly within the economy—until they reach the consumer and disappear. The worker, on the other hand, plays other roles besides his occupational role. He interacts in the economy, but *not only* in the economy. To go back to some of the issues discussed in Chapter 1, workers have *role conflicts;* commodities do not.[12] These role conflicts explain why labor markets are, in the words of the economist, "imperfect," why workers are reluctant to move from an economically stagnant community to a growing community paying higher wages. A worker may have relatives and friends whom he does not wish to leave behind; he may want his children to continue in the same school; he may enjoy his home and garden. Unlike the economist, the sociologist must consider the consequences for the worker's *other* roles of his participation in the occupational system.

The United States Bureau of the Census measures with precision the occupational involvement of various population segments. So do the statistical offices of other industrial countries. Table 6.3 shows the differential participation in the labor force of men and women and of adolescents, adults, and the elderly. A much higher percentage of males than of females was in the labor force in 1960 at every age. The explanation of the difference is partly that many women, especially married women with young children, devote their full-time efforts to homemaking. Nine-tenths of American *males* between the ages of 25 and 55 were in the labor force. The remaining tenth included the mentally ill and deficient, the permanently disabled, and inmates of prisons and other institutions. For practical purposes, therefore, all American men between 25 and 55 who *could* pursue an occupation in 1960 did belong to the labor force. (Note that the labor force, as defined in Fig. 6.1, includes those people who are unemployed but looking for work.) Going to school kept many younger males out of the labor force. As for men over 55, retirement and the increasing incidence of disabilities pushed large numbers out of the labor force, especially after 65, when they became eligible for Social Security payments.

As with all statistical tabulations, Table 6.3 becomes more meaningful when the definitions used in classifying the population are thoroughly understood. The Census Bureau classified a person as a member of the labor force even though he happened to be unemployed during the calendar week in April 1960 preceding the enumerator's visit (the "census week"). A person uninterested in working or unable to work was not considered unemployed and was not classified as a member of the labor force. The Census Bureau clearly defined what it meant by "employed," "unemployed," "in the labor force," and "not in the labor force" (Fig. 6.1). It applied these concepts to a series of questions on the census schedule asked by enumerators (Fig. 6.2).

---

[12] Karl Polanyi speaks of "the commodity fiction." See his *The Great Transformation*, New York: Farrar and Rinehart, 1944.

Employed. Employed persons comprise all civilians 14 years old and over who were either (1) "at work"—those who did any work for pay or profit, or worked without pay for 15 hours or more on a family farm or in a family business; or (2) "with a job but not at work"—those who did not work and were not looking for work but had a job or business from which they were temporarily absent because of bad weather, industrial dispute, vacation, illness, or other personal reasons.

Unemployed. Persons are classified as unemployed if they were 14 years old and over and not "at work" but looking for work. A person is considered as looking for work not only if he actually tried to find work during the reference week but also if he had made such efforts (i.e., within the past 60 days) and was awaiting the results of these efforts. Examples of looking for work are:

1. Registration at a public or private employment office.
2. Meeting with or telephoning prospective employers.
3. Being on call at a personnel office, at a union hall, or from a nurses' register or other similar professional register.
4. Placing or answering advertisements.
5. Writing letters of application.

Persons waiting to be called back to a job from which they had been laid off or furloughed were also counted as unemployed. . . .

Labor force. The labor force includes all persons classified as employed or unemployed, as described above, and also members of the Armed Forces (persons on active duty with the United States Army, Air Force, Navy, Marine Corps, or Coast Guard). The "civilian labor force" comprises only the employed and unemployed components of the labor force. The experienced civilian labor force comprises the employed and the unemployed who have had previous work experience.

Not in labor force. This category consists of all persons 14 years old and over who are not classified as members of the labor force and includes persons doing only incidental unpaid family work (less than 15 hours during the week). Most of the persons in this category are students, housewives, retired workers, seasonal workers enumerated in an "off" season who were not looking for work, inmates of institutions, or persons who cannot work because of long-term physical or mental illness or disability.

FIGURE 6.1 **Labor force concepts underlying questions on employment and unemployment in the 1960 Census.** Source: Bureau of the Census, *United States Census of Population: 1960, United States Summary,* Washington, D.C.: Government Printing Office, 1962, pp. xxvii-xxviii.

The "labor force" concept is useful for describing the economically active segment of the population only in industrial societies. In preliterate societies where food gathering, agriculture, or hunting are not specialized activities but aspects of kinship or communal roles, the concept is irrelevant. The market test of labor force participation—remuneration for services—does not apply. As an approximate measure of the development of a labor market in a society moving toward industrialization, Wilbert Moore suggested computing the pro-

TABLE 6.3

Labor-Force Participation in the United States, by Age and Sex, 1960

Age	Male Population, Age 14 and over: Total of Specified Age	In Labor Force Number	Per-centage	Female Population, Age 14 and over: Total of Specified Age	In Labor Force Number	Per-centage
14–15	2,823,032	452,943	16.0	2,697,727	186,902	6.9
16–17	2,891,892	1,064,523	36.8	2,791,152	581,791	20.8
18–19	2,337,550	1,548,520	66.2	2,406,632	1,114,666	46.3
20–24	5,236,986	4,510,798	86.1	5,492,006	2,462,697	44.8
25–29	5,298,596	4,975,113	93.9	5,506,465	1,933,693	35.1
30–34	5,805,617	5,562,577	95.8	6,078,049	2,156,467	35.5
35–39	6,055,047	5,802,969	95.8	6,386,767	2,569,986	40.2
40–44	5,619,690	5,360,030	95.4	5,893,104	2,667,149	45.3
45–49	5,349,759	5,052,877	94.5	5,535,365	2,624,207	47.4
50–54	4,744,298	4,372,149	92.2	4,917,741	2,253,086	45.8
55–59	4,167,829	3,656,323	87.7	4,399,358	1,744,365	39.7
60–64	3,374,074	2,618,958	77.6	3,719,035	1,096,055	29.5
65–69	2,876,754	1,261,842	43.9	2,297,013	546,732	16.6
70–74	2,133,158	611,429	28.7	2,517,769	241,122	9.6
75 and over	2,280,630	352,939	15.5	3,068,168	129,411	4.2
Total, all ages	60,994,912	47,203,990	77.4	64,706,351	22,308,329	34.5

Source: Bureau of the Census, *United States Census of Population: 1960, United States Summary, Detailed Characteristics,* Washington, D.C.: Government Printing Office, 1963, p. 499.

portion of all males 15 to 64 years of age who were wage and salary earners.[13] He showed, for example, that the Philippines had 35.7 per cent of its eligible males working for wages or salaries in 1939 as compared with 65.5 per cent in the United States in 1940. He concluded that "the goal of economic growth in undeveloped areas may be expressed as the attempt to create a 'labor force' in the technical sense."[14]

Social Consequences of Occupational Role Differentiation. The meaning of work in industrial societies is different from the meaning of work in preindustrial societies partly as a consequence of the physical separation of work and residence. Commuting is more than exposure to rush hour traffic jams; it dramatizes the independent existence of the community of residence and the work community. Typically now the worker's *home,* the place of his kinship roles, is distinct from his *job* location. This physical separation of work and

[13] Wilbert E. Moore, "The Exportability of the 'Labor Force' Concept," *American Sociological Review,* Vol. 18, February 1953, pp. 68-72.

[14] Moore, "The Exportability of the 'Labor Force' Concept," p. 72.

P22. Did this person work at any time last week?

Include part-time work such as a Saturday job, delivering papers, or helping without pay in a family business or firm. Do not count own housework.

Yes_____☐   No_____☐

P23. How many hours did he work last week (at all jobs)? (if exact figure not known, give best estimate)

1 to 14 hours_____☐   40 hours_____☐
15 to 29 hours_____☐   41 to 48 hours_____☐
30 to 34 hours_____☐   49 to 59 hours_____☐
35 to 39 hours_____☐   60 hours or more_____☐

P24. Was this person looking for work, or on layoff from a job?

Yes_____☐   No_____☐

P25. Does he have a job or business from which he was temporarily absent all last week because of illness, vacation, or other reasons?

Yes_____☐   No_____☐

FIGURE 6.2   **Questions from the Household Questionnaire of the 1960 Census.** Source: Bureau of the Census, *United States Census of Population: 1960, United States Summary,* Washington, D.C.: Government Printing Office, 1962, p. xxvii.

residence is the essence of what economic historians call "the factory system." A factory is commonly thought to be a building containing specialized machinery for manufacturing products. But the history of the **factory** shows that the emphasis should not be placed on equipment but on social organization.

The work role on a family farm or in a family business is a consequence of family membership, but most jobs today are not obtained on this basis. Indeed, giving a relative a job rather than filling it on the basis of impersonal qualifications may be considered reprehensible. Congressmen charged with nepotism in filling positions on their staff find themselves at a disadvantage at election time. And the late President Kennedy was accused of attempting to establish a dynasty because of the political offices held by his brothers and his brothers-in-law. Not every industrial society separates the occupational realm from family life as completely as does the United States. Japan, for example, has a strong familistic tradition which seems to be compatible with industrial development. Thomas Wilkinson has shown that the proportion of unpaid family workers in the Japanese labor force is far larger than in the United States or Great Britain.[15]

[15] Thomas O. Wilkinson, "Family Structure and Industrialization in Japan," *American Sociological Review,* Vol. 27, October 1962, p. 681.

Ken Heyman

Apparently the family is more frequently the unit of economic activity in Japan than in Western industrial countries. Nevertheless, even in this familistic society, the forces of industrialization tend to separate the occupational from the kinship roles. The development of the British wool industry is a good illustration of this process:[16]

> Factory workers are gathered together in buildings or rooms wholly devoted to their work; the establishment does not serve as a home for either employer or employee. The aggregation of workers created new problems of discipline. When work was done in the household no regularity of hours was necessary. The craft worker enjoyed considerable freedom as to the manner and time of doing such work as was necessary for his support. Even when the putting-out system had become elaborately organized it was not possible to exert much pressure on the workers as to the time of finishing the work allotted to them. The aggregation of the workers in factories made it possible to improve the timing of the productive process; the work could be made to flow along without interruptions; no group of workers need be obliged to wait for the group engaged on the earlier stages of the work. The division of labor that existed under the putting-out system could thus be more effectively carried out, but on one condition — the subjection of the whole body of workmen to a systematic schedule.

[16] Reprinted by permission. From Abbott Payson Usher, *The Industrial History of En* Boston: Houghton Mifflin, 1920, pp. 350-351.

The organization of factories thus gave a different meaning to the relation between the capitalist employer and the workman. The dependence of the worker on the capitalist was not increased; under the putting-out system every possible degree of dependence existed: at an early date it became common for the capitalist to own the machines or tools, and in the later phases of this system the capitalists owned the entire establishment. The Hand-Loom Weavers' Commissioners reported that a firm at Newark, Notts, employed about one hundred weavers in cottages; "the system is for the manufacturer to build cottages adapted for weavers, and filled up with looms, and to let these cottages at a moderate weekly rental: every weaver taking a house and not having a family sublet portions of the cottage." The gathering together of such cottage workers into a factory involved only one change: the introduction of discipline. The capitalist employer became a supervisor of every detail of the work; without any change in the general character of the wage contract, the employer acquired new powers which were of great social significance. He acquired authority which was irksome to the men and almost certain to become the source of much friction.

It is doubtless possible to exaggerate the extent of the increased authority of the employer under the factory system; the small master of the earlier periods undoubtedly exercised some supervision over his journeymen and apprentices, but in theory his authority was that of a parent or fellow-workman, and it seems likely that in actual practice supervision amounted to nothing that would imply a different relation between master and journeyman. The capitalist employer of the putting-out system certainly exercised no powers of supervision. It was therefore an essentially new thing for the capitalist to be a disciplinarian.

Although we cannot be certain, there is reason to believe that the factory system did not afford a significant margin of profit as compared with the putting-out system until machinery became relatively elaborate. The factory thus held out little hope of special profits to the capitalist in the early period, and, as it was bitterly opposed by the men, there was no general tendency to substitute the factory for the organization of cottage industry under the putting-out system. Unfortunately, we cannot determine the relative importance of these two factors in the postponement of the factory development; but the late evidence makes it clear that factories developed slowly even after they had become profitable to the capitalist. This was notably the case with weaving factories; the handloom weavers could not be induced to forsake the freedom of the old system under which they had enjoyed more independence even than farm laborers.

Speaking of the conditions in Coventry, the special commissioner writes:

"With all its usual distress and degradation, the trade of single hand weaving (requiring a minimum of strength and skill) offers half the liberty of savage life, for which the uninstructed man is almost tempted to sacrifice half the enjoyments of the civilized. Thus, there is a well known feeling among the farm laborers, the brick-layers, and other ordinary artizans in this district, that it is very hard on them to be turned out at early hours every day instead of being able to take what hours they please, like the ribbon weaver, and like him, take saint Monday, and saint Tuesday too if they choose. Precisely the counterpart of these feelings is also found in the other sex. Notwithstanding the wretched state in which, until recently, the trade had long been, it was impossible for respectable families to procure domestic servants. There is the greatest difficulty in prevailing upon

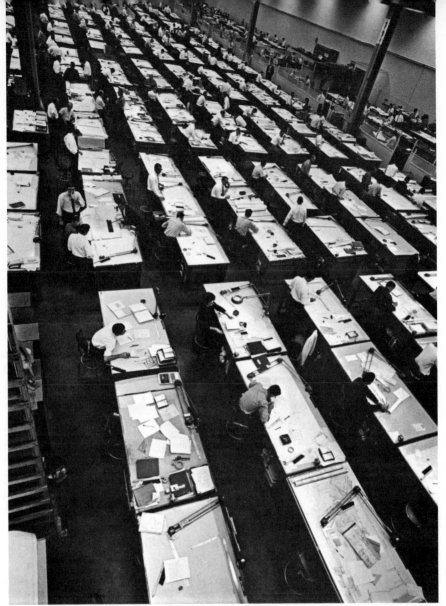

parents to let their children come to service. The young women look down with scorn upon it, and prefer the liberty of the Monday and Saturday, the exemption from confinement, and the little finery, with the liberty to wear it, which the loom furnishes them."

From all sections of England there came similar testimony. The great attraction of hand-loom weaving was the degree of freedom enjoyed, the weavers refusing to leave their cottages for the factory even when the factory offered higher wages. It would seem that the discipline of the factory was not merely a distinguishing feature, but an obstacle to the introduction of the system. Machinery became important in the development of the system because its introduction ultimately forced the workman to accept the discipline of the factory. As long as there were some measure of freedom of choice between cottage and factory the workman preferred the cottage. The general development of the factory thus required the existence of commanding economic advantages, advantages so great as to destroy any real freedom of choice on the part of the worker. The development of the factory is thus closely associated with the introduction of machinery, but it would inevitably distort one's conception of the rise of the system if the use of machinery were made the characteristic test of the existence of a factory. Machinery made the factory a successful and general form of organization, but there can be a factory "without machinery."

If the factory consists of premises controlled by the employer to which employees come to work for pay, a hospital, a school, a post office, and a jet airplane are factories no less than a manufacturing establishment.

Clearly, the factory method of organizing production had to be invented to make possible a modern economy. The extensive division of labor in automobile production, for example, presupposes rigid adherence to specifications in manufacturing each of thousands of parts. Quality control is feasible in *factory* production, but not under the **domestic system.** Imagine the frequency of breakdowns in automobile assembly lines if the home production of parts were attempted. Not only would parts fail to arrive on time; they would also vary so much from specifications that unlikely coincidences would be required in order to assemble a complete automobile. Another feature of contemporary industrial economies, large investments in plant and equipment, depends on factory production. True, *some* investment in machinery occurred even during the cottage-industry phase of British economic history. But elaborate, bulky, expensive, and easily damaged machines can prove profitable only if the employer can supervise their operation and maintenance, and can keep them busy. Beyond a relatively primitive stage of industrial development, this requires factory production. A steel mill, for instance, or an oil refinery requires such tremendous investment in plant and equipment that less than full-scale production tends to be unprofitable.

Before the development of the factory system, human and animal brawn were the main sources of energy for production. The factory system was conducive to the development of *inanimate* sources of energy: coal, oil, natural gas, electricity, and, most recently, atomic energy. Utilization of these inanimate sources of energy enormously increased productivity per worker. Table 6.4 shows how rapidly the per capita consumption of inanimate energy increased in the United States over the past century. The high American standard of living is made possible by this harnessing of inanimate energy. Of course, other industrial societies are also high-energy societies.[17] And they likewise enjoy high standards of living. Recall Table 6.1, which provides statistical documentation of the proposition that high-energy societies tend to be high-income societies and, conversely, that societies with primitive technologies are low-income societies.

---

[17] Fred Cottrell, *Energy and Society: The Relationship between Energy, Social Change, and Economic Development.* New York: McGraw-Hill, 1955.

TABLE 6.4

Growth in the Horsepower of Prime Movers in the United States, 1850 to 1960 (in thousands)

Year	Factories	Mines	Railroads	Merchant Ships, Powered	Sailing Vessels	Farms	Windmills	Electric Central Stations
1850	1,150	60	586	325	400	—	14	—
1860	1,675	170	2,156	515	597	—	20	—
1870	2,453	380	4,462	632	314	—	30	—
1880	3,664	715	8,592	741	314	668	40	—
1890	6,308	1,445	16,980	1,124	280	1,452	80	447
1900	10,309	2,919	24,501	1,663	251	4,009	120	2,443
1910	16,697	4,473	51,308	3,098	220	10,460	180	6,228
1920	19,422	5,146	80,182	6,508	169	21,443	200	17,050
1930	19,519	5,620	109,743	9,115	100	28,610	200	43,427
1940	21,768	7,332	92,361	10,094	26	42,488	130	53,542
1950	32,921	9,167	110,969	11,032	11	63,090	59	87,965
1960	37,360	34,000	46,856	23,890	2	201,756	44	217,173

Year	Aircraft	Work Animals	Automobiles, Trucks, Buses, Motorcycles	Total Horsepower	Population	Total Horsepower per 100,000 Population
1850	—	5,960	—	8,495	23,191,876	37
1860	—	8,630	—	13,763	31,443,321	44
1870	—	8,660	—	16,931	39,818,449	43
1880	—	11,580	—	26,314	50,155,783	52
1890	—	15,970	—	44,086	62,947,714	70
1900	—	18,730	100	65,045	75,994,575	86
1910	—	21,460	24,686	138,810	91,972,266	151
1920	—	22,430	280,900	453,450	105,710,620	429
1930	3,382	17,660	1,426,568	1,663,944	122,775,046	1,353
1940	7,455	12,510	2,511,312	2,759,018	131,669,275	2,095
1950	22,000	7,040	4,403,617	4,747,871	150,697,361	3,151
1960	36,534	2,790	10,366,880	10,967,285	178,464,236	6,145

Sources: Bureau of the Census, *Historical Statistics of the United States, Colonial Times to 1957,* Washington, D.C.: Government Printing Office, 1960, p. 506; Bureau of the Census, *Statistical Abstract of the United States: 1962,* Washington, D.C.: Government Printing Office, 1962, pp. 5, 528.

Thus the invention of the factory method of production ultimately helped to raise the standard of living in Western industrial countries beyond the expectations of all but utopians. In the early stages of the factory system, however, the transformation of the *social* aspects of the work situation was more obvious. Workers did not like the long hours and the harsh discipline. They reacted to factory discipline, first, by preferring lower wages in the cottages to higher wages in the factories; then, after factories became the wave of the future, they expressed their frustration by sporadic riots and sabotage. (The

Lewis W. Hine—George Eastman House

derivation of "sabotage" is the French word, *sabot,* meaning wooden shoe; apparently considerable damage resulted when *sabots* were thrown into machinery.) Karl Marx and his followers put this resentment into words. Communism developed in direct opposition to the "exploitation of the working class"—illustrated from official reports of working conditions in British factories and mines during the first half of the nineteenth century.[18] Marx recognized the inequality of bargaining power within the enterprise, a power differential not appreciated sufficiently by economists of his day, and he attributed the low level of wages to the weakness of bargaining power of workers. He did not anticipate that the trade union movement would redress the balance of power and that wage and salaried workers would share in the rising standard of living made possible by rising productivity.

Instead of the increasing misery of the working class, which Marx believed inevitable, the standard of living of workers in capitalist countries rose steadily.[19] Equally important, instead of the polarization of society into a mass of downtrodden proletariat and a tiny stratum of oppressors, an increasing proportion of the population in industrial societies consists of neither *manual workers* nor *capitalists* but *white-collar* administrative, professional, technical, clerical,

---

[18] Karl Marx, *Capital: A Critique of Political Economy,* New York: Modern Library, no date, Chaps. 10 and 15.

[19] Simon Kuznets, "Economic Growth and Income Inequality," *American Economic Review,* Vol. 45, March 1955, pp. 1-28.

or sales persons.[20] Marx did not foresee the tremendous need for engineers, teachers, secretaries, clerks, technicians, and supervisory employees in industrial societies. In the early stages of industrialism, the wretchedness of factory workers made their future appear hopeless, and this, combined with Marx's commitment to radical change, led him to underestimate the possibilities of more equitable distribution of economic benefits under capitalism.

Marxist criticism of capitalism has had important intellectual as well as practical consequences. Much scholarly work in economics and sociology during the past century was undertaken in order to reformulate Marxist theory.[21] And the sense of mission of many pioneering trade unionists derived, directly or indirectly, from Marxism. Marx was influential despite some polemical exaggerations, perhaps because he recognized the changing character of industrial societies. Once work shifted from the home to the factory, its meaning changed. Regardless of the shares of income received by the worker and by the owner, a central question for Marx, the factory worker interacts for a considerable portion of his waking life with other workers instead of with his family. Before the separation of work and residence, *work* satisfaction was entangled with *marital* and *family* adjustment and with the more general problem of *life* satisfaction. Marx was right to call attention to work satisfaction as a problem in its own right. But he *assumed* that the meaning of factory work in a private ownership system had to be dehumanization and frustration **(alienation),** as it was during the early stages of industrialization. But empirical studies of work satisfaction in contemporary societies show that "the vast majority of workers, in virtually all occupations and industries, are moderately or highly satisfied, rather than dissatisfied with their jobs."[22] This does not mean that all workers are satisfied to the same extent. Table 6.5 shows that workers vary considerably in their responses to the question, "What type of work would you try to get into if you could start all over again?" Most professional workers said they would choose the same occupation; most manual workers, especially unskilled workers, chose some other occupation. What interests sociologists are the reasons underlying this variation. Robert Blauner, an industrial sociologist, identified four major reasons: the varying prestige of occupations, the varying solidarity of occupational communities, the morale of the work group, and the degree of freedom from supervisory control enjoyed by the worker. Here is Blauner's discussion of these four factors:

1. OCCUPATIONAL PRESTIGE

Occupational prestige is the one best explanatory factor in the sense that if all

[20] Lewis Corey, "The Middle Class," *Antioch Review,* Vol. 5, Spring 1945, pp. 1-20.

[21] See, for example, Max Weber, *General Economic History,* New York: Collier, 1961.

[22] Robert Blauner, "Work Satisfaction and Industrial Trends in Modern Society," in Walter Galenson and Seymour M. Lipset, Eds., *Labor and Trade Unionism: An Interdisciplinary Reader,* New York: Wiley, 1960, p. 353. The reading that follows is condensed from this article and reprinted by permission.

TABLE 6.5

Proportion in Various Occupations Who Would Choose Same Kind of Work if Beginning Career Again

Professional Occupations (Per Cent)		Working Class Occupations[d] (Per Cent)	
Mathematicians[a]	91	Skilled printers	52
physicists[a]	89	Paper workers	52
Biologists[a]	89	Skilled automobile workers	41
Chemists[a]	86	Skilled steelworkers	41
Lawyers[b]	83	Textile workers	31
Journalists[c]	82	Unskilled steelworkers	21
		Unskilled automobile workers	16

[a] "The Scientists: A Group Portrait," *Fortune,* October 1948, pp. 106-112.

[b] "The U.S. Bar," *Fortune,* May 1939, p. 176.

[c] Leo Rosten, *The Washington Correspondents,* New York: Harcourt, Brace, 1938, p. 347.

[d] These are unpublished data which have been computed from the IBM cards of a survey of 3000 factory workers in 16 industries, conducted by Elmo Roper for *Fortune* magazine in 1947. A secondary analysis of this survey is being carried out by the Fund for the Republic's Trade Union Project. The general findings of the original study appeared in "The Fortune Survey," *Fortune,* May 1947, pp. 5-12, and June 1947, pp. 5-10.

Source: Blauner, "Work Satisfaction," p. 343.

occupations (for which sufficient data are available) were ranked in order of extent of typical job satisfaction, and these ranks were compared with the rank order in which they partake of public esteem, the rank-order correlations would be higher than those resulting from any other factor. This is because the prestige of any occupation depends on the level of skill the job entails, the degree of education or training necessary, the amount of control and responsibility involved in the performance of the work, the income which is typically received — to mention the most readily apparent factors. Since occupational prestige as a kind of composite index partly subsumes within itself a number of factors which contribute heavily to differences in satisfaction, it is not surprising that it should be itself the best individual measure of satisfaction.

In addition, jobs that have high prestige will tend to be valued for their status rewards even when "objective" aspects of the work are undesirable; similarly, low-status jobs will tend to be undervalued and disliked. . . .

2. OCCUPATIONAL COMMUNITIES

The nature of the association among workers *off-the-job* is also a factor in work satisfaction. The evidence of the work literature supports the notion that levels of work satisfaction are higher in those industries and in those kinds of jobs in which workers make up an "occupational community." One such industry is mining. Not only is the actual work carried out by solidary work groups, but, in addition, miners live in a community made up largely of fellow workers. This kind of "inbreeding" produces a devotion to the occupation which is not characteristic of many other working class jobs. . . .

3. INTEGRATED WORK GROUPS

A third factor that is important in explaining occupational differences in work satisfaction is the nature of on-the-job social relations. The technological structure of certain industries such as steel production and mining requires that the work be carried out by *teams* of men working closely together, whereas in industries such as automobile assembly the formation of regular work groups is virtually prohibited by the organization of production. There is much evidence to support the proposition that the greater the extent to which workers are members of integrated work teams on the job, the higher the level of job satisfaction.

In a steel mill in which 85 per cent of sixty-two workers interviewed were satisfied with their jobs, Charles Walker found that "the source of satisfaction most often articulated or implied was that of being part of, or having membership in, the hot mill crew." . . .[23]

4. CONTROL

In a perceptive passage, the Belgian socialist Henri DeMan remarks that "all work is felt to be coercive." The fact that work inherently involves a surrender of control, a "subordination of the worker to remoter aims," is probably what makes the relative degree of control in work so important an aspect of job attitudes. As Max Weber, the German sociologist, suggested long ago, "no man easily yields to another full control over the effort, and especially over the amount of physical effort he must daily exert."

a. Control over Time, Physical Movement and Pace of Work. Assembly line work in the automobile industry is a good example of the almost complete absence of this aspect of control.[24]

Its coerced rhythms, the inability to pause at will for a moment's rest, and the need for undeviating attention to simple routines made it work to be avoided if possible and to escape from if necessary. So demanding is the line that one worker, echoing others, complained: "You get the feeling, everybody gets the feeling, whenever the line jerks everybody is wishing 'break down, baby!' "

The consensus of the work literature is that assembly line work, especially in the automobile industry, is more disliked than any other major occupation, and the prime factor in dissatisfaction with the assembly line is the lack of control over the pace of production. Workers in assembly line plants have strong preferences for jobs off the line. A study of the job aspirations of 180 men on the line found that the "workers' motivations were not what might normally be expected.

---

[23] Charles R. Walker, *Steeltown,* New York: Harper, 1950.

[24] Ely Chinoy, *Automobile Workers and The American Dream,* Garden City, N.Y.: Doubleday, 1955, p. 71.

It was not promotion or transfer in order to improve one's economic status. Rather, it was primarily a desire 'to get away from the line.'" *Only 8 per cent* were satisfied, in the sense of not preferring to get an off-line job. . . .

b. *Control over the Technical and Social Environment.* In those occupations in which the physical environment or the technological work process is particularly challenging, control over it seems to be an important aspect of job satisfaction. Coal-miners have "a very personal sense of being pitted against their environment" and express "feelings of accomplishment and pride at having conquered it." That steel production is found fascinating is suggested by a mill worker: "It's sort of interesting. Sometimes you have a battle on your hands. You have to use your imagination and ability to figure out what move to make." Similarly, it has been noted that railroad workers derive a sense of power in "the manipulation of many tons of railroad equipment." Engineers derive more pleasure in running large engines rather than small ones; switchmen and brakemen "give the signals that move fifty or so freight cars back and forth like so many toys."

c. *Control as the Freedom from Direct Supervision.* On a slightly different level of analysis is this third dimension, which refers not to the aspects of the work process under control, but rather to the locus of control. One of the most consistent findings of work research is that industrial workers consider light, infrequent supervision, "foremen who aren't drivers," a crucial element in their high regard for particular jobs and companies.

The absence of close supervision in the mines has been considered an important determinant of the miners' high level of satisfaction. And truck drivers and railroad workers, in explaining their preference for their own trades, stress the independence they experience in these jobs where the contact between employees and supervisor is so much less frequent than in factory work.

Blauner went on to consider whether the mix of occupational roles in modern America (and in other mature industrial societies) is shifting to produce a larger proportion of dissatisfied workers. Is the dissatisfied assembly-line worker becoming the prototype of industrial man? Blauner did not think so; the myth of the dehumanized robot was not supported by hard data.

An indication that the actual proportion of assembly line workers is quite small is suggested by figures of the automobile industry, the conveyor belt industry par excellence. If we consider total employment in the industrial groupings involved in the manufacture, sales, repair, and servicing of automobiles, we find that assembly line workers make up less than 5 per cent of all workers in this complex. There are approximately 120,000 automobile workers who are line assemblers, yet the number of skilled repair mechanics in all branches of the industry, a job which in many ways resembles the craft ideal, exceeds 500,000. In addition, the 120,000 assemblers are outnumbered by 400,000 managers who own or operate gas stations, garages, new and used car lots, and wrecking yards, and by 200,000 *skilled* workers in automobile plants. Recent developments, especially automation, have served further to decrease the proportion of assembly line operatives in the industry.

If the situation in the automobile industry is at all typical, research might well show that those kinds of job contexts which are associated with high work satisfaction and control over one's time and destiny, such as skilled repair work and self-employment, are more representative than is commonly believed, and are even increasing over the long run. Such a prospect should bring considerable satisfaction to all those in the diverse intellectual traditions who have been concerned with what happens to human beings in the course of their major life activity, their work. And yet, this would not necessarily mean that the problem of the lack of fulfillment in work had become less serious. For as one industrial sociologist has suggested, this problem *may become more acute,* not because work itself has become more tedious, fractionated, and meaningless, but because the ideal of pride in creative effort is shared by an increasingly large proportion of the labor force as a result of the rise of democratic education and its emphasis on individualism and occupational mobility.

In the closing sentences of the preceding article, Blauner calls attention to what has been called the **revolution of rising expectations.** The phrase, in its more usual application, refers to the rising economic and political aspirations of people in underdeveloped countries. Curiously enough, although the twentieth century has witnessed progress in the standard of living in backward countries and great increases in their political autonomy, aspirations have arisen *faster* than changes. A similar phenomenon has been noted in affluent, democratic, industrial societies. Blauner's suggestion that rising expectations applies to the work situation is intriguing. Rising expectations for the work situation could account for increases of dissatisfaction despite objective improvements in some or all of the four factors that, according to Blauner, bear a relationship to work satisfaction.

For instance, Blauner argues persuasively that the closer the supervision over the worker and the less the choice he can exercise over the timing of his operations, his physical movements, and the pace of his work, the less is his work satisfaction. Is worker control over the work situation *decreasing?* Not clearly so; this is a complicated problem. Some technological developments in machine-line operations seem to reduce worker autonomy; other technological developments seem to increase it. Apart from technology, two industrial developments *favor* worker control over the work situation. One is a change in managerial ideology.

Partly as a result of studies conducted by Elton Mayo of the Harvard Business School and his colleagues, business executives are aware of "human relations in industry."[25] They recognize that the character of supervision is an important factor in worker morale and therefore, indirectly, in productivity. For instance, take the oft-cited study of absenteeism and labor turnover in a California aircraft factory during the Second World War.[26] In a new factory, some

---

[25] Reinhard Bendix, *Work and Authority in Industry: Ideologies of Management in the Course of Industrialization,* New York: Wiley, 1956, pp. 308-340.

[26] Elton Mayo and George F. Lombard, *Teamwork and Labor Turnover in the Aircraft Industry of Southern California,* Boston: Harvard Graduate School of Business Administration, Business Research Studies, No. 32, 1944.

inexperienced foremen had natural talent for leadership; others thought that a foreman was supposed to bark orders at underlings. The researchers discovered that variation in supervisory skill accounted for the tremendous rate of absenteeism and labor turnover in certain departments and the negligible rate in others. Government and industry learned from such wartime experiences that supervisory skill can be developed through training. More than a million foremen were taught methods of handling workers in the Training Within Industry Program of the War Manpower Commission.[27] And since the end of the war, industry has continued the stress on human relations in its training programs for supervisory personnel. The human-relations climate in many large corporations means that management tries to exercise supervision *tactfully*. An industrial corporation can never be as democratic as the ideal New England town meeting, but the feelings of subordinates can be considered or ignored in the communication of decisions from the top. Insofar as the new human-relations ideology has permeated the company, workers experience a *less* coercive atmosphere.

The second change, the power of giant unions to limit managerial authority, tends to increase worker influence in the work situation. In 1966 more than 19 million American workers were enrolled in 190 unions, three of which contained more than a million members each[28] (see Table 6.6). In the steel, coal, automobile, and electrical industries, giant corporations bargain with giant unions.[29] In the garment and coal industries, the unions are more powerful than individual corporate employers and have on occasion loaned money to employers to save tottering businesses. This strength of unions has resulted in contracts with employers which customarily provide protection for the worker against arbitrary actions on the part of management. Two officials of the Steelworkers Union went so far as to explain the appeal of unions largely in terms of worker desire for a Bill of Rights. "Labor unions have their origin in the desire of workers for self-protection against arbitrary acts of management in layoff, promotions, wage distributions, speed-ups, and other matters that vitally affect them."[30] The main thrust of this statement is *not* on wage benefits but on what is known in constitutional law as "due process." "Due process" is what a leading labor economist was emphasizing when he called collective bargaining a system of "industrial jurisprudence."[31]

Union contracts place limitations on the authority of the employer to hire, fire, promote, and make work rules. Some employers resent this. They feel

[27] Stuart Chase, *The Proper Study of Mankind,* rev. ed., New York: Harper, 1956, p. 166.

[28] Bureau of the Census, *Statistical Abstract of the United States: 1969,* Washington, D.C.: Government Printing Office, 1969, p. 237.

[29] John Kenneth Galbraith, *American Capitalism: The Theory of Countervailing Power,* Boston: Houghton Mifflin, 1952.

[30] Clinton S. Golden and Harold J. Ruttenberg, *The Dynamics of Industrial Democracy,* New York: Harper, 1942, p. 255.

[31] Sumner H. Slichter, James J. Healy, and E. Robert Livernash, *The Impact of Collective Bargaining on Management,* Washington, D.C.: Brookings Institution, 1960.

that promotions based on seniority, for example, prevent them from rewarding the best workers and thereby reduce overall efficiency. On the other hand, seniority provisions in the contract give workers a feeling of job security; they are less likely to suspect that favoritism or discrimination underlies management decisions. In Blauner's terms, seniority gives workers more *control* over the work situation. If morale of the work force thereby improves, seniority might *increase* productivity even though it is a demonstrable violation of the logic of efficiency.

Giant unions do not guarantee the individual worker greater control over his immediate work situation. If the union is undemocratic, the worker may feel subjected to two tyrannies, that of union bureaucrats and that of his supervisors, instead of one.[32] The likelihood is, however, that even in undemocratic unions, shop stewards and other union officials cannot ignore their members' concern over the work situation.

Thus the power of big unions as well as current human relations ideology on the part of management may have increased worker independence over the past generation. As Blauner points out, however, worker satisfaction depends not only on the objective work situation, but also on the aspirations of the worker. Therefore improvements in the work situation and increases in worker dissatisfaction could be compatible. But as Table 6.5 indicates, job dissatisfaction is not necessarily a problem for workers today.

For the majority of workers in contemporary societies, and especially for executives and professionals, "work" has assumed a new significance. Talcott Parsons notes that the English language implicitly assumed that the residential community is the paramount commitment of the worker: " . . . the place of residence, the 'home' is said to be the place where the person 'lives,' as though, when away from home, he were not alive."[33] This assumption was approximately correct in the preindustrial era when work was a necessary accompaniment to kinship obligations, as on a family farm. It may be correct even today among unskilled, highly supervised workers whose job satisfaction is minimal; they put up with work for the money it provides and expect their main satisfactions to come from home, family, and friends. But for most workers today, particularly for professionals and executives, the assumption that the worker does not "live" until he returns to his place of residence sounds quaint. Contemporary man not only *lives* when away from home; he may feel that his life away from home, his **career,** is as important to him as his family. The term "career" is usually applied to an orderly sequence of prestige occupational roles in government, business, or the professions; manual workers have "jobs," not "careers." Role conflict can arise in industrial societies between family and manual work roles, but conflicts in allegiance between work and family are most conspicuous on upper career levels of the occupational struc-

---

[32] Chapter 10 takes up the problem of bureaucracy at greater length.

[33] Talcott Parsons, *Structure and Process in Modern Society*, Glencoe, Ill.: Free Press, 1960, p. 252.

TABLE 6.6

National and International Labor Unions Reporting 100,000 Or More Members in 1966.

Name of Union	Number of Members
1. International Brotherhood of Teamsters, Chauffeurs, Warehousemen, and Helpers of America (Independent)	1,651,000
2. United International Union of Automobile, Aircraft, and Agricultural Implement Workers of America	1,403,000
3. United Steelworkers of America	1,068,000
4. International Brotherhood of Electrical Workers	875,000
5. International Association of Machinists	836,000
6. United Brotherhood of Carpenters and Joiners of America	800,000
7. Retail Clerks International Association	500,000
8. International Hod Carriers', Building, and Common Laborers' Union of America	475,000
9. International Ladies' Garment Workers Union	455,000
10. Hotel and Restaurant Employees and Bartenders International Union	450,000
11. Amalgamated Clothing Workers of America	382,000
12. Amalgamated Meat Cutters and Butcher Workmen of North America	353,000
13. Building Service Employees' International Union	349,000
14. International Union of Operating Engineers	330,000
15. Communications Workers of America	321,000
16. International Union of Electrical, Radio, and Machine Workers	320,000
17. United Association of Journeymen and Apprentices of the Plumbing and Pipe Fitting Industry of the United States and Canada	285,000
18. American Federation of State, County, and Municipal Employees	281,000
19. Brotherhood of Railway and Steamship Clerks, Freight Handlers, Express and Station Employees	270,000
20. American Federation of Musicians	252,000
21. International Union of Dist. 50, United Mine Workers of America	232,000
22. Brotherhood of Painters, Decorators, and Paperhangers of America	201,000

ture. Newspaper accounts of divorce actions among film stars, for instance, hint that career problems underlie many of the legal charges. Husbands are away from home for months at a time to make movies in foreign countries; wives are more interested in nightclubbing with other film celebrities than in home-making. Commitments to careers are especially disruptive when *both* spouses have strong career commitments, as in the entertainment world. For business

TABLE 6.6 (continued)

Name of Union	Number of Members
23. American Federation of Government Employees	200,000
24. National Association of Letter Carriers of the United States of America	190,000
25. Brotherhood of Railroad Trainmen	185,000
26. Textile Workers Union of America	182,000
27. International Brotherhood of Pulp, Sulphite, and Paper Mill Workers	171,000
28. Retail, Wholesale, and Department Store Union	171,000
29. United Rubber, Cork, Linoleum, and Plastic Workers of America	170,000
30. United Electrical, Radio, and Machine Workers of America (Independent)	167,000
31. Oil, Chemical, and Atomic Workers International Union	165,000
32. International Association of Bridge, Structural, and Ornamental Iron Workers	162,000
33. Bricklayers, Masons, and Plasterers' International Union of America	149,000
34. United Papermakers and Paperworkers	144,000
35. United Federation of Postal Clerks	143,000
36. Brotherhood of Maintenance of Way Employees	141,000
37. International Brotherhood of Boilermakers, Iron Shipbuilders, Blacksmiths, Forgers, and Helpers	140,000
38. United Packinghouse, Food, and Allied Workers	135,000
39. Transport Workers Union of America	135,000
40. Brotherhood of Railway Carmen of America	126,000
41. American Federation of Teachers	125,000
42. International Association of Firefighters	115,000
43. International Printing Pressmen and Assistants' Union of North America	114,000
44. International Typographical Union	107,000
45. Amalgamated Transit Union	103,000
46. Sheet Metal Workers' International Association	100,000

Source: Bureau of the Census, *Statistical Abstract of the United States,* 1969, Washington, D.C.: Government Printing Office, 1969, p. 237.

executives, on the other hand, the husband's commitment to his career need not disrupt the marriage because the wife is often willing to subordinate family life to the demands of her husband's workload. In the colorful words of a former *Fortune* editor, William H. Whyte, Jr., home is not a sanctuary but a "branch office":[34]

[34] William H. Whyte, Jr., *The Organization Man,* New York: Doubleday Anchor, 1957, P. 162.

To the executive there is between work and the rest of his life a unity he can never fully explain, and least of all to his wife. One of the few secrets many an executive manages to keep from his wife is how much more deeply he is involved in his job than in anything else under the sun. Thus he can never really explain to his wife that what he is doing is not overwork, for the explanation would be tactless. "Overwork as I see it," says one company president, "is simply work that you don't like. But I dearly love this work. You love only one time and you might as well do something you like." He was not talking about his wife.

Whyte implies that the executive invests too much of himself in his career and not enough in his family. But Whyte is honest enough to admit that the executive is happy in his work, so happy "that he cannot distinguish between work and the rest of his life. . . ." For the organization man, work is *fun*. To eliminate the value judgment from Whyte's argument and yet retain his data, one might say that certain interesting and prestigious occupational roles attract major commitments of time and energy. A corresponding *decrease* is possible in the *family* commitments of persons in such executive roles. This assumes that a man has a finite amount of psychic energy to invest. If more goes into his job, less is available for his family and local community. On the other hand, it is possible that some people have more energy and ability than others and that these fortunate individuals bring more to every sphere of life. Or perhaps success in one context makes for increased motivation in the other.

These empirical questions have been studied to some extent. Harold Wilensky examined the relationship between work history and community participation in a Detroit sample of 678 white male workers from 21 to 55 years of age.[35] The sample was deliberately restricted to white workers of higher-level manual occupations and lower-level white-collar occupations (so as to eliminate race as a confounding variable and to reduce the influence of economic status). Furthermore, Wilensky controlled statistically on the income, education, and age of respondents in analyzing his interview data. He concluded that men with more successful careers, successful in the sense of an orderly succession of increasingly prestigeful jobs in a related field, tended to have stronger attachments (1) to community organizations and (2) to relatives, friends, and neighbors. Wilensky interpreted the correlation as due to the following causal sequence: education led to better chances for an orderly career, which in turn generated motivation and opportunities for community participation. The converse was also true: men with chaotic experiences in the economic order had less motivation and opportunity for social participation. In short, role conflict between family and career *can* occur, but the more usual situation is mutual support. Successful performance in one context is associated with successful performance in the other.

---

[35] Harold L. Wilensky, "Orderly Careers and Social Participation: The Impact of Work History on Social Integration in the Middle Mass," *American Sociological Review*, Vol. 26, August 1961, pp. 521-539.

THE STYLE OF LIFE OF INDUSTRIAL POPULATIONS

The division of the world into industrialized and developing societies[36] pertains not only to the distribution of goods but also to the opportunities for health and for life itself. The American people had in 1966 a crude death rate (deaths, exclusive of stillbirths, per thousand population) one-half the rate of the Guatemalan people.[37] The American infant mortality rate (deaths of children under 1 year per 1000 live births) was in 1966 one-fourth the Guatemalan rate—23.7 per 1000 compared to 91.5 per 1000.[38] Such striking differences in life expectancies are decreasing with the introduction of insecticides and other techniques of disease control. However, the difference in living standards between industrialized and developing societies has widened in recent years.[39] How does living in a rich society that is getting richer affect the way its members think about the world? Are they likely to be more optimistic, generous, and reasonable than members of an impoverished society? How is their **style of life** distinctive?

Economic abundance does not rigidly determine the thought processes or behavior of a population, but it makes possible options not available to people living in an economy of scarcity.[40] For example, early retirement from the labor force and an extended period of formal education for children are hardly conceivable in agricultural societies. In such societies scarcity exerts pressure on the bulk of the population to make an economic contribution. Industrial societies *can* forgo the economic contribution of the young and the old, and, as Table 6.7 shows, tend to do so. Industrial societies also permit newlyweds to establish separate households from their parents. This expensive arrangement incidentally undermines the solidarity of the extended family and the authority of grandparents. Furthermore, the size of homes in industrial societies can be large enough to permit a child from an ordinary family to have a room of his own, a luxury in a preindustrial economy. "It seems clear beyond dispute that the household space provided by the economy of abundance has been used to emphasize the separateness, the apartness, if not the isolation, of the American child."[41] The economy of abundance contributes to the child's conception of

---

[36] Robert Theobald, *The Rich and the Poor: A Study of the Economics of Rising Expectations,* New York: New American Library, 1961; Robert L. Heilbroner, *The Great Ascent: The Struggle for Economic Development in Our Time,* New York: Harper & Row, 1963.

[37] Bureau of the Census, *Statistical Abstract of the United States: 1968,* Washington, D.C.: Government Printing Office, 1968, p. 838.

[38] Bureau of the Census, *Statistical Abstract: 1968.*

[39] Suphon Andic and Alan T. Peacock, "The International Distribution of Income, 1949 and 1957," *Journal of the Royal Statistical Society,* Series A (General), Vol. 124, Part 2, 1961, pp. 214-215.

[40] The rest of this paragraph leans on the analysis of the effects of affluence on the American character in David M. Potter, *People of Plenty: Economic Abundance and the American Character,* Chicago: University of Chicago Press, 1954, Chap. 9.

[41] Potter, *People of Plenty,* p. 197.

TABLE 6.7

Labor Force Participation of Males in Countries with Different Levels of Industrialism (Percentage economically active among male population of given age group)

Degree of Industrialization	Age (Years)							
	10-14	15-19	20-24	25-34	35-44	45-54	55-64	65 and over
Industrialized countries[a]	4.1	72.4	91.5	96.7	97.6	95.9	85.6	37.7
Semi-industrialized countries[b]	13.2	70.3	91.8	96.2	97.1	95.9	88.9	61.0
Agricultural countries[c]	23.9	78.4	91.2	96.3	97.5	96.3	91.6	70.1

[a] The following 21 countries have less than 35 per cent of active males engaged in agriculture and related activities:
Argentina
Australia
Austria
Belgium
Canada
Denmark
France
Germany, Eastern
Germany, Federal
    Republic of
Israel
Japan
Malta and Gozo
Netherlands
New Zealand
Norway
Sweden
Switzerland
United States
United Kingdom:
    England and Wales
    Northern Ireland
    Scotland

[b] The following 30 countries have 35 to 59 per cent of active males engaged in agriculture and related activities:
British Guiana
British Honduras
Ceylon
Chile
Cuba
Cyprus
Finland
Greece
Hungary
Iceland
Ireland
Italy
Jamaica
Malaya, Federation of
Martinique
Mauritius
Panama
Poland
Portugal
Puerto Rico
Réunion
Ryukyu Islands
South West Africa—
    all races
Spain
Union of South Africa—
    Bantu population
Union of South Africa—
    colored population
United Arab Republic—
    Egyptian region
Venezuela
West Indies
Yugoslavia

[c] The following 21 countries have 60 per cent or more of active males engaged in agriculture and related activities:
Algeria—Moslems
Bolivia
Brazil
Bulgaria
Colombia
Costa Rica
Ecuador
El Salvador
Fiji Islands
Guatemala
Haiti
India
Korea, Republic of
Morocco—indigenous
    population
Mozambique—
    indigenous population
Nepal
Paraguay
Philippines
Thailand
Tunisia
Turkey

Source: United Nations, Department of Economic and Social Affairs, *Sex and Age Patterns of Participation in Economic Activities*, Population Studies No. 33, New York: 1962, pp. 12, 77.

himself as an individual in yet another way: it frees his mother to lavish on him what are, by preindustrial standards, inordinate care and guidance.

The idea of the importance of the individual (**individualism**) is congenial to industrial societies because affluence makes *individuality* more feasible. Industrial societies tend to be individualistic for another reason. They are highly differentiated societies in which roles in the economy or in government are assigned to persons as individuals rather than as representatives of families or tribes. Thus an *occupational* role can be played well or poorly quite independently of the person's role in his *family*. A woman, for example, can get a job and support herself and her children if she is not satisfied with the way her husband treats her. The possibility of employment for women does not automatically lead to a high divorce rate or to an equalitarian ideal for married couples, but the role structure is conducive to female independence. For the same reason a differentiated role structure is also conducive to *adolescent* independence. If Johnny leaves home, he has a place to go and the means of supporting himself. The individualistic organization of industrial societies therefore is an obstacle to patriarchal domination. Unlike the situation in biblical times, wives and children can survive socially and economically if they do not obey the would-be patriarch.

Affluence, Leisure, and Individual Fulfillment. In industrial societies, inanimate sources of energy—coal, oil, natural gas, electricity, and, most recently, atomic energy—are the basis of productivity, not human or animal brawn. The term "horsepower" is a survival of the preindustrial era when horses and other animal sources of power kept farms and cottage industry going. The increasing utilization of inanimate energy sources is a major factor in the increasing productivity per worker and therefore in the rising standard of living. Recall that Table 6.4 demonstrated the decline in the relative importance of work animals in the American economy over the past century along with the astronomical growth of total horsepower. One sociologist calls industrial societies "high-energy societies" to call attention to the relationship between the high standard of living and the high per capita consumption of inanimate energy.[42] Table 6.1 demonstrated this relationship statistically. Generally, the higher the per capita income in a country, the higher the per capita consumption of energy.

As productivity per worker rose in industrial societies, real income per family rose, and new goods and services were added to the standard of living. At the same time, the average work week declined. People in affluent societies wanted more *leisure* to enjoy their high standard of living. No longer compelled to work long hours for the bare necessities of life, they preferred more leisure to more luxuries. To put this another way, the Industrial Revolution took the worker out of the home and put him in the factory; the high level of productivity made possible by industrialism is sending him back. There is, however,

---

[42] Cottrell, *Energy and Society*.

an important difference between the preindustrial and the contemporary family situation. In the preindustrial era the worker shared his *work* with his family; in industrial society he shares his *leisure*. In preindustrial societies a small leisure class was common. But not until the industrial era did mass leisure appear — and with it an ideology of individual fulfillment, a pursuit of happiness and good times alien to the stress on obligations of preindustrial societies. Some commentators have gone so far as to call contemporary individualism "the emergence of fun morality."[43] Indeed, there seems to be in the contemporary United States what amounts to a moral obligation to "enjoy, enjoy." On returning from a vacation, only a courageous or an unpleasant character asked the question, "Did you have a good time?" will reply, "No, wretched."

One reason for the ideology of individual fulfillment lies in social organization. The individual is the unit of social participation far more than in preindustrial societies. Thus he tends to think in individual terms not only about his *contributions* to society but also about his *rewards.* Since fun and the leisure to enjoy it are rewarding, the contemporary individual is prone to ask whether he is getting his fair share of them. He worries about not having as much fun on Saturday evenings as others do. A second reason for the ideology of individual fulfillment is that fun in industrial societies has become purchaseable in the market place. Commercialized recreation offers the possibility of enjoyable leisure through classes in ballroom dancing, skiing weekends, sailboat charters, a flight to Las Vegas, a visit to Disneyland — as well as by watching television, seeing movies, playing golf, and bowling. As *Life* put it in a survey of the $40 billion Americans spend on recreation, "Never have so many been so determined to get so much out of *everything.*"[44]

Perhaps part of this determination is stimulated by advertising campaigns on behalf of Caribbean vacations and by other commercial promises of joy-filled leisure. Commercialized recreation is partly a response to the restlessness and boredom produced by mass leisure. On the other hand, some of the restlessness, some of the taste for new recreational kicks, is deliberately stimulated by salesmen for the leisure industry.

Not everyone approves of the mass leisure made possible by industrialization. Some social critics are pessimistic about the capacity of the average man to spend his leisure wisely. They point out that he litters the countryside and the public beaches with empty Coca-Cola cans, that his search for kicks sometimes leads him to marijuana or to drinking himself numb in taverns and cocktail lounges and perhaps ends in auto accidents. These critics do not rejoice even when mass leisure turns toward the arts; they point out that the mass market for the novel, the motion picture, and the television play has tended to lower artistic standards. Mass appeal is obtained by a preoccupation

[43] Martha Wolfenstein, "The Emergence of Fun Morality," *Journal of Social Issues,* Vol. 7, No. 4, 1951, pp. 15-24.

[44] Robert Coughlan, "A $40 Billion Bill Just for Fun," *Life,* Vol. 47, December 28, 1959, p. 74.

Bob Smith—Rapho Guillumette

with sex and violence.[45] Other social critics argue that the talent for using leisure to enrich life can be developed. The trick is to avoid the boredom that often accompanies leisure because flight from boredom leads as often to self-destruction as to wholesome recreation. And boredom can be avoided by putting passion and commitment into leisure, by working at fishing or photography or some other avocation with the same dedication that professionals put into their careers. [46]

Although there is pessimism in some quarters about the uses to which the new leisure is put, this pessimism is as nothing beside the pessimism of those who fear that the new leisure cannot be made available to the bulk of the world's population. This fear goes back nearly two centuries to the beginnings of the Industrial Revolution in Europe. The pessimists of that day pointed out that the productivity of industrial societies did not necessarily raise the standard of living and increase leisure. In 1798 Thomas Robert Malthus published *An Essay on the Principle of Population* in which he warned that population growth might wipe out the gains of productivity and keep the standard of

[45] For a discussion of the effect of Mass Culture on High Culture, see Dwight Macdonald, "A Theory of Mass Culture," *Diogenes,* No. 3, 1953, pp. 1-17; Bernard Rosenberg and David M. White, Eds., *Mass Culture: The Popular Arts in America,* Glencoe, Ill.: Free Press, 1956.

[46] Russell Lynes, "Time on Our Hands," *Harper's Magazine,* Vol. 217, July 1958, pp. 34-39.

living low.[47] Malthus assumed that people would have as many children as they could afford to support. This did *not* happen during the nineteenth century in industrializing countries. Birth rates *fell* in such countries as Sweden, France, Switzerland, and the United States.[48] Even though industrialization made possible more children per family and declining mortality rates ensured the survival of more children, what actually happened was conscious family limitation. Why? Because people changed their behavior:[49]

> Regardless of nationality, language, and religion, each industrializing nation tended to postpone marriage, to increase celibacy, to resort to abortion, to practice contraception in some form, and to emigrate overseas.

What was the motivation for these demographic changes? The cruel check of hunger and disease? Malthus, who was pessimistic about rational planning, might have thought so. He wrote the first edition of his *Essay* in response to the radical ideas generated by the French Revolution. Condorcet in France and William Godwin in England argued that the corrupting influence of social institutions led to human misery; hence they advocated **anarchy**. Condorcet and Godwin believed that men were basically reasonable and good and that therefore anarchy would produce social harmony, prosperity, and happiness. Malthus was horrified. He sought to justify social institutions, and he used the danger of overpopulation as an argument in support of the status quo. Marriage is necessary so that a man cannot escape the responsibility to provide for the children he brings into the world. Private property gives him the resources to discharge this responsibility. Without familial and economic institutions, men would have no incentive for procreative restraint and would multiply like fruit flies. Since the food supply of the world is limited, eventually population growth would be checked by war, disease, and famine.[50] The logic of Malthus' position drove him not only to support existing social institutions but to oppose higher wages for working men. He assumed that higher wages would be translated into a continuing population explosion, and society would be worse off than before.

The weakness of the Malthusian theory was its underestimation of human intelligence and foresight. If Malthus had known in 1798 that industrial populations would produce better-educated, higher-income, white-collar, and urbanized segments that would practice family limitation before the pattern spread to the poorer-educated, lower-income, blue-collar, and rural segments, he might have formulated his theory of population pressure more

[47] Thomas R. Malthus, *An Essay on the Principle of Population as It Affects Future Improvement of Society,* London: Macmillan, 1926.

[48] Dennis H. Wrong, *Population,* New York: Random House, 1956, p. 53.

[49] Kingsley Davis, "The Theory of Change and Response in Modern Demographic History," *Population Index,* Vol. 29, October 1963, p. 351.

[50] See the discussion of Malthus in Talcott Parsons, *The Structure of Social Action,* New York: McGraw-Hill, 1937, pp. 102-107.

optimistically. But accurate demographic data were only beginning to become available in Malthus' time; his theory did not have to grapple with such hard and stubborn facts. On the basis of these facts, demographers now realize that human beings do not necessarily multiply as rapidly as the food supply permits, as fruit flies do. Human beings are capable of entertaining a concept of a "decent standard of living." Once they are committed to maintaining a particular standard, they tend to protect it from decline. A large family is a threat to their standard of living, especially under urban industrial conditions. So, unless other values (such as religious convictions) deter them from practicing family limitation, they are motivated to practice it. Note that the motivation for family limitation in industrial societies is not hunger or even fear of hunger; it is to obtain a share of the rising standard of living.

Nineteenth-century experience in Western Europe and the United States suggested that the population growth associated with industrialization was temporary. **Mortality** rates declined as public health practices and nutritional standards improved; but **fertility** rates also declined. There was an initial spurt of population, but after a while a new balance was achieved between births and deaths. Instead of the cruel balance of preindustrial societies, where a high birth rate was matched by an equally high death rate, industrial societies achieved a balance with low death rates and low birth rates. Demographers call the passage from a high birth rate-high death rate balance to a low birth rate-low death rate balance the **demographic transition,** represented graphically in Fig. 6.3.

Malthus was unduly pessimistic about population growth in the nineteenth century, but he has been more nearly correct in the twentieth. The contem-

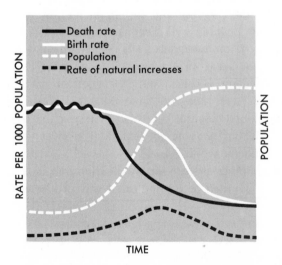

FIGURE 6.3 **Vital rates and population growth during the demographic transition.** Source: Kingsley Davis, "The Demographic Consequences of Changes in Productive Technology: An Essay on the Problem of Measurement," in Georges Baladier et al., *Social, Economic and Technological Change: A Theoretical Approach,* Paris: Conseil International des Sciences Sociales, 1958, pp. 195-227.

porary situation seems to be this: although industrialization offers hope of a better standard of living to underdeveloped societies, industrialization can produce this happy result *only if these societies succeed in passing through "the demographic transition."* Japan is virtually alone in having done this in the twentieth century. Why should it be more difficult for societies to pass through the demographic transition in the twentieth century than it was in the nineteenth? The main obstacle is modern science. In the nineteenth century the death rate declined slowly instead of plunging downward as it has in the twentieth. For example, in Ceylon the control of malaria resulting from DDT spraying raised the life expectancy from 43 years in 1946 to 52 years in 1947, as big an increase as most Western countries experienced in half a century.[51] In Mexico the crude death rate dropped from 26.6 per 1000 in 1930 to 11.7 per 1000 in 1960.[52] These precipitous declines in the death rate produce a population explosion—growth much greater than that experienced by countries in the nineteenth century. Mexico's population increased between 1953 and 1960 at the rate of 3.1 per cent per year, fast enough to double Mexico's population every 23 years.[53] Extrapolation of the current rate of growth of *world* population yields a prediction of 50 billion people in less than 200 years.[54] Explosive population growth, by consuming the increase in productivity made possible by industrialization, destroys hope that the standard of living can rise. This undercuts the motivation for family limitation (Malthus would have said "destroys the incentive for moral restraint") and thereby the basis for population stability at low birth and death rates. In short, under twentieth-century conditions, developing countries must reduce fertility *quickly;* in the nineteenth century there was more time. Perhaps fertility *can* be reduced quickly in the underdeveloped countries. Just as new knowledge has quickly reduced the death rate, so the development of new techniques of contraception may make possible swift declines in the birth rates of underdeveloped countries. If so, improvements in their standards of living are possible, including shorter hours of work and mass leisure, as in Western countries. The gap in living standards between industrialized and underdeveloped societies—between the haves and the have nots—can begin to narrow. Because the underdeveloped countries have so far been unable to bring birth rates down quickly, Malthus' gloomy predictions of war, famine, and pestilence may return to haunt the world.

Within industrial countries there is also a division into haves and have nots: between persons adjusted to the industrial way of life, who function

[51] William Peterson, *Population,* New York: Macmillan, 1961, p. 468.

[52] Peterson, *Population,* p. 37, gives the Mexican death rate in 1930. For the 1960 Mexican death rate, see Bureau of the Census, *Statistical Abstract of the United States: 1962,* Washington, D.C.: Government Printing Office, 1962, p. 913.

[53] Bureau of the Census, *Statistical Abstract of the United States: 1962,* Washington, D.C.: Government Printing Office, 1962, p. 911.

[54] Philip M. Hauser, *Population Perspectives,* New Brunswick, N.J.: Rutgers University Press, 1960, p. 7.

adequately in the complex role structure of a highly differentiated society, and persons who do not understand the cultural values of industrialism. The latter group are a large portion of those with minimal economic rewards, thus constituting a welfare and dependency problem for the former group. However, unlike the division between industrial and underdeveloped countries, the proportion of the population adjusted to the industrial way of life is increasing as larger numbers of people are upgraded educationally and economically. One indication of better adjustment to industrial culture is the tendency for consumer goods to be distributed more equitably in rich industrial societies. "It is, indeed, a regular occurrence endowed almost with the dignity of an economic law that the poorer the country, the greater the difference between poor and rich."[55]

In short, the division of industrial societies into **in-group** and **out-group** cultures may be transitional. Welfare-minded Sweden has moved far enough toward a homogeneous culture that slums are nonexistent in Swedish cities. For the time being, however, an advanced industrial country like the United States should be thought of as having two cultures: that of the industrially oriented in-group (haves) and that of the demoralized out-group (have nots).[56]

In what sense do industrially oriented segments of the population in an advanced society constitute an in-group? They are not linked by such obvious characteristics as skin color or the absence of physical handicaps. Their unity depends on sharing certain skills in coping with the problems of life in a complex society. For example, they utilize the media of mass communication for information and for entertainment; they regard formal education as an important asset in adjusting to their society; they are able to relocate easily in other communities to provide a better environment for children or better occupational opportunities for the breadwinner. If acceptance of the institutions of their society is inferred from active participation in them, they are conformists. Obviously, some members of the in-group exemplify its values

[55] Gunnar Myrdal, *An International Economy,* New York: Harper, 1956, p. 133. Quoted in Seymour Martin Lipset and Reinhard Bendix, *Social Mobility in Industrial Society,* Berkeley: University of California Press, 1959, p. 108, along with supporting United Nations data.

[56] An *in-group consists of persons linked to one another by feelings of solidarity.* An in-group can be small in size: a family or a squad of soldiers. It can also include an entire nation, as when Americans emphasize their common allegiance, which excludes all "foreigners." Thus the in-group concept is relevant to many levels in a complex society: wherever a feeling of solidarity unites some people and excludes others. The *out-group is defined residually, by subtracting the in-group from a larger category.* Sometimes members of an out-group are drawn together by the bond of their common exclusion; sometimes they feel rejected in isolation. Racial discrimination in the United States creates a Negro out-group, but Negro protest organizations like the National Association for the Advancement of Colored People, the Urban League, the Black Panthers, the Black Muslims, and the Congress of Racial Equality help to create *esprit de corps* among victims of racial discrimination, thus transforming an out-group into a kind of in-group. For an excellent discussion of the in-group concept, see Robert Bierstedt, *The Social Order: An Introduction to Sociology,* New York: McGraw-Hill, 1957, pp. 263-268.

Ken Heyman

more strongly than others. Since many values and skills are involved, it might be argued that no sharp separation occurs between the in-group and the out-group, that instead there is continuous variation from those most at home in the society to the totally maladjusted. There is some evidence, however, that poverty is more painful psychologically in rich societies and that therefore a bridge between the cultures of affluence and of poverty is as difficult to build internally as internationally. In the next section, we consider the economic and psychological aspects of poverty within affluent industrial societies.

Poverty and the Feeling of Failure. Poverty is nothing new. But the *meaning* of poverty is different in affluent industrial societies from its meaning in the underdeveloped countries of Asia, Africa, and South America. In these pre-industrial societies, poverty means physical deprivations: hunger, cold, disease, premature death. Poverty is the condition of the majority of the population in these societies, and it is not usually interpreted as a sign of personal failure. In affluent industrial societies, where poverty is the exception rather than the rule, self-respect is less compatible with poverty. One of the two major reasons for poverty in industrial societies is catastrophe: severe illness in the family, unemployability of the breadwinner, uninsured losses. Economists call such circumstances "case" poverty. Welfare payments are designed to remedy the resulting physical deprivations but not the damaged self-esteem of such "cases." The second reason for poverty is that certain categories of persons are *excluded* from economic opportunities: the elderly, the uneducated, the migrant worker, members of a rejected minority group. Because such people cannot obtain adequate income from occupational roles, they find themselves dependent on welfare assistance. In some groups (American Negroes, the *Burakumin* in Japan) resentment at exclusion is as frequent a reaction as gratitude for aid.[57] The American "war on poverty" (initiated by the Economic Opportunity Act of 1964) is an attempt to bring more of the American population, especially Negroes and other disadvantaged ethnic minorities, into the economic mainstream.

Whether it be case poverty or backwater poverty, poverty in industrial societies, being exceptional, is often interpreted as a sign of intellectual or moral failure. Thus the poor in industrial societies must carry the stigma of personal inadequacy in addition to not having the spacious housing, the air conditioners, and the new cars possessed by the more affluent. In short, the meaning of poverty in modern societies is as much psychological as economic. The absence of certain household furnishings helps to define the identity of the householder—to himself as well as to others. Materialistic preoccupations are partly a consequence of this identity-defining function of possessions in societies rich enough to use them in this way.

This means that poverty in contemporary societies is as much a state of mind as an economic condition. No simple relationship exists between objective deprivation and subjective dissatisfaction, in part because objective deprivation rarely proceeds to the limits of biological endurance. The Hollywood writer who said, "In this town, I'm snubbed socially because I only get a thousand a week. That hurts," *felt* poor. That he ate regularly and wore fashionable clothes did not protect him from *feeling* deprived. The concept of **relative deprivation** was invented during the Second World War to explain the causes of seemingly groundless feelings of deprivation—specifically, the greater dissatisfaction of unpromoted soldiers with available opportunities for promotion in the Air Corps (where promotions were frequent) than in the Military Police (where promotions were rare).[58] The researchers interpreted the data in Fig. 6.4 by hypothesizing that a private in the MPs did not feel as bad about not being promoted because he had lots of company. In the Air Corps, on the other hand, the table of organization permitted a larger percentage of noncoms; consequently a private in the Air Corps was more prone than a similarly unpromoted man in the Military Police to suspect that *he* had failed. Criticiz-

[57] The similarities between the psychological responses of the excluded *Burakumin* and the excluded Negro in two outwardly dissimilar societies is remarkable. See George DeVos and Hiroshi Wagatsuma, *Japan's Invisible Race: Caste in Culture and Personality,* Berkeley: University of California Press, 1966.

[58] Samuel A. Stouffer et al., *The American Soldier,* Vol. 1, Princeton, N.J.: Princeton University Press, 1949, pp. 124-130.

Ken Heyman

ing the promotion system by choosing responses other than "a very good chance" was an alternative to blaming himself. The concept of relative deprivation, broadly relevant to the social psychology of invidious comparisons, is especially useful in explaining dissatisfactions in affluent industrial societies, where people seem more concerned with the distribution of goods and services in this world than with eternal salvation in the next. Here economic dissatisfactions, which are usually defined relatively, are prominent partly because the mass media — to which television has been an important addition — stimulate desires for a luxurious style of life among all segments of the population. In short, the psychic sting of socioeconomic deprivation is probably greater for the poor in affluent industrial societies than for the more deprived poor in less affluent societies.

Relative deprivation can be thought of as a new dimension of poverty, a

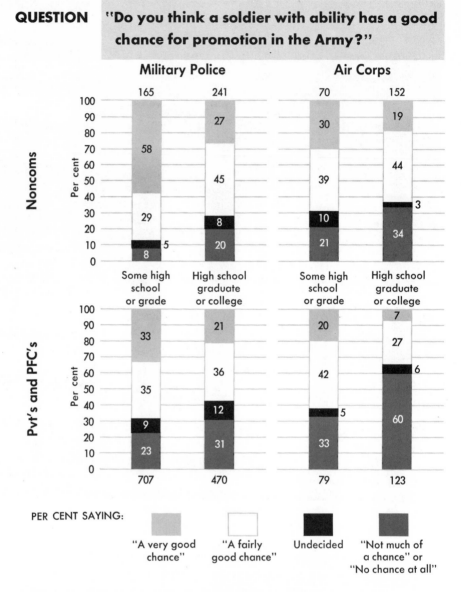

FIGURE 6.4 **Opinions about promotion opportunity — comparisons by education and rank between Military Police and Air Corps. (White enlisted men in the Army 1 to 2 years, continental United States.)** Source: Samuel A. Stouffer et al., *The American Soldiers,* Vol. 1, Princeton, N.J.: Princeton University Press, 1949, p. 252.

dimension that will remain no matter how affluent industrial societies become. But old-fashioned deprivation continues also, not only in regional and educational backwaters that have not experienced the full impact of industrialization and among the catastrophe cases, but also among preindustrial minorities — the Negro in the United States, the Untouchables in India, the *Burakumin* in Japan, the Irish and the nonwhites in England — ethnic groups that do not participate fully in the economic and social lives of their societies. Unlike the elderly, whose lack of participation can be justified by physical incapacities, ethnic barriers to full participation can be explained only by historical accidents. Gypsy and Slav, white and Negro, Jew and Hindu, all racial and ethnic groups *can* participate in an industrial society because all are potentially literate; all can adapt to the factory system; all are willing to live in cities. The requirements of industrialism tend to transform industrial societies into gigantic melting pots in which ethnic origin is becoming less and less important. However, a society is a prisoner of its ethnic history. Although slavery has not existed in the United States for more than a century, the place of Negroes in contemporary American cities is affected by the circumstance that black slaves were brought here to work as farm laborers. To varying degrees, the Lapps in Scandinavia, the Burakumin in Japan, the Irish in England, the Moslem North Africans in France, and the Indonesians in Holland are also barred from full participation in economic and social life. Cultural pluralism sounds workable, and ethnic cleavages lead to demonstrable inefficiencies and problems. Nevertheless, prejudice and discrimination do not automatically disappear.

Minority problems are more serious in the United States than in other industrial societies. The task of integrating into American society a Negro minority composing 11 per cent of the population is vastly more difficult than the problem Sweden faces with Lapp reindeer herders in the Arctic region. Nevertheless, most industrial countries and developing societies contain ethnic minorities—although the logic of industrialism makes for their gradual assimilation just as the logic of industrialism is incompatible with a rural peasantry. Temporarily, however, ethnic minorities live within affluent industrial societies but are less likely to share their cultural **values** and material rewards. The tendency is for these minorities to live in a different cultural world from the majority—a meaner, smaller world. This is what anthropologist Oscar Lewis calls the **culture of poverty.**[59] A family that has become impoverished does not necessarily share the culture of poverty; the members may continue to hold the same values and aspirations as before. The culture of poverty refers to a climate of hopelessness arising either from generations of deprivation or from personal defeats so crushing that the future holds no further promise. Long-term unemployment can generate such hopelessness.[60] Professor Lewis suggests that poverty produces essentially the same attitudes and values whether it appears among the Untouchables in India, among detribalized natives in the slums of Johannesburg, among dwellers in the *vecindades* of Mexico City, or among migrant laborers in the United States. Do people react with the same quiet desperation regardless of geography or national culture? Lewis maintains that they

---

[59] Oscar Lewis, *Five Families: Mexican Case Studies in the Culture of Poverty,* New York: Basic Books, 1959, p. 2.

[60] Mirra Komarovsky, *The Unemployed Man and His Family,* New York: Dryden, 1940; E. Wight Bakke, *Citizens without Work,* New Haven, Conn.: Yale University Press, 1940.

do and has published a variety of case studies compatible with this interpretation. On the other hand, Lewis recognizes that the culture of poverty presents a different problem in societies where "it represents a relatively small segment of the population and those in which it constitutes a very large one."[61] In industrial societies where it affects a small segment of the population, programs to break the cycle of poverty (from one generation to the next) are *economically* feasible. But the culture of poverty in such societies may be more deeply rooted *psychologically;* it is fed not only by economic deprivation but by social rejection and derivatively by the loss of self-respect.

To identify ethnic minorities with the "culture of poverty" would be an oversimplification even in the United States. Large numbers of American Negroes, Puerto Ricans, Mexican-Americans, Indians, and Orientals have completed high school; they work at white-collar jobs and own their homes. Large numbers of white Protestants can be found in the worst slums, living on welfare allowances. Still, there can be no doubt that the underdogs of American society (as of other industrial societies) come disproportionately from visible ethnic minorities. In 1960 more than 60 per cent of nonwhite families had less than $4000 a year income as compared with less than 30 per cent of the white families.[62] Furthermore, income does not tell the complete story; discrimination in rental housing, hotel and restaurant accommodations, recreational facilities, and educational opportunities foster the cultural isolation of many nonwhites. The incredible congestion and dilapidation of the Negro neighborhoods of New York, Chicago, Cleveland, and other large American cities reflects not only Negro poverty but also the resistance to Negro **invasion** of white neighborhoods. The *Report* of the commission appointed by President Johnson to investigate the causes of the summer riots of 1967 pointed to the explosive consequences of excluding an ethnic minority from the material benefits and the cultural values of the industrial way of life:[63]

> To continue present policies is to make permanent the division of our country into two societies; one, largely Negro and poor, located in the central cities; the other, predominantly white and affluent, located in the suburbs and in outlying areas.

The race riots in American cities — in the Watts section of Los Angeles in 1965, in Detroit and Newark in 1967 — shocked not only white America but the world. Yet the ethnic grievances that produced them are present in most industrial societies. Indeed, although the *Burakumin* constituted less than 2 per cent of the Japanese population in 1918, they played a leading role in the Japanese riots of that year protesting the increase in the price of rice:[64]

[61] Oscar Lewis, *La Vida: A Puerto Rican Family in the Culture of Poverty — San Juan and New York,* New York: Vintage Books, 1968, p. lii.

[62] Conference on Economic Progress, *Poverty and Deprivation in the U.S.: The Plight of Two-Fifths of a Nation,* Washington, D.C.: Conference on Economic Progress, April 1962, p. 48.

[63] National Advisory Commission on Civil Disorders, *Report,* New York: Bantam Books, 1968, p. 22.

[64] De Vos and Wagatsuma; *Japan's Invisible Race,* p. 41.

The first riot began in August, 1918, in a little fishing village in Toyama Prefecture on the Japanese sea coast and quickly spread to neighboring villages. Soon after, Burakumin rioted in Kyoto; they were joined by more Burakumin and the poor in general. The riots spread through almost all the cities in Japan (they were especially violent in Osaka, Kobe, Wakayama, Okayama, and Hiroshima), and from the cities, disturbances spread to the outlying farming and fishing villages. Coal miners also went on strike. In all of these riots the Burakumin were particularly active, often taking the initiative and leadership.

The problem of integrating ethnic minorities into the social and economic mainstream is perhaps more difficult in the United States than in European countries because blacks and Spanish-speaking people constitute such a large minority. But the problem is not unique. All of the industrial countries have similar tendencies to polarize into two or more peoples instead of one: Canada tries to bridge the gulf between the English and the French; Holland has her Indonesians. In Rhodesia and South Africa, the white minority, dominant for the present, has tyrannized the black majority in a deliberate attempt to maintain two societies, separate and unequal. These white supremacist regimes make the implicit assumption that an industrial society can remain viable while containing an unreconciled ethnic group of considerable size. Even with modern weapons to control riot and repress dissent, this seems unfeasible.

CONCLUSION

In every society, production and distribution of goods and services pose a major problem of adaptation to the environment. An industrial society is unusual in possessing an "economy" differentiated from other institutions. A necessary condition for this **differentiation** is the commercialization of exchange. A further condition is the separation of work and residence. Once separation occurs, the organization of production becomes fundamentally different. Occupational roles emerge. The ratio of capital to labor grows along with the increased utilization of inanimate sources of energy. Provided that population growth is not too rapid, the standard of living of the average family rises, and the disparity of income between the rich and the poor decreases. Recreational industries develop, one aspect of the emerging cultural expectation of individual fulfillment.

The economic aspects of the industrial way of life are the expansion of the market, the differentiation of occupational roles, the growth in affluence. The ecological aspect of the industrial way of life will be discussed in Chapter 7: the concentration of population in urban areas.

The population of an industrial society can be roughly divided into a majority that shares its cultural values and material rewards and a minority that does not understand the urban industrial way of life and is excluded from its benefits. In the United States, the industrially oriented majority consists largely of urbanized whites. Majority Americans usually have stable families, a low death rate, and high educational aspirations. They live in pleasant homes, often in the suburbs of large cities, but many are willing to move at short notice to distant parts of the country in order to advance the career of the male breadwinner. These moves are not disorganizing, partly because neighborhood roots are shallow in industrial societies and partly because American communities have remarkably similar social organization and cultural characteristics.

The nonindustrial minority of the American population includes both rural and urban segments. The rural poor, including migrant laborers, may ultimately disappear as the demand for unskilled farm workers declines. Rural Negroes and Mexicans move to cities where they join the slum-dwelling remnants of previous migrations, including the failures left behind by the transAtlantic migration of European peasants. This nonindustrial population of American cities has a higher incidence of broken families and illegitimacy, a higher death rate, more welfare problems, and lower educational attainment, on the average, than the industrially oriented majority. Whether these malintegrated elements of American cities will maintain a permanent culture of poverty or be assimilated into the mainstream of urban industrial life is not clear; massive rural-to-urban population shifts are still being absorbed by metropolitan areas. The test will come (1) when rural areas are industrialized and no longer export surplus unskilled labor and (2) when city slums begin to be dominated by second-generation and third-generation natives of the cities. Meanwhile, the nonindustrial poor exist within American society but are not of it.

SOME SIGNIFICANT LITERATURE ON ECONOMIC DIFFERENTIATION

Theodore Caplow and Reece J. McGee, *The Academic Marketplace,* New York: Basic Books, 1958. The authors studied 237 professorial vacancies that occurred in the liberal-arts departments of 10 major American universities between June 30, 1954, and July 1, 1956. They were concerned with professors as *employees* in a competitive labor market rather than with their academic duties or achievements. Hence the book concentrates on the motivations of the professor for leaving his position and the motives of department chairmen and other recruiters in searching for replacements. Prestige considerations are perceived as of major importance to both the professor and the recruiters, especially at leading universities. Thus a department is often more interested in hiring a well-known scholar, who adds to the reputation of the university, than a good teacher. Although professors are paid to teach, they are evaluated mainly on the basis of research contributions (publications); hence professors preoccupied with career advancement are tempted to put more of their energies into research than into teaching. At secondary universities, teaching ability, service to the university, and acceptability to the local community are weighed more heavily in the evaluation of professors both for initial recruitment and for promotion. For a more general treatment of the labor market, see Gertrude Bancroft, *The American Labor Force: Its Growth and Changing Composition,* New York: Wiley, 1958, one of a series of studies of the 1950 census sponsored by the Social Science Research Council.

Conference on Economic Progress, *Poverty and Deprivation in the United States: The Plight of Two-fifths of a Nation,* Washington: Conference on Economic Progress, 1962. Certain groups within the American population are more likely than others to have inadequate incomes: non-whites, the disabled, the aged, the unemployed, the farm population, the poorly educated, the unskilled, families headed by women (broken homes), and families with teen-age heads. This monograph estimates that in 1960 38 million Americans lived in poverty and 39 million in some deprivation out of a total population of 180 million people. Persons in social categories vulnerable to poverty are likely to live in blighted areas; low income usually forces families and even un-attached individuals to accept substandard housing in the less desirable neighborhoods. In 1960 out of 58 million dwelling units in the United States, about 9½ million were seriously deficient according to Census Bureau standards—5 million inside large metropolitan areas and 4½ million outside. These social and ecological concentrations of low-income people provide a favorable climate for the development and maintenance of the culture of poverty. For a comprehensive view of the sociology as well as the economics of poverty, see Margaret S. Gordon, Ed., *Poverty in America,* San Francisco, Calif: Chandler, 1965.

William J. Goode, "Community within a Community: The Professions," *American Sociological Review,* Vol. 22, April 1957, pp. 194-200. Occupational roles are a feature of industrial societies. Professions are high-prestige occupations having some of the characteristics of communities, although not a physical center: (1) Members of a profession have a sense of identity and share common values. (2) Within the scope of professional action, members communicate by means of a common language only partially comprehensible to outsiders. (3) The profession has power over its members. (4) "Though it does not produce the next generation biologically, it does so socially through its control over the selection of professional trainees, and through its training processes it sends these recruits through an adult socialization process." Furthermore, like a community a profession exists within and depends on a larger society, and this circumstance gives rise to interesting sociological problems of the relationship between the contained community and the society.

Clark Kerr, "Changing Social Structures," in Wilbert E. Moore and Arnold S. Feldman, Eds., *Labor Commitment and Social Change in Developing Areas,* New York: Social Science Research Council, 1960. This article interprets industrialism as a new way of life toward which all underdeveloped societies are moving. Four stages of commitment of workers to industrial life may be distinguished: In Stage 1 the *uncommitted* worker takes a job in order to earn money for a specific purpose; when he accumulates enough, he quits. In Stage 2 the *semicommitted* worker has a regular job, but he also maintains connections with a nonindustrial way of life, usually in rural areas. In Stage 3 the *committed* worker has severed his connections with his rural or tribal roots; he is permanently resident in a city, and it is not unusual for his wife to enter the labor market. In Stage 4 the *overcommitted* worker has tied himself so closely to a particular occupation or to a particular employer that he cannot easily move to another job. Kerr concludes that differences in cultural backgrounds are less important to an understanding of the process of industrial commitment than might be supposed.". . . The future into which workers are going is much more determinative of what happens to them than the past from which they are drawn."

Elliot Liebow, *Tally's Corner: A Study of Negro Streetcorner Men,* Boston: Little, Brown, 1967. This field study of two dozen black men who "hang" on a street corner in the Washington, D.C., ghetto depicts the way of life of people marginal to urban industrial society. Although an anthropologist himself, Liebow does not subscribe to the view that the ghetto is a "self-contained, self-generating, self-sustaining" culture. He thinks of it rather as an adaptation — and a painful one — to failure in the larger society:

> Although he wants to get married, he hedges on his commitment from the very beginning because he is afraid, not of marriage itself, but of his own ability to carry out his responsibilities as husband and father. His own father failed and had to "cut out," and the men he knows who have been or are married have also failed or are in the process of doing so. He has no evidence that he will fare better than they and much evidence that he will not. However far he has gone in school he is illiterate or almost so; however many jobs he has had or hard he has worked, he is essentially unskilled. Armed with models who have failed, convinced of his own worthlessness, illiterate and unskilled, he enters marriage and the job market with the smell of failure all around him. Jobs are only intermittently available. They are almost always menial, sometimes hard, and never pay enough to support a family (pages 210-211).

For a comparative perspective on a submerged minority in a very different society (Japan), see George DeVos and Hiroshi Wagatsuma, *Japan's Invisible Race: Caste in Culture and Personality,* Berkeley: University of California Press, 1966. An interesting feature of the Japanese caste problem is that the pariah group is not racially distinct from the majority.

C. Wright Mills, *White Collar: The American Middle Classes,* New York: Oxford University Press, 1951. The United States has experienced a decline in the relative proportion of the labor force composed of small manufacturers, retailers, farmers, and self-employed professionals and an increase in the relative proportion of executives, salaried professionals, salespeople, and office workers. This new middle class is distinguished from other strata not only by a generally middle position with reference to income, prestige, and power but also by the fact that it works with symbols and with other people. Mills interprets the situation of white-collar people as being rather bleak, but this interpretation rests on certain value judgments of the author; other reputable sociologists disagree with him. This summary is based on a review by Paul K. Hatt, *American Sociological Review,* Vol. 16, October 1951, pp. 727-728.

William Peterson, *Population,* New York: Macmillan, 1961. The culture of poverty referred to in the text has qualitative aspects not reflected in birth rates, death rates, migration statistics, marriage and divorce rates, sex and age composition, and so forth. Nevertheless, demographic data are the quantitative expression of sociological, social psychological, and cultural factors; hence such relatively precise indices of the culture of poverty or of the culture of the industrial in-group should be consulted wherever possible. To take advantage of opportunities to use demographic data for index purposes one must understand demographic *concepts* and the *sources* of population data — as well as some substantive facts about preindustrial, industrializing, and fully industrialized populations. Peterson's textbook is an excellent treatment of these topics.

W. G. Runciman, *Relative Deprivation and Social Justice: A Study of Attitudes to Social Inequality in Twentieth-Century England,* Berkeley: University of California Press, 1966. Subjective feelings of satisfaction in a population do not correlate perfectly with objective indicants of deprivation. This book attempts to explain these discrepancies in twentieth-century England. A historical analysis of the period between 1918 and 1962 shows that various circumstances reduced the likelihood that manual workers would compare their wealth and income with that of the non-manual stratum and therefore did not feel *economically* deprived. Nor did they feel *politically* deprived because, although they had less power than the nonmanual stratum, they recognized that the Labour Party was giving increasingly effective representation to their interests. They did, however, feel *socially* deprived—despite the objective decrease of status distinctions in British society: ". . . [A]s greater equality was attained, the awareness of such inequalities as remained was heightened" (page 113). In short, the historical analysis generated a prediction that feelings of relative deprivation would be most evident with regard to status. This prediction was tested in a 1962 survey of 1415 respondents who constituted a stratified random sample drawn from voting lists in England and Wales. The findings of this survey throw considerable light on the relationship between institutionalized inequalities and awareness and resentment of them.

Max Weber, *General Economic History,* New York: Collier, 1961. When Max Weber died in 1920, he had just finished giving a course of lectures on economic history. His colleagues decided that his insights should not be lost, and they put together this volume from his fragmentary notes and from the lecture notes of his students. The last section of the book, "The Origin of Modern Capitalism," is particularly interesting to sociologists. It discusses not only the economic and political conditions necessary for the development of capitalism, but also "the capitalist spirit." Weber denies that capitalists are as rapacious as, say, oriental traders. He argues that the acquisitive impulse is disciplined under capitalism so as to produce "a regulated economic life with the economic impulse functioning within bounds." The early entrepreneurs possessed some of the ascetic inclinations and the religious anxieties of monks, but unlike monks they labored in the world. The concept of a "calling"—an occupation to which one felt called by God—reflected these motivations.

Harold L. Wilensky and Charles N. LeBeaux, *Industrial Society and Social Welfare: The Impact of Industrialization on the Supply and Organization of Social Welfare Services in the United States,* New York: Russell Sage Foundation, 1958. Industrial development has led to changes in the character of the welfare problems in advanced societies. In addition to an over-all discussion of American conceptions of social welfare and the scope of existing welfare programs, the authors consider in detail two fields, family services and agencies designed to cope with juvenile delinquency. They also deal with social work as a profession and with the social agency as a bureaucratic organization. This summary is based on a review by Zena Smith Blau, *American Sociological Review,* Vol. 23, August 1958, pp. 461-462.

THE URBAN COMMUNITY

Constantine Manos—Magnum

Every interactive system must have boundaries defining who is and who is not a member. Sometimes these social boundaries coincide with spatial boundaries, as in a Sicilian village. Under modern conditions of rapid transportation and communication, however, membership in an interactive system is not narrowly circumscribed by spatial limits. As noted in Chapter 2, the American Sociological Association is an interactive system even though members, scattered through 50 states and Canada, are not in continuous physical contact. In an industrial society the local **community** remains a spatially bounded interactive system, but the local community has become less important because of the proliferation of interactive systems less rooted in geography: schools, factories, political organizations, voluntary associations like the American Red Cross.

The territorial location of persons and their activities structures interactive systems in special ways. Hence a community, though it must cope with the four basic problems—adaptation to its environment, socialization of new members, policy making, and mutual integration of its members—also imposes a distinctive meaning on both members and nonmembers. Territorial location implies a *place* where role players interact and therefore a place where they are especially vulnerable to social pressure.[1] Unlike interactive systems lacking a definite territorial location, the community has access to the person of a member in a physical sense and on an ongoing basis. Neighbors are people who cannot be avoided because they are physically *there*. The ability of a community to influence the attitudes and the behavior of its members depends to an extent on their mutual entrapment in a territorial location. Although members of industrial societies change their places of residence rather easily from one community to another, they ultimately reside somewhere. The word "entrapment" may exaggerate their bondage to a *particular* residence, but it correctly emphasizes the fact of their spatial location.

The ability of a community to influence the attitudes and behavior of its members rests also on its relation to government. Governments are concerned with policy making, and policies cannot be effective unless they can be enforced. Since enforcement depends on a territorial jurisdiction within which coercion is used if necessary, the political process always operates in a demarcated area. Must the jurisdiction of a unit of government coincide with the territorial base of a community? Not necessarily, but there is a strong tendency for it to do so. The reason for this tendency is that government, though reserving the right to utilize force in the area of its jurisdiction, is most effective if its authority is recognized as *legitimate* by those bound by its decisions. (Chapter 9 will discuss the topic of the legitimation of political authority at greater length.) On the national level, the failure of the Greek majority and the Turkish minority on the island of Cyprus to form one community underlies recurrent governmental breakdown. On local levels also, effective government

---

[1] Talcott Parsons, "The Principal Structures of Community," in *Structure and Process in Modern Societies*, Glencoe, Ill.: Free Press, 1960. Chap. 8.

is difficult to maintain without the consent of the bulk of the governed. By definition, a community is an area whose population demonstrates a willingness to live together within a framework of rules. Political boundaries tend to follow the consensual boundaries of an existing community. When that happens, the territorial base of a community is not mere geography; it is the jurisdiction within which political power can be mobilized to support the moral order. One of the serious problems of modern urban communities is that they embrace so large an area and so heterogeneous a population that they lack a unitary community base for political organization. This is what students of municipal government mean when they cry that New York City may be "ungovernable."[2]

Despite the long list of urban problems, large cities somehow survive. Insofar as a city is a viable interactive system, it must cope with the four organizational requirements of interactive systems. Since the form that these organizational requirements take in the large city is unique, let us examine the specific social structures developed by the city to fulfill the basic organizational requirements.[3]

1. *Adaptation.* Since the city is, by definition, a densely populated area, city residents cannot raise crops to provide their own food. Therefore, a basic adaptive problem of the city is to persuade or force residents of rural areas to donate food and other raw materials. The human race took a long time to solve this problem. Only comparatively recently—between 6000 and 4000 B.C.—did the invention of the ox-drawn plow and wheeled cart, the sailboat, metallurgy, irrigation, and the domestication of new plants make possible an agricultural surplus large enough to support a population concentration of nonfarmers.[4] From then on, the inventions facilitating larger settlements—writing and accountancy, bronze, rudimentary science, a solar calendar, bureaucracy—were probably developed in cities and towns. There were technological limitations on the size of these early cities; before iron came into use in Asia Minor about 1300 B.C. it took 50 to 90 cultivators to support one city dweller. Transportation and storage of the agricultural surplus were problems. Conditions of public health made city life perilous. Thus cities developed 7000 years ago, but they were small by modern standards, and only 1 or 2 per cent of the population of the ancient world lived in them. The true urban society did not emerge until the nineteenth century, as Kingsley Davis points out:[5]

---

[2] Wallace Sayre and Herbert Kaufman, *Governing New York City,* New York: Russell Sage Foundation, 1960.

[3] The analysis in the following paragraphs is heavily indebted to John E. Bebout and Harry C. Bredemeier, "American Cities as Social Systems," *Journal of the American Institute of Planners,* Vol. 29, May 1963, pp. 64-76.

[4] Kingsley Davis, "The Origin and Growth of Urbanization in the World," *American Journal of Sociology,* Vol. 60, March 1955, pp. 429-437, is the source of the historical data on urbanism contained in the rest of the paragraph.

[5] Davis, "Origin and Growth of Urbanization," p. 432.

The cities of Mesopotamia, India, and Egypt, of Persia, Greece, and Rome, had all been tied to an economy that was primarily agricultural, where handicraft played at best a secondary role and where the city was still attempting to supplement its economic weakness with military strength, to command its sustenance rather than to buy it honestly. In western Europe, starting at the zero point, the development of cities not only reached the stage that the ancient world had achieved but kept going after that. It kept going on the basis of improvements in agriculture and transport, the opening of new lands and new trade routes, and, above all, the rise in productive activity, first in highly organized handicraft and eventually in a revolutionary new form of production—the factory run by machinery and fossil fuel. The transformation thus achieved in the nineteenth century was the true urban revolution, for it meant not only the rise of a few scattered towns and cities but the appearance of genuine urbanization, in the sense that a substantial portion of the population lived in towns and cities.

Contemporary urban communities are better adapted to the *physical* environment than the city of the ancient world. But their adaptation to the *social* environment is more precarious. The environment of a contemporary city includes sidewalks, buildings, parks, sewers, the smog-filled air, corporations, trade unions, professional associations—and also the suburban communities surrounding the city and their resident populations. A considerable part of the adaptive effort of the city is applied to the physical environment: to importing vast amounts of food and raw materials, to maintaining streets, to purifying water, to eliminating sewage, to preventing the level of sulfur dioxide in the air from killing off the population. Some adaptive effort goes into cajoling or persuading residents of suburban communities to take jobs in the city's industries despite morning and evening commuting—and also to shop in the city's stores and to utilize the city's recreational facilities. Some adaptive effort is expended on government officials of suburban communities because their cooperation is necessary for the solution of metropolitan problems like water and air pollution, traffic control, and crime. One aspect of the financial crisis of American cities is their weak bargaining position vis-à-vis the populations and the governments of environing suburbs. The resources that the city has available to motivate voluntary cooperation are usually insufficient to the task. The result is often failure to adapt to the suburban environment; a symptom of this failure is a flight of families and businesses that the city needs for financial and social health.

Governmental agencies deal with many of the adaptive problems of the city: public health, zoning, sewage disposal, economic development. But businessmen are also concerned with the adaptation of the city. Manufacturing and trade with rural areas and with other urban communities are conducted in the United States mainly by business firms.

2. *Socialization.* The school system and organized programs of adult education constitute the main formal socialization structure of cities as well as of rural and suburban areas of contemporary societies. The city has, however, a unique problem: the socialization of rural migrants into the industrial

Ken Heyman

culture. In industrial societies population growth is greater in metropolitan areas than in rural areas, despite a higher birth rate in the rural areas, because of the endless flow of migrants (largely young adults) from nonmetropolitan areas attracted by the economic opportunities and the glamor of the cities. These young adults, brought up in rural areas relatively isolated from industrial culture, need to be socialized anew for industrial occupations and urban living patterns. Formal retraining programs are rare. (One such program, the American Indian Relocation Program of the Bureau of Indian Affairs, U. S. Department of the Interior, was discussed in Chapter 5.) Nevertheless, city people in various roles—social workers, policemen, foremen, building superintendents, neighbors—informally socialize the newcomers. Immigrants were socialized for life in their adopted country in the same way during the era of large-scale international migration.[6]

[6] Oscar Handlin, *The Uprooted: The Epic Story of the Great Migrations That Made the American People,* Boston: Little, Brown, 1951.

Human migrants to the city obviously require socialization. But corporate and governmental newcomers require socialization too. When the national headquarters of a corporation moves from El Paso to New York City, its relation to the community changes. Successful businessmen are expected to contribute their time and talent to community chest drives and to voluntary associations in small communities as well as in the metropolis, but technical competence is more necessary as the scale of the community enlarges. The community chest drive is more complicated in New York than in El Paso; participation must be on a more specialized basis.

3. *Policy Making.* Decisions must be made regarding the allocation of the city's resources. Should education receive increased budgetary support at the cost of curtailing police and fire protection? Should welfare recipients receive more money even if this means an increased tax on retail sales? Who makes these decisions on behalf of the city? Some policies are made by decision makers in more inclusive jurisdictional units—in the United States by federal and state officials. Other decisions are made locally by elected or appointed city officials. Still others are made by influential persons in the community although they may not hold formal offices. Robert Dahl studied the initiation or vetoing of policies in New Haven, Connecticut, on such matters as public education and urban redevelopment; he concluded that the decision-making group, though small compared to the total population, shifts appreciably from issue to issue.[7] Chapter 9 will return to the topic of policy-making roles in terms of the political process in entire societies. On the level of the local community it is enough to keep in mind (1) that policy making is a basic process in all interactive systems and (2) that the city, being an interactive system, must have policy-making roles, formal and informal.

4. *Integration.* Although all interactive systems must check tendencies to disunity, the city faces this problem in an especially tangible way. A geographic entity, the city must be concerned about traffic flow, about telephone and postal service, and (ultimately) about the speed and convenience with which people can get from one location to another. The early twentieth-century sociologists at the University of Chicago were right: whatever else the city is, it is people and their activities spread over a land surface. Movement of people and communication of messages between them, even with the help of electronic equipment, takes time and costs money. Thus the city must expend resources to reduce traffic congestion, to promote public transportation, and to maintain the flow of communications. Without a viable transportation system a city obviously cannot function as an integrated community. Without the communications media—radio, television, newspapers, magazines, telephone service—residents and commuters to the city would not receive the inputs of information they require to play

---

[7] Robert A. Dahl, *Who Governs? Democracy and Power in an American City,* New Haven, Conn.: Yale University Press, 1961.

their roles. The continuing operation of the city as a unified interactive system depends as much on citizens obtaining data concerning movies and other cultural events, business opportunities, apartment rentals, funerals, and background information about public affairs, as it does on transportation. On June 30, 1945, the deliverymen of eight major New York City newspapers went on strike, thereby giving sociologists the opportunity to observe by their absence how newspapers help to integrate a large literate community.[8]

The integrative problems of the large city are only partially solved when the transportation and communications systems are reasonably adequate. The free flow of people and messages does not guarantee solidarity of the community. While it has proved possible to mobilize loyalty to the national state, it is harder to develop emotional commitments to the large city. To give one's life for one's country may be noble, but to offer the "supreme sacrifice" for Elizabeth, New Jersey, sounds faintly ridiculous. As long as this is true, it will be easier to integrate a small community or a national society than to integrate a large city.

A case can be made for treating urbanism as coextensive with contemporary society. Industrial populations have been living in an urban society for some time. Fifty-eight per cent of the population of England and Wales, admittedly in the vanguard of urban development, lived in cities of 20,000 and over as early as 1901.[9] Demographers predict that the world may well become "as urbanized as the most urbanized countries today—with perhaps 85-90 per cent of the population living in cities and towns of 5,000 or more and practicing urban occupations."[10] On the other hand, even in advanced industrial countries differences remain in the problems and the ways of life of central cities, suburbs, and rural areas. The cultural gap has narrowed, but it has not disappeared yet, and it probably will never completely disappear. Even in a still more urbanized world, the city will remain the seedbed of innovation, the symbol of glamor, the locus of social problems, and the center of power.

THE BLURRING OF RURAL-URBAN DIFFERENCES IN CONTEMPORARY SOCIETIES

Industrialization of agriculture has tied together the rural and urban economies. Commercial farming is a business resembling urban businesses in its consciousness of costs, its orientation to the market, its investment in capital

---

[8] Bernard Berelson, "What 'Missing the Newspaper' Means," in Paul Lazarsfeld and Frank N. Stanton, Eds., *Communications Research, 1948-1949,* New York: Harper, 1949, pp. 111-129.

[9] Davis, "Origins and Growth of Urbanism," p. 433.

[10] Davis, "Origins and Growth of Urbanism," p. 437.

equipment, and even in its use of modern accounting. One author has called commercial farms "factories in the field," and others talk about "agribusiness" instead of "agriculture."[11] The average size of commercial farms in the United States is growing. In 1920 the average size was 147 acres; in 1968, 369 acres.[12] Small farms cannot use power machinery efficiently; economic pressure forces the small farmer to sell out or expand. From 1920 to 1968 the number of farms *decreased* from 6,518,000 to 3,059,000 and the proportion of the American population living on farms decreased from 30.1 per cent to 5.4 per cent.[13] Over a 30-year period, however, the average value of farmland and buildings (not including equipment) *increased* from $7313 to $35,578.[14] The United States and Canada are unusual cases; these countries contained vast open spaces during much of their recent history. None of the urban industrial societies of Western Europe has been able to utilize agriculture power machinery on the same scale.[15] And the problem of fractionated, inefficient farms is even more acute in the developing countries. In 1968, 5 per cent of the American work force was able to feed a total population of 200 million people—as well as to produce a politically embarrassing food surplus. The swift urbanization of the United States cannot be fully understood without an awareness of the special circumstances facilitating the industrialization of agriculture.

The industrialization of agriculture in the United States helps to explain the narrowing of the difference between the style of life of city and farm families. Rural populations in all of the urban industrial societies are deeply involved in the money economy, but the integration of rural and urban economies is closer in the United States, thus accounting for some of the increased homogeneity. For instance, not only has rural electrification eliminated such laborious tasks as pumping water and milking cows by hand; it has also enabled farm families to listen to the same radio programs and see the same television programs as urban families.[16] Good roads not only enable farmers to transport their crops speedily to distant markets; they also make urban recreational and educational facilities accessible. Farm families dispose of their incomes much as city people do. Like city people, they talk on telephones and ride in airplanes. They live in the same culture.

[11] Carey McWilliams, *Factories in the Field: The Story of Migratory Farm Labor in California,* Boston: Little, Brown, 1939; John H. Davis and Roy A. Goldberg, *A Concept of Agribusiness,* Boston: Division of Research, Graduate School of Business Administration, Harvard University, 1957.

[12] Bureau of the Census, *Statistical Abstract of the United States: 1968,* Washington, D.C.: Government Printing Office, 1958, p. 594.

[13] Bureau of the Census, *Statistical Abstract of the U.S.: 1968, p. 594.*

[14] Bureau of the Census, *Statistical Abstract of the United States: 1962,* Washington, D.C.: Government Printing Office, 1962, p. 608.

[15] Fred Cottrell, *Energy and Society: The Relationship between Energy, Social Change, and Economic Development,* New York: McGraw-Hill, 1955, pp. 110-165, especially p. 128.

[16] U. S. Department of Agriculture, "Farming in the United States," Agricultural Information Bulletin No. 246, Washington, D.C.: Government Printing Office, 1961.

The line between rural and urban has been blurred in yet another way in urban industrial societies: by the emergence of suburbs. From one point of view, suburbs are the inevitable consequence of urbanization. An urbanized society cannot develop without booming city growth. Such growth usually means spilling over beyond original political boundaries. Even with high-rise apartment houses, there are limits to population density. From this point of view, then, suburbs are political accidents. They represent urban growth occurring outside the boundaries of the city. Had the annexation of outlying areas kept pace with the functional growth of cities, there would be less need to talk about "suburbs." However, suburbs emerge for another reason: improved transportation and communication makes a larger area accessible to the central business district. This accessibility of the hinterland necessitates greater transportation costs, but industrial societies are affluent societies. Many people are willing to pay the cost in time and money which commutation involves in order to escape high population density. Suburbia is a compromise between urban work and rural residence. In the United States, for example, large cities are not merely increasing the scope of their influence over larger and larger areas; the population density at their centers is *decreasing*.[17] Cities are not as concentrated as they once were; they sprawl. For instance, Boston's population decreased from 801,444 in 1950 to 697,197 in 1960, a loss of 13 per cent.[18] Most of these people fled to communities in the Boston commuting zone: to Cambridge, Chelsea, Everett, Lynn, Malden, Medford, Melrose, Quincy, Revere, Waltham, or Woburn.

In1950, the Census Bureau defined 168 population clusters called **standard metropolitan areas** to measure the new kind of sprawling urbanism emanating from large cities. A standard metropolitan area consists of one or more central cities containing at least 50,000 population and surrounding built-up areas in close economic and social communication with the central city (or cities). By 1960, the Census Bureau identified 212 metropolitan areas containing nearly 113 million persons, out of a total American population of 180 million.[19] While the American population as a whole rose 18.5 per cent between 1950 and 1960, metropolitan population increased 26.4 per cent, whereas the suburban segments of metropolitan areas alone increased 48.6 per cent.[20]

Despite the blurring of differences between rural and urban areas as a result of common participation in industrial development, some distinctive characteristics remain, even in the United States where **metropolitan dom-**

[17] Amos H. Hawley, *The Changing Shape of Metropolitan America: Deconcentration since 1950,* Glencoe, Ill.: Free Press, 1956.

[18] Bureau of the Census, *Statistical Abstract of the United States: 1962,* Washington, D.C.: Government Printing Office, 1962, p. 13.

[19] Bureau of the Census, *Statistical Abstract of the U.S.: 1962,* p. 13.

[20] Bureau of the Census, *Statistical Abstract of the U.S.: 1962,* pp. 12-13.

inance is far advanced because cities lead and rural areas follow.[21] Table 7.1 demonstrates the concentration of college-educated males in urban areas. Whereas 22.7 per cent of urban white males, 25 years old or older, had completed at least one year of college in 1960, only 7.4 per cent of white males living on farms had done so. Nonwhite males were much less likely to have completed one or more years of college than white males, and nonwhite males were even more concentrated in urban areas than white males in 1960. The chances were better than 1 in 11 in cities that a nonwhite male had completed some college, but only about 1 in 59 on farms. Other differences between urban and rural communities persist. Women are less likely to seek gainful employment outside of the home and birth rates are higher in rural areas.[22] Cities have a preponderance of females and rural areas a preponderance of males.[23] Rural farm people are much more likely to have lived in the same house for five years or more than rural nonfarm or urban people.[24] Nonetheless, these are differences of degree; in the urban society, rural communities are *not* isolated; they respond to the influences arising in urban areas.

THE URBANISM STIMULATED BY INDUSTRIALISM

Although the urban society emerged only after industrialization, it would be an oversimplification to regard it as arising from industrialization only. Preindustrial cities have been trade centers, centers of handicrafts, centers of administration, educational centers, fortresses, and religious communities.[25] In industrial societies, too, some cities are organized around functions unrelated to industrial activities, for example, resort cities.[26] Furthermore, the underdeveloped countries of the contemporary world contain many large cities. Three-quarters of the world's population lives in underdeveloped countries, and these countries have slightly more people living in cities of 100,000 or more than do the industrialized nations.[27] To put it the other way around, of the

[21] "Metropolitan dominance" refers to the fact that a large territory outside the central city is directly under the influence of the metropolitan center for trade and employment. See Donald J. Bogue, "Urbanism in the United States, 1950," *American Journal of Sociology,* Vol. 60, March 1955, pp. 471-486.

[22] Bureau of the Census, *United States Census of Population: 1960, United States Summary,* Washington, D.C.: Government Printing Office, 1962, pp. 212, 214.

[23] Bureau of the Census, *U.S. Census: 1960, Summary,* p. 200.

[24] Bureau of the Census, *U.S. Census: 1960, Summary,* p. 204.

[25] Gideon Sjoberg, "The Preindustrial City," *American Journal of Sociology,* Vol. 60, March 1955, pp. 438-445.

[26] Albert J. Reiss, Jr., "Functional Specialization of Cities," in Hatt and Reiss, *Cities and Society: The Revised Reader in Urban Sociology,* Glencoe, Ill.: Free Press, 1957.

[27] Kingsley Davis and Hilda Hertz Golden, "Urbanization and the Development of Pre-Industrial Areas," *Economic Development and Cultural Change,* Vol. 3, October 1954.

TABLE 7.1

Comparison of Urban, Rural Nonfarm and Rural Farm Males, Age 25 and Over, Who Completed One or More Years of College, United States, 1960

Residence	White Males (Per Cent)	Nonwhite Males (Per Cent)
Urban	22.7	9.5
Rural nonfarm	13.4	3.7
Rural farm	7.4	1.7

Source: Bureau of the Census, *United States Census of Population: 1960, United States Summary, General Social and Economic Characteristics,* Final Report PC(1)-1C, Washington, D.C.: Government Printing Office, 1962, p. 208.

897 cities in the world with more than 100,000 population, only 434 are in industrial societies. But the large cities of preindustrial societies and the large cities of industrial societies are fundamentally different. In a preindustrial society the city is the headquarters for a minority of the population, sometimes a powerful minority. In an industrial society a majority of the population lives in cities, which serve as the cultural center and exemplify basic societal values.

Until the Industrial Revolution, cities constituted an occasional clustering of population in essentially rural societies. With industrialization came the *urbanized society* in which clustered population is the dominant pattern. Figure 7.1 documents this development in the United States. Of course, many parts of the contemporary world are still preindustrial ("underdeveloped").

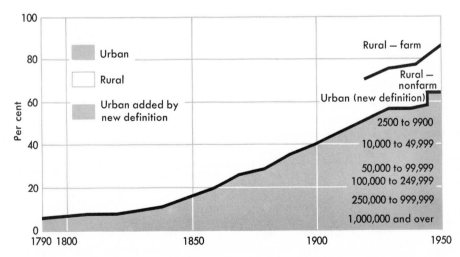

FIGURE 7.1 **Population of the United States by size of place of habitation, 1790–1950.** Source: Donald J. Bogue, "Urbanism in the United States, 1950," *American Journal of Sociology,* Vol. 60, March 1955, p. 472.

This circumstance provides an opportunity to examine the relationship between *degree* of industrialization and *degree* of urbanization. Table 7.2 shows that the *lower* the percentage of the gainfully employed males in agriculture, the *larger* the percentage of the population in cities of over 100,000 population. This is not a tautology. Industrialization makes an impact in rural areas, too. The tremendous increase in productivity per farm worker results from the application of power-driven machinery, from scientific methods of fertilizing the soil, rotating crops, and checking erosion, and from more efficient farm management. Conceivably, industrialization could occur without much clumping of population. Workers not needed for industrialized farming might remain in rural areas in manufacturing or other nonfarming occupations. This has not happened. Of the 17,513,086 manufacturing workers enumerated in the 1960 census in the United States, 13,348,151 lived in cities.[28] And a considerable proportion of the remaining manufacturing workers, though technically "rural nonfarm," probably lived in the suburban fringes of metropolitan areas.[29] Modern industrialism, accompanied as it is by technological advances in transportation and communication as well as by great increases in productivity, created the *urbanized society*.

The Relative Pace of Urbanization and Industrialization. When sociologists examine the history of urbanization in Western Europe and the United States, they relate it to economic development. They do not mean, of course, that all urbanites are engaged in manufacturing or that all manufacturing is done in cities. Nor do they mean that the fabrication of goods is more crucial to an industrial society than the wide variety of activities that develop concomitantly: transportation, communication, public utilities, wholesale and retail trade, banking, insurance, real estate, public administration, health, education, and other professional services. As a matter of fact, while a predominantly manufacturing city like Manchester, England, could grow fairly large, the real giants (New York, London, Paris) were also commercial, financial, and administrative centers. Nevertheless, the major impetus for urban growth in the Western world for the past three centuries has been industrial development. Urban populations grew because rural people were attracted to urban areas by occupational opportunities. When sociologists concern themselves with urbanization in the underdeveloped countries of Asia, Africa, and South America, however, they face a new situation: a larger flow of population into cities than is necessary to keep up with economic growth or increased administrative functions.

This new situation arose largely because the underdeveloped countries

---

[28] Bureau of the Census, *United States Census of Population: 1960, United States Summary,* Washington, D.C.: Government Printing Office, 1962, p. 221. The Census Bureau definition of the urban population is complicated. Essentially it includes persons living in incorporated places of 2500 population or more and also persons living in the densely settled fringe of large cities.

[29] Vincent H. Whitney, "Changes in the Rural-Nonfarm Population, 1930–1950," *American Sociological Review,* Vol. 25, June 1960, pp. 363-368.

TABLE 7.2

Degree of Urbanization in World's Countries and Territories Classified by Degree of Agriculturalism

Percentage of Gainfully Occupied Males in Agriculture	Number of Countries	Percentage of Population in Cities of 100,000-plus
0-19	11	32.3
20-29	11	23.6
30-39	7	23.2
40-49	7	21.9
50-59	16	17.7
60-69	17	8.9
70-plus	86	6.3

Source: Kingsley Davis and Hilda Hertz Golden, "Urbanization and the Development of Pre-Industrial Areas," *Economic Development and Cultural Change,* Vol. 3, October 1954, p. 8.

have been strongly influenced by Western industrial countries. For instance, during the nineteenth century, when Burma was politically as well as economically dominated by Great Britain, the city of Rangoon grew because it served as an economic link between Burma and the world market.[30] Imported European manufactured products and Burmese raw materials exported in exchange passed through Rangoon. Shanghai, Hong Kong, Karachi, and Djakarta also flourished because they served as centers of Western influence.[31] For similar reasons, swift urbanization is now taking place in Central and West Africa. By 1950 Nairobi had grown to 119,000 population, Leopoldville to 211,000, Lagos to 230,000, Dakar to 209,000, and Accra to 136,000.[32] "This sudden juxtaposition of twentieth-century cities and extremely primitive cultures (virtually stone-age in their organization and technology) gives rise in some respects to a sharper rural-urban contrast than can be found anywhere in the world."[33]

In short, some underdeveloped countries are undergoing more rapid urbanization than is necessary for the level of economic differentiation. This is partly because of the pull of Western consumption standards that are visible but not easily attainable in the cities and partly because of the impoverishment of the rural population.[34] Demographers have pointed out, for example, that 19.3 per cent of the Egyptian population lived in cities of 100,000 population or more in 1947—about the same proportion of the population as in France, Switzerland,

[30] Bert F. Hoselitz, *Sociological Aspects of Economic Growth,* Glencoe, Ill.: Free Press, 1960, pp. 204-205.

[31] Hoselitz, *Economic Growth,* p. 223.

[32] Davis and Golden, "Urbanization and Development," p. 21.

[33] Davis and Golden, "Urbanization and Development," p. 20.

[34] Hoselitz, *Economic Growth,* p. 202.

and Sweden, which are far more industrialized.[35] The Egyptian system of absentee landlords living in the cities heightens the contrast between rural and urban standards of living and contributes to what may be called "overurbanization." A similar explanation accounts for overurbanization in Latin America. The Spanish and Portuguese settlers of Latin America regarded life in the port cities as providing contact with the center of civilization, Europe.[36] They regarded life in the rural interior of the South American continent as culturally barren and physically uncomfortable. Those owning land in the interior lived in the cities through choice, attracting retainers to serve them. Thus Latin American cities have been population magnets for reasons unrelated to industrial development. Overurbanization, though historically understandable, is an example of societal maladaptation to the physical and cultural environment.

The Growth Pattern of Industrial Cities. *Advanced* industrial countries like Great Britain and the United States offer the best opportunities to study the growth process of modern cities. Cities like Manchester and Chicago developed gradually—as contrasted with the explosive growth of Buenos Aires or Johannesburg. In the decade following the First World War, sociologists from the University of Chicago theorized that the study of differential land use in the city would ultimately lead to an explanation of the changing character of neighborhoods as the city grew. They therefore mapped the distribution of various kinds of activities and events throughout the metropolis: the location of rooming houses and retail stores, cases of juvenile delinquency and mental illness, etc. They identified *competition for scarce space* as a natural tendency in the crowded city, and they demonstrated how the economic expression of this competition resulted in concentric rings with characteristic land uses.[37]

The inner ring, being most accessible to people from all parts of the city, is a favorable location for department stores and office buildings. Therefore, such business enterprises are willing to outbid all other potential users of land in the central business district. Anyone who did not mind the expense and congestion could still reside in a one-family house in Chicago's Loop. However, most people are not willing to pay ten times the taxes the same land use would cost on the fringe of the city. Rational economic calculation induces a flow of business enterprises into the central business district as it becomes accessible to an increasingly larger population. Simultaneously, it produces a flow of residential users out of the area. Thus, as the metropolis expands, so too does the central business district. To draw upon one of the ecological concepts which the Chicago sociologists borrowed from biology, business *invades* a residential area and, because business firms are willing to pay more than residential users for the available space, one land use succeeds another.

---

[35] Davis and Golden, "Urbanization and Development," p. 16.

[36] From Kingsley Davis and Ana Casis, "Urbanization in Latin America," *Milbank Memorial Fund Quarterly,* Vol. 24, April 1946, pp. 186–207.

[37] Robert E. Park, Ernest W. Burgess, and Roderick D. McKenzie, *The City,* Chicago: University of Chicago Press, 1925.

Invasion and **succession** take time, however. Between the anticipation of the expansion of the central business district and the actual razing of residential structures to make way for stores and offices is a period of uncertainty for the neighborhood in question. The land is beginning to appreciate in value, but the structures on it have no future; the owners hardly see the practicality of making repairs. This **zone in transition,** as the University of Chicago ecologists called it, is the second concentric ring; it is a **slum.** Into its deteriorating structures crowd those who can pay least for living space: first-generation immigrants and their families, ethnic minorities, alcoholics and petty criminals, elderly persons on small pensions.

The third concentric ring is the "zone of workingmen's homes." Unlike the zone in transition, it is *not* a slum; often it is the next step for those who have escaped from the slum and are on the way "up." Cheap rents and proximity to work are important considerations for the factory workers who live in this zone, but this is an area of thrift rather than of deprivation and public welfare. The fourth concentric ring is a middle-class residential zone, and the fifth concentric ring contains the spacious homes of affluent commuters.

The zonal theory developed by Ernest Burgess and his colleagues fitted large American cities fairly well. It was predicated on realistic assumptions for a free-enterprise industrial society:

1. Cities will continue to grow.
2. The centers of cities will continue to be accessible for these larger populations.
3. The real-estate market will continue to be the main mechanism determining land use.
4. Business uses will continue to outbid residential uses in the central neighborhoods of maximum accessibility.
5. The demand for spacious residential uses and the costs of commutation will continue to push the "best" residential neighborhoods into remote suburbs.

Although obviously irrelevant to preindustrial cities, these assumptions were reasonably descriptive of American society. On the other hand, the zonal theory was never fulfilled *in its entirety* even in American cities. For example, Beacon Hill remains a high-rent, high-prestige area in the heart of Boston instead of turning into a slum.[38] Some Bostonians are willing to pay the economic premium that residing on Beacon Hill requires. Some of the assumptions of the theory are less true today than when the theory was developed. Zoning laws and other planning efforts of local governments are interfering with the free play of the real-estate market. Moreover, as the metropolis spreads, centers develop in outlying areas, thus reducing the dominance of the main business district. Finally, as suburbia recedes further into the countryside and as commuting traffic becomes a more and more serious problem, élite residential neighbor-

[38] Walter Firey, *Land Use in Central Boston,* Cambridge, Mass.: Harvard University Press, 1947.

hoods have returned to the heart of the city. These changes may explain why a recent survey of the New York metropolitan area described the evolution of neighborhoods in terms only faintly reminiscent of the University of Chicago ecologists.[39]

One reason the concentric-zone theory does not seem to fit contemporary urban life is the continued explosive growth of metropolitan areas. Such explosive growth reduced to an absurdity preexisting city boundaries, but boundaries are political facts and difficult to redraw. Consequently most metroplitan areas are a political mess. A large American metropolitan area may include more than 1000 separate governments (including school districts). In 1950 the 162 Standard Metropolitan Areas of the United States included over 16,000 governmental units with powers to tax and spend.[40] The London metropolitan area included the City Corporation, London County, 28 metropolitan counties, 5 administrative counties, 42 boroughs, 15 urban districts, and 5 special authorities; the Rome metropolitan area included 100 communes.[41] If it were always possible for the central city to annex suburban rings as population moves toward the periphery, the zonal model would fit better. But suburban communities are jealous of their political autonomy. Especially in the United States, they are usually successful in resisting annexation. The result: administrative variations — including different property-tax structures and different zoning codes — are superimposed on the market factors affecting land use.

The political heterogeneity of metropolitan areas disrupts their community character and forces constituent political units to try to solve problems that can be handled only by a more inclusive interactive system. The slum problem illustrates this political failure. When University of Chicago ecologists described the emergence of the "zone in transition," they considered slums a temporary phenomenon, a **natural area** in the growing metropolis. Private enterprise could be counted on to raze blighted areas and build office buildings, factories, and department stores when the central business district expanded to service a larger metropolitan population. However, in the polycentric metropolitan area containing a multiplicity of governmental jurisdictions, the central business district need not expand much, certainly not proportionately to the growth of metropolitan population. Under these circumstances, blight can persist and spread, fostered rather than checked by the uncontrolled operation of the real estate market. These "natural" market forces are so powerful that massive urban renewal efforts are necessary to reverse the process of urban decay. Although the government of a city like Newark may be

---

[39] Edgar M. Hoover and Raymond Vernon, *Anatomy of a Metropolis: The Changing Distribution of People and Jobs within the New York Metropolitan Region,* Cambridge, Mass.: Harvard University Press, 1959, pp. 191-204.

[40] Philip M. Hauser, *Population Perspectives,* New Brunswick, N. J.: Rutgers University Press, 1960, p. 136; see also Robert C. Wood, *1400 Governments,* Cambridge, Mass.: Harvard University Press, 1961.

[41] Robert C. Wood, "Metropolitan Government," *International Encyclopedia of the Social Sciences,* Vol. 2, New York: Macmillan, p. 461.

eager to undertake such efforts, so much of Newark is low-revenue slum neighborhoods that the tax base cannot finance a massive campaign against blight.
Like Newark, many central cities cannot cope with deteriorating housing
without federal or state subsidies.

Such inability is partly the result of growth that has spilled beyond the original jurisdiction of the central city. The poor live mostly within the political
boundaries of the central city and the affluent dwell for the most part beyond
its taxing power. This American and Western European pattern is related to the
production orientation of cities in industrial societies. Manufacturing and commercial uses of the central city create employment opportunities that attract
the rural poor. Many new arrivals dwell in congested areas near their work and
avoid the costs of commutation. The occupational opportunities of the central
city, including financial and administrative activities, also attract the well
educated. However, professional and business workers come to the city for
occupational activities; they can afford to make their homes in the pleasanter
environment of suburbia. One result is that suburban parents who are concerned about the education of their own children are not forced to be concerned about the education of the children of slum dwellers in the central
city.[42] They are not part of the same educational system. In terms of the organizational requirements of a metropolitan area as an interactive system, ecological segregation of the affluent and the poor jeopardizes integration. The
prejudice and discrimination faced by ethnic minorities exacerbates integrative problems by concentrating the minorities in slums. Although Negroes
constituted only a small proportion of the suburban population of American
metropolitan areas in 1966 (4 per cent), they constituted 20 per cent of the
population of central cities.[43] When the suburbs are inhabited overwhelmingly
by whites and the slums mainly by blacks, solidarity of the metropolitan community becomes more difficult to achieve. Ethnic cleavages add to the political cleavages.

THE CULTURAL BASIS OF URBANISM

Even though it is difficult to describe the difference precisely, the character
of interaction in an urban society differs from interaction in rural societies.
Rural societies are more traditional, slower to change their patterns of interaction.[44] In addition, they tend to be oriented to the local community in con-

[42] James B. Conant, *Slums and Suburbs: A Commentary on Schools in Metropolitan Areas,*
New York: McGraw-Hill, 1961.

[43] National Advisory Commission on Civil Disorders, *Report,* New York: Bantam, 1968, p.
250.

[44] Robert Redfield, "The Folk Society," *American Journal of Sociology,* Vol. 52, January 1947,
pp. 293-308; Fredrik Barth, "Subsistence and Institutional System in a Norwegian Mountain
Valley," *Rural Sociology,* Vol. 17, March 1952, pp. 28-38.

trast to the more cosmopolitan orientation of urban societies. A city is inter-dependent with the rural area supplying it with food; a rural community, on the other hand, can be self-sufficient. Even in predominantly rural societies, then, cities are dramatic evidence of the economic and social division of labor. Urban societies push interdependence further; they represent an in-crease in the *scale* of social organization beyond the local community. The individual still interacts extensively within a limited space, a neighborhood, but he also has commitments to economic, political, educational, and relig-ious organizations that transcend the local community. Unlike the peasant in a preindustrial rural society, who has no alternative but to immerse himself psychologically in the world of the village, the individual in an urban society can orient himself toward the diffuse solidarities of family and neighborhood (primary groups) or toward narrower, more specialized relationships in more inclusive social structures (secondary groups). Primary groups are character-ized by intimate face-to-face association among members. They are primary in the sense that they form the "social nature and ideals of the individual" and also in the sense that the *first* groups the child joins are of this type: the fam-ily, the play group, the neighborhood.[45] The adult continues to crave the **diffuse roles** available in primary groups, and he finds them in his family, his friendship group, and his clique at work. However, the adult in contemporary societies also participates in the purposive, specialized, segmental associations afforded by **secondary groups.**

Cosmopolitanism and Individual Striving. Members of an urban society who orient themselves consistently toward primary groups may for compara-tive purposes be described as **local** types.[46] Those who orient themselves con-sistently toward secondary groups may be described as **cosmopolitans.** But the logic of urban societies is to induce most people to adopt both orientations at different times depending on social context. Within urban societies some com-munities contain more local types and others more cosmopolitans. Generally, the smaller, rural communities are more likely to contain locals than cosmo-politans, while cosmopolitan types are more likely to be represented in the metropolis. But research has demonstrated that some neighborhoods within the supposedly impersonal metropolis are in actuality a mosaic of local communi-ties permeated with primary group relationships. Herbert Gans coined the apt phrase "urban villagers" to describe the dominant orientations of the people in such communities.[47] Urban villagers (locals) are more prone than cosmopoli-tans to confine their interaction to the immediate neighborhood. They know more about the local community partly because of their more active participa-tion in it and partly because they have different sources of information. Locals are likely to rely for information on relatives, friends, and neighbors; cosmo-politans are more prone to rely on newspapers, radio and television, and na-

---

[45] Charles Horton Cooley, *Social Organization,* New York: Scribner's, 1929.

[46] Robert K. Merton "Patterns of Influence: Local and Cosmopolitan Influentials," in Merton, *Social Theory and Social Structure,* rev. ed., Glencoe, Ill.: Free Press, 1957.

[47] Herbert Gans, *The Urban Villagers,* New York: Free Press of Glencoe, 1962.

Marc Riboud — Magnum

tional magazines. Gresham Sykes explored the differential distribution of knowledge concerning the local community in a study of a small city on the periphery of the New York metropolitan area.[48] In the summer of 1949, Professor Sykes conducted a questionnaire survey of white male wage earners in Plainfield, New Jersey. The questionnaire consisted of three parts: a test of knowledge of the community, a set of questions dealing with political participation, and background information (income, occupation, education, length of residence in the community, home ownership, and so forth). On the basis of the background information some respondents could be categorized as being oriented to the local community by virtue of long residence, location of work in the community, children in the schools, and other characteristics. Others worked outside of the community, rented their homes, lived only a short time in Plainfield, and did not have children in the schools; these were presumably less oriented to the local community. Sykes found that *locals* had much greater community knowledge than *nonlocals* (cosmopolitans).

Even in a peasant village in Turkey, a cosmopolitan can develop. Daniel Lerner of the Massachusetts Institute of Technology, in the course of directing a study of the modernization of Turkey, was surprised to find an earlier interview with such a cosmopolitan. He was a grocer, an urban type before urban values had reached the village. Although he was not considered a prophet in his own

---

[48] Gresham M. Sykes, "The Differential Distribution of Community Knowledge," *Social Forces,* Vol. 29, May 1951, pp. 376-382.

lifetime, after the road from Ankara had made his village of Balgat accessible, the values of the community shifted sufficiently toward the cosmopolitan to credit the grocer for his vision. This is the way the grocer was described by a Turkish interviewer, Tosun, in the spring of 1950:[49]

> The respondent is comparatively the most city-like dressed man in the village. He even wore some sort of a necktie. He is the village's only grocer, but he is not really a grocer, but so he is called, originally the food-stuffs in his shop are much less than the things to be worn, like the cheapest of materials and shoes and slippers, etc. His greatest stock is drinks and cigarettes which he sells most. He is a very unimpressive type, although physically he covers quite a space. He gives the impression of a fat shadow. Although he is on the same level with the other villagers, when there are a few of the villagers around, he seems to want to distinguish himself by keeping quiet, and as soon as they depart he starts to talk too much. This happened when we were about to start the interview. He most evidently wished to feel that he is closer to me than he is to them and was curiously careful with his accent all during the interview. In spite of his unique position, for he is the only unfarming person and the only merchant in the village, he does not seem to possess an important part of the village community. In spite of all his efforts, he is considered by the villagers even less than the least farmer. Although he pretended to take the interview naturally, he was nervous and also was proud to be interviewed although he tried to hide it.

The interviewer contrasted the grocer with the Chief of Balgat, who exemplified traditional Turkish virtues:

> With his life in Balgat, as with the Orphic wisdom that supplies its rationale, the Chief is contented. At sixty-three his desires have been quieted and his ambitions achieved. To Tosun's question on contentment he replied with another question. "What could be asked more? God has brought me to this mature age without much pain, has given me sons and daughters, has put me at the head of my village, and has given me strength of brain and body at this age. Thanks be to Him."
>
> The Grocer is a very different style of man and, though born and bred in Balgat, lives in a different world — an expansive world, populated more actively with imaginings and fantasies, hungering for whatever is different and unfamiliar. To Tosun's probe, the Grocer replied staccato: "I have told you I want better things. I would have liked to have a bigger grocery shop in the city, have a nice house there, dress nice civilian clothes." He perceives his story as a drama of Self *versus* Village. "I am not like the others here. They don't know any better. And when I tell them, they are angry and they say that I am ungrateful for what Allah has given me."
>
> Clearly, from the readiness and consistency of his responses to most questions, the Grocer had in fact brooded much over his role. At one point in the in-

[49] Reprinted by permission. From Daniel Lerner, "The Grocer and the Chief," *Harper's Magazine,* Vol. 211, September 1955, pp. 47-56. An expanded version of the article appears in Daniel Lerner, *The Passing of Traditional Society: Modernizing the Middle East,* New York: Free Press (paperback edition), 1968, pp. 19-42.

terviews, after asking each respondent to state the greatest problem facing the Turkish people, Tosun was obliged by the questionnaire to ask what the person would do about this problem if he were the president of Turkey. Some were shocked by the impropriety of the very question. "My God! How can you say such a thing?" gasped the shepherd. "How can I . . . I cannot . . . a poor villager . . . master of the whole world."

The Chief, Balgat's virtuoso of the traditional style, summarized prevailing sentiment by his laconic reply to this question with another question: "I am hardly able to manage a village, how shall I manage Turkey?" When Tosun prodded him (by rephrasing the question to ask "What would you suggest for *your village* that you can not handle yourself?"), the Chief said he would ask for "help of money and seed for some of our farmers." When the turn of the Grocer came, he told what he would and would *not* do, if he were president of Turkey, without embarrassment or hesitation: "I would make roads for the villagers to come to towns to see the world and would not let them stay in their holes all their life."

To get out of his hole the Grocer even declared himself ready—and in this he was quite alone in Balgat—to live outside of Turkey. This came out when Tosun asked: "If you could not live in Turkey, where would you want to live?" The standard reply of the villagers was simply that they *would not* live anywhere else. When Tosun persisted by asking, "Suppose you *had* to leave Turkey?" the shepherd replied finally that he would rather kill himself.

The Chief again responded on this issue with the clear and confident voice of traditional man. "Nowhere," said the Chief, and then added, with a calm assurance that this was all the reason required, "I was born here, grew old here, and hope God will permit me to die here." To Tosun's further probe, the Chief responded firmly: "I wouldn't move a foot from here." Only the Grocer found no trouble in imagining himself outside of Turkey, living in a strange land. Indeed he seemed fully prepared, as a man does when he has already posed a question to himself many times. "America," said the Grocer, and, without waiting for Tosun to ask him why, stated his reason, "because I have heard that it is a nice country, and with possibilities to be rich even for the simplest persons."

The vivid sense of cash displayed by the Grocer was perhaps his most grievous offense against Balgat ideas of taboo talk. In the code regulating the flow of symbols among Anatolian villagers, cravings for blood and sex are permissible but not for money. To talk of money at all—possibly because so little of it exists—is an impropriety. To reveal a *desire* for money is—Allah defend us!—an impiety. The Grocer, with his "city-dressed" ways and his "eye at the higher places" and his visits to Ankara, provoked the Balgati to wrathful and indignant expressions of this code. But occasional, and apparently trivial, items in the survey suggested that some Balgati were talking loud about the Grocer to keep their own inner voices from being overheard by the Chief—or even by themselves.

As we were interested in knowing who says what to whom in such a village as Balgat, Tosun had been instructed to ask each person whether others ever came to him for advice, and if so what they wanted advice about. Naturally, the Balgati whose advice was most sought was the Chief, who reported: "Yes, that is my main duty, to give advice. [Tosun: *What about?*] About all that I or you could imagine, even about their wives and how to handle them, and how to cure their sick cow." But this conjunction of wives and cows, to illustrate all the Chief could imagine, runs the gamut only from A to B. Tosun discovered that some Balgati went for advice also to the disreputable Grocer. What did they ask his advice about? "What to do when they go to Ankara, where to go and what to buy, how much to sell their things. . . ."

The cash nexus, this suggested, was somehow coming to Balgat and with it a new role for the Grocer as cosmopolitan specialist in how to avoid wooden nickels in the big city. Also, how to spend the nickels one got, for the Grocer was a man of clear convictions on which coffee houses played the best radio programs for their customers and which were the best movies to see in Ankara. While his opinions on these matters were heterodox as compared, say, to the Chief's, they had an open field to work in, since most Balgati had never heard a radio or seen a movie and were not aware of what constituted orthodoxy with respect to them.

At the time of Tosun's visit, there was only one radio in Balgat, owned by no less a personage than the Chief. In the absence of a standard doctrine on radio inherited from the great tradition, the Chief—who was also of course the large land-owner of Balgat—had bought a radio to please his sons. He had also devised an appropriate ceremonial for its use. Each evening a select group of Balgati forgathered in the Chief's guest room as he turned on the newscast from Ankara. They heard the newscast through in silence and, at its conclusion, the Chief turned the radio off and made his commentary. "We all listen very carefully," he told Tosun, "and I talk about it afterwards."

Tosun inquired of the Grocer, a frequent attendant at the Chief's salon, how he liked this style of radio session. Without complaining directly about the Chief's exclusive preoccupation with Radio Ankara news of "wars and the danger of wars"—which turned out in fact to be a rather single-minded interest in the Korean War to which a Turkish brigade had just been committed—the Grocer indicated that after all *he* had opportunities to listen in the coffee houses of Ankara where the audiences exhibited a more cosmopolitan range of interests. "It is nice to know what is happening in the other capitals of the world," said the Grocer. "We are stuck in this hole, we have to know what is going on outside our village."

The Grocer had his own aesthetic of the movies as well. Though the Chief had been to the movies several times, he viewed them mainly as a moral prophylactic: "There are fights, shooting. The people are brave. My sons are always impressed. Each time they see such a film they wish more and more their time for military service would come so that they would become soldiers too." For the Grocer, movies were more than a homily on familiar themes; they were his avenue to the wider world of his dreams. It was in a movie, he told Tosun, that he had first glimpsed what a *real* grocery store could be like—"with walls made of iron sheets, top to floor and side to side, and on them standing myriads of round boxes, clean and all the same dressed, like soldiers in a great parade."

This fleeting glimpse of what sounds like the Campbell Soup section of a supermarket had provided the Grocer with an abiding image of how his fantasy world might look. No petty pedantries obstructed his full sensory relationship to the movies; he delivered clear net judgments in unabashedly hedonist categories. "The Turkish ones," he said, "are gloomy, ordinary. I can guess at the start of the film how it will end. . . . The American ones are exciting. You know it makes people ask what will happen next?"

Four years after the Turkish interviewer visited Balgat, Professor Lerner hired a car in Ankara and drove with two interviewers to the village he knew only from reports. He discovered to his surprise that Balgat was only a 20-minute drive from his hotel.

> We looked puzzled at each other until Tosun's words of 1950 recurred to us: "It could have been half an hour to Ankara if it had a road." Now it did have a road. What was more, a *bus* was coming down the road, heading toward us from the place our driver had called Balgat. As it passed, jammed full, none of the passengers inside waved or even so much as stuck out a tongue at us. Without these unfailing signs of villagers out on a rare chartered bus to celebrate a great occasion of some sort, we could only make the wild guess that Balgat had acquired a regular bus service. And indeed, as we entered the village, there it was—a "bus station," freshly painted benches under a handsome new canopy. We got out and looked at the printed schedule of trips. "The bus leaves every hour, on the hour, to *Ulus* Station. Fare: 20 Kurus." For about 6 cents Balgati could now go, whenever they felt the whim, to the heart of Ankara.
>
> The villagers were getting out of their holes at last. . . .
>
> Galvanized by the intelligence now suddenly put before us (even Tahir S. [a member of the original interview team] had reawakened promptly upon discovering that there were hardly any farmers left in Balgat), we started to fire a battery of questions of our own. As this created a din of responding voices, Tahir S.—once again the American-trained interviewer—restored order by asking whether each man around the circle would tell us, in turn, what he was now working at and how long he had been at it. This impromptu occupational census was never quite completed. As it became clear that most of the male population of Balgat was now in fact working in the factories and construction gangs of Ankara—*for cash*—our own impatience to move on got the better of us.
>
> How did they spend the cash they earned? Well, there were now over a hundred radio receivers in Balgat as compared to the lone receiver Tosun had found four years earlier. There were also seven refrigerators, four tractors, three trucks, and one Dodge sedan. Also, since there was so little farming in Balgat now, much of the food came from the outside (even milk) and had to be bought in the grocery stores (of which there were now seven in Balgat). Why milk? Well, most of the animals had been sold off during the last few years. What about the shepherd? Well, he had moved to a village in the east a year or so ago, as there were no longer any flocks for him to tend. How was the Grocer doing? *"Which one?"* The original one, the great fat one that was here four years ago? *"Oh that one, he's dead!"*
>
> Tahir S. later told me that my expression did not change when the news came (always the American-trained interviewer). I asked a few more questions in a normal way—"What did he die of?" "How long ago?"—and then let the questioning pass to Tahir. I don't recall what answers came to my questions or to his. I do recall suddenly feeling very weary and, as the talk went on, slightly sick. The feeling got over to Tahir S. and soon we were saying good-by to the group of Balgati, relieved that the ritual for leave-taking is less elaborate than for arriving. We promised to return and said our thanks. *"Güle, güle,"* answered those who remained ("Smile, smile" signifying farewell). . . .

I slept late the next morning and was tired when I awoke. While dressing slowly and ingesting a full-scale breakfast, I decided that the Grocer was—and, to face right up to it, had been right from the start—*my* man.

I recalled Tosun's unflattering sketch of him as a pretentious phony, as "the only unfarming person in the village . . . who is even less than the least farmer." But I had never minded this about the Grocer, nor Tosun's disgust that "he even wore some sort of a necktie." What had located all these details in a context I could understand, what had made the Grocer a man I recognized, was Tosun's acid remark: "He most evidently wished to feel that he is closer to me than he is to the other villagers and was curiously careful with his accent all during the interview."

There was something in this sentence that had sounded to me like History. Maybe it was the eighteenth-century field hands of England who had left the manor to find a better life in London or Manchester or Liverpool. Maybe it was the nineteenth-century French farm lad, who, wearied by his father's burdens of the *taille* and the *tithe* and the *gabelle,* had gone off to San Francisco to hunt gold and finding none, tried his hand as a mason, mechanic, printer's devil; though none of these brought him fortune, as he cheerfully wrote home (in a letter noted by the perspicacious Karl Marx), he was going to stay in this exciting new city where the chance to try his hand at anything made him feel "less of a mollusk and more of a man."

The Grocer of Balgat stood for some part of all these figures as he nervously edged his psyche toward Tosun, the young man from the big city. I'm like you, the Grocer might have been feeling, or I'd like to be like you and wish I could get the chance. It was harsh of Tosun, or perhaps only the antibourgeois impatience of a consecrated young scholar looking for the suffering poor in a dreary village, to cold-shoulder this fat and middle-aged man yearning to be comfortably rich in an interesting city. But the Grocer had his own sort of toughness. He had, after all, stood up to the other villagers and had insisted, even when they labeled him infidel, that they ought to get out of their holes.

This time I was going out to Balgat by bus instead of taxi, to see how the villagers traveled. The way the villagers traveled, it turned out, was in a shiny new bus from Germany that held three times as many passengers as there were seats. The bus was so new that the signs warning the passengers not to smoke or spit or talk to the driver (while the bus is moving) in German, French, and English had not yet been converted into Turkish. There was, in fact, a great deal of smoking (some Turkish tobacco is used *in* Turkey) and several animated conversations between the driver and various passengers occurred, in the intervals between which the driver chatted with a crony whom he had brought along for just this purpose.

In Balgat I reported directly to the Chief. He was out on his land but appeared after a few minutes, steaming and mopping his large forehead. He had been pruning some trees and, in this warm weather, such work brought the sweat to his brow. This was about the only work he did any more, he explained, as he had sold or rented most of his land in the last few years, keeping for himself only the ground in which he had planted a small grove of trees that would be his memorial on earth. The Chief agreed to show me his trees and as we strolled away from the house he resumed his discourse of yesterday.

Things had changed, he repeated, and a sign of the gravity of these changes was that he—of a lineage that had always been *Muhtars* and land-owners—was no longer a farmer. Nor was he long to be *Muhtar*. After the coming election, next month, the incorporation of Balgat into Greater Ankara was to be completed and thereafter it would be administered under the general municipal system.

"I am the last *Muhtar* of Balgat, and I am happy that I have seen Balgat end its history in this way that we are going."

The new ways, then, were not bringing evil with them? "No, people will have to get used to different ways and then some of the excesses, particularly among the young, will disappear. The young people are in some ways a serious disappointment; they think more of clothes and good times than they do of duty and family and country. But it is to be hoped that as the *Demokrat* men complete the work they have begun, the good Turkish ways will again come forward to steady the people. Meanwhile, it is well that people can have to eat and to buy shoes they always needed but could not have."

And as his two sons were no longer to be farmers, what of them? The Chief's voice did not change, nor did his eyes cloud over, as he replied: "They are as the others. They think first to serve themselves and not the nation. They had no wish to go to the battle in Korea, where Turkey fights before the eyes of all the world. They are my sons and I speak no ill of them, but I say only that they are as all the others."

I felt at this moment a warmth toward the Chief which I had not supposed he could evoke. His sons had not, after all, learned to fight bravely and die properly. These two sons through whom he had hoped to relive his own bright dreams of glory had instead become *shopkeepers*. The elder son owned a grocery store and the younger one owned Balgat's first clothing store. As we turned back to the house, the Chief said we would visit the shops after lunch and his sons would answer all my questions.

That afternoon we went first to the elder son's grocery store, just across the road from the Chief's house and alongside the village fountain. The central floor space was set out with merchandise in the immemorial manner—heavy, rough, anonymous hemp sacks each laden with a commodity requiring no identity card, groats in one and barley in another, here lentils and there chicory. But beyond the sacks was a distinct innovation, a counter. What is more, the counter turned a corner and ran parallel to two sides of the square hut. Built into it was a cash drawer and above each surface a hygienic white porcelain fixture for fluorescent lighting. Along the walls was the crowning glory—a case of shelves running from "top to floor and side to side, and on them standing myriads of round boxes, clean and all the same dressed, like soldiers in a great parade." The Grocer's words of aspiration came leaping back to mind as I looked admiringly around the store. His dream house had been built in Balgat—in less time than even he might have forecast—and by none other than the Chief!

The irony of the route by which Balgat had entered History stayed with me as we walked in quartet, the Chief and I ahead, the sons behind, to the clothing store of the younger son. This was in the newer part of the village, just across the new road from the bus station. The stock inside consisted mainly of dungarees, levis, coveralls—all looking rather like U. S. Army surplus stocks. There was a continuous and growing demand for these goods, the Chief stated solemnly, as more and more men of Balgat went into the labor market of Ankara, first discard-

ing their *shalvars* (the billowing bloomers of traditional garb in which Western cartoons always still portray the "sultan" in a harem scene). In a corner of the store there was also a small stock of "gentleman's haberdashery" — ready-made suits, shirts, even a rack of neckties.

The younger son, who maintained a steady silence in the presence of the Chief, replied to a direct question from me that he had as yet sold very few items from this department of the store. The Balgat males by and large were still reticent about wearing store-bought clothes. A few, however, had purchased in a *sub rosa* sort of way neckties which remained to be exhibited in public. But wearing them would come, now that several owned them, as soon as an older man was bold enough to wear his first. The owners of the neckties had only to get used to them in private, looking at them now and then, showing them to their wives and elder sons, and some one of them had to show the way. I remembered Tosun's rather nasty comment, as though this was his most telling evidence against the Grocer's preposterous pretences, *"He even wore some sort of a necktie."* As one saw it now, the Grocer *had* shown the way, and it was now only a hop, skip, and jump through history to the point where most men of Balgat would be wearing neckties.

The Grocer's memory stayed with me all afternoon, after I had expressed intense satisfaction with the shops, wished the sons good fortune, thanked the Chief again and, with his permission, started out to walk among the alleys and houses of Balgat. On the way, I absently counted sixty-nine radio antennas on the roofs and decided that yesterday's estimate of "over a hundred" was probably reliable. And only four years ago, I reminded myself, there was but a single radio in this village. The same theme ran through my recollection of the numbers of tractors, refrigerators, and "unfarming persons." That was what Tosun had called the Grocer—"the only unfarming person in the village." . . .

Weary of walking, I turned back to the cofee house. The ceremony of welcome was warm and the coffee was again on the house, but the conversational group was smaller. Only eleven Balgati appeared to praise the weather and hear my questions. The group got off on politics, with some attention to the general theory of power but more intense interest in hearing each other's predictions of the margin by which the *Demokrat* party would win the elections next month. There was also general agreement, at least among the wiser heads, that it would be better to have a small margin between the major parties. "The villagers have learned the basic lesson of democratic politics," I wrote in my notebook.

The afternoon was about over before I got an appropriate occasion to ask about the Grocer. It came when the talk returned to the villagers' favorite topic of how much better life had become during the past four years of *Demokrat* rule. Again they illustrated the matter by enumerating the new shops in Balgat and the things they had to sell that many people could buy. "How are these new grocery shops better than the old grocery shop of years ago owned by the fat grocer who is now dead?" I asked. The line of response and the examples cited were obvious in advance, but the question served to lead to another. What sort of man had the Grocer been? The answers were perfunctory, consisting mainly of *pro forma* expressions of good will toward the departed. I tried to get back of these ritual references to the Grocer by indirection. How had he dressed? Why had he been so interested in the life of Ankara? The light finally shone in one of the wiser heads and he spoke the words I was seeking: "Ah, he was the cleverest of us all. We did not know it then, but he saw better than all what lay in the path ahead. We have none like him among us now. He was a prophet."

To the Grocer, urbanization was not a threat but an opportunity. The Chief was not so sure. This difference in the interpretation of the meaning of urbanization can be duplicated in the industrial cities of the West. Many persons regard the city as the place for the development of cultural potentialities: art museums, universities, symphony orchestras, theater, ballet, libraries, book stores. Because transportation of persons requires time and money, a considerable concentration of persons is required in order to develop a following for an activity with limited appeal, such as concert going.[50] The infinite variety of New York, London, or Tokyo results from the size and heterogeneity of their populations. In a city of 7,000,000 persons, probability favors the emergence of constituencies for the most esoteric and bizarre interests.[51]

Competition and Individual Choice. The notion that urban life gives rise to a distinct personality draws on a long tradition, counting among its proponents such founding fathers of sociology as Max Weber, Georg Simmel, and Robert E. Park. But certainly it is not the paving stones of the city that produce cosmopolitans. Nor is it congestion alone. Rather it is the character of interaction

[50] Hans L. Zetterberg, *Social Theory and Social Practice,* New York: Bedminster Press, 1962, Chap. 4.

[51] Karl W. Deutsch, "On Social Communication and the Metropolis," in Lloyd Rodwin *The Future Metropolis,* New York: Braziller, 1961, pp. 129-143.

Bruno Barbey — Magnum

resulting partly from elaborate division of labor and a competitive method of role allocation.

Every interactive system has the problem of allocating its personnel to roles on some basis. Urban societies allow the individual considerable discretion as to what roles he will play. From the viewpoint of the individual this is freedom of choice; from the societal standpoint it is a competitive method of allocating people to roles. A role filled by competition among potential candidates for it on the basis of their supposed capacities to play it (e.g., an occupational role) is called an **achieved role.** In all societies, however, many roles are filled by assigning the individual to a role on the basis of qualities he possesses without considering how well he can play that role or whether he wishes to play it. Age and sex roles are examples of noncompetitive assignment to roles on the basis of a biological characteristic. The technical term for assignment to roles because of *qualities* rather than performance is **ascription.** As soon as an infant arrives in the world, he is assigned to the "boy" or the "girl" role on the basis of a genital examination. The assignment determines how he will be defined and what people will expect from him. Sometimes a male child prefers to play with dolls and sew rather than wrestle, but he cannot compete with female children for feminine roles.

Achieved roles are more prominent in urban industrial societies than in preliterate societies. Modern societies carry role differentiation too far for a mechanical transmission of roles from father to son. The peculiar combination of talent and training entering into a brain surgeon must be mobilized afresh in each generation. An advantage of a competitive system of role allocation is obvious: it increases the chances of finding adequate candidates, particularly for roles requiring special abilities. The disadvantage is that the preferences of the population and the role structure of the society may not match. More people aspire to be business tycoons than there are openings in top management. On the other hand, dirty, dangerous, or menial jobs have to be filled but are intrinsically unattractive.

Urban industrial societies face a dilemma: the more attractive they make roles at the top of the occupational hierarchy, the more eager will people be to play them and the less eager to play roles at the bottom. The labor market provides a partial solution to the problem. Since the average person has to find employment to support himself and his family, he is driven by economic considerations to take less attractive jobs if he cannot compete for better jobs. The economist can demonstrate by supply and demand analysis how impersonal market mechanisms induce people to take jobs.

The ideal in competitive role allocation is the filling of roles with those most capable of performing them. Candidates for attractive roles vie with one another in the labor market until the supply is brought into balance with available vacancies. The price of unattractive roles, on the other hand, is bid up until sufficient applicants appear to satisfy the demand. Logical though this process may be, it creates a situation of happy winners and disappointed losers. The losers may deal with their disappointments by accepting the fact that the winners were better qualified. Yet a competitive system does not always choose the best man. Sometimes the boss promotes a "yes-man" instead of the most competent worker. This makes it easy for failures to suspect that the ideals of the system are violated rather than to concede their own incompetence. Such suspicion may lead to rebellious behavior (what will be called deviance in Chapter 13). If the unsuccessful competitor is forced to admit that the competition was fair, the tensions are likely to be internalized. Management of these tensions is a problem for the individual personality but not usually a threat to the stability of the interactive system.

The complex, rapidly changing role structure of an urban industrial society necessitates a competitive method of role allocation not only in the occupational system, but also in such personal contexts as friendship and marriage. The individual competes for a wife as well as for a job. The *pervasiveness* of competition in industrial societies makes for widespread feelings of inadequacy because everyone is an unsuccessful competitor in one context or another. Ruth Benedict suggested that race prejudice, the belief that persons of different racial or ethnic stock were *inferior,* served to quell doubts about competitive adequacy:[52]

---

[52] Ruth Benedict, *Race: Science and Politics,* rev. ed., New York: Viking, 1945, p. 99.

Racism is essentially a pretentious way of saying that "I" belong to the Best People. For such a conviction it is the most gratifying formula that has ever been discovered, for neither my own unworthiness nor the accusations of others can ever dislodge me from my position—a position which was determined in the womb of my mother at conception. It avoids all embarrassing questions about my conduct of life and nullifies all embarrassing claims by "inferior" groups about their own achievements and ethical standards.

In spite of this drawback, competition is characteristic of urban industrial societies because it is the most feasible mechanism for filling the roles in a dynamic, fluid society. That same dynamism contributes to the anonymity of urban life, which stems partly from the sheer numbers of people but partly from the specialized kind of interaction required by an industrial society. In the preliterate society, where role differentiation is at a minimum, interaction is more personal.

As anthropologist Robert Redfield put it, "the personal and intimate life of the child in the family is extended, in the **folk society,** into the social world of the adult and even into inanimate objects."[53] In contemporary urban societies, social participation is often organized around specific functions and therefore is less personal than in preliterate societies. The supermarket customer interacts with the checker over such limited segments of their respective personalities that calling their relationship "personal" would distort reality. In the same way, in a subway train during the morning rush-hour, the other riders are *bodies* rather than *people*; they are physically close but psychologically re-

[53] Redfield, "Folk Society."

mote. The interactions that take place in these specialized contexts are efficient, but they tend to be emotionally unsatisfying. Gordon Allport, the social psychologist, has suggested that *participation* (in the sense of psychic commitment) is a crucial problem of urban life.[54] This problem was also discussed by Louis Wirth, who, in a classic article, deduced the anonymity and impersonality of urban life from population density and heterogeneity.[55]

> The multiplication of persons in a state of interaction under conditions which make their contact as full personalities impossible produces that segmentalization of human relationships which has sometimes been seized upon by students of the mental life of the cities as an explanation for the "schizoid" character of urban personality.

Urban anonymity does not mean that personal, emotionally significant relationships are disappearing, even for cosmopolitan types. Primary groups persist in the metropolis, most notably in the family, but also in the neighborhood, the work situation, and in voluntary associations. In recent years, sociologists have rediscovered the primary group, embedded though it often is in **formal organizations.**[56] The enormous number of secondary groups, an organizational necessity given the scale of urban societies, makes it possible for an adult to *survive* without much primary group involvement. He can live in a hotel, eat in restaurants, and work as a solitary street cleaner. In short, urban society permits one to lead the life of a hermit without residing in a wilderness. For the overwhelming majority of urban people, however, this opportunity is not attractive. Hence they live in two worlds, "the world of physically close but socially distant strangers" and the world of primary groups.[57]

The existence of the two worlds means that the individual can escape primary group controls if he wishes. He can escape them to join the American Civil Liberties Union, to wear a beret, to eat with chopsticks at an oriental restaurant, or to paint abstract pictures. He can also escape them to rob a bank. It is difficult for a local resident to rob a bank successfully in a rural community because (1) he would be recognized by the tellers and (2) he would be unable to spend the proceeds of the robbery without drawing attention to himself. This is not an argument for the general superiority of less urbanized communities over the metropolis. The looser control of the big city makes it easier for vice and crime to escape detection, but it also makes more likely creditable adventures of the human spirit. The balance sheet is a complicated one.

Urban industrial societies combine diminished social control over the individual with increased freedom for him to choose his own role commitments.

[54] Gordon W. Allport, "The Psychology of Participation," *Psychological Review,* Vol. 53, May 1945, pp. 117-132.

[55] Louis Wirth, "Urbanism as a Way of Life," *American Journal of Sociology,* Vol. 44, July 1938, pp. 1-24.

[56] William F. Whyte, "Social Organization in the Slums," *American Sociological Review,* Vol. 8, February 1943, pp. 34-39.

[57] Kingsley Davis, *Human Society,* New York: Macmillan, 1948, p. 331.

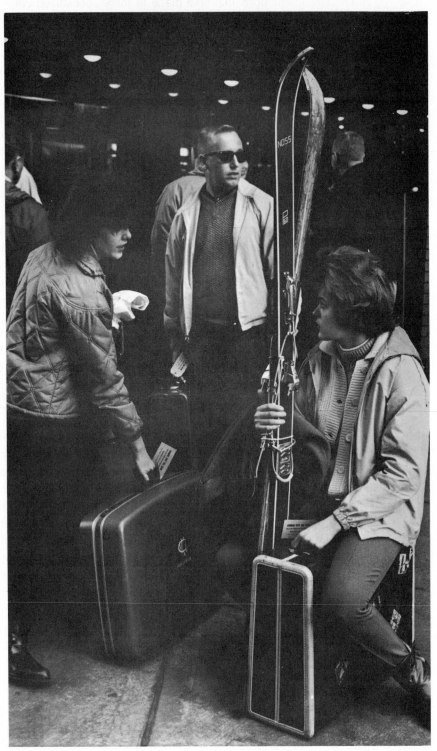

Burk Uzzle — Magnum

(Chapter 13 returns to the problem of social control in contemporary societies.) True, some urban industrial societies are more individualistic than others. Contrast the United States, for example, with Japan, where family obligations are still considered more important than personal happiness. And large cities are generally more individualistic than the rural hinterland. But an individualistic **ideology** tends to permeate every part of all the urban industrial societies because the individual is the unit of social organization in these societies, and ideologies cannot be too remote from social reality. The achievement of individual "success"—meaning accomplishments, material possessions, power over others, and prestige—is as important to many people in urban industrial societies as marriage, children, and friendship, which are more prominent values in preindustrial societies.

Television, radio, and movies, themselves products of industrial technology, reinforce an individualistic ideology. The glimpses provided in the mass media of impeccably groomed men and women dining in expensive restaurants, living in luxurious homes, and riding in sleek new automobiles arouse aspirations for individual "success." These aspirations are reinforced by the explicit temptations of advertising. The appetite for fame is also whetted by the mass media—for example, by their implicit suggestion that individuals whose activities are chronicled in newspapers and magazines are more valuable than "ordinary" people. Envy was certainly not invented by urban industrial societies, but envy is stimulated more systematically in them. This is partly an unintended consequence of the existence of mass media, which make visible the rewards of success. It is also the result of relying on envy as the motivational basis for a competitive system of role allocation.

The scientific focus of contemporary societies also contributes to concern with individual potentialities. The ability of science and technology to harness the forces of nature cannot be forgotten when human problems arise. Whatever the explicit religious commitments of industrial societies, to Christianity, to Judaism, to Buddhism, to Islam, or to Marxism, an implicit value is the importance of the here and now, and an implicit faith is activism. Frustrations need not be borne with resignation in a scientific age. Rational thinking and hard work may lead to a solution. Thus the individual dissatisfied with his lot is prone to do something about it. This helps to explain the hunger for fame of a musician or painter—and also the lure of "easy money" for the professional criminal.

There are many ways in which the urban society molds personality. We no longer regard the city as the embodiment of progress or the symbol of sin. The virtues of the city are real, but the problems of the city stem from these same virtues. The freedom of choice which urban life offers is obtained at a price. The more choices people have as to what roles they will play and what goals they will pursue, the less certain it is that everyone will be included in the web of community. For example, boys are free to seek out for dating girls who are pretty, well poised, and good conversationalists and to ignore those who are not. Freedom to choose is freedom to ignore. The probability is that the more ignored one is, the less adequate will one feel. A person cannot easily maintain a good opinion of himself if nobody wants him as a friend or if he finds it much more difficult than the average person to obtain a job. And when he begins to agree that he is worthless, he becomes a problem not only to himself but also to the community. He may withdraw into a world of his own where he does not get pushed around; and even a skilled psychiatrist may not be able to induce him to leave it. Or he may turn for consolation to liquor or drugs.[58]

CONCLUSION

Modern industrialism, accompanied as it is by technological advances in transportation and communication as well as by scientific methods of farming, makes possible the urban society. In the urban society, cities are the rule rather than the exception. A majority of the population lives in metropolitan areas and depends on the labor market for income, on the real-estate market for housing, on the retail store for food and clothing, and on commercial entertainment for recreation. Even in rural areas, the style of life is radically different from that of subsistence agriculture; rural areas in the urban society are more closely integrated with cities than are rural areas in preindustrial societies.

Robert E. Park assumed that the urban community reflected a moral order in its spatial pattern.[59] He and his disciples at the University of Chicago conducted meticulous studies of human ecology because they considered these data reflections of underlying social and cultural meanings. Today sociologists are less convinced that the territorial location of persons and activities is fundamental to an interactive system. Systems of interaction can function without a permanent territorial base. Nevertheless, an important type of interactive system (the community) has a territorial basis, and sociologists interested in urban or rural communities must consider the special requirements of interaction spread over a land surface. Transportation and communication over a considerable area not only impose economic costs; they take time, and time is valuable, especially in an industrial society.

The pattern of growth of industrial cities reflects the salience of economic activities. Competition for scarce space is reflected in sales prices, rental costs, and property taxes. Through the market mechanism, commercial uses typically preempt accessible locations in the center of the city — even though the expansion of the central business district spreads blight in surrounding residential areas.

[58] Harry C. Bredemeier and Jackson Toby, *Social Problems in America: Costs and Casualties in an Acquisitive Society,* New York: Wiley, 1960.

[59] Robert E. Park, "The Urban Community as a Spatial Pattern and a Moral Order," in Ernest W. Burgess, Ed., *The Urban Community,* Chicago: University of Chicago Press, 1962.

An urban industrial society is a fluid society. Although age and sex roles continue to be *ascribed,* a wide range of occupational and other roles are *achieved,* that is, filled through competitive processes, which necessarily involve some freedom of choice—and also some disappointed aspirations. The individual continues to find meaningful relationships in primary groups (particularly in the family). But he also interacts in more specialized relationships in political organizations, professional societies, churches, and schools. The distinction between *cosmopolitan* and *local* types hinges on the extent to which the individual utilizes specialized secondary groups as the basis for his values, opinions, and goals.

An urban industrial society is an individualistic society. The individual (rather than the kinship unit) is the unit of social participation. The individual enrolls in school, votes at election time, looks for a job, and gets married. An individualistic ideology reflects this social fact. No one should be startled by the competitive striving or by the freedom of choice of urban industrial societies. Both preoccupations are nourished by the belief in individual fulfillment. And the belief in fulfillment, though not an inevitable consequence of industrialism, is promoted by an individualistic, competitive social organization.

SOME SIGNIFICANT LITERATURE ON THE URBAN COMMUNITY

Theodore R. Anderson, "Comparative Urban Structure," *International Encyclopedia of the Social Sciences,* Vol. 2, New York: Macmillan, 1968, pp. 466-472. Some of the characteristics of cities in Europe and the United States stem from historical circumstances. For example, the emergence of a central business district and the dense concentration of population resulted from the simultaneous development of the large-scale factory and the predominance of rail transportation. The shift to automotive transportation (with a resulting dispersal of residences and business enterprises into the suburbs) is changing the character of modern cities even in the West. Other characteristics of cities are more basic and appear in all historical periods and in various cultures. Anderson attempts a comparative perspective on cities to identify these universal characteristics.

James S. Coleman, "Community Disorganization," in Robert K. Merton and Robert A. Nisbet, Eds., *Contemporary Social Problems,* 2nd ed., New York: Harcourt, Brace and World, 1966, pp. 670-722. Partly for historical reasons—the piling up of newly arrived immigrants in the slum neighborhoods of big cities—urbanism is closely identified in the sociological literature with such social problems as poverty, crime, suicide, alcoholism, and mental illness. Coleman discusses the underlying theoretical issue: the processes that make communities of geographic localities. These processes are more complicated in the metropolis than in isolated rural hamlets. For discussions of the social pathology that emerges when communities become disorganized, see the following collections of articles: Jack P. Gibbs, Ed., *Suicide,* New York: Harper and Row, 1968; Robert D. Herman, Ed., *Gambling,* New York: Harper and Row, 1967; David J. Pittman, Ed., *Alcoholism,* York: Harper and Row, 1967; and James F. Short, Jr., Ed., *Gang Delinquency and Delinquent Subcultures,* New York: Harper and Row, 1968.

Otis Dudley Duncan and Albert J. Reiss, Jr., *Social Characteristics of Urban and Rural Communities,* 1950, New York: Wiley, 1956. This volume is part of the Census Monograph Series which was sponsored by the Social Science Research Council to take advantage of data made available by the 1950 census. The authors use detailed tabulations of census data by size of place to find out whether there is a sharp discontinuity between rural and urban communities or a continuous variation suggested by the concept of a rural-urban continuum. The findings of the authors are relevant to the interpretive problem of users of census statistics in dealing with the "rural" and "urban" categories. See also Raymond Vernon, *The Changing Economic Function of the Central City,* New York: Committee for Economic Development, 1959.

Philip M. Hauser, *Population Perspectives,* New Brunswick, N.J.: Rutgers University Press, 1960, Chap. 4 and 5. These chapters present data on the explosive growth of metropolitan areas in the world generally and in the United States in particular. Hauser considers the consequences and implications of this explosion. For example, metropolitan growth has reduced to an absurdity many existing political boundaries; in 1950 the 162 Standard Metropolitan Areas of the United States included over 16,000 governmental units with powers to tax and spend (including school districts). Hauser discusses briefly the physical problems of metropolitan housing and transportation and the human-relations problems resulting from a new ethnic mix in the central cities. For a broader perspective, see Philip M. Hauser, *Urbanization in Asia and the Far East,* Calcutta: UNESCO, 1957. This volume consists of papers contributed to a conference on urbanization in Asia and the Far East at Bangkok in August 1956.

Sheridan T. Maitland and Reed E. Friend, *Rural Industrialization: A Summary of Five Studies,* Agricultural Information Bulletin No. 252, Washington: Government Printing Office, November 1961. This report summarizes the results of five surveys on the effects of industrial plants in economically depressed rural areas—two in Utah, one in Mississippi, one in Louisiana, and one in Iowa. The survey method included two random samples in each community: (1) of the employees of the industrial plant recently established in the community and (2) of all rural households in the community. A major finding was that older rural workers and workers with little industrial experience were least likely to seek and find jobs in the new plant. Nevertheless, the new plant provided rural workers an opportunity to shift from farm to factory work without migrating to distant industrial centers. Even if it only postpones the migration, it gives the worker some industrial experience which may facilitate his later adjustment to urban life.

Walter T. Martin, *The Rural-Urban Fringe: A Study of Adjustment to Residence Location,* Eugene: University of Oregon Press, 1953. A random sample of residents of the unincorporated countryside contiguous to the cities of Eugene and Springfield, Oregon, was interviewed concerning satisfaction with the locations of its homes. It was hypothesized that ". . . the extent of satisfaction of family members varies directly with the degree of accessibility of the center (of the city) to that location," but this hypothesis was not borne out by the data. Other factors did distinguish the more satisfied from the less satisfied. Males were more satisfied with the location of their homes than females, high-income persons than low-income persons, persons with a large number of memberships in formal associations than persons with few such memberships. This summary is based on a review by Richard Dewey, *American Sociological Review,* Vol. 19, December 1954, pp. 799-800.

Horace Miner, *The Primitive City of Timbuctoo,* Princeton, N.J.: Princeton University Press, 1953. Sociological study of cities suffer from a sampling bias. Most of the cities studied have been deeply influenced by the culture of Western Europe; hence it is difficult to know whether the urban characteristics that have been identified are the inevitable result of population concentration or the result of population concentration under special cultural conditions. Miner's study of the African city of Timbuctoo was undertaken ". . . to see whether such phenomena as crime, secularization, and group conflict are products of city life per se or whether they are the products of our particular type of urban civilization." Timbuctoo dates back to the eleventh century, and it was not until the twentieth century that appreciable European influence appeared. Thus it proved a crucial case in which to examine the hypothesis that certain phenomena of city life are independent of culture. This summary is based on a review by D. B. Stout, *American Sociological Review,* Vol. 19, June 1954, pp. 367-368.

David W. Plath, *The After Hours: Modern Japan and the Search for Enjoyment,* Berkeley: University of California Press, 1964. The emphasis on fun, on personal fulfillment, is usually considered a result of cultural developments peculiar to the western world. This study of leisure in modern urban Japan shows, however, a similar pattern of commercially fostered hedonism, although with some Oriental variations. Men in Japan frequently take "the long way home" stopping in bars for refreshment and sociability with male colleagues or friends rather than returning directly after work and taking their recreation with wives and children. In response, Japanese women have mounted an ideological offense called the Go Home Quickly movement. For a broader view of the urban context of modern Japan, see Ezra F. Vogel, *Japan's New Middle Class: The Salary Man and His Family in a Tokyo Suburb,* Berkeley: University of California Press, 1963, and Ronald P. Dore, *City Life in Japan: A Study of a Tokyo Ward,* Berkeley: University of California Press, 1958.

Peter H. Rossi, *Why Families Move: A Study in the Social Psychology of Urban Residential Mobility,* Glencoe, Ill.: Free Press, 1955. This study is based on depth interviews in high-income and low-income neighborhoods and in neighborhoods of high and low rates of residential mobility. Change of residence has long been thought about by sociologists as due to a double motivation: rejection of the old neighborhood and attraction for the new one (a push and a pull). This study shows the relationship of pushes and pulls to the family's stage in the life cycle. Specifically, the tendency to move is greatest during the period when the family is increasing in size. Lack of adequate space overshadows objectionable qualities of the neighborhood as a "push." The relationship between mobility and stage of the family cycle explains an otherwise puzzling finding: Families are more mobile than unattached persons even in areas of high mobility containing large numbers of single, divorced, or widowed persons. This summary is based on a review by Donald O. Cowgill, *American Sociological Review,* Vol. 21, June 1956, pp. 395-396.

Max Weber, *The City,* Glencoe, Ill.: Free Press, 1958. In these essays, the famous German sociologist considered the historical evolution of cities and city life. Weber attempted to formulate an inductive definition of the city based on his historical research. "To constitute a full urban community a settlement must display a relative predominance of trade-commercial relations, with the settlement as a whole displaying the following features: (1) a fortification; (2) a market; (3) a court of its own and at least partially autonomous law; (4) a related form of association; and (5) . . . an administration by authorities in the election of whom the burghers participated." Obviously a rather restrictive definition, in terms of which only the Occident produced urban communities, it is not useful for contemporary urban research. This summary is based on a review by Albert J. Reiss, Jr., *American Sociological Review,* Vol. 24, April 1959, pp. 267-268.

THE RELIGIOUS STRUCTURE OF SOCIETY

United Press International

The family of orientation is the representative of society and transmits elements of its culture to the child, much of which he internalizes. However, socialization in the family, even if successful in every respect, is only a beginning of the motivational regulation of the child. He does not internalize the explanations his culture offers as to the meaning of life because family interaction does not usually force a small child to recognize such a problem. As he grows older, he develops the intellectual capacity and emotional detachment to question whether life has meaning — human life in general and his life in particular. Western psychiatrists term questioning the significance of the individual's own life the **identity crisis** and associate it with adolescence. On the more general level of uneasiness about the significance of human existence or of society, the problem is considered philosophical or religious. Both the identity crisis and the broader philosophical issue involve justification or repudiation of *motivational commitment to values embodied in the role structure.*[1] Religious ideas and practices may provide reassurance for the individual. From the standpoint of society, they channel commitment to normative behavior.

Small interactive systems usually do not have religions, but they have myths and rituals that are functional equivalents of religion. A student's commitment to his school may be reinforced by the vision of events in which heroic figures performed great deeds for the glory of alma mater. Thus Rutgers students can never forget that Rutgers won the first football game with Princeton in 1869 and the centennial game in 1969. A football game, besides being an athletic contest, may be thought of as a religious service. The cheerleaders may believe that the role commitment they are encouraging applies only to the contest, but the sociologist assumes that the enthusiasm generated at the game carries over into pride in being a student and willingness to accept the responsibilities of the student role. In short, the small interactive system has the same need as a self-sufficient society to develop a symbol system that reinforces the motivation of its members to commit their energies to their roles.

On the societal level, Christianity or Buddhism can provide reinforcing motivation, but so can symbol systems not usually considered religious. Political ideologies such as Marxism and democracy are secular equivalents of religion. Philosophies sometimes take on the appearance of religions, especially if religion is defined broadly enough to include both the animistic faiths of preliterate peoples and Eastern religions like Confucianism, which lack the Western concept of a personal God. To distinguish religions from philosophies and political ideologies, many sociologists insist that a religious symbol system contain the following features:[2]

1. Beliefs concerning sacred entities which are "set apart" from the workaday world and on which the meaning of life depends, for example, God.

[1] Robert N. Bellah, "The Sociology of Religion," *International Encyclopedia of the Social Sciences,* Vol. 13, New York: Macmillan, 1968, pp. 406-414.
[2] This list was drawn up by Talcott Parsons in "Religious Perspectives of College Teaching in Sociology and Social Psychology," New Haven, Conn.: Hazen Foundation, 1952, pp. 7-8.

2. Symbols for expressing the emotional states appropriate to this supernatural sphere, for example, the cross for Christians.
3. Prescribed activities for a believer, although they are not supposed to help him realize secular goals, for example, attendance at church services.
4. A conception of a moral community, a universe of persons who subscribe to the beliefs and participate in the activities and thereby constitute a solidary group. (In nonliterate societies, the boundaries of the tribe and of the religious community coincide; in contemporary societies, many religious communities exist side-by-side depending on the number of separate **denominations.)**
5. A faith that the sacred entities in the supernatural world have prescribed certain rules of conduct and moral values for believers, for example, the Ten Commandments.

These five facets of religion reflect the particular interests of sociologists. Sociologists are not concerned with the validity of religion but with the consequences an accepted religion has on the operation of a society. Insofar as it addresses *successfully* universal anxieties about human existence, it helps the members of the society to continue fulfilling their social obligations. Insofar as its answers to these universal anxieties are *unsatisfactory* or widely disbelieved, it undermines the motivation for conformity and promotes demoralization. Now let us turn to a consideration of the anxieties to which religions implicitly address themselves.

RELIGION AND THE AFFIRMATION OF MEANING

Every society faces a morale problem. Human experience produces evidence that life is "a tale told by an idiot, full of sound and fury, signifying nothing." The inevitability of physical death, the unpredictability and uncontrollability of events in whose outcomes people have emotional investments, and the failure of events to fulfill moral expectations all seem to prove that existence is meaningless.

In the course of socialization human beings develop the capacity to treat themselves as objects. Once self-awareness develops, the individual loves himself or hates himself, is proud of himself or ashamed of himself; his emotional investment in himself is too great for him to be indifferent to the possibility of oblivion. His intellectual awareness that the organism must perish creates a chronic feeling of anxiety. We are born; we suffer; and we die—to what purpose? The French sociologist Émile Durkheim demonstrated in his classic study that this feeling of purposelessness increases the probability of suicide; the best insurance against self-destruction is the belief that life has meaning.[3] However,

---

[3] Émile Durkheim, *Suicide,* Glencoe, Ill.: Free Press, 1951.

the act of self-destruction can fulfill life's meaning instead of negating it, as, for example, the Kamikaze pilots during the Second World War who dived their planes laden with explosives into American battleships because they believed that self-destruction, under these circumstances, would win them eternal glory. Similarly, Buddhist monks and nuns in Vietnam have immolated themselves to affirm their convictions in the face of government harassment, as has a Czechoslovak youth, Jan Palach, to protest the Soviet invasion of his country in 1968.

A second threat to the meaning of life is the uncertainty of human efforts and plans. As the poet Robert Burns put it:

> But, Mousie, thou art no thy lane,
> In proving foresight may be vain;
> The best laid schemes o' mice an' men
>   Gang aft agley,
> An' lea'e us nought but grief an' pain
>   For promised joy.

In preliterate societies, the exposure of agriculture to unpredictable and uncontrollable weather illustrates the limitation of human planning. Hard work makes a good crop more likely, but hard work cannot guarantee it. The anthropologist Bronislaw Malinowski suggested that the greater the uncertainty of human effort, the more likely would supernatural means be sought to increase the *feeling* of control.[4] He cited the difference between lagoon fishing and open-sea fishing in the Trobriand Islands. Lagoon fishing is safe and sure, and no rituals are associated with it; open-sea fishing is dangerous, the yields are uncertain, and rituals abound. In contemporary industrial societies, science and technology have provided greater control over crops and even weather. But the future continues to be unpredictable. The threat of war and economic crises—as well as personal problems of health and unemployment—remind us that the investment of hope and effort is a gamble.

A third threat to the meaning of life is the partial failure of **moral determinism** in all societies.[5] "The good die young while the wicked flourish as the green bay tree." This biblical statement exaggerates the actual state of affairs. Every society makes an effort to balance the moral economy: to reward the virtuous and punish the wicked. But all societies fail to some extent because social control is never complete. In every society, good people can be found who fare badly and corrupt people can be found who seem to be enjoying life immensely. This partial failure of moral determinism suggests that social life is little better than a jungle. If those who abide by ethical principles are pushed

---

[4] Bronislaw Malinowski, "Magic, Science and Religion," in Joseph Needham, Ed., *Science, Religion and Reality,* New York: Macmillan, 1925, pp. 31-32.

[5] The phrase "moral determinism" is used by Kingsley Davis in *Human Society,* New York: Macmillan, 1948, pp. 530-531, in the course of a penetrating chapter on religious institutions. In lectures and writings, Talcott Parsons has repeatedly pointed out the discrepancies between conformity to moral standards and secular rewards.

aside by those who have no principles, might makes right, and life is a tale told by an idiot, signifying nothing.

Religious Regulation of Individual Commitment. Unless human beings are somehow reassured that life has meaning, demoralization ensues. Émile Durkheim introduced the term **anomie** into sociology to describe a demoralized society—without goals or norms. Several centuries earlier, Thomas Hobbes tried to imagine life in a demoralized society ("a state of nature"); he emphasized the insecurity which would result from "a war of all against all." Neither Durkheim nor Hobbes could accurately describe a demoralized society because reorganization occurs before demoralization becomes unbearable; thus *anomie* is the hypothetical result of a process that is never carried to its conclusion.

What prevents demoralization from becoming total? The efforts of the society to affirm its ultimate values. On the most concrete level, these efforts underlie child socialization. Suppose a five-year-old raises his metal shovel menacingly over the head of a playmate. The child's mother happens to be near enough to avert the disaster. "You must not do that!" she cries. "Why not?" he might ask as she pulls the shovel out of his hands. "Because I do not want you to," is a polite way of saying, "Shut up and do what you are told." It settles the issue in power terms rather than by asserting the existence of ultimate values. However, the mother can justify her determination to prevent bloodshed by citing religious tradition and thereby obtaining transcendental justification for her peaceful policy. "Because God is up there watching, and He does not want you to beat up anyone with a shovel." Perhaps the mother could have gotten the child to accept a more mundane justification this time, but, sooner or later, ultimate questions call for ultimate answers. If the child keeps asking, "Why?" as children have been known to do, his mother must either resort to naked force or justify secular rules in moral terms. On those occasions when the question "Why?" is a challenge to the arrangements that make possible the peaceful coexistence of people in a society, religion can step into the breach. Voltaire is reported to have said, "If God doesn't exist, we must invent him."

Adults are more prone than children to ask difficult questions. When a loved one is killed in an automobile collision and his relatives exclaim, "Why did it happen to *him?*" they are not satisfied with a detailed explanation of the technology of the accident. A reasonably satisfactory answer is possible for bereaved relatives who have faith in the goodness of God and the inscrutability of His ways. They may be consoled for their loss by the thought that the victim is going to his reward in a better world.

The efforts of a society to affirm its ultimate values are evident not only in the crises of socialization and death but also in day-to-day applications of social norms. Religion supports the social order on this level, too. Some 70 years before the birth of Jesus, Rabbi Hillel provided a classic statement of such support in reply to a challenge that he sum up all of the rules of conduct in the Torah and the Talmud while standing on one foot. He said, "Do not do to others what you would not want others to do to you." Hillel was saying that God forbade men to commit aggressions against one another. The abstractness of the formulation makes it equally applicable to cannibal as to Hebrew society: every society prohibits aggressive behavior within the group, and religious beliefs sanctify these prohibitions. The variation arises from what is considered aggression and who is included within the group. Wife beating is grounds for divorce in American society; among some peasant groups in Eastern Europe, a woman whose husband did not slap her occasionally would have reason to fear he had lost interest.

Every society must prohibit behavior which is divisive. But social solidarity does not result from the absence of rape, murder, and theft. True, solidarity could not exist if these harms were freely perpetrated, but lack of them or any overt aggression is not solidarity. Solidarity is the feeling of mutual obligation among members of a group. A family in which each member "minds his own business" has no solidarity even though no arguments or fistfights take place; it has the atmosphere of a rooming house. Family solidarity requires that parents be actively concerned about the welfare of their children and that children consider the feelings of their parents. Religion promotes social solidarity by prescribing positive obligations as well as by prohibiting aggression. The classic statement of religious support of group solidarity is that of Jesus: "Do unto others as you would have others do unto you." The phraseology is reminiscent of Hillel, but emphasis has changed. To put the difference crudely, Hillel was forbidding "bad" acts, Jesus was prescribing "good" ones.

Note that the Golden Rule, because it requires *universal* solidarity, depends on guilt rather than shame to motivate conformity. Violations of the commandment "Honor thy father and thy mother" are easy to detect. If one does not treat one's parents according to the customs of the community, the parents are likely to be resentful, and one may become a subject for neighborhood gossip. On the other hand, the failure to manifest universal love is difficult to measure. Therefore, the **universalistic** norms of religions that prescribe human brotherhood depend on conscience rather than on social pressure. Since urban industrial societies are too fluid for informal group pressure to achieve solidarity, a universalistic religion is more necessary in contemporary than in nonliterate societies.

Religion and Group Integration. Since no one can prove scientifically that life is worth living, an act of faith is necessary to affirm the meaningfulness of life. When this act of faith is anchored to a belief in a supernatural world, a belief shared by a group of persons and symbolized by prescribed collective activities, the individual receives help in dealing with the crises of existence. Concomitantly, *society* is better integrated because it is protected against the demoralization of its members. The death of a loved one, a universal experience, is demoralizing in all societies. In industrial societies life expectancy is relatively long, so bereavement usually occurs later in the life cycle. The psychotherapeutic aspect of funeral ceremonies is more necessary for preliterate peoples, whose death rates are much higher. In the following account anthropologist Bronislaw Malinowski describes how the funeral ritual in a preliterate community helps the bereaved to accept the meaningfulness of life despite his loss:[6]

> Let us start with the religious act par excellence, the ceremonial of death. Here the call to religion arises out of an individual crisis, the death which threatens man or woman. Never does an individual need the comfort of belief and ritual so much as in the sacrament of the viaticum, in the last comforts given to him at the final stage of his life's journey — acts which are well-nigh universal in all primitive religions. These acts are directed against the overwhelming fear, against the corroding doubt, from which the savage is no more free than the civilized man. These acts confirm his hope that there is a hereafter, that it is not worse than present life; indeed, better. All the ritual expresses that belief, that emotional attitude which the dying man requires, which is the greatest comfort he can have in his supreme conflict. And this affirmation has behind it weight of numbers and the pomp of solemn ritual. For in all savage societies, death, as we have seen, compels the whole community to forgather, to attend to the dying, and to carry out the duties towards him. These duties do not, of course, develop any emotional sympathy with the dying — this would lead merely to a disintegrating panic. On the contrary, the line of ritual conduct opposes and contradicts some of the strongest emotions to which the dying man might become a prey. The whole conduct of the group, in fact, expresses the hope of salvation and immortality; that is, it expresses only one among the conflicting emotions of the individual.
>
> After death, though the main actor has made his exit, the tragedy is not at an end. There are the bereaved ones, and these, savage or civilized, suffer alike, and are thrown into a dangerous mental chaos. We have given an analysis of this already, and found that, torn between fear and piety, reverence and horror, love and disgust, they are in a state of mind which might lead to mental disintegration. Out of this, religion lifts the individual by what could be called spiritual cooperation in the sacred mortuary rites. We have seen that in these rites there is expressed the dogma of continuity after death, as well as the moral attitude towards the departed. The corpse, and with it the person of the dead one, is a potential object of horror as well as of tender love. Religion confirms the second part of this double attitude by making the dead body into an object of sacred duties. The bond of union between the recently dead and the survivors is maintained, a fact of immense importance for the continuity of culture and for the safe keeping of tradition. In all this we see that the whole community carries out the biddings of religious tradition, but that these are again enacted for the benefit of a few individuals only, the bereaved ones, that they arise from a personal conflict and are a solution of this conflict. It must also be remembered that what the survivor goes through on such an occasion prepares him for his own death. The belief in immortality, which he has lived through and practiced in the case of his mother or father, makes him realize more clearly his own future life.
>
> In all this we have to make a clear distinction between the belief and the ethics of the ritual on the one hand and on the other the means of enforcing them, the

[6] Reprinted by permission. From Bronislaw Malinowski, "Magic, Science and Religion," in Joseph Needham, Ed., *Science, Religion and Reality* New York: Macmillan, 1925, pp. 57–62.

technique by which the individual is made to receive his religious comfort. The saving belief in spiritual continuity after death is already contained in the individual mind; it is not created by society. The sum total of innate tendencies, known usually as "the instinct of self-preservation," is at the root of this belief. The faith in immortality is, as we have seen, closely connected with the difficulty of facing one's own annihilation or that of a near and beloved person. This tendency makes the idea of the final disappearance of human personality odious, intolerable, socially destructive. Yet this idea and the fear of it always lurk in individual experience, and religion can remove it only by its negation in ritual.

Whether this is achieved by a Providence directly guiding human history, or by a process of natural selection in which a culture which evolves a belief and a ritual of immortality will survive and spread—this is a problem of theology or metaphysics. The anthropologist has done enough when he has shown the value of a certain phenomenon for social integrity and for the continuity of culture. In any case we see that what religion does in this matter is to select one out of the two alternatives suggested to man by his instinctive endowment.

This selection once made, however, society is indispensable for its enactment. The bereaved member of the group, himself overwhelmed by sorrow and fear, is incapable of relying on his own forces. He would be unable by his single effort to apply the dogma to his own case. Here the group steps in. The other members, untouched by the calamity, not torn mentally by the metaphysical dilemma, can respond to the crisis along the lines dictated by the religious order. Thus they bring consolation to the stricken one and lead him through the comforting experiences of religious ceremony. It is always easy to bear the misfortunes—of others, and the whole group, in which the majority are untouched by the pangs of fear and horror, can thus help the afflicted minority. Going through the religious ceremonies, the bereaved emerges changed by the revelation of immortality, communion with the beloved, the order of the next world. Religion commands in acts of cult, the group executes the command.

But, as we have seen, the comfort of ritual is not artificial, not manufactured for the occasion. It is but the result of the two conflicting tendencies which exist in man's innate emotional reaction to death: the religious attitude consists merely in the selection and ritual affirmation of one of these alternatives—the hope in a future life. And here the public concourse gives the emphasis, the powerful testimony to the belief. Public pomp and ceremony take effect through the contagiousness of faith, through the dignity of unanimous consent, the impressiveness of collective behavior. A multitude enacting as one an earnest and dignified ceremony invariably carries away even the disinterested observer, still more the affected participant.

Although funerals in contemporary societies perform the same function as in nonliterate communities, science has made it difficult for industrial man to accept the reassurances offered by these traditional religious observances. When astronomers can calculate the number of light-years separating the earth from various stars and rocket experts send men to the moon, people find it harder to believe in a supernatural world. The natural universe seems so immense that supernatural phenomena are crowded out. In previous generations, children thought that heaven lay above the clouds. Where do they imagine it to be in the space age?

Scientific advances coupled with the individualism characteristic of urban industrial societies have increased commitment to secular alternatives to religion and have shifted the emphasis from Christian existentialism to atheistic existentialism. Christian existentialists gave meaning to their lives by making a "leap into faith" in order to accept supernatural religious beliefs. Existentialists today do not make this leap but define the meaning of their lives through their actions, a way of life consistent with the individualism of urban societies of today.

Secular commitments—for example, identification with spouse and children—enable the individual to ignore the inevitability of his own death. His death does not necessarily imply extinction of the self; he is linked to life through loved ones who survive him. On the other hand, the individual who makes such commitments runs the risk that disasters will befall the persons with whom he is identified. As Francis Bacon put it, a wife and children are "hostages to fortune." The fire in a Boston nightclub in which scores of persons lost their lives showed how shattering premature death can be on the bereaved.[7] Dr. Erich Lindemann, the psychiatrist who tried to get the survivors to accept their loss, found **morbid identification** with the victims a serious obstacle. That is, some survivors were so emotionally entangled with persons lost in the fire that they regarded life without them as meaningless. They developed psychosomatic symptoms, including ulcerated colitis, as well as emotional disturbances. Dr. Lindemann was able to treat some "morbid grievers" successfully, especially those who were oriented to traditional religion and were responsive to the condolences offered by ministers, priests, or rabbis.

Other kinds of secular commitments are functional equivalents of religious faith. Some scientists have a quasi-religious devotion to the pursuit of truth, some artists to the creation of beautiful paintings. Nationalistic fervor is another secular religion. In its milder version, commitment to one's country is called patriotism. In its fanatical version, nationalism can inflame mobs against foreigners in Cairo, Caracas, or Calcutta—and explain arrogant political speeches in Moscow and Washington. Nationalism enables the individual to identify with something that existed before he was born and will presumably last forever: his country. For the nationalist, this identification adds meaning to life. Thus the coronation of Queen Elizabeth contributed to the solidarity of the British community by including the entire population in a secular ritual. A pair of sociologists summed up their interpretation of the coronation ceremony as follows:[8]

> A society is held together by its internal agreement about the sacredness of certain fundamental moral standards. In an inchoate, dimly perceived, and sel-

---

[7] Erich Lindemann, "Symptomatology and Management of Acute Grief," *American Journal of Psychiatry,* Vol. 101, September 1944, pp. 141-148.

[8] Edward A. Shils and Michael Young, "The Meaning of the Coronation," *Sociological Review,* Vol. 1, December 1953, pp. 63-81.

dom explicit manner, the central authority of an orderly society, whether it be secular or ecclesiastical, is acknowledged to be the avenue of communication with the realm of the sacred values. Within its society, popular constitutional monarchy enjoys almost universal recognition in this capacity, and it is therefore enabled to heighten the moral and civic sensibility of the society and to permeate it with symbols of those values to which the sensitivity responds. Intermittent rituals bring the society or varying sectors of it repeatedly into contact with this vessel of the sacred values. The Coronation provided at one time and for practically the entire society such an intensive contact with the sacred that we believe we are justified in interpreting it . . . as a great act of national communion.

Queen Elizabeth reigns but does not rule. No one fears her, although many of her subjects are extraordinarily devoted. Politically powerless but far more permanent than heads of state in republics, she is an uncontroversial national symbol. In dictatorial countries the opposite situation prevails: leaders have enormous political power. Stalin was probably more feared than loved. Nevertheless, dictators can also serve as national symbols. Nasser is the focus of quasi-religious adulation in Egypt.

Nationalism is a secular religion that requires little or no intellectual justification. The least educated Egyptian peasant can respond fervently to the nationalistic appeals broadcast by Radio Cairo. Communism is a secular religion with more of an intellectual tradition, an ideology. It began as an international protest movement against working conditions in nineteenth-century factories and mines. The *Communist Manifesto,* the bible of this religion, was partly political propaganda—Marx and Engels' protest against exploitation of the workers—and partly an analysis of the mechanisms by which the proletariat's suffering would inevitably lead to a revolution that would establish a glorious society. In social psychological terms, the appeal of Communism resembles the appeal of religious movements: for some people, it is a vehicle that transmutes frustrated expectations in the present into extravagant hopes for the future.[9]

The religious aspect of Marxism bears some similarity to the millenarian tradition leading from Persian Zoroastrianism, through the messianic religious hopes of prophetic Judaism, into Christianity and a branch of Islam, and finding contemporary expression in the Seventh Day Adventists, Jehovah's Witnesses, and the Black Muslims.[10] No one would have been more horrified than Marx and Engels to have heard Communism likened to a religious movement; they thought of organized religion as a reactionary force, a bulwark of a social order they wished to supplant. Yet attainment of the society they visualized after the revolution has many parallels with the dreams of salvation entertained by the

[9] Gabriel A. Almond, *The Appeals of Communism,* Princeton, N.J.: Princeton University Press, 1954.

[10] Yonina Talmon, "Millenarism," *International Encyclopedia of the Social Sciences,* Vol. 10, New York: Macmillan, 1968, pp. 349-362.

adherents of **millenarian** cults. Consider the five characteristics of millenarian dreams:[11]

1. Salvation is to be enjoyed by the faithful as a group.
2. Salvation is to be realized on earth.
3. Salvation will come soon and suddenly.
4. Life on earth will be transformed into a state of perfection, not merely improved.
5. This will be accomplished through the intervention of supernatural agencies.

By the first four criteria, Communism qualifies as millenarian. It differs from traditional millenarian movements mainly in denying the necessity of supernatural intervention. Thus a dimly foreseen Revolution takes the place of a Judgment Day of the millenarian sect. The sacred writings of the Communist movement are the works of Marx, Engels, Lenin, and Stalin and are not assumed to be divinely inspired. The society to be established on the other side of the Revolution is, like Paradise, rather vague, but it will be enjoyed collectively by the faithful. And what happens to the faithful when the Revolution comes and the world remains grey and inglorious? Some suffer demoralization similar to that experienced by adherents of a millenarian sect when Judgment Day fails to arrive on schedule.[12] Many adherents of Communism faced demoralization and bitter personal disillusionment after the Bolshevik revolution of 1917.[13] The bloody Soviet purges of the 1930s culminating in the Moscow trials, the Nazi-Soviet alliance of 1939, and the repression of intellectual and artistic freedom caused spiritual turmoil among Communists. However, the failure of Russian reality to live up to the Marxist dream has not destroyed Communism any more than revisions in the schedule for Judgment Day have destroyed Jehovah's Witnesses.

A mechanism of psychological defense helps to explain why the adherent redoubles his efforts after the original goal begins to slip away. When an individual commits himself to a religion, secular or supernatural, he derives initial benefits in terms of relieving some of the intellectual and emotional stresses of his life. But he also makes personal sacrifices, which would themselves be frustrating did they not have meaning in terms of his faith. Such sacrifices are an obstacle to admitting to himself that his faith might be idolatrous, even in the face of disillusioning experiences. The life of poverty and chastity of the priest becomes by this psychological mechanism a secondary defense of his religious beliefs. A similar defense mechanism may account for the insistence of the Chinese Communists on ideological purity; they also have subordinated personal pleasure and family life for their creed. To admit its inadequacies is to

---

[11] Sylvia L. Thrupp, Ed., *Millenial Dreams in Action,* Supplement II to *Comparative Studies in Society and History,* The Hague: Mouton, 1962.

[12] Leon Festinger, Henry W. Riecken, and Stanley Schacter, *When Prophecy Fails,* Minneapolis: University of Minnesota Press, 1956.

[13] Richard Crossman, *The God That Failed,* New York: Harper, 1950.

deny the significance of their commitment. The Russian Communists, unlike the Chinese, have been in business for a half century. The Old Bolsheviks, who bled and labored to bring the dream into being, are mostly dead. The new leaders, having given fewer hostages to fortune, can afford to be more flexible. They are willing to believe that peaceful coexistence with capitalist countries is possible.

The Emergence of New Religions. This comparison between the doctrinaire Chinese Communists and the more pragmatic Russians suggests the distinction between the **sect** and the **church.** According to sociologists of religion, the sect is a religious group that rejects its social environment, whereas the church comes to terms with it.[14] Rejection is a matter of degree; many religious groups accept some aspects of the secular world and condemn others. But clear-cut extremes exist. Jehovah's Witnesses believe that the modern world is hopelessly corrupt; they refuse to salute the flag of any nation or to serve in any army because this would be trafficking with the Devil.[15] On the other hand, the Anglican Church, the official Church of England, is deeply implicated in British social organization. Other characteristics of sects and churches are understandable in terms of their defining stance toward the secular world. Members of sects tend to be less educated and less prosperous than members of churches. Members of sects are not only more critical of society but also of other religions. Church members are readier to believe in alternative paths to God. The church includes the infant offspring of members because grace can be dispensed routinely by ecclesiastical specialists. The sect often insists on a spiritual call to membership not heard until adolescence or adulthood.

In short, the sect gives its members a definition of reality as fundamentally depraved, and it makes life bearable by offering a redemptive vision. If, however, the sect persuades large numbers of people that its vision is correct, it runs the risk of becoming part of the power structure of the society. As it gains power and prestige, it cannot easily maintain an attitude of thoroughgoing rejection of the society; it has unwittingly become a pillar of that society. Thus sects either die out or show a tendency to evolve into more conservative religious organizations, churches.[16] Christianity, from its beginnings as a millenarian offshoot of Judaism, illustrates this process.[17] Early Christians had no thought of dominating the Roman world. They assumed that the Second Coming was imminent, and they prepared for this event by spreading the Gospel. Even if they had presumed to think that their humble fellow-believers could shake the Roman state, there was no point in doing so for the little time that was left. In the fourth century, however, the Emperor Constantine embraced Christianity as the official religion of the Roman state. Moreover, the Second

---

[14] Benton Johnson, "On Church and Sect," *American Sociological Review,* Vol. 28, August 1963, pp. 539-549.

[15] Royston Pike, *Jehovah's Witnesses,* New York: Philosophical Library, 1954.

[16] H. Richard Niebuhr, *The Social Sources of Denominationalism,* New York: Holt, 1929.

[17] Parsons, "Religious Perspectives," pp. 21-28.

United Press International

Coming seemed less imminent. Consideration began to be given by church leaders—it was by this time a church rather than a sect—to long-run relations with a going society.

Though the Catholic Church retained a suspicion of wealth and power inherited from its millenarian past, by the Middle Ages it possessed both wealth and power. Cathedrals and monasteries, though devoted to religious purposes, also constituted wealth in the economic sense. At its zenith the Church held title to about a third of the land of Europe.[18] This being so, the Church could not avoid being an economic force in medieval society. When monks raised crops on Church lands, they contributed significantly to Europe's food supply. Similarly, the Church could not avoid exercising secular power. Even as late as 1431 when Joan of Arc was burned at the stake by the English, she was first tried in a Church court and convicted of heresy, witchcraft, and sorcery. Only then was she given to secular authorities for execution; Bishop Cauchon knew well that excommunication of Joan was equivalent to a death sentence. In

[18] Parsons, "Religious Perspectives," p. 26.

short, the Church wielded secular power not only because it had land and soldiers but because its advice on political matters was heeded by kings and
nobles. From the point of view of a radical insistence on the redemptive value
of poverty and meekness, the medieval Church was corrupted by its own success. It gained universal acceptance of its ideas but in doing so prevented their
realization in its own organization. "It is not possible to influence the lives of
men . . . without being involved in the moral dilemmas of power."[19]

But this is true not only of the Middle Ages. Once institutionalized, churches
invariably become implicated in secular activities — even though their doc-
trines explicitly repudiate the things of this world. A church thereby becomes
less capable of rationalizing realistic frustrations and reassuring alienated elements of the society. Norman Vincent Peale's "power of positive thinking" is
attractive to successful sales executives but not to those whose discouragement
with life reflects a hopeless situation. Contemporary Christian theologians are
well aware of the tendency for churches to blunt the radical implications of
the biblical message and to settle back into complacency. Paul Tillich entitled his Terry Lectures at Yale "The Courage To Be" because he felt that
affirmation of the meaningfulness of life requires an act of courage.[20] Similarly, Reinhold Niebuhr has insisted that religion must come to grips with the
tragedy of human existence or subside into sentimentality and irrelevance.[21]

> Moral sensitivity inevitably leads to pessimism. Only callous men can be
> consistent optimists. Social intelligence likewise leads to pessimism. Only ig-
> norant men are optimists. The sensitive man recognizes the extent of human mis-
> ery, and the intelligent man knows how many hopes for a world in which in-
> justice and human brutality would be eliminated have been disappointed. He
> knows that a terrible inertia frustrates, or seems to frustrate, every redemptive
> effort. . . .
>
> Certainly nothing that is worth doing can ever be completed in the life of one
> generation. Every Moses perishes outside of the promised land and can behold
> it only through the eyes of faith. Religion is the hope that grows out of despair.
> It is the ultimate optimism which follows in the wake of a thorough pessimism.
> One reason why our generation is not religious is that it has been too senti-
> mental to be thoroughly pessimistic. It has never looked into the bottomless
> abyss, on the edge of which all citadels of faith are built. . . . If progress be re-
> garded as automatic, there is no real place for religion, however diligent may be
> the effort to read God into the evolutionary process.

The efforts of theologians like Niebuhr and Tillich to retain the prophetic
character of the biblical message have partially succeeded. Ministers, priests,
and rabbis have been in the forefront of the struggle for civil rights in the United

---

[19] Parsons, "Religious Perspectives," p. 25.

[20] Paul Tillich, *The Courage To Be*, New Haven, Conn.: Yale University Press, 1952.

[21] Reinhold Niebuhr, *The Contribution of Religion to Social Work*, New York: Columbia
University Press, 1932, pp. 72-74.

States. Official statements of major denominations have vigorously supported programs of racial reconciliation. Theologians have been less successful in drawing the attention of conservative church *memberships* to the radical implications of the Judeo-Christian tradition. The conservative tendencies of existing churches is especially unsatisfying in periods of social turmoil. New evidence of the relevance of religious values are needed at these times, especially for persons whose lives are most severely disorganized. In these terms, the growth of the Black Muslim movement among American Negroes reflects the readjustments faced by a population, largely rural in experience, in an urban industrial environment. The Christian sects and churches that adequately interpreted the frustrations of *rural* life were less successful than the Muslims with the underprivileged and undereducated in the *urban* ghettoes.[22]

> By redefining one's racial identity, by repudiating the white man's religion and attacking him as a knave, the 100,000 or more members of [the Muslim] movement seek for salvation from their soul-crushing lives. Most of the members are recent migrants into large cities, where their old accommodative patterns of life have been destroyed, their aspirations raised, their sense of power enhanced. Yet the painful facts of disprivilege and discrimination remain. It is in this context that the young, mostly male, mostly lower-class, often functionally illiterate Negroes join the Black Muslims.

When suffering cannot be justified by traditional religious ideas, the sufferer may be attracted by a new religion offering a simple and (to him) convincing explanation. The Black Muslims tell ghetto Negroes that their frustrations result from the fact that white men are devils. This makes sense of the tantalizing combination of aroused expectations and capricious degradation. Consider the experience of Cassius Clay, a Negro school dropout from Louisville, who won an Olympic medal for the United States in boxing and a Golden Gloves championship. He had some reason to believe that a boxing champion would be treated by his fellow Americans as "the greatest." As a Negro, however, he was still, in 1960, subject to the racial etiquette of a Southern city. "He was walking down a Louisville street when a large car pulled alongside and a white man leaned out. 'Hey, boy, hey, you boy, get on over heah,' the man shouted. 'I want yoah autograph.'"[23] Not long after, Clay won the world heavyweight boxing championship and made public his membership in the Black Muslim sect. He had found a religion with a simple explanation of his complex identity problem.

In short, new sects proliferate when the churches fail to satisfy the need for meaningful interpretation of life problems. In pointing this out, sociologists do not presume to evaluate the validity of the religious ideas that become popular. Both demonic movements like Naziism and creative innovations in cul-

---

[22] J. Milton Yinger, *Sociology Looks at Religion,* New York: Macmillan, 1961, p. 47.

[23] Robert Lipsyte, "Cassius Clay, Cassius X, Muhammad Ali," *The New York Times Magazine,* October 25, 1964, p. 110.

Robert Malloch—Magnum

tural development are responses to social psychological strains. Nor do new
religions emerge only in advanced societies. The **cargo cult** of Melanesia and
the peyote cult of American Indians in the Southwest are examples of the religious responses of preliterate societies. In contemporary Japan the *Soka
Gakkai* sect has grown fantastically since the Second World War and includes
more than ten million Japanese. "Soka Gakkai" means "the value-creating
academy"—an appropriate name for a religious movement that strives to
make sense of a society transformed first by defeat in war and subsequently by

rapid economic growth. Ivan Morris' description of the movement emphasizes its usefulness in reducing the disorganizing impact of social and cultural change:[24]

> It is an evangelistic, well-knit politico-religious group that promises, and indeed provides, solutions for many of the difficulties that beset the less favored elements of the population, notably unorganized members of the urban working class. For increasing millions of Japanese people it satisfies needs that other religious and political parties seem unable to meet. . . .
>
> The main aim is to secure man's happiness. This can be done by the creation of proper "values," of which the most important is private and social "gain." The philosophical transcendental and mystical aspects of religion are disregarded; everything is focused on finding the most practical answers to mundane problems: keeping sober, making friends, getting a job.

[24] Ivan Morris, "Soka Gakkai Brings 'Absolute Happiness,'" *The New York Times Magazine*, July 18, 1965, pp. 9, 36.

Typical Soka Gakkai activities are not church services but group meetings in which members unburden their problems to each other's sympathetic ears. In addition to these therapeutic discussions there are body-building clubs, singing circles, culture festivals and rallies of a type especially popular in Japan. Through activities such as these, Soka Gakkai helps to relieve people—especially the poorer members of the community—from their dissatisfactions and achieve the goal of a "bright home" in accordance with the group's slogan: "The home community as a vehicle of salvation."

The Soka Gakkai and Black Muslim movements show how sects function to satisfy a society's needs. In preliterate societies, an individual has only one religion available if he requires the comfort of supernatural faith in the crises of existence. The same situation prevailed in medieval Christendom. In these circumstances the religious organization is a church rather than a sect. It supports the existing institutional framework because it is inextricably involved in that framework by dint of its monopolistic character. As societies became more differentiated, different needs were satisfied by the growth of religious sects. In modern societies where legitimate competition for communicants exists among religious organizations religion is not clearly conducive to social integration. Some sects are savagely critical of secular society as well as of competing sects. A case can be made for the divisive role of religion in pluralistic societies.[25] But it can be argued that religious cleavages are often forerunners of social change, which may be necessary for including an increasing proportion of the society in the web of solidarity. If social integration is thought of in ultimate rather than immediate terms, religious *sects* may promote integration by calling attention to needs unmet by the more conservative *churches.* A society with an established church—like Sweden—may find that a large proportion of the population cannot utilize the church to cope with problems of identity and meaning. This is less likely to happen in a religiously pluralistic society where Holy Rollers are as legitimate as Episcopalians.

THE DIFFERENTIATION OF RELIGION IN INDUSTRIAL SOCIETIES

Like the family and the economy, religion in an industrial society is different from religion in a nonliterate community. Religion is a more specialized part of the cultural tradition in modern societies. In preliterate societies religious traits cannot easily be distinguished from artistic or technological traits. In industrial societies the culture is differentiated into subcultures (as Chapter 3 pointed out). In the course of Western history, art, science, and education, all of which were closely associated with the church, became independent realms

[25] Allan W. Eister, "Religious Institutions in Complex Societies: Difficulties in the Theoretic Specification of Function," *American Sociological Review,* Vol. 22, August 1957, pp. 387-391.

of ideas and practice. The relationship between religious behavior and other activities is looser in industrial societies than in less differentiated societies. Whereas in a nonliterate community a religious dimension permeates every aspect of life from agriculture to warfare, in an industrial society religion tends to be segregated from economic, political, educational, artistic, and scientific activities and embodied in a special-purpose organization, the church. Furthermore, the local church is usually affiliated with a larger organization having national and sometimes international interests.

An organized religion, like other special-purpose organizations, must compete for societal resources and support. In American society, this means going into the market and buying land for a church, paying a contractor to put up a structure, and hiring a minister to lead the congregation. Thus religious organizations cannot be indifferent to money because money is a means for realizing religious as well as secular goals. Organizational requirements have a logic of their own. Some evangelical sects condemn drinking, smoking, dancing, and gambling despite the likelihood that this ascetic attitude will alienate potential support. Instead of having full-time, salaried ministers, who attended divinity school in order to achieve professional status, they may rely on unpaid, part-time "ministers" with meager religious education and much enthusiasm. On the other hand, established denominations are more likely to sponsor dances for young people and bingo for their elders, and to counsel long-winded ministers that "no souls are saved after 15 minutes." The compromise which a particular denomination strikes between traditional values and the necessities of gaining support from secular society helps explain the differences in the values of adherents of various religious groups.

Sociologists have long been interested in empirical studies showing the social consequences of differentiated religious organizations with a variety of value commitments. For instance, Robert Merton showed that the Puritan contribution to English scientific development in the seventeenth and eighteenth centuries was disproportionately great. Professor Merton's explanation of the disproportion is that the Puritan value complex demanded " . . . the systematic, rational, and empirical study of Nature for the glorification of God in His works and for the control of the corrupt world."[26] Merton, like Max Weber before him, showed that Karl Marx was mistaken in his belief that organized religion necessarily supported the status quo. Weber's studies in the sociology of religion demonstrated through comparative analysis of Europe, China, India, and ancient Judea that the Protestant attitude toward economic activities made Western Europe more receptive to capitalism than otherwise comparable societies.[27] Weber did not maintain that the growth of Protestantism in Western

[26] Robert K. Merton, "Puritanism, Pietism and Science," in *Social Theory and Social Structure,* rev. ed., Glencoe, Ill.: Free Press, 1957, pp. 574-606.

[27] Max Weber, *The Protestant Ethic and the Spirit of Capitalism,* New York: Scribner's, 1930; Max Weber, *The Religion of China: Confucianism and Taoism,* Glencoe, Ill.: Free Press, 1951; Max Weber, *Ancient Judaism,* Glencoe, Ill.: Free Press, 1952; Max Weber, *The Religion of India: The Sociology of Hinduism and Buddhism,* Glencoe, Ill.: Free Press, 1958.

Euope *caused* capitalism to develop, but he showed that certain religious values were a necessary ingredient. He showed further that early entrepreneurs in Western Europe and the United States were likely to be members of Protestant sects that encouraged members to look for signs of divine favor in entrepreneurial success. For instance, the Calvinist belief in predestination was coupled with the notion that God would not permit members of His Elect to fare poorly in this world. Calvinists therefore desired secular achievements for genuinely religious reasons. They needed financial accomplishments to validate their presumption of Election; they were usually ascetic in their personal behavior and had no interest in using the proceeds of success for high living. In short, Weber demonstrated the connection between these religious attitudes (the **Protestant Ethic**) and self-disciplined work conducive to economic development.

A recent study in the Weber tradition sought to discover whether membership in Protestant denominations continues to differentiate the population in a mature industrial society. Do economically successful Americans come disproportionately from certain denominations? Table 8.1, based on survey data from Detroit, shows considerable variation in the socioeconomic composition of denominations. This variation can be explained in one of three ways:

1. Belonging to a denomination that encourages hard work in a secular calling makes economic success more likely.
2. Members of some denominations start out with competitive advantages over members of other denominations.
3. Individuals who achieve economic success convert to high-prestige denominations *after* their rise.

The study of the Detroit population from which Table 8.1 is taken contains no data on changes in denominational affiliation, but it takes account of three variables that might affect *initial* opportunities for economic success: rural birth, foreign birth or parentage, and length of residence in Detroit.[28] The researchers show that these three ascribed factors alone or in combination cannot account for all of the variability in the economic achievements of the religious denominations included in the survey. Unless it is assumed that the remaining variability can be explained by changes in denominational affiliations subsequent to economic advancement, the Weber thesis continues to be relevant to industrial societies.

In positing the Protestant Ethic as an independent variable, Weber assumed that members of the Protestant sects were concerned enough about eternal salvation to be influenced profoundly by theological definitions of the possibilities in the next world. Recent American surveys show that 25 per cent of Catholics, 35 per cent of all Protestants, and half the members of liberal Protestant denominations (Congregationalists, Methodists, and Episcopalians) are

---

[28] Albert J. Mayer and Harry Sharp, "Religious Preference and Worldly Success," *American Sociological Review,* Vol. 27, April 1962, pp. 218-227.

TABLE 8.1

Socioeconomic Composition of Religious Groups, Detroit, 1954–1959

Religious Group and Race	Median Income $2,000 and Above (Per Cent)	Self-Employed (Per Cent)	High-Status Occupations (Per Cent)	Median School Year Completed
White				
Catholic	27	7	19	10.0
Episcopalian	35	9	42	12.5
Lutheran	30	6	28	12.2
Calvinist	35	11	37	12.5
Methodist	32	8	27	12.3
Baptist	21	6	15	9.8
Small sects	16	11	17	9.5
No denomination	29	11	26	12.0
Semi-Christian	24	15	39	12.4
Jewish	42	41	62	12.5
Eastern Orthodox	35	15	13	9.3
No preference	23	9	28	10.0
Negro				
Catholic	6	4	7	10.0
Methodist	7	5	6	9.8
Baptist	8	3	3	9.1
Other	12	10	15	9.8

Source: Albert J. Mayer and Harry Sharp, "Religious Preference and Worldly Success," *American Sociological Review*, Vol. 27, April 1962, p. 224.

doubtful about "life beyond death."[29] This skepticism is likely to increase in the decades ahead, particularly in the liberal denominations. Two researchers in the sociology of religion concluded on the basis of American surveys that there is a general decline in commitment to the Christian religion:[30]

> While many Americans are still firmly committed to the traditional, super-natural conceptions of a personal God, a Divine Savior, and the promise of eternal life, the trend is away from these convictions. Although we must expect an extended period of doubt, the fact is that a demythologized modernism is over-whelming the traditional Christ-centered, mystical faith.

If traditional faith declines, membership in denominations will cease to have predictive value for economic and social behavior. The denominational

---

[29] Charles Y. Glock and Rodney Stark, "Is There an American Protestantism?" *Trans-action*, Vol. 3, November-December 1965, p. 11.

[30] Rodney Stark and Charles Y. Glock, "Will Ethics Be the Death of Christianity?" *Trans-action*, Vol. 5, June 1968, p. 7.

tag will not reflect value commitments but accidents of family history. Under these circumstances the function of providing meaning would shift from supernatural religion to secular faiths and to private systems of ultimate significance.[31] But in the contemporary United States religious organization is still a pervasive factor in society.

Denominational Pluralism in the United States.[32] Organized religion has influence on secular society in the United States but no power over it. American denominations cannot claim the support of the state to propagate their religious ideas or to penalize dissidents. Moreover, although religious groups are free to set up parochial schools, public education, from primary school to college, is a secular matter. Further, unlike the medieval Church, American denominations have no formal *right* to regulate private morals. For instance, a man whose sexual habits were unusual might be condemned by his neighbors and possibly arrested by the police; his conscience might trouble him. But he could not be called to account by a religious organization except voluntarily. True, his friends might advise him to talk the matter over with his minister. But he would just as likely be advised to consult a psychiatrist. Behavior that would surely have been considered sinful in medieval times is more likely in contemporary America to be regarded as a symptom of mental illness amenable to secular treatment or as the individual's private concern. Thus criminality is usually conceived of as personal wickedness, sometimes as a symptom of mental illness, but rarely as sinful.[33] Some students of religion believe this trend can be extrapolated to suggest that organized religion is on the way out in America.

Jurisdictional retreat is regarded as one sign of the twilight of organized religion. Another is the loss of faith in the supernatural underpinnings of Judaism and Christianity. Recall that Stark and Glock concluded from their survey of American denominations that there was growing skepticism toward traditional beliefs. They inferred from the erosion of faith "that this *may* very well be the dawn of a post-Christian era."[34] Another scholar contrasted the flourishing outward forms of religiosity in America—church attendance, church membership, prayer, religious instruction for children—with the secular values of Protestants, Catholics, and Jews.[35] He concluded that the old forms remain but without biblical content; the real religion of America is the American Way of Life. In short, religion has succumbed to secularism. Denominations should be thought of not as fellowships of believers but as private clubs providing weekly meetings and neighborliness for a mobile population.

---

[31] Thomas Luckman, *The Invisible Religion: the Problem of Religion in Modern Society,* New York: Macmillan, 1967.

[32] The analysis in this section leans heavily on Talcott Parsons, "Some Comments on the Pattern of Religious Organization in the United States," in *Structure and Process in Modern Societies,* Glencoe, Ill.: Free Press, 1960, pp. 295-321.

[33] Richard V. McCann, *Delinquency: Sickness or Sin?,* New York: Harper, 1957.

[34] Stark and Glock, "Will Ethics Be the Death of Christianity?" p. 7.

[35] Will Herberg, *Protestant, Catholic, Jew,* Garden City, N.Y.: Doubleday, 1955.

Talcott Parsons interprets the same data differently. Parsons agrees that religion in America has struck a new balance with secular society. But he interprets the separation of religion from government, from education, and from science not as atrophy but as part of a process of institutional specialization characteristic of industrial societies. According to this conception, religious organizations have given over some activities to specialized secular agencies, for example, education to public schools, in a process parallel to the one transferring economic activities from the household to the factory. It can be argued that the loss of economic functions has weakened the family just as it can be argued that loss of control over secular education weakened organized religion in America. Yet organized religion may remain viable without power over government, education, or science and with a reduction in the supernatural grounding of its dogmas if the critical issue is *its capacity to provide meaning for the individual communicant.*

From this point of view, the values of secular society and organized religion are not necessarily incompatible. They share values because both have emerged from the same tradition. According to Parsons, American society and the Judeo-Christian tradition share a faith in **activism,** a philosophy of mastery over physical or social obstacles as opposed to passive acceptance or mystical escape. Unlike the Confucian, who adapts to the world with oriental resignation, or the Hindu, who seeks to attain peace through personal improvement in successive incarnations, those in the Judeo-Christian tradition have the ideal of transforming the world in accordance with the divine will. American society, partly because of its religious heritage, partly because of the exuberance bred of successful achievement, is also confident that the world can be made over. One of the explicit goals of the First World War was "making the world safe for democracy." And a sign appearing in war plants and military installations during the Second World War read: "The difficult we do immediately. For the impossible, give us 24 hours." American enthusiasm for science, which is at bottom an effort to *force* nature to give up her secrets, continues this activistic tradition. A secular activist may have a different image of the world he wishes to bring into being from that of the committed Christian, but they share an assumption that the world need not be accepted as it is but can be transformed. They are rivals in interpreting the meaning of life, but they understand one another and tolerate the competition. The Chinese Communists, on the other hand, regard the Confucian religion as opposed to society because of the incompatibility of Confucian resignation and Communist activism.

American society and the Judeo-Christian tradition also share a faith in the *importance of the individual.* This religious tradition stresses the dignity of the human being created in the image of God. The brotherhood of man derives from the fatherhood of God; in the eyes of the Father, all of His children are of *equal* worth. The eighteenth-century ideas concerning the natural rights of man, so evident in the Declaration of Independence, were fully compatible with this religious egalitarianism. Equality of educational and economic opportunity, equality before the law, the right of the individual to express his opinions and to participate in the political process, his right to privacy — these rights and privileges considered fundamental in a democratic society are also fundamental to the religious belief in the importance of the individual. Thus many persons who are agnostic or otherwise alienated from organized religion may be impressed with such "democratic" behavior as the efforts of church-men to secure equal rights for Negroes. True, there are militant atheists who regard organized religion as a menace, and there are fundamentalist sects that regard secular society as an instrument of the Devil. But the broad picture of American society shows a feeling of tolerance between religious organiza-tions and secular institutions, and part of the explanation for this harmony is consensus on key values.

Another reason for harmony is organizational. The separation of church and state provided for in the Constitution was partly an accident of history. The religious diversity of the thirteen colonies was too great to permit any one the privileges of an Established Church. Separation of church and state was therefore a necessary compromise. The equality among an indefinite plurality of competing denominations, none of which received government support, means that religion had been entrusted to voluntary associations. Individuals were free to join and support a church or sect just as they were free to join a political club or a learned society — and free not to join any if they were so inclined. Religion was relegated to the sphere of private affairs.

Denominational pluralism may have reduced the cleavage between religion and secular society. Since there was a multiplicity of denominations, each with its own dogmas and practices, it was not a simple matter to identify "the" religious position. Lack of consensus among denominations prevented them from uniting to impose religious ideals on society. Moreover, since equally legitimate religious organizations took quite different stances, it be-came hard to deny *any* group the right to call itself a religion. Thus the Mor-mons were at first persecuted but eventually accepted as fully legitimate. At the present time, the Black Muslim sect is not recognized as a religious group in most American prisons, but if past examples can be used to predict the future, Black Muslim prisoners will eventually obtain the right to hold religious services.

What about *private* religiosity? Given the legitimacy of almost any religious group, it seems arbitrary to maintain that an individual can be religious only if he formally affiliates with a congregation. (Arbitrary or not, the Selective Serv-ice System used to take this position in judging the validity of conscientious objection to bearing arms.) The next step beyond recognizing the legitimacy of personal religiosity is recognizing the legitimacy of secular morality un-supported by supernatural commitments. Many Americans have already taken it. It is still a political liability to be agnostic or atheistic, but such beliefs are increasingly regarded as private preferences that do not interfere with social respectability.

The pluralistic organization of American religious life softens the areas of conflict between religion and secular society. Another organizational factor, the similarity between the self-governing structures of most denominations and those of secular voluntary associations, also serves to allay conflict. Such structural parallelism facilitates mutual understanding. An exception is the Catholic Church, which, unlike most Protestant and all Jewish congregations, is not organized as a self-governing voluntary association. Unlike the minister and the rabbi, who are religious teachers and enjoy no special authority in matters of faith or morals, the priest wields such authority by virtue of his office. This authoritarian stance of the Catholic Church runs counter to the more equalitarian approach to policy making in secular voluntary associations. Furthermore, Protestants and Jews are prone to interpret priestly intermediaries between man and God as an encroachment on the dignity and freedom of the individual. The hierarchial structure of the Catholic Church not only reduces individual autonomy but it seems to enable the Church to be more consistent throughout the country and more effective in influencing the secular community than self-governing religious groups. In short, value conflicts and organizational frictions between the Catholic Church and secular America make for a sharper cleavage between religion and society than would obtain if the United States contained only Jews and Protestants.

In Catholic countries like France and Italy the cleavage between religion and society is more serious than in the United States. In these countries religiously based political parties tend to polarize the society. The middle classes, the preindustrial élites, and a majority of the peasants support the Catholic parties; workers, socialists, and Communists support anticlerical parties. The identification of the Catholic Church and the political parties associated it with conservatism, though not entirely accurate, has historical justification. The Church has not used its power to press for rapid change even when rapid change seemed necessary. The United States, unlike European countries with the tradition of an Established Church, succeeded in keeping religion in the private rather than in the public sphere. Hence *political* cleavages were not reinforced by preexisting *religious* cleavages and denominations or between believers in supernatural religion and militant secularists. This explains how denominational pluralism minimized conflict between religion and secular society in the United States and thus promoted political stability. The only recent issue on which religious groups took a public stand, race relations, was one on which secular democrats and religious leaders agreed.[36]

> The great practical impact of the moral pronouncements of religious leaders about racial integration stems in part from the fact that they are so completely in accord with the democratic values of the American culture. Religious and political motivations are mutually supportive—the politician can use scripture to confirm constitutional arguments, and the religious spokesman can use the principles of democracy to confirm the need for brotherhood under God.

[36] Joseph H. Fichter, "American Religion and the Negro," *Daedalus,* Vol. 94, Fall 1965, p. 1094.

Harmony between the religious community and secular society depends on the greater strength of the forces working toward consensus than of those making for cleavage. One of the forces making for cleavage has been mentioned, namely, the discrepancy between the hierarchial organization of the Catholic Church and the self-governing organization of Protestant and Jewish congregations. Ethnic differences have magnified this organizational tension. The Protestant denominations contain ethnic groups whose ancestors came to America long ago; the Catholic Church contains persons of Irish, Italian, Polish, and Puerto Rican background whose forebears arrived within the past century. Not only are Protestants of colonial stock prone to look down on recent arrivals for ethnic reasons; they also have a socioeconomic basis for snobbery. White Protestants are usually upper class or middle class, whereas the recent immigrants are usually working class. Thus ethnic and socioeconomic prejudice magnifies the organization tensions between Catholic and Protestant.

Within Protestantism the chief ethnic cleavage is between whites and Negroes. At the national level every major Protestant denomination has gone on record in favor of desegregation of its own congregations.[37] Still, the bulk of American Negroes are Protestants worshiping in segregated congregations. Part of the reason for this is residential segregation within the city as well as economic pressure on blacks to live in inner-city areas rather than in suburbs. Another factor is the racial prejudice of white congregations. However, unlike the situation in South Africa, American Protestantism does not justify segregation; it officially condemns it.

[37] Fichter, "American Religion and the Negro," p. 1090.

The cleavage between Christians and Jews is partly religious and partly ethnic. Some Christians blame the Jews for the death of Jesus and resent the unwillingness of Jews to acknowledge his divinity.[38] On the other hand, Unitarians, who also deny the divinity of Jesus, are theologically close to the Reform Jews. Other liberal Protestant denominations (Congregationalists, Methodists, Episcopalians) have rejected literal interpretations of the Bible and therefore do not find Jewish disbelief of New Testament miracles religiously disturbing. In short, there are Protestant fundamentalists and conservative Catholics who are religiously troubled by Jews, but no unanimous religious hostility among Christians.

One final threat to religious equilibrium should be mentioned: the social inequality among denominations. Not only is the membership of the Catholic Church of generally lower status than the membership of white Protestant churches; *within* Protestantism some churches are more affluent and socially élite than others; and within Judaism some congregations also have a reputation of socioeconomic distinction. A system in which congregational membership is voluntary implies that religious organizations reflect the socioeconomic inequalities of secular society. Despite religious concerns, denominations are also voluntary associations in competition with one another for membership. Thus some shifts are due to a desire to belong to a more élite denomination. Sometimes families will affiliate with a congregation to facilitate the moral education and guidance of their children.[39] And some shifts are due to changing religious needs in accordance with the individual's unique experiences and his stage in the life cycle. The existence of alternative affiliations may promote social inequality, but it means that diverse solutions to religious problems are more readily available to the population.

While shifts in affiliation create some denominations with a larger proportion of well-educated business and professional families and others with a working-class flavor (see Table 8.1), the socioeconomic range within each denomination is considerable. The socioeconomic differences *within* denominations exceed the differences *between* denominations. This loose relationship between religious affiliation and other social characteristics actually facilitates the integration of American society. Instead of reinforcing cleavages between the well-educated and the poorly educated or between businessmen and manual workers, religious affiliation cross-cuts such cleavages and thereby blunts their divisive impact. The potential for conflict among adherents of different religions is greatest when religious differences are reinforced by other distinctions: ethnic background, education, geographic location, social class. On the other hand, a religious difference is less likely to generate conflict when people divided by religious affiliation are united by other solidarities. Religious har-

---

[38] Charles Y. Glock and Rodney Stark, *Christian Beliefs and Anti-Semitism,* New York: Harper and Row, 1966.

[39] Dennison Nash and Peter Berger, "The Child, the Family and the 'Religious Revival' in Suburbia," *Journal for the Scientific Study of Religion,* Vol. 2, Fall 1962, pp. 85-93.

mony in American society can therefore be explained partly in terms of cross-cutting solidarities:[40]

> ... Catholics have diffused upwards in the economic structure, and outward geographically to the suburbs; Jews similarly are less concentrated in particular economic roles and geographic locations than before; Protestants who grew up in one sect in a community are dispersed and recongregated in communities where sects must combine to survive. In sum, economic and geographic mobility is imposing new conditions of association and group identification on persons of different religious groups.

The harmony among denominations in the United States and between religious organizations and secular society has proved stable thus far. The factors making for cleavage—the different organizational principles of the Catholic Church and of Protestant and Jewish congregations, ethnic and religious prejudice, and the socioeconomic stratification of congregations—are becoming less divisive with the passage of time. Protestantism is now less fundamentalist in orientation. The Catholic Church is modifying its hierarchical principle in the direction of greater consultation with laymen and with parish priests. Except for black-white differences, which remain highly visible, ethnic differences are growing less important. Intermarriage has been increasing between Jews and Christians as well as between Catholics and Protestants.[41] Meanwhile the common values underlying consensus—especially the concern for the individual both in secular society and in the Judeo-Christian tradition—continue to bind American society together.

Denominational pluralism has succeeded in the United States in two senses. First, it prevented a sharp cleavage between clerical and anticlerical groups, as occurs in some countries. Second, it enabled organized religion to flourish in terms of membership and of the absence of opposition. If attendance at religious services is not as great as ministers, priests, and rabbis would like, attendance is not good at union meetings, public lectures, and other voluntary associations either. Success is a limited one; the United States is not a theocracy. On the other hand, the United States is not militantly atheistic in the style of Communist China or the Soviet Union. The supernatural aspect of organized religion may decrease as the population grows more sophisticated, scientifically oriented, and better educated. The "death of God" theology reflects this trend. The complete disappearance of supernatural religion is less likely. The stalwarts of most congregations will continue to be those whose religious needs are greatest. It is doubtful whether secular faiths or abstract modern theologies

---

[40] James S. Coleman, "Social Cleavage and Religious Conflict," *Journal of Social Issues,* Vol. 12, No. 3, 1956, p. 47.

[41] John L. Thomas, S.J., "The Factor of Religion in the Selection of Marriage Mates," *American Sociological Review,* Vol. 16, August 1951, pp. 487-491; David M. Heer, "The Trend in Interfaith Marriage in Canada: 1922–1957," *American Sociological Review,* Vol. 27, April 1962, pp. 245-250.

address these needs as satisfactorily as supernatural religion. Furthermore, sophisticated modernism and fundamentalism have learned to live together within congregations just as secular and religious organizations coexist within the larger society. Although it is unlikely, one issue that might precipitate a knock-down, drag-out fight between supernatural religion and secularism is the religious education of children.

Religious Socialization in a Pluralistic Society. Denominational pluralism is well suited to peaceful coexistence between religion and secular interests. One cost of this peace, however, is the difficulty of distinguishing religious from secular viewpoints. In particular, the socialization of children into the religious tradition of their parents is problematic in the United States, partly because state support for religious education is prohibited, partly because religion is neither passionately attacked nor resolutely defended. Ignorant friends may be as dangerous to religion as prejudiced enemies. In a society where many are "for" religion, communicating the content of particular religions to the young is difficult. And this problem is complicated by the tacit agreement among religious factions of one another's legitimacy. In a recent survey, only 12 per cent of American Catholics and 25 per cent of Protestants thought that "being of the Jewish religion" definitely or possibly prevented salvation.[42] Slightly larger proportions (15 per cent of Catholics and 32 per cent of Protestants) thought that "being of the Hindu religion" prevented salvation.

This tolerance is the American answer to religious diversity; it makes harmony possible. But tolerance, as G. K. Chesterton remarked, may be the easy virtue of people who do not believe in anything. It is difficult to believe strongly in one's religious convictions and simultaneously to admit that other religions can be equally valid. Particularly in troubled times—and what times are not troubled?—it is tempting to foist one's religious ideas on others "for their own good."

Parents do this with their own children as part of a general responsibility for socialization. They can do this with other people's children only through a near-universal socializing agency like the public school. The disestablishment principle—the separation of church and state—prevents any denomination from prescribing the content of religious education in public schools. But concern with the problem of the religious socialization of children, especially other people's children, has tempted some politicians and secular educators to look for a least-common-denominator religion that *can* be taught in the public schools. William Lee Miller of the Yale Divinity School reports the instructive outcome of this search in New York City more than a decade ago:[43]

> "These troubled times," declared the New York Board of Regents in 1954,
> ". . . call for the teaching of 'Piety and Virtue' in the schools, and of that depen-

---

[42] Glock and Stark, "Is There an American Protestantism?" p. 13.

[43] Reprinted by permission. From William Lee Miller, "The Fight over America's Fourth 'R,'" *The Reporter,* Vol. 14, March 22, 1956, pp. 20-26.

dence upon Almighty God so clearly recognized in the Declaration of Independence, the Constitution of the United States, the Constitution of the State of New York, and in the pronouncements of the great leaders of our country." Just where the Federal Constitution so clearly recognizes dependence on Almighty God the Regents did not say, but in these troubled times that may not be the kind of question one should ask. . . .

[In June, 1955,] after a series of very devotional recommendations by the State Board of Regents, the New York City superintendents issued their proposed "guiding statement." This document explained how and why teachers should inculcate the ubiquitous "moral and spiritual values." That much was all right. But along with unexceptionable affirmations about the worth of the individual were others: ". . . the public schools must reinforce the program of the home and church in strengthening belief in God," and ". . . identify God as the ultimate source of natural and moral law." These caused an uproar.

The statement went on to suggest how teachers in the various disciplines could get these points across to students, and it found opportunities all over the place. In science and mathematics, for example, " . . . consideration of the vastness and the splendor of the heavens, the marvels of the human body and mind, the beauty of nature, the mystery of photosynthesis, the mathematical structure of the universe . . . cannot do other than lead to humbleness before God's handiwork. . . ." In industrial arts, "the composition of metals, the grain and the beauty of woods, the ways of electricity and the characteristic properties of the materials used, invariably give rise to speculation about the planning and the orderliness of the natural world and the marvelous working of a Supreme Power."

The response of the "three faiths" to this guiding statement must have come as something of a jolt to those who want a common American religious front. The Roman Catholic Archdiocese promptly supported the statement; the Protestant Council of the City of New York, representing a constituency that ranged from strong supporters to strong opponents, debated awhile and finally made some comments that were partly appreciative but mostly critical; the New York Board of Rabbis solidly opposed it, issued a negative analysis of it, and organized concerted preaching against it in the city's temples and synagogues.

In New York City the number of Catholics and Jews is so large (fifty-two and twenty-five per cent of the population, respectively) that the nature of the major religious groups is made inescapably apparent. It is possible to see very clearly that each of the "three faiths" is really a quite different phenomenon from the others. They are not, as tolerance literature sometimes suggests, just three indiscriminable outlets selling three slightly different brands of the one basic product, religion. They differ, to continue this unfortunate metaphor, not only in brand names but also in marketing and packaging, and even in the contents of the packages.

Many Christians, accustomed to a more or less doctrinal religion and to a more or less dominant status in society, had a hard time understanding the Jewish opposition to the New York guiding statement—particularly because the opposition was unanimous. Orthodox, Conservative, and Reform Jews stood side by side, and rabbis of quite widely differing positions in other matters joined together, five hundred strong, to preach against the statement throughout the city. "And they say *we* are monolithic!" remarked a bemused Catholic priest.

The universal and doctrinal character of Christianity, especially Catholicism, bumped squarely against the communal and ritualistic character of Judaism. A Catholic, with his commitment to a fully worked-out, intellectually formulated truth for all men, may try to get as much of that truth as possible taught wherever he can—as for example to every child in the schools: "Because we are convinced that moral and spiritual values have their ultimate source in God and are meaningless without God," said the Archdiocesan statement, "we are anxious to see God given due recognition in our public schools." But for a Jew, the formulations of theology do not have the same authority, and religious words are not so easily separated from the context of the ritual and history of the group. The Jew's faith centers instead in a whole fabric of historic observances of a particular law by a particular community. "We deny," said the rabbis, "that a non-Jewish teacher, however deeply devoted he may be to his own faith, can conscientiously and properly teach Jewish children the fundamentals of their faith . . ."

The New York controversy made plain another important fact, overlooked in much interfaithism: There is a big difference between being in the majority and in the minority. It is easier to settle for a religious stew if the meat of one's own faith determines the dominant flavor. In the nineteenth century, when Roman Catholics were a small minority, they led the fight against religion in the public schools because they knew it would have a Protestant taste to it. Their situation has changed. But the Jewish community has an ancient awareness of the situation of a religious minority from long years of experience with Christian majorities and their "truth." It knows that public religion tends to include more what Christians think Jews believe than what Jews do in fact believe. In this period when religion is surrounded with a rosy glow of popularity, the Jew may enter the reminder that for a child in the minority, religion can be a very uncomfortable business.

Plenty of others joined in opposition to the New York City guiding statement: the Society for Ethical Culture, some Unitarian ministers, the United Parents Association, the New York Civil Liberties Union, Americans for Democratic Action, and the Teachers Guild. . . .

The liberal Catholic magazine *Commonweal* said it doubted whether a "religion of the least common denominator" could fill the religious vacuum in the schools; the New York Civil Liberties Union predicted that the result would be a "vague theism"; the New York Board of Rabbis said, ". . . some teachers are bound to become missionaries for their own religious convictions. . . . Other teachers will, no doubt, become advocates of a watered, meaningless 'public school religion,' glossing over differences among religious groups which stem from vitally important convictions. . . . [making] little more than a collection of platitudes and truisms."

A supporter of "common American beliefs" might say that thin soup is better than none, but that's one of the chief mistakes: to think any "religion" whatever is good. If what one seeks is depth, then teaching shallowness won't help.

The public school cannot possibly rise any higher in teaching of religion than the general opinion of the community: Its religious platitudes would become an official ideology. Teachers, untrained in religion, would be called upon to teach or "recognize" it; political agencies, chosen on nonreligious grounds, would formulate the core religion. Of the results of that process we already have a sample in the Regents' literature, and it's not encouraging.

Professor Miller was arguing deductively in the foregoing article. That is, he hypothesized that the kind of religion which could be taught in a pluralistic society would not satisfy anybody. It would have to be least-common-denominator religion. Several years after Professor Miller wrote his article, a journalist reported in *The New York Times* the experience of one high school with a non-sectarian ritual. It turned out to be a case study of least-common-denominator religion:[44]

As not every schoolboy knows, the fourth stanza of "America," as originally written by Samuel Francis Smith, goes as follows:

> Our fathers' God to thee
> Author of liberty,
> To thee I sing;
> Long may our land be bright
> With freedom's holy light;
> Protect us by thy might,
> Great God, our King!

If our schoolboy lives anywhere in the city of New York, however, he ought to know these words, because every day—from the moment he enters the lower grades until the day he graduates—he is required by law to sing stanza four. On Nov. 30, 1951, the State Board of Regents adopted a "Statement of Moral and Spiritual Training in the Schools" recommending that "at the commencement of every school day the Pledge of Allegiance to the Flag be joined with an Act of Reverence to God." And on Jan. 15, 1953, the Board of Education of the City of New York resolved that "at the commencement of each school day the Pledge of Allegiance to the Flag be followed by the singing in unison of the fourth stanza of 'America'"—selected for its reverent quality. . . .

In view of the great emphasis given stanza four, one might assume that by the time our schoolboy gets to high school, he would know the words—if not backward, at least forward. One New York City high school principal who had his doubts decided to test this assumption and had pupils in half a dozen assorted English classes write down their versions of the fourth stanza—as recollected in tranquillity.

Some were able to reproduce a reasonable facsimile—with the expected variations in punctuation and spelling. Several didn't know the words at all and merely wrote: "I don't no the words," or "I don't now the words." (The second seems to give promise of future commitment.)

The others? The variations of and deviations from the original—the improvements—were legion.

The first line ("Our fathers' God to thee") appeared in such various guises as:

> Our father art to thee
> Our father's gone to thee
> Our father's guard to thee
> Our father's scout to thee
> Our fathers guide to thee

---

[44] Reprinted by permission. From Maxwell Nurnberg, "Of Thee I Sing—Maybe," *The New York Times Magazine*, Nov. 26, 1961, p. 86.

The second and third lines were comparatively free of mutilation with only "Offer, thy liberty," and "All thou of liberty," "To thee we see" and "To thee we sign" appearing as variants.

Line four ("Long may our land be bright") offered some interesting opportunities:

Law made our land be bright
Lord make our land be bright
Lord made our land be bright
Lord maid our land be bright

There was still some restraint shown in their treatment of line five:

With freedom's holly light
With freedom's holey light
With freedom hold thy night
With freedom's whole delight
With freedom all delight

With line six the floodgates opened wide:

Protect us by thy mite
Protect us by the night
Protect us from thy might
Protect us spy die might
Protect us spy they might
Protect us spy thy might

Line seven closed on a minor note with:

Gray God our King
Grant God our King
Pray God our key
God save the Queen

A few of the girls and boys confusing stanza one with stanza four came up with:

Land of the pilgrim's bride
Land of the pilgrim sprite
Land where the pilgrims pried

One or two, thinking that a line or two from "America the Beautiful" would somehow add something, gave us the lovely line:

God shed His grease on thee

So—to recapitulate—here, with only some punctuation added, are the "best" lines of stanza four in a composite reconstruction worthy of a Pogo or a James Joyce (sing along with me):

Our father's gone to thee,
Offer thy liberty,
To thee we sign.
Lord made our land be bright
With freedom's whole delight;
Protect us—spy they might—
God save the Queen!

CONCLUSION

During the nineteenth century and the early years of the twentieth, readers of Darwin, Freud, Marx, Pareto, and Spencer tended to consider traditional religion an anachronism and an obstacle to scientific progress. The Civil War hero and former Attorney General of Illinois, Colonel Robert G. Ingersoll, denounced the Judeo-Christian tradition as superstitious nonsense during successful lecture tours of the United States. "Everybody talks about the Bible," said Colonel Ingersoll, the son of a Congregational minister, "and nobody reads it; that is the reason it is so generally believed. I am probably the only man in this United States who has read the Bible through this year. I have wasted that time. . . ."[45] Many of the thinking men of the era agreed that religion was unnecessary in a scientifically advanced society.

Contemporary sociology cannot evaluate the truth or falsity of nonempirical religious ideas. However, most sociologists believe that scientific knowledge is insufficient to give meaning to human existence. Life raises ultimate questions, and science provides partial and provisional answers. Religion interprets the human situation in ways that protect the believer against the threat of meaninglessness. For this reason and because group support reinforces supernatural interpretations of the crises of existence, sociologists anticipate that religious organizations will persist—even in industrial societies in which the development of science has shaken faith in miracles. New religious sects will arise to bring emotionally satisfying answers into the lives of marginal members of society, members not adequately served by existing churches.

Karl Marx assumed that religion was an obstacle to change. Study of the relationship between Protestantism and the development of a market economy demonstrates that religion is not necessarily conservative.[46] When sociologists talk of religious support of the social order, they refer to the basic values inculcated during the socialization process. Considerable variation in economic and political arrangements can occur within the same value framework.

Secular equivalents of religion exist in contemporary society: commitments to family, country, art, and science. These secular commitments are a substitute for traditional religion in an age of skepticism about the supernatural world. They are capable of helping the individual transcend his own existence and perceive a pattern of meaning greater than himself. But secular equivalents of religion, since they are anchored to human beings or to human institutions, are vulnerable to the vicissitudes of human life. Supernatural religion has, *for the believer,* greater possibilities for reassurance.

The differentiation of religious organizations in industrial societies poses additional tendencies to secularization. To begin with, the religious organization must obtain support from the larger society. Its supporters are necessarily

---

[45] Robert Green Ingersoll, *Colonel Robert G. Ingersoll's 44 complete Lectures,* New York: Donohue, 1924, p. 10.

[46] Weber, *The Protestant Ethic and the Spirit of Capitalism.*

persons who interact mainly in secular contexts, and its **facilities** depend on secular resources. Second, the multiplicity of religious organizations in large, heterogeneous societies limits the support any one of them can receive from the state and from other secular institutions. A necessary condition for religious freedom and religious tolerance is that no religious organization may have a predominant advantage over others. In the United States, this condition is formalized in the constitutional principle of separation of church and state. But even in England and Sweden, countries with established churches, education is firmly under secular control, a good indication of the limitations on state support. Under these conditions, each denomination must struggle to win *voluntary* support and enthusiasm; this is an additional reason for compromising with secular values.

Nevertheless, the secularization of traditional religions may be self-limiting. Even after organized religion has withdrawn from politics, education, art, and science, some still find it an effective bulwark against the meaninglessness of life. Especially in industrial societies like the United States, where the values of the religious tradition and of secular society are congruent, peaceful coexistence is possible. Talcott Parsons goes further. He perceives the religious-secular equilibirum as analogous to the balance of political parties in a two-party system. Each is a kind of "loyal opposition" to the other because each regards the other point of view as legitimate, albeit mistaken.

SOME SIGNIFICANT LITERATURE ON RELIGION

N. J. Demerath, III, and Phillip E. Hammond, *Religion in Social Context: Tradition and Transition,* New York: Random House, 1969. Among other topics considered in this wide-ranging discussion of religion in contemporary society is the tension between the integrative function of religion (stressed by Durkheim) and the innovative function of religion (stressed by Weber). This summary is based on a review by Paul M. Harrison, *American Sociological Review,* Vol. 34, December 1969, pp. 1104-1105. An empirical investigation of this problem, based on analysis of questionnaire data from bishops, priests, and laity of the Protestant Episcopal Church, is contained in Charles Y. Glock, Benjamin B. Ringer, and Earl R. Babbie, *To Comfort and To Challenge: A Dilemma of the Contemporary Church,* Berkeley: University of California Press, 1967.

Joseph H. Fichter, S. J., *Dynamics of a City Church: Southern Parish,* Vol. 1, Chicago: University of Chicago Press, 1951. Father Fichter, a Ph.D. in sociology from Harvard University as well as a priest, describes in this book St. Mary's parish, a Cathol c congregation located in a city within the American Bible Belt. The study is largely descriptive: the numbers attending mass, going to confession, taking communion, giving donations, and the like. Forrest E. LaViolette reported in his review (*American Sociological Review,* Vol. 17, April 1952, p. 255) that the remaining volumes of Father Fichter's study might not be published. High officials in the Catholic Church feel that confidences of the Church were violated in the study. Although the remainder of Father Fichter's study has not yet appeared, he did publish a collection of essays on various aspects of

Catholic parish life: *Social Relations in the Urban Parish*, Chicago: University of Chicago Press, 1954.

Charles Y. Glock and Benjamin B. Ringer, "Church Policy and the Attitudes of Ministers and Parishioners on Social Issues," *American Sociological Review*, Vol. 21, April 1956, pp. 148-156. In 1951–1952, questionnaires were filled out by a sample of American ministers and laymen of the Protestant Episcopal Church, the latter being randomly selected from the parishes of the ministers included in the study. The questionnaires gathered attitude data on nine public issues ranging from the acceptability of war as an instrument of international policy to permissiveness toward intermarriage with Roman Catholics. Since the Episcopal Church passed resolutions on public questions at its triennial denomination meetings, it was possible to compare the attitudes of ministers and laymen with the official position of the Church. "Ministers' attitudes clearly tend to reflect church policy. Where the church has elected to compromise on an issue, the minister also has compromised with the view of his parishioners. However, where the church has taken a partisan point of view, the minister generally identifies with this view despite the opposition of a substantial segment of his parishioners."

Benton Johnson, "On Church and Sect," *American Sociological Review*, Vol. 28, August 1963, pp. 539-549. The usefulness of a typology of religious organizations explains the popularity of Ernst Troeltsch's distinction between *church* and *sect*. Troeltsch defines the sect as a small, voluntary fellowship of converts constituting a community apart from the world around it; he defined the church as a more conservative religious community "that seeks to dominate all elements within society, to teach and guide them, and to dispense saving grace to them by means of sacraments administered by ecclesiastical office holders." Unlike the sect, the church regularly includes the infant offspring of members. Johnson analyzes the Troeltsch definitions, which were derived from a study of Christian Europe prior to 1800, and concludes that they have limited relevance to the contemporary world. He suggests the following unidimensional criterion for distinguishing between church and sect: "A sect is a religious group that rejects the social environment in which it exists." A church accepts the secular milieu. Johnson recognizes that his criterion defines a continuum rather than a polarity, and he tests its utility by applying it to the American religious scene. He points out that Methodists, Presbyterians, Congregationalists, and Episcopalians are close to the church end of the continuum; Reform and Conservative Jews are intermediate as are Mormons, Seventh Day Adventists, Orthodox Presbyterian, and Christian Reformed; Roman Catholics and Orthodox Jews are the most sectarian of American religious organizations. Notwithstanding these distinctions, Johnson contrasts the American religious situation with that in other parts of the world. "The most striking fact about the American religious situation is that the vast majority of religious bodies seems to accept the dominant value system."

Gerhard E. Lenski, "Social Correlates of Religious Interest," *American Sociological Review*, Vol. 18, October 1953, pp. 533-544. Individual interest in religion in urban industrial societies varies from fanatical zeal at one extreme to utter indifference at the other. This Indianapolis study of 860 native-white married couples of Protestant background explores possible explanations of the variation in religious interest in this population. Based on intensive interviews conducted with husbands and wives separately in 1941, the findings are as follows: (1) Women are more interested in religion than men. (2) Couples with children are more interested in religion than couples without children. (3) Middle-income families express more interest in religion than either upper-income or lower-income families. (4) The greater the educational attainment, the less is the interest in religion. (5) Greater interest in religion is expressed by persons who have suffered large income *losses* since marriage, and the least interest is expressed by those with the largest income *gains*. (6) Husbands and wives from different denominations are less interested in religion than couples from the same denominational background. Despite these relationships, Lenski feels that the relationships between social factors and religious interest are not strong enough for sociologists to make more than tentative generalizations about underlying causal factors. For a study by the same author of the *effects* of religious interest rather than its causes, see *The Religious Factor: A Sociological Study of Religion's Impact on Politics, Economics and Family Life,* Garden City, N.Y.: Doubleday, 1961.

Gary T. Marx, "Religion: Opiate or Inspiration of Civil Rights Militancy among Negroes?" *American Sociological Review,* Vol. 32, February 1967, pp. 64–72. In a nationwide survey of Negroes living in metropolitan areas in the United States, questions about religious behavior and beliefs were asked along with some questions about civil rights. The civil-rights questions were combined into an index of civil-rights militancy, and the study went on to examine the relationship between various types of religious behavior and belief among blacks and their approach to civil rights. Members of fundamentalist sects were less likely to be militant than members of liberal denominations, but even for blacks belonging to more conventional churches, the greater the religious involvement, the less militancy. This relationship stood up regardless of whether religious involvement was measured by frequency of church attendance, orthodoxy of religious belief, the subjectively defined importance of religion, or all three taken together. For a fuller account of the study, see Gary T. Marx, *Protest and Prejudice: A Study of Belief in the Black Community,* New York: Harper and Row, 1968. For a similar finding concerning the American population more generally, namely, that social protest is more usually fed by secular than religious orientations, see Charles Y. Glock and Rodney Stark, *Religion and Society in Tension,* Chicago: Rand McNally, 1965.

Dennison Nash and Peter Berger, "The Child, the Family and the 'Religious Revival' in Suburbia," *Journal for the Scientific Study of Religion,* Vol. 2, Fall 1962, pp. 85–93. The authors interviewed a sample of adults who recently joined one of three churches of the Congregational-Christian denomination in a rapidly growing suburb of Hartford, Connecticut. "For most of these people the decision to join was prompted by the prospect or presence of children in the family." In general, joining was *not* preceded by a conversion experience of the sort described by William James in *The Varieties of Religious Experience,* nor was it motivated by crises in their personal lives. Joining appears to have been a rational decision connected with the religious education and moral guidance of their children.

Thomas F. O'Dea, *The Mormons,* Chicago: University of Chicago Press, 1957. In the first five chapters O'Dea traces the rise and expansion of the Mormon Church. He then turns to a consideration of Mormon theology, the organizational structure of the Mormon Church, the social ethic of the church, and, finally, the sources of strain and conflict within the church and between Mormons and other Protestants. The continued vitality of Mormonism is puzzling in view of characteristics that might be expected to reduce its appeal in a scientifically oriented democracy where women approximate equality of status with men. Mormonism is a fundamentalist religion with an authoritarian priesthood that excludes women. One implication of this study is that religious beliefs and values have consequences for the secular behavior of communicants. This summary is based on a review by Kimball Young, *American Sociological Review,* Vol. 23, February 1958, pp. 103-104. For a study showing the relevance of Zoroastrian values for the economic behavior of present-day Zoroastrians in India, see Robert R. Kennedy, Jr., "The Protestant Ethic and the Parsis," *American Journal of Sociology,* Vol. 68, July 1962, pp. 11-20.

Rodney Stark and Charles Y. Glock, *Patterns of Religious Commitment,* Berkeley: University of California Press, 1968. Using two samples, a sample of 3000 church members in four counties of Northern California and a 1976-member sample of the adult population of the United States, the authors seek to demonstrate the changing meaning of religious commitment for Christian Americans. On the one hand, there exist religious conservatives who adhere to conventional dogmas (e.g., a life after death) as revealed truth. On the other hand, there exist religious liberals who are much more flexible on matters of belief and who stress the ethical implications of religious commitments rather than doctrinal purity. Stark and Glock foresee a shift from the conservative to the liberal position in the American population and the ultimate emergence of a post-Christian society. This summary is based on a review by Roland Robertson, *American Sociological Review,* Vol. 34, April 1969, pp. 281-283. For a point of view that goes even further along the path of separation between religiosity and church affiliation as it has been known in Judeo-Christian societies, see Thomas Luckman, *The Invisible Religion: The Problem of Religion in Modern Society,* New York: Macmillan, 1969.

W. Lloyd Warner, *The Living and the Dead: A Study of the Symbolic Life of Americans,* New Haven, Conn.: Yale University Press, 1959. Warner brings his anthropological background to bear on the ceremonial and symbolic activities of a modern community (Newburyport, Massachusetts) in this, the sixth and concluding volume of the Yankee City series. He starts with a living symbol: the career of a mayor and political boss who is a hero to some and a villain and clown to others. Warner moves on to a discussion of the ritualization of the past: Memorial Day, Lincoln as a patriotic symbol, Catholic and Protestant symbolism, and the place of the cemetery in the community. The generality of the conclusions of this book as well as the other five Yankee City books has been questioned. Is the symbolic life of a small American city typical of the large metropolis? This summary is based on a review by Orrin E. Klapp, *American Sociological Review,* Vol. 25, October 1960, p. 757.

THE POLITICAL STRUCTURE
OF INDUSTRIAL SOCIETIES

Lynn Pelham—Rapho Guillumette

The **political process** is the policy-making mechanism of interactive systems. Its two primary concerns are redistribution and the achievement of consensus. Many activities of government are involved in determining who gets what, when, and how.[1] The graduated income tax is clearly redistributive; less obviously redistributive are decisions of agencies like the Interstate Commerce Commission, the Veterans Administration, and the Food and Drug Administration.[2]

Equally fundamental to the political process is the achievement of consensus necessary for effective collective action.[3] Policy decisions that bind members of the interactive system are arrived at through political processes. This is clearly true at the governmental level, but it is equally true in small interactive systems like families.

Any ongoing interactive system faces the need to organize collective action effectively, to set goals and mobilize resources necessary to attain these goals. Usually such organization means a leadership role (the father in a patriarchal family) or a complex of leadership roles (the Federal government). In an informal group, leadership may shift from one member to another depending on the activity; under these circumstances political *processes* proceed without a stable political *structure*. This unstructured arrangement is unusual because of the difficulties of solving political problems when everyone has equal responsibility for dealing with them. Leadership roles (political structures) are almost universal. The difference between democratic and autocratic political processes lies less in the existence of leaders than in the basis for justifying their authority.

THE LEGITIMATION OF LEADERSHIP ROLES

The most familiar examples of leadership roles are government officials in modern societies. However, the same justifications of authority apply to the incumbents of nongovernmental leadership roles. There are four basic ways to legitimize a leadership role.

1. *Legal-bureaucratic authority.* The *authority of office* confers certain rights upon the officeholder. He enjoys this authority by virtue of his position in

---

[1] Harold D. Lasswell, *Politics: Who Gets What, When, How,* New York: McGraw-Hill, 1936.

[2] Blair Bolles, *How to Get Rich in Washington: Rich Man's Division of the Welfare State,* New York: Norton, 1952.

[3] Seymour Martin Lipset, "Political Sociology," in Merton, Broom and Cottrell, Eds., *Sociology Today: Problems and Prospects,* New York: Basic Books, 1959, pp. 81-114; Talcott Parsons, "'Voting' and the Equilibrium of the American Political System," in Burdick and Brodbeck, Eds., *American Voting Behavior,* Glencoe, Ill.: Free Press, 1959, pp. 80-120; Talcott Parsons, "On the Concept of Political Power," *Proceedings of the American Philosophical Society,* Vol. 107, June 19, 1963, pp. 232-262.

an organization. Although this legal-bureaucratic authority is held by an individual, it is delimited by universalistic rules that make for procedural uniformity and hopefully are regarded as "fair." In British schools rules permit teachers, who possess legal-bureaucratic authority, to administer corporal punishment to unruly students; in American schools they generally do not. The incumbent of an office usually does not make the rules himself; they are established by higher authority. But in all cases rules are established to give the person in authority the right to exert authority.

2. *Authority stemming from the cultural tradition.* This is quite different from the authority of office. It is a voluntary acceptance of authority based on a cultural value. For example, students accept the teacher's authority not only because he is employed by the school as their teacher but also because he is, as an older person, entitled to respect from the young.

3. *Authority stemming from technical competence.* This type of authority, stemming from presumed competence in a particular subject matter, is the authority of the expert. Authority of the physician or the lawyer or the teacher depends on what nonexperts think he knows. Since it is always difficult for nonexperts to evaluate the technical competence of experts, *professional reputation* is usually a substitute for personal judgment of technical competence.

4. *Charismatic authority.* The term "stimulating" is a pale expression of what is called **charisma** in its fully developed form. It is a force so powerful that its possessor may almost mesmerize his audience into accepting his authority. Exceptionally forceful politicians (e.g., Hitler) are the most obvious examples of charismatic authority.

These four theoretically distinct justifications of authority may blend together in an actual situation. They are rarely mentioned explicitly (or even thought about), but they justify the classroom leadership of the teacher. In conservative school systems, teacher authority will depend more on traditional and legal-bureaucratic justifications. In school systems dedicated to progressive education, technical competence and perhaps even personal charisma will more often legitimate the authority of the classroom teacher.

The legitimation of authority is not always successful. If the student refuses to keep quiet when the teacher tries to lead a discussion, the order of the classroom threatens to collapse. The teacher may ask the student to go to the principal's office for a scolding, but students have been known to refuse to leave. Faced with such defiance, the teacher either calls for help (ultimately from the police) or he might resort to force to sustain the authority he was not able to sustain through symbolism alone. Conceivably, some teachers might maintain order in their classrooms by letting it be known that they carry a pearl-handled revolver and a switchblade knife. Why does this sound farfetched? First, because the legitimation of teacher authority is generally successful; the bulk of students, however much they may dislike an individual teacher or hate their studies, do not challenge his *right* to dominate the classroom. Second, those few students so alienated that they disregard the teacher's authority can be extruded from the interactive system (suspended, expelled, or brought to juvenile court). Their extrusion makes force unnecessary in the classroom — although physical force *can* be called upon from the larger society in emergencies. One reason why police use naked force more often than teachers is that the police have no one to call when their authority is disregarded; they cannot "pass the buck." Third and finally, teachers do not use revolvers (force) to maintain their authority because they have not been authorized by the state to do so.

An Alternative to Legitimation: Force. It is no accident that the state seeks to control the use of force within its territorial jurisdiction. If the political arm of the society, the state, permitted subsystems like schools to resort freely to force, subsystems could use force to sabotage collective action on the part of the larger society. Thus a basic condition of political viability for a society is to *monopolize the legitimate use of organized force within its borders* (and to keep the illegitimate use of force to a minimum).[4] The state is reluctant to delegate the right to use force because each delegation is a potential threat to its political effectiveness. The instrumentalities of the state, for example, the police, use force because they have no higher authority to which they can appeal. If the leadership structure of the society itself is challenged, that is, if legitimation is unsuccessful, leadership disintegrates or shifts from symbolic appeals to intrinsic coercion — but challenges are rare in a functioning society.

By definition, a leader has an institutionally justified right to make decisions on behalf of the group. The acceptance of his leadership by those members of the group without leadership responsibility rests on its symbolic legitimation. It depends on **power,** too. Power is not force; it is *symbolic* rather than physical coercion. Power depends on a right to mobilize punitive sanctions if the expected compliance is not forthcoming. Suppose the dean of a college came to the office of the chairman of the sociology department, whipped out a .45 caliber pistol, and insisted that two additional sections of introductory sociology be added to the fall offerings. That would be force. If, on the other hand, the dean telephoned the chairman of the department, pointed out that additional sections of introductory sociology would help solve the problem of finding courses for all students at registration, and suggested that two sections be added, he would be using power. The dean has a right to expect compliance from department chairmen in matters of course offerings, but he also has budgetary and other punishments available for uncooperative chairmen. A legitimized expectation of compliance and the resources to punish noncompliance are necessary ingredients of power, as it is used here.

The consensual aspect of power — the legitimized expectation of compliance — depends on one or more of the legitimations of authority: legal-bureaucratic, cultural, charismatic, or technical competence. In modern so-

---

[4] Talcott Parsons, *Structure and Process in Modern Societies,* Glencoe, Ill.: Free Press, 1960, pp. 261-262.

cieties legal-bureaucratic legitimation is especially prominent because of the proliferation of large-scale organizations. (Chapter 10 considers the place of large-scale organizations in contemporary industrial societies at length.) An interesting aspect of the right of *organizational* leaders to expect compliance is that the obligations of subordinates are voluntarily assumed, usually as part of the contract of employment. The worker need not accept employment by a particular organization, but once he does so, he assumes the obligation not only to submit to specific directives of his supervisor but also to express general loyalty to the organization. Similarly, Americans need not become committed to the Democratic or Republican party. Having done so, however, the individual feels an obligation to vote for and verbally support members of "his" party.

Private Governments. Large-scale organizations within modern societies can be thought of as private governments.[5] What is the relation between the multiplicity of private governments and the paramount political authority of the society, the state? For example, can a democratically organized state tolerate undemocratically organized trade unions or corporations? One answer is that it can tolerate a quite different pattern of internal organization by private governments if they are truly *private, voluntary, limited-purpose* associations.[6] Most organizations in modern societies do not satisfy this test. Take, for instance, county medical societies in the United States. If membership in such societies is a practical necessity for the practice of medicine, a physician can properly argue that calling membership "voluntary" is stretching the meaning of the word. Similarly, participation of state and county medical societies in the licensing of physicians by the state blurs the line between public and private.

One implication of this blurring is that so-called private governments cannot be autonomous. Directly or indirectly, they depend for legitimation and enforcement of authority on the society in which they are imbedded. The relationship to society may be formalized, as when a board of trustees of a state university is the legal-bureaucratic link between the citizens of the state and the educational organization.[7] Charters of incorporation provide another formal link; they give legal standing to organizations, including the important right to seek redress of grievances through the courts. Such charters explicitly provide for internal operations according to accepted cultural norms. Even where the relationship between society and the subgroup is less formal, as in the case of individual families, cultural norms from the larger society seep into the subgroup and influence its internal organization. Of course, these norms differ from one society to another. Thus Soviet society will not permit a newspaper the same freedom to criticize public officials and their policies as newspapers enjoy in the United States, Great Britain, Holland, Denmark, France, Italy, or

---

[5] Grant McConnell, "The Spirit of Private Government," *American Political Science Review,* Vol. 52, September 1958, pp. 754-770.

[6] McConnell, "The Spirit of Private Government."

[7] Parsons, *Structure and Process,* p. 65.

Japan. In addition to legitimizing private governments, the state (logically enough) supports them. When a university or a labor union feels threatened with illegitimate disruption, it can appeal to the courts or to the police.

Private governments' coexistence with state governments illustrates the tendency for every society to be integrated politically. Some societies (usually called totalitarian) are so highly integrated that all organizations are directly controlled by the state. Even in **pluralistic societies,** however, some degree of political integration exists between the paramount political authority and the various subgroups and organizations. Without such integration social existence could easily degenerate into chaos. The seventeenth-century social philosopher Thomas Hobbes called this "a war of all against all"; he concluded that human life under these circumstances would be "solitary, poor, nasty, brutish, and short."[8] Hobbes' solution to the problem of the precariousness of social order was strong central government, which in his time meant monarchy. He believed in despotism because he saw no alternative; the consensual basis of political integration was not then understood.

Political integration between the paramount political authority and, say, educational organizations is unavoidable in a viable society. In a pluralistic society, however, integration is looser than in a totalitarian one. Universities in Great Britain, Sweden, and Japan support some governmental activities, but they possess enough influence to challenge others—even though universities in these countries depend on government financing to a greater extent than do American universities. Recall that many American colleges and universities participated in protests against their government's Viet Nam policy on October 15, 1969. The charge that universities or labor unions or religious denominations are the lackeys of the central government is more false the more pluralistic the society.

THE IDEOLOGICAL ROOTS OF CONSENSUS

The larger and more differentiated the society, the more necessary is central leadership (government). The character of the leadership structure can, however, be despotic or democratic, depending on historical circumstance and on the ideas to which the population subscribes. Based on some 5000 interviews conducted in the United States, Great Britain, Germany, Italy, and Mexico, two political scientists found that the attitudes of American and British citizens are more compatible with a stable democratic process than the atti-

---

[8] Thomas Hobbes, *Leviathan; or the Matter, Forme and Power of a Commonwealth, Ecclesiasticall and Civill,* Cambridge, England: Cambridge University Press, 1904; Talcott Parsons, *The Structure of Social Action,* New York: McGraw-Hill, 1937, pp. 89–94.

tudes of people in the other three countries.[9] Why? Because Americans and Britons have more confidence in the ability of their political systems to surmount temporary crises. Without such a reservoir of loyalty, a war or a depression can bring about governmental collapse, as happened in Germany in 1933 when democracy crumbled and the Nazis came to power.[10] The *ideology*—the system of beliefs about collective action—of Americans and Britons gives their governments a margin for error necessary for political stability. The Viet Nam war, unpopular though it became, did not destroy the American political system. Thus ideology influences the viability of political structures.

Political ideologies include a variety of beliefs, some true, some false, and some involving values and aspirations not susceptible to the true-false criterion. Hobbes believed in despotism because he assumed (1) that *consensus* is so difficult to achieve that freedom must be sacrificed to order and (2) that *justice* is so easy to achieve that ultimate power can be entrusted to an absolute ruler. Ideological fashions have changed since Hobbes' day, but assumptions about the possibilities of consensus and justice still underlie political thinking. Democratic ideologies tend to be optimistic about the possibilities of consen-

[9] Gabriel A. Almond and Sidney Verba, *The Civic Culture: Political Attitudes and Democracy in Five Nations,* Princeton, N.J.: Princeton University Press, 1963.

[10] " . . . [A] backlog of success in the use of democratic institutions has been lacking wherever totalitarian movements have been successful." Reinhard Bendix, "Social Stratification and Political Power," *American Political Science Review,* Vol. 46, June 1952, p. 375.

sus. The faith of the eighteenth-century "Enlightenment" in the power of human reason justified democracy for men like Thomas Jefferson. As we shall see later in this chapter, recent research into the political process has shown less individual rationality than eighteenth-century thinkers believed necessary. It has also shown that societal consensus can be achieved without such high levels of voter rationality.

Democratic ideology, at least in the American version embodied in the Constitution, is mildly pessimistic about the possibilities of justice. Fear of injustice underlay the Bill of Rights and the system of checks and balances between federal and state governments and among the executive, legislative, and judicial branches. Despotic ideologies are more optimistic about the possibilities of achieving justice. Insofar as he thought about the problem at all, Hobbes assumed that a wise and benevolent ruler would be equally fair (or equally oppressive) to all of his subjects. Similarly, the confidence of Marxists that a one-party dictatorship results in greater social justice than capitalist democracy rests on the Hobbesian assumption that despotism can be permanently and indiscriminately benevolent. As Reinhold Niebuhr put it, "Marxism expects men to be as tame and prudential on the other side of the revolution as Adam Smith and Jeremy Bentham thought them . . . on this side of the revolution."[11] The internal operation of Communist governments has refuted this Hobbesian notion; the dictatorship of the proletariat has, in practice, proven oppressive.[12]

Ideology provides a cultural definition of the political system. Although all large-scale societies concentrate power in leadership roles to some degree, in some this concentration is taken for granted; in others it is regarded as a betrayal of equalitarian ideals. *Objectively* speaking, equal treatment by government officials for all citizens is more nearly realized in democratic than in despotic societies. But the *subjective* feeling of political deprivation varies in accordance with ideological commitments. It may be minimal in a Communist country where the Party is culturally defined as benevolent. It may be intense among some Americans who feel alienated from the political system because they observe that its benefits are not equally available to rich and poor, white and Negro. This is another cultural interpretation of reality discussed in Chapter 3: "If men define situations as real, they are real in their consequences."

Law and the Implementation of Justice. In complex societies, the execution of policy decisions poses integrative problems. The effective coordination of the efforts of persons who administer such decisions requires large-scale organization (and will be considered in Chapter 10). However, the execution of policy is not only a matter of effective coordination of human effort. Conflicts

---

[11] Reinhold Niebuhr, *The Children of Light and the Children of Darkness: A Vindication of Democracy and a Critique of Its Traditional Defence,* New York: Scribner's, 1944, p. 60.

[12] Arthur Koestler, *The Yogi and the Commissar and Other Essays,* New York: Collier, 1961; Milovan Djilas, *The New Class,* New York: Praeger, 1957.

arise in the carrying out of collective action just as they arose during the process of arriving at initial decisions. The legal system is assigned the task of resolving these conflicts in conformity with popular notions of *justice*. This is an especially thorny task in pluralistic societies where many different interests must be balanced against one another.[13] Failure to resolve them threatens the unity of the society.

Two distinct types of conflict arise: between private parties (including organizations) and between the state and private individuals. Civil law is concerned with the first type of conflict, criminal law with the second. Settling conflicts between private parties is necessary because such conflicts interfere with productive cooperation.[14] If two automobiles collide, a court decides who must bear the financial costs of the accident. If a labor union and a corporation disagree about renewing a contract, an arbitrator may settle the terms of the new contract. Without settlements, private conflicts would disrupt the orderly cooperation essential to a functioning society. Society also has an interest in settling private disagreements "fairly." If private parties feel that their legitimate interests were disregarded in a settlement, they withdraw some of their loyalty from the interactive system. "Fairness" in civil matters is not radically different in democratic and despotic societies; it depends on applying uniformly the established standards of equity. The greater the uniformity in the settlement of disagreements, the more successful are lawyers in predicting the results of trials in advance and the fewer are the cases that have to be litigated.

Criminal law operates differently in democratic and despotic societies. In despotic societies, the judicial system tends to be a branch of executive authority. Where the state is pitted against the defendant, as in criminal cases, the state is both accuser and adjudicator. In democratic societies, the judicial system, though dependent on executive authority for enforcement of decisions, has genuine independence. This means that the accused has a better chance of having his guilt or innocence objectively evaluated in a democratic society. It also means that the guilty have a better chance of escaping punishment. How this works in practice can be illustrated by the elaborate procedures for dealing with those accused of crime in the United States.

Take the matter of burglary. Since Americans do not want thieves breaking into homes and places of business, laws prohibit such behavior and specify maximum periods of incarceration following conviction. Policemen patrol the streets to deter the potential thief and to apprehend persons who actually "break and enter." But what happens when a policeman discovers an 18-year-old boy trying to open the safe in the back office of a supermarket? Does he whip out his gun and execute the young burglar on the spot? Or does he talk to him like a Dutch uncle and send him home? Neither, if he follows American

---

[13] Talcott Parsons, "Law and Social Control," in William M. Evan, *Law and Sociology,* New York: Free Press of Glencoe, 1962, pp. 56-72.

[14] Harry C. Bredemeier, "Law As an Integrative Mechanism," in Evan, *Law and Sociology,* Chap. 4.

legal procedures. He arrests the suspect and takes him to police headquarters. The accused is held in a lockup until he can be formally charged with "breaking and entering" in a hearing before a magistrate. The accused has a right to have a lawyer represent him in this hearing and to advise him whether to plead "guilty" or "not guilty." If he pleads "not guilty," he is entitled to release on bail until the time of trial—on the assumption that his guilt has not yet been established. If he pleads "guilty," he is also entitled to release on bail until he is sentenced by a judge having jurisdiction over his case. When and if he comes before a judge for sentencing, the judge ordinarily has discretion as to whether to imprison the convicted offender or to place him on probation—and, if to imprison him, for how long. But the judge does not have limitless discretion; he cannot sentence a person to the electric chair for "breaking and entering." The range of possible penalties for this offense have been established by the legislature of the state in which the prohibited act took place.

Why this time-consuming fuss? The boy was caught in the act. The process of evaluating guilt or innocence is more complicated than a despotic society assumes. Maybe the boy had some other reason for fondling the safe besides an intention to steal its contents. Unlikely, but unlikely events sometimes happen. A jury trial gives him an opportunity to tell his story to people who have less reason to disbelieve it than the arresting officer. The process of *punishing* a convicted burglar is also anchored with rules of procedure. The alternative is to allow a hasty reaction to burglary to be more severe than a calm consensus of community judgments would favor. Recall that urban industrial populations are heterogeneous. The range of values among policemen and judges is sufficiently great that their spontaneous reactions to a suspected offender may not coincide with the **collective conscience.** A legal system limits official discretion. It provides some protection against brutal policemen and prejudiced judges.

Laws must still be administered by human beings with parochial biases; hence the democratic ideal of equal treatment under the law is never fully achieved. For example, the sentencing practices of judges in criminal courts show wide variation within the same jurisdiction.[15] And those punished relatively severely for crimes that are leniently handled in other cases feel unfairly treated. But existing resentment of "injustice" is mild compared with the indignation that would result if the legal system did not limit variations in police and court practices.

Law helps to justify the naked force behind political decisions in other ways besides guaranteeing some uniformity in the processing of individual cases. The American Constitution forbids *ex post facto* laws because the American conception of fairness requires the state to specify in advance what acts will be punished and how severely. This means that if someone thinks up a type of

---

[15] F. J. Gaudet, G. S. Harris, and C. W. St. John, "Individual Differences in the Sentencing Tendencies of Judges," *Journal of Criminal Law and Criminology,* Vol. 23, January-February 1933, pp. 811-818.

crime that existing laws do not forbid, he cannot be punished for it—even though it outrages his society. Of course, legislatures constantly add to the criminal code so as to keep brief the periods during which crime pays.

The American Constitution also protects substantive rights: freedom of speech and assembly, security in one's home against unreasonable searches by law-enforcement personnel, the right to petition public officials. Sometimes these rights of citizens are regarded by officials as obstacles to carrying out their jobs. Police often have well-founded suspicions about the identity of an armed robber or a murderer. They believe that they could get a confession from the suspect, complete with corroborative evidence (like a gun), if only the law permitted them to use "third degree" methods. The law does not permit the police to torture suspects, no matter how convincing the suspicions, and therefore the courts are required to protect the citizenry *against their own officials*. The seeming inefficiency of legal procedures and the opportunities which they offer for the guilty to escape punishment are a by-product of the attempt to persuade the citizenry that a miscarriage of justice is unlikely.

In short, a legal system can help a complex society to keep going by satisfying popular notions of justice. The legal system is concerned with procedural niceties because procedural niceties prevent hasty resolution of social conflicts. From the point of view of "getting things done" politically, the legal system is a brake on progress. From the point of view of protecting legitimate interests that might otherwise be alienated from the society, the legal system is necessary because it is an integrative force. Especially in a heterogeneous society like the United States, ethnic and other interest groups must be reconciled with one another in order for a unified society to endure. We shall return to a fuller discussion of the integrative problems of modern societies in Chapter 15.

THE BASIS OF SOCIETAL LEADERSHIP:
CONSENT AND COERCION

In contemporary industrial societies, consensus is at least as problematic as it was in Hobbes' lifetime. Whenever alternatives confront a community, regardless of whether they are economic, educational, religious, or military, disagreement over them is a possibility. Hence there is a political dimension to every issue that can potentially divide or disrupt a society. Whether individuals should be allowed to select their own pattern of religious behavior is a political question. So is the extent to which people are permitted to buy, sell, and produce goods. Americans do not ordinarily think of these as political questions because they were settled long ago. The American solution was to place the authority (and the coercive force) of government behind individual freedom in both religious and economic behavior. The Soviet solutions to these political questions are obviously different.

The **political institutions** of a society are mechanisms for reevaluating previous policies in the light of recent experience and for making decisions about newly presented alternatives. At one time, parents could decide whether to send their children to school and for how long. Today, all of the industrial countries have compulsory school-attendance laws, and the number of years of compulsory attendance continues to rise. Compulsion is implicit in every governmental policy because a policy cannot be effective unless opponents are prevented from interfering with its execution. Ultimately, this may involve force. Sometimes people have to be physically removed from homes condemned under the right of eminent domain for a new highway or school.

Usually, though, governmental decisions are complied with, half because they are felt to be just, half because of an awareness that resistence is useless.

Industrial societies are too complicated to permit everybody to participate in every policy decision. Part of the political process consists of the selection of persons authorized to make decisions on behalf of the society: legislators, judges, administrators. Even in despotic political systems, where government officials are less dependent on popular support, leaders need acceptance of the legitimacy of their **authority** as well as fear of their *power*. Authority, a pivotal concept in political sociology, refers to a recognition of the policy maker's *right* to make a binding decision on behalf of the group.[16]

Parsons has suggested an analogy between the division of labor in the economic realm and leadership in the political realm. Just as the individual worker in an industrial society forgoes the self-sufficiency of a subsistence farmer, so the individual citizen forgoes immediate control over collective decisions. He delegates his share of political power to a leader, and he hopes that the particular decisions in which he is personally interested will be satisfactory. The worker receives compensation in exchange for his sacrifice of independence in the form of a higher standard of living than he would otherwise enjoy. Similarly, the citizen is compensated for his delegation of power by enjoying more effective societal direction than would be possible under conditions of participatory democracy.[17]

The most conspicuous difference between democratic and despotic societies is that in the former leadership roles are filled by genuine contests between rival groups of potential leaders. In this situation the incumbents have a limited grasp on policy-making roles. A system with parties presenting opposing viewpoints, prescribed intervals between elections, rules limiting the number of terms in office, and certain conditions of equilibrium among the groups and organizations within the society helps keep elections vehicles for the transfer of power instead of mere rituals, as they are in despotic societies. Democratic countries have thus solved the problem of succession, whereas despotic societies cannot ensure an orderly transfer of power because they do not permit meaningful elections. The death of Stalin created a more serious crisis than the death of President Kennedy. Since there was no legitimized way to select Stalin's successor, the dissatisfactions that built up were expressed in a struggle for power. This problem sometimes culminates in revolution. In democratic countries, elections are safety valves that usually prevent pressures of dissatisfactions from building up to a revolutionary explosion. From the anti-democratic viewpoint, however, free elections are regarded as institutionalized chaos.

In spite of the variety of political systems and the differences within demo-

---

[16] Robert M. MacIver, *The Web of Government,* New York: Macmillan, 1947, p. 83; Chester I. Barnard, *The Functions of the Executive,* Cambridge, Mass.: Harvard University Press, 1938, p. 163.

[17] Parsons, "'Voting' and the Equilibrium of the American Political System."

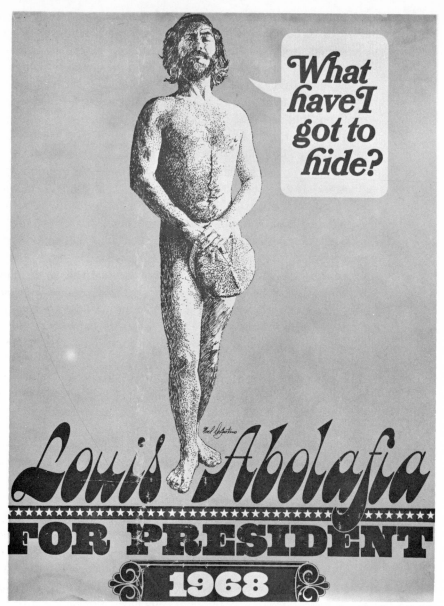

Courtesy of Louis Abolafia

cratic systems, many people simply assume that political institutions identical to their own are necessary for *any* democracy. Is this mere ethnocentrism? May not democracy be compatible with a one-party system or with a multi-party system? What about Mexico, where one party has held power for 40 years, but where elections seem to be meaningful?[18] The seeming incompatibility between a one-party state and democracy stems from the difficulty of

[18] Joseph A. Kahl, *Comparative Perspectives on Stratification: Mexico, Great Britain, Japan,* Boston: Little, Brown, 1968, pp. 1-4.

transferring power in an orderly way. If an organized group of policy makers (a party) is so powerful that its voice in the decision-making process cannot be effectively challenged, a revolution is necessary in order to change leadership. The despotism of a ruling party may be benevolent, but the question is one of power transferability, not of benevolence.

Orderly transfer of power is also difficult when three or more parties vie with one another for the support of voters, as in France, Italy, or Israel. Far from concentrating power too much, government by coalition disperses it too widely. Comparative analysis of stable and unstable democracies has shown that a two-party system is more conducive to stability than a multiparty system.[19] But there is the danger that a two-party system may achieve stability by minimizing the opportunities for minority viewpoints to participate in the political process. Thus in the 1968 American presidential election, the effective contest was between two moderates, Hubert Humphrey and Richard Nixon. The right-wing candidate, George Wallace, and the candidates of various splinter groups of the New Left and of the black militants had no chance of coming into leadership positions. If the two-party system is flexible, political minorities may have some influence, but the normal channels are frequently unresponsive to them. A two-party system is committed to expressing and implementing the consensus of a majority. The tactics of confrontation politics may be a road to political influence for minorities unable to obtain what they want from the system but it is a dangerous tactic that may produce repression instead of response.

A two-party or multiparty political system institutionalizes the legitimacy of opposition to current decision makers. Thus in democratic countries, parties not in power are permitted (and even encouraged) to criticize the incumbents of political office and to solicit support to "throw the rascals out" at the next election. The British have a phrase that epitomizes the legitimacy of dissent from the policies of current decision makers. The party out of power is known as Her Majesty's *Loyal* Opposition. Note the word "loyal." If a party in power manages to define opposition parties, or the policies of opposition parties, as illegitimate, disloyal, and, ultimately, illegal, elections become empty ceremonials, and democracy is dead.[20] This is the situation today in the Soviet Union, Spain, Portugal, Yugoslavia, Egypt, Communist China, Nationalist China (Taiwan), and several South American countries.

Legitimacy of opposition implies that the government does not dominate all groups within the society. Churches, universities, labor unions, business firms, youth organizations, and other voluntary associations have some independence. Normal though this may be in democracies, and even in conservative oligarchies like Portugal and Saudi Arabia, it is intolerable in totalitarian

---

[19] Seymour Martin Lipset, "Party Systems and the Representation of Social Groups," *European Journal of Sociology,* Vol. 1, No. 1, 1960, pp. 3-38.

[20] Morton Grodzins, *The Loyal and the Disloyal: Social Boundaries of Patriotism and Treason,* Chicago: University of Chicago Press, 1956.

societies because independent groups might become the nucleus for opposition to the regime. Thus in the Soviet Union, not only is the *economy* controlled by the state; so are universities, labor unions, youth organizations, professional associations, and so forth. One reason totalitarian leaders get into conflict with organized religion — a struggle with the Catholic Church proved the downfall of Perón in Argentina — is that the churches are notoriously reluctant to surrender their independence to secular authorities. Yet totalitarian leaders cannot help but be jealous of independent associations; independence means potential opposition, and opposition is, by definition, subversive in the totalitarian society.

Totalitarian leaders seek to dominate all groups within the society as insurance against loss of power. They go further, however. They demand *ideological* conformity to the regime as well as obedient *actions*. For instance, in the Soviet Union, there is a Communist Party "line" on political and economic issues — and also on art, music, literature, history, genetics, architecture, pedagogy. Those who do not express the "correct" ideas, or do not shift ground rapidly enough when the "line" changes, are looked upon with suspicion. Why should Soviet leaders care about artistic, musical, or literary ideas? Because it is difficult to deny intellectual freedom on political and economic issues and permit it on other topics. Totalitarian leaders fear that people free to think independent thoughts may start thinking about new leaders.

The lack of freedom of association and of intellectual freedom in a totalitarian society does not necessarily produce political stability. True, organized opposition is difficult. But covert disaffection is more likely than in democratic societies because so little of life is permitted to be nonpolitical. Whereas American painters, writers, scientists, musicians, ministers, physicians, and architects can ignore politics, comparable professionals in the Soviet Union cannot. The Communist Party "line" in their field forces them to take stands, to pass endless loyalty tests, to risk punishment for intellectual "unreliability." These restrictions on professional freedom undoubtedly alienate some Soviet citizens who, in a democratic society, would not care who governs the country. Bear in mind that only a minority of Soviet citizens are enrolled in the Communist Party or its subdivisions. Consensus is difficult to attain in complex societies, totalitarian or democratic, but it may be easier in democracies.

Informed Consent. Is consensus really so difficult to obtain in contemporary societies? After all, mass literacy exposes the majority of the population to a fairly narrow range of political messages, even in democratic countries. In totalitarian countries, government control of press, radio, and television gives the party in power an opportunity to repeat its propaganda messages without fear of contradiction. Monopoly of the instruments of mass communication enables a totalitarian regime to put across "the big lie." Even when the regime is not perpetrating an outright lie, its ability to determine what information to allow the citizenry to receive, and in what context, may enable it to engineer consensus instead of allowing consensus to develop naturally. In democratic countries, the mass media are not monopolized by the state, but neither does a free market in ideas exist. People wealthy enough to own a newspaper have a better chance than less affluent citizens to influence public opinion. In the United States, for instance, the Republican Party has enjoyed greater support in the editorial columns of newspapers and magazines than the Democratic Party.[21] This does not, however, give an insuperable advantage to Republican candidates.

Are the mass media, then, irrelevant to the political process in a democracy? They are not irrelevant, but their influence is indirect. Their initial impact is on the opinion leaders of the community.[22] Due to the personal influence of these leaders on politically apathetic segments of the population, ideas about issues and candidates percolate through the electorate. Therefore, even though the mass media *are* influential, no one should expect votes to be exactly proportional to the linage of political propaganda. Professional politicians have a saying that reflects the uncertainty of efforts at mass persuasion: "Half of the money spent on campaigns is wasted. But which half?"

Mass communication has aroused *fears* about mass manipulation of voters. Research has shown that these fears have been based on a wrong assumption: that all citizens are oriented to the political messages of mass media. Only a minority is interested in campaign oratory and devotes the time and effort necessary to understand the issues involved. Mass communication has also aroused *hopes* for a more enlightened electorate. Nineteenth-century liberals thought that the rise in the educational level in democratic countries was bound to make a better world. H. G. Wells spoke for his generation when he remarked, "Human history becomes more and more a race between education and catastrophe." These hopes for an enlightened electorate have also proved illusory. Universal education resulted in mass literacy, but mass literacy has not produced greater reason and good will in politics. Teaching people to read does not guarantee that they will prefer to read speeches rather than comic books. Educational television has proved far less popular than cowboy dramas.

The concept of "the consent of the governed" is not as simple as it may first appear. Consent can be explicit and the result of political concern. Consent can also be a result of the *absence* of political concern. A voter preoccupied with making a living, the health problems of himself or members of his family, marital conflict, or disciplining the children is often willing to trust officials to take care of the "big" decisions. He is poorly informed and politically oblivious. In the summer of 1954, for instance, when American television and radio networks buzzed with excitement over the "cold war" with the Soviet Union and with Senator Joseph McCarthy's charges of Communist traitors in the American government, two public-opinion research organizations could not

---

[21] Frank Luther Mott, "Newspapers in Presidential Campaigns," *Public Opinion Quarterly,* Vol. 8, Fall 1944, pp. 348-367.

[22] Robert K. Merton, *Social Theory and Social Structure,* rev. ed., Glencoe, Ill.: Free Press, 1957, pp. 387-420.

discover much concern on the part of the citizenry with either issue.[23] A national cross section of Americans was asked, "What kinds of things do you worry about most?" Eighty per cent responded *solely* in terms of personal or family problems. Less than 1 per cent said they were worried about the threat of Communists in government or about civil liberties. With private concerns more salient to most voters than public issues, the meaning of "consent of the governed" is ambiguous. It may be an informed consent or acquiescence steeped in ignorance and indifference.

Even the minority of citizens interested in and knowledgeable about public issues cannot be represented exactly on all issues. Whereas there are hundreds of public issues, there are only a few political parties. Supporting a political party consequently requires the citizen to give a blank check in the sense that he cannot expect the party to faithfully reflect his views on every issue. The individual citizen in a two-party system may even protest that he is not offered a real choice. Neither of the candidates reflects his views on those issues over which he is most concerned. There is no help for it. Voter consent has to be generalized from a multitude of specific issues into a broad base of party support. In the process of generalization, individual citizens cannot all be satisfied in detail. The best that the individual can hope for is a favorable compromise within the coalition of other supporters of his party. Of course, the more involved the individual is with his private affairs, the more readily will he accept such compromises. Thus **privatism** provides leeway necessary for vigorous competition between the parties.

[23] Samuel A. Stouffer, *Communism, Conformity, and Civil Liberties,* Garden City, N.Y.: Doubleday, 1955, pp. 58-70.

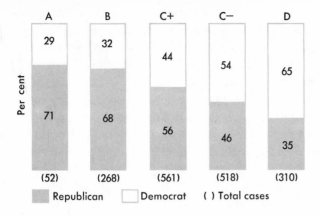

FIGURE 9.1 **Voting behavior by socioeconomic status.** Source: Paul F. Lazarsfeld, Bernard Berelson, and Hazel Gaudet, *The People's Choice: How the Voter Makes Up His Mind in a Presidential Campaign,* New York: Duell, Sloan and Pearce, 1944, p. 19.

"Vigorous competition" does not mean irreconcilable differences between the parties. In the United States, for instance, the Republican Party has leaned toward the interests of the business community and the Democratic Party toward the interests of labor unions and ethnic minorities, but these tendencies are blurred by efforts of both parties to appeal to as broad a population base as possible. Figure 9.1 shows the relationship between socioeconomic status and voting behavior in Erie County, Ohio, in 1940. Subsequent studies have confirmed the findings of Fig. 9.1 that a tendency for voters of high socioeconomic status to favor the Republicans and those of low socioeconomic status to favor the Democrats.[24] Note, however, that the Erie County electorate was *not* **polarized** into two groups—with the poor unanimously favoring the Democrats and the rich unanimously Republican. This looseness of the relationship between socioeconomic status and political predisposition is duplicated in the relationship between political predisposition and religious affiliation, rural-urban residence, and ethnicity. In short, social differences largely cross-cut political differences. The result is to reduce the fervor of political partisanship. It is less easy to regard all Republicans as angels and all Democrats as devils when some of your neighbors and co-religionists, if not of your family, support the Democrats.

Tolerance for political disagreement is a benefit in democratic societies. Commitment to a policy or a candidate or a party without recognition of possible merit on the other side leads to fanaticism, which would endanger the democratic process (1) by tempting the losing side to resort to violence to reverse

[24] Seymour Martin Lipset, *Political Man: The Social Bases of Politics,* Garden City, N.Y.: Doubleday Anchor, 1963, p. 304.

the verdict of the electorate and (2) by tempting the winning side to define opposition as disloyal. A few fanatics add color to the political scene, but an entire electorate that regards elections as life or death issues makes for trouble. A limited amount of **political apathy** is desirable in a democracy to prevent internal cleavages from destroying the society.

The same social heterogeneity that threatens industrial societies with sharp political conflict indirectly generates political apathy. Recall the discussion of role conflict in Chapter 1. Something analogous to role conflict occurs in the realm of politics when an individual belongs to groups pushing him in different political directions. Catholics tend to support the Democratic Party in the United States; the more affluent strata of the population tend to support the Republican Party. What do *affluent Catholics* do? Caught in cross-pressures, they often vacillate. Like the starving mule standing midway between two bales of hay and unable to decide which to eat first, the cross-pressured voter usually makes up his mind later in the campaign than a voter whose group member- ships mutually support one party. The cross-pressured voter expresses less in- terest in the campaign than the voter not subject to inner conflicts. He is less informed on the issues. Thus a heterogeneous, mobile society indirectly pro- duces the necessary cushion of political apathy; the portion of the electorate subject to inconsistent political predispositions is less involved in electoral outcomes.

The flexibility that enables the political system to adapt to changed circum- stances stems from this less involved, less informed portion of the electorate. Cross-pressured voters are more susceptible to shifts from one party to another than are voters whose loyalty to party is firmly anchored in social roots. Thus democratic consent is not quite the informed consent the eighteenth-century rationalists thought it had to be. Democratic consent requires citizen participa- tion but not too much participation.[25] It requires some dispassionate rationality, but not from everybody and certainly not all the time. Classical democratic theorists exaggerated the importance of concerned and knowledgeable voters because they assumed that majority rule could not be based on anything less. Recent research dealing with voting decisions has demonstrated widespread voter apathy and ignorance as well as powerful tendencies to vote in response to the influence of friends, family, and political predisposition rather than in response to arguments presented during the campaign.[26] This being so, a feebleminded deaf-mute running on the Democratic or Republican ticket would have a good chance of polling 40 per cent of the votes cast in most American communities. How then can the viability of the American political system (or of any contemporary democracy) be explained?

Nonrational Consent. On the surface, the political process in an industrial

[25]Morris Janowitz and Dwaine Marvick, *Competitive Pressure and Democratic Consent,* Ann Arbor: Bureau of Government, Institute of Public Administration, University of Michigan, 1956.

[26] Bernard R. Berelson, Paul F. Lazarsfeld, and William N. McPhee, *Voting: A Study of Opinion Formation in a Presidential Campaign,* Chicago: University of Chicago Press, 1954.

society depends on millions of individuals arriving independently at voting decisions. In actuality, people vote their social loyalties most of the time. They vote as their family members vote, as their neighbors vote, as their fellow workers vote, and as members of their ethnic group have traditionally voted. These nonrational loyalties stabilize the political process by ensuring that shifts in political direction take time. During an election campaign in a democracy, the voter receives two distinct messages. One is from the candidates and the political parties; it is concerned with the policy decisions proposed for the society and with the personalities of those who aspire to leadership roles. The other is the silent tug of his group loyalties. For voters who have been unable to make up their minds on the basis of the issues and the personalities, the campaign reaffirms the political predispositions of the solidary groups to which they are attached and determines their vote. But all voters are influenced by both rational considerations and nonrational loyalties. The outcome of a particular election — and more generally the balance between stability and change in a society — depends on the outcome of these tendencies in the electorate.

Note the implications of this line of reasoning: the strength of a democratic political system lies not so much in the *individual voter* as in the balance it achieves in the *society*. The stability of the system as a whole could not be predicted from examining the characteristics of the average voter because stability depends on competition among various pressure groups for voter support. Even when the majority of voters are ignorant of the issues or apathetic toward them, the democratic process may be working well. Apathy in a democracy means that some people are satisfied enough with the status quo to ignore the opportunity to change leaders presented by the ballot box. The importance of an election is not how many people vote but how many *could* vote if they were motivated to. As long as that potentiality exists, current decision makers must tremble during an election campaign even though they are aware that most people pay little attention to campaign oratory and that half of the eligible voters may not bother to vote. Table 9.1 shows the proportion of eligible voters who cast ballots in presidential and congressional contests from 1920 to 1968.

Given widespread apathy and ignorance, many voters cast their ballots for reasons that might have horrified Thomas Jefferson. In particular, political machines in large cities appeal to voters on a personal basis or as reciprocation for past favors. The following article shows how votes used to be controlled in a Negro slum community in Nashville, Tennessee:[27]

> The other day the [Nashville] police raided a Negro barbecue and beer joint and arrested nine people. The raid and the arrests came as something of a shock to the owner. "I don't know why they're bothering me," said Henry ("Good Jelly") Jones, restaurateur, bootlegger, and politician, "It ain't election time." But bother him they did, and because Good Jelly (or just "Jelly" to his

---

[27] Reprinted by permission. From David Halberstam, "'Good Jelly's' Last Stand," *The Reporter,* Vol. 24, Jan. 19, 1961, pp. 40-41.

TABLE 9.1

Percentage of Eligible Voters Voting in Presidential and Congressional Elections, 1920–1968

Election Year	Presidential Elections Eligible Voters Voting for Presidential Electors (Per Cent)	Congressional Elections Eligible Voters Voting for U.S. Representatives (Per Cent)
1920	43.5	
1922		32.1
1924	43.9	
1926		29.8
1928	51.9	
1930		33.7
1932	52.5	
1934		41.4
1936	57.0	
1938		44.1
1940	59.2	
1942		33.9
1944	52.9	
1946		37.4
1948	51.3	
1950		41.6
1952	62.6	
1954		42.4
1956	60.1	
1958		43.4
1960	64.0	
1962		46.7
1964	62.9	
1966		46.3
1968	61.8	

Source: Bureau of the Census, *Statistical Abstract of the United States: 1969,* Washington, D.C.: Government Printing Office, 1969, p. 368.

friends) is something of a local celebrity these days, there was a sizable press section on hand for his trial.

The reporters were not disappointed. Good Jelly's wife, when asked whether a gallon jug was the same jug found during the raid, answered, "I don't know. Jugs don't have no names." Later the white prosecuting attorney asked her why she found it so easy to answer defense questions and so hard to understand his. "Mr. City Attorney," said Robert Lilliard, her Negro attorney, "she's a little confused by all your high-class words. You just talk like we talk down at Good Jelly's and we'll be all right." "High-class words," snorted the city attorney. "What's so high-class about the words 'white corn'?"

The case came out as everyone knew it would: the charges against Good Jelly and his friends were dismissed. For if Good Jelly has a striking ability to get into trouble, he has an even more remarkable ability to get out of it. Fifteen times he has been called before the bar of justice in recent years, fourteen times he has been set free. The explanation of this enviable batting average lies deep in the structure of Southern politics, the Negro's role in it, and the specific power structure of Nashville. Henry Jones, with his golfer's cap, big flashing smile, and long police record, is a power. He is among the last of the ward heelers. Very simply, he controls the votes of a large number of unbelievably poor people, and for a minimum of service, protection, and financial reward, he delivers these same votes without the slightest concern for ideology.

In Nashville, he is the Negro whom many Negroes like least to think about; he is the Negro whom many whites like most to think about. In his own blunt word, he is a "nigger"; what is worse, that is all he wants to be. Respectable Negro society shuns him, yet to some of the Negro poor he is perhaps the only truly big man in their lives.

Good Jelly first became interested in politics at an early age. Because he was an uneducated Negro there were distinct limitations to the ambitions he might reasonably entertain and yet many people who govern his city and who dedicate schools and other buildings in the highest of ideals are perfectly willing to deal with him. "Call him a backdoor Negro," said one white leader; "they won't have their picture taken with him, and they won't pose with him, even at Negro functions. But they know how to get hold of him." When a white man once complained about Jelly's police record and about his bootlegging and the fact that he has many friends among politicians, a Negro answered: "That's the way you people really want him."

It is hardly surprising, then, that the complexities of playing the system at both ends have produced two Jellies. They are separate but equal Jellies. There is a Jelly for whites and a Jelly for Negroes. The whites' Jelly is an ingratiating Uncle Tom, laughing, smiling, hiding from any slightly serious question or threat behind the big smile and a joke (in which old Jelly is always the butt). The Negroes' Jelly is something different. He is kind: he has clothed many of his people, housed more, and fed them all. If he calls one and gives him the key to the big black Cadillac and says it's time to move the Caddy, the man is honored by the assignment; if he calls eight of them together and says that the newspaper wants their picture and that he, Jelly, approves of the idea, then a picture of eight smiling faces is taken; if he tells them to vote this way or that, they vote this way or that.

"I carry a lot of weight around here," Jelly admits. "'Bout half the people in this precinct I control. Two hundred, three hundred people. They're my people."

"I DON'T TURN THEM DOWN"

Good Jelly is a dark, stocky man of about fifty, whose use of minstrel-show techniques in front of whites is a legitimate heritage. As a young man he left his Nashville home and joined the cast of the Mandy Green from New Orleans Minstrel Show (the poor man's version of the famous Silas Green show). For Mandy Green he traveled the South as what he calls "one of those black-face comedians, and I was pretty good." Then he returned to Nashville, where he became associated with the then ruling Negro ward heeler, "Pie" Hardison. "I was Pie's chauffeur. He thought I was a pretty good fellow, and I was a good driver and a good talker, and so he got me into politics. One time Pie said I ought to be in there pitching for the mayor, and I said: 'If you want the mayor, then I'm pitching one hundred per cent,' and so I got him the votes."

Pie Hardison is gone now and his heir does his pitching from a small hut off a dark alley deep in the Negro slums. In a small half-masonry, half-wooden café, he cooks, bootlegs, and politicks. There is one small sign over the door—it is upside down—and it says "BEST." Jelly says this is not the name of the café, that the name is "Jones Barbecue." It is a small café and there are no menus, only signs on the walls. At one end of the café white beans cost twenty-five cents, at the other they cost twenty-one cents. There, with regular violations of local whiskey laws ("We have some whiskey but we don't have no beer—we have to send out for the beer"), he operates his machine: the restaurant is essential to his success as a politician.

For Good Jelly's machine has been described by one reporter as "the lame, the sick, the poor, and a few of the penniless." Good Jelly himself says: "Down in this part folks don't have but a little money and so they come over here when they have a little and we feed them, and they come over here when they don't have any money and we still feed them. I don't turn them down. I always feed them and I get them a place to sleep, most times right here, and get them to a hospital, and even a job sometimes. They get what I got, these folks, and they don't forget."

If the voters don't forget, neither does Good Jelly. He keeps a thorough file on each of his debtors: name, favors granted, address—or frequently the address of someone who will know where to find the debtor. Before election day Good Jelly will make sure all his friends are registered; he will also send out cards reminding them of their civic responsibility. Come election day and Good Jelly takes out his big Cadillac and herds his people to the polls. He likes to start early; it gives him more time later in the day for rounding up slackers. "I'll tell you why Good Jelly has got so many friends," said Robert Lilliard, the Negro attorney who is also a city councilman. "A lot of these politicians just like him: you can really count on Jelly. If he's for you, why you can check his precinct the next day and his votes will be there. If you treated him right."

Good Jelly himself says that he asks little for his interest in politics. "I'm for any man that's a good man," he is fond of saying. How does he tell who's a good man? "I read about this man, see, and I can tell if he's for me. I want to know all the issues."

Is that all? What issues? "A lot of these men, they want to be politicians and so they come and see Jelly and I see how friendly they are, and they're pretty friendly. They're good men. We talk about these issues. All of these issues." He repeated emphatically: "I'm for any man that's a good man."

Other interpretations of Good Jelly's political motivations have been offered from time to time. "I'd say he gets an average of about $300 for an election," one white politician told me. "It depends. On a close local election with a lot at stake I expect he's gotten $500 or more. Maybe a thousand."

"How much money did you get for the sheriff's race?" I asked him point-blank.

"Money? Money? I wouldn't do none of that," he said. "The man, he come down here and he was a good man and he said how he wanted to do right . . ."

It is not without a touch of regret that many white politicians, worried by the new power of the sit-in leaders and the young Negro ministers, foresee the

demise of Good Jelly and his kind. "You make the deal with Jelly," one politician said, "and that's it. You don't have to worry about him coming downtown
with a bunch of his damn people and sitting down at some nice restaurant, or
calling the damn newspapers and announcing he's going to picket some company for better jobs. Jelly's all right. Take care of him on the drunk and disorderly and that kind of thing, and that's it."

"He comes through?" I asked.

"We take care of him and he takes care of us," the man answered. . . .

Jelly's lack of concern about civil rights galls many young Negroes in Nashville. "If John Kasper [a white supremacist] were running against Thurgood
Marshall and it was a local race and the right people went to see Jelly for Kasper,
that's all it would take," said one Negro bitterly. Jelly himself has said: "My
folks, they're not the integration type. They're not interested in all that. All they
want is a little food." Attorney Robert Lilliard has explained Jelly's continuing
popularity in just about the same terms: "Those folks, they aren't going to eat at
Woolworth's or Grant's or anything like that. But they got to eat. Jelly's the only
thing those people have, and he looks mighty good to them."

But even Lilliard concedes that sooner or later other political leaders will supplant Good Jelly Jones and his kind among the Negroes. "You take this city,
growing all the time, and the city limits going out, and the Negro making a little
more money all the time—a thing like Jelly got, it's getting to be less and less
important all the time. Five, ten years from now there probably won't be any
Good Jelly. Pretty soon both sides [will be] too busy worrying about this middle-
class vote to pay for Jelly. That's where the next battle will be."

The significance of precinct leaders like Good Jelly Jones is that they involve
people in the political process who are too apathetic to participate on their own
initiative. Good Jelly's friends do not vote in response to television debates or
to paid political advertisements in the newspaper. They vote the way Good
Jelly tells them to vote because that is how they reciprocate his kindnesses.
Whether Good Jelly's constituency is a burden to the democratic process in
Nashville is not clear. Perhaps a **political machine** offers the best chance for
poorly educated minorities to have a voice in the community. However, with
the breakup of ethnic ghettoes and the educational upgrading of the population, political machines are declining in importance. American democracy
survived the first three decades of the twentieth century during which political
machines controlled cities like New York, Chicago, Philadelphia, Jersey City,
Memphis, and Boston, and were a factor on state and national levels. It will
certainly survive Good Jelly Jones.

Coerced Consent: The Theory of the Power Élite. Marxists never accepted
the theory that societal leadership rests ultimately on value consensus. Marx
regarded governments as instruments of the dominant class in capitalist societies, as the executive committee of the bourgeoisie. But the Marxist view
seemed overdrawn to many political scientists as industrial societies became
increasingly pluralistic. Pluralistic theories of societal leadership deny the
existence of a unified "ruling class." Instead of a ruling class, they hypothesize
within capitalist democracies a constant struggle for power among shifting

coalitions of interest groups, each of which perceives the others as limiting its opportunities to make societal policy. David Riesman went so far as to argue that no group has much power in the contemporary United States except the ability to veto the suggested policies of other groups.[28] He suggested the term **veto groups** to describe this fluid situation. Some empirical studies of power in the local community support pluralistic theories. For instance, Robert Dahl studied party nominations, educational policy, and planning for urban redevelopment in New Haven, Connecticut.[29] He concluded that participation in the political process is fairly widespread, not controlled by a ruling élite of social and economic notables. Community studies in this pluralistic tradition also find that power lies in one realm or another, rather than manifesting itself uniformly in governmental, business, and educational fields.

Within the past dozen years, however, there has been a resurgence of interest in theories of a ruling class. In particular, C. Wright Mills popularized the concept of "the power élite" in an influential book:[30]

> The power elite is composed of men whose positions enable them to transcend the ordinary environments of ordinary men and women; they are in positions to make decisions having major consequences. Whether they do or do not make such decisions is less important than the fact that they do occupy such pivotal positions: their failure to act, their failure to make decisions, is itself an act that is often of greater consequence than the decisions they do make. For they are in command of the major hierarchies and organizations of modern society. They rule the big corporations. They run the machinery of the state and claim its prerogatives. They direct the military establishment. They occupy the strategic command posts of the social structure, in which are now centered the effective means of the power and the wealth and the celebrity which they enjoy.

Mills' central thesis is that a small, homogeneous group mans the political, economic, and military "command posts" of American society and has increased its relative power over the past generation:[31]

> As the requirements of the top places in each of the major hierarchies become similar, the types of men occupying these roles at the top—by selection and by training in the jobs—become similar. This is no mere deduction from structure to personnel. That it is a fact is revealed by the heavy traffic that has been going on between the three structures, often in very intricate patterns. The chief executives, the warlords, and selected politicians came into contact with one another in an intimate, working way during World War II; after that war ended, they continued their associations, out of common beliefs, social congeniality, and coinciding interests. Noticeable proportions of top men from the military, the eco-

---

[28] David Riesman, *The Lonely Crowd,* New Haven, Conn.: Yale University Press, 1951, pp. 242-255.

[29] Robert A. Dahl, *Who Governs? Democracy and Power in an American City,* New Haven, Conn.: Yale University Press, 1961.

[30] C. Wright Mills, *The Power Elite,* New York: Oxford University Press, 1956, pp. 3-4.

[31] Reprinted by permission. From Mills, *The Power Elite,* pp. 287-288.

nomic, and the political worlds have during the last fifteen years occupied positions in one or both of the other worlds: between these higher circles there is an interchangeability of position, based formally upon the supposed transferability of "executive ability," based in substance upon the co-optation by cliques of insiders. As members of a power elite, many of those busy in this traffic have come to look upon "the government" as an umbrella under whose authority they do their work.

As the business between the big three increases in volume and importance, so does the traffic in personnel. The very criteria for selecting men who will rise come to embody this fact. The corporate commissar, dealing with the state and its military, is wiser to choose a young man who has experienced the state and its military than one who has not. The political director, often dependent for his own political success upon corporate decisions and corporations, is also wiser to choose a man with corporate experience. Thus, by virtue of the very criterion of success, the interchange of personnel and the unity of the power elite is increased.

Although Mills is becoming increasingly popular, there are arguments against the power-élite thesis.[32] First, Mills offers a limited conception of power. He perceives only the exploitative aspect of it: how one group, the holders of power, obtains advantages by keeping the powerless from participating in the decision-making process. He does not consider power as the capacity of a society to mobilize its resources in order to realize common goals. To put it another way, Mills views power as inherently "bad" rather than as a resource available to the leadership of an interactive system, a resource that can serve good or evil ends. Parsons, on the other hand, believes that political power is more necessary as societies grow larger and more differentiated. Parsons considers the nostalgia for the individualism of eighteenth-century rural America a form of romanticism. The Jeffersonian option is not open to contemporary society. The choice is rather between pluralistic systems in which power is wielded by governmental as well as private organizations and monolithic systems in which governmental bureaucracies enjoy a power monopoly.

Mills—like the liberals of 150 years ago—conceives of man as naturally good but observes war and injustice and prejudice. In the tradition of Jean Jacques Rousseau, he solves the paradox of moral man in immoral society by pointing to the source of corruption in social institutions. The machinations of the power élite explain to Mills' satisfaction how a democratic society falls short of human potentialities. Mills is too sophisticated to advocate anarchy, yet his distrust of power points him in that direction. His followers in the New Left extend his logic to a general attack on political authority; they advocate destruction of this "hopelessly corrupt" society. They assume that something better will emerge from the ashes because philosophic anarchists believe in the

---

[32] The discussion to follow leans heavily on a review article dealing with *The Power Elite* by Talcott Parsons, "The Distribution of Power in American Society," *World Politics*, Vol. 10, October 1957, pp. 123-133.

spontaneous goodness of man. The communes brought into being by the hippie movement share with the New Left suspicion of leaders and romantic confidence that social organization is unnecessary and corrupting.

Mills thinks of American business, military, and governmental leaders not as policy makers on behalf of society but as a military-industrial coalition that increasingly dominates society. Office holders (including members of Congress) are perceived as *junior* partners whose main function is to manipulate the electoral process so as to distract attention from the exploitative activities of their *senior* partners. Mills speaks of "cumulative advantage" to refer to the process by which the rich grow richer and more powerful. By virtue of high salaries, bonuses, and stock options, executive employees become wealthy. The typical pattern is the separation of ownership and control—with control (power) securely in the hands of well-educated, well-paid employees.[33] These nonowners wield greater economic power than can be exerted by richer men not in the seats of corporate authority. Mills believes their independence decreases at this stage because they now acquire interest in their corporations and begin to think as owners do.

Mills' inability to recognize corporate management as a center of power only loosely coordinated with ownership of great wealth is paralleled by his overestimation of the power of "big business" over government. Probably business leaders have greater influence on government than labor leaders, civil rights advocates, lawyers, civil servants, or university professors. But this is not the same thing as saying that other interest and professional groups have no influence at all. Or that politicians do not balance the economic power wielded by big business against the direct political power represented by blocs of voters who may, as individuals, have insignificant visibility. If this were not true, the passage of the National Labor Relations Act in 1935—against the bitter opposition of the business community—would be inexplicable. The National Labor Relations Act forced large business firms to bargain collectively with labor unions winning the allegiance of a majority of their employees.[34] Hailed by organized labor as the Magna Carta of the working class, this legislation illustrates governmental regulation of economic activities despite strident objections from business interests.

In coining the phrase "power élite" Mills connects the concept of power with the concept of prestige; most sociologists think of them as overlapping domains but logically distinct from one another. Mills recognizes the existence of professional celebrities, those whose achievements are in the entertainment

---

[33] Adolph A. Berle, Jr., and Gardiner C. Means, *The Modern Corporation and Private Property*, Chicago: Commerce Clearing House, 1932; Adolph A. Berle, Jr., *The Twentieth Century Capitalist Revolution*, New York: Harcourt, Brace, 1954.

Chapter 10 considers the separation of ownership and control further—as an aspect of the development of large-scale formal organizations.

[34] Sumner H. Slichter, James J. Healy, and E. Robert Livernash, *The Impact of Collective Bargaining on Management*, Washington, D.C.: Brookings Institution, 1960.

world, professional sports, or other activities unrelated to economic, political, or military matters. Nevertheless, he says explicitly that true prestige is ultimately derived from power:[35]

> Yet prestige is the shadow of money and power. Where these are, there it is. Like the national market for soap or automobiles and the enlarged arena of federal power, the national cash-in arena for prestige has grown, slowly being consolidated into a truly national system. Since the men of the higher political, economic, and military circles are an elite of money and power, they accumulate a prestige that is considerably above the ordinary; all of them have publicity value and some of them are downright eminent; increasingly, by virtue of their position and by means of conscious public relations, they strive to make their names notable, their actions acceptable, their policies popular. And in all this, they tend to become national celebrities.

Power does give rise to prestige, but power is not the only path to élite status. As Mills himself shows in a discussion of the mingling of celebrities from many realms in cafe society, "the success, the champion, . . . is one who mingles freely with other champions to populate the world of the celebrity."[36] The professor of surgery at a leading medical school does not have political power; he may not have a particularly large income; but he possesses élite status in American society. In neglecting such a case, Mills fails to evaluate properly a major occupational category in modern societies: the professions. Not only physicians but scientists, engineers, teachers, writers, actors, and accountants represent this emerging leadership category in modern societies.[37] The influence of members of the professions stems less from their political or economic power than from their technical competence gained from mastery of intellectual disciplines. Emphasis on rationality and technical competence reflects the achievement values of industrial economies as well as the new importance of universities in the mainstream of society. Chapter 11 will return to this latter point in the context of a discussion of formal education. The power-élite theory draws attention to the possibility that consent can rest on coercion as well as on value consensus. In a family, in a business corporation, or in society at large, a strong leader may impose his will on those vulnerable to the power under his control regardless of whether they share his assessment of the collective interest. Sometimes this is unavoidable even in a democratic family or a democratic government. Consensus is not always possible—although discussion is frank and prolonged. Whether consensus is achieved or not, integration of the interactive system may require *one* policy. To take a familiar example, in 1860 consensus could not be achieved within the United States on the slavery question, and Lincoln was unwilling to accept the secession of

---

[35] Mills, *The Power Elite,* p. 83.

[36] Mills, *The Power Elite,* p. 74.

[37] Talcott Parsons, "The Professions," *International Encyclopedia of the Social Sciences,* New York: Macmillan, 1968, Vol. 12, pp. 536-547.

southern states. The Civil War was necessary in order to impose by force the policy that slavery was illegitimate in all parts of the society. In short, consent may have to be coerced despite the preference of leaders to avoid coercion. Like Lincoln, they may have to choose between coerced consent and the dissolution of the interactive system. Chapter 15 returns to the problem of societal integration and to its ultimate reliance on political power — even in democratic societies.

Nevertheless, the power-élite theory distorts the fluid complexities of the political process in capitalist democracies. It serves as a corrective for the evaluation of power as totally benign, but it dashes to the pessimistic extreme of viewing power as chronically exploitative. The power-élite theory appeals to suspicions that power is invariably abused. But it does not do justice to leaders motivated (at least partially) by a desire to serve their society, by what Walter Lippman called "the public philosophy."[38]

CONCLUSION

Even in small interactive systems like families, there is a recognizable political process. Parents play political roles insofar as they make binding decisions on behalf of families. Like governmental decisions, parental decisions are binding in a twofold sense: children recognize the *right* of parents to make family policy. But apart from the children's recognition of the legitimacy of parental leadership, parents can *enforce* their decisions within the family. They have power — not just the possibility of using physical coercion but also the reward of approval and the punishment of material deprivation. A political process in the family differs from the political process in the larger society in at least two respects. In the first place, policy makers within the family depend on policy makers in the larger society for the ultimate enforcement of their decisions. Thus, if a child refuses to heed the rules of his parents, they are not permitted to put him in a dungeon for disobedience; they must appeal to a juvenile court on the grounds that he is "ungovernable." They may hit him, of course, but the extent of the beating is limited by statutes protecting children even against their own parents. Second, membership in the family is compulsory for children. Whereas an adult can usually withdraw from an organization or community with an uncongenial leadership structure, children can only rebel. Despite these differences, it is useful to keep in mind that the problem of collective action arises in small interactive systems as well as in self-contained societies.

In every society conflicts must be resolved and decisions made. In less differentiated societies, this political function can be handled informally. Leader-

[38] Walter Lippman, *Essays in the Public Philosophy,* Boston: Little, Brown, 1955.

ship exists but not necessarily government. Industrial societies are sufficiently large and differentiated that formal political institutions are inevitable. The differences between democratic and despotic government hinge on the method of *selecting current policy makers, the extent to which opposition to them is legitimate, and the degree of independence of the legal system from them or their administrative subordinates.* In both types of society, consent of the governed rests on a mixture of value consensus and political coercion. In a democracy the mix is richer in value consensus; in a despotism, consent is more often coerced by those in authority.

On a more philosophical level, the difference between democracy and despotism hinges on different conceptions of human nature and of social life. Despotic political philosophies tend to make either or both of two extreme assumptions:

1. *Consensus* is so difficult to achieve that freedom must be sacrificed to order.
2. **Justice** is so easy to achieve that political authority can be entrusted to a wise man or to a benevolent party.

Democratic political philosophies tend to be mildly optimistic about the possibilities of consensus and mildly pessimistic about the possibilities of justice. The Protestant theologian Reinhold Niebuhr put it very well when he said, "Man's capacity for justice makes democracy possible; but man's inclination to injustice makes democracy necessary." [39] That is, belief in the viability of democracy rests on faith that man is a moral animal and not a jungle cat. Being moral, human beings have the capacity to transcend their own partial perspectives and partisan interests—at least sometimes. Hence, democratic policy making approximates a moral consensus and not a triumph of the most powerful interest group. On any given issue, interest groups contend with each other for a favorable decision, but no group is dominant, so that all interest groups must ultimately appeal to the disinterested and somewhat apathetic majority. Belief in democracy rests on hope that the verdict of this majority will be just. The theory of the power élite holds that such hope is illusory.

Hope that the democratic process will result in a just consensus has not blinded democratic theorists to potentialities for injustice. The framers of the American Constitution were careful to build checks and balances into the system because they were afraid of the tyranny of a temporary majority. For the same reason, influential leaders in the thirteen colonies opposed ratification of the Constitution until a Bill of Rights was tacked on (the first ten amendments). When Professor Niebuhr says " . . . man's inclination to injustice makes democracy necessary," he is echoing the pessimism of the Founding Fathers about political authority generally, and he is asserting that *self*-government is the best protection against tendencies to injustice. He suggests that it is an inconsistency of totalitarian political philosophies to place so little faith in the

[39] Niebuhr, *Children of Light,* p. xi.

citizen and so much in the rulers. "If men are inclined to deal unjustly with their fellows, the possession of power aggravates this inclination. That is why irresponsible and uncontrolled power is the greatest source of injustice."[40] That, argues Niebuhr, is why democracy is *necessary*. It is not an argument in favor of anarchy.

SOME SIGNIFICANT LITERATURE ON THE POLITICAL STRUCTURE OF INDUSTRIAL SOCIETY

Daniel Bell, *The End of Ideology: On the Exhaustion of Political Ideas in the Fifties,* rev. ed., New York: Collier Books, 1961. Ideologies that once gave intellectuals a sense of political direction have lost the power to arouse passion.

> Few serious minds believe any longer that one can set down "blueprints" and through "social engineering" bring about a new utopia of social harmony. . . . Few "classic" liberals insist that the State should play no role in the economy, and few serious conservatives, at least in England and on the Continent, believe that the Welfare State is "the road to serfdom." In the Western world, therefore, there is today rough consensus among intellectuals on political issues: the acceptance of a Welfare State; the desirability of decentralized power; a system of mixed economy and of political pluralism.

Bell hopes that a new age has dawned in which political goals will be chosen more rationally rather than on the basis of "apocalyptic fervor." What Bell did not foresee, as a phase succeeding the loss of ideological fervor, is political alienation in the absence of concrete objectives such as the coming to power of a socialist government. For a description of this apolitical alienation, see James McEvoy and Abraham Miller, Eds., *Black Power and Student Rebellion,* Belmont, Calif.: Wadsworth, 1969.

William A. Faunce, "Size of Locals and Union Democracy," *American Journal of Sociology,* Vol. 68, November 1962, pp. 291-298. At the 1959 convention of the United Automobile Workers, 1815 delegates representing 753 U.A.W. locals filled out questionnaires dealing with participation in union affairs. After the convention, 108 delegates from locals in Lansing and Flint, Michigan, were interviewed at length not only about their participation in the national convention but also about politics in the U.A.W. locals. Delegates from *small* locals were less likely than delegates from *large* locals to take an active part in convention proceedings and to express concern about representing rank-and-file views at the national level. Although delegates from small locals reported a higher proportion of members voting in local elections than delegates from large locals, they also reported fewer contested elections and less well-developed opposition parties. Faunce concludes that large locals appear to contribute more than small locals to democratic processes in unions both on the national and on the local levels. For other studies of the conditions favoring democratic processes in trade unions, see Seymour Martin Lipset, Martin A. Trow, and James S. Coleman, *Union Democracy: The Internal Politics of the International Typographical Union,* Glencoe, Ill.: Free Press, 1956; and Seymour Martin Lipset, "The Law and Trade Union Democracy," *Virginia Law Review,* Vol. 47, January 1961, pp. 1-50.

[40] Niebuhr, *Children of Light.*

William A. Gamson, *Power and Discontent,* Homewood, Ill.: Dorsey, 1968. In this theoretical analysis of power, Gamson contrasts the influence perspective from the social control perspective. The social control perspective looks at power and discontent from the viewpoint of *authorities,* those who make binding decisions on behalf of an interactive system. It "emphasizes the process by which they attempt to achieve collective goals and to maintain legitimacy and compliance with their decisions" in a situation in which some of their constituents are not fully satisfied (page 2). The influence perspective takes the point of view of actors in the system rather than the system as a whole. These participants have wants and demands that conflict to some extent with other participants. Thus they tend to become *partisans,* system members who attempt to influence the decisions of authorities on behalf of their own goals. When there is widespread consensus within the system about values and concrete goals, the social control activities of authorities do not arouse serious discontent; authorities tend to be perceived as the servants of the system rather than its tyrants. When, on the other hand, consensus does not exist or when there are large dissenting groups, the necessary attempt on the part of authorities to control partisans generates discontent and sometimes social change. For a similar analysis of power which distinguishes between power problems in small interactive systems and in large-scale societies, see Edward W. Lehman, "Towards a Macrosociology of Power," *American Sociological Review,* Vol. 34, August 1969, pp. 453-465.

Morton Grodzins, *The Loyal and the Disloyal: Social Boundaries of Patriotism and Treason,* Chicago: University of Chicago Press, 1956. Democratic and totalitarian nations have different methods of sustaining loyalty. In a democracy, loyalty is a by-product of satisfaction achieved within the family, the economic system, the church, and other non-national solidarities that the nation is implicitly assumed to symbolize: "The democratic system of limited government presupposes that national loyalty will be a limited loyalty." In a totalitarian society, all identifications that the ruling party might not be able to control are regarded as signs of disloyalty: "Every effort is made to blast the individual from his non-national identifications. Then he is offered the single identification with the state." Grodzins illustrates these contrasting conceptions of loyalty by citing the more than 6000 American citizens of Japanese descent who, during the Second World War, formally declared that they were not loyal to the United States. The government program of evacuation and relocation of West Coast Japanese had so disturbed their primary group relations as to make the United States a negative symbol instead of the positive symbol it had been before. Therefore, when they were registered and forced to reply to a question, "Will you swear unqualified allegiance to the United States of America . . . and forswear any form of allegiance to the Japanese emperor?" 6000 out of the 37,000 Japanese-American citizens in relocation centers said, "No." Grodzins implies that this loyalty test implicitly assumed a totalitarian rather than a democratic concept of loyalty. This summary is based on a review by S. Frank Miyamoto, *American Sociological Review,* Vol. 21, October 1956, p. 657.

Joseph R. Gusfield, "Mass Society and Extremist Politics," *American Sociological Review,* Vol. 27, February 1962, pp. 19-30. Some sociologists maintain (1) that traditional solidarities — family, class, neighborhood, ethnic group — have little significance in societies characterized by mass communications, bureaucratized relationships in large-scale organizations, and equalitarian ideologies and (2) that the resulting rootlessness of degrouped individuals creates opportunities for demagogues and extremist political parties. Gusfield criticizes this theory on both theoretical and empirical grounds: (1) The mass society theorists emphasize only the disruptive consequences of urban industrial culture. Homogeneous experiences with mass media and with formal education may *increase* consensus and integration — particularly on the national level. (2) The chief source of political extremism seems to be the population elements most isolated from the institutions and the values of mass society as, for example, in the desegregation crisis. "Opposition to a national culture of race relations is found most intensively among those most localistic, least educated, least urban, least exposed to mass media, and least integrated into the national economy." For an exposition of the views Gusfield is criticizing, see William Kornhauser, *The Politics of Mass Society,* Glencoe, Ill.: Free Press, 1959; and Philip Selznick, *The Organizational Weapon: A Study of Bolshevik Strategy and Tactics,* New York: McGraw-Hill, 1952.

Morris Janowitz and Dwaine Marvick, *Competitive Pressure and Democratic Consent,* Ann Arbor: Bureau of Government, Institute of Public Administration, University of Michigan, 1956. The authors assess American voting behavior in the 1952 presidential election in terms of a theory of "democratic consent." Five criteria are suggested in terms of which the election can be evaluated: (1) competition among rival candidates is sufficiently intense to generate widespread citizen participation; (2) the citizenry is concerned about the outcome but is willing to accept the verdict of the electoral process; (3) the campaign stimulates effective deliberation on the candidates and the issues; (4) no party or candidate monopolizes the mass media; (5) mass-media influences and personal influences of friends and relatives are independent. Although the authors identify segments of the electorate which did not participate in 1952 in a process of democratic consent (Negroes and lower-class persons), they conclude that in general the 1952 election fulfilled their criteria. This summary is based on a review by Duncan MacRae, Jr., *American Sociological Review,* Vol. 22, April 1957, p. 238.

Seymour Martin Lipset, "Party Systems and the Representation of Social Groups," *European Journal of Sociology,* Vol. 1, No. 1, 1960, pp. 3-38. Even when social and economic conditions are conducive to a stable democratic system, formal political institutions may contribute to stability or to instability. Lipset demonstrates by means of comparative analysis of stable and unstable democracies that a two-party system is more conducive to stability than a multiparty system except when the society is polarized by class, race, or religion. If under these circumstances "the political lines follow those of social cleavage, a two-party system may intensify internal conflict rather than help integrate the society." But how is a two-party system developed? Lipset shows that proportional representation favors the development of a multiparty system, whereas an electoral system wherein the candidate wins who receives a plurality of the votes tends to be a two-party system. The reason for this tendency in a plurality system is that voters are reluctant to "waste" their votes on a weak party. Lipset explicitly credits political scientists with this insight and chides sociologists for assuming that underlying social cleavages must result in multiparty instability.

Seymour Martin Lipset, *Political Man: The Social Bases of Politics,* Garden City, N.Y.: Doubleday, 1960. A major concern running through the various essays included in the book is the conditions conducive to stable democracy. Lipset considers, for example, whether high voter turnout is desirable. On the one hand, a low voting rate usually means that the socially and economically disadvantaged groups are underrepresented in government. On the other hand, an extremely high turnout is usually a symptom of political crisis and the decline of consensus. He concludes that it is the *sudden* introduction of previously apathetic nonvoters into politics that is dangerous for democracy. "To the extent that the lower strata have been brought into [the] electoral process *gradually* (through increased organization, an upgrading of the educational system, and a growth in their understanding of the relevance of government action to their interests), increased participation is undoubtedly a good thing for democracy." In another section of his book Lipset considers the relationship between economic development and democracy by comparing more democratic and less democratic countries by indices of wealth, industrialization, education, and urbanization. He concludes from the statistical correlations that stable democracy is difficult to attain before a minimum level of economic development is reached.

Nelson W. Polsby, "The Study of Community Power," *International Encyclopedia of the Social Sciences,* Vol. 3, New York: Macmillan, 1968, pp. 157-163. Two different interpretations of community power can be found in the sociological literature: the stratification interpretation and the pluralist interpretation. According to the stratification interpretation, political and civic leaders are subordinate to the dominant economic class; this upper class deals with a wide variety of community issues in accordance with its own economic interests. According to the pluralist interpretation, different small groups in the community have decisive influence on different community problems; their size, cohesiveness, state of mobilization, and range of interests are empirical questions. For a review of empirical studies of decision making in local communities, see Peter H. Rossi, "Community Decision Making," *Administrative Science Quarterly,* Vol. 1, March 1957, pp. 415-443. An example of a recent study of local community leadership is Linton C. Freeman, *Patterns of Local Community Leadership,* Indianapolis, Ind.: Bobbs-Merrill, 1968.

Ralph H. Turner, "The Public Perception of Protest," *American Sociological Review,* Vol. 34, December 1969, pp. 815-831. In this, his Presidential address to the American Sociological Association in September 1969, Ralph Turner analyzed the meaning of collective acts of disruption and violence. He was interested not so much in the motivations of the participants (or even in the causes of the violence) but in the public interpretation of the significance of the acts. In particular, he sought to understand why civic disorders were interpreted sometimes as criminal deviance and sometimes as social protest. He suggested that one factor in the public interpretation of disorder as protest is the credibility of the event as the expression of justified grievances. Thus the grievance tends to be credible to groups in a more advantageous situation than the disrupters, which explains why middle-class whites are more ready to interpret violence in the black ghetto as protest than are working-class whites. Among the other conditions for the interpretation of civic disorder as protest, Turner mentions an optimal balance between appeal and threat. That is to say, there should be enough threat so that the community pays attention to the disorder, and enough appeal so that the moral claim is recognized. Too much threat produces repression, and too little threat, inattention. For an analysis of violent confrontation (including burning and looting) as political protest, see Jerome H. Skolnick, *The Politics of Protest: Violent Aspects of Protest and Confrontation,* Washington, D.C.: Government Printing Office, 1969.

LARGE-SCALE FORMAL
ORGANIZATIONS

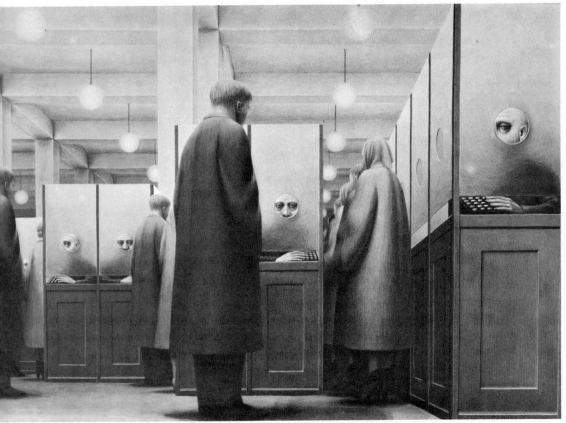

The Metropolitan Museum of Art, George A. Hearn Fund, 1956

Organized interaction in industrial societies is characterized by elaborate division of labor. In a university, for example, the activities of teachers and students are facilitated by an army of specialists: accountants, switchboard operators, secretaries, librarians, maintenance men, housemothers, policemen, postal clerks, editors, physicians, architects, scheduling officers, cooks, receptionists, and dozens more. Specialization by task promotes efficiency because specialists are usually faster and more skillful than generalists. However, this differentiation of an interactive system into highly specific roles poses a difficult problem of coordination. Who or what will see to it that the many activities mesh?

Informal communication integrates a small social system like a family, but it is not reliable enough to ensure the continued operation of General Motors, Rutgers University, the United States Bureau of Prisons, the Roman Catholic Church, or the Ford Foundation. Therefore, large organizations formalize the coordination of activities. Sociologists use the term "bureaucracy" to refer to the way large-scale administrative tasks tend to be organized. For the sociologist, "bureaucracy" is not an evil word. Once political mechanisms have set goals, **bureaucracy** is an efficient way to implement them on a large scale.

Bureaucratic organizations are not a modern invention. The emperors of ancient China governed with the aid of a bureaucracy composed of Confucian scholars.[1] The Romans utilized bureaucracies to administer their empire. Nevertheless, until recent times bureaucracy was not a predominant form of social organization. In contemporary societies it is everywhere. A direct cause of the spread of bureaucracy is the increase in the scale of operations in urban industrial society. An indirect cause is the knowledge explosion. As Chapter 11 will show, the scientific viewpoint permeates modern culture, thereby sensitizing role players to the possibility that traditional practice is not necessarily efficient or rational. Faced with the problem of coordinating human effort on a large scale, the contemporary response tends to be bureaucracy: a relatively efficient way to realize objectives defined by those who occupy policy-making positions.

Bureaucratic authority is rational authority in the sense that bureaucrats ideally execute policy efficiently. The bureaucracy may not seem rational to those who deal with it as customers or clients. However, a student who charges the administration of his college with not being responsive, flexible, or imaginative (with regard to student concerns) is not considering whether it manifests these virtues in relation to the board of trustees. Bureaucracies are established to carry out orders from the top, not to transmit upward complaints from the bottom.[2] To put the same point in another way, bureaucracies are naturally asymmetrical. They do not pay as much attention to those at the bottom of the

---

[1] H. H. Gerth and C. Wright Mills, *From Max Weber: Essays in Sociology,* New York: Oxford University Press, 1946, pp. 416-444.

[2] Burleigh B. Gardner, "The Factory as a Social System," in William Foote Whyte, Ed., *Industry and Society,* Chicago: University of Chicago Press, 1946, pp. 4-20.

hierarchy (or to those outside the organization) as to those at the top. Especially in a democratic society, where the political ideology suggests that every member of the society has an equal claim to attention, this asymmetry makes lower-level participants and clients feel dehumanized and indignant. They object to being treated like IBM cards because political socialization taught them to expect a share in "the action."

Bureaucracies are the major type of formal organization in modern societies but not the only type. Professional organizations, for instance, are formally structured and emphasize technical competence (rationality) but are collegial rather than hierarchical in structure. The university is a hybrid: a bureaucracy and a professional association cohabiting uneasily together. From the point of view of a dean, the department chairman is the representative of the administration and is responsible for securing the cooperation of his subordinates in the execution of university policy. From the point of view of faculty members within a department, the chairman is the representative vis-à-vis the administration of a group of professional equals, the fellow who obtains secretarial assistance, leaves of absence, classroom space, and salary increases so that they may teach their classes and engage in scholarly research. Professional organizations belong to a larger social category, voluntary associations. Like bureaucracies, voluntary associations are increasingly numerous in modern societies — although for different reasons. Voluntary associations bind together in solidary groups individuals whose common interests are a basis for interaction. Voluntary associations embody the principle of individual choice on the basis of these interests. Since individual choice is basic to achieved roles and achieved roles are increasingly prominent in industrial societies, voluntary associations flourish.

Bureaucracy is a compromise between the freedom of choice of voluntary associations and the constraints of ascribed solidarities such as kinship, neighborhood community, and ethnicity. The organizational recruit typically contracts freely to become a member of the bureaucracy, be it General Motors or the Catholic priesthood. Especially when the organization is a business firm, monetary inducements are a major factor in his decision to join. Once a member of the organization, however, the recruit is expected to carry out lawful assignments from his administrative superiors. Unless he elects to leave the organization, which is not always an option, his duty is to carry out the assignment without regard for his preferences, his own assessment of the situational requirements, or the monetary rewards available to him or to the unit of the organization to which he is attached. In short, he is subject to the authority of the top management of the organization in much the same way a citizen is subject to the authority of the political leadership of his society or a child to the authority of his parents. Thus all formal organizations are political structures. They carry out their tasks by delegating authority to realize their goals from the top down. The other internal characteristics of bureaucracy are designed to implement organizational goals with maximum efficiency.

THE INTERNAL CHARACTERISTICS OF BUREAUCRATIC ORGANIZATIONS

One of the most obvious—and most irritating—characteristics of bureaucracy is formality. Positions in the organization are precisely defined, meaning, in practice, that an outsider must know with *whom* to get in touch in the organization to get action. Bureaucracies also promulgate highly specific procedural rules and do not allow idiosyncratic variations—even when justice or efficiency would seemingly be better served by stretching them. Thus the individual may fuss and fume, but he must conform to an arbitrary procedure in order to enable this centralized system to work.

Formal roles and precise definition of functions make the operation of a bureaucracy predictable. For instance, at one college a student must have an overall average no higher than 3.25 in order to graduate. (The grades of this college are reminiscent of golf scores: the lower the numerical grade, the higher the achievement it represents.) Is there something so sacred about 3.25 that a student with a cumulative average of 3.4 should be denied his diploma? The particular average used to qualify for graduation is not crucial, but it is crucial to have a cutoff point. The 3.25 requirement is sufficiently clear that students, faculty, and the clerical personnel in the various offices concerned with academic bookkeeping know precisely *who is entitled to graduate and who is not.* Without the rule, there would be endless wrangling between students and parents, on the one hand, and college personnel, on the other. The outcomes of these controversies would not be uniform. Persuasive or persistent students might graduate with a 3.4 average. Timid students or students unfortunate enough to talk to grouchy administrators might *fail* to graduate despite a 3.1 average. However arbitrary they may seem, formal rules make organizational behavior predictable. Furthermore, they increase the likelihood that everyone will be treated uniformly.

The codification of bureaucratic rules, often found in bulky manuals, is a helpful device. In the long run, we are all dead; hence the organization must take measures to maintain efficiency despite loss of personnel through death, illness, marriage, military service, firing, and promotion. A file clerk who uses her own system—say, one who files material under the second letter of the main topic rather than the first—thereby makes herself indispensable; nothing can be found in the files unless she locates it personally. But she violates the bureaucratic ideal of continuity. A bureaucracy assumes not merely that everyone is replaceable, but also that everyone's task can be routinized and codified in standard operating procedures, thus permitting a replacement to take over on short notice.

Just as bureaucratic formalism is criticized, so is bureaucratic impersonality. The *coldness* of bureaucracies is contrasted with the friendliness of a small group. Yet impersonality is the best insurance against either favoritism or discrimination. The prison administrator knows that the guard who is friendly with the inmates he supervises is bound to be *more* friendly with some than with others. Where will this lead? To a letter smuggled *out* without going through normal prison censorship? To a gun smuggled *in* to be used in an escape attempt? Prison administrators do not want friendly guards because they are aware, from bitter experience, that friendship corrupts the integrity of a guard more often than money.[3] This does not imply that prison administrators want unfriendly or cruel guards; they want guards who apply the rules *fairly,* and this means *impersonally.*

Bureaucracies are not only formalistic and impersonal; they are also hierarchical. Hierarchy is necessary because the number of persons an individual can direct is limited. Large numbers of subordinates have to be coordinated through a smaller number of supervisors who are themselves supervised. The hierarchy in a bureaucratic organization is graphically represented in a table of organization, like that of the National Office of the Boy Scouts (Fig. 10.1). The table of organization shows who reports to whom at each echelon — not, of course, the names of individuals but rather the formal roles (offices). Although policy is set at the top of the hierarchy, decisions augmenting policy have to be made at every level in the organization. The *responsibility* for policy making remains with the top bureaucrats, but they cannot know in detail all the collective problems of the organization. If something goes wrong, however, the top bureaucrats cannot claim ignorance of what is occurring five echelons down. They are supposed to know. This pressure to make rational decisions on the basis of what is at best partial knowledge is one of the strains of the executive role.

In short, bureaucracy is a technique for systematic, rational planning of the contributions of members.[4] From this point of view, bureaucracies should be contrasted with voluntary associations where participation depends on individual interest: a Baptist congregation, a chess club, a trade association, the League of Women Voters. The leaders of voluntary associations can request help from members, but they depend on *influence* to secure cooperation, not on *authority.* They cannot coordinate the efforts of members in as disciplined a fashion as an executive in a bureaucracy because they have no right to *order.* They have followers but not subordinates. In contrast, Philip Selznick emphasizes the authority structure of bureaucratic organizations:[5]

> The mobilization of technical and managerial skills requires a pattern of coordination, a systematic ordering of positions and duties which defines a chain of command and makes possible the administrative integration of specialized functions. In this context *delegation* is the primordial organizational act, a precarious venture which requires the continuous elaboration of formal mechanisms

[3] Lloyd W. McCorkle and Richard R. Korn, "Resocialization within Walls," *Annals of the American Academy of Political and Social Science,* Vol. 293, May 1954, pp. 88-98.

[4] Arthur L. Stinchcombe, "Formal Organization," in Neil J. Smelser, Ed., *Sociology: An Introduction,* New York: Wiley, 1967, p. 154.

[5] Philip Selznick, "Foundations of the Theory of Organization," *American Sociological Review,* Vol. 13, February 1948, p. 25.

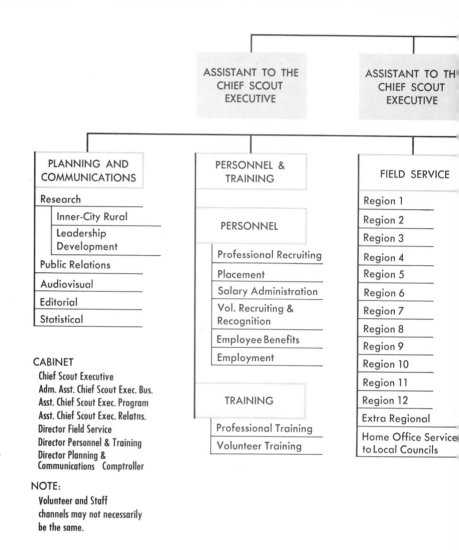

ASSISTANT TO THE
CHIEF SCOUT
EXECUTIVE

ASSISTANT TO TH'
CHIEF SCOUT
EXECUTIVE

PLANNING AND COMMUNICATIONS

Research

Inner-City Rural
Leadership
Development

Public Relations

Audiovisual

Editorial

Statistical

CABINET
Chief Scout Executive
Adm. Asst. Chief Scout Exec. Bus.
Asst. Chief Scout Exec. Program
Asst. Chief Scout Exec. Relatns.
Director Field Service
Director Personnel & Training
Director Planning &
Communications   Comptroller

NOTE:
Volunteer and Staff
channels may not necessarily
be the same.

PERSONNEL & TRAINING

PERSONNEL

Professional Recruiting

Placement

Salary Administration

Vol. Recruiting &
Recognition

Employee Benefits

Employment

TRAINING

Professional Training

Volunteer Training

FIELD SERVICE

Region 1

Region 2

Region 3

Region 4

Region 5

Region 6

Region 7

Region 8

Region 9

Region 10

Region 11

Region 12

Extra Regional

Home Office Service
to Local Councils

FIGURE 10.1   **Organizational chart of the National Office of the Boy Scouts of America, 1968.**

of coordination and control. . . . In this way, the formal structure becomes subject to calculable manipulation, an instrument of rational action.

Formality, impersonality, and hierarchy are characteristic of bureaucratic organizations whatever the societal needs served by the organization. Thus a business firm, a hospital, a news service, an army, and a philanthropic foundation are similar in the way they coordinate the efforts of members of the organization. They are different only in their objectives. Talcott Parsons has suggested that differences in operational procedures can be explained by considering

ADMINISTRATIVE ASSISTANT TO THE CHIEF SCOUT EXECUTIVE

COMPTROLLER

RELATIONSHIPS

LOCAL COUNCIL FINANCE

BOYPOWER '76 CAMPAIGN

INSTITUTIONAL RELATIONSHIPS
- Religious
- School
- Community
- Organization

INTERNATIONAL RELATIONS

PROGRAM

PROGRAM IMPLEMENTATION
- Cub Scouting
- Boy Scouting
- Camping & Conservation
- Activities
- Health & Safety
- Engineering

EXPLORING

NATIONAL EVENTS

BUSINESS

SUPPLY
- Merchandising
- Advertising
- Purchasing
- Warehousing

ADMINISTRATIVE SERVICES
- Data Processing
- Registration & Fulfillment
- Office Equipment & Supplies

BOYS' LIFE
- Printing & Production
- Circulation
- Promotion
- Advertising
- Editorial

PROPERTIES
- Phillips Properties
- Home Office Building
- Schiff
- Canoe Bases

objectives in terms of the societal problems the organization addresses.[6] The business corporation is concerned with the adaptation of the society to its environment. The university is concerned with socialization, as are prisons and mental hospitals. One bureaucracy concerned with integration is the state employment service, which seeks to integrate workers into the job market. And governmental bureaucracies implement collective policies of a society. There

[6] Talcott Parsons, *Structure and Process in Modern Societies*, Glencoe, Ill.: Free Press, 1960, p. 54.

353

is some evidence that the internal character of these bureaucracies reflects their function. For example, socializing organizations generally are more humane than business corporations. However, there has not been enough research comparing various bureaucracies to confirm this thesis. The critical questions that still must be studied are the range of variation (1) within organizations dealing with the same functional problem and (2) between organizations dealing with different functional problems.

BUREAUCRATIZATION OF THE ECONOMY

Formal organizations in industrialized societies produce outputs for their society: a business firm produces goods and services; a university produces knowledge and educated men. In highly differentiated societies, this characteristic of formal organization comes to characterize other forms of social organization. Thus the nuclear family specializes in the production of socialized adolescents.[7] Even though parents may not consider themselves in this light, the contemporary family has evolved as a result of structural differentiation toward a specialized output. A well-known demographer suggested during the 1930s that the fall in the birth rate might be checked by deliberately promoting this tendency to specialize; he advocated paying some women to raise very large families on behalf of the society.[8] Such a suggestion was conceivable because the family was already producing a specialized product. He went a step further and proposed a more efficient organization.

The efficiency of bureaucratic organizations in channeling the production of specialized outputs and the convenience of corporations as a device for pooling venture capital have led to the striking development of bureaucracy in the economy. When the business corporation was invented several hundred years ago in response to the problems of British trade, no one anticipated that it would transform economic behavior. The building and operation of sailing vessels was costly, and the investment was risky. In order to encourage this form of enterprise, the Crown chartered trading corporations and endowed them with certain attractive characteristics, the most important of which was that owners were not liable for debts of the corporation.[9] The most they could lose was their investment. Some of these corporations became rich and famous like the East India Company. On the other hand, Adam Smith wrote in his

[7] "Social function refers to *observable objective consequences,* and not to *subjective dispositions* (aims, motives, purposes)." Robert K. Merton, *Social Theory and Social Structure,* rev. ed., Glencoe, Ill.: Free Press, 1957, p. 24.

[8] Kingsley Davis, "Reproductive Institutions and the Pressure for Population," *Sociological Review,* Vol. 29, No. 3, July 1937, pp. 1-18.

[9] Scott Buchanan, "The Corporation and the Republic," New York: Fund for the Republic, 1958.

Wealth of Nations (published in 1776) that corporations could never be a major force in the economy; no man pays as much attention to his employer's affairs as to his own, and therefore the corporation is necessarily inefficient.[10]

Karl Marx also underestimated the corporation. When he predicted the division of capitalist society into a tiny group of owner-managers ("exploiters") and a vast majority of propertyless employees ("proletarians"), it was impossible to foresee the enormous growth of corporate size and power. When a company gets to be the size of General Motors— it had more than *half a million* employees in 1969— large numbers of managerial, technical, and professional employees fit neither the capitalist nor the proletarian stereotype.

The Declining Importance of Ownership. As Reinhard Bendix showed in a historical survey of business management, there was a shift from owner-managers to bureaucratic employees in the course of the industrialization of Western countries:[11]

> The most useful, single index of the internal bureaucratization of economic enterprises is the proportion of salaried employees in the occupational structure of a country. With industrialization the proportion of independent individual proprietors declines and that of economically dependent employees increases. Among dependent employees the proportion of salaried workers increases more rapidly than that of manual workers wherever the number of large-scale economic enterprises increases rapidly. In the United States, for instance, the total gainfully occupied population increased by 49 per cent from 1910 to 1940. During this period individual proprietors increased by 17 per cent, manual workers by 49 per cent, and salaried employees by 127 per cent. These illustrative figures point to significant changes in the occupational structure, which are relatively recent. The bureaucratization of economic enterprises, however, began with the Industrial Revolution.
>
> At one time individual entrepreneurs performed a large variety of routine administrative tasks in addition to their "distinct economic function of undertaking new things" which Schumpeter has singled out for special emphasis.[12] Seen historically, bureaucratization may be interpreted as the increasing subdivision of the functions which the owner-managers of the early enterprises had performed personally in the course of their daily routine. These functions may be divided into labor management, technical staff work, administrative management, and mercantile functions of purchasing, sales, and finance. As the work involved became more extensive and complex with the development of economic enterprises, it came to be delegated to subordinates both with regard to routine work and with regard to selected aspects of the entrepreneurial function proper. During

[10] Adolph A. Berle, Jr., "Economic Power and the Free Society," New York: Fund for the Republic, 1957, pg. 4; Adolph A. Berle, Jr., *The Twentieth Century Capitalist Revolution,* New York: Harcourt, Brace, 1954; Edward S. Mason, Ed., *The Corporation in Modern Society,* Cambridge, Mass.: Harvard University Press, 1959.

[11] Reprinted by permission. From Reinhard Bendix, *Work and Authority in Industry: Ideologies of Management in the Course of Industrialization,* New York: Wiley, 1956, pp. 211-216, 226-236.

[12] Joseph A. Schumpeter, *Capitalism, Socialism, and Democracy,* New York: Harper, 1950, p. 132.

TABLE 10.1

Number of Administrative and Production Employees in Industry for Selected Countries and Selected Years

Year	(A) Administrative Employees[a]	(P) Production Employees	A/P (Per Cent)
I. United States				
1899	348,000	4,496,000	7.7
1909	750,000	6,256,000	12.0
1923	1,280,000	8,187,000	15.6
1929	1,496,000	8,361,000	17.9
1937	1,518,000	8,553,000	17.7
1947	2,578,000	11,916,000	21.6
II. France				
1901	425,000	3,609,000	11.8
1906	392,000	3,772,000	10.4
1921	671,000	4,650,000	14.7
1926	699,000	5,458,000	12.8
1931	762,000	5,496,000	13.9
1936	635,000	4,355,000	14.6
III. Great Britain				
1907	408,000	4,755,000	8.6
1924	627,000	4,708,000	13.0

[a] The figures for administrative employees *exclude* owners and top executives.

[b] The German and French series were not extended beyond the 1930s because the more recent figures cannot be put on a basis comparable with the earlier figures. Taken independently, however, the more recent data also show an increasing bureaucratization.

Sources: *United States:* Recomputed from Seymour Melman, "The Rise of Administrative Overhead in the Manufacturing Industries of the United States, 1899–1947," *Oxford Economic Papers,* Vol. III, 1951, p. 66.

France: Ministère du Travail et de la Prévoyance Sociale, *Resultats du Recensement Général de la Population 1906,* Vol. I, 2nd section, p. 187, Table IV (for 1901 and 1906); *ibid.,* 1927, Vol. XLVII, pp. 11, 13 (for 1921). Sous-secretariat d'état et d'Economie Nationale, Bureau de la

the initial period of growth, the most important subordinates were likely to be relatives of the founder or persons who had earned his confidence and who frequently married into his family. The administrative and managerial work of early entrepreneurs, the importance of family ties, and the rather gradual increase of salaried employees in the early period (compared with the increase of workers) are reflected in [Table 10.1].

TABLE 10.1 (cont'd)

Year	(A) Administrative Employees[a]	(P) Production Employees	A/P (Per Cent)
III. Great Britain (cont'd)			
1930	589,000	4,286,000	13.7
1935	676,000	4,482,000	15.0
1948	1,126,000	5,651,000	20.0
IV. Germany[b]			
1895	266,000	5,530,000	4.8
1907	606,000	7,922,000	7.6
1925	1,122,000	9,463,000	11.9
1933	802,000	5,718,000	14.0
V. Sweden			
1915	25,000	374,000	6.6
1920	37,000	417,000	8.9
1925	34,000	392,000	8.7
1930	45,000	455,000	9.9
1935	54,000	471,000	11.5
1940	76,000	555,000	13.7
1945	111,000	639,000	17.3
1950	140,000	663,000	21.0

Statistique Générale, *Recensement Général de la Population,* Vol. I, 3rd section, 1931, p. 95 (data for 1926), p. 94 (data for 1931); Institut National de la Statistique et des Etudes Economiques, Statistique Générale de la France, *Annuaire Statistique,* Vol. LVI, 1946, pp. 17, 19 (for 1936).

Great Britain: Seymour Melman, *Dynamics of Industrial Productivity,* Chap. 11, Table 1, unpublished manuscript, by permission of the author.

Germany: Statistik des Deutschen Reichs, Berlin, Vol. 466, 1937, Table 7, p. 194.

Sweden: Fritz Croner, *Die Angestellten in der Modernen Gesellschaft,* Frankfurt: Humboldt, 1954, pp. 120-121.

Great care has been taken to make the figures for each country internally consistent and to make them as comparable as possible for all five countries. Success in this respect, however, can only be approximate, and it is best to think of comparisons among several countries in terms of orders of magnitude and overall trends.

With the increase of salaried employees, Western business management no longer rested mainly on *ownership* but on *employment* in professional and executive occupational roles. Peter Drucker calls this an employee society,[13] emphasizing that the highly paid top-level executives are also employees. For

[13] Peter F. Drucker, *The New Society,* New York: Harper, 1959.

those American executives who are not sizable stockholders in the company, ownership is almost as remote as it is for the factory manager in the Soviet Union. A Soviet citizen who strode airily into a Leningrad factory and explained that he was one of the owners would be ejected as quickly as a United States Steel stockholder who arrived unannounced to inspect one of "his" plants.

The bureaucratization of business management and the separation of *ownership* from *control* mutually reinforce one another in giant corporations. The stockholders own the corporation, but they are usually too numerous to take an active part in the management of its affairs. They are entitled to profits, which they receive in the form of dividend checks. They are entitled also to vote in proportion to their stock holdings for or against the incumbent board of directors. But ordinarily, stockholders have little choice but to mail in their proxies to the hands that feed them, and the incumbent board is overwhelmingly reelected. Occasionally, a large stockholder tries to wrest control from the existing management in a costly proxy fight. The late financier Robert Young took control of the New York Central Railroad in this way. Such contests are so rare that they generate enormous excitement. As A. A. Berle, Jr., put it, "In practice, institutional corporations are guided by tiny self-perpetuating oligarchies. These in turn are drawn from and judged by the group opinion of a small fragment of America—its business and financial community."[14]

Karl Marx had in mind entrepreneurs and heirs, not bureaucrats, when he talked about bourgeois exploiters. If he had anticipated the development of bureaucratic management, he would probably have recognized that *ownership* of the means of production was less important than *control*. Bureaucrats tend to control the means of production in all industrial societies. Communist as well as "free-enterprise" societies give high pay and some autonomy to professional managers.[15] The managerial revolution has eroded the organizational differences between "capitalist" and "Communist" societies. The main economic difference lies in the method of control at the top level of enterprises; in Communist countries there are direct political controls; in capitalist countries there is greater reliance on semi-automatic market controls supplemented by political regulation.[16] However, the great majority of workers in both types of society have their tasks planned for them by administrative superiors in essentially the same way. At least in the realm of economic organization, industrial societies have converged—despite mutual denial of such convergence on the ideological level.[17]

The Growth of Procedural Safeguards. As bureaucracies became the dom-

---

[14] Berle, *The Twentieth Century Capitalist Revolution,* p. 180.

[15] James Burnham, *The Managerial Revolution,* New York: John Day, 1941; Alex Inkeles, "Social Stratification and Mobility in the Soviet Union, 1940-1950," *American Sociological Review,* Vol. 15, August 1950, pp. 465-479.

[16] Parsons, *Structure and Process,* pp. 100-101.

[17] As the previous chapter made clear, no such convergence has occurred as yet in the realm of political organization.

inant form of economic organization, means to control their power were coming into existence. Government agencies were created to protect both the consumer and the worker. Another limitation on big business occurred through the unionization movement.

At the start of the factory system (Chapter 6), the owner-entrepreneur controlled the work situation despotically. Eventually unions developed, first as illegal conspiracies, then as the legitimate expression of employee interests. With the growth of large, bureaucratically organized unions capable of bargaining with corporate employers on equal terms, business enterprises lost some of their despotic power over individual employees. Grievance machinery was routinely established as part of the contract between the union and the employing organization. It became less possible for a foreman to fire a worker for capricious reasons or for union activity.

Although these developments increased the likelihood that workers would receive fair treatment from corporate employers, unions grew and became bureaucracies that could be as arbitrary as a business bureaucracy. Thus unions present two faces: they are voluntary associations that dues-paying members join for their own benefit, but in the internal administration of their own employee operations unions are much like the corporate bureaucracies they bargain with:[18]

[18] Reprinted by permission. From Seymour M. Lipset, "The Political Process in Trade Unions," in Walter Galenson and Seymour M. Lipset, Eds., *Labor and Trade Unionism: An Interdisciplinary Reader,* New York: Wiley, 1960, p. 217.

Unions, like all other large-scale organizations, are constrained to develop bureaucratic structures, that is, a system of rational (predictable) administration. The need for bureaucracy comes from both internal and external sources. In dealing with their members or locals, unions must set up administrative systems with defined patterns of responsibility and authority. Subordinate officials and administrators must operate within the given rules for dealing with commonly met situations. The larger the size of a local union, or an international, the greater is the need to establish a bureaucratic hierarchy. A large local, for example, may be involved in handling workmen's compensation, apprentice schools, pension plans, hospitalization, insurance, and assignment of workers to jobs, besides the usual trade union tasks of collective bargaining, handling of worker's grievances, and keeping basic records on all members.

On the international level, these problems are often magnified by the increased size and complexity of operations, and require the creation of a specialized staff which is appointed by and under the control of the officials. And so the knowledge and skill of union operation gradually become available only to members of the administrative elite.

In addition to the need for bureaucracy which is inherent in the sheer problem of administration — a determinant largely related to the size of the organization — the degree of bureaucratic centralization in unions is influenced by the extent of centralization in the outside groups with which they must deal. I would suggest as a research hypothesis that the more centralized an industry, the more need there is for a union to be bureaucratic. A union such as the steelworkers', which bargains with a few gigantic corporations, must set up a union authority-structure which parallels that of the corporations. Grievance procedures or wage rates must be comparable in every part of the industry. The union cannot permit a local leader in one plant to reach an agreement that may be used as a precedent for the handling of grievances in other parts of the country.

Thus the union helps the worker gain fair treatment from his corporate employer, but he sometimes needs help to secure fair treatment from his union. Especially when union membership is essential to employment, as in some skilled trades or when there are union-shop agreements with employers, expulsion from the union means loss of livelihood. Under these circumstances, public opinion is intolerant of an autocratic union in which dissident elements are intimidated or expelled. When the McClellan Committee Hearings of 1957 and 1958 revealed gangster control of some unions, public opinion was aroused to the need for governmental protection of the right of union members to oppose the bureaucracy. Congress enacted the Labor-Management Reporting and Disclosure Act of 1959 which gave the Secretary of Labor and the Federal courts authority to guarantee some democratic procedures in unions.[19] At about the same time (1957), the United Auto Workers established *voluntarily* a system of appeal from decisions of the executive board of the UAW to a board

[19] Walter E. Oberer, "Union Democracy and the Rule of Law," in *Democracy and Public Review: An Analysis of the UAW Public Review Board,* Santa Barbara, Calif.: Center for the Study of Democratic Institutions, 1960, p. 50.

[20] Oberer, "Union Democracy," pp. 7-32.

of eminent outsiders.[20] Although the United Auto Workers pays the cost of operating the Public Review Board, six of the 29 initial cases carried to the Board were decided against the leadership of the UAW. Neither existing laws nor voluntary programs have transformed American trade unions into models of democratic decision making, but they place limits on the power of union officials over members.

Large corporations have also established machinery to guarantee procedural rights to workers. Sometimes this machinery is established to forestall government intervention, sometimes as a direct result of collective bargaining with unions, and sometimes as a by-product of bureaucratization. Thus procedures to ensure fair treatment have seeped into the large corporation as an unintended consequence of the establishment of personnel administration as a staff function:[21]

> Personnel administration as a specialized staff function has arisen, in part, out of the functional necessities of large-scale bureaucratic enterprises and partly as a result of certain historical circumstances.
>
> As industrial enterprises have increased in size and complexity, they have become characterized by what Max Weber described as the characteristics of bureaucracy in its "ideal type." Among these characteristics is functional specialization and impersonality in the relationship of top management to employees at the lowest levels of the organizational hierarchy. Impersonality in the employment relationship has necessitated specialized personnel agencies which are charged with the function of establishing uniform personnel practices to integrate employees into an impersonalized organizational context. Specialization of the personnel function has proceeded along the same lines as specialization of other functions in the enterprise; e.g., finance, public relations, purchasing, transportation, etc.
>
> Among the historical conditions that particularly contributed to the establishment of staff personnel and industrial relations departments in American industrial enterprises are: the concern with efficient utilization of manpower arising out of the scientific management movement and developments in World War I; labor legislation in the 1920's and 1930's that imposed special conditions of employment and employee treatment upon affected organizations; the growth of the trade union movement and resultant management concern with the "divided loyalty" of employees; and the human relations movement, emphasizing employee counseling procedures and attention to the "human" element in production.
>
> Personnel offices may operate under a number of different titles. Among these titles are "labor relations office," "industrial relations office," "employment office," "manpower management office," and "employee relations office." A distinction frequently is made between "personnel" functions, as those concerned with intra-firm problems of personnel administration, and "labor relations" functions, as those concerned with union-management relations. Only intra-firm problems of personnel administration are considered in this paper.

[21] Reprinted by permission. From Howard M. Vollmer and Patrick J. McGillivray, "Personnel Offices and the Institutionalization of Employee Rights," *Pacific Sociological Review*, Vol. 3, Spring 1960, pp. 29-34.

A study by Dale Yoder in 1954 reported that at least 70 per cent of firms surveyed reported the following functions for their "employment relations" departments: (1) administration of the **staff** division; (2) planning of personnel policy, programs, and organization; (3) job analysis, recruitment, and selection; (4) training of personnel; (5) promotion, transfer, and release; (6) labor relations; (7) employee benefits and services; (8) medical and safety functions; (9) wage and salary administration; (10) personnel records and reports; and (11) personnel research.

Regardless of what functions personnel offices perform, their formal position within the managerial structure is usually conceived of by management as a *staff* position. Nevertheless, in actual practice it may be maintained that personnel departments in many cases exercise **line** functions; that is, *direct* control over personnel management affairs within the firm, in spite of their formal position as staff agencies.

This control over personnel matters is manifested in the written personnel policies of some firms. In the Jones and Laughlin Steel Company, for example, the Director of Personnel Relations is responsible for continuous review of the personnel relations activities in the various operations of the corporation and for compliance with corporation-wide objectives, policies, and programs in this regard. Similarly, a personnel executive in a large railroad transportation company told the authors:

"We have an enlightened management as far as labor relations is concerned. Our president has pointed out repeatedly that anything that affects labor relations must be approved by the personnel department. He has also said that in doubtful matters the personnel department will determine whether the particular matter affects labor relations or not." . . .

The managerial rationale behind the establishment of personnel offices in most firms has given prominent emphasis to the promotion of employee morale, harmony, and loyalty to the goals of the organization. The Carborundum Company, for example, includes the following statement among its personnel policies in regard to the functions of its personnel department:

"To maintain high morale, enthusiasm, and loyalty to the interests of the company. To promote good understanding and cooperation among the company's personnel. To create a sense of belonging, so that all employees are working toward a common goal."

This orientation is expressed also in the personnel policies of the Lukens Steel Company, S. C. Johnson and Son, and others.

In such policies, high value is placed upon cooperative effort. The means proposed to achieve this objective is manipulation of employee attitudes toward the firm. Involved here is the assumption that it is within the ability of personnel specialists, using the technical skills of their trade, to select and motivate employees toward a high degree of harmonious cooperation and productive effort.

This manipulative orientation, however, is also reacting upon the character of industrial enterprises through the actions of the very agencies which were established with the explicit objectives of specializing in manipulation—personnel departments. Personnel specialists have operated in many firms to promote an attitude of adaptation to the presumed rights and interests of individual employees. The emergent concept of employee rights in personnel philosophy has perhaps been expressed most aptly by James Worthy of Sears, Roebuck and Company:

"These ideals are usually expressed in terms of 'rights'—the very word 'rights' implying their essentially moral and ethical nature . . . we may summarize some of the more significant of these rights as follows:

1. The right of every man to be treated as an individual and respected as a person;
2. The right of every man to a voice in his own affairs, which includes his right to contribute to the best of his ability to the solution of common problems;
3. The right of every man to develop and make use of his highest capacities;
4. The right of every man to fairness and justice in all his relationships with his superiors."

Mutual recognition of employee rights concepts, which is promoted by the activities of personnel specialists, may be rationalized and expressed verbally in different ways. For example, a personnel executive in a chemical firm stated what he believed to be a relationship between employee rights concepts and "the American way of life":

"Because of the type of country we live in, where the individual is more important than any company, a man carries this idea about his rights into his work—this idea of his 'dignity.' Employees are particularly concerned with their rights to job security, fair treatment, and being respected by management and their fellow workers."

A personnel executive in a food processing and packing firm mentioned the relevance of employee rights concepts to the implicit meaning of the employment relationship to the parties concerned:

"There are actual rights and there are implied rights. Actual rights are overtly expressed in company policies and practices. Implied rights are implicit in the expectations of the mutual parties to a relationship—like the employment relationship. Usually, when employees talk about their rights, they are not referring to contract provisions. Employees use the term in a broader sense. For example, if an employee feels his supervisor has treated him ill, he speaks of his rights as an individual with human dignity. For an instance of this, an employee who is publicly reprimanded in front of other employees is likely to feel that his rights as a human being with dignity have been violated by the supervisor."

The value orientations expressed in the previous comments of personnel specialists, however, tend to be merely ideological statements, rather than expressions of actual policy, if they lack institutionalized support. There seem to be three general sources of institutionalized support for the continued recognition of employee rights and their expanded acceptance in the future: (1) further formalization of the "line" authority of personnel offices in personnel management matters; (2) professionalization of personnel specialists; and (3) establishment of formal personnel policies that specify safeguards for employee rights.

Melville Dalton has pointed out that staff-line conflict is to be expected in industrial enterprises as a result of the differing personal backgrounds and organizational functions of staff and line managerial personnel. The additional point may be made that everyday conflicts between personnel specialists and line managerial officers are especially likely to occur because of confusion between "line" and "staff" responsibilities.

Arguments about proper personnel management practices are especially likely to occur in regard to disciplinary actions. Such disagreements were often indicated in the authors' survey of personnel executives. The personnel executives interviewed frequently reported that they see it as their responsibility to "sell" line management on what personnel specialists believe to be the proper procedures in disciplinary practices. Where their selling techniques are unsuccessful, they see it as their duty to take their cases to higher management for policy decisions. A personnel executive in the regional division of a large steel corporation reported:

"There are times when we believe line management at the plant level is wrong. Then they say, 'God damn you, you're selling us down the river.' Then we must sell them on the right way to handle discipline. We may even have to go to the company president if we have a firm disagreement with plant managers." (Steel manufacturing)

A personnel director in a shipyard stated:

"I have as many arguments with the back office (line management) as I do with union leaders. Yesterday I had a fight with one of our managers to get him to give an employee adequate notice before discharging him." (Marine construction and repair)

A personnel executive in a petroleum company reported:

"I'm employed by the company, but my responsibility is to the employee as well as to the company. Sometimes I have to fight for an employee with management. I have to ward off the impulsive actions of division heads. Believe me, one has to have the courage of his convictions to do this." (Petroleum products)

Insofar as personnel specialists "win" their arguments on personnel matters of these types, particularly in regard to disciplinary procedures, they act to limit the arbitrary powers of line management officials over employees. They promote a new orientation within the firm directed toward the acceptance of what has come to be considered the legitimate "rights" of employees.

Also, to the degree to which personnel specialists become professionalized and identified with status considerations with regard to their occupational associates in local communities and even nationally, they become more committed to standards of practice and codes of ethics which emphasize fair treatment and "due process" principles in dealing with employees. Several of the national professional personnel societies, such as the personnel section of the American Management Association and the Society for Personnel Administration, have been concerned with the establishment and general recognition of ethical codes that emphasize employee rights concepts. Where such codes are accepted, the activities of personnel specialists within firms become less attributable to the individual ideas of individual personnel specialists and more referable to commonly accepted standards of personnel practice.

What is perhaps the most significant and potent mechanism for the institutionalized recognition of employee rights concepts has been the development of formalized personnel policies within industrial enterprises. In the Yoder study referred to earlier, it was indicated that "employment relations divisions" participate in the planning of policy programs and organization in eighty-six per cent of the firms surveyed. The formal policies which result from this planning activity not only may give personnel specialists considerable authority in "line" personnel management functions, but also may specify in considerable detail the safeguards established to protect employee rights, particularly in disciplinary actions.

The Bureau of National Affairs has reported that about three-fourths of business firms have such written disciplinary regulations in the form of "plant rules." Many companies in the remaining fourth operate under rules that are well known to employees, even though they are not in written form. The outlook for the future was summarized by a personnel executive in a paper products company in the following terms:

"In the future I see a continuing trend toward specifying and tightening disciplinary policies. Employees like to have a tight-run ship. They like to know that their supervisor will take the same action each day. They like to have rules and to have a part in creating them. They expect their discipline to be fair."

Formal disciplinary regulations not only have become more likely to specify causes for discipline but also more likely to define the severity of disciplinary action permitted in specified circumstances. Many plant rules have specific penalties attached to the violation of certain regulations. A high proportion of these simply state, "The following offenses may result in immediate dismissal."

In other cases, however, plant rules may list certain types of actions for which an employee ordinarily is not subject to discharge in a first offense. For example, the rules of an electronics firm studied by the authors state:

"For offenses against safety, plant working, and employee conduct rules, other than those specifically mentioned under Section B below, an employee shall not be discharged without first having been notified that repetition of the offense will be cause for dismissal. The record of this notification shall be incorporated in the personnel record at the time it is given. . . ."

In a shipyard, the disciplinary regulations make the following distinctions:

"Any employee committing any of the following violations shall be subject to discharge: (thirteen types of offenses are listed). . . .

"For any of the following offenses an employee will be given a pink (reprimand) slip: (six types of offenses are listed). . . .

"Any employee issued a second pink slip will be given five days off. . . .

"Any employee issued a third pink slip for any of the above violations shall be discharged."

In the procedure for disciplinary action of a small parts manufacturing company, offenses are classified into three types with correspondingly greater severity of discipline: "minor offenses," "major offenses," and "intolerable offenses." In the same company the following instructions, written by the personnel director, are given to supervisors regarding discharge policy:

"Not every rule violation justifies dismissal. But there is a point at which discharge becomes proper by reason of either a single serious infraction or an accumulation of minor infractions. The following 'yardstick' is suggested to determine whether this point has been reached:

1. Has the employee seriously or irreparably damaged the employer's trust and confidence in him? The importance of this test depends on the type of work done by the employee.
2. Does it seem likely that the employee will correct his deficiencies within a reasonable period of time if he is not fired?
3. What effect would retaining the employee have on the discipline and morale of other employees?
4. What about the individual himself? Does he have a long period of good

service and, therefore, deserve special consideration? How would a discharge affect his job prospects elsewhere?

5. Finally, does discharge seem fair, all things considered? In other words, does the punishment fit the crime, taking into account any mitigating circumstances that might be present?"

The existence of such gradated penalties for different types of offenses and a discharge policy such as that just cited both tend to restrain management from arbitrary disciplinary action.

The Bureau of National Affairs study reported that among larger firms which have written plant rules about fifty per cent spell out the penalties for breaking each rule. According to this study, penalties for chronic absenteeism most frequently take the form of one or two warnings, then suspension, and then discharge—although in many firms suspension is not used and employees are discharged after one or two warnings. Insubordination is the basis of immediate discharge in about one-third of larger companies, although about the same proportion of companies report they do not discharge an employee until after one warning about insubordination. The penalty for fighting is immediate discharge in about half of the companies studied, whereas other companies treat a first offense with a warning or suspension. As these disciplinary procedures are formalized, they become part of the pattern of legitimate expectations for both employers and employees. They establish standards of fair treatment that have become institutionalized.

BUREAUCRATIZATION OF SERVICE

The production of goods is not the only goal of an industrial society: efficient provision of health, welfare, and educational services is also a goal. Hence there is a tendency to utilize large-scale formal organization to provide *services* as well as *goods*. But the bureaucratic delivery of service differs from the bureaucratic production of goods, and these differences affect the character of service bureaucracies.

One difference is that the output of service organizations—schools, hospitals, and casework agencies—must be generated in the context of a social relationship with consumers. As Parsons puts it, the performance of services requires the cooperation of the recipients of the service, whether it be teaching students or nursing patients:[22]

> This cooperation cannot always be taken for granted; it has to be motivated. Witness . . . the problem of truancy in schools, to say nothing of passive resistance to learning and the commonness with which patients leave hospitals contrary to medical advice. Since sheer coercion is not adequate, the service-performer must *offer* something to induce adequate cooperation, and the readi-

[22] Parsons, *Structure and Process*, pp. 72-73.

ness to do this has to be included in the terms by which the cooperative relationship is set up. . . . The physical producer does not have to offer his raw materials anything.

In order to ensure this essential cooperation, service organizations do not usually treat beneficiaries of their service as General Motors treats purchasers of its automobiles, namely, as outsiders. Students in a school (or patients in a hospital) are given a kind of membership in the organization. It is not full membership. A student is not a paid employee of the school; the authority of the teacher over him is not the same kind of authority as that of the principal over the teacher. But the student bears a closer relationship to the school than the Chevrolet owner bears to General Motors. The relationship is stronger when the recipients of service live and work in premises controlled by the organization, as in the residential college, the hospital, or the prison. The nomenclature of service organizations reflects the necessity of maintaining a relationship of continuing cooperation with recipients of service; they are called "clients," "patients," "students," "inmates," never "customers."

When quasi-membership in a live-in service organization is involuntary, as in an army, a prison, or a mental hospital, the staff may behave as though the recipients of service have no more choice than raw materials in a factory. The term "total institution" has been coined to call attention to the helplessness and potential humiliation of inmate-clients in coercive service organizations:[23]

> In **total institutions** there is a basic split between a large managed group, conveniently called inmates, and a small supervisory staff. Inmates typically live in the institution and have restricted contact with the world outside the walls; staff often operate on an eight-hour day and are socially integrated into the outside world. Each grouping tends to conceive of the other in terms of narrow hostile sterotypes, staff often seeing inmates as bitter, secretive, and untrustworthy, while inmates often see staff as condescending, high-handed, and mean. Staff tends to feel superior and righteous; inmates tend, in some ways at least, to feel inferior, weak, blameworthy, and guilty.

The extent to which the cooperation of inmate-clients can be motivated through coercion is an empirical question. Studies of concentration camps show that cooperation of a minimal sort can be guaranteed if the decision-makers in control of the organization observe no limits in using force.[24] But in democratic societies prison and hospital administrators presumably have been socialized to hold values incompatible with limitless coercion. Furthermore, their organizations are dependent on the larger society for support; even if their own values permit brutality, they are deterred by the likelihood of unfavorable publicity. As a result, prisons and mental hospitals in the United States and Western Europe depend considerably on voluntary cooperation from nominally helpless inmate-clients. A tiny group of conscientious objectors in American prisons were sometimes able by threatening noncooperation to win concessions from correctional administrators during the Second World War.[25]

For a quite different reason, coercion is not necessarily relied on to secure cooperation even in "total institutions." If the goal of a prison or mental hospital is to prevent inmates from escaping, then the minimal cooperation extracted by threat of force may be adequate. But if correctional administrators are concerned with *changing the anti-social values of prisoners* and mental hospital personnel *want patients to recover from their illnesses,* inducements to

---

[23] Erving Goffman, *Asylums: Essays on the Social Situation of Mental Patients and Other Inmates,* Garden City, N.Y.: Anchor, 1961, p. 7.

[24] Donald R. Cressey and Witold Krassowski, "Inmate Organization and Anomie in American Prisons and Soviet Labor Camps," *Social Problems,* Vol. 5, Winter 1957-58, pp. 217-230; Eugen Kogon, *The Theory and Practice of Hell: The German Concentration Camps and the System behind Them,* New York: Berkley, 1960.

[25] Alfred Hassler, *Diary of a Self-Made Convict,* Chicago: Regnery, 1954.

cooperate are more necessary; threats are not effective enough. In short, the goals of the service organization must be explicitly considered in order to assess its need for voluntary cooperation — and to predict its reliance on coercion or inducements.

A common goal of service bureaucracies, socialization of quasi-members, sets them apart from economic bureaucracies. *The more the goals of the organization emphasize socialization of its quasi-members, the more likely it is that the organization relies on professional employees.* The professional (psychiatrist, teacher, social worker) is assumed to have the expertise necessary for carrying out successful socialization. Staffing the organization with such technical experts has certain consequences. First, professionals have a dual loyalty: to the organization that employs them but also to the professional group that validates their technical competence.[26] This means that they are less dependent on the organization for approval and more likely to oppose organizational directives if they run counter to professional norms. Moreover, professionals base their authority as much on their technical competence as on their positions within the organization. Thus psychologists or social workers in the prison speak sometimes as therapists and sometimes as prison officials with custodial responsibilities. The psychiatrist in the mental hospital is in precisely the same position. For both reasons professionals tend to be less devoted to the "chain of command" of the organization and less impersonal than the bureaucratic ideal suggests.

The university is a good example of a large-scale organization dedicated to socialization and employing a high proportion of professionals. How does this differentiate the university from the business firm? An obvious difference is that the top leadership of the university treats professors more gingerly than top management in General Motors treats junior executives and manual workers. The greater the scholarly eminence of the faculty, the more the university administration serves merely to provide facilities for teaching and research. The less distinguished the faculty, the more closely the relationship of administration to professors approximates that of corporate employers to employees. A 1955 survey of 2451 faculty members at 165 American colleges and universities found that the more scholarly faculties tended to be treated more deferentially by academic administrators.[27] They participated in policy making, and their freedom to express heterodox ideas was protected. The trustees, the president, and the deans cannot themselves undertake a major part of the teaching and research operations, nor can they replace leading scholars easily. University administrations depend on professional employees because technical competence is a scarce resource. It is also a resource that administrative superiors have difficulty evaluating. These circumstances help to explain the aca-

[26] William Kornhauser, *Scientists in Industry: Conflict and Accommodation,* Berkeley: University of California Press, 1962.

[27] Paul F. Lazarsfeld and Wagner Thielens, Jr., *The Academic Mind: Social Scientists in a Time of Crisis,* Glencoe, Ill.: Free Press, 1958.

demic custom of lifetime job tenure for senior faculty, a labor force consisting of professional experts:[28]

> The professor is a technical expert in an organization where his administrative superiors are almost always lacking in technical ability to evaluate the quality of his work. Denial to administrations of the right to "fire" him, except for cause involving grave professional or personal misconduct, protects him against arbitrary intervention in his work by persons who . . . possess . . . power but who do not possess the competence to exercise it wisely on the basis of their personal knowledge and experience alone.

The scarcity of professional talent and the ease with which such talent can move to other organizations justifies lifetime job tenure for college professors. But teachers in the public schools enjoy similar job security without comparable professional distinction. Why? Tenure protects the teacher when his immediate responsibilities generate frustration and rebellion, as attempts at socialization sometimes do. If students and their parents complain about a teacher, school administrators might, in the absence of tenure rules, find it easier to fire the teacher than to investigate the merits of the charge. Tenure improves teacher morale—a teacher need not fear for his job when he gives a low grade to a poor student or applies pressure to a lazy one to motivate greater efforts. The disadvantage of tenure is that it protects incompetents too: tenure not only protects the teacher against community pressure but also against his administrative superiors. Such security befits the dignity of a professionally trained person committed to a code of professional ethics; a problem arises when presumed professional commitment does not produce ethical or competent service. At the college level, the tradition of academic freedom protects the professor against parents, students, alumni, and administrators who might blame him for the ferment produced when cherished beliefs are challenged, when religious faith wavers, when grooming deteriorates. The tenure custom reinforces the protection afforded by the principle of intellectual freedom by making it almost impossible to fire a senior professor.

There are differences between service and production bureaucracies in the remuneration of employees as well. Remuneration of employees in a production bureaucracy is ideally in terms of their contribution to the marketability of the organization's products. Remuneration in a service bureaucracy cannot be geared to marketability because health, education, and welfare services are not made available by the mechanisms of market supply and demand. These services are typically subsidized by government or private philanthropy so that beneficiaries do not pay for them in full if at all. As a result, there exists a lower level of remuneration of employees in service bureaucracies than in production organizations and a greater reliance on nonmonetary rewards, including the prestige obtained from working in a socially valued occupation: teachers get more community respect and less cash.

[28] Parsons, *Structure and Process*, p. 54.

Recruitment, like remuneration and job security, tends in a service bureaucracy to reflect procedures suitable for professional employees. Since judging professional competence is difficult for those not in the profession, in recruiting reliance is placed on professional peers who recognized the technical character of the service to be rendered. Thus, in universities, faculty recruitment is the responsibility of specific departments, not of deans. Where professional recruitment rests with the central administration, as in the public school system and some small colleges, faculty expertise cannot be adequately assessed. The implicit assumption is that professional standing is less important than other aspects of the faculty role, for example, teaching.

The professionalization of the organizational staff is partly a function of the goal of the organization. A socializing bureaucracy is more likely to consist of professionals than is a production bureaucracy or a governmental bureaucracy. But factors other than the organizational purpose influence professionalization. For example, a study of American Army and Navy officers from 1910 to 1950 showed that changing social backgrounds and skill distributions affected the character of the professional soldier and the nature of his authority.[29] Many occupational groups in industrial societies are professionalizing as part of an educational upgrading and career building process.[30]

Since this proceeds to a different extent in various kinds of organizations, professionalization influences the character of organizations independently of the specific organizational purpose. As organizations of professionals, the New York City Ballet Company and Bellevue Hospital are sisters under the skin.

THE THREAT OF ORGANIZATIONAL TYRANNY

In industrial societies, permeated as they are by large-scale formal organizations, the autonomy of the individual seems threatened. Marxists have long maintained that factory workers find their work meaningless—and as a result feel resentful at being coerced by forces over which they have no control. But recent critics of bureaucracy have pushed the argument further. The author of *The Organization Man* maintains that the corporate *executive* has been seduced by power and money into leading a meaningless life.[31] The executive is not *ordered* to take work home; he does so voluntarily (in order to keep up in the scramble for advancement). He wears conservative clothes and expresses

[29] Morris Janowitz, *The Professional Soldier: A Social and Political Portrait*, Glencoe, Ill.: Free Press, 1960.

[30] William J. Goode, "Community within a Community: The Professions," *American Sociological Review*, Vol. 22, April 1957, pp. 194-200; Nelson N. Foote, "The Professionalization of Labor in Detroit," *American Journal of Sociology*, Vol. 58, January 1953, pp. 371-373.

[31] William H. Whyte, Jr., *The Organization Man*, Garden City, N. Y.: Doubleday Anchor, 1957.

conventional opinions because to do otherwise might place a roadblock across his path into top management. He accepts the intrusion of the corporation into his private life—some companies have "wife programs"—just as he accepts transfers from one job location to another. The tyranny is masked by a "human relations" ideology; hence the executive does not recognize it as tyranny at all. Talk about teamwork, getting along with others, group dynamics, conference sense, and sensitivity training disguises corporate possessiveness as benevolence:[32]

> Held up as the end-all of organizational leadership, the skills of human relations can easily tempt the new administrator into a tyranny more subtle and more pervasive than that which he means to supplant. No one wants to see the old authoritarian return, but at least it could be said of him that what he wanted primarily from you was your sweat. The new man wants your soul.

These are strong words. Equally strong words have been applied to educational bureaucracies. In the course of the 1964 student disruption of the Berkeley campus of the University of California, a leader of the Free Speech Movement expressed his feelings of outrage at the "educational factory":[33]

> In our free-speech fight at the University of California, we have come up against what may emerge as the greatest problem of our nation—depersonalized, unresponsive bureaucracy. We have encountered the organized status quo in Mississippi, but it is the same in Berkeley. Here we find it impossible usually to meet with anyone but secretaries. Beyond that, we find functionaries who cannot make policy but can only hide behind the rules. We have discovered total lack of response on the part of the policy makers.
>
> One conception of the university, suggested by a classical Christian formulation, is that it be in the world but not of the world. The conception of Clark Kerr [the president of the University of California in 1964] by contrast is that the university is part and parcel of this particular stage in the history of American society; it stands to serve the need of American industry; it is a factory that turns out a certain product needed by industry or government. Because speech does often have consequences which might alter this perversion of higher education, the university must put itself in a position of censorship. It can permit two kinds of speech, speech which encourages continuation of the status quo, and speech which advocates changes in it so radical as to be irrelevant in the foreseeable future. Someone may advocate radical change in all aspects of American society, and this I am sure he can do with impunity. But if someone advocates sit-ins to bring about changes in discriminatory hiring practices, this cannot be permitted because it goes against the status quo of which the university is a part. And that is how the fight began here. . . .
>
> Many students here at the university, many people in society, are wandering aimlessly about. Strangers in their own lives, there is no place for them. They are

---

[32] Whyte, The Organization Man, p. 440.

[33] Reprinted by permission. From Mario Savio, "An End to History," Humanity, December 1964. Reprinted in Seymour Martin Lipset and Sheldon S. Wolin, Eds., The Berkeley Student Revolt: Facts and Interpretations, Garden City, N. Y.: Doubleday Anchor, 1965, pp. 216-219.

people who have not learned to compromise, who for example have come to the university to learn to question, to grow, to learn—all the standard things that sound like clichés because no one takes them seriously. And they find at one point or other that for them to become part of society, to become lawyers, ministers, businessmen, people in government, that very often they must compromise those principles which were most dear to them. They must suppress the most creative impulses that they have; this is a prior condition for being part of the system. The university is well structured, well tooled, to turn out people with all the sharp edges worn off, the well-rounded person. The university is well equipped to produce that sort of person, and this means that the best among the people who enter must for four years wander aimlessly much of the time questioning why they are on campus at all, doubting whether there is any point in what they are doing, and looking toward a very bleak existence afterward in a game in which all of the rules have been made up, which one cannot really amend.

Is a bureaucratized society necessarily oppressive? Whether it is or not, the free speech demonstrators at the University of California felt oppressed. But the reason for this feeling may be higher aspirations for individual fulfillment rather than the objective tyranny of large-scale formal organizations. The former president of the University of California, Clark Kerr, may have been a casualty of the revolution of rising expectations rather than a deposed autocrat.

Another way of looking at the problem of individuality in the bureaucratized society is to ask whether limits exist on the loyalty that the organization can exact from members. Does anything prevent the large-scale formal organization from demanding absolute loyalty, as does the state in totalitarian societies? Yes, there are limiting factors derived from the fact that organizations are not independent interactive systems but subsystems of larger societies. As subsystems, organizations must embody values compatible with those institutionalized in the larger society.[34] Thus, in Western democracies, one limitation on the domination of the individual by the organization is the positive valuation of human freedom and autonomy. The Bill of Rights may not be formally subscribed to by American business corporations, schools, and hospitals, but notions of individual rights are embedded in the psyches of organizational members. When organizations establish autocratic procedures for dealing with employees or customers, they arouse resentment because they violate the value placed on individual autonomy. This limits the power of American organizations over the individual. For example, Catholic colleges and universities in the United States, though perhaps less responsive to student and faculty wishes than secular colleges, cannot centralize decision making as fully as Catholic schools in some countries because American students and faculty have internalized expectations of democratic procedure. Other values place similar limits on organizations; the use of physical force to secure compliance is disapproved. Prisons and mental hospitals sometimes resort to physical coercion anyway, but it is illegitimate, and publicity causes a scandal.

A second limitation on the domination of the individual by the organization

---

[34] Parsons, *Structure and Process*, pp. 35-41.

lies in the societal norms governing the use of authority. The norms governing authority are more specific than the general values of the society. Authority norms explain how hierarchical relations operate in any organization, that is, the ways a bureaucratic superior may relate to a subordinate. In American society, for example, a bureaucratic superior is not supposed to yell at subordinates for their mistakes or slap their faces; he may in fact be on reciprocal first-name terms with his subordinates, although he need not be. In Japanese society, a subordinate bows to his bureaucratic superior and would be shocked by the suggestion of reciprocal use of first names. Such authority norms mean that a large-scale formal organization within a given society cannot depart too far from the general pattern of wielding authority.

Like the norms governing authority, the norms governing *contract* limit the domination of the individual by the organization. The institution of contract defines the terms on which human services and nonhuman facilities are made available to the organization. Thus the contract of employment specifies not only the hours during which the employee is subject to the authority of the organization but the specific services it is entitled to receive. The specificity of contractual services protects the employee. The boss may *solicit* sexual favors from his secretary, but he cannot claim that his position in the organization *entitles* him to them. In the Western democracies, employment contracts are based on mutual consent and are terminable on short notice. They presuppose competence to perform the work on the part of the employee, not a previous **particularistic** relationship. In Japan, on the other hand, there is still a tendency for the relationship between employing organization and employee to be permanent; workers do not expect to quit, and they know they will never be fired. Under these conditions (where the work relationship resembles a marriage contract), it is understandable that particularistic factors like kinship are given consideration.

CONCLUSION

Large-scale formal organization is *not* the antithesis of democracy. Democracy is a procedure for achieving consensus through free competition among opposing interest groups. Democracy is contrived to be somewhat unstable because it is predicated on the assumption that current decision makers are temporary. Bureaucracy, on the other hand, is a structure for carrying out decisions with maximum efficiency; it is predicated on the assumption that a best way exists, irrespective of who administers it, to realize current objectives. Peter Blau put the contrast well: "When people set themselves the task of determining the social objectives that represent the interests of most of them, the crucial problem is to provide an opportunity for all conflicting viewpoints to be heard. In contrast, when the task is the achievement of given social objectives, the essential problem to be solved is to discover the efficient, not the popular, means for doing so."[35] In short, large-scale formal organization is compatible with democracy.

But formal organization is also compatible with tyranny. The political indifference of bureaucratic procedures explains why administrative structures in the Soviet Union and in the United States are so similar. In both societies, large-scale organizations exist characterized by formal rules of procedure, impersonality, and a hierarchy of authority, and members of both societies complain about bureaucratic "red tape."

Large-scale formal organization came to dominate the economies of Western countries partly because the corporation is a convenient way of pooling venture capital and partly because economic activities are efficiently performed by highly differentiated organizations. Concomitantly, corporations became increasingly autonomous of their nominal owners; control passed into the hands of self-perpetuating managements. Accompanying the separation of ownership and control was the emergence of a new middle class consisting of managerial, professional, and clerical employees. A rule of internal law developed within the corporation. "Due process" was one of the demands of unions, and therefore it can be argued that the rule of internal law was grudgingly granted when unions developed sufficient strength to compel its institutionalization. It can also be argued that the logic of bureaucratic rationality independently worked toward the rule of law and that the arbitrary treatment of employees was incompatible with personnel administration as a staff function.

Large-scale formal organizations deliver service as well as goods. Schools, hospitals, social work agencies, and philanthropic foundations tend to be organized bureaucratically in industrial societies. Similar though production and service bureaucracies are with respect to formal rules of procedure and impersonality, their authority structures differ. The hierarchical pattern characteristic of production bureaucracies is modified in service bureaucracies, especially those whose goals are socialization. Teaching of students or nursing of patients requires a cooperative relationship between the provider and the recipient of service, and this requirement has consequences both for the relationship between policy makers and operating personnel and for the relationship between the organization and the beneficiaries of its service. *Within* the organization, the necessity of maintaining cooperative relationships with students, patients, or clients makes for a staff consisting of professional workers: teachers, physicians, nurses, social workers, psychologists. Professional workers, because of their technical competence and their lateral relations with colleagues in other organizations, are more independent of their bureaucratic superiors than manual or clerical workers. Professionals may receive orders, but the orders are likely to follow consultation; their area of autonomy is recognized by their nominal superiors. In its *external* relations, the necessity of maintaining cooperative relationships results in a quasi-membership in the organiza-

---

[35] Blau, *Bureaucracy in Modern Society,* p. 107.

tion on the part of students, patients, or clients. They have a voice in the organization stronger than that of customers of a business firm, who are plainly outsiders.

The proliferation of large-scale formal organizations in industrial societies has raised questions about the dehumanization of the individual. It has been charged that manual workers become cogs in a meaningless production line and that students are punch cards in educational factories. But organizations are not independent entities. They are subsystems of the larger society and must embody values and operating procedures compatible with those of the society supporting them. General values govern interpersonal relationships, and specific institutions regulate the exercise of authority and the scope of contracts. This societal guidance over organizations militates against the University of California evolving into Murder, Incorporated.[36]

SOME SIGNIFICANT LITERATURE ON LARGE-SCALE ORGANIZATIONS

Morroe Berger, *Bureaucracy and Society in Modern Egypt: A Study of the Higher Civil Service,* Princeton, N.J.: Princeton University Press, 1957. In 1954, 249 higher civil servants in the Egyptian ministries of Agriculture, Education, Finance and Economy, and Municipal and Rural Affairs responded to questions asked them in Arabic by trained interviewers. Through analysis of the replies, Berger discovered . . .

. . . the social origins of higher civil servants [in Egypt] today; the reasons for the attraction this career has for so many of the educated élite; the changing socioeconomic status of the higher civil servants; their loyalties and the extent of their professionalization; and their attitudes toward such norms of bureaucratic behavior as impartiality, impersonality, subordination to one's superior, and the exercise of the permitted degree of initative.

In particular, Berger was interested in finding out how the public bureaucracy in Cairo differed from that of most Western countries. ". . . The study of bureaucracy in a non-Western setting points to the limitation of current bureaucratic theory, developed mainly in the West." This summary is based on a review by George L. Harris, *American Sociological Review,* Vol. 23, April 1958, pp. 223-224.

Peter M. Blau, *The Dynamics of Bureaucracy: A Study of Interpersonal Relations in Two Government Agencies,* Chicago: University of Chicago Press, 1955. Blau studied the behavior of lower officialdom in a state employment agency to test the hypothesis that informal interactions need not constitute idiosyncratic deviations from bureaucratic regulations but may instead be work-facilitating innovations. He found that change in patterns of informal activities followed the introduction of statistical performance records. He concluded that bureaucracy did not inevitably resist change; it did so only under specific conditions. For example, workers whose statuses are

---

[36] Joseph Freeman, "The Inside Story of a Crime Trust, *The Nation,* Vol. 150, May 25, 1940, pp. 645-649.

insecure tend to resist change, but job tenure arrangements, professionalization, established work groups, and the absence of basic conflict between work group and management reduce this insecurity and thereby the opposition to change. This summary is based on a review by Sheldon L. Messinger, *American Sociological Review*, Vol. 21, February 1956, pp. 102-103.

Erving Goffman, "On the Characteristics of Total Institutions," in Donald R. Cressey, Ed., *The Prison: Studies in Institutional Organization and Change*, New York: Holt, Rinehart, and Winston, 1961, pp. 15-106. Although institutional differentiation is characteristic of urban industrial societies — people usually work, play, and sleep in different places — some organizations existing within modern societies concentrate these activities in common locations: prisons, homes for the aged, mental hospitals, military bases, and monasteries. Goffman calls such organizations "total institutions" and describes the systematic invasion of privacy that becomes possible when all spheres of the individual's life are subject to the same authority. In the course of his discussion, he comments perceptively on the mortification of newcomers, the personal reorganization that occurs within the privilege system of the total institution, staff-inmate relations, the inmate culture, and the individual's loss of, or failure to acquire, some of the habits currently in use in the larger society. Goffman highlights the similarities among a wide variety of people-processing organizations, and he stresses the dehumanizing aspects of their social control activities. For a study of *variation* among one type of total institution, training schools for delinquent boys, see David Street, Robert D. Vinter, and Charles Perrow, *Organization for Treatment*, New York: Free Press, 1966. For a study of a total institution showing that inmate cultures depend not only on the enforced setting but on the preinstitutional characteristics of the inmate population, see Rose Giallombardo, *Society of Women: A Study of a Women's Prison*, New York: Wiley, 1966.

Robert H. Guest, "Managerial Succession in Complex Organizations," *American Journal of Sociology*, Vol. 68, July 1962, pp. 47-54. This paper compares two studies of the succession of a new leader at the top of bureaucratic hierarchy. In one case, Alvin Gouldner's study of a small gypsum plant, the new manager felt under pressure from his superiors in the central office of the corporation to institute more bureaucratic routines and to use disciplinary measures to make the organization more efficient. He instituted what Gouldner called "punishment-centered" discipline, and the result was an increase in internal organizational tensions. In the other case, Guest's own study of succession in one of six identical plants of a large corporation, the new manager felt free to use a more democratic technique of wielding authority; he permitted the initiation of interaction from lower levels in the hierarchy, and he established group meetings at all levels of the organization to cope with problems. Quantitative indices showed that this democratic leader made a significant improvement in the productive efficiency of the plant. ". . . [T]here emerges from both studies encouraging evidence suggesting that it is possible for democratic processes to function in an otherwise authoritarian bureaucratic social system." For a more detailed description of the studies compared in this paper, see Alvin W. Gouldner, *Patterns of Industrial Bureaucracy*, Glencoe, Ill.: Free Press, 1954; and Robert H. Guest, *Organizational Change: The Effect of Successful Leadership*, Homewood, Ill.: Irwin-Dorsey, 1962.

Morris Janowitz, *The Professional Soldier: A Social and Political Portrait*, Glencoe, Ill.: Free Press, 1960. Janowitz traces the changes among American professional soldiers over the past half century: the changing social backgrounds, skill distribution, and career patterns. Concomitantly, the basis of discipline in the military establishment has shifted from domination by arbitrary command toward authority maintained by persuasion, manipulation, and concern with morale. Janowitz used historical, documentary, and biographical sources in analyzing a historical sample of 760 generals and admirals covering the years 1910, 1920, 1935, and 1950. He also obtained questionnaire data from contemporary members of his sample, and he interviewed 113 Army, Navy, and Air Force officers on duty at the three Service headquarters. One of his most interesting conclusions is that the careers of the most distinguished military leaders deviate from the pattern of advancement by seniority usual in the military establishment. This summary is based on a review by Hans Speier, *American Sociological Review,* Vol. 25, December 1960, pp. 970-971.

Sheldon L. Messinger, "Organizational Transformation: A Case Study of a Declining Social Movement," *American Sociological Review,* Vol. 20, February 1955, pp. 3-10. This case study of the Townsend Movement, a voluntary association created during the late 1930s to help old people maintain economic independence, is a contribution to understanding organizational adaptation to decline of support. With increasing lack of public concern for the original organizational mission, the preoccupation of the leadership shifts from the implementation of values the organization is taken to represent to maintaining the organizational structure. Sometimes this involves finding a new mission. An interesting example of a shift in mission occurred when polio was, in effect, conquered through the development of vaccines, and the National Foundation for Infantile Paralysis had to adapt, not to failure, but to success. It chose to take on a broader mission and continue in business. For a careful study of this successful organization, see David M. Sills, *The Volunteers,* Glencoe, Ill.: Free Press, 1957.

Arthur L. Stinchcombe, "Institutions of Privacy in the Determination of Police Administrative Practice," *American Journal of Sociology,* Vol. 69, September 1963, pp. 150-160. Police bureaucracies started little more than a century ago when Sir Robert Peel organized the London Metropolitan Police (thenceforth called "bobbies" after Sir Robert). Stinchcombe shows that the character of police administrative practices is influenced by the tasks assigned to the police by increasingly urbanized societies. For example, rural police depend much more on complaints from people who are injured by a crime or who observe it than do urban police who rely heavily on patrol of public places. This difference in administrative practice is a consequence of the greater intensity of use of public places in big cities and the greater feasibility of police surveillance of public places. Stinchcombe goes on to suggest (1) that different types of crimes have varying probabilities of being committed in public places where they are vulnerable to police intervention and (2) that persons occupying different positions within an urban industrial society have varying opportunities to escape police observation by entering private places. (By definition, the police cannot penetrate private places except under special circumstances — for instance, if they have a search warrant.) Stinchcombe hypothesizes that some of the difference between the arrest rates of lower-class and middle-class persons may be the result of differential observability of their behavior by the police.

Arthur L. Stinchcombe, "Bureaucratic and Craft Administration of Production: A Comparative Study," *Administrative Science Quarterly,* Vol. 4, September 1959, pp. 168-187. In mass production manufacturing industries, bureaucratic administration is economically feasible; work flow is sufficiently stable that it pays to hire clerks to maintain the communication system between continually functioning officials. In the construction industry, on the other hand, the seasonal nature of the work flow usually militates against bureaucratic organization of production. Under these circumstances, craft unions are more than labor organizations. They constitute a form of rational administration under the peculiar conditions of the construction industry. They entrust decision making largely to a professionalized manual labor force, thus relying more on previous socialization than on detailed supervision. For another approach to the relationship between a professional and a bureaucratic organization, see the study of eight international accounting firms in Paul D. Montagna, "Professionalization and Bureaucracy in Large Professional Organizations," *American Journal of Sociology,* Vol. 74, September 1968, pp. 138-145.

James D. Thompson, "Organizations and Output Transactions," *American Journal of Sociology,* Vol. 28, November 1962, pp. 309-324. "Classic bureaucratic theory is preoccupied with behavioral relations ordered by a single, unified authority structure from which the client is excluded. . . ." In point of fact, though, purposive organizations distribute the organization's ultimate product, service, or impact to nonmembers through persons who occupy what Thompson calls *output roles,* as, for example, salesmen, caseworkers, checkout clerks in supermarkets. He develops a typology of output transactions and analyzes for each one the interactive possibilities between nonmembers and persons in the output roles. Four types of output transactions are generated (1) by the degree of control by the organization over the behavior of the member in the output role and (2) by the degree to which the nonmember finds interaction with the organization optional. Maximum organizational control over the member in the output role occurs when "the member is equipped with a single, complete program—a standard procedure which supposedly does not vary, regardless of the behavior of the nonmember." An example of minimum nonmember discretion about interacting with the organization is the prisoner who must deal with his guard.

Stanley H. Udy, Jr., "Administrative Rationality, Social Setting, and Organizational Development," *American Journal of Sociology,* Vol. 68, November 1962, pp. 299-308. Members of bureaucratic organizations are supposed to behave rationally. (Social behavior is rational "in so far as it is purposefully directed toward explicit empirical objectives and planned in accordance with the best available scientific knowledge.") On the basis of a study of formal organizations engaged in the production of material goods in 34 nonindustrial societies, Udy suggests that administrative rationality involves a cumulative emphasis on the following characteristics: (1) central management; (2) compensatory rewards for participation; (3) the concurrent performance of three or more qualitatively different operations by different members ("specialization"); (4) continuous job assignment by management of particular people to particular roles; (5) rewards contingent on the amount and quality of the work done ("performance emphasis"); (6) explicit definition of the terms of participation by mutual agreement ("segmental participation"); and (7) limited organizational objectives. By a cumulative emphasis, Udy means that organizations with characteristic (4) will tend to possess characteristics (1), (2), and (3) and that organizations with characteristic (7) will tend to possess all of the other rational characteristics.

FORMAL EDUCATION: SOCIAL ALLOCATION THROUGH CULTURE TRANSMISSION

The New York Times

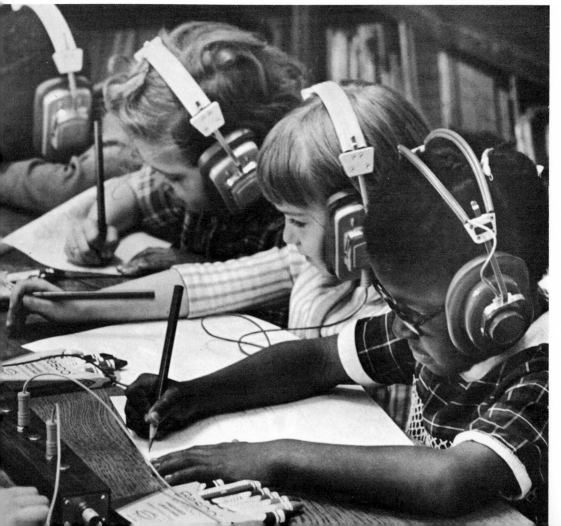

All societies must cope with the task of transmitting their cultural traditions to the new generation. In preliterate societies, this task is handled informally by the family and the community. In industrial societies, the family starts the education of the young, but a specialized organization, the school, soon assumes the main responsibility. Modern societies were compelled to create *formal* educational institutions because the universal problem of culture transmission is more difficult under urban industrial conditions. The tremendous size of the culture base means that no one has detailed knowledge of the entire culture. Members of the society share a common culture in a composite sense: Each person has a general idea of the contents of the culture and also has detailed knowledge of small portions of it. The cultural mosaic is further differentiated (1) by ethnic, regional, and class subcultures and (2) by a rapid rate of cultural change. Under these difficult conditions the school attempts to provide a guaranteed minimum of useful knowledge for everybody as well as specialized education for particular subgroups.

CULTURE TRANSMISSION AND SOCIAL INTEGRATION

Suppose there were no schools, and parents educated their children in accordance with their own notions of what a child ought to know. Would a child who depended on the version of the cultural tradition transmitted by his parents learn enough basic ideas and skills to function in a complicated society? All industrial countries have implicitly assumed a negative answer to this question. They have established systems of mass education at the primary school level to teach basic literacy, arithmetic, and some common knowledge and beliefs.

The ability to read and write is hardly a luxury in urban industrial societies. An illiterate gets lost more often than persons who can read street signs and house numbers. He does not understand notices posted on a bulletin board at his place of employment. He probably is not able to get a driver's license. He has trouble making employment applications, signing contracts, and paying bills. Not knowing how to read labels, he has difficulty shopping in the supermarket. He has difficulty in finding a job.[1] The emphasis in primary schools on basic literacy is plainly dictated by necessity.

Arithmetic is also a necessity in urban industrial communities. In a society in which nearly everyone at some stage of his life (1) sells his services in the labor market and (2) consumes the goods and services it produces, monetary transactions are inescapable. A person who cannot add and subtract is at a serious disadvantage in such transactions. Arithmetic is also required in other

[1] Eli Ginzberg and Douglas W. Bray, *The Uneducated,* New York: Columbia University Press, 1953.

TABLE 11.1

Illiteracy in Developed and Underdeveloped Countries, 1950[a]

| Geographical Division | Percentage of Illiterates in the Population Aged 10 and Over | | |
	All Countries	Developed Countries	Underdeveloped Countries
World	47	6	70
North America[c]	2	2	[b]
Europe	8	3	20
Oceania	11	1	88
U.S.S.R.[d]	11	11	[b]
South America	42	17	51
Middle America[e]	48	20	52
Asia	70	2	75
Africa	88	55	91

[a] Developed countries are those with less than 50 per cent of their economically active males in agricultural pursuits, including hunting, fishing, and forestry; underdeveloped countries are those with 50 per cent or more of their economically active males in these pursuits.

[b] No country in this category.

[c] U.S.A., Canada, and Alaska.

[d] The U.S.S.R. is a borderline case but has been classed here among the developed countries, since today its agricultural labor force is probably slightly below 50 per cent.

[e] The Central American republics and the islands of the Caribbean.

activities, although not as obviously as in exchange. A carpenter must know how to add and subtract fractions, or his measurements will not be correct. Inventory control requires endless counting. Personal budgeting requires arithmetic, and so does a checking account.

The importance of reading, writing, and arithmetic skills can also be appreciated by comparing education in industrialized and underdeveloped societies. Hilda Hertz Golden has demonstrated (1) that literacy is correlated with industrialism and (2) that *mass education* is a necessary condition for industrial development:[2]

> If those countries in which 50 per cent or more of the gainfully occupied males are engaged in agriculture are regarded as underdeveloped, we find, as expected, that the underdeveloped countries are highly illiterate, with the striking exception of those in Europe (Table 11.1). But even the latter are far more illiterate than the industrial nations. Despite exceptions, then, Table 11.1 demonstrates the close association between the levels of educational achievement and of industrialization.

[2] Reprinted by permission. From Hilda Hertz Golden, "Literacy and Social Change in Underdeveloped Countries," *Rural Sociology*, Vol. 20, February 1955, pp. 1-7.

. . . . Literacy and industrialization in 1950 correlate closely: the coefficient of correlation is .87 when industrialization is measured by the proportion of gainfully occupied males in nonagricultural pursuits, and .84 when measured by per-capita income. The closeness of these relationships is further substantiated by historical data for individual countries. In England and Wales, for example, the growth of literacy has been closely associated with that of industrialism, as is confirmed here by a coefficient of correlation of .98.

Establishing the close interrelation of the diffusion of literacy and industrialization invites speculation on why it should exist: Literacy is not essential in the training for or the practice of traditional agriculture and its related handicraft occupations. These occupations can be learned through apprenticeship, by watching an experienced person, by attempting to imitate him by trial and error. The knowledge required for such work can be stored in a person's memory; the principles can be transmitted verbally as part of the apprenticeship process. Since neither business documents nor accounts need be kept, and since the work requires no blueprints, reading and writing are not essential to everyday life.

When most parents follow these traditional occupations, they feel no strong incentive to send their children to school or to arrange somehow that the children acquire literacy skills; they view with indifferent skepticism the practical benefits to be derived from literacy and education. They are easily discouraged by lack of funds, by long distances from school, by their need for their children's labor. Therefore, unless local governments or outside agents push a program of formal education with unusual vigor or attempt with great persistence to diffuse literacy skills, their prospects of success are slight.

Besides the agriculturalist's apathy toward formal education and his poverty, lack of government funds is an additional obstacle to the diffusion of literacy, since governments of underdeveloped countries cannot provide adequate educational facilities even when they want to. Many impoverished governments, for example, exempt rural children from school attendance because providing school facilities for them is too costly.

In peasant-agricultural countries, literacy begins to diffuse beyond a few traditional occupations (such as the scribe's) and beyond the confines of a literate élite when the society is starting to change in its occupational structure. Since urban-industrial occupations require reading and writing for their acquisition and practice, literacy appears as a skill that leads the individual out of traditional agriculturalism. Education begins to be regarded as a passport from the hard and primitive life of the subsistence farmer to the haven of nonagricultural employment. When parents are no longer employed in traditional agriculture but instead have become unskilled industrial laborers, occupational training of children requires time and skills beyond the power of parents to provide. Parents thus acquire incentives to send their children to school; they acquire some notion of the usefulness of primary education and are less likely to demand their children's services at an early age. They may view education as a channel of mobility from unskilled to skilled occupations, from agriculture to industry. Furthermore, with increasing industrialization governments become more able to provide educational facilities and to enforce school attendance. In brief, the growth and diffusion of literacy in underdeveloped countries is closely tied to the growth and diffusion of an urban-industrial civilization.

TABLE 11.2

Graduates from Public and Private Secondary Schools in the United States, 1870–1965

School Year Ending	Secondary School Graduates	
	Number	Percentage of 17-Year-Olds in Population
1870	16,000	2.0
1880	23,634	2.5
1890	43,731	3.5
1900	94,883	6.4
1910	156,429	8.8
1920	311,266	16.8
1930	666,904	29.0
1940	1,221,475	50.8
1950	1,199,700	59.0
1960	1,864,000	65.1
1965	2,638,000	71.9

Source: Bureau of the Census, *Historical Statistics of the United States, Colonial Times to 1957,* Washington, D.C.: Government Printing Office, 1960, p. 207; *Statistical Abstract of the United States: 1968,* Washington, D.C.: Government Printing Office, 1968, p. 127.

CULTURE TRANSMISSION AND SOCIAL DIFFERENTIATION

As important as is basic literacy, the need for it does not alone explain mass formal education in industrial societies. If reading, writing, and arithmetic were sufficient, mass education would not have reached the secondary school level — and in the United States, the college level. Table 11.2 shows the increasing proportion of 17-year-old Americans who graduate from high school in the twentieth as compared with the nineteenth century. Mass secondary education began in the United States and is spreading to Western European countries. Table 11.3 shows that a substantial proportion of youngsters 14 to 18 are enrolled in school in various European countries. Secondary education was originally thought of as preparation for humanistic or professional education in the universities, but the philosophy of secondary education has changed.[3] With advancing industrialization, an increasing proportion of jobs require technical skill or the mastery of a body of accumulated knowledge.[4] The re-

[3] A. D. C. Peterson, *A Hundred Years of Education,* rev. ed., New York: Collier, 1962, pp. 145-177.

[4] Burton R. Clark, *Educating the Expert Society,* San Francisco: Chandler, 1962, pp. 45-58.

TABLE 11.3

Percentage of age group enrolled in secondary education, 1965 or latest year

Percentage Enrolled	Country	Age Group	Year
Over 80	United States	14–18	1960
	Japan	15–18	1964
60–80	Netherlands	14–18	1964
	Canada	15–18	1961
40–60	France	14–18	1964
	Belgium	14–18	1964
	Austria	14–18	1965
	Germany (incl. part-time)	14–18	1965
	Denmark	14–18	1960–1962
	Sweden	14–18	1963
	Yugoslavia	15–18	1965
20–40	Italy	14–18	1965
	Germany (full-time only)	14–18	1965
	England and Wales	14–18	1965
	Greece	12–17	1960–1961
Less than 20	Spain	14–17	1960
	Portugal	14–18	1963
	Turkey	15–19	1960

Source: *Development of Secondary Education: Trends and Implications,* Paris: Organisation for Economic Co-operation and Development, 1969, p. 32.

sponsibility for preparation for these jobs was gradually assumed by secondary and advanced education. Thus secondary education in the technological society helps prepare youngsters to assume adult occupational roles. This preparatory function means that education must "keep up" with a *changing* culture base. As anthropologist Margaret Mead maintains, under these conditions education can never be completed; the concept of a completed education belongs to a bygone era.[5] For contemporary industrial societies education must be augmented in varying amounts and at various stages during the individual's lifetime. Since this is so, it cannot be the *old* teaching the *young* but the more knowledgeable teaching the less knowledgeable. Professor Mead calls this "lateral transmission of knowledge."

Lateral education, in this sense, is already well developed. The proliferation of educational upgrading programs in industry, of extension courses offered by universities, and of adult education under a variety of sponsorships

[5] Margaret Mead, "Thinking Ahead: Why Is Education Obsolete?," *Harvard Business Review,* Vol. 36, November-December 1958, pp. 23-30.

shows that education in the technological society tends to continue throughout the life cycle. Adult education goes by different names in different countries (in Japan it is called "social education"[6]), but all industrial societies attempt to cope with a rapidly changing technology, which prevents children from learning in school all they must know on the job. Adult education does not, however, solve the problems of how much and what kind of education to give the young. More secondary education and college attendance may be desirable to prepare modern youth for the occupational requirements of industrial societies.

The occupational role structure has been changing in industrial countries. For example, the American economy upgraded its manpower requirements over the past half century in the direction of professional, technical, managerial, clerical, and sales occupations.[7] These demand greater formal education than most blue-collar occupations. Partly in response to financial rewards available to the better educated, educational levels have been rising. The proportion of American youngsters graduating from high school has grown astoundingly. But *educational upgrading has been insufficient to satisfy the occupational demand for the better educated.* And, conversely, too many youngsters for the economy to absorb drop out of school to seek unskilled laboring jobs. Unemployment statistics show more unemployment among blue-collar workers than among white-collar workers and more among dropouts than among high school graduates. In March 1968, 5.1 per cent of the blue-collar civilian labor force of the United States was unemployed compared with 1.9 per cent of white-collar workers; in 1966, 12.8 per cent of the civilian labor force 16 to 21 years of age who dropped out of high school was unemployed as compared with 9.8 per cent of high school graduates in that age group.[8] Youngsters who leave school as soon as they can legally do so enter an overcrowded labor market where the pay is low and the work menial.

The technical and scientific manpower needs of an industrial society are not satisfied automatically. The school system attempts to teach youngsters the skills and attitudes appropriate for the places in the occupational system which they want to occupy. Or, to put it the other way around, those youngsters who learn at school the intellectual content and the associated values of white-collar jobs tend to get such jobs. Those youngsters who rebel against the authority of teachers, fail to learn verbal skills, or for some other reasons drop out before graduating from high school lose out in the competition for better-paid white-collar occupations. The individual student and his parents may see this result in terms of personal success or failure. The *social* consequences of dif-

[6] Ronald S. Anderson, *Japan: Three Epochs of Modern Education,* Bulletin No. 11, United States Office of Education, Washington, D.C.: Government Printing Office, 1959, pp. 187-204.

[7] Seymour L. Wolfbein, "Education and Employment," in Eli Ginzberg, Ed., *The Nation's Children,* Vol. 2, New York: Columbia University Press, for the White House Conference on Children and Youth, 1960, pp. 138-157.

[8] Bureau of the Census, *Statistical Abstract of the United States: 1968,* Washington, D.C.: Government Printing Office, 1968, pp. 217, 114.

ferential educational achievement is the allocation of the society's human resources to its adult role structure.[9]

Socialization in Primary School. When the child starts school, he enters a world fundamentally different both from his family milieu and from his peer group. It is his first experience with explicit, long-term goals—in this case the transmission of neatly packaged units of "education." Even though kindergarten provides a transition, cushioning somewhat the shock that is to come, the child has good reason to resist socialization into the student role. The discipline of school is imposed on him by adults. It is not the schoolboy who decides that 9 o'clock is a good time to arrive and 3 o'clock a good time to go home. Nor is his interest in shouting, jumping, or pinching his neighbor given much consideration. Is it any wonder that the early grades are filled with chatterers and squirmers, controlled by the eternal vigilance of their teachers? But socialization takes hold: If you walk through a school, visiting first the lower grades and then the higher grades, you are likely to observe the gradual decrease of fidgeting and the increasing concentration.

The student role is a difficult one to learn because school represents a curtailment of the freedom of the child for the sake of goals he only dimly understands. Another difficulty is that the student role requires a relationship between adults and children quite different from the one learned in the family. The teacher's reaction to her student is qualitatively different from the mother's reaction to her child. The teacher does not love her students; there are too many of them. The size of classes and the necessity of communicating prescribed lessons militate against diffuse personal relationships between teacher and students. Instead of giving students love, the teacher gives them approval (or disapproval), which is a far more contingent reaction. The teacher's reaction to a child depends preponderantly on what he *does:* on how fast he learns, on how often he throws spitballs, on how readily he raises his hand to volunteer an answer to her questions. At home, on the other hand, his mother's response to him is preponderantly based on the fact that he is *hers*. His beauty, intelligence, and even his naughtiness are secondary considerations. This is not to say that the student role is the child's first experience with contingent reactions. On the contrary, as Chapter 4 tried to show, the contingency of maternal responses is crucial to internalization. But there is a difference between contingency that is a small part of a basically uncontingent relationship and a relationship that is predicated on contingency. The student role is of the second type. So are other roles of industrial societies, notably occupational roles. But the student role comes earlier in the life cycle. This is part of the explanation for the incidence of problems in the first few grades.

In the classroom the child faces an inherently competitive situation. He and his classmates are supervised by an adult whose job it is to judge comparative intellectual performance. The teacher also judges nonintellectual be-

---

[9] Talcott Parsons, "The School Class as a Social System: Some of Its Functions in American Society," *Harvard Educational Review,* Vol. 29, Fall 1959, p. 309.

Susanne Szasz

havior, expressing approval of neatness and punctuality and disapproval of insolence and irresponsibility based on the teacher's own values, usually those of the middle class. The superior student is one who performs well on both these tests of comparative achievement.[10] Whether a student's performance is superior or inferior, he learns to *value* achievement—to believe that rewards *should* be given to those who outperform others in a competitive contest. Thus classroom socialization prepares the student to compete later for occupational roles and to accept competitive failure with some grace. Unless internalization of a competitive spirit occurred, urban industrial societies would have difficulty in attracting the talent and the discipline required of brain surgeons or novelists, as the section on Competition and Individual Choice (in Chapter 7) suggested.

It is easy for *successful* students to internalize the competitive values of the classroom. However, unsuccessful students also must internalize the principle of differential reward for differential performance. Lack of such commitment

---

[10] Parsons argues that the high achiever in elementary school "... is evaluated in diffusely general terms; a *good* pupil is defined in terms of a fusion of the cognitive and the moral components...." Parsons, "The School Class," p. 304.

creates disinterest and learning problems, and threatens the authority of the teacher, who must rely on power rather than respect to maintain order if the values underlying class activities are not shared. But the cost of sharing achievement values is high for the unsuccessful student—he has to judge his own performance as inadequate. Rather than accept this blow to his self-concept, the unsuccessful student may reject achievement values—in the classroom at any rate. Thus delinquents frequently have a prior history of school maladjustment.[11]

When parents support the achievement values of the classroom, the student is likely to accept them and to perform as successfully as possible. Some parents reinforce the authority and prestige of the teacher, encouraging the child to respect her and compete for her approval. The teacher makes a good parent-surrogate for him if his parents accept her in this role and urge him to value her opinion of him. Although the child initially may be motivated to cooperate with the teacher by parents, motivation autonomous of parental pressure usually develops later. Part of this new motivation may be growing interest in the subject matter. *Learning* to read may be a disagreeable chore; but the time soon comes when interesting stories are made accessible by the development of reading skill. Another source of motivation favorable to school is the symbolic recognition a student gets in the form of high marks. He learns that he enjoys success in the achievement contest: to secure the approving attention of the teacher, to skip grades, and to remain always in the "bright" classes. In grade school the "bright" and the "dull" classes take approximately the same work, but pupils and teachers have no difficulty in separating the high-prestige groups. In high school, "commercial," "trade," and "general" courses have different curricula from the high-prestige "college" course. Again, there is consensus among the students as well as the teachers that the noncollege courses are for those who are not "college material."

Although parental support of achievement values *decreases* the likelihood of school failure, differences in innate ability and in personal circumstances make for some failure among children of parents who subscribe to achievement values. For such children, rejection of achievement values is difficult because it involves conflict not only with the school but with their parents. This helps to explain why internalization of achievement values is more widespread than the frequency of scholastically successful children. There are other reasons. For one, the unsuccessful student may have distributed some eggs in other baskets. True, he reads slowly and has no mind for arithmetic, but he is fine at baseball, and he was marvelous in the class play. Thus intellectual achievement is not the only realm in which the principle of differential rewards for differential achievement applies. In a pluralistic society, individuals do not have

---

[11] Walter E. Schafer and Kenneth Polk, "Delinquency and the Schools," in The President's Commission on Law Enforcement and the Administration of Justice, *Juvenile Delinquency and Youth Crime,* Washington, D.C.: Government Printing Office, 1967, pp. 222-227.

to stake their self-respect on a single area of achievement, even one as important as academic accomplishment.[12]

A second reason that internalization of achievement values occurs even among those who fail is that initially the nonachievers *expect* success. The first grader and his parents do not know that he will never learn to read. By the time he realizes that he is unlikely to succeed in school, he may have already internalized the achievement principle. Some societies—England and Japan, for example—have examination systems that testify rather early to the educational prognosis for the student. A Japanese schoolboy who cannot pass the entrance examination to the junior high school of his choice cannot aspire to enter a leading high school and ultimately Tokyo University.[13] In the United States, on the other hand, marks are given, but **streaming** does not occur until high school. Furthermore, ''general'' students and ''college prep'' students usually attend the same public high school and take some classes together. This makes it psychologically and administratively easier for ''general'' students to switch to a ''college prep'' curriculum or to attend a college without having taken the college preparatory course. Hope for educational success can remain alive longer in the American educational system than in the British or the Japanese because the implications of poor performance are not spelled out so dramatically. Thus American high school seniors replied to the question, ''How bright do you think you are in comparison to the other students in your grade?'' as follows:[14]

12%	Among the brightest
35%	Above average
45%	Average
3%	Below average
1%	Among the lowest
4%	No answer to the question
100%	Total high school seniors

[12] Howard S. Becker, ''Notes on the Concept of Commitment,'' *American Journal of Sociology*, Vol. 66, July 1960, pp. 32-40.

[13] Ezra F. Vogel, *Japan's New Middle Class: The Salary Man and His Family in a Tokyo Suburb*, Berkeley: University of California Press, 1963, Chap. 3, ''The Gateway to Salary: Infernal Entrance Exams.''

[14] This question was part of a national survey undertaken by the United States Office of Education in 1965 ''concerning the lack of availability of equal educational opportunities for individuals by reason of race, color, religion, or national origin. . . .'' James S. Coleman et al., *Equality of Educational Opportunity*, Washington, D.C.: Government Printing Office, 1966, p. 287.

TABLE 11.4

Percentage Distribution of Replies of Twelfth-Grade Pupils to the Question, "Every time I try to get ahead, something or somebody stops me," for White and Negro Pupils in Metropolitan and Nonmetropolitan Areas by Region, and for Selected Minority Groups for the United States, Fall 1965

Race and Area	Agree	Not Sure	Disagree	No Response
White, nonmetropolitan:				
South	16	22	61	2
Southwest	14	19	64	4
North and West	14	20	64	2
White, metropolitan:				
Northeast	13	19	65	2
Midwest	15	22	62	2
South	14	19	65	3
Southwest	13	20	63	4
West	12	18	65	5
Negro, nonmetropolitan:				
South	22	22	44	12
Southwest	26	21	42	12
North and West	24	22	49	5
Negro, metropolitan:				
Northeast	21	20	48	12
Midwest	23	22	47	8
South	19	17	43	21
Southwest	23	22	42	13
West	21	19	41	20
Mexican Americans, total	23	22	46	10
Puerto Ricans, total	30	20	36	14
Indian Americans, total	27	28	39	7
Oriental Americans, total	18	31	47	4
Other, total	29	23	38	10
Total, all races	16	20	59	5

Source: James S. Coleman et al., *Equality of Educational Opportunity*, Washington, D.C.: Government Printing Office, 1966, p. 289.

Since only 4 per cent of the seniors considered themselves below average and 47 per cent considered themselves above average, some students were unduly optimistic about their intellectual abilities. Whatever the consequences of illusions for the individual student, the consequence for the educational system is to make it easier to inculcate a competitive spirit into schoolchildren.

A third reason for internalization of achievement values even among unsuccessful students is a cultural definition of school competition as *fair*. As long as students and their parents have faith in equality of educational opportunity, they blame themselves for stupidity or lack of diligence rather than the educational system for discrimination when failure occurs. Correct or incorrect, a cultural definition of school competition as fair helps socialize school

children to achievement values. Yet it may be difficult for many students to accept this definition. This partly accounts for the suspicion on the part of some nonwhite parents that ghetto schools are not equal to those outside the ghetto and that their youngsters do not get a fair chance to learn.[15] Rejection of the definition of school competition as fair has two consequences. One is the attempt to decentralize big city school boards and give communities control of their schools.[16] A second effect is an undermining of the motivation to achieve on the part of nonwhite students. If they are playing in a rigged game, why try? Table 11.4 suggests that substantial proportions of minority-group students in the United States have their incentive to achieve undercut in this way.

Most children internalize in primary school faith in the legitimacy of differential rewards for differential achievement. High grades mean competitive success, and children learn to define competitive success as pleasurable as well as moral. As Chapter 3 pointed out, meanings have to be *learned*. In school the child has an early experience with the meaning of differential achievement. Note that the internalization of this value is not the objective of schools. Some school systems, in fact, stress the virtues of cooperation and express faith in "progressive education," based on the ideas of John Dewey. Sociological

[15] Jonathan Kozol, *Death at an Early Age: The Destruction of the Hearts and Minds of Negro Children in the Boston Public Schools,* Boston: Houghton-Mifflin, 1967.

[16] Wallace Robert, "The Battle for Urban Schools," *Saturday Review,* November 16, 1968, pp. 97-117.

analysis suggests, however, that (1) the classroom situation is inherently competitive, (2) the internalization of achievement values is necessary for successful progress through the educational system, and (3) the internalization of these values prepares the individual for the system of competitive **role allocation** in the occupational realm of industrial societies. Other values are internalized as a result of socialization to the student role. Self-control is one. Sensitivity to temporal scheduling is another. Split-second scheduling is more important in railroading than in most other industrial occupations, but many crucial operations of an industrial society cannot be coordinated unless workers and materials arrive predictably (as scheduled).[17] So nonrational devotion to punctuality is necessary; and it is usually inculcated in the course of the praise and scolding of primary school teachers. In short, while the teaching of cognitive culture (arithmetic, vocabulary) proceeds in the forefront of the classroom, the teaching of expressive and moral values goes on implicitly.

Differential Educational Opportunities. Even if all children successfully internalized the relevant values of the student role and even if schools were entirely universalistic in their treatment of students, some students would learn more than others. Differential performance is inherent in differences in native intellectual ability and in the idiosyncratic interactions of students and teachers. Furthermore, in contemporary industrial societies merit is rewarded; effort and intellectual abilities tend to result in educational achievement. The socioeconomic status of the family is another consideration.

If plans for college attendance on the part of high school seniors are considered an index of achievement (plans are highly correlated with actual attendance), the socioeconomic status of the family and the measured intelligence of the student have a roughly equal effect on educational achievement, as Table 11.5 shows. Students of meager intelligence who come from families of low socioeconomic status rarely plan to attend college; students of high intelligence coming from high-status families mostly plan to go to college. Students low on one factor and high on the other are intermediate in their college plans. Table 11.5 reflects not only the *direct* effects of measured intelligence and family status on college plans but indirect effects as well. The important indirect effect is through the intervening variable of *parental encouragement*. High school seniors participating in the study reported on in Table 11.5 were asked to check one of the following four statements:

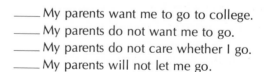

_____ My parents want me to go to college.
_____ My parents do not want me to go.
_____ My parents do not care whether I go.
_____ My parents will not let me go.

Those students who checked the first statement were considered "encouraged" by their parents; those who checked the other three statements were

---

[17] W. F. Cottrell, "Of Time and the Railroader," *American Sociological Review,* Vol. 4, April 1939, pp. 190-198.

TABLE 11.5

Percentage of High School Seniors Planning To Go To College by Sex, Socioeconomic Status, and Measured Intelligence, Wisconsin, 1957

| Socioeconomic Status of Family | Measured Intelligence | | | | | Number of Cases |
	Low	Low Middle	Upper Middle	High	All	
Males						
Low	4.0	13.0	21.7	34.9	14.6	(1,150)
Lower middle	8.4	19.4	33.6	49.6	26.3	(1,298)
Upper middle	17.6	25.8	46.2	64.0	38.8	(1,298)
High	29.0	48.3	68.7	85.6	66.4	(1,245)
All	11.7	25.4	44.7	65.4	36.9	(4,991)
Females						
Low	2.7	5.0	10.0	25.4	7.7	(1,330)
Lower middle	10.4	16.9	22.9	34.8	19.8	(1,349)
Upper middle	15.5	23.7	27.3	50.6	29.4	(1,346)
High	28.0	44.0	65.5	71.7	59.4	(1,302)
All	10.5	20.6	33.2	53.0	28.9	(5,327)

Source: Adapted from William H. Sewell and Vimal P. Shah, "Social Class, Parental Encouragement, and Educational Aspirations," *American Journal of Sociology*, Vol. 73, March 1968, p. 569.

considered "not encouraged." Of the 2906 boys who perceived their parents as encouraging college attendance, 58.6 per cent planned to attend; of the 2085 boys who perceived their parents as not encouraging college attendance, only 6.5 per cent planned to go. The corresponding figures for girls were 55.6 per cent and 6.2 per cent.[18] Parental encouragement clearly was strongly related to student plans.

Why did some parents encourage college attendance and others not? Apparently, parents encouraged intellectually able children on all socioeconomic levels, but, in addition, families of high socioeconomic status were more likely than families of low socioeconomic status to encourage college attendance, as Table 11.6 shows. Table 11.6 looks quite similar to Table 11.5 because much of the relationship between measured intelligence and college plans and between family status and college plans can be explained by the intervening variable of parental encouragement.[19] Close study of the two tables

[18] William H. Sewell and Vimal P. Shah, "Social Class, Parental Encouragement, and Educational Aspirations," *American Journal of Sociology*, Vol. 73, March 1968, p. 569.

[19] Some of the relationship is *direct*, rather than through an intervening relationship with perceived parental encouragement. That is, among students *not* encouraged by their parents to attend college, there existed a positive relationship between both measured intelligence and family status with college plans. And a similar relationship held for the group of students *encouraged* by their parents.

TABLE 11.6

Percentage of High School Seniors Encouraged by Their Parents to Attend College by Sex, Socioeconomic Status, and Measured Intelligence, Wisconsin, 1957

Socioeconomic Status of Family	Measured Intelligence					Number of Cases
	Low	Low Middle	Upper Middle	High	All	
Males	17.9	32.7	40.0	54.4	31.8	(1,150)
Lower middle	32.1	42.8	59.3	65.0	48.8	(1,298)
Upper middle	44.2	59.4	69.5	85.0	64.8	(1,298)
High	64.9	80.4	85.9	94.9	85.6	(1,245)
All	35.2	52.3	65.8	80.4	58.2	(4,991)
Females						
Low	10.4	16.1	19.7	32.3	16.6	(1,330)
Lower middle	23.3	34.6	45.5	48.8	36.6	(1,349)
Upper middle	38.8	44.5	50.7	64.8	50.7	(1,346)
High	62.7	71.3	83.8	88.1	80.6	(1,302)
All	26.0	39.1	52.1	68.0	45.9	(5,327)

Source: Adapted from William H. Sewell and Vimal P. Shah, "Social Class, Parental Encouragement, and Educational Aspirations," *American Journal of Sociology*, Vol. 73, March 1968, p. 569.

reveals a difference: socioeconomic status of the family is more closely associated with *parental encouragement* of college attendance than with the student's own plans. To put it another way, the roughly equal effect of the student's intelligence and his family status on college plans (shown in Table 11.5) arises by different processes. *Intelligence* affects college plans about equally through the direct raising of student aspirations and through the indirect influence of parental encouragement. *Socioeconomic status* affects college plans primarily as an indirect result of greater parental encouragement and only secondarily by directly raising student aspirations.

Both Table 11.5 and Table 11.6 contain percentages in the cells of the tables without providing the number of cases on which the percentages are calculated; this avoids clutter in the cells but obscures the relationship between measured intelligence and socioeconomic status. If there were *no* relationship between measured intelligence of students and the socioeconomic status of their families, each cell of the table would be based on approximately equal numbers of cases (somewhat over 300). Table 11.7 shows the *actual* distribution of cases; cases tend to pile up on the diagonal formed from low intelligence-low socioeconomic status to high intelligence-high socioeconomic status. This means that measured intelligence is correlated with family status. What accounts for this relationship? In order to consider possible explanations, one must first understand the operational definitions of "socioeconomic

TABLE 11.7

The Relationship between the Measured Intelligence of High School Seniors and the Socioeconomic Status of Their Families, Wisconsin, 1957

Socioeconomic Status of Families	Measured Intelligence				
	Low	Lower Middle	Upper Middle	High	All
Males					
Low	430	321	230	169	1,150
Lower middle	345	367	312	274	1,298
Upper middle	312	310	357	319	1,298
High	148	265	339	493	1,245
Females					
Low	512	378	279	161	1,330
Lower middle	386	390	323	250	1,349
Upper middle	278	371	377	320	1,346
High	150	261	371	520	1,302

status" and of "intelligence." In this study, intelligence is measured by scores on the Henmon-Nelson Test of Mental Ability administered annually to all high school juniors in Wisconsin. The socioeconomic status of a student's family is based on a weighted combination of father's occupation, father's educational attainment, mother's educational attainment, an estimate of the funds the family can provide if the student is to attend college, the degree of sacrifice this would entail for the family, and the approximate wealth and income of the family.[20]

What do these six components have to do with the *native* intellectual ability of children? Very little. But the correlation shown in Table 11.7 is not between the native intellectual ability of students and the socioeconomic status of their families. It is between Henmon-Nelson test scores of high school juniors and questionnaire data concerning their families supplied by these students during their senior year. Scores on the Henmon-Nelson Test of Mental Ability, as on every intelligence test to greater or lesser degree, depend not only on the innate intelligence of the respondent but on his familiarity with the cultural universe from which the items are drawn. A Navaho boy who scores 90 on the Henmon-Nelson may be unusually bright; the test was not standardized on Navaho children; hence a score of 100 does not constitute a valid reference point around which to assess his intellectual superiority or inferiority. This does not mean that intelligence tests in general or the Henmon-Nelson in particular are invalid. An intelligence test is a valid predictor of academic ac-

[20] William H. Sewell and Vimal P. Shah, "Socioeconomic Status, Intelligence, and the Attainment of Higher Education," *Sociology of Education,* Vol. 40, Winter 1967, p. 8.

complishment but is not a pure measure of innate intelligence. Paradoxically, it would not predict school accomplishment so well if it were a perfect index of native intelligence. Adjustment in the educational system depends not only on innate ability but on familiarity with the cultural milieu and on interest in competing with other students in solving abstract problems. The student who does not try to get as high a score as possible on the intelligence test is likely to be similarly apathetic in the classroom.

From these considerations emerges the explanation of the superior performance on intelligence tests of students from families of high socioeconomic status. It is not necessarily their innate intelligence but the mobilization of whatever intellectual abilities they possess to the problems of the tests. To begin at the beginning, it cannot be taken for granted that any child, whatever the socioeconomic status of his family, will perceive school as pleasant. Starting school is a shocking obligation imposed on him by adults. Forced to come at set times, to restrain his conversation so that the teacher may instruct the class as a group, he cannot easily see a relationship between current or future gratification and what the teacher insists that he learn. In this situation of problematic school adjustment, parents of high socioeconomic status are usually more successful than parents of low socioeconomic status at inculcating in their children a willingness to accept academic discipline. They have probably graduated at least from high school, and their child is aware that they expect him to do the same or better. If he has difficulty with his studies, they are eager (and competent) to help him. And not only do his *parents* expect him to apply himself to his studies, so do his *friends* and *their* parents. He is caught in a neighborhood pattern of academic achievement in much the same way some lower-class boys are caught in a neighborhood pattern of truancy and delinquency.[21] This concern with education is insurance against the child's fall in social status. Middle-class parents convey to their children subtly or explicitly that they must make good in school if they want to go on being middle class. This may be phrased in terms of preparation for a "suitable" occupation (an alternative to a stigmatized occupation such as manual labor), in terms of a

---

[21] Statisticians call this a **contextual effect.** That is, children from schools with a high concentration of well-motivated students have a stronger commitment to academic achievement than would be expected from knowledge of individual characteristics (such as intelligence) alone. See, for example, Ralph H. Turner, *The Social Context of Ambition: A Study of High School Seniors in Los Angeles,* San Francisco: Chandler, 1964. However, some sociologists argue that neighborhood context adds little to correct prediction of the college plans of high school students beyond that predicted from their sex, family socioeconomic status, and measured intelligence. See William H. Sewell and J. Michael Armer, "Neighborhood Context and College Plans," *American Sociological Review,* Vol. 31, April 1966, pp. 159-168. This objection is compatible with the view that neighborhood context causes higher aspirations indirectly. The statistical effect of social context may be through raising measured intelligence in neighborhoods of high socioeconomic status. By attracting into such neighborhoods disproportionate numbers of families of high socioeconomic status concerned that their children receive a good education, a cultural climate favorable to educational aspirations is created.

correlation between a "comfortable" standard of living and educational level, or in terms of the honorific value of education for its own sake.

Actually, the superior performance on intelligence tests of children from families of high socioeconomic status begins before they arrive at school. Parents of such children mingle with lawyers, accountants, businessmen, and others who in their day-to-day activities manipulate symbols. In the course of conversation these people use a sizable vocabulary including many abstractions of high order. The child unconsciously absorbs these concepts in an effort to understand his parents and their friends. He is stimulated in this endeavor by the praise he receives from his parents when he shows verbal precociousness. The attention he receives as a result of a remark insightful beyond his years and the pride his mother shows in repeating a bright response of his to her friends motivate further development of the verbal skills valued in school and measured on intelligence tests.

The other side of the coin is the failure of some blue-collar children to develop the kind of orientation which will enable them to overcome the initial frustration of school discipline. To begin with, the parents of the blue-collar child may not support the school as do middle-class parents. His parents probably do not have much education themselves, and, if not, they cannot very well make meaningful to him subjects that they do not themselves understand. Even more important, they lack the incentive to encourage him in and praise him for school accomplishment at that critical early period when he finds school new and strange and distasteful. Almost the same reasoning can be applied to the inculcation of a cooperative attitude toward school in the child as has been applied to an acceptant attitude toward toilet training. If the parents convey to the child their eagerness to have him adjust to irksome school discipline, he will probably accept it to please them and retain their love just as he learned to urinate and defecate at appropriate times and places. But toilet training and school adjustment training differ in an important particular. Parents *must* toilet train the child because permitting him to soil himself at will is a constant and immediate nuisance.

The consequences of a child's disinterest in school may also be unpleasant, both for him and for his parents, but it is not immediate. In the short run, allowing him to neglect school may be the least troublesome course for his parents to take. If they are neutral or antagonistic toward school, a result (1) of the esoteric nature of the curriculum from the point of view of skills cultivated and appreciated in their cultural milieu and (2) of their failure to see the relevance of education to occupational advancement into a higher socioeconomic class, they do not have to give the kind of support to the school given by middle-class parents. There is no reason to assume that the value of education is self-evident. For those working-class or lower-class people who have lost hope in social mobility, the school is a symbol of a competition in which they do not believe they can succeed. If they themselves have given up, will they necessarily encourage their children to try to strive harder?

Moreover, coming as he does from a social stratum where verbal skills are not highly developed, such a child finds school more difficult than does his middle-class contemporary. His father, a carpenter or a factory worker, manipulates concrete objects rather than symbols in his occupational role. Insofar as he learns from his father, he is more likely to learn how to "fix things" than the importance of a large vocabulary. This learning does not help him with his schoolwork, for school tends to give a competitive advantage to those with verbal facility.

American educators use the term **cultural deprivation**[22] to explain why minorities like Negroes and Puerto Ricans are disproportionately represented among schoolchildren with low records of achievement. Cultural deprivation results from two disadvantages: the socioeconomic status of their parents and the demoralization produced by prejudice. But the disadvantages of working-class children in school have been noted in all industrial societies, including the most welfare minded. In Denmark, for example, the Danish National Institute of Social Research divided 16- to 19-year-olds into 5 social classes and examined the distribution of youngsters on educational activities.[23] Whereas 77 per cent of the youngsters in the *highest* socioeconomic group were enrolled in academic schools, 13 per cent were in vocational schools, and 10 per cent were not enrolled in school; only 11 per cent of the youngsters in the *lowest* socioeconomic group were enrolled in academic schools, 39 per cent were in vocational schools, and 50 per cent were working or unemployed.

An English sociologist has suggested that the linguistic subculture of the British working class incapacitates many working-class children from succeeding in school.[24] Although the reasoning was developed to explain British experience, it is relevant to all urban industrial societies. Working-class linguistic usages form a relatively condensed language supplemented by gestures and implicit meanings. Such language is adequate "for expressing and receiving concrete, global, descriptive relationships organized with a relatively low level of conceptualization." It is adequate, however, only in a community "in which complex verbal procedures are made irrelevant by the system of nonverbal, closely shared identifications which serve as a backdrop to the speech." Formal education requires a shift of emphasis from nonverbal resources to verbal signals and therefore to greater conceptual resources for expressing applications of the general case to the specific instance. Many working-class children find this shift difficult to make.

One possible response of the blue-collar child to his disadvantages in the school situation is to increase his efforts. But his initial orientation may drive him in the opposite direction: to respond to competitive failure by going on

[22] Frank Riessman, *The Culturally Deprived Child,* New York: Harper, 1962.

[23] Danish National Institute of Social Research, *The Educational Situation of Danish Youth of 14 to 20 Years in 1965* (in Danish), Copenhagen: Teknisk Forlag, 1968.

[24] Basil Bernstein, "Social Structure, Language and Learning, *Educational Research,* Vol. 3, June 1961, pp. 163-176.

strike psychologically, neglecting his homework, paying no attention in class, annoying the teacher. Uninterested in the curriculum, he learns as little as he can. Instead of a situation where the student and the teacher work toward a common goal, the development of the student's understanding of certain ranges of problems, he and his teacher are oriented antagonistically to one another. The teacher tries to stuff into his head as much of the curriculum as possible; he tries to absorb as little as is consistent with his own safety in terms of sanctions mobilized by the school and his parents.

But school subjects are cumulative. Within a few years he is retarded in basic skills, such as reading, necessary for successful performance in the higher grades. Whether he is promoted along with his age-mates, "left back," or shunted into "slow" programs makes relatively little difference. For whatever is done, he finds himself at the bottom of the school status hierarchy. He is considered "dumb" by the more successful students and by the teachers. This makes school still more uninteresting, if not unpleasant, and he neglects his work further. The same effect is sometimes observed in teachers. They may feel that students in "slow" programs will not learn, and they therefore become lax in teaching them. Eventually the student realizes he can never catch up.

Without realizing what he was doing, he had cut himself off from the channels of social ascent. In those crucial early grades where the basis for school adjustment was being laid, he had not yet known that he wanted a higher socioeconomic status than his parents. Or, if he knew, he did not realize that school achievement and high occupational status are related. And he was not lucky enough to have parents who realized it for him and urged him on until he was old enough to identify with the school through choice. The student can hardly decide at 18 that he wants to become a lawyer if he is five years retarded in school. It is no longer possible for him to "catch up" and use school as a means to realize his ambitions. Sometimes working-class men will rue their failure to take advantage of the opportunities presented by the school. James T. Farrell captures the flavor of this regret in the following passage from one of his novels:[25]

> Walking on, seeing the lights of Randolph Street before him, he wondered if they were college football players [referring to the young men walking in front of him]. That was what Studs Lonigan might have been. Even if he did admit it, he had been a damn good quarterback. If he only hadn't been such a chump, bumming from school to hang around with skunky Weary Reilley and Paulie Haggerty until he was so far behind at high school that it was no use going. It wouldn't have been so hard to have studied and done enough homework to get by, and then he could have set the high school gridiron afire, gone to Notre Dame and made himself a Notre Dame immortal, maybe, alongside of George Gipp, the Four Horsemen, Christie Flannagan and Carideo. How many times in a guy's life couldn't he kick his can around the block for having played chump.

[25] James T. Farrell, *Judgment Day,* New York: Vanguard Press, 1935, p. 24.

These considerations do not mean that all children from families of high socioeconomic status get high scores on intelligence tests and adjust well to school or that all children of low socioeconomic status are doomed to fail at school. Innate intellectual ability and idiosyncratic experiences greatly affect school adjustment. The point of the foregoing discussion is to throw light on the social psychological mechanisms that make it more *likely* that a child from a middle-class family than from a working-class family will make a successful school record. Table 11.8 demonstrates that the median number of years of school completed by white boys from 7 to 17 is higher the higher the socioeconomic status of their families. (The lower the median years of school completed by an **age cohort,** the more members of that cohort are in grades below the normal placement for their age.) The social psychological mechanisms leading to superior scholastic performance on the part of children from middle-class families start operating in the early grades, and the gap widens with each passing year. In the special report of the United States census of 1940 from which Table 11.8 is taken are other tables showing that this relationship between the socioeconomic standing of families and the school achievement of their children holds for girls as well as for boys and for small communities as well as for large cities. Subsequent as well as previous studies show the same relationship. It shows up in the contrasting atmospheres of slum and suburban schools, as the former president of Harvard University, James B. Conant, observed.[26] In slum schools, dropping out is normal at the age when the law no longer compels attendance *regardless of intellectual potentialities*; in suburban schools, college attendance is expected *regardless of abilities or interests*. Thus in suburbia the school failure has a serious problem of self-respect. In the slum, the school failure finds company on every street corner.

To sum up, the middle-class child has the following advantages in school compared with the blue-collar child:

1. His parents are probably better educated and are therefore more capable of helping him with his school work if this should be necessary.
2. His parents are more eager to make his school work seem meaningful to him by indicating, implicitly or explicitly, the occupational applications of long division or history.
3. The verbal skills which he acquires as part of child training on the middle-class status level prepare him for the type of training that goes on in school and give him an initial (and cumulating) advantage over the working-class child in the classroom learning situation.
4. The coordinated pressure of parents, friends, and neighbors reinforce his motivation for scholastic success and increase the probability of good school adjustment.

[26] James B. Conant, *Slums and Suburbs: A Commentary on Schools in Metropolitan Areas,* New York: McGraw-Hill, 1961.

TABLE 11.8

Median Years of School Completed by Native White Boys by Monthly Rental Value of Home and by Age in Cities of 250,000 Inhabitants or More, 1940

Age	Monthly Rental Value of Home						
	Under $10	$10– $14	$15– $19	$20– $29	$30– $49	$50– $74	$75 and Over
7 years	1.3	1.5	1.6	1.7	1.7	1.7	1.7
8 years	2.1	2.4	2.4	2.5	2.6	2.6	2.7
9 years	2.8	3.2	3.3	3.4	3.5	3.7	3.7
10 years	3.6	4.0	4.2	4.4	4.5	4.6	4.7
11 years	4.4	4.9	5.1	5.3	5.5	5.6	5.6
12 years	5.4	5.7	6.0	6.2	6.5	6.6	6.7
13 years	6.0	6.7	7.1	7.2	7.5	7.7	7.8
14 years	7.2	7.8	7.9	8.2	8.5	8.7	8.8
15 years	8.3	8.5	8.8	9.2	9.4	9.6	9.8
16 years	8.6	9.3	9.6	9.8	10.3	10.5	10.6
17 years	9.4	9.9	10.2	10.7	10.7	11.3	11.5

Source: Bureau of the Census, *Sixteenth Census of the United States (1940), Monograph on Population Education: Educational Attainment of Children by Rental Value of Home,* Washington, D.C.: Government Printing Office, 1945, p. 3.

Educational opportunities, according to the United States Supreme Court, must be formally equal. But the economic disabilities of families of low socio-economic status frequently instill in children *attitudes* not conducive to scholastic success. Failure confirms the initial disinterest and often breeds resentment and rebellion. A child thus victimized seems to imply by his behavior, "If I learn nothing but how to fail here, I won't cooperate." Unfortunately, school achievement is related to later occupational placement. Failure to cooperate with the teacher cuts this child off from a business or professional career. August Hollingshead describes what happened to working-class boys from a small town in Illinois who withdrew from school:[27]

> The withdrawees' job skills are limited to what they have learned from contact with parents, relatives, friends, and through observations and personal experience, largely within the community; no withdrawee has any technical training for any type of job; furthermore, few have plans to acquire it in the future. . . . The boys have some acquaintance with working on farms, washing cars, loading and unloading grain, repairing cars, driving trucks, doing janitor work, clerking in stores, and odd jobs, but their lack of training, job skills, and ex-

[27] Reprinted by permission. From August B. Hollingshead, *Elmtown's Youth,* New York: Wiley, 1949, pp. 368-369, 387-388.

perience combined with their youth and family backgrounds severely limit their job opportunities. These factors, along with need, force them to take whatever jobs they can find. . . . Menial tasks, long hours, low pay, and little consideration from the employer produce discontent and frustration, which motivate the young worker to seek another job, only to realize after a few days or weeks that the new job is like the old one. This desire for a more congenial job, better pay, shorter hours, and a better employer gives rise to a drift from job to job. . . .

The association between education, job levels, and prestige in the social structure is so high that the person with more education moves into the high-ranking job and the person with little education into the low-ranking job. Furthermore, and this is the crucial fact from the viewpoint of the person's relation to the social structure, each tends to remain in the job channel in which he starts as a young worker. This is especially true if he has less than a high school education; then he starts as an unskilled menial and has few opportunities in later years to change to skilled labor, business, or the professions. Therefore, his chances to be promoted up through the several levels of the job channel in which he functions are severely limited. As the years pass, his position in the economic system becomes fixed, and another generation has become stable in the class structure.

EDUCATIONAL ORGANIZATIONS

A system of formal education exemplifies the large-scale organizations that comprise the larger society. The explicit goals of formal educational organizations are (1) transmitting the cultural tradition and (2) adding to it, especially adding cognitive culture (knowledge). Primary and secondary schools emphasize the first goal, culture transmission, whereas universities emphasize the second goal, research. What goes on in schools can be understood further by analyzing the functioning of schools and colleges in terms of the four requirements of interactive systems. How these requirements apply to a university was discussed in Chapter 1, and Chapter 10 contained a general discussion of the needs of socializing bureaucracies.

In the remaining two sections of this chapter, we shall consider two major educational organizations of industrial society, the secondary school and the university. In particular, we shall be interested in the separate cultures that develop within each of these organizations and their effect on the opportunities for intellectual achievement.

The Secondary School and Its Differentiated Cultures. One component of the cultural tradition of the school is contributed by teachers. Through the concepts and values absorbed in the course of professional training, through reading professional journals, and through continuing contact with their colleagues, teachers contribute professional values to the culture of the school. Profes-

United Press International

sional values are not necessarily concerned with the ultimate occupational placement of students; professional values depend on the central concerns of the leading educational philosophers and the ideologies of the centers of teacher training. Thus American educators have been as much concerned about the *social* adjustment of students ("life adjustment") as about occupational preparation.[28] Some try to promote wholesome family living, less juvenile delinquency, and better citizenship. But these are peripheral concerns of formal education and success or failure in this area should not be used to evaluate an educational system.

Whatever reasons teachers have for entering the profession, they are full-time employees of large-scale formal organizations. As such, they receive salaries and prefer larger to smaller remuneration, so school systems compete among themselves for superior teachers. School systems that pay high salaries attract more recruits and thus may select better-qualified teachers. Moreover, the educational system competes collectively for the services of superior college graduates against other industrial and governmental employers. American evidence shows that the teaching profession recruits less able college graduates than other occupations; furthermore, a considerable proportion of young teachers leave the profession for other fields, and these tend to be the better

[28] Martin Mayer, *The Schools,* New York: Harper, 1961, Chaps. 2 and 3. Myron Lieberman, *Education as a Profession,* Englewood Cliffs, N. J.: Prentice-Hall, 1956.

educated.[29] The lack of success of educational organizations in the competition for college graduates means that high schools must hire teachers who are inadequately prepared for the subjects they teach:[30]

> A study conducted by the National Council of Teachers of English of over 7000 high school English teachers, whose average experience was nine years, reports that "only 50.5 per cent had majored in English. One-third majored in a field with no relationship to English. Two-thirds rated themselves as poorly prepared to teach composition and oral skills, 90 per cent said they were poorly prepared to teach reading, and almost 50 per cent said they were poorly prepared to teach literature." A national study of junior and senior high school science and mathematics teachers sponsored by the National Science Foundation in 1960 and 1961 concludes that "a teacher who has less than eighteen semester hours of college work in a science does not have a substantial education in it, and we have seen that two-thirds of the physics classes, a third of the chemistry classes and upper level mathematics classes are taught by such teachers."

The frequency of poorly prepared teachers explains why the 1966 survey of educational opportunity in the United States turned up a correlation between the quality of teachers in a school and the intellectual achievement of its students.[31] Poor quality of teachers lowers the intellectual climate of the school as well as interfering with the transmission of information. The failure of school systems to attract and keep more qualified teachers has led to efforts to improve American education regardless of the competence of the average classroom teacher. University professors have worked to reshape the curriculum, initially in mathematics and the sciences, more recently in foreign languages, English, and the social sciences.[32] Thus, with the financial support of the National Science Foundation, the American Sociological Association sponsored Sociological Resources for Secondary Schools; S.R.S.S. prepared a complete course in sociology for high school as well as forty two-week units for use in a variety of social studies courses. Educational television, team teaching, and the use of such technological aids as computers and programmed instruction make it possible to have better education without necessarily having better teachers—not in every classroom anyway.

B. F. Skinner, the inventor of the teaching machine, puts the case for teacher-proof instruction diplomatically.[33] He argues that schools must become more "efficient" in order to cope with the problems of mass education, and he describes programmed instruction (the fundamental part of the teaching machine) as a step in this direction. The instructional program is a cunningly designed series of questions presented in such a way that the student must

[29] Martin Trow, "Two Problems in American Public Education," in Howard Becker, Ed., *Social Problems: A Modern Approach,* New York: Wiley, 1966, pp. 101-106.

[30] Reprinted by permission. From Trow, "Two Problems in American Public Education," p. 102. The quotations are from the original sources.

[31] Coleman, *Equality of Educational Opportunity,* pp. 316-319.

[32] Trow, "Two Problems in American Public Education," p. 100.

[33] B. F. Skinner, "Teaching Machines," *Science,* Vol. 128, October 1958, pp. 969-977.

learn the correct answer to one question before he is permitted to go on to the next. What are the advantages of teaching machines?

1. They make possible individualized instruction; the slow student and the bright student each learns at his own pace — something impossible in large classes. Thus teaching machines can cope with a common reason for educational failure: differences in learning speeds.
2. Teaching machines encourage the student to take an active part in the instructional process. The student must respond to the program correctly in order to advance to the next question; hence he cannot remain a passive recipient of information as he could if he lolled in front of a television set or sat inertly in a large classroom.
3. Teaching machines reinforce the student's correct response immediately — unlike the ordinary test situation where the student must wait several days to find out whether his answers are correct. This immediate feedback facilitates retention.

Skinner argues that a teaching machine is an approximation to an individual tutor. "Like a good tutor the machine presents just that material for which the student is ready. It asks him to take only that step which he is at the moment best equipped and most likely to take. Like a skillful tutor the machine helps the student to come up with the right answer. It does this in part through the orderly construction of the program and in part with techniques of hinting, prompting, suggesting. . . ." In short, the teaching machine is, according to Skinner, the least painful way to communicate most kinds of information to large numbers of students. But Skinner makes clear that programmed instruction is no mere presentational aid for the teacher — or even a way to multiply the impact of superior teachers (like closed-circuit television). He thinks that programmed instruction can do better what teachers now do in the classroom.

Secondary school teachers are not universally enthusiastic about the efforts of university professors to improve the curriculum and to make educational methods more efficient. They have their professional status at stake. If education can be improved while teacher quality remains the same and the educational level of the general population rises, the prestige and pay of teachers cannot rise appreciably. On the other hand, some evidence exists that beginning teachers do not think of teaching as a professional career anyway. A 1957 study of 7150 beginning American teachers showed that relatively few of them planned to remain in teaching. The women intended to leave teaching for homemaking responsibilities, and the men aspired to becoming educational administrators.[34]

A second component of the cultural tradition of the school is contributed by the agency defining the goals of the school. In most European coun-

---

[34] Ward S. Mason, Robert J. Dressel, and Robert K. Bain, "Sex Role and Career Orientations of Beginning Teachers," *Harvard Educational Review,* Vol. 29, Fall 1959, pp. 370-383.

tries, schools are extensions of the central government. In the United States, schools are controlled through locally elected (or appointed) boards of education.[35] Different as are these methods of channeling societal support to the school, both involve policy dilemmas. An obvious dilemma is the proportion of societal resources to be devoted to education rather than to other desirable goals. The agency defining these goals is particularly important because a school budget that may be considered satisfactory by one group may be totally inadequate to another. Professional educators have attempted to influence local communities, but the community does not always accept the definition of the problem offered by professionals, especially in the United States where educators are a weak professional group. This is partly because so many teachers are women, partly because many of them have been trained in teachers' colleges rather than in prestigious universities, and partly because local control over education encourages laymen to set educational goals.

Although formal education is a public responsibility in all industrial societies, at issue is the relative strength of the various voices claiming to speak on behalf of the public. Different societies allow the professional educator varying degrees of influence over educational policy. In England the teaching profession has a greater voice than in the United States both in setting educational goals and in their application.[36] The main reason for this difference is that the British system of national control over education minimizes parental influence over their children's education, whereas the American system of local control enables nonprofessionals in the community to interpret the educational task to the teacher. Another factor reinforcing the authority of teachers in England vis-à-vis parents is that British teachers are more likely than American teachers to be better educated than the parents of their students. A much greater proportion of the American population than of the British enroll in institutions of higher learning; this automatically makes for greater educational parity between American parents and teachers.[37]

Since the goals of schools depend on who controls formal education, the schools may be used to advance special purposes. One possibility is to use schools to compensate for the deficits in child motivation created by the family and the neighborhood. This has been suggested as a way to equalize the educational performance of children from different socioeconomic levels. Plans for compensatory education assume a commitment on the part of the society (as well as of the educational bureaucracy) to equality of educational *results* for social groups rather than to equality of educational *opportunity* for individuals. Even in the United States, where ethnic inequalities of educational

[35] Neal Gross, Ward S. Mason, and Alexander W. McEachern, *Explorations in Role Analysis: Studies of the School Superintendency Role,* New York: Wiley, 1958.

[36] George Baron and Asher Tropp, "Teachers in England and America," in A. H. Halsey, Jean Floud, and C. Arnold Anderson, *Education, Economy, and Society: A Reader in the Sociology of Education,* New York: Free Press of Glencoe, 1961, pp. 545-557.

[37] A. H. Halsey, Ed., *Ability and Educational Opportunity,* Paris: Organization of Economic Cooperation and Development, 1961, pp. 191-192.

results have aroused much concern, public support for this change in educational goals is problematic. Not only would compensatory education be vastly more expensive, if indeed it is possible for the school to equalize initial differences regardless of cost. It necessarily means more favorable treatment to children who seem least able. Although some people oppose this principle (many of George Wallace's ten million votes in the 1968 presidential election represented people who felt blacks were being treated too well by the government), New York City has conducted an experiment in compensatory education which has proven fairly successful. The More Effective Schools Program was started in 1964 in ten ghetto schools. These schools received extra teachers, social workers, and psychologists and more funds for supplies. A United States Department of Health, Education and Welfare study[38] has shown that students in these enriched schools learned somewhat more than students in other ghetto schools, although at a per pupil cost nearly twice that of ordinary schools. The Board of Education has increased the number of More Effective Schools; there are now 21. The existence of this compensatory program is encouraging to members of minority groups who felt that education in ghetto schools discriminated *against* them, but the implementation of the program depends on whether those who set educational goals are willing to discriminate *in their favor* until they can catch up.

The third component of the culture of the school is contributed by the students themselves. In the United States, college preparatory students, future dropouts, and youngsters whose formal educations will end with high school graduation interact within the comprehensive high school. This creates a different type of student subculture from Great Britain where a two-track system persists; "grammar" schools contain the academic youngsters and "secondary modern" schools contain vocationally oriented youngsters, largely of working-class origins. The student subculture in the American high school must cover a wider range of student backgrounds and interests than in European school systems where the two-track system is common. This necessity helps to explain why the student subcultures of American secondary schools often promote athletic and social success more ardently than academic success. In one major study, the student status systems in ten Midwest high schools were examined, five schools in small towns, one in a working-class suburb, one in a wealthy suburb, and three in cities of various sizes.[39] In answer to the question, "How would you most like to be remembered in school: as an athletic star, a brilliant student, or most popular?," a majority of boys in all the schools were more interested in being remembered as athletic or popular than as a brilliant student. The researcher explained the emphasis on athletic values as partly due to the fact that an outstanding athlete represents his school and not

[38] United States Department of Health, Education, and Welfare, *It Works: More Effective Schools, New York City,* Washington, D.C.: Government Printing Office, 1969.

[39] James S. Coleman, "The Adolescent Subculture and Academic Achievement," *American Journal of Sociology,* Vol. 65, January 1960, pp. 337-347.

himself alone when he plays on a varsity team. "The outstanding student, in contrast, has little or no way to bring glory to his school. His victories are always personal, often at the expense of his classmates, who are forced to work harder to keep up with him." Professor Coleman inferred from his research that the student culture tends to deemphasize academic achievement because academic achievement is *individual;* therefore the superior performance of one student necessarily involves the relative failure of others.[40] Especially in a comprehensive high school containing a heterogeneous mix of intellectual potentialities, consistent emphasis on academic achievement would be divisive, a threat to social integration. Athletic achievement, on the other hand, occurs within a framework of interschool competition. The athletic triumph of an individual does not belong to him alone; the entire school, including nonathletes, participates in it vicariously. Hence *interschool* athletic competition promotes the social integration of the school as *intraschool* competition for grades does not. Coleman has suggested that establishing *academic* contests between schools would enable the brilliant student to contribute to the glory of his school and thereby make it possible for even unsuccessful students to identify with scholastic success. The divisiveness of intraschool competition for grades might diminish because intellectual achievement would be evaluated in collective as well as individual terms. Under such a structural arrangement the student culture could shift toward greater emphasis on intellectual values.

For Coleman, the anti-intellectual character of student culture is a reaction against a threat to school solidarity posed by academic competition *as presently organized.* For Talcott Parsons, the anti-intellectual character of student culture is due to a more fundamental aspect of contemporary society.[41] According to Parsons, high school students realize that their occupational futures depend on their academic records. From an instrumental point of view, they are allowing athletic or extracurricular activities to distract them from mobilizing their full intellectual potentialities toward attaining their goal. This cold-blooded rationality does not take account of their emotional uncertainties ("hang-ups"). Some students fear they are not performing well enough to get into college (or into the college of their choice); popularity seems more attainable. Other students, the intellectually able offspring of parents of low socioeconomic status, may be tempted by the occupational opportunities offered by higher education, yet be reluctant to repudiate parental and neighborhood values. Athletic interests enable them to keep a foot in both camps. In short, Parsons suggests that, far from being indifferent to the school's effect on their futures, many high school students are so deeply concerned with the competition that they cannot afford consciously to admit it. Surface preoccupation with sports and popularity in the student culture is necessary to ease the emotional strain. They are sidebets for most students and are recognized

---

[40] James S. Coleman, "Academic Achievement and the Structure of Competition," *Harvard Educational Review,* Vol. 29, Fall 1959, pp. 330-351.

[41] Parsons, "The School Class."

as ephemeral. For a very few, professional sports, the entertainment world, or politics might offer a career.

Thus Parsons, like Coleman, argues that the academic achievement value is too threatening to be given unlimited scope. The difference between them is that Parsons stresses the intrapsychic threat to the individual of staking everything on scholastic success, whereas Coleman stresses the threat to community solidarity of providing only one path to social recognition. They agree that the student culture helps cope with some of the emotional strains of the student role. This explanation of the anti-intellectual current in *high school* culture gains added force from studies of students who drop out of *college*.[42] A surprisingly large number of college casualties are students with the intellectual capacity to do college work who are "unmotivated." Seeming lack of motivation often conceals ambivalence. A student wants to please his parents, who expect him to become an engineer; he is interested in philosophy, not engineering; he compromises by flunking out. Another student goes to a first-rate college after a high school career during which he established his self-concept as a brilliant student. Even though he worked hard during his freshman year, his grades place him at the middle, not the top, of his class. His identity collapses, and he withdraws from college to think things over.[43] Sometimes the stakes can be *too* high.

The Rise of Multiversities. The university was an invention of medieval Europe; the multiversity is the emerging educational institution of industrial societies. "University" is a term stressing the unity of knowledge, an assumption of the medieval curriculum. Considering that the modern university no longer makes this assumption—its curriculum ranges from geophysics to hotel management—Clark Kerr, former president of the University of California, suggested that "multiversity" is the more appropriate name. In order to understand how the University of Bologna, an association of students founded in the eleventh century, and the University of Paris, an association of teachers founded in the twelfth century, evolved into highly differentiated multiversities like the University of California, which enrolled about 36,000 undergraduates and 15,000 graduate students on various separate campuses in 1960, it is necessary to understand the changing functions of higher education over the centuries.[44] Originally the pope brought universities into being as self-governing scholastic corporations; faculty and students were considered clerics whether they had taken holy orders or not; and the local bishop exercised only minimal

[42] John Summerskill, "Dropouts from College," in Nevitt Sanford, Ed., *The American College,* New York: Wiley, 1962, pp. 627-657.

[43] Arthur L. Stinchcombe calls this identity crisis of the superior student "the prodigy syndrome." See his article, "On Getting 'Hungup' and Other Assorted Illnesses," *Johns Hopkins Magazine,* Vol. 18, Winter 1966, pp. 25-30.

[44] A. H. Halsey, "The Changing Functions of Universities in Advanced Industrial Societies," *Harvard Educational Review,* Vol. 30, Spring 1960, pp. 119-127; Joseph Ben-David and Awraham Zloczower, "Universities and Academic Systems in Modern Societies," *European Journal of Sociology,* Vol. 3, Spring 1962, pp. 45-84.

supervision.[45] The medieval university concerned itself with theological and humanistic scholarship, but unlike the modern secular university, its scholarship assumed that Christian faith and the power of reason led directly to truth. Empirical investigations were inconceivable. The universities produced a tiny class of professionals: mainly theologians, lawyers, and physicians.

The secularization of learning proceeded slowly, facilitated by the corporate autonomy of universities and their theory of academic freedom. During the eighteenth century, higher education and theological training were still intertwined. In the American colonies a majority of the early graduates of Harvard, Yale, and the other colonial colleges became clergymen.[46] But even after universities and colleges gained a measure of independence vis-à-vis the church, they remained conservative. University attendance was less an opportunity for the intellectually able than an ascriptive right for members of the aristocracy. Oxford and Cambridge aimed at producing gentlemen, persons whose conduct and ideas were suitable for the station on which they were destined to live. This meant familiarity with the languages, the literature, and the ideas that gentlemen were expected to know. It meant extracurricular education also: an accent from Oxford or a dueling scar from Heidelberg. Grades were not important because the young men who attended a university had a place waiting for them in the top rank of their society; it was their birthright. The "gentleman C" dates from an era in the history of higher education when *who* one was overshadowed *what* one learned.

The scientific revolution gave the universities a new function — although the universities did not wish to embrace it. As a distinguished historian of education put it, "the scientific revolution occurred not through, but in spite of, the English universities.[47] Because developments in physics, chemistry, biology, and mathematics are intimately related to economic and technological change, industrial societies needed *the systematic production of new knowledge*. When established universities were not prepared to satisfy this demand, new universities, institutes, and research centers were created. While Oxford and Cambridge wavered between being cloistered finishing schools for the élite and the means whereby new knowledge was transmitted to the administrative, professional, and research personnel required in an advanced society, the universities of London, Manchester, Birmingham, Leeds, and Liverpool came into being. Oxford and Cambridge at first failed to recognize the legitimacy of illuminating a scientific and technological age. But eventually they joined the academic procession.

The English universities did not embrace science and technology as en-

---

[45] Joseph Ben-David, "Universities," *International Encyclopedia of the Social Sciences,* New York: Macmillan, 1968, Vol. 16, pp. 191-199.

[46] Richard Hofstadter and C. De Witt Hardy, *The Development and Scope of Higher Education in the United States,* New York: Columbia University Press, 1952, pp. 6-9.

[47] Sir Eric Ashby, *Technology and the Academics: An Essay on Universities and the Scientific Revolution,* New York: Macmillan, 1958, p. 13.

Charles Rotkin — Photography for Industry

thusiastically as did the German or the American universities, but by the middle of the *nineteenth* century, Oxford and Cambridge had both humanistic and scientific commitments. By the middle of the *twentieth* century, Sir Charles Snow created an intellectual stir by writing about "the two cultures" (the humanities and the sciences) and the chasm between them.[48] Some English and French universities are still prisoners of their pasts. They give less emphasis than American or Soviet universities to applied science and to organized research because they are dominated by scholars who underestimate the relevance of science or who have exclusively humanistic interests.[49] As a result, English and French business executives and engineers are less likely to have university degrees than their American or Soviet counterparts.[50] The Soviet Union has gone farther than any other industrial society in establishing a scientific-technological ideal for higher education.[51] This vocational emphasis

[48] Charles P. Snow, *The Two Cultures and the Scientific Revolution,* Cambridge, England: Cambridge University Press, 1959.

[49] Ben-David and Zloczower, "Universities and Academic Systems in Modern Societies," p. 82.

[50] Seymour Martin Lipset and Reinhard Bendix, *Social Mobility in Industrial Society,* Berkeley: University of California Press, 1959, pp. 40-42.

[51] Nicholas DeWitt, "Soviet Science Education and the School Reform," *School and Society,* Vol. 88, Summer 1960, pp. 297-300.

in Soviet education stems from a belief on the part of Soviet leaders that industrial managers and government officials need such training. In Western Europe and in the United States, a liberal arts education is more acceptable as preparation for executive roles and government service.

Before assuming that the Soviet Union is correct in its rejection of liberal education, recall that for 2000 years Chinese emperors selected ministers, generals, and government officials from candidates who had passed examinations in *Confucian literature*.[52] It was assumed that cultivated minds could apply their wisdom to a wide range of problems. Recall further that Julius Caesar and other military geniuses of the Ancient World did not attend military academies. Possibly industrial societies have evolved to the point where native talent and humanistic education are not enough and therefore specialized training is crucial. Certainly, technical education is necessary for *some* industrial occupations—chemical engineering, for example. Certainly, too, the *belief* that a technical or scientific education is essential for factory managers can result in their being selected on the basis of training in engineering. But this is an illustration of the self-fulfilling prophecy and not proof that such training improves performance in the role. Urban industrial societies need more scientists and technicians than previous generations dreamed of producing, but whether they require a monolithic emphasis remains an open question.

In the United States, where undergraduate enrollments reached 38 per cent of the 18- to 21-year-old population in 1966, the emphasis on applied subjects is great.[53] American educational institutions can be classified in terms of their postures toward vocational preparation. The small, selective liberal-arts colleges teach the arts and sciences for their educational value and assume that a well-educated man is not disadvantaged in the labor market. (A study of the careers of a large number of graduates from a variety of American colleges provides empirical support for this assumption; graduates of Ivy League colleges earned more than graduates of other colleges—even with the economic background of the family controlled.[54]) Community junior colleges try to be "practical"; they teach an array of service and vocational courses. The large state universities are committed both to liberal and to vocational education, usually in different divisions, but with much overlapping. Generally speaking, students from working-class backgrounds are more likely than students from middle-class families to perceive higher education as vocational education, to choose applied curricula and courses, and to attend municipal commuting colleges or state universities, where this type of education is available. Thus the increasing rate of college·and university attendance—an average increase

[52] H. H. Gerth and C. Wright Mills, *From Max Weber: Essays in Sociology,* New York: Oxford University Press, 1946, pp. 416-444.

[53] Bureau of the Census, *Statistical Abstract of the United States: 1969,* Washington, D.C.: Government Printing Office, 1969, p. 124. See also Martin Trow, "The Democratization of Higher Education in America," *European Journal of Sociology,* Vol. 3, Fall 1962, pp. 231-262.

[54] Patricia Salter West, "Social Mobility among College Graduates," in Reinhard Bendix and Seymour Martin Lipset, Eds., *Class, Status and Power,* Glencoe, Ill.: Free Press, 1953, p. 476.

of 1 per cent per year of the age cohort in the United States since the end of the Second World War—means that American higher education is increasingly serving vocationally oriented students.

Vocational training is not a new function of higher education. Universities have long been responsible for training physicians, lawyers, and the clergy. What is new is the proportion of the age cohort (1) who seek higher education and (2) who regard higher education as vocational preparation—not only in the traditional professions, the pure sciences, or technical specialties like aeronautical engineering, but in applied fields like business administration and elementary education. Some critics of the heavy emphasis on vocational applications of higher education have pointed out that such emphasis may delude students into thinking they are being perpared for high-level occupations when they are not. In a changing culture, *general* education may be better vocational preparation than elaborate specialization. One implication of Margaret Mead's point that education must continue throughout life is that premature specialization does not produce an individual who can make all the readjustments demanded by a changing culture. Perhaps so. Perhaps the multiversity overdoes the effort to be practical. But no one advocates returning to the conception of education for an established élite. Not everyone who attends the multiversity will achieve high socioeconomic status, but higher education does increase the likelihood—partly because knowledge is instrumentally valuable, partly because of a widespread cultural definition of knowledge as valuable.

We have been speaking about the multiversity as though it were synonymous with higher education. In fact, of 5,570,000 students enrolled in degree programs in the United States in the fall of 1965, only 2,304,000 were attending universities.[55] The rest were in junior colleges, in liberal arts colleges not affiliated with universities, and in independent professional schools (teachers colleges, technological schools, theological academies, art colleges, and the like). Although more students are enrolled in other institutions of higher education than in universities, the university is the heart of modern higher education in several senses. First, universities, not independent colleges or even professional schools, are centers of the knowledge explosion. Surveys show that the priority goal of the modern university is research, the training of future researchers, and providing conditions that facilitate scholarly productivity.[56] This priority means less attention of the faculty to the general education of undergraduates enrolled in arts and sciences colleges of universities, and faculty neglect has been one grievance of student rebels.[57] But priority on

[55] Bureau of the Census, *Statistical Abstract of the United States: 1968,* Washington, D.C.: Government Printing Office, 1968, p. 128.

[56] Edward Gross, "Universities as Organizations: A Research Approach," *American Sociological Review,* Vol. 33, August 1968, pp. 518-544.

[57] See, for example, Seymour M. Lipset and Sheldon S. Wolin, Eds., *The Berkeley Student Revolt: Facts and Interpretations,* Garden City, N. Y.: Doubleday Anchor, 1965, and The Cox Commission, *Crisis at Columbia,* New York: Vintage, 1968.

the production of knowledge is not the arbitrary preference of administrators and faculty. It stems from the increasing appreciation that government and industry have for new ideas. Ever since the New Deal of Franklin Roosevelt, the American government has made increasing use of scientific consultants from the universities, not only in the natural sciences but in the social sciences. Industry, too, treats knowledge as a scarce resource; 361,000 engineers and scientists were employed by American industry *in research and development activities alone* in 1966.[58] This was a third of the total number of engineers and scientists employed by American industry in all capacities. Yet industry looks beyond its own laboratories and personnel toward researchers at universities, so much so that a factor in the location of new plants, often more important than low taxes or cheap labor, is proximity to universities. Clark Kerr cites industrial development in the Boston and San Francisco Bay areas as a concrete illustration of this point and goes on to argue that the university is undergoing a transformation in response to governmental and industrial requests for advice:[59]

> Basic to this transformation is the growth of the "knowledge industry," which is coming to permeate government and business and to draw into it more and more people raised to higher and higher levels of skill. The production, distribution, and consumption of "knowledge" in all its forms is said to account for 29 per cent of gross national product...; and "knowledge production" is growing at about twice the rate of the rest of the economy.... What the railroads did for the second half of the last century and the automobile for the first half of this century may be done for the second half of this century by the knowledge industry: that is, to serve as the focal point for national growth. And the university is at the center of the knowledge process.

Multiversities are at the center of the knowledge industry because they represent a fusion of the traditional teaching function (culture transmission) with the *development* of scholarly disciplines through research. In societies oriented to the instrumental value of knowledge, it makes sense to select teachers who are also contributors to the process of the advancement of knowledge.[60] Thus the graduate departments of universities provide the standards of disciplinary competence used to evaluate academic people in independent colleges and professional schools. It may be that undergraduate teaching is less good at universities than at independent liberal arts colleges, but without the universities to set academic standards, professors at liberal arts colleges would not be as good as they are.

Just as there are separate cultural strands in the secondary schools, so there are differentiated cultures at colleges and universities. Within the student body

---

[58] *Statistical Abstract of the United States: 1968,* p. 529.

[59] Clark Kerr, *The Uses of the University,* Cambridge, Mass.: Harvard University Press, 1963, pp. 87-88.

[60] Talcott Parsons, "New Roles for Academic Facilities," Unpublished address at the 21st National Conference on Higher Education, Chicago, March 15, 1966.

alone, sociologists have identified four distinct meanings of education.[61] For vocationally oriented students (probably the majority), higher education is preparation for middle-class jobs. For academically oriented students, college is a chance to master a body of knowledge. For "collegiate" types of students, higher education is an opportunity to enjoy sociability, sports, and sex without parental supervision. For nonconformist students, higher education offers a chance to develop a rebellious identity in a relatively permissive environment. The character of a particular college owes much to the mix of student subcultures within it, although faculty and administration subcultures are also relevant.

In view of the knowledge explosion and the contribution of higher education to it, collegiate and nonconformist subcultures seem to interfere with the long-run (adult) interests of students. Pot smoking and varsity athletics jeopardize one's studies equally, and grades assume greater importance as larger proportions of college graduates go on to graduate and professional schools. On the other hand, the pressure becomes unbearable when there are no side-bets. Even for above-average students—and only half the student body can be above average—the dating game or the football team may constitute psychologically necessary safety valves. The following fictitious letter is a satire on the lack of intellectual values on the part of football coaches, but it is also an indirect commentary on the failure of some professors to appreciate the high stakes of academic competition:[62]

Department of English
October, Any Year

Dear Coach Musselman:

Remembering our discussions of your football men who are having troubles in English, I have decided to ask you, in turn, for help.

We feel that Paul Spindles, one of our most promising scholars, has a chance for a Rhodes Scholarship, which would be a great thing for him and for our college. Paul has the academic record for this award but we find that the aspirant is also required to have other excellences, and ideally should have a good record in athletics. Paul is weak. He tries hard, but he has trouble in athletics.

We propose that you give some special consideration to Paul as a varsity player, putting him, if possible, in the backfield of the football team. In this way, we can show a better college record to the committee deciding on the Rhodes Scholarships. We realize that Paul will be a problem on the field, but—as you have often said—co-operation between our department and yours is highly desirable and we do expect Paul to try hard, of course. During intervals of study we shall coach him as much as we can. His work in English Club and on the debate team will force him to miss many practices, but we intend to see that he carries an old football around to bounce (or whatever one does with a football) during in-

---

[61] Burton R. Clark and Martin Trow, "Determinants of the Sub-Cultures of College Students: The Organizational Context," in Theodore M. Newcomb and Everett K. Wilson, Eds., *College Peer Groups,* Chicago: Aldine, 1967, pp. 17-70.

[62] Reprinted by permission. From William E. Stafford, (untitled), *College English,* Vol. 16, April 1955, p. 453.

tervals in his work. We expect Paul to show entire good will in his work for you, and though he will not be able to begin football practice till late in the season, he will finish the season with good attendance.

Benjamin Plotinus
Chairman, English Department

CONCLUSION

In an urban industrial society, the cultural tradition is so vast and it is being augmented so rapidly that informal methods of transmitting ideas and skills to the younger generation are insufficient to the task. Formal educational institutions have been established in the industrial societies to guarantee that all children know how to read, write, and do simple computations. Mass elementary education has not been enough to equip children for adult roles, however, and therefore educational levels are still rising. Moreover, adult education under a wide variety of sponsorships—industry, the armed services, voluntary associations—attempts to compensate for the continuing obsolescence of childhood education. A system of formal education develops traditions of its own, which sometimes interfere with learning and, therefore, with producing sufficient numbers of highly educated youngsters to fill managerial, technical, and professional roles. An anti-intellectual working-class culture is such an interference. So are student cultures in certain schools.

The occupational structure of an industrial society requires, as industrialization advances, increasing proportions of better-educated white-collar workers and less unskilled labor. But an industrial society does not require high levels of education for all workers. Hence the school system attempts to guarantee that all children possess a minimum of useful knowledge and skills; above this minimal level, the population is increasingly differentiated in accordance with additional educational accomplishment. Differential educational achievements is the major mechanism for allocating youngsters to various status levels in industrial societies. Education has been related to social status in preindustrial societies also, but the educational horse followed the status cart. Preindustrial educational differentiation was either humanistic or dogmatic; special education was defined as suitable for the élite—the gentry in feudal China or preindustrial England. Industrial education, on the other hand, tends to be pragmatic, technical, vocational; it *generates* social status instead of being a *result* of it.

The rise of multiversities reflects institutionally the dynamic role of knowledge in contemporary societies. Multiversities are places where intellectually able students learn what they need to know in order to play high-level occupational roles, where social allocation occurs in the process of culture transmission. But they are also places where the knowledge explosion is occurring. And the knowledge explosion has provided a built-in predisposition for social change, as we shall see in Chapter 14 where social change will be discussed at greater length.

SOME SIGNIFICANT LITERATURE ON FORMAL EDUCATION

David P. Ausubel, *Maori Youth,* Wellington, New Zealand: Victoria University of Wellington Publications in Psychology, No. 14, 1961. Although New Zealand makes great efforts to achieve racial equality, interviews with 50 white and 50 Maori secondary school boys in two communities, one rural and the other urban, show that Maori youths are educationally disadvantaged in both. They have as high vocational and educational aspirations as white youngsters, but they are less likely to implement their ambitions through successful school performance, partly because of white prejudice and partly because the Maori culture does not prepare them adequately to compete successfully in school. Apparently, different as New Zealand is from the United States in many ways, the educational difficulties of racial minorities are similar in the two countries. This summary is based on a review by Richard Robbins, *American Sociological Review,* Vol. 27, February 1962, pp. 106-107.

Howard S. Becker, Blanche Geer, and Everett C. Hughes, *Making the Grade: The Academic Side of College Life,* New York: Wiley, 1968. This study of the undergraduate college of the University of Kansas focuses on grades as a reward for academic effort. It concludes that the pursuit of grades is an obstacle to learning and recommends the elimination of cumulative averages and perhaps of grades. In a skeptical review, Eldon Wegner points out (1) that the field study technique (utilizing a handful of observers) seems inappropriate for studying a population of 7000 students who probably vary considerably in their attitudes toward grades, (2) that the recommendation to eliminate grades seems to rest on other considerations than their ineffectiveness as a motivator of academic effort, and (3) that there seems to be little reason to suppose that students would curtail the extracurricular activities that they say they enjoy "for the austere life of a scholar" in the absence of a system of institutional recognition. See the review by Eldon L. Wegner, *American Sociological Review,* Vol. 34, August 1969, pp. 591-592. An eminent clinical psychologist, David McClelland, has independently concluded that the American educational system searches for too narrow a range of achievement capacity through grades and scores on standardized tests: "Overstressing academic merit can discourage young people with types of talent that are very important for our society and can create in them a discontent and sense of frustration that lasts a lifetime." David C. McClelland, "Encouraging Excellence," *Daedalus,* Vol. 90, Fall 1961, p. 714. See also Christopher Jencks and David Riesman, *The Academic Revolution,* Garden City, N.Y.: Doubleday, 1968, for a discussion of the impact of graduate schools on undergraduate education. Because graduate schools serve to train professional experts (an occupational élite), a growing proportion of undergraduates seek to enter them, thus fostering preoccupation with grades as well as a choice of courses attractive to admissions committees in the graduate schools.

Orville G. Brim, Jr., *Sociology and the Field of Education,* New York: Russell Sage Foundation, 1958. "Education has the inescapable problem of somehow integrating the various aims of its two major bodies of personnel, the educators and the students." Thus begins this survey of sociological research in the fields of education. After examining the *goals* that have been assigned to educational institutions, Dr. Brim considers research on the *allocation of societal resources* to educational systems, including differential allocation depending on the clientele served. In these areas research is scarce, and Dr. Brim points out gaps that need filling. When he comes to discuss the *allocation of personnel,* which includes selection and promotion both of teachers and students, research is more plentiful. The *role prescriptions* for teachers include expectations governing community behavior, classroom interaction with students, and professional associations. All of these have been studied. The *role prescriptions* for students include classroom behavior and community participation—although neither of these aspects of the student role has been investigated systematically. On the other hand, the third aspect of the student role, relationships with fellow students, has received much attention. Dr. Brim concludes with a consideration of the consequences of different types and quantities of education on the student.

Burton R. Clark, "The 'Cooling-Out' Function in Higher Education," *American Journal of Sociology,* Vol. 65, May 1960, pp. 569-576. According to Clark, the major function of the junior college in the United States is to reconcile students of mediocre intellectual ability but high ambitions to *not* completing a four-year college. Of course, the junior college also provides a second chance for students who did poorly in high school because of economic or social deprivation or because of personal circumstances. But its major social role, according to Clark, is the cooling-out one: gradually persuading the mediocre student, partly through counseling, partly through the experience of course failure, partly through the provision of alternative goals, that he should surrender the dream of completing a four-year college and settle for something else. Instead of the short, sharp shock of refusal to admit the student who seems destined to fail or the equally traumatic dismissal for academic failure, the junior college has mechanisms for delaying the denial and thereby cushioning the blow to the individual ego. Although Clark discusses mainly the junior college, his analysis is relevant to four-year colleges that shunt less able students into "less demanding" programs and to the process by which high school guidance counselors seek to allocate students into college prep, business, or general courses. For a more complete account of Clark's study of junior colleges, see Burton R. Clark, *The Open Door College: A Case Study,* New York: McGraw-Hill, 1960.

Neal Gross, *Who Runs Our Schools?,* New York: Wiley, 1958. Lengthy interviews with 105 superintendents of school and 508 school-board members in Massachusetts show the professional and lay pressures on school superintendents in the United States. Cross-pressures are analyzed from the point of view of the school superintendent, from the point of view of the school-board member, and, finally, from the point of view of the researcher. This summary is based on a review by Robert J. Havighurst, *American Sociological Review,* Vol. 24, August 1959, p. 605. See also Neal Gross, Ward S. Mason, and Alexander W. McEachern, *Explorations in Role Analysis: Studies of the School Superintendency Role,* New York: Wiley, 1958.

Morris Janowitz, *Institution Building in Urban Education,* New York: Russell Sage Foundation, 1969. This book utilizes sociological theory to examine the effectiveness of school systems in American cities and especially in slum neighborhoods. The conclusion reached by Professor Janowitz is that urban school systems are not well organized to accomplish their new mission in a contemporary society: "to accept responsibility for all youngsters who are not college bound until they develop levels of personal maturity sufficient for them to enter the labor market" (p. 9). The reason for this failure is that reforms have been piecemeal rather than informed by an overall plan for the reorganization of a social institution. Janowitz shows how a model based on a greater recognition of socialization responsibilities as well as academic goals has better prospects for success than current practice. Among the implications of this model are the following:

1. The classroom teacher should be the paramount classroom authority rather than surrendering functions to curriculum specialists or disciplinarians. The justification for this emphasis on a generalist rather than on specialists is (a) that the organization of materials is less important than the mobilization of student interest in subject matter and (b) that socializers are more effective if they have continuing personal relations with those they are socializing.
2. Programs of compensatory education should utilize "intensive human effort rather than

elaborate but impersonal technology" (p. 49). The motivation to learn, especially for a young-ster who is falling behind, is enormously strengthened when he believes that the teacher cares about him. Therefore individual tutoring tends to be more effective than instruction in groups, even small ones.

3. The teaching style in the classroom should maximize peer group support and utilize subpro-fessionals and volunteers rather than emphasizing solo virtuosity.
4. The boundary between the school and the community should be permeable, partly on the assumption that the classroom is not the sole locus of learning, partly to increase the account-ability of teachers and principals for the authority they wield over children.

James McEvoy and Abraham Miller, *Black Power and Student Rebellion: Conflict on the American Campus,* Belmont, Calif.: Wadsworth, 1969. This book of readings describes disruptions on several campuses—San Francisco State, Columbia, the University of Chicago, Duke, Stanford, and the University of California at Berkeley. In addition to these descriptions, other articles provide analysis of the forces making for campus confrontations: the ideology of the New Left, the in-creasing militance of black college students, and the widespread resentment of college students of paternalistic supervision of their private lives. The editors deliberately sought to include a wide spectrum of value commitments among their contributors. Radicals and conservatives are repre-sented, as are blacks and whites, students and professors.

David Riesman, "The Influence of Student Culture and Faculty Values in the American College," *Year Book of Education, 1959,* Yonkers-on-Hudson, N.Y.: World, 1959, Chap. 2. Riesman reviews a number of researches directly or indirectly concerned with the influence of student subcultures on the values of college students. He concedes that student subcultures may work at cross-purposes with faculty values, especially at large universities. School spirit "is all too easily achieved at those big American state universities of the second and third rank where student solidarity, enshrined in fraternities and sororities, confronts a faculty culture so comparatively feeble and unprotected that nothing the latter would do could readily influence the former; students at such colleges, when asked to read a book they think beyond them, or which is not a free text, will turn in blank pages on the exam." On the other hand, Riesman notes, public-opinion polls make clear that the values of the college educated differ from the values of the rest of the population. Unless it is assumed that these differences can be entirely attributed to self-selection among youngsters who go to college, student cultures do not prevent the faculty from wielding some influence. For an examination of the student subculture in medical schools, see Everett C. Hughes, Howard S. Becker, and Blanche Geer, "Student Culture and Academic Effort," in Nevitt Sanford, Ed., *The American College: A Psychological and Social Interpretation of the Higher Learning,* New York: Wiley, 1962, pp. 515-530.

Robert Singleton and Paul Bullock, "Some Problems in Minority-Group Education in the Los Angeles Public Schools," *Journal of Negro Education,* Vol. 32, Spring 1963, pp. 137-145. During the 1959–1960 and 1960–1961 academic years four Los Angeles high schools enrolled predom-inantly Negro students, and two high schools enrolled mainly Mexican-American youngsters. In each of those years, the proportion of enrollees who left these six schools without indicating an intention of entering another school was more than 20 per cent of the total enrollment. In Los Angeles high schools as a whole, however, the dropout rate was 10.5 per cent in 1959–1960 and 11.1 per cent in 1960–1961. Thus Negro and Mexican-American high school students attended school in a milieu where dropping out rather than graduating was a more common expectation. Students expecting to quit school probably lack motivation to do homework conscientiously or attend regulary. In such a situation discipline problems are chronic. A negativistic student sub-culture is also characteristic of secondary modern schools in Great Britain, not because the students are predominantly from ethnic minorities but simply because most of them leave school to go to work at the age of 15. See John Webbs, "The Sociology of a School," *British Journal of Sociology,* Vol. 13, September 1962, pp. 264-272. For a study showing that the sociocultural climate in a secondary school influences the grades and the aspirations of youngsters beyond what could be expected from knowledge of *individual* student characteristics, see Alan B. Wilson, "Residential Segregation of Social Classes and Aspirations of High School Boys," *American Sociological Review,* Vol. 24, December 1959, pp. 836-845.

William H. Whyte, Jr. "The Training of Organization Man," in *The Organization Man,* Garden City, N.Y.: Doubleday, 1957, pp. 69-152. Whyte argues in this section of his book that American colleges are trying too hard to prepare youngsters to take their places in a technological society. He deplores the growth of enrollments in vocationally oriented curricula like business adminis-tration not only because he believes that a liberal-arts education is intellectually "liberating" but also because he does not agree that future business men need "... more and more ... training in the minutiae of organization skills ... " To be sure, he notes (with obvious sadness) (1) that corporate recruiting procedures penalize the liberal-arts major as against the vocationally "trained" undergraduate and (2) that the growing vocational emphasis of the colleges is helping to reduce the discontinuity between education and work. "For the senior who is headed for the corporation [to join its training program] ... the locale shifts; the training continues, for at the same time that the colleges have been changing their curriculum to suit the corporation, the corporation has responded by setting up its own campuses and classrooms."

Part IV

SOCIAL PROCESSES IN URBAN INDUSTRIAL SOCIETIES

What is social process? A process is a change, and indeed the topics considered here are more closely related to change than to stability. But social processes have been discussed in every chapter because they are the dynamic aspect of social structures. It is a matter of emphasis. The roles discussed in Chapters 6 to 11 stressed stability over flux. In Chapters 12 to 15, on the other hand, flux is more prominent.

Chapter 12 (Social Stratification and Mobility) considers the evaluative processes of industrial societies and how these generate (1) various levels of prestige and (2) upward and downward flow of individuals from one level to another. Chapter 13 (Deviance and Social Control) treats the failure of initial and later socialization to produce fully conforming role players. Chapter 14 (Social Change) discusses how individuals react to cultural developments in such a way as to alter established patterns of interaction. Finally, Chapter 15 (Social Integration and Disintegration) seeks to call attention to those processes that unify contemporary societies as well as those that disrupt them.

An important social process is role allocation: the assignment to the individual of obligations in an interactive system. No one chapter deals with role allocation; it is analyzed at various places throughout the book. For example, a society's emphasis on ascription or achievement (discussed in Chapter 7) really is an implicit decision about personnel allocation. Industrial societies give unusual weight to performance criteria (achievement) compared to preindustrial societies. Industrial societies also give unusual weight to individual preferences. Marriages, fraternity membership, and jobs are contracted for in a selection process involving mutual choice. A combination of voluntary choice of the role on the part of the role seeker and of freedom on the part of the role allocator to accept or reject the role seeker in terms of the abilities the role calls for is characteristic of industrial societies. What is called "competition" includes situations where qualities are being sifted (as in a beauty contest) as well as those where role allocators judge performance, but qualities tend to be a less important basis of role allocation as societies modernize. The erosion of an "ascriptive base" of role allocation in urban industrial societies is what makes the process a "rat race":[1]

> [Competition] expands enormously the range of alternative roles available to the individual but, by the same token, he cannot claim a role merely by virtue of being born. He must earn the right to a role. He must demonstrate qualities or perform actions which are then evaluated by society and compared with the qualities and performances of all the other people who wish to occupy that role. In short, a competitive system is a little like a jungle. Only the fittest obtain the highest rewards of the system. You live in a world filled with rivals and potential rivals, with persons who want your job, your reputation in the community, your girl friend. Lewis Carroll might have been describing a competitive system when he had the Red Queen say in Through the Looking Glass, "Now, here, you see, it takes all the running you can do, to keep in the same place. If you want to get somewhere else, you must run at least twice as fast as that!" In a competitive society, every aspect of life tends to be defined as a contest, and one's sense of adequacy, of worthiness, of security, and even of pleasure hinges on whether one is a winner or a loser.

The concept of role allocation calls attention to the requirements of the role structure. From the individual's viewpoint, role allocation is choice. From the societal viewpoint, it is a little like putting billiard balls into pockets in a game of pool. The passage of personalities through the role structure as people are born, grow to maturity, and die changes society in a sense. Different mixes of personalities give a different character to an interactive system. But sociologists do not regard the mere passage of personnel through the role structure as social change, however much individuals moving from role to role feel that the world is changing, unless the role structure itself changes. Role allocation, social mobility, and deviance that is contained are social processes that do not transform the role structure. Thus some social processes perpetuate an existing role structure, whereas other processes tend to change it. Both tendencies exist in every society.

One important change in industrial societies is increasing social differentiation. Although occupations were already differentiated a century ago, they are today more radically segregated from kinship, partly because

---

[1] Harry C. Bredemeier and Jackson Toby, *Social Problems in America*, New York: Wiley, 1960, p. 105.

the separation of work and residence is more widespread now than it was then, partly because a higher proportion of the labor force works for bureaucratic organizations oblivious of the kinship ties of their employees, and partly because a greater proportion of the activities of society are carried on in occupational rather than family contexts.[2] For example, the college professor role in 1870 was less specialized than it is today, not only because there are many more academic disciplines than existed a century ago but also because the professor was expected to relate to students on a more personal basis. Corresponding to the college obligation to act *in loco parentis* was the expectation that the professor would inculcate morals as well as ancient history. The term "college community" accurately reflected these primary group relations between faculty and students. Today, the roles of the professor and of the student are more segmental; each brings a smaller proportion of his total self to the classroom. This social change in higher education is paralleled in the occupational structure generally. A necessary accompaniment of increased differentiation is more emphasis on social integration; we shall return to this problem in Chapter 15.

[2] Talcott Parsons and Winston White, "The Link between Character and Society," in Seymour Martin Lipset and Leo Lowenthal, Eds., *Culture and Social Character: The Work of David Riesman Reviewed,* New York: Free Press of Glencoe, 1961, pp. 109-111.

SOCIAL STRATIFICATION
AND MOBILITY

The *content* of expected behavior—what the individual does or is supposed to do in a role—is the *instrumental* side of social organization. There is also an *expressive* side: how the person feels about what he is doing in the role and how other people feel about him. Erving Goffman has analyzed with great sensitivity the expression of these feelings.[1] He calls the individual's expression of *his own* feelings about his role **demeanor;** he calls the expression of reactions to the role player (on the part of those with whom he interacts) **etiquette;** and he distinguishes deferential from contemptuous reactions. This sounds rather complicated—especially in industrial societies with thousands of different roles. And a further complication has yet to be mentioned: a person normally occupies dozens of roles, some of them sequentially, some of them simultaneously. This multiplicity of roles sometimes places the individual under cross-pressures; he may be forced to resolve a "role conflict."[2] Multiplicity of roles also poses a choice for the community. How is an adult male regarded in a particular situation: as a college professor, as a parent, as a taxpayer in the local community? Or does he receive a composite evaluation based on all of his roles simultaneously? Which roles of the individual are the basis for his social evaluation? For many sociologists, this issue is central to the system of social stratification prevailing in a society.

STRATIFICATION AS A PROCESS OF INTERPERSONAL EVALUATION

Social stratification, by definition, refers to some kind of inequality within a society. Inequality with respect to what? Some sociologists believe that stratification can most fruitfully be thought of in multidimensional terms: variations in economic power, variations in political authority, and variations in societal prestige.[3] Others prefer a unidimensional conception of stratification, even though they are aware that a high position in one dimension is correlated in the real world with a high position in another. In this book, social stratification is defined unidimensionally as *the organization of deference.* An individual's *status* is his level of societal **prestige,** the approximate consensus prevailing in his society as to how much deference he is entitled to receive and from whom. This conception of stratification is deliberately valueless; it treats the religious, educational, economic, or political characteristics

[1] Erving Goffman, "The Nature of Deference and Demeanor," *American Anthropologist,* Vol. 58, June 1956, pp. 474-502.

[2] Jackson Toby, "Some Variables in Role Conflict Analysis," *Social Forces,* Vol. 30, March 1952, pp. 323-327.

[3] Reinhard Bendix and Seymour Martin Lipset, *Class, Status and Power: A Reader in Social Stratification,* Glencoe, Ill.: Free Press, 1953.

associated with certain positions in the hierarchy as an open question, to be settled by empirical research.

Implicit in such a conception of social stratification is the assumption that a hierarchy of social honor is an inescapable feature of human life, however variable its basis in different societies. Most sociologists would agree that social inequality *is* inevitable. Certainly it is ubiquitous, arising even in societies dedicated to the ideal of classlessness. The emergence of social inequality despite egalitarian ideals reflects the strength of the forces tending to produce *in*equality.[4] What are these forces? First must be mentioned the tendency for members of a society to evaluate one another's behavior in the course of interaction. "Social stratification" is the end-product of an *evaluative process:* the giving and receiving of deference. Although "stratification" may suggest rigidity instead of dynamism, the evaluation of interaction creates the stratification system anew every day. One reason social stratification is universal is that human beings make value judgments, for example, whether role *A* is being played well and whether role *A* is more valuable to the society than role *B*.[5] These judgments depend on implicit standards (values) about which consensus exists.

Another factor in the universality of stratification is that these value judgments are not confined to roles but generalized to *people*. For example, suppose Mr. Jones, a banker, is evaluated by his neighbors exactly as they evaluate Mr. Smith, a factory worker living on the same street. They ignore differences between Mr. Jones and Mr. Smith in education, income, wealth, and occupational achievement and respond to Jones and Smith as "neighbors." If specific reactions were the rule in a society, Mr. Jones would have no consistent worth; he would be judged quite differently depending on the role he occupied at the moment. The concept of social stratification assumes a tendency for all of the people who interact with Mr. Jones to evaluate him in approximately the same way, to judge him as a composite which transcends momentary roles. Hence many specific role evaluations are generalized to a rating of the person as a whole and, by extension, of other persons closely related to him. Thus Talcott Parsons defines a **social class** as "an aggregate of kinship units of approximately equal status in the system of stratification."[6] Not only does Mr. Jones enjoy the same deference (or contempt) from a variety of persons who interact with him; his *children* also share his status and thereby possess life chances in American society different from those of the children of other parents.

[4] Eva Rosenfeld, "Social Stratification in a 'Classless' Society," *American Sociological Review,* Vol. 16, December 1951, pp. 766-774; Alex Inkeles, "Social Stratification and Social Mobility in the Soviet Union: 1940–1950," *American Sociological Review,* Vol. 15, August 1950, pp. 465-479.

[5] Talcott Parsons, *Essays in Sociological Theory: Pure and Applied,* Glencoe, Ill.: Free Press, 1949, Chap. 7, pp. 166-184; Kingsley Davis and Wilbert E. Moore, "Some Principles of Stratification," *American Sociological Review,* Vol. 10, April, 1945, pp. 242-249; Melvin Tumin, "On Inequality," *American Sociological Review,* Vol. 28, February 1963, pp. 19-26.

[6] Talcott Parsons, *The Social System,* Glencoe, Ill.: Free Press, 1951, p. 172.

This transmission of status from one generation to the next (inherited inequality) violates the ideal of equality of opportunity.[7] The inequality does not result from individual qualities and achievements.

Yet transmission of status advantages from one generation to the next results from the solidarity of the family of orientation. Given a situation where some parents and their dependent children enjoy more prestige in their society than others and given strong emotional ties between parents and their children, it is natural for parents to try to pass advantages on to the next generation. Only if children are removed from their parents at birth and brought up communally, as Plato suggested, can radical equality of opportunity be guaranteed. But since Plato's suggestion has generally not been adopted, and stratification has always been present in society, sociologists have frequently concerned themselves with the inequitable life-chances inherent in social stratification.[8] From the scientific point of view the personal feelings of sociologists about equality of opportunity do not matter; their task is to describe how the stratification system operates in a given society. The specific form that stratification takes depends ultimately on *values* and more immediately on the role considered important by members of that society. In industrial societies, high productivity is considered important. Thus it is safe to expect that strategic roles in the *economy* will carry high status.

TECHNIQUES FOR MEASURING STATUS

Sociologists have used a variety of techniques for allocating people to social classes. Studies in the field of social stratification show that, by and large, *different* techniques are used in small communities and in the **mass society** of big cities. **Reputational** measures, for instance, are common in community studies like the Elmtown study carried out a generation ago in a small city in Illinois.[9] Elmtown contained only about 6200 people when August Hollingshead was studying its system of social stratification. Neat ranking of community

---

[7] Seymour Martin Lipset and Reinhard Bendix, *Social Mobility in Industrial Society,* Berkeley: University of California Press, 1960, Chap. 3, pp. 76-113.

[8] Walter Buckley, "Social Stratification and the Functional Theory of Social Differentiation," *American Sociological Review,* Vol. 23, August 1958, pp. 369-375; Kingsley Davis, "The Abominable Heresy: A·Reply to Dr. Buckley," *American Sociological Review,* Vol. 24, February 1959, pp. 82-83.

[9] August B. Hollingshead, *Elmtown's Youth: The Impact of Social Classes on Adolescents,* New York: Wiley, 1949. The following are other examples of community studies: W. Lloyd Warner and Paul S. Lunt, *The Social Life of a Modern Community,* New Haven, Conn.: Yale University Press, 1941; Harold F. Kaufman, "Prestige Classes in a New York Rural Community," Ithaca, N.Y.: Cornell University Agricultural Experiment Station, Memoir 260, 1944, pp. 3-46; John Useem, Pierre Tangent, and Ruth Useem, "Stratification in a Prairie Town," *American Sociological Review,* Vol. 7, June 1942, pp. 331-342.

prestige is more feasible in a small community than in an anonymous metropolis. After all, standards of evaluation may not be fully shared by all members of the society. And the larger the society, the more probable is lack of consensus; Detroiters are more likely than Elmtowners to disagree as to who belongs where. Second, status ratings necessarily refer to a particular moment. This would not constitute a serious problem in feudal or caste societies where the standing of the individual does not change much during his lifetime. But industrial societies permit considerable upward and downward movement on the prestige scale. Hence an assessment of the status of an individual in an industrial society is like taking a photograph of a moving object with a slow lens. The faster it moves, the worse the picture. And there is evidence that upward and downward movement is faster (more common) in large cities than in small ones.[10] Finally, in a highly differentiated society, the individual's multiplicity of roles cannot be fully known to all of the persons with whom he interacts. Yet global status evaluations depend on such knowledge.

Sociologists at the University of Michigan threw light on the rank systems of mass society by surveying a random sample of residents of the Detroit metropolitan area.[11] Lenski and Landecker examined the positions of 749 respondents on four characteristics identified in the sociological literature as underlying community standing: income level, educational attainment, occupational prestige, and racial or ethnic origins. Although three-quarters of their respondents had consistent ratings on all four characteristics, one-quarter had markedly inconsistent standings in two or more of them; for example, some well-educated Negroes had low-paid jobs. Lenski and Landecker hypothesized that these persons whose status had not *crystallized* would have distinctive political attitudes, and they found evidence supporting their hypothesis. Even if we ignore what Lenski and Landecker were most interested in studying, the *effect* of lack of **class crystallization,** the *existence* of inconsistent evaluations in the large city means that the position of the individual in the status hierarchy is unclear. Class lines are not as simple to draw in Detroit as they are in Elmtown.

Despite the difficulties of status measurement in fluid industrial societies, hundreds of studies have been carried out in which individuals are allocated to social classes and their differential behaviors compared. Table 12.1, an example of such studies, reports data collected in 1947 on the value placed on higher education by different social classes in a national sample of approximately 3000 persons. Several different techniques for breaking the sample into social classes lead to the same result: persons in the lower echelons of the

[10] Seymour Martin Lipset and Reinhard Bendix, *Social Mobility in Industrial Societies,* Berkeley: University of California Press, 1960, pp. 204-213.

[11] Gerhard E. Lenski, "Status Crystallization: A Nonvertical Dimension of Social Status," *American Sociological Review,* Vol. 19, August 1954, pp. 405-413; Werner S. Landecker, "Class Crystallization and Its Urban Pattern," *Social Research,* Vol. 27, August 1960, pp. 308-320; Werner S. Landecker, "Class Crystallization and Class Consciousness," *American Sociological Review,* Vol. 28, April 1963, pp. 219-229.

TABLE 12.1

The Differential Emphasis among Economic Classes upon College Education as an Essential to Advancement

Various Measures of Class Status	Percentage Recommending College Education	N
Interviewer's rating of economic level		
Wealthy and prosperous	68	512
Middle class	52	1,531
Lower class	39	856
Occupation		
Professional	74	301
Businessmen and proprietors	62	421
White collar workers	65	457
Skilled labor	53	392
Semiskilled	49	416
Domestic and personal service workers	42	194
Farmers	47	417
Nonfarm laborers	35	132
Highest education achieved		
Attended college	72	564
Attended high school	55	1,411
Attended grammar school	36	926
Among renters, monthly rental		
Above $60	70	327
$40-60	64	666
$20-40	54	990
Below $20	37	403

Source: Herbert H. Hyman, "The Value Systems of Different Classes: A Social Psychological Contribution to the Analysis of Stratification," in Bendix and Lipset, Eds., *Class, Status and Power,* Glencoe, Ill.: Free Press, 1953, p. 430.

American stratification system are less likely than persons in higher echelons to consider college education essential for young people.[12] This result reflects the tendency for the different status levels of a society to develop different sub-cultures, different societal goals, and different judgments about the relative importance of specific roles. If this tendency goes far enough, communication of shared meanings between social classes is minimized. The Marxian notion of

[12] Herbert H. Hyman, "The Value Systems of Different Classes: A Social Psychological Contribution to the Analysis of Stratification," in Bendix and Lipset, Eds., *Class, Status and Power,* Glencoe, Ill.: Free Press, 1953, pp. 426-442.

class consciousness becomes relevant.[13] Class consciousness may begin with an awareness that different classes have different economic resources and different values. If these differences are defined as unfair ("exploitation"), such a definition of the situation causes class conflict. However, although the breakdown of value consensus between social classes may be the fore-runner of divisive cleavage in the society, class subcultures do not necessarily produce class conflict. (The conditions under which cleavages emerge constitute an integrative problem we shall return to in Chapter 15.) Objective differences between social classes must be culturally defined before they influence interaction. Defined in one way, they lead to alienated youth and predatory crime; defined differently, they lead to radical political movements or eschatological religions.

Reputational Ratings. In a reputational study, the status rating for an individual hinges on the votes he receives from other members of his community in a poll conducted by the researcher. In the Elmtown study, Hollingshead adopted the following procedure:[14]

1. He asked 12 Elmtowners to assign a control list of 20 well-known families to different status levels.
2. Since most of the 12 judges distributed the 20 well-known families among 5 levels, Hollingshead assigned his 20 control families to these 5 levels.
3. He then used 31 Elmtowners (other than the 12 original raters) to assign each of the 535 families in the study to one of the 5 prestige levels established by the 20 control families.

Since the 31 raters were carefully chosen on the basis of long residence in Elmtown (and other criteria) and since at least two well-known families from the control list exemplified each status level, the raters did not have difficulty assigning the families to status levels. Some families were identified by as many as 22 raters; 10 families were identified by only 7 of them. In general, the status level assigned the family by Hollingshead was the average assignment given to it by those who rated it. Complicated though Hollingshead's procedure was, it amounted to having 31 residents of Elmtown serve as *representatives* of the community for the purpose of assigning ratings. Hollingshead might equally well have asked *all* Elmtowners instead of 31 to rate the 535 families; he devised an ingenious short-cut to avoid asking every member of the community about everyone else. The 20 control-list families functioned as a single pretested question. Essentially, then, Hollingshead delineated the deference hierarchy in a small city in Illinois by asking representatives of the community to answer the following question about every family that they recognized: "Is the community standing of this family more like that of families A and B, of families C, D, and E, of families F, G, H, and I, of families J, K, L, M, N, and O, or of families P, Q, R, S, and T?"

---

[13] Talcott Parsons, "Social Classes and Class Conflict in the Light of Recent Sociological Theory," *American Economic Review,* Vol. 39, May 1949, p. 23.

[14] Hollingshead, *Elmtown's Youth.*

Self-Placement in the Class Structure. The reputational method of measuring status has obvious limitations. If the community is large, no rater can evaluate more than a tiny fraction of the total population. Furthermore, ratings from *different* communities within the same society are not comparable. These drawbacks of reputational methods do not apply to techniques that permit the respondent to assess his *own* standing **(self-placement).** One of the best self-placement measures of status was developed by a social psychologist, Richard Centers, for inclusion in surveys conducted by polling organizations.[15] Respondents are assigned to socioeconomic classes on the basis of their replies to the following question: "If you were asked to use one of these four names for your social class, which would you say you belonged in: the middle class, lower class, working class, or upper class?" Table 12.2 shows how a national sample of white American men answered this question in 1945. Very few respondents defined themselves as "upper class" or "lower class"; "working class" and "middle class" were the attractive choices.

The self-placement method of measuring status has limitations of its own. For example, the class with which the respondent identifies himself may represent his aspirations rather than his current interactions. The self-placement technique relies on the honesty as well as on the class awareness of the respondent. Neither of these limitations destroys the validity of the self-placement method. The problem of obtaining truthful answers to potentially embarrassing questions is not unique to studies of stratification; some respondents lie in order to increase their sense of self-importance, but not many. And most people are aware of the existence of a hierarchy of prestige and power in their community. Interestingly enough, self-placement did not look like a promising technique

TABLE 12.2

Class Identifications of a National Cross Section of White Males (July 1945)

Response	Percentage
Upper class	3
Middle class	43
Working class	51
Lower class	1
Don't know	1
"Don't believe in classes"	1
Total	100

Source: Richard Centers, *The Psychology of Social Classes: A Study of Class Consciousness,* Princeton, N.J.: Princeton University Press, 1949, p. 77.

[15] Richard Centers, *The Psychology of Social Classes: A Study of Class Consciousness,* Princeton, N.J.: Princeton University Press, 1949.

before Centers added "working class" to the "upper class, middle class, lower class" choices. Faced with "upper class, middle class, lower class," 88 per cent of American respondents said they were "middle class."[16] This was interpreted to mean that Americans were not aware of class differences. A better interpretation would have been that Americans did not like the ideological implications of calling themselves "lower class." The fact is that subjectively determined class identifications correlate strongly with more objective indices: educational attainment, occupation, and income—and also with economic

TABLE 12.3

Differential Identification with the Middle and Upper Classes on the Part of Respondents from Various Occupational, Educational, and Income Levels

	Number	Percentage Identifying with Middle and Upper Classes
Occupational and educational levels		
Business, professional, and white collar		
Graduate school	49	92
College graduate	68	90
Some college	81	83
High school graduate	96	71
Some high school	69	64
All grade school levels	53	58
Manual workers		
All college levels	18	—
High school graduate	75	28
Some high school	97	22
Seventh and eighth grades	134	22
Sixth grade or less	84	7
Interviewer Rating of Economic Status		
Wealthy	49	86
Average plus	135	84
Average	345	60
Poor plus	275	30
Poor	292	19

Source: Richard Centers, *The Psychology of Social Classes: A Study of Class Consciousness,* Princeton, N.J.: Princeton University Press, 1949, pp. 164, 110.

[16] George Gallup and S. F. Rae, *The Pulse of Democracy,* New York: Simon and Schuster, 1940, p. 169.

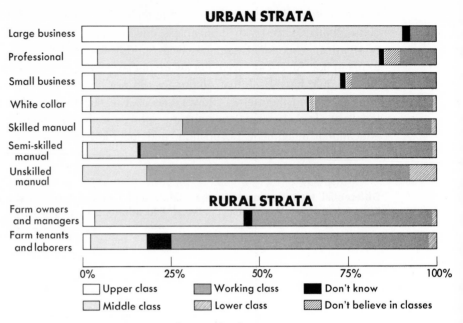

FIGURE 12.1   **Class identifications of occupational strata.**

and political attitudes. Table 12.3 and Fig. 12.1 present data tabulated by Centers which illustrate this point.

The Evaluation of Cultural Artifacts by the Observer. In some research projects, people are classified in one social rank or another, not on the basis of what they say about themselves or of what others say about them, but because of cultural symbols associated with them. **(evaluation of cultural artifacts).** Public-opinion polls often use interviewer ratings of the socioeconomic status of respondents. On the basis of their style of dress, the furnishings of their homes, their manner of speech, and other symbols known to be associated with socioeconomic status, respondents are rated A, B, C+, C, or D.[17] Figure 9.1 (p. 329) showed that such ratings of socioeconomic status bear a consistent relationship to voting behavior.

Despite the training that interviewers receive from the polling organization to achieve consistency in their ratings, much discretion is necessarily left to the interviewers. A generation ago F. Stuart Chapin constructed a less intuitive scale of socioeconomic status, which also used interviewer assessment of cultural symbols. Professor Chapin's Living Room Scale of status depended on notations made by an interviewer of the furnishings and appearance of a family's living quarters.[18] A schedule of questions was supplied the interviewer;

[17] Paul F. Lazarsfeld, Bernard Berelson, and Hazel Gaudet, *The People's Choice: How the Voter Makes Up His Mind in a Presidential Campaign,* New York: Duell, Sloan and Pearce, 1944, pp. 17-18.

[18] F. Stuart Chapin, *Contemporary American Institutions,* New York: Harper, 1935, pp. 373-398; Louis Guttman, "A Revision of Chapin's Social Status Scale," *American Sociological Review,* Vol. 7, June 1942, pp. 362-369.

his task was to check on various items, such as whether there was a rug on the living room floor. Once the interviewer handed in his filled-out schedule, previously determined weights were applied, and a status score for the family emerged. Although none of the items on the schedule dealt with the interaction of one family with another (or the prestige of one family vis-a-vis another), Chapin meant the status scores generated by his Scale to be compared with one another. He developed the Living Room Scale because interactive evaluations struck him as more difficult to measure than the possession of certain cultural objects and because he assumed that such possessions reflected the social standing of their owners.

Status Ratings Based on Occupation, Education, or Income. The most common measures of social class used by contemporary sociologists are, as might be expected, the simplest and the cheapest. Research has demonstrated that status ratings based on occupation, education, or income correlate with reputational and self-placement ratings as well as with exposure to cultural symbols. For example, Table 12.4 shows that higher-status people are more likely to read *Life* magazine whether status is measured by educational achievement or by annual household income.

TABLE 12.4

Differential Readership of Life Magazine by Education and Annual Household Income (Percentage)

Repeat Audiences of *Life* by Education (People Age 20 and Older)

Number of Issues Read out of Six Issues	0–4th Grade	5–7th Grade	Finished Grade School	1–3rd Year High School	Finished High School	1st Year College or beyond	All People 20 Years Old and Older
Audience coverage							
One or two	18.2	21.1	27.3	33.8	30.6	25.1	27.3
Three or four	2.3	9.6	7.6	11.9	14.6	21.6	12.1
Five or six	2.2	3.0	4.7	6.8	11.0	22.7	9.0
Total: read one or more	22.7	33.7	39.6	52.5	56.2	69.4	48.4

Repeat Audiences of *Life* by Annual Household Income

Number of Issues Read Out of Six Issues	Under $2,000	$2,000–$2,999	$3,000–$4,999	$5,000–$6,999	$7,000 or More	All People
Audience coverage						
One or two	18.8	34.2	30.4	29.1	27.9	29.1
Three or four	4.9	11.7	12.9	17.9	20.0	12.7
Five or six	4.5	4.3	8.5	13.0	22.0	8.8
Total: read one or more	28.2	50.2	51.8	60.0	69.9	50.6

Source: Alfred Politz Research, Inc., *A Study of Four Media: Their Accumulative and Repeat Audiences,* New York: Time, Incorporated, 1953, pp. 21, 23.

Implicit in the use of occupation, education, or income to rank a population into strata is some *theory* of social stratification. In this book, stratification is defined unidimensionally: as a gradient of prestige. A theory is required to account for the emergence of this gradient and to explain why status ratings (of prestige) correlate with ratings based on occupation, education, and income. The theory of stratification in industrial societies presented in the next section tries to fit known facts and succeeds in fitting some better than others.

STRATIFICATION IN INDUSTRIAL SOCIETIES[19]

One key to social stratification in industrial societies is the occupational structure and specifically the place of adult males in it. The value industrial societies place on economic production makes the occupational structure crucial as a determinant of status. In social organization terms, roles associated with production usually carry higher prestige than otherwise comparable roles associated with socialization, policy making, or integration. The high value placed on conquering the environment through production is responsible for a preoccupation with possessions, the tangible outcome of production, and

[19] The analysis that follows leans heavily on Talcott Parsons, "A Revised Analytical Approach to the Theory of Social Stratication," in Bendix and Lipset, Eds., *Class, Status and Power*, Glencoe, Ill.: Free Press, 1953, pp. 92-128.

with money, the all-purpose possession. True, possessions are desired partly for the intrinsic sensual enjoyment afforded by good food, fine clothing, and an air-conditioned house, but more importantly for the *symbolic* meaning of possessions for the possessor. As Chapter 3 pointed out, cultural meanings are consensual; they depend on shared definitions of the situation. Within a society the meaning of possessions is widely shared. Thus most members of industrial societies interpret control over possessions as a measure of a man's contribution to the social product.

There are two contexts in which possessions convey this meaning: the occupational and the familial. In the occupational context, a large office, an expensive rug on the floor, and a private secretary suggest that the possessor is important to the organization making these facilities available to him. In the familial context, a swimming pool reflects the large monetary rewards available to this (presumably important) family. In the first context, possessions are mainly instrumental to the performance of an occupational role, in the second, they are usually rewards for that performance. Nevertheless, control over possessions conveys the same meaning in both contexts: the prestige of the possessor. This meaning sometimes makes seemingly irrational behavior comprehensible. The executive who insists on a private secretary even though the typing pool is adequate for his correspondence is searching for a status symbol. He does not need the secretary for typing; he needs her to communicate his position in the company.

If one key to social stratification in industrial societies is the occupational structure, the other is the family. Social stratification is a ranking of family units. Therefore, it is necessary to discover the relationship between the occupation of the husband-father and the status of the family collectively. What happens when both parents work and they occupy different status levels in the occupational system? Perhaps the situation will change with greater equality between the sexes, but heretofore it has been the occupational status of the husband-father that establishes the status of the family in society. Gainful employment of women, including married women, is a continuing trend, but the married woman derives her social status more from her husband's job than from her own. That is why women tend to be wary about marrying men of lower status whereas men can afford to be more democratic.[20] The socially prominent woman who marries a laborer falls in status; the socially prominent man who marries a showgirl pulls her up to his station in life. What about children? Adolescent and preadolescent children derive their status from that of their fathers just as married women derive their status from that of their husbands. Of course, once they become adults, marry, and establish their own households, their status no longer depends on that of their parents. Occu-

[20] August B. Hollingshead, "Cultural Factors in the Selection of Marriage Mates," *American Sociological Review,* Vol. 15, October 1950, pp. 625-626; Zick Rubin, "Do American Women Marry Up?" *American Sociological Review,* Vol. 33, October 1968, pp. 750-760, finds that ". . . daughters of white collar workers were more likely than their brothers to marry the children of professionals and managers."

Burk Uzzle—Magnum

pation becomes the status determinant for sons; for daughters, the main criterion is the men they marry.

The occupational role is crucial to social stratification in industrial societies for two reasons, one direct, the other indirect. What a man *does* occupationally tends to define him to himself as well as to others—and therefore to provide a *direct* basis for social assessment. In addition, the occupational role of the adult male is the main source of money income for most families. Since money income influences the neighborhood in which the family lives, the type of car it can afford, and the clothing its members wear (as well as its expenditures for food and recreation), the occupational role of the breadwinner is an indirect determinant of the style of life of the family. And the style of life of a family is interpreted by members of the family as well as by outsiders as a symbolic reflection of community esteem. The pervasiveness of this interpretation has sometimes helped turn adolescents into delinquents, perhaps spending thousands of stolen dollars on clothing, cars, and tips in an effort to "make an impression."[21] In short, the occupational role has two meanings: (1) what the worker *produces* for society and (2) the remuneration he receives for his productive contribution, and thus what he and his dependents *consume.*

The educational attainment of a man, like his occupation, is correlated with the class position of his family, but the meaning of the relationship is quite different. An unskilled laborer with a college degree may not have much more prestige in industrial societies than a laborer with less education. But educational achievement is highly predictive of occupational achievement, so that educational attainment is almost as good an index of social status as is direct evaluation of occupations. (In view of the difficulty of avoiding classificatory errors in assessing thousands of occupational categories, an index of social status based on education may be more valid than one based on occupation.[22]) This is not to minimize the relationship between education and social stratification. Education is the single most important factor in the class position of adult males, as Chapter 11 has shown. But the significance of education lies in its preparatory value for middle-class occupational roles, not in its direct contribution to status. Education is the bridge between the individual's status past and his status future.

Stratification in the United States. The rank order of prestige of 90 occupations was measured in a study conducted by the National Opinion Research Center (N.O.R.C.) in 1947. The N.O.R.C. field staff interviewed a United States sample containing 2920 respondents. Each respondent was asked to select the number on a card (handed to him by the interviewer) corresponding to his evaluation of each occupation.[23] The card looked like this:

For each job mentioned, please pick out the statement that best gives *your own personal opinion* of the *general standing* that such a job has.

1. *Excellent* standing
2. *Good* standing
3. *Average* standing
4. *Somewhat below average* standing
5. *Poor* standing
X. I don't know where to place that one

---

[21] For a brilliant fictional treatment of this phenomenon, see Willa Cather, "Paul's Case," in Grant Overton, Ed., *Great Modern Short Stories,* New York: Modern Library, 1930, pp. 193-217.

[22] For a study of the relationship between the educational requirements of various American occupations and their prestige ratings, see Otis Dudley Duncan, "A Socioeconomic Index for All Occupations," in Albert J. Reiss, Jr., *Occupations and Social Status,* New York: Free Press of Glencoe, 1961, pp. 109-138.

[23] Reiss, *Occupations and Social Status,* pp. 18-19.

TABLE 12.5

Comparison of the N.O.R.C. Prestige Ratings and the 1949 Incomes of 45 Occupations

Census Occupational Title (N.O.R.C. title in parentheses)	N.O.R.C. Prestige Rating[a]	1949 Income[b]
Accountants and auditors (accountant for a large business)	82	62
Airline pilots and navigators (airline pilot)	83	72
Architects (architect)	90	75
Authors (author of novels)	76	55
Chemists (chemist)	90	64
Clergymen (minister)	87	21
College presidents, professors, and instructors (college professor)	93	64
Dentists (dentist)	90	80
Editors and reporters (reporter on a daily newspaper)	52	67
Engineers, civil (civil engineer)	88	72
Funeral directors and embalmers (undertaker)	57	42
Lawyers and judges (lawyer)	89	76
Physicians and surgeons (physician)	97	76
Social and welfare workers, except group (welfare worker for a city government)	59	41
Teachers (instructor in the public schools)	73	48
Conductors, railroad (railroad conductor)	38	76
Managers, officials, and proprietors: Construction (building contractor)	76	53
Manufacturing (owner of a factory that employs about 100 people)	81	60
Retail trade (manager of a small store in a city)	45	42
Banking and other finance (banker)	92	78
Bookkeepers (bookkeeper)	39	29
Mail carriers (mail carrier)	34	48
Insurance agents and brokers (insurance agent)	41	55
Salesmen and sales clerks, retail trade (clerk in a store)	16	29
Carpenters (carpenter)	33	21
Electricians (electrician)	53	47
Locomotive engineers (railroad engineer)	67	81
Machinists (trained machinist)	57	36

TABLE 12.5 (cont'd.)

Census Occupational Title (N.O.R.C. title in parentheses)	N.O.R.C. Prestige Rating[a]	1949 Income[b]
Mechanics and repairmen, auto- mobile (automobile repairmen)	26	22
Plumbers and pipe fitters (plumber)	29	44
Attendants, auto service and park- ing (filling-station attendant)	10	15
Mine operatives and laborers, coal mining (coal miner)	15	7
Motormen, street, subway, and ele- vated railway (streetcar motorman)	19	42
Taxicab drivers and chauffeurs (taxi driver)	10	9
Truck and tractor drivers (truck driver)	13	21
Operatives and kindred workers, manufacturing (machine operator in a factory)	24	21
Barbers, beauticians, and manicurists (barber)	20	16
Bartenders (bartender)	7	16
Bootblacks (shoe shiner)	3	9
Cooks, except private household (restaurant cook)	16	14
Counter and fountain workers (soda fountain clerk)	6	12
Guards, watchmen, and doorkeepers (night watchmen)	11	17
Janitors and sextons (janitor)	8	7
Policemen and detectives, govern- ment (policemen)	41	34
Waiters and waitresses (restaurant waiter)	10	8

[a] Percentage of respondents rating occupation "excellent" or "good"; base of percentages excludes "don't know" responses.

[b] Percentage of males in the 1950 experienced civilian labor force with incomes of $3500 or more in 1949, adjusted by age of respondents.

Source: Albert J. Reiss, Jr., *Occupation and Social Status,* New York: Free Press of Glencoe, 1961, pp. 122–123, in a chapter prepared by Otis Dudley Duncan.

Table 12.5 compares the prestige ratings of 45 of these occupations with the levels of remuneration they afford. Note that high-prestige occupations like architects and bankers usually had high incomes; and low-prestige occupations like bootblacks and counter and fountain workers usually had low incomes. On the other hand, clergymen had high prestige and low incomes;

and railroad conductors had low prestige and high incomes. Which is more relevant to social status: occupational prestige or money income?

Money income is certainly a *convenient* index of social status; it generates an unequivocal rank order without elaborate attitude surveys. Furthermore, prestigeful consumption patterns are correlated with money income. Although ostentatious displays of wealth by *nouveaux riches* prove that purchasing power is not sufficient to maintain a prestigeful style of life, most of the symbols of high-prestige consumption are expensive. The difficulty with money income as an index of status is that industrial societies contain parallel rank systems within the occupational realm with comparable prestige and different levels of remuneration.[24] Within business and professional occupations, for example, the self-employed restaurateur or dentist may earn more than a middle-level executive or a research scientist in a large corporation, yet the standing of the executive and the scientist in the community is at least as high. Second, there exists a class of occupations dependent on philanthropy or taxation rather than on the sale of products or services in the market place. The level of remuneration in government service (including the Armed Forces), in churches, in hospitals, and in social-work agencies reflects the subsidized character of these occupations, not necessarily low prestige. That a Metropolitan opera star earns less than Elvis Presley and a Supreme Court justice less than a corporation lawyer is ironic; but it does not prove who outranks whom in social status.

In short, the level of remuneration of an occupation sets the standard of living for the worker's family. In a perfectly integrated society the standard of living of his family should correspond to his occupational prestige. But such integration is prevented by the existence of parallel **rank systems** providing different levels of remuneration for jobs of comparable prestige. Thus families of public school teachers and clergymen are given more *deference* in the community than money with which to purchase possessions that convey the *demeanor* appropriate for their status levels.[25] What saves the United States from serious role conflicts over these discrepancies is social fluidity, especially in large cities. Such a wide range of goods and services is for sale in the market place in an affluent industrial society that consumers have an enormous range of discretionary expenditures. Even a laborer can buy a Rolls-Royce if he can scrape up enough cash for a down-payment. In feudal Europe, on the other hand, only a noble could participate in knightly tournaments. This difference means that in industrial societies status comparisons frequently are not made and status credentials are not scrutinized too closely.

[24] Paul K. Hatt, "Occupation and Social Stratification," *American Journal of Sociology,* Vol. 55, May 1950, pp. 533-543; Richard T. Morris and Raymond J. Murphy, "The Situs Dimension in Occupational Structure," *American Sociological Review,* Vol. 24, April 1959, pp. 231-239.

[25] Goffman, "Deference and Demeanor," p. 489, defines demeanor as "that element of the individual's ceremonial behavior typically conveyed through deportment, dress, and bearing, which serves to express to those in his immediate presence that he is a person of certain desirable or undesirable qualities."

The looseness of the relationship between the **occupational prestige** of the husband-father and the style of life of the family is promoted by other aspects of industrial society. Multiple-breadwinner families constitute a growing trend: since it is now acceptable for women to seek paid employment, the income of the household need not depend on the husband's pay alone. Further, the free choice of residential location, the possibility of private schooling for children, and membership in voluntary associations, including political and religious organizations, all reduce the correspondence between the occupational prestige of the husband-father and the style of life of the family.

Fluidity of the class structure helps to explain why the precise *number* of social classes is a matter of dispute among sociologists. W. Lloyd Warner counts six, Hollingshead five, and so on.[26] In most contexts, especially for males, occupational prestige is the crucial factor in social ranking. In some contexts, especially for females, style of life is more important. An element of arbitrariness necessarily enters into any classification of social classes because the scientific observer must settle questions that interaction leaves unsettled. Furthermore, a complex society is a mosaic of separate worlds. The university professor lives in a world of university professors, a businessman in a world of businessmen. These worlds may be physically close, as when a professor and a businessman are neighbors, but they have divergent standards of evaluation. Thus a university professor can drive a ten-year-old car without the slightest loss of status in his reference group, whereas his entrepreneurial neighbor *must*

[26] Warner and Lunt, *The Social Life of a Modern Community*; Hollingshead, *Elmtown's Youth*.

drive a later-model car to maintain *his* standing in the business community.[27] In sum, the many rank systems of an industrial society do not fully coalesce — except in sociological analyses of stratification. People tend to care more about the judgments of their immediate neighbors or work associates than they do about their overall standing in the larger society. This reference-group aspect of stratification further blurs an already fluid class system.

Fluidity is not, however, complete independence. Stratification implies *consensus* on who stands high and who stands low. If bankers looked down on garbage collectors, and garbage collectors reciprocated by looking down on bankers, no clear-cut hierarchy of prestige could emerge. A slight tendency was observed in the 1947 N.O.R.C. survey for members of an occupational category to evalute their own category more favorably than other respondents did; but this tendency was dwarfed by a much more powerful tendency for respondents to *agree* on the relative prestige of particular occupations regardless of the region of the country they came from, the size of the place they lived in, their own occupational group, their age, sex, educational attainment, or economic position.[28]

Stratification in Other Industrial Societies. Consensus on relative occupational prestige prevails in all industrial societies. Surprisingly, the occupational prestige hierarchies are similar from one industrial society to another despite differences in history and culture. The following article shows how this came about.[29]

> During the latter part of the nineteenth and the first half of the twentieth centuries the factory system of production was introduced, at least on a small scale, to most areas of the world. The factory has generally been accompanied by a relatively standard set of occupations, including the factory manager (sometimes also owner) and his administrative and clerical staff, engineering and lesser technical personnel, foremen, skilled, semi-skilled, and unskilled workers. In the factory, authority and responsibility are allocated largely according to the degree of technical or administrative competence required for the job. In addition, the allocation of material and social rewards, the latter generally in the form of deference, is closely adjusted to levels of competence and degrees of authority and responsibility. The pattern of differentiation of authority is undoubtedly functionally necessary to the productive activity of the factory, and it may be that the associated pattern of reward differentiation is also functionally necessary.
>
> There is, however, no clear-cut imperative arising from the structure of the factory as such which dictates how the incumbents of its typical statuses should be *evaluated* by the population at large. One possibility is that in popular esteem

---

[27] A reference group is the group setting the individual's behavioral standards and expectations whether or not he is a member. For a classic discussion of the social psychology involved in reference groups, see Robert K. Merton and Alice S. Rossi, "Contributions to the Theory of Reference Group Behavior," in Merton, *Social Theory and Social Structure*, rev. ed., Glencoe, Ill.: Free Press, 1957, pp. 225-280.

[28] Reiss, *Occupation and Social Status*, Chap. 8, pp. 162-237.

[29] Reprinted by permission. From Alex Inkeles and Peter H. Rossi, "National Comparisons of Occupational Prestige," *American Journal of Sociology*. Vol. 61, January 1956, pp. 329-339.

the typical occupations will stand relative to one another in a rank order strictly comparable to their standing in the formal hierarchy of competence, authority, and reward in the factory. It is also possible, however, that the popular evaluation of these occupations will be quite different. Indeed, where the factory system has been introduced into societies like those of Spain or Japan, with well-established values based on tradition and expressive of the culture, one might expect significant differences between an occupation's standing in the formal hierarchy of the industrial system and its position in the popular ranking scheme.

Thus the interaction of the two systems—the standardized modern occupational system and the individual national value pattern for rating occupations—presents an interesting and important problem in comparative sociology.

We may posit two extreme positions in this interaction, while granting that it might be difficult to find live exponents of either. The extreme "structuralist" would presumably insist that the modern industrial occupational system is a highly coherent system, relatively impervious to influence by traditional culture patterns. Indeed, he might go so far as to insist that the traditional ranking system would in time have to be subsumed under, or integrated into, the industrial system. Consequently, his argument would run, even such occupations as priest, judge, provincial governor, not part of the modern occupational system and often given unusual deference, would come in time to have roughly the same standing relative to one another and to other occupations, no matter what their national cultural setting.

By contrast, an extreme "culturalist" might insist that within each country or culture the distinctive local value system would result in substantial—and, indeed, sometimes extreme—differences in the evaluation of particular jobs in the standardized modern occupational system. For example, he might assume that in the United States the company director would be rated unusually high because of our awe of the independent businessman and large corporations or that in the Soviet Union the standing of industrial workers would be much higher relative to managerial personnel than in Germany, with its emphasis on sharply differentiated status hierarchies. Furthermore, he might argue that the more traditional occupational roles assigned special importance in particular cultures would continue to maintain their distinctive positions in the different national hierarchies. Indeed, he might hold that the characteristic roles of the modern industrial system would come to be subsumed within the traditional rating system, each factory occupation being equated with some traditional occupation and then assigned a comparable rank.

A systematic test of these contrasting positions is not beyond the capacity of contemporary social research. A standard list of occupations—say thirty or forty in number—might be presented for evaluation to comparable samples from countries presenting a range of culture types and degrees of industrialization. The list should contain both standard industrial occupations and the common, but differentially valued, traditional roles (e.g., priest, legislator, etc.).

Data are available which, though far from completely adequate, will carry us a long way beyond mere speculation on these matters. In the postwar years studies of occupational ratings have been conducted in and reported on five relatively industrialized countries: the United States, Great Britain, New Zealand, Japan, and Germany. In addition, the authors have available previously unpublished data for a sixth country, the Soviet Union.

Since these six studies were, on the whole, undertaken quite independently, our ideal research design is clearly far from being fulfilled. Nevertheless, the data do permit tentative and exploratory cross-national comparisons.

I. THE COMPARABILITY OF RESEARCH DESIGNS

The elements of similarity and difference in the six studies may be quickly assessed from the following summary of their essential features:

A. *Population Studied. United States:* National sample of adults fourteen years and over; 2,920 respondents. *Japan:* Sample of males twenty to sixty-eight years of age in the six large cities of Japan; 899 respondents. *Great Britain:* Written questionnaires distributed through adult-education centers and other organizations; 1,056 returns (percentage returned unspecified). *U.S.S.R.:* Sample of displaced persons, mostly in DP camps near Munich, Germany, and some former DP's now residing on eastern seaboard of U.S.; 2,100 written questionnaires. *New Zealand:* Sample collected mainly by interviews with inhabitants of town of 2,000, partly by mailed questionnaires (12 per cent returns) sent out to town of 4,000; 1,033 questionnaires and interviews used. *Germany:* 1,500 Schleswig-Holsteiners: vocational-school students, university students, and male adults (not otherwise specified); adult sample only used here.

B. *Overlap Among Occupations Studied.* Each study involved a different number of occupations, ranging from 88 in the case of the National Opinion Research Center American study to 13 in the Soviet research. Only the New Zealand and the British groups studied exactly the same occupations. Each of the remaining four studies used a different, but partially overlapping, set of occupations. In order to make comparisons between pairs of countries, each occupation studied in each research was matched, when possible, with an occupation in the data gathered in the other country. In many cases it was necessary to disregard the information about an occupation in one of the paired countries because no comparable occupation was studied in the other. In other instances, in order to increase the number of occupations which could be compared for any given pair of countries, occupations were matched which were only very roughly comparable, e.g., Buddhist priest and minister, or collective farm chairman and farm owner and operator. In most cases, however, a direct correspondence characterizes the pairs of occupations which are being equated. The reader is invited to

TABLE 12.6

Number of Identical or Similar Occupations Rated among Six Industrial Countries

	U.S.	Great Britain	U.S.S.R.	Japan	New Zealand	Germany
United States	—	24	10	25	24	20
Great Britain	—	—	7	14	30	12
U.S.S.R.	—	—	—	7	7	8
Japan	—	—	—	—	14	19
New Zealand	—	—	—	—	—	12
Total occupations studied	88	30	13	30	30	38

turn to Table 12.7 (below), where the lists of occupations used from each of the researches are printed. The occupations listed on any row or line were matched. The number of pairs of similar or identical occupations for each cross-national comparison is shown in Table 12.6.

C. *Nature of Rating Task. United States:* Respondents were asked: ". . . Please pick out the statement that best gives your own *personal opinion* of the *general standing* that such a job has. Excellent standing, good standing, average standing, somewhat below average, poor standing." *Japan:* Respondents were given a set of thirty cards and asked: " . . . Think of the general reputations they have with people, and sort them into five or more groups, from those which people think highly of to those which are not thought so well of." *Great Britain:* Respondents were told: "We should like to know in what order, *as to their social standing,* you would grade the occupations in the list given to you. [Rate them] . . . in terms of five main social classes . . . ABCDE." *U.S.S.R.:* Respondents were asked: "Taking everything into consideration, how desirable was it to have the job of (— — —) in the Soviet Union? Very desirable? Desirable? So-so? Undesirable? Very undesirable?" *New Zealand:* Same as in Great Britain. *Germany:* The source is unfortunately not very specific about the rating task assigned. The respondents were apparently asked to rank-order a list of 38 occupations presented as one slate.

D. *Computing Prestige Position.* With the exception of the German study, each research presents a "prestige score" for each of the occupations studied. These scores, computed variously, represent in each case the "average" rating given to each of the occupations by the entire sample of raters used. The German study presented only the rank-order positions of the occupations.

One is not sure whether differences between nations are generated by the differences in the questionnaires or the differences in the nations themselves. However, similarities in the prestige hierarchies, particularly when they are striking, are somewhat strengthened by the same lack of comparability in research designs and in the occupations matched to one another. Similarities may be in-

TABLE 12.7[a]

Correlations between Prestige Scores (or Ranks) Given to Comparable Occupations in Six National Studies

	U.S.S.R.	Japan	Great Britain	New Zealand	U.S.	Germany[b]
U.S.S.R.	—	.74	.83	.83	.90	.90
Japan	—	—	.92	.91	.93	.93
Great Britain	—	—	—	.97	.94	.97
New Zealand	—	—	—	—	.97	.96
United States	—	—	—	—	—	.96
Av. correlation	.84	.89	.93	.93	.94	.94

[a] See Table 12.6 for numbers of occupations involved in each comparison.

[b] All coefficients are product-moment correlations, with the exception of those involving Germany, which are rank-order coefficients.

terpreted as showing the extent to which design and other differences are overcome by the comparability among the prestige hierarchies themselves.

II. COMPARABILITY OF OCCUPATIONAL PRESTIGE HIERARCHIES

Since each study included some occupations used in another study, it is possible to compare the prestige hierarchies of occupations in pairs of countries by computing correlation coefficients for the scores (or ranks) of occupations. The fifteen correlation coefficients which result are presented in Table 12.7. It will be seen immediately that the levels of correlation are considerably higher than the magnitude to be expected if there were only rough agreement on placement in the top and bottom halves of the prestige hierarchy. Indeed, twelve of the fifteen coefficients are above .9, and only one is below .8. The three coefficients below .9 all concern the Soviet ratings, which, it will be recalled, involve only a very small number of occupations, maximizing the chances for lower correlations arising from merely one or two "mismatches."

For most of the comparisons, furthermore, the findings go beyond establishing mere comparability of rank orders. With the exception of the correlations involving Germany, each coefficient represents the relationships between prestige *scores* given to the same occupations in two different nations. Hence there is a high relationship between the relative "distance" between occupations, as expressed in score differences, as well. In other words, if, of two occupations, one is given a much lower score than the other by the raters in one country, this difference in prestige scores and not merely crude rank order also obtains in another country.

It should also be noted that these high correlations were obtained by using samples of occupations which were not strictly identical from country to country, including such very crude comparisons already mentioned as that of collective farm chairman and farm owner and operator. One may anticipate that if the occupations studied were more uniform, the similarities of prestige hierarchies from country to country would be even higher.

In other words, *despite the heterogeneity in research design, there exists among the six nations a marked degree of agreement on the relative prestige of matched occupations.* To this extent, therefore, it appears that the "structuralist" expectation is more nearly met than is the expectation based on the culturalist position.

Each of the six nations differs in the extent to which its prestige hierarchy resembles those of other nations. The average of the correlations for each nation, contained in the bottom row of Table 12.7 expresses these differences among nations quantitatively. Thus we may see that the American and German occupational prestige hierarchies are most similar to those of other nations, while the Soviet and Japanese hierarchies are most dissimilar. When we consider that the Soviet Union and Japan are, of the six, the more recently industrialized cultures, we may see there some small degree of evidence for the culturalist position. . . .

IV. INTERNATIONAL COMPARABILITY OF TYPES OF OCCUPATION

. . . Perhaps if we classify occupations according to the features of social structure or culture to which they are most closely related, we may gain further insight into the interaction between culture, social structure, and occupational prestige hierarchies. To explore this question, we grouped all the occupations into seven basic types: industrial, clerical and commercial, professional, political, traditional crafts, agricultural and service occupations. In Table 12.8 we have indicated the number of international comparisons between pairs among the five countries, again excluding Germany, which could be made involving the occupations in each class of occupations. We have also indicated the proportions of those comparisons which yielded disagreements. . . .

Because our findings so far have so strongly supported the structuralist expectation concerning the influence of industrialization in producing uniformity, our initial expectation may well be that occupations closely allied to the industrial system will enjoy highly comparable standings from country to country, while occupations more remotely connected would be the focus of international discrepancies. Table 12.8 indicates that industrial occupations do enjoy comparable standing in all five countries. Nevertheless, the *lowest* proportion of disagreements is shown by the professions. In addition, other occupational types, such as the political occupations and the traditional crafts, which are not necessarily closely allied to the industrial system, manifested levels of disagreement as low as that enjoyed by the industrial occupations. Only the agricultural and service occupations yield a degree of disagreement which sets them apart from the other occupational groups.

Accounting for these discrepancies appears to require a combination of arguments. In the first place, some types of non-industrial occupations are easily assimilated to the industrial system. The traditional crafts serve as the prime example here, since the skills involved in such occupations as bricklayer, carpenter, and plumber have a close resemblance to the skills of industrial workers. Indeed, some crafts have been partly incorporated into the industrial system, and, it may be argued, such occupations are easily placed within the hierarchy of in-

TABLE 12.8

Discrepancies in Prestige Position According to Type of Occupation

Occupation Types[a]	Proportion of Discrepancies (Per Cent)	Number of Comparisons
Professional	16	31
Industrial	24	29
Political	25	16
Traditional crafts	27	11
Clerical and commercial	32	37
Agricultural	50	16
Service	63	20

[a]Examples of occupations included in each type are as follows: *Professional:* doctor, minister, teacher, etc.; *industrial:* industrial worker, company director, factory manager, engineer; *political:* judge, civil servant, etc.; *traditional crafts:* bricklayer, carpenter, fisherman; *clerical and commercial:* accountant, bookkeeper, salesman, small entrepreneur, etc.; *agricultural:* farm owner and operator, farm hand; *service:* shoe shiner, barber, porter, streetcar conductor, etc.

dustrial occupations and may tend to assume roughly the same position vis-à-vis industrial occupations. Likewise, some professions, such as engineering and applied scientific research, have a most immediate connection with the industrial system, and others, such as architecture, are easily equated with it.

However, closeness or assimilability to the industrial system will not suffice to explain the relatively stable position of other professions, such as doctor. Nor will it serve to explain the low proportion of disagreement concerning the political occupations. We must recognize that the nations being compared have certain structural and cultural features in common, in addition to the presence of industry. For example, they share certain needs, as for socialization, and values, such as health and systematic knowledge, which insure relatively comparable standing to doctors, teachers, and scientists. Furthermore, all the countries compared have in common the national state, with which is associated a relatively standardized occupational structure ranging from ministers of state to local bureaucrats. In addition, both the professions and the political occupations are highly "visible," and agreement as to their standing is probably facilitated by the relatively objective and easily perceived indexes of power, knowledge, and skill manifested by their incumbents.

The types of occupation which generate the greatest amount of disagreement are highly variant and unstandardized or difficult to assimilate to the industrial structure. Agriculture may be conducted, as in Japan, on relatively small holdings, on collective farms as in the U.S.S.R., or, as in the western plains of the United States, in "agricultural factories." Being a farmer means very different things in each of the five countries, quite unlike the standardized image of the machinist or the factory manager. It can be anticipated, however, that as agriculture tends to be similarly organized in different countries, agricultural occupations will achieve more uniform standing.

The "service" occupations—barber, shoe shiner, chef, street sweeper—show the greatest amount of variation. Many of them antedate the industrial system and are in agrarian as well as industrial societies. They have no fixed position relative to the industrial order, nor are they similar to typical industrial occupations, as are many of the traditional crafts. They therefore appear to be most easily evaluated according to the traditional culture. Personal service in countries like Japan and Great Britain, in which a servant class was historically well developed and benefited from intimate association with an aristocratic upper class, may still be regarded as not so degrading as in the more democratic societies, such as the United States and New Zealand. In fact, the greatest discrepancy to be found among all the comparisons involves the differences in prestige position accorded to chef in Great Britain as compared with either the United States or New Zealand, although in the case of the former the match was poor, since the comparable occupation was "restaurant cook." As these services come to be organized and mechanized—as in modern laundries or restaurants—they will become more thoroughly integrated into the larger economic order and may in time achieve more strictly comparable status from country to country.

All told, it would appear from this examination of international discrepancies that a great deal of weight must be given to the cross-national similarities in social structure which arise from the industrial system and from other common structural features, such as the national state.

The similarity in the prestige ratings of specific occupations in six countries with different histories and cultures suggests that occupational structure is constitutive of status in all industrialized countries. Even the exceptions tend to reinforce this conclusion. Note the low prestige of "small independent farmer" in Japan (in Table 12.9) as compared to the relative standing of this occupation in the United States, Great Britain, and New Zealand. (Similarly, farm laborers rank relatively lower in Germany and in the Soviet Union than in the United States, Great Britain, and New Zealand.) The people of Japan, Germany, and the Soviet Union have not yet forgotten the *peasant* status with which farming was traditionally associated in these countries. In the United States and New Zealand, on the other hand, a feudal past cannot be remembered because it did not exist, and in Great Britain it is not as recent as in Japan, Germany, and the Soviet Union.

No society completely escapes its history. Just as agricultural work has a *lower* status in an industrial society with a feudal past, so some occupations have *higher* status due to historical associations which may be irrelevant to the current functioning of the society. The samurai tradition in Japan probably inflates the prestige of military officers; this occupation was unfortunately not rated in the Japanese survey, so this guess cannot be put to the test with the data at hand. The United States does not have a feudal past, but the distribution of prestige in contemporary American society is also affected by historical circumstances. The disadvantaged status of Negroes is partly the result of Negro enslavement during the eighteenth and nineteenth centuries.

Historical and cultural circumstances, then, distort the hierarchy of prestige in an industrial society from what it would be if occupational structure were the only factor in social stratification. Moreover, the history of individuals as well as the history of the society affects the distribution of prestige. The son of class I parents in Elmtown would retain some prestige directly by virtue of his origins even if he became an unskilled laborer. Although family connections also count in more dynamic urban areas, the son of middle-class parents in New York City who became an unskilled laborer would probably be upgraded *indirectly* by his family background—because of his taste in clothing and home furnishings, his hobbies, his childhood friends, and the educational history reflected in his speech. The *direct* assessment of family background is less likely in the more anonymous city.

SOCIAL MOBILITY

In all societies, children start life on the social level occupied by their parents. In traditional societies they usually remain on that level throughout their lives. In industrial societies, the child initially shares the status of his family, but by late adolescence he moves into social limbo. His social evaluation becomes unclear because his own activities in school or in the labor market

TABLE 12.9

The Comparative Prestige of Occupations in Six Industrial Societies

Occupation	Score	Occupation	Rank	Occupation	Score	Occupation	Score	Occupation	Score	Occupation	Score
United States:		*Germany:*		*Great Britain:*		*New Zealand:*		*Japan:*		*U.S.S.R.*	
Physician	93	Doctor	2	Medical officer	1.3	Medical officer	1.4	Doctor	7.0	Doctor	75
State governor	93							Prefectural gov.	3.8		
College professor	89	Univ. professor	1					Univ. professor	4.6	Scientific worker	73
Scientist	89										
County judge	87							Local court judge	4.7		
Head of dept. in state government	87	High civil servant (Regierungsrat— höherer Beamter)	4	Civil servant	6.0	Civil servant	7.0				
								Section head of a government office	7.2		
Minister	87	Minister (Pfarrer)	6	Non-conformist minister	6.4	Non-conformist minister	5.9				
								Priest of a Buddhist temple	12.5		
Architect	86	(Elec. engineer)	10					(Architect)	9.5		
Lawyer	86										
Member of board of directors of large corporation	86	Factory director (Fabrikdirektor)	5	Country solicitor	2.6	Country solicitor	3.8	Officer of large company	5.5	Factory manager	65
				Company director	1.6	Company director	3.6				
Civil engineer	84	Elec. engineer	10					(Architect)	9.5	Engineer	73
Owner of factory that employs about 100 people	82							Owner of a small or medium-sized factory	10.2		
Accountant for a large business	81			Chartered accountant	3.2	Chartered accountant	5.7	(Company office clerk)	16.1	Bookkeeper	62
Captain in regular army	80	Major (in armed forces)	8								
Building contractor	79			Jobbing master builder	11.4	Jobbing master builder	10.7			Officer in the armed services	58
Instructor in public schools (teacher)	78	Elem.-school teacher (Volksschullehrer)	11	Elem.-school teacher	10.8	Elem.-school teacher	10.3	Elem.-school teacher	11.7	Teacher	55

United States:		Germany:		Great Britain:		New Zealand:		Japan:		U.S.S.R.	
Farm owner and operator	76	Farmer (Bauer—mittelgrosser Betrieb)	13	Farmer	7.3	Farmer	8.1	Small independent farmer	16.4	Chairman of collective farm	38
Official of international labor union	75							Chairman of national labor federation	10.8		
Electrician	73			Fitter (elec.)	17.6	Fitter (elec.)	15.8				
Trained machinist	73	Skilled industrial worker (Industriefacharbeiter)	24								
Reporter on daily newspaper	71			News reporter	11.8	News reporter	13.8	Newspaper reporter	11.2		
Bookkeeper	68	Bank teller (bookkeeper in bank)	19	Routine clerk	16.1	Routine clerk	16.4	Company office clerk	16.1	(Bookkeeper)	62
Insurance agent	68	Insurance agent	20	Insurance agent	14.6	Insurance agent	16.1	Insurance agent	20.2		
Traveling salesman for wholesale concern	68			Commerical traveler	12.0	Commerical traveler	14.1				
Policeman	67			Policeman	16.1	Policeman	15.5	Policeman	16.4		
Mail carrier	66	Postman	23								
Carpenter	65	Carpenter	18	Carpenter	18.6	Carpenter	17.0	Carpenter	20.2		
Corporal in regular army	60	Non-commissioned officer	31								
Machine operator in factory	60	Machine operator (Maschinenschlosser-Geselle)	26	(Composite of fitter, carpenter, bricklayer, tractor driver, coal hewer)	20.5	(Composite of fitter, carpenter, bricklayer, tractor driver, coal hewer)	20.9	Latheman	21.1	Rank-and-file worker	48
Barber	59	Barber	16					Barber	20.5		
Clerk in a store	58	Store clerk (Verkäufer im Lebensmittel geschäft)	28	Shop assistant	20.2	Shop assistant	20.2	Department-store clerk	19.8		
Fisherman who owns own boat	58							Fisherman	22.0		
Streetcar motorman	58	Conductor	33					Bus driver	20.9		

Table 12.9 (continued)

Occupation	Score	Occupation	Rank	Occupation	Score	Occupation	Score	Occupation	Score	Occupation	Score
United States:		*Germany:*		*Great Britain:*		*New Zealand:*		*Japan:*		*U.S.S.R.*	
Restaurant cook	54			Chef	13.8	Chef	21.8				
Truck driver	54			Carter	25.8	Carrier	20.2				
Farm hand	50	Farm laborer (worker)	36	Agricultural laborer	25.5	Agricultural laborer	24.4			Rank-and-file collective farmer	18
Coal miner	49			Coal hewer	23.2	Coal hewer	24.7	Coal miner	23.7		
Restaurant waiter	48	Waiter (Kellner)	30								
Dock worker	47			Dock laborer	27.0	Dock laborer	28.3				
Bartender	44			Barman	26.4	Barman	28.3				
Street sweeper	34	(Unskilled laborer)	38	Road sweeper	28.9	Road sweeper	28.9	Road worker	24.8		
Shoe shiner	33							Shoe shiner	26.9		
		Bricklayer	27	Bricklayer	20.2	Bricklayer	19.3				
		Clothing-store owner	12	Business manager	6.0	Business manager	5.3	Owner of a retail store	15.3		
		Tailor	14	Works manager	6.4	Works manager	7.9	Tailor	17.7		
		Street peddler	35	News agent and tobacconist	15.0	News agent and tobacconist	15.4	Street-stall keeper	24.9		
				Tractor driver	23.0	Tractor driver	22.8				
				Railway porter	25.3	Railway porter	25.3				

Sources: (1) A. A. Congalton, "The Social Grading of Occupations in New Zealand," *British Journal of Sociology*, Vol. 4, March 1953 (New Zealand data); (2) John Hall and D. Caradog Jones, "The Social Grading of Occupations," *British Journal of Sociology*, Vol. 1, January 1950 (British data); (3) National Opinion Research Center, "Jobs and Occupations: A Popular Evaluation," in Reinhard Bendix and Seymour Martin Lipset, Eds., *Class, Status and Power*, Glencoe, Ill.: Free Press, 1953 (United States data); (4) *Der Spiegel*, June 30, 1954 (German data); (5) Research Committee, Japan Sociological Society, "Report of a Sample Survey of Social Stratification and Mobility in Six Large Cities of Japan," December 1952 (Japanese data); and (6) Unpublished materials from the Project on the Soviet Social System of the Russian Research Center at Harvard University (U.S.S.R. data).

foreshadow his future status about as well as the social standing of his parents. By adulthood, the impact of parental status has receded further. Family origins affect social status *indirectly* by influencing opportunities for educational and occupational achievement, but this is a far cry from the *direct* inheritance of status that occurs in aristocratic societies, when a title passes from father to son, and in countries like India, where **caste** is similarly passed on.[30] Inheritance of status in industrial societies occurs mainly because high-status parents help and low-status parents hinder their children in preparing educationally for white-collar employment.

This generalization is, of course, a statistical one. Some working-class youngsters go to college, presumably with the help and encouragement of their families, and some youngsters from economically advantaged backgrounds do not. Table 12.10 presents data from a survey of a national sample of American households; these data show a greater rate of college attendance for the children of parents in the higher occupational strata. Nevertheless, about three-tenths of working-class high school graduates went to college in 1960, and the absolute number of youngsters from white-collar backgrounds going to college (363,000) was only a little more than the number of youngsters from all other backgrounds (293,500).

TABLE 12.10

1960 High School Graduates Enrolled in College, by the Occupations of the Household Heads in 1959

Occupations of the Household Heads in Families of 1960 High School Graduates	1960 Graduates Who Attended College in 1960		Total Number of 1960 High School Graduates
	Number	Percentage	
White-collar workers	363,000	62.7	579,000
Manual or service workers	220,000	29.3	752,000
Farm workers	40,500	27.0	150,000
Unemployed or not in labor force	33,000	33.3	99,000
Total	656,500	41.6	1,580,000

Source: Bureau of the Census, "Factors Related to College Attendance of Farm and Non-Farm High School Graduates: 1960," Series P-27, No. 32, Washington, D.C.: Government Printing Office, June 1962, p. 16.

[30] The caste system, a rigid, permanent division of society, sanctified by the Hindu religion, is still prevalent in India and other Far Eastern countries. A good study of how this is changing is Bryce F. Ryan, *Caste in Modern Ceylon: The Sinhalese System in Transition*, New Brunswick, N. J.: Rutgers University Press, 1953.

The concept of "social mobility" spreads like an umbrella, covering several distinct departures from the rigidity of a caste system. One is **vertical mobility:** upward and downward changes of status. Another is the sidewise movement from one social system to another within the same society. Rural-urban population flow is one example of this **horizontal mobility;** another is a worker changing employers but keeping the same job, say, a typist. Sometimes geographic mobility accompanies vertical mobility. However, vertical mobility is clearest when the community setting is unchanged. When *different* social systems are involved, as, for example, when a person moves from one community to another, precise evaluation of vertical movement is difficult.

Vertical mobility can be defined (1) in terms of comparisons between members of one generation and the next—**intergenerational mobility**—or (2) in terms of comparisons between different stages in the life of members of the same generation—**intragenerational mobility.** An infant starts life on the same status level as his parents, but in urban industrial societies an individual begins to create his own status in adolescence. Some individuals enjoy their highest status in middle age; others enjoy it in youth, and others in old age. This is intragenerational mobility. A study of labor mobility in the East Bay section of metropolitan San Francisco found that a large proportion of the family heads whose work histories were surveyed had "worked in different communities, in different occupations, and in many different jobs."[31] The greater the intragenerational mobility, the more complicated is the task of measuring intergenerational mobility. The stage of the life cycle at which comparisons are made is bound to affect the result. Gunnar Boalt faced this difficulty in his comparison of the occupations of 24-year-old Stockholm men in 1949 with the occupations of their fathers in 1936.[32] The fathers were more than 24 years old in 1936. Thus sons at an early stage of their careers were compared with their fathers at a later stage, which minimized the extent of *upward* mobility and exaggerated the incidence of *downward* mobility.

When sociologists speak of vertical mobility, they sometimes mean **gross mobility:** the proportion of persons in a society who have been *either* upwardly or downwardly mobile. At other times, however, they mean **net mobility:** the *difference* between the amounts of upward and downward changes in status. A society could have no net mobility at all and still have a high rate of gross mobility, the upward moves of some members being balanced by the downward moves of others. In point of fact, industrial societies are characterized by appreciable net upward mobility. This is due partly to the changing occupational structure, which permits an increasing proportion of the population to enjoy middle-status levels, and partly to the tendency for white-collar families to have a lower birth rate than blue-collar families, thus creating more room at mid-

---

[31] Seymour Martin Lipset and Reinhard Bendix, *Social Mobility in Industrial Society,* Berkeley: University of California Press, 1960, p. 180.

[32] Gunnar Boalt, "Social Mobility in Stockholm: A Pilot Investigation," in *Transactions of the Second World Congress of Sociology,* Vol. 2, London: International Sociological Association, 1954, pp. 67-63.

dle- and top-status levels.[33] Net mobility could be the main component of gross mobility, but it apparently is not. Joseph A. Kahl has estimated that net mobility accounted for only about 40 per cent of the gross mobility in the United States between 1920 and 1950.[34]

Net mobility is related to occupational changes tied to processes of industrialization and urbanization. *Gross* mobility reflects a society's mechanisms for social ascent and descent as well as its net mobility. Presumably, societies differing in values will also differ in readiness to accept radical redistributions of status from generation to generation. All the more interesting, therefore, are the conclusions of a comparative study of gross mobility in six industrial countries which suggest that gross mobility rates are about the same in all industrial countries.[35] Table 12.11 shows Germany with slightly more gross mobility than the United States—with Sweden, Japan, France, and Switzerland close behind.

Gross mobility rates may be about the same in different industrial countries. Yet within any society opportunities for mobility may vary for particular

TABLE 12.11

Comparative Indices of Upward and Downward Mobility (Percentages)

Country	*Nonfarm Populations*		
	Upward Mobility (Nonmanual Sons of Manual Fathers)	*Downward Mobility (Manual Sons of Nonmanual Fathers)*	*Total Vertical Mobility (Nonfarm Population Mobile across the Line between Working and Middle Class)*
United States	33	26	30
Germany	29	32	31
Sweden	31	24	29
Japan	36	22	27
France	39	20	27
Switzerland	45	13	23

Source: Seymour Martin Lipset and Reinhard Bendix, *Social Mobility in Industrial Society,* Berkeley: University of California Press, 1960, p. 25.

[33] Elbridge Sibley, "Some Demographic Clues to Stratification," *American Sociological Review,* Vol. 7, June 1942, pp. 322-330.

[34] Joseph A. Kahl, *The American Class Structure,* New York: Rinehart, 1957, pp. 251-262. Lipset and Bendix, *Social Mobility in Industrial Society,* pp. 86-88, refer approvingly to Kahl's technique for partitioning total mobility into gross and net mobility.

[35] Seymour Martin Lipset and Hans L. Zetterberg, Chap. 2, in Lipset and Bendix, *Social Mobility in Industrial Society.* Later studies generally support the conclusions of Lipset and Zetterberg. See Peter M. Blau and O. Dudley Duncan, *The American Occupational Structure,* New York: Wiley, 1967.

groups. For example, the Negro population of the United States amounts to 11 per cent of the total population, and the bulk of Negroes cannot easily obtain white-collar work. Minorities sharing the culture of poverty are immobile not because of legal restrictions but because of traditional prejudice and discrimination and the hopelessness engendered by such experience. In an average mobility rate for the United States as a whole, the immobility of these minorities is combined with the high mobility rate of white Americans. Even if sons of working-class Negroes in the United States are more likely to go to college than sons of European workers, they cannot be mobile, in accordance with an occupational criterion of mobility, without obtaining white-collar jobs. Hence a crucial question is whether a college education gives them better opportunities for white-collar employment than sons of European workers have without higher education. (It probably does.)

In all industrial societies formal education tends to allocate people to occupational levels. In contemporary Japan, for example, educational attainment is important enough in personnel recruitment so that educational attainment and occupational status correlate extremely well in the large factory.[36] Whether the relationship between educational and occupational attainment implies intergenerational *mobility* depends on the correlation between *parental status* and the *education* of offspring. Data from the Boalt study of social mobility in Stockholm (Table 12.12) show a strong relationship between the occupational status of fathers and the educational attainment of sons.[37] More than half of the sons of high-status fathers (173 out of 282) graduated from college.[38] Sons of fathers of medium or low occupational statuses were much less likely to have gone this far in school. On the other hand, *some* of the sons of fathers of medium or low occupational statuses also attained this educational level, and the majority of them (138 out of 208) had high occupational status at the time of the study. In short, higher education may be the normal expectation on middle- and upper-class levels, but higher education is also a socioeconomic escalator for intellectually able youngsters from working-class backgrounds. If Stockholm is typical of contemporary large cities, formal education is a genuine channel of social mobility in industrial societies — and probably an increasingly important one. Bureaucratized economies can deal more rationally with qualifications like education than they can with personal factors like family connections. Besides, the size of urban societies creates staggering problems of social sifting; educational criteria offer a simple approach to screening.

[36] James C. Abegglen, *The Japanese Factory: Aspects of Its Social Organization,* Glencoe, Ill.: Free Press, 1958, p. 28.

[37] Boalt, "Social Mobility in Stockholm."

[38] The labels in Table 12.12 attempt to translate levels of the Swedish educational system into their closest American equivalent. Thus "college graduate" is the closest approximation of passing the student examination, which is required for university attendance in the Scandinavian countries. "Some college" refers to attendance at the *gymnasium* but without passing the student examination.

TABLE 12.12

Education of Sons Related to the Occupational Status of Their Fathers in 1936 and Their Own Occupational Status in 1949, Stockholm

Occupational Status of Sons	Education of Sons				
	College Graduate	Some College	Secondary School Graduate	Some Secondary School	Primary School Only
Fathers of high occupational status:					
High	135	1	—	—	—
Medium	38	52	15	31	6
Low	—	—	—	2	2
Fathers of medium occupational status:					
High	115	—	—	—	—
Medium	49	65	96	99	143
Low	—	2	7	24	116
Fathers of low occupational status:					
High	23	—	—	—	—
Medium	21	11	101	61	404
Low	—	2	21	37	515
Fathers of all occupational statuses:					
All statuses	381	133	240	254	1186

Source: Gunnar Boalt, "Social Mobility in Stockholm: A Pilot Investigation," in *Transactions of the Second World Congress of Sociology,* Vol. 2, London: International Sociological Association, 1954, p. 68.

Are the systems of formal education in contemporary societies sufficiently alike to account for the similarities in mobility rates? A recent study has shown that university students are less likely to come from working-class backgrounds in Germany, France, The Netherlands, Switzerland, and Austria than in Great Britain or the United States.[39] That is, industrial societies differ in the extent to which they approach equality of educational opportunity. They probably differ also in the extent to which educational achievement and occupational achievement are correlated. All the more puzzling, therefore, is the observed similarity in mobility rates reported in leading industrial countries. If such similarities persist in comparative studies conducted under the same auspices and using the same methods, this would suggest that industrial societies dip into lower strata to the same extent for persons of ability. Very likely, educational systems serve to provide opportunities for social ascent to such persons in all the industrial societies, although not to *all* young persons of talent.

[39] David V. Glass and René Koenig, *Soziale Schichtung und Soziale Mobilität,* Cologne: Westdeutcher Verlag, 1961, reviewed by Kurt B. Mayer in *American Sociological Review,* Vol. 28, August 1963, pp. 638-639.

But educational achievement need not guarantee high occupational status. In the United States, for example, one out of five 24-year-olds in 1960 completed one year of college or more.[40] It is unlikely that all of these persons will achieve high occupational status, partly because there are not sufficient opportunities, partly because the American educational system is not as selective of talent as some of the European systems.

High rates of gross mobility involve social *descent* as well as social *ascent*. Systems of formal education in all industrial societies alert parents to the prospect of downward mobility for their children; school failure conveys the same meaning in the suburbs of Tokyo, Paris, London, and New York: the likelihood of a *fall* in social status.

For several reasons, vertical mobility tends to be greater in large cities than in small towns or rural areas.[41] Large cities are characterized by far more elaborate division of labor than small towns. This means that youngsters are presented with more potential choices as to the roles they will play. Second, the anonymity of the metropolis allows the youngster who is unwilling to accept the same status as his parents more chance to avoid community pressures favoring status inheritance. Third, the concentration of high-quality educational institutions in large cities gives ambitious youngsters a better chance to utilize educational channels of mobility than they would have in smaller communities. Finally, the demographic characteristics of cities make for *net* upward mobility; the *growth* of cities creates new occupational opportunities—including high-level positions. And apart from the effect of growth, the larger the city, the greater is the proportion of the labor force in white-collar jobs.

Whether these additional opportunities for vertical mobility make city dwellers more ambitious depends, as Lipset and Bendix point out, on the ideology of the society. A society may discount small moves upward or downward and consider only meteoric careers as examples of mobility.[42] If, however, situations in which the son of a machinist becomes a mechanical engineer or the son of a salesman becomes an electrician are discounted, the citizen may recognize fewer possibilities for mobility than the sociologist. In the United States, one result of the tradition of celebrating meteoric careers and paying less attention to the more prosaic, step-by-step mobility is a counterideology of disbelief in the possibilities of social ascent.

Ideological Interpretations of Opportunities for Mobility. The objective situation never speaks for itself; it must always be interpreted by participants. Let us apply this sociological axiom to social mobility. Even if mobility rates of industrial societies are comparable, they may be interpreted as "high" or "low," "good" or "bad," depending on the cultural values of a particular tradition. Lipset and Bendix argue that the American belief in "opportunity" can

---

[40] Bureau of the Census, *United States Census of Population: 1960, United States Summary, Detailed Characteristics,* Washington, D.C.: Government Printing Office, 1963, p. 398.

[41] Lipset and Bendix, *Social Mobility in Industrial Society,* pp. 203-226, is the source of the data on which this paragraph is based.

[42] Lipset and Bendix, *Social Mobility in Industrial Society,* p. 117.

be better understood in terms of the equalitarian ideas of a new country than in terms of greater objective opportunities for social mobility on this side of the Atlantic Ocean:[43]

> We can only speculate when we assess the absence of a feudal past in America. Clearly it has not meant the absence of status distinctions, which have frequently been every bit as insidious on this side of the Atlantic as on the other. But it has led, among other factors, to an ideological equalitarianism, which is not any the less important because it has been contradicted throughout and on every side by the existence of status differences. No act is perhaps as symbolic of this persuasion as Thomas Jefferson's order to have a round table replace the rectangular one at the White House, because this would relieve him of the necessity to stipulate the order of precedence at official receptions. The implication of this act was not to deny the existing differences in rank and authority; it was rather a testimony to the belief that these were the accidental, not the essential, attributes of man. Among men of equal worth, it is not good form to insist on the accidental distinctions which divide them.
>
> Such ideological equalitarianism has played, and continues to play, an important rôle in facilitating social mobility in the United States. It enables the person of humble birth to regard mobility as an attainable goal, for himself or for his children. It facilitates his acceptance as an equal, if he succeeds in rising socially and economically. It mitigates the emotional distance between persons of different social rank. And it fosters in any existing elite the persuasion (however mistaken this may be in fact) that its eminence is the result of individual effort, and hence temporary. The point worth emphasising is not that these beliefs are often contradicted by the experience of those who hold them and that distinctions of status exist in fact. What calls for analysis is the persistence of this equalitarian ideology in the face of facts which contradict it. We would suggest that the absence of hereditary aristocracy has aided in this respect. Americans have rarely been exposed to persons whose conduct implies their own inherited and God-given superiority as well as the demand that others demonstrate their recognition of this fact by deferential behaviour.

The American ideological emphasis on equality provides a lens through which American mobility is viewed. Insofar as it is possible, mobility is interpreted as evidence of an open society. This optimistic interpretation of mobility in America perhaps explains why Horatio Alger found 50 million readers for his 135 novels—despite devastating criticism of his literary talents.[44] On the other hand, European traditions of élitism fostered disbelief in the reality of mobility on their side of the Atlantic Ocean. European observers were more prone to notice *immobility* because they were ideologically prepared to see it.

---

[43] Reprinted by permission. From Seymour Martin Lipset and Reinhard Bendix, "Ideological Equalitarianism and Social Mobility in the United States," *Transactions of the Second World Congress of Sociology*, Vol. 2, London: International Sociological Association, 1954, pp. 34-54.

[44] R. Richard Wohl, "The 'Rags to Riches Story': An Episode of Secular Idealism," in Bendix and Lipset, Eds., *Class, Status and Power: A Reader in Social Stratification*, Glencoe, Ill.: Free Press, 1953, pp. 388-395.

If ideological considerations exaggerate the actual differences in mobility rates between Europe and America, they also exaggerate the differences between mobility in nineteenth-century America and mobility in the contemporary United States. What schoolboy has not learned to associate the frontier with opportunity and the closing of the frontier with increasing social rigidity? Yet careful studies have not succeeded in demonstrating a tendency for mobility to decrease since 1900.[45] Even though opportunities have not decreased, it is what people *believe* to be true about mobility rather than the actual distribution of opportunities to rise or fall in status which produces satisfaction or discontent. We come back again to the principle of relative deprivation mentioned in Chapter 6.

Legitimate and Illegitimate Mobility Aspirations. Disbelief in the existence of occupational opportunities is especially pronounced in slum neighborhoods. The culture of poverty generates apathy and resentment rather than faith in the existence of legitimate opportunities (ambition). Dissatisfaction leads to ambition only when it is coupled with hope. When dissatisfaction occurs in conjunction with disbelief in legitimate opportunities, it promotes a willingness to utilize illegitimate opportunities. The slum boy sees the urban industrial economy from a peculiar perspective. He and his family have a low standard of living. Many of the people he observes in films and reads about in newspapers live more comfortably, and he would like to move up to their level. He has little chance to see the educational achievements and the occupational responsibilities that make a luxurious standard of living possible. The mass media do not, it is true, portray the idle rich to the exclusion of business and professional men, but élite occupational roles are represented vaguely and romantically. The middle-class child can "fill in" the details from observations in his milieu; he has some notion of what a lawyer or a business executive does at work and the preparations such careers entail. But a boy with few sources of information about high-status people may think that their only talent is a talent for spending money. Besides, illegitimate opportunities may seem accessible; legitimate opportunities may not.[46]

Social psychological research is capable of specifying how an objectively disadvantaged youngster perceives the alternative between legitimate and **illegitimate opportunities** *subjectively*. For a start, Richard Stephenson studied the occupational aspirations and expectations of 1000 ninth-grade students in New Jersey high schools.[47] He demonstrated that the occupational aspirations of ninth graders were uniformly high even though their concrete educational and job goals were correlated with their fathers' occupational status. They dream, but they know the difference between dream and reality. And Arthur Stinchcombe, in a study of a California high school, found that young-

---

[45] Lipset and Bendix, *Social Mobility in Industrial Societies,* p. 90.

[46] Richard A. Cloward, "Illegitimate Means, Anomie and Deviant Behavior," *American Sociological Review,* Vol. 24, April, 1959, pp. 164-176.

[47] Richard M. Stephenson, "Mobility Orientation and Stratification of 1,000 Ninth Graders," *American Sociological Review,* Vol. 22, April 1957, pp. 204-212.

sters who could not perceive education as leading anywhere were likely to feel resentful and to act rebellious.[48] Neither of these studies was specifically concerned with economically deprived or socially stigmatized adolescents. Yet such studies provide insights into the subjective reactions of slum youth. Nevertheless, many gaps remain in our knowledge of their assessment of legitimate and illegitimate opportunities.

Is the slum boy likely to believe that the way to a higher standard of living than his parents enjoy is through starting a business of his own? A careful study of the work histories of 935 wage earners in Oakland, California, showed that self-employment was one of the few positions of higher status attainable by manual workers.[49] Although the number of self-employed businessmen at any given time is small, a considerable number of manual workers have tried at some time in their lives to become self-employed. Most of them do not succeed because they are swimming against the tide. The trend in industrial societies is toward more bureaucratic organization of economic activity, greater capital investment per enterprise, and high mortality rates for new businesses.[50] But many try, and some thrive. Whether a slum youngster thinks about owning a gas station or a bar or about starting some other small business probably depends on whether people he has known have ventured into self-employment. If he is a Negro, the chances of his knowing someone with this kind of experience are small because so few American Negroes are self-employed businessmen; the maldistribution is self-perpetuating.

The slum boy not optimistic about starting a business of his own will not aspire to a managerial position in a large corporation either. This is feasible only for a youngster who plans to complete high school and then go on to college or engineering school. Working one's way up is no longer common.[51]

> Today fewer men rise from the bottom to the top places in industry and business than did a generation ago . . . more and more top jobs are being filled by men coming from the technical and engineering schools or from the universities. The route up for them is no longer through a hierarchy of increasing skill to management and ownership as it was two generations ago. The prudent mobile man today must prepare himself by education . . .

A personnel officer recruits executives for the large corporation and selects only those working-class youngsters who have demonstrated their potentialities by educational achievement. For the slum boy who lacks scholastic aptitude, becoming a business executive may be as difficult as becoming a physician or a lawyer.

For low-status youngsters with special talents, careers in professional sports

---

[48] Arthur Stinchcombe, *Sources of Rebellion in a High School,* Chicago: Quadrangle, 1964.

[49] Lipset and Bendix, *Social Mobility in Industrial Society,* pp. 156-181.

[50] Kurt B. Mayer, "Business Enterprise: Traditional Symbol of Opportunity," *British Journal of Sociology,* Vol. 4, June 1953, pp. 160-180.

[51] W. Lloyd Warner, Marcia Meeker, and Kenneth Eells, *Social Class in America,* Chicago: Science Research Associates, 1949, p. 24.

or entertainment offer possibilities for high prestige and income. For instance, for three-quarters of a century boxing has reflected the aspirations of disadvantaged minority groups in American cities. Sixty years ago, the leading boxers were Irish, German, and English; 40 years ago, they were Italian and Jewish; today they are Negro.[52] Boxing shares with careers in acting, singing, and baseball an emphasis upon performance rather than upon formal educational qualifications. But boxing differs from most careers in professional sports or in the entertainment field because the physical dangers are greater. Weinberg and Arond report that a majority of boxers sustain brain injuries which leave them mildly or severely "punch-drunk." The risks of a boxing career, its necessary brevity, and the handful of boxers who earn substantial money serve to discourage middle-class competition. This explains why professional boxers are recruited disproportionately from the minority currently on the socioeconomic floor—and why managers believe that a "hungry" boxer is better motivated.

Lower-class boys are not disadvantaged in competing for baseball careers, either. Although preadolescent boys dream of becoming baseball players (in the United States and Japan), middle-class parents smile benignly and refuse to regard baseball as a potential career. How can one plan on doing something that depends in part on muscular maturation? Since it is easier to predict that a 12-year-old boy has the aptitude for law school than the muscular coordination and the timing of a Joe DiMaggio, middle-class parents prefer to regard sports as recreation and school as vocational preparation. Professional football and tennis are more likely to recruit from the ranks of college players, thus restricting opportunities for nonacademic youngsters; but even in these sports, circumstances and talent sometimes catapult an unlikely person to fame and fortune.

Success in sports and entertainment depends on abilities that few youngsters possess; legitimate success without higher education is rare. This realization makes illegitimate opportunities more attractive to children who have educational difficulties. A slum boy may think of the money he would have by robbing a bank, a lower-class girl of the pretty clothes she could wear if she made herself sexually available to men with money. The slum youngster hears that gamblers are not strictly legitimate, but he observes that they suffer less for their sins than honest laborers for their virtues. He may disregard parental advice because he does not wish to forego the good things of life as his parents have done. On the other hand, his parents may be oriented to short-cut methods of making money also. The numbers racket and other forms of gambling flourish in slum neighborhoods.[53] The poor "waste" money on longshots because they believe that the gulf between what they have and what they would like to have can be bridged only by luck. They gamble even though they

[52] S. Kirson Weinberg and Henry Arond, "The Occupational Culture of the Boxer," *American Journal of Sociology,* Vol. 57, March 1952, pp. 460-469.

[53] Edward C. Devereux, "Gambling and the Social Structure," unpublished Ph. D. dissertation, Harvard University, 1950, Part V.

are aware of the odds against winning.[54] As a professional gambler testifying before a Congressional investigation put it, gambling gives substance to their daydreams. Armed robbery, like gambling, is a way of getting money by techniques that repudiate the exchange principle embodied in the economic institutions of industrial societies.

Lower-class youngsters, then, who are not able to utilize the educational escalator, may seek illegitimate means to avoid entrapment at the bottom of the socioeconomic heap. The values of the particular subculture in which they are socialized affects the choice between legitimate and illegitimate courses. Comparison of delinquency rates of second-generation Jewish and southern Italian boys in 1930 illustrates this.[55] The southern Italians had traditionally rejected education: their dialect was different from the Italian taught in schools, they needed their children's help in the fields, education could not help in their farming communities in any case. These attitudes were brought to the United States by many Italian immigrants, and they continued to be held by this close-knit subculture. Jewish tradition, on the other hand, stresses the value of education. Thus while the Jewish youngsters were encouraged to go to school, their Italian counterparts were told to go out and earn a living. These cultural differences explain why Jewish boys who were dissatisfied with poverty became ambitious and pursued legitimate roads to success, whereas Italian boys in the same circumstances were more likely to become delinquents.

How can delinquency be a substitute for respectability? What is the connection between the petty, crudely executed thefts of a hoodlum and success even of an illegitimate variety? Delinquents typically force open the back door of a grocery store and rifle the cash register; they drive off a car and "strip" it of radio, heater, and tires; they break into a darkened house and look for valuables; they beat up a drunk on the street and take his wallet. A professional con-man or safecracker would be ashamed to "pull jobs" so lacking in craftsmanship. The businessmen of crime, who operate lucrative rackets, have political friends to intercede with police and prosecutors, and hire top-notch lawyers, bear slight resemblance to hoodlums who gain little from crime but daredevil escapades to recall during incarceration.

Yet there is a connection. Although some juvenile delinquents remain the unskilled workers of crime, enjoying a trifling income and spending most of their lives in custody, a few graduate into the ranks of organized crime, as Al Capone did. In the annals of illegitimate opportunity, Al Capone was a Horatio

---

[54] In an experiment directed by Professor Frederick Mosteller of the gambling behavior of Harvard undergraduates (middle class) and National Guardsmen (lower class), Mosteller provided all visitors to his experimental gambling casino with precise odds before taking bets. Nevertheless, the National Guardsmen bet more heavily than the college students. See James Olds, "Gambling and the Value of Money," *Lab Bulletin,* Vol. 2, October 1949, Laboratory of Social Relations, Harvard University, pp. 1-5.

[55] Jackson Toby, "Hoodlum or Business Man: An American Dilemma," in Marshall Sklare, Ed., *The Jews,* Glencoe, Ill.: Free Press, 1958, pp. 542-550.

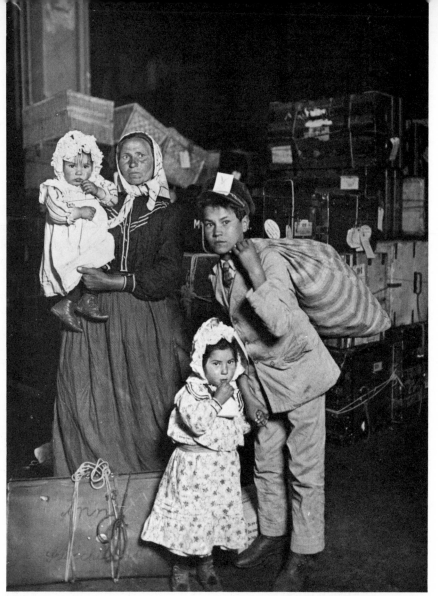

Alger story, a Brooklyn boy who made good in Chicago.[56] Organized crime has to staff openings in its ranks without the benefit of formal educational preparation. Important racketeers do not write books explaining their recruiting methods, but they probably look for promising youngsters among alumni of reformatories and prisons. Organized crime, because its operations are conspicuous, must also have collaborators in politics and law enforcement. Thus the slum boy who joins the local political club, working first as a precinct captain, then as a ward leader, may develop a close relationship with local gambling interests. This relationship may be even closer if the racketeers and the politicians are members of the same disadvantaged ethnic group striving to

[56] Frank Tannenbaum, *Crime and the Community,* New York: Columbia University Press, 1938.

move up the ladder. Daniel Bell lays great emphasis on the parallel strivings of racketeers and politicians in his analysis of the relationship between politics and crime in American cities.[57]

CONCLUSION

Members of a society evaluate one another's role behavior, partly because judgment is inherent in human interaction, partly because performance in one role is a basis for admission to, or exclusion from, another role. Industrial societies are especially prone to base role allocations on the evaluation of past performances.

Some sociologists believe that mutual evaluations can occur without generating a system of social stratification, but the majority of sociologists assume that a hierarchy of deference emerges in all societies. The religious, educational, economic, or political characteristics associated with particular positions in the hierarchy in particular societies is an empirical matter. Several factors account for the crystallization of status in the form of social strata.

1. Judgments tend to be generalized to the *person* instead of remaining confined to specific *roles*. Thus the individual receives a composite prestige rating based on his social participation in all of his roles.
2. Judgments tend to be generalized to the kinship unit instead of remaining confined to the individual. Thus infants automatically occupy the status possessed by their parents.
3. The advantages inherent in a hierarchy of prestige and rewards are often transmitted from one generation to the next because high-status parents can provide better opportunities for their children than lower-status parents.

Social classes can be distinguished in industrial societies despite the fluidity resulting from heterogeneous populations, geographic mobility, and opportunities to rise or fall in status during one's lifetime. Sociologists have developed several techniques for measuring class membership: (1) reputational ratings, (2) self-placement, (3) evaluation of cultural artifacts, and (4) indirect ratings based on the correlation between social honor and occupation, education, and income. Implicit in these various techniques are assumptions about the process of status determination in industrial societies. Reputational ratings assume that members of a community are sufficiently aware of the prestige hierarchy that they are able to place their friends and acquaintances in it. The self-placement technique assumes that a respondent's *identification* with a social class is a good indication of his objective position in the stratification

---

[57] Daniel Bell, "Crime as an American Way of Life," *Antioch Review,* Vol. 13, Summer 1953, pp. 131-156.

system. Evaluation of cultural artifacts is based on the premise that different symbols are used at different levels of the deference hierarchy. Status ratings based on occupation rest on the theory that the occupational role is the main determinant of status in industrial societies, directly for adult males, indirectly for women and children. Status ratings based on educational achievement rest on the correlation observed between occupational and educational attainments. Finally, status ratings based on income rest on the assumption that the more luxurious style of life made possible by a large income is positively valued in industrial societies and must therefore be at least roughly related to judgments of social worth.

An increase in family income may be used to claim higher social standing in the community. A newer car, a coat of paint on the house, and fashionable clothes symbolize this claim. From a narrow economic point of view the expressive use of income is *wasteful;* a famous economist called this "conspicuous consumption" and "conspicuous waste."[58] This assumes that symbolic meanings are less valuable than intrinsic ones. From the point of view of maximizing human satisfactions, use of income to acquire and display symbols of social status is like any other voluntary expenditure. Money satisfies wants— in this case, it is used to help maintain a demeanor appropriate for the level of community deference the family thinks is its due.

Some evidence exists that classes are generated by the occupational system in essentially the same way in all industrial societies despite differences in historical and cultural circumstances. This increases the confidence of sociologists in the generality of the conclusions reached on the basis of stratification studies done in a few countries. If, however, social stratification in industrial societies depends mainly on occupational achievement, population elements not integrated into the occupational system cannot be rank ordered. W. Lloyd Warner dealt with this classificatory problem by attaching the label "lower-lower" to low-status people which Chapter 6 identified with the culture of poverty and the label "upper-upper" to élites whose high status transcended occupational considerations. An alternative approach would be to recognize that some people live in an industrial society but have little stake in its institutions or its system of social stratification.

Despite difficulties in measuring social mobility with precision, many studies of mobility have been made in industrial countries. They show (1) that all industrial societies are characterized by high rates of social mobility and (2) that all industrial societies have approximately the *same* mobility rates. This latter finding is especially surprising in view of the variety of histories and values. Perhaps more precise methods of comparing mobility rates will reveal differences in mobility patterns which we do not now appreciate. If it turns out, however, that industrial societies from varying cultural backgrounds have the same mobility rates, this would suggest that industrialization and urbanization are making developed countries more similar to one another than might be inferred from superficial differences in language and customs.

[58] Thorstein Veblen, *The Theory of the Leisure Class,* New York: Random House, 1931.

A high rate of gross mobility does not imply either a harmonious or a disharmonious society. If, however, a high rate of mobility is regarded by the members of a society as a sign of strength and flexibility, its consequences will be less disruptive than if mobility is considered an indication of societal disintegration. Interestingly enough, both the United States and the Soviet Union are proud of high rates of social mobility. To a lesser extent, so are the countries of Western Europe. In India, on the other hand, the high mobility rates resulting from industrialization can be achieved only by breaking down the caste organization of Indian society and the isolation of Indian villages; hence, mobility is regarded as a mixed blessing. Nevertheless, the leaders of India are pushing industrial development as fast as an impoverished economy and an overpopulated country can go.

Educational upgrading can be regarded as a crude index of the commitment of a society to high rates of mobility. Even for the sociologically unsophisticated, it is apparent that the system of formal education is the main mechanism of social mobility in contemporary societies. Of course, there are other reasons for the worldwide effort to upgrade education besides acceptance of high mobility rates. It has been argued that some underdeveloped countries put more resources into education than is necessary for their level of economic development and that therefore educational upgrading can be a form of conspicuous consumption. Education can also be valued for its own sake without concern for pragmatic consequences. The likelihood is, however, that the tremendous expansion of educational facilities throughout the world would not have take place without an acceptance of its logical consequences: increased utilization of education as a mechanism of social designation.

High rates of mobility tend to generate a belief in an open society. However, mobility may be defined in terms of meteoric careers; hence, it is possible for a society to have high rates of step-by-step mobility without ideological recognition of it. Some research has shown that mobile individuals have a greater tendency than the immobile to break down psychologically (possibly because mobility disconnects the mover from some of his primary groups) and to be politically apathetic (possibly because the mover must choose between the values of the group he has left and the values of the group he has joined).[59] A special case of immobility are those members of the society trapped at the bottom of the socioeconomic pile. Slum-dwelling minorities are less likely to believe that they can move up—except by a stroke of luck. Among minorities immersed in the culture of poverty, the principle of relative deprivation helps to explain a counter-ideology of disbelief in legitimate mobility. Skeptical about legitimate opportunities, minority group members may become demoralized, may use deviant means of social ascent, or may support social change to increase equality of opportunity.[60]

---

[59] For a summary of these studies, see Lipset and Bendix, *Social Mobility in Industrial Society*, pp. 64-72.

[60] Robert K. Merton, "Social Structure and Anomie," and "Continuities in the Theory of Social Structure and Anomie," in *Social Theory and Social Structure*, Glencoe, Ill.: Free Press, 1957, pp. 131-194.

SOME SIGNIFICANT LITERATURE ON SOCIAL STRATIFICATION AND MOBILITY

Otis Dudley Duncan and Robert W. Hodge, "Education and Occupational Mobility: A Regression Analysis" *American Journal of Sociology,* Vol. 68, May 1963, pp. 629–644. Data collected for a six-city survey of labor mobility in 1951 are reanalyzed to throw light on social mobility. The Chicago cases, consisting of 1105 male workers ranging from 25 to 64 years of age at the time of the original survey, are examined on four bases: (1) the number of years of school completed by the respondent, (2) the longest job held during 1950, (3) the job held in January 1940, and (4) his father's longest job. The analysis shows that fathers' occupational statuses were only weakly related to the occupational statuses of their sons. Educational attainment of the respondents was a more important factor in occupational status. In fact, part of the relationship between the occupational levels of fathers and sons is explainable through an intervening tie between the occupational statuses of fathers and the educational opportunities of sons. The authors are cautious in interpreting one of their most interesting findings: that the relationship between educational attainment and occupational status was stronger in 1950 than in 1940. If this finding is not due to peculiarities in their data or to artifacts of their data processing, it means that formal education is becoming *more important* as a mechanism of social placement. For a definitive study of American occupational stratification based on a 1962 survey of more than 20,000 males between the ages of 20 and 64, see Peter M. Blau and Otis D. Duncan, *The American Occupational Structure,* New York: Wiley, 1967.

Norval D. Glenn, "Negro Prestige Criteria: A Case Study in the Bases of Prestige," *American Journal of Sociology,* Vol. 68, May 1963, pp. 645–657. Many studies have shown that educational achievement is the most important single factor in prestige rankings among American Negroes. In the general American community, on the other hand, occupational attainment and educational achievement are correlated with prestige to about the same extent. Why should Negroes give education greater weight as a determinant of prestige than whites? Glenn offers three possible explanations: (1) Negroes may value education more than whites do, perhaps because higher education is rarer among Negroes than among whites. Higher education *is* rarer among Negroes: in 1950 nonwhites constituted 10.5 per cent of the American population and had about 7.6 per cent of the total years of school completed by persons 25 years old and older. (2) Education is more unequally distributed among Negroes than among whites, and relative scarcity may make for prestige. In 1950 the best-educated tenth of the white population had completed 16.8 percent of the years of school completed by whites, whereas the best-educated tenth of the nonwhite population had completed 21.4 per cent of the schooling completed by nonwhites. (3) Because higher education is rarer among Negroes, higher education may make a greater difference for Negroes than for whites in opening up high-level jobs. Actually, nonwhite college graduates get far better jobs than nonwhites who have had some college but have not graduated; graduation is less crucial to whites. For a study of the social origins of Negro professionals in the Washington, D. C., area, see G. Franklin Edwards, *The Negro Professional Class,* New York: Free Press, 1959.

August B. Hollingshead and Frederick G. Redlich, *Social Class and Mental Illness: A Community Study,* New York: Wiley, 1958. The authors investigated psychiatric cases active in New Haven, Connecticut, between June 1, 1950, and December 1, 1950, in order to find out whether the differing life circumstances of various social classes generate differing amounts and types of mental illness. They reported much higher prevalence of mental illness in lower strata than in higher strata. The concept of *prevalence* refers, however, to all cases known during the period of observation, not to new cases alone (*incidence*). The prevalence of mental illness during this five-month period was much greater than the incidence because mental illness typically requires lengthy treatment. In fact, the prevalence of psychosis was 21 times the incidence of psychosis in the lowest class but only seven times the incidence in the highest. One explanation of this class difference in the ratio of prevalence to incidence is that psychiatric treatment was less successful among lower-class persons, probably because of communication difficulties with middle-class psychiatrists. Variation in incidence by class level was by no means as sharp, but the data supported the hypothesis that lower-class persons were more likely than persons at higher social levels to break down psychologically. This summary is based on a review by Herbert Goldhamer, *American Sociological Review*, Vol. 24, August 1959, pp. 579–581. A careful review of the research literature on child development, however, indicates that the relationship between social class and personality is small. Insofar as personality tests reveal differences between middle-class and lower-class children, they show that middle-class children are somewhat *better* adjusted. See William H. Sewell, "Social Class and Childhood Personality," *Sociometry*, Vol. 24, December 1961, pp. 340–356.

Ruth R. Kornhauser, "The Warner Approach to Stratification," in Bendix and Lipset, Eds., *Class, Status and Power: A Reader in Social Stratification,* Glencoe, Ill.: Free Press, 1953, pp. 224–255. This analysis of W. Lloyd Warner's approach to social stratification is a careful, yet readable, summary of what Warner himself reports about his research methods in half a dozen books. In addition, the article contains a searching discussion of the methodological problems in Warner's researches, most of them gleaned from critical discussions in the sociological literature. For example:

1. Warner's definition of social class is based mainly on community prestige, but it takes too seriously what the members of the community *say* are the reasons for differential prestige. This tempts him to lump together (in his concept of class) prestige, economic power, political influence, and style of life instead of exploring empirically the relationships among these factors.
2. Since the places studied by Warner and his collaborators were small, well-integrated communities, findings based on them are not applicable to highly urbanized, more anonymous communities. In the metropolis, stratification may be thought of more fruitfully in terms of power hierarchies and interest groups than in terms of a prestige hierarchy.
3. Warner's analysis is essentially static, ignoring the immigration of the foreign-born and the emigration of ambitious youngsters to large cities.
4. Warner's portrayal of the prestige structure of the communities he studied gives heavier weight to the *social* values of upper- and middle-class residents than to the *economic* values of lower-class residents. Class differences in the criteria of allocating persons to strata forced Warner to construct a composite prestige hierarchy built from the varied perspectives of local residents. But he paid disproportional attention to the values of high-prestige respondents.

Daniel Kubat, "Social Mobility in Czechoslovakia," *American Sociological Review,* Vol. 28, April 1963, pp. 203–212. When the Communists came into power in Czechoslovakia in 1948, their ideological and administrative policies tended to restrict opportunities for mobility: (1) The Communist Party denied the existence of class differences and ridiculed the acquisition of a car and other symbols of success. (2) Income differences between manual and nonmanual occupations narrowed, thus reducing the incentive to leave manual occupations. (3) Since small business careers no longer existed, the main channel of mobility for children of manual workers became higher education. In addition to the financial and cultural obstacles similar to those experienced by children of workers in other industrial societies, higher education became unpalatable to workers' children in Czechoslovakia because it required verbalization of an ideological commitment to the regime. "We would thus hazard a conclusion — however tenuous because of the inaccessibility of many data — that the command economy of totalitarian societies discourages processes of social mobility once the rank order of the social structure has been set."

Eva Rosenfeld, "Social Stratification in a 'Classless' Society," *American Sociological Review,* Vol. 16, December 1951, pp. 766–844. Ideologically committed to social equality, collective farms in Israel (*kibbutzim*) are deliberately organized so that economic rewards are minimized. Food is eaten in a communal dining room. Children are brought up from birth in communal child-care arrangements. Room allocations have nothing to do with the importance of the individual's job. Nevertheless, in these small agricultural settlements — averaging 200 members — a managerial stratum and a rank-and-file stratum occupy distinct prestige levels. Eva Rosenfeld explains the emergence of prestige ranks as due to a scarcity of administrative talent in the pioneering days of the settlements. The survival of the settlements required continuity of management, and successful managers tended to be reelected. It is not clear what happened to the earlier glorification of manual labor. The pioneers insisted on turnover in managerial positions, which they considered unproductive, but this attitude must have changed subsequently to one of deference, which is apparently the present sentiment toward managers. For an impressionistic view of the personality consequences of *kibbutz* life, see Bruno Bettelheim, *The Children of the Dream,* New York: Macmillan, 1969.

Melvin Seeman, "Social Mobility and Administrative Behavior," *American Sociological Review,* Vol. 23, December 1958, pp. 633–642. Seeman calls attention to the possibility that occupational advancement is not necessarily due to a desire for upward mobility; sometimes it is the unintended consequence of intrinsic interest in one's work. He constructed a Mobility-Achievement scale to identify those whose social strivings take precedence over more intrinsic interests in health, family, community, and the like. Forty-four school executives filled our a questionnaire containing the scale and a job history, thus enabling Seeman to place them in one of four categories: " (1) the mobile status-seeker, (2) the unsuccessful status-seeker, (3) the mobile non-striver, and (4) the stable non-striver. The crucial point is that this typology, derived exclusively from the executive's standpoint, is related to the behavioral descriptions of him provided by the staff members and school board members." The scale succeeds in predicting administrative behavior.

Ralph H. Turner, "Sponsored and Contest Mobility and the School System," *American Sociological Review,* Vol. 25, December 1960, pp. 855–867. Industrial societies with the same *rate* of upward social mobility may nevertheless be characterized by different modes of recruitment into the élite. Specifically, Turner contrasts British "sponsored mobility" with American "contest mobility." *Sponsored mobility* "involves controlled selection in which the élite or their agents choose recruits early and carefully induct them into élite status." Thus the British educational system selects from the population of 11-year-old students those who will attend "grammar schools" and receive the education appropriate for those in high-status occupations. In *contest mobility* "élite status is the prize in an open contest, with every effort made to keep lagging contestants in the race until the climax." The American educational system (and specifically the comprehensive high school) avoids sharp social separation between superior and inferior students and enables youngsters to transfer into the college preparatory curriculum at a fairly late stage of their education. Hope for future success is kept alive much longer than in a system of sponsored mobility. Individual rebellion occurs (the hippie or the criminal), but organized opposition to the system is less likely. The delinquent's complaint is less that the system is unjust than that he has not gotten what he wanted out of it.

Y. C. Wang, "Western Impact and Social Mobility in China," *American Sociological Review,* Vol. 25, December 1960, pp. 843–855. Until the end of the nineteenth century, civil-service examinations offered broad opportunities to rural youth. "Education was relatively inexpensive, and once a scholar passed the examination at the provincial or national level, he joined the privileged group and assumed a leadership role in society." However, in 1902 the Chinese government established a modern educational system based on Japanese and Western models, and in 1905 civil-service examinations were abolished. Study abroad and a diploma from American or European universities became the most efficient route to fame and power. Prestigious education had become expensive; " . . . the opportunity to receive a higher education was virtually limited to men from official, professional, and mercantile families . . . . The only way a peasant could rise into officialdom was within a channel of violence—banditry or soldiery." Wang believes that the lack of mobility opportunities for rural youth and the resulting preponderance of urban-born officials in the central government helped create political instability in twentieth-century China. "The needs of the rural masses were neglected . . . ."

Harold L. Wilensky and Hugh Edwards, "The Skidder: Ideological Adjustments of Downwardly Mobile Workers," *American Sociological Review,* Vol. 24, April 1959, pp. 215–231. In 1951 the Survey Research Center of the University of Michigan obtained questionnaire responses on occupational history from 495 male manual workers of urban backgrounds in two plants of a manufacturing company in a midwestern city. Of these, 20 per cent were *worklife skidders:* workers who entered the factory from a previous white-collar occupation; and 19 per cent were *intergenerational skidders:* blue-collar sons of white-collar fathers. Both types of skidders were more likely than nonskidders to reject identification with the working class, to believe in ability rather than seniority as a proper basis for promotion, to aspire to middle-class positions, to anticipate leaving the factory soon, to say they would accept the job of foreman if it were offered to them, and to expect middle-class positions for their children. Apparently early socialization was a more important influence than subsequent or anticipatory socialization. "The ideological conservatism of skidders can be explained almost entirely by the presence of . . . *older* worklife skidders and . . . *young* intergenerational skidders." [Emphasis added]. However, in a study of high school seniors from ten high schools in Los Angeles and Beverly Hills (1352 boys and 1441 girls), status prospects had more influence on the achievement values of the individual than his status origins. See Ralph H. Turner, *The Social Context of Ambition,* San Francisco: Chandler, 1964. Similarly, a study of alienation and rebellion among high school students showed status prospects a better predictor of conformity or rebelliousness than status origins. See Arthur L. Stinchcombe, *Rebellion in a High School,* Chicago: Quadrangle, 1964.

DEVIANCE AND SOCIAL CONTROL

Courtesy of Columbia Pictures

The more heterogeneous the culture and the more swiftly its norms change, the less consensus about right and wrong exists within the society. In the United States, for instance, moral values differ in upper and lower classes, among blacks and whites, and in various regions, occupations, religions, and ethnic groups. This social heterogeneity of industrial societies implies value pluralism, and value pluralism makes for conflict, not consensus.[1] For example, twelve million Americans have used marijuana despite severe penalties for those who are caught.[2] Instead of overwhelming consensus that marijuana smoking is wrong, even on the part of marijuana smokers themselves, and just a sprinkling of individuals who believe that smoking pot is legitimate, American society is polarized into a large group, probably a majority, who consider marijuana smoking *wrong* and a smaller group (but a substantial proportion of adolescents and young adults) who consider pot harmless and are *indignant* at societal interference. The results of the Asch experiment (Chapter 1) show that a non-conformist is immensely strengthened by having even one ally. And in contemporary societies allies for illegal behavior are not too difficult to locate. Polarization implies that this process has gone far enough so that "group conflict" better describes the situation than the consensus-oriented concept of **social control.**

Yet moral polarization does not characterize American society on every topic. A fairly strong consensus exists that persons who smell and persons who force others to participate in sexual relations are reprehensible. Body odor and rape seem an incongruous combination. One is informally disapproved; the other is a statutory crime punishable by the state. From the sociological point of view, this difference is less important than that both deviate from the moral order. **Deviance** is the *purposive* evasion or defiance of a normative consensus. If no normative consensus exists, the concept of deviance is inappropriate. Thus political opponents of American military involvement in Viet Nam, even those who express their dissent by engaging in illegal confrontations with the military forces or the police, consider their behavior morally justified, and a sizable portion of the American people agree. They are law violators but not deviants.

Other acts are illegal without being deviant. Drunken driving, even when it results in injuries to persons or in property damage, does not arouse the same moral indignation as theft or assault. Neither do **white-collar crimes,** which are offenses committed by business and professional people against laws regulating their activities—for example, patent infringement. The term **folk crime** has been coined to tag violations of law tolerated by the general public. Drunken driving may come to be regarded with the same indignation as theft; morality will have caught up with the laws required in a complex indus-

---

[1] Dennis Wrong, "The Oversocialized Conception of Man in Modern Sociology," *American Sociological Review,* Vol. 25, April 1961, pp. 183-193; Ralf Dahrendorf, *Class Conflict in Industrial Society,* Stanford, Calif.: Stanford University Press, 1959.

[2] James L. Goddard, "Marihuana: Should It Be Legalized?" *Life,* Oct. 31, 1969, p. 34.

trial society. H. Laurence Ross offers the following hypotheses explaining the emergence of illegalities that are at least temporarily not considered immoral.[3]

(a) Major increments to the complexity of a society, of which the automobile is a technological example, create a need for regulation where none was previously necessary.

(b) Legislation to regulate the conditions brought about by increasing complexity reclassifies certain prevalent non-criminal behavior as crime.

(c) Especially where the harmful effect of the proscribed behavior is indirect or improbable in most instances, the novel legislation may not be related to previously existing norms.

(d) Criminal behavior in folk crime is rooted, not necessarily in lower-class culture, but in the culture of groups most affected by the social or technological changes that the legislation attempts to control. White-collar crime is the special case of folk crime resulting from legislation regulating business and finance. The automobile, with its impact on all social classes, generates more pervasive forms of folk crime.

(e) In particular instances, large numbers of people, including those of high status, will be involved in law violations related to major social changes.

(f) The lack of congruence between the new laws and established mores, the generally higher social status of the violators, and the possibly large size of the group of violators among the total population, will tend to be associated with preferential treatment of folk criminals in the public image and in the judicial process.

Figure 13.1 shows the relationship between deviance and **crime.** Rape is both deviant and illegal; a parent punishing his child is neither. Bear in mind that these are evaluations of behavior, in the one case by the general public in terms of a moral consensus, in the other by officials in terms of the criminal law. Behavior adjudged acceptable in terms of both criteria may nevertheless be anti-social by other standards. Until quite recently water and air pollution

Evaluation by the criminal law	Evaluation by the public	
	Deviant	Acceptable
Criminal	RAPE	DRUNKEN DRIVING
Legal	BODY ODOR	PARENT PUNISHING HIS CHILD

FIGURE 13.1   **Evaluation of behavior by the public at large and evaluation by the legal system.**

[3] H. Laurence Ross, "Traffic Law Violation: A Folk Crime," *Social Problems,* Vol. 8, Winter 1960–1961, pp. 236–237.

did not arouse public indignation and was usually not illegal. On the other hand, witchcraft was illegal and deviant in seventeenth-century Massachusetts.[4]

DEVIANT ACTS, DEVIANT ROLES, DEVIANT SUBCULTURES

The perpetrator of a deviant act, be it homosexuality, drug use, or overtime parking, is not necessarily labeled a homosexual, a drug addict, or an overtime parker. However, if conforming members of society do assume that someone is playing a deviant role, they expect continued deviant acts from him; often he expects them of himself. Thus socialization into deviant roles occurs. The likelihood that a deviant act will be diagnosed by the author of the act and by the rest of society as symptomatic of a deviant identity depends on the cultural definition of the meaning of the act, not on its intrinsic qualities. One can get innumerable parking tickets without becoming socially defined as an overtime parker. On the other hand, public discovery of a single homosexual act may be enough to label a person a deviant forever:[5]

> One of the factors that materially contributes to the development of exclusively homosexual histories is the ostracism which society imposes upon one who is discovered to have had perhaps no more than a lone experience.

Once this label is affixed, the bearer is subject to arrest in some localities, may be unofficially discriminated against in hiring practices, and is often mocked or abused.

The likelihood that a deviant act will recur and become organized in the form of a social role is usually increased when supported by a deviant subculture. For example, the homosexual subcultures found in most large cities give encouragement to informal social groups, bars, private clubs, and magazines.[6] The individual rejected by the heterosexual community because of a homosexual experience finds acceptance and opportunities for additional homosexual activity in this subculture. A subculture also may prevent a deviant act from developing into a deviant role. In a study of schoolboys between 12 and 17 years of age in Nashville, Tennessee, Albert Reiss found that homo-

---

[4] Kai T. Erikson, *Wayward Puritans: A Study in the Sociology of Deviance,* New York: Wiley, 1966.

[5] Alfred C. Kinsey, Wardell B. Pomeroy, and Clyde E. Martin, *Sexual Behavior in the Human Male,* Philadelphia, Pa.: Saunders, 1948, p. 663.

[6] Evelyn Hooker, "Male Homosexuals and Their 'Worlds,' " in Judd Marmor, Ed., *Sexual Inversion: The Multiple Roots of Homosexuality,* New York: Basic Books, 1965, pp. 83-107; Maurice Leznoff and William A. Westley, "The Homosexual Community," *Social Problems,* Vol. 4, April 1956, pp. 257-263.

United Press International

sexual behavior defined as predatory was condoned by the peer group.[7] Delinquent cliques encouraged members to "make money off queers" by engaging in sexual acts, as long as these acts were simply a way of raising money and were not considered enjoyable. The boys did not regard themselves as either prostitutes or homosexuals, and they anticipated giving up this "racket" when they were old enough to obtain "good" jobs. In this case homosexual acts occurred without tending to develop into homosexual roles.

The preceding examples indicate that the meaning of a deviant act is redefined in a deviant subculture. The homosexual subculture glorifies homosexual love; delinquent subcultures legitimize adolescent stealing, fighting, and drug use. These contracultures are collective solutions to the problem of stigma. They are more satisfactory to the individual than is either alternative: engaging in deviant acts without social support or striving to conform to an institutionalized rule which may be difficult or frustrating.[8] Two theorists of

[7] Albert J. Reiss, Jr., "The Social Integration of Queers and Peers," *Social Problems,* Vol. 9, Fall 1961, pp. 102-120.

[8] Albert K. Cohen, "The Study of Social Disorganization and Deviant Behavior," in Robert K. Merton, Leonard Broom, and Leonard S. Cottrell, Jr., Eds., *Sociology Today: Problems and Prospects,* New York: Basic Books, 1959, pp. 461-484.

gang delinquency have described the sequence by which lower-class adolescents build delinquent subcultures out of individual alienation.[9] The underlying maladjustment of recruits to criminal, fighting, or drug-using gangs is an inability to find legitimate means to realize their aspirations for money and the things money will buy. They are resentful because the equalitarian ideology of American society seems to promise them a fair share of the good things of life, and they realize that ethnic or class barriers will prevent them from attaining these goals. The feeling of unjust deprivation underlies alienation, "a process of withdrawal of attributions of legitimacy from established social norms." When youngsters become disenchanted with conventional society, they seek support from others who are similarly alienated, and they evolve a collective solution to their common problem. Not only do they join in delinquent acts, they also develop in concert "a supporting structure of beliefs and values that provide advance justification for deviant conduct." If these groups of alienated adolescent boys live in a slum community containing opportunities to learn and practice criminal skills under the guidance of older thieves, their gang crystallizes around stealing. If they live in a disorganized neighborhood where neither legitimate nor illegitimate opportunities for financial gain are plentiful, they stage gang wars to establish neighborhood hegemony. If the criminal or fighting opportunities disappear—or were never available—the focus of gang activity becomes drug use or heavy drinking. In short, delinquent subcultures may be interpreted as collective solutions to the problems experienced by many lower-class boys.

The concept of the deviant subculture supplements the explanation of Chapter 5 for the attraction of a deviant role, namely, an impaired capacity to play legitimate roles or a self-concept of such incapacity. The deviant subculture gives these individuals a chance to prove their worth to themselves and to a limited circle of significant others: failures in conventional society may be successes here. This may lead to a radical break with conventional institutions. Homosexual subcultures, for example, have relatively few points of contact with family life. Delinquent gangs, too, usually are isolated from the influence of schools, churches, and business firms. But there are other deviant subcultures that are virtually institutionalized.

Organized crime is one deviant subculture indirectly supported by society. Although the "rackets" are not legitimate, they enjoy *covert* support and protection from *overtly* conforming members of the community. For instance, in a slum neighborhood where there is considerable betting on horse races, a bookie may be an object of envy to the youth of the community. He wears new and expensive clothes, drives a flashy car, and always has money in his pocket. He is by no means a social outcast: not only do people of the neighborhood place bets with him, not only are ambitious youngsters eager to work for him as "runners"; he is also on familiar terms with local police—he pays

[9] Richard E. Cloward and Lloyd E. Ohlin, *Delinquency and Opportunity: A Theory of Delinquent Gangs,* Glencoe, Ill.: Free Press, 1960.

them off on a regular basis. A boy may find this bookie a more attractive role model than his own father, a day laborer. Here an illegitimate role offers potential recruits rewards greater than or at least equal to the rewards of a legitimate role. Gambling—only part of which is illegal bookmaking—is one of America's largest industries. The complex operations which bookmaking requires means that bookmaking must be operated "in a goldfish bowl." Police cannot help being aware of such activities. Therefore organized crime spends large sums to induce law enforcement officials to ignore their illegal transactions.[10]

THE FIRST LINE OF DEFENSE AGAINST DEVIANCE: INTERNALIZED VALUES

There is a complex relationship between legal norms and collective morality. The legislators and judges who make and interpret the law are, by and large, well-educated, high-status persons. No matter how hard they try to be merely spokesmen of collective sentiments, they cannot help reading the parochial morality of their milieu into their conception of the public conscience. Thus the administration of the criminal law is not simply the enforcement of morality—except perhaps for middle-aged, middle-class, male, white Protestants. For members of other groups, the intentional commission of a crime is not synonymous with evasion or defiance of the **collective conscience.** Everyone perceives morality from the vantage point of his own place in the social structure. Drunken driving, nonsupport of spouse and children, stealing from large corporations, and cheating on income-tax returns are not condemned to the same extent by different segments of a heterogeneous industrial society, but they are all condemned by the state as illegal and punishable.

Violations of the value consensus by people who have been brought up to believe that drunken driving, theft, assault, and other prohibited acts are wrong is a problem we wish to explain. Persons engage in what is for them deviant behavior because socialization is never fully successful. Since human beings do not have the social rules imbedded in their biological makeup, as ants and bees do, the individual must *learn* the group pattern. On any subsequent occasion when he experiences envy, hatred, fear, or other strong emotions, he faces a choice between his own deviant inclinations and his internalized desire to obey the rules of his society. The collective conscience formulates universal prohibitions. Yet circumstances occur in the lives of *most* people when they wish to drive an automobile at 80 miles an hour, beat

[10] President's Commission on Law Enforcement and Administration of Justice, *Task Force Report: Organized Crime,* Washington, D. C.: Government Printing Office, 1967, pp. 61-79, 114-126.

up an enemy, or take something without paying for it. The fact that the rules have to be *learned* makes crime possible; the fact that situations of extraordinary temptation or **strain** arise makes crime inevitable. It is a commonplace of criminology that quite ordinary people embezzle large sums of money from their employers or kill close relatives in the course of a quarrel.[11]

Situations of strain impinge on everyone. Some people succumb; others do not. During the siege of Leningrad from 1941 to 1943 more than a million Russians died, a considerable portion of starvation; yet cannibalism was rare.[12] Differential internalization of norms helps to explain why some hungry people resorted to cannibalism while most did not. In short, peculiarities of *socialization* help explain the incidence of deviant behavior. Chapter 4 called attention to socialization experiences that engender resentment against parents and weak internalization of the norms they seek to inculcate (inadequate socialization). Chapter 5 called attention to socialization experiences that prepare the individual for roles in subgroups but handicap him for participating in the central institutions of the larger society (inappropriate socialization). Inappropriate socialization is common in highly differentiated industrial societies. By smoking pot, a jazz musician becomes an "insider" to his colleagues and an "outsider" to law enforcement officials and to "squares."[13]

Inadequate and inappropriate socialization help explain the incidence of deviant behavior because deviant *behavior* is an outcome of deviant *motivation*. But deviant motivation is not necessarily acted out in behavior. Whether it is or not depends on the cultural definitions and social controls of the society. If cannibalism is defined by the culture as horrifying, extreme hunger may not be sufficient to evoke it. If the prohibited behavior must take place under public scrutiny in order to occur at all, the individual may restrain his deviant motivations rather than risk sanctions. More generally, social control should be thought of not only as a response to deviance but as a filter between deviant motivation and deviant behavior.[14]

It is not difficult to understand why crime and other forms of deviance exist. It is harder to explain conformity. Yet conformity is so commonplace that explanations for criminality are thought to be necessary. Do the police forces of organized society explain conformity? The potential thief may refrain from stealing because he is afraid he will be caught and punished. The classic demonstration of the validity of this argument was provided by the Nazis during the Second World War; they deported all of Denmark's police force and crime in-

---

[11] Donald R. Cressey, *Other People's Money: A Study in the Social Psychology of Embezzlement,* Glencoe, Ill.: Free Press, 1953; Marvin E. Wolfgang, *Patterns in Criminal Homicide,* Philadelphia: University of Pennsylvania Press, 1958.

[12] Harrison E. Salisbury, *The Siege of Leningrad,* New York: Harper & Row, 1969.

[13] Howard S. Becker, *Outsiders: Studies in the Sociology of Deviance,* New York: Free Press, 1963, Chaps. 3, 4, 5, and 6.

[14] Albert J. Reiss, Jr., "The Study of Deviant Behavior: Where the Action Is," *Ohio Valley Sociologist,* Vol. 32, Autumn 1966, p. 6.

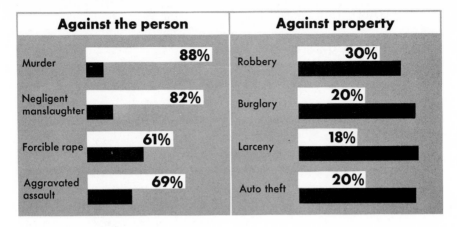

Against the person		Against property	
Murder	**88%**	Robbery	**30%**
Negligent manslaughter	**82%**	Burglary	**20%**
Forcible rape	**61%**	Larceny	**18%**
Aggravated assault	**69%**	Auto theft	**20%**

☐ CLEARED
■ NOT CLEARED

FIGURE 13.2 **Crimes cleared by arrest, 1967.** Source: Federal Bureau of Investigation, *Uniform Crime Reports — 1967,* Washington, D.C.: Government Printing Office, 1968, p. 31.

creased greatly.[15] This demonstration notwithstanding, laymen exaggerate the **deterrent** value of the police. In industrial societies, a thief has at least an even chance of not getting caught. For example, in 1967 less than 30 per cent of the property crimes reported to the police in American cities were cleared by the arrest of suspects, as Fig. 13.2 shows. The police do better in solving crimes against the person: murder, rape, aggravated assault. Apparently the conditions of life in industrial societies — the mobility, the anonymity, the ready marketability of valuables — are not conducive to catching thieves. Since urbanization and industrialization are increasing in the contemporary world, stealing will become *less* risky in the decades ahead — barring an unanticipated breakthrough in police science. Table 13.1 shows that in American cities a smaller proportion of serious crimes are cleared by the arrest of suspects than used to be the case. Although small cities tend to be somewhat more successful than large cities in solving crimes, the decrease in police efficiency afflicts small as well as large cities. Another way of looking at police effectiveness is to examine the number of known crimes in various jurisdictions in proportion to population. Table 13.2 shows that there are many more serious crimes reported in large cities in proportion to population than in small cities. In short, the police are necessarily inefficient under contemporary conditions. If the police were the only reason that the temptation to steal did not eventuate in thefts, indus-

[15] Jörgen Trolle, *Syv Maneder uten politi* (Seven Months without Police), Copenhagen, 1945, quoted in Nils Christie, "Scandinavian Criminology," *Sociological Inquiry,* Vol. 31, Winter 1961, p. 101. A one-day strike of the Montreal police force taught the same lesson. See Gerald Clark, "Black Tuesday in Montreal: What Happens When the Police Strike," *The New York Times Magazine,* November 16, 1969, pp. 45, 176-196.

TABLE 13.1

Percentage of Crimes Cleared by the Arrest of Suspects in American Cities, 1947–1967, by Size of City

Type of Crime	Year	Under 10,000	10,000– 25,000	25,000– 50,000	50,000– 100,000	100,000– 250,000	250,000 and over
Murder	1947	88.9	91.1	89.6	92.2	90.1	85.6
	1957	85.0	94.8	94.7	95.0	93.8	90.1
	1967	87.1	91.1	89.1	89.3	91.7	87.9
Robbery	1947	48.1	40.3	40.1	34.0	33.8	43.5
	1957	48.4	42.1	44.5	40.8	39.9	42.9
	1967	35.0	33.1	30.5	28.9	29.9	28.6
Aggravated assaults	1947	89.3	88.3	82.0	83.8	72.8	77.4
	1957	89.5	87.1	88.3	81.3	71.3	75.9
	1967	76.0	74.3	69.6	69.2	73.6	66.8
Burglary	1947	35.6	28.3	27.5	27.4	25.1	31.2
	1957	33.8	31.8	29.8	28.4	27.6	29.6
	1967	21.8	20.2	20.3	19.9	20.8	20.1
Auto theft	1947	39.7	33.2	26.9	24.9	24.8	30.4
	1957	46.0	40.5	30.1	28.5	29.7	28.2
	1967	36.7	28.3	22.4	20.0	21.2	18.6

Note: Rape and larceny are not included in this table because the definition of these offenses changed between 1947 and 1967, making data incomparable.

Source: Federal Bureau of Investigation, *Uniform Crime Reports,* various years.

trial societies would need a policeman for every ten citizens and special police to watch the police.

Criminologists are prone to stress another factor to explain why the temptation to steal only infrequently results in thefts or attempted thefts. It takes skill to steal successfully. Trying to learn shoplifting or safecracking through trial-and-error methods is likely to result in swift apprehension. In point of fact, few youngsters steal without previous contact with more sophisticated delinquents. They serve an informal apprenticeship, learning what things are worth stealing and how to dispose of them, what techniques to use to gain entrance unobtrusively to stores, factories, and private homes, and how to answer the questions of detectives to avoid self-incrimination. This training is not available for the asking. Nor do motion pictures or television programs provide sufficiently detailed instruction. Neighborhoods differ greatly in the opportunities they present for training in deviant activities.[16] High-delinquency neighborhoods, for example, are not only neighborhoods where theft and violence are

[16] Richard A. Cloward and Lloyd E. Ohlin, *Delinquency and Opportunity: A Theory of Delinquent Gangs,* Glencoe, Ill.: Free Press, 1960, Chaps. 6 and 7.

TABLE 13.2

**Differential Crime Rates in American Cities, by Size of Community, 1967
(Major Crimes Known to Police, Rate per 100,000 Population)**

Type of crime	Size of City					
	Under 10,000	10,000– 25,000	25,000– 50,000	50,000– 100,000	100,000– 250,000	Over 250,000
Murder	3	3	4	4	7	12
Forcible rape	5	7	8	10	14	27
Robbery	15	26	45	69	108	330
Aggravated assault	76	79	85	101	160	257
Burglary	456	574	668	821	1,111	1,474
Larceny—$50 and over	329	416	560	626	692	913
Auto theft	123	181	259	371	485	776

Source: Adapted from Federal Bureau of Investigation, *Uniform Crime Reports—1967*, Washington, D.C.: Government Printing Office, 1968, pp. 100-101.

likely to occur; they are also neighborhoods where a growing boy has a better chance than in other neighborhoods to become friendly with persons who will teach him how to steal or to look for "kicks" in gang fighting or drug use. The theory of **differential association** attempts to explain socialization into criminal roles in terms of a preponderance of criminal over noncriminal associations,[17] thus facilitating the learning of criminal skills.

Crime is not mere negativism; it usually requires a repertoire of skills that have to be learned in a social context. Yet the infrequency of deviance cannot be accounted for solely by lack of opportunity to learn illegitimate skills. Persons who happen to live in communities where deviant activities are infrequent are mobile enough in industrial societies to find models for deviant roles in other communities. The *raggare* gangs of Stockholm are a case in point. They recruit youngsters from all over the city. This is necessary because of a deliberate policy (by officials charged with allocating scarce housing) to distribute multiproblem families as widely as possible instead of concentrating them in certain neighborhoods as occurs in the United States and Great Britain. Perhaps the *raggare* youths' tremendous emphasis on automobiles is an adaptation to the difficulties of getting into contact with other deviantly oriented adolescents under Swedish conditions.

[17] Edwin H. Sutherland and Donald R. Cressey, *Principles of Criminology*, 6th ed., New York: Lippincott, 1960, p. 78; several articles in the summer 1960 issue of *Social Problems* were devoted to theory and research on differential association.

Some people conform because they are afraid of being caught and punished, and others conform because they have not located models to show them
how to carry out their deviant impulses. However, neither of these factors,
singly or in conjunction with one another, seems adequate to explain widespread resistance to ever-present temptations. A better explanation of conformity lies in the *internal* resources for resisting illicit motives, namely, guilt and
shame.

Guilt: The Internalized Policeman. To the extent that the individual has
incorporated within his own personality the "do's" and "don'ts" of the collective conscience, society has mobilized his self-respect on the side of conformity. He feels that stealing and murder are *wrong,* not merely acts which
might arouse the police force. Suppose, for example, a woman shopper sees in
a jewelry store a bracelet which she would like to own but cannot afford; she
thinks she could put it in her pocketbook without anyone seeing her. But the
norms within her psyche prevent her from taking advantage of this opportunity. She knows that she could not respect herself if she thought of herself as a
"thief."

Most conforming behavior can be understood as part of the individual's
attempt to maintain his self-conception intact. If the conscience of every member of society were precisely the same, **guilt** feelings would always work in
favor of conformity. In fact, however, the agents of socialization (parents,
friends, neighbors, teachers) stress different norms and apply them with varying
degrees of pressure. The result is that within the same society (1) notions of
right and wrong differ from personality to personality, and (2) even though
there may be consensus that certain behavior is wrong, individuals differ in the
extent to which they can engage in such behavior without guilt reactions incompatible with their self-conceptions. Some people have such strict consciences that they suffer remorse over deviations which most members of the
society would consider trifling. On the other hand, psychiatrists occasionally
encounter individuals who have hardly been touched by the socialization
process. They are egocentric and amoral (like the infant); they respond to
their impulses, oblivious of social rules. Apparently, anything they may wish to
do is compatible with their self-conceptions. (Chapter 4 discussed psychopaths
as an instance of inadequate socialization.)

Psychopaths get into trouble frequently and spend much time in prisons and
mental hospitals. However, the perpetrator of a crime is not necessarily a psychopath. A professional burglar may well consider rape to be *wrong* and may
therefore be incapable of such behavior. The concept of crime, geared as it is
to the predictability of state sanctions, obscures the motivational distinction
between acts compatible with the offender's self-image and acts which are not.
Offenders do not challenge the rules on principle. They find laws an obstacle to
getting what they want, and, if the particular offense is not too guilt provoking,
they take a chance that they will not be caught. Crime is an abstraction; rob-
beries, assaults, auto theft, embezzlements, arsons, forgeries, and so forth, are
the concrete realities. Thus a man with a long criminal record may be psycho-

logically incapable of engaging in 90 per cent of the offenses defined by the criminal code. His conscience is operative, and it prevents most antisocial behavior.

Guilt reactions are exceedingly complex. Even when criminal behavior is entered upon without overt guilt, closer study usually reveals that strong motivation to engage in prohibited behavior overcomes a norm in the psyche. Sometimes the victory of the deviant impulse is temporary, and subsequently remorse overwhelms the offender. Psychiatrists claim that some offenders are so effective at self-condemnation that they unconsciously seek out punishment in order to expiate their guilt feelings. A guilt-ridden offender may confess his crime—and sometimes others he did not commit. One well-publicized and ghastly Los Angeles murder gave rise to 38 "confessions" to the police over a ten-year period. The Black Dahlia mystery is still unsolved.

Those who denounce themselves to the police for other people's crimes are probably psychotic. Offenders who are not psychotic have guilt problems too—as the following techniques for chloroforming the conscience suggest:

1. Liquor is frequently an accompaniment of crime—as well as of lesser forms of misbehavior. This is partly because consciences can be put out of commission by alcohol.
2. Much crime is executed in groups—from burglary to lynching. Social support stills the self-condemnations which the individual might suffer alone.
3. Convicted offenders offer elaborate justifications for their crimes.

Two sociologists systematically questioned juvenile delinquents in a state training school about these justifications. They were persuaded by their research that rationalizations that neutralized guilt were part of the explanation of juvenile delinquency. They identified five types of rationalization capable of explaining how boys knowingly commit crimes without feeling like criminals. They describe one of the five, "condemnation of the condemners," as follows:[18]

> The delinquent shifts the focus of attention from his own deviant acts to the motives and behavior of those who disapprove of his violations. His condemners, he may claim, are hypocrites, deviants in disguise, or impelled by personal spite. This orientation toward the conforming world may be of particular importance when it hardens into a bitter cynicism directed against those assigned the task of enforcing or expressing the norms of the dominant society. Police, it may be said, are corrupt, stupid, and brutal. Teachers always show favoritism and parents always "take it out" on their children. By a slight extension, the rewards of conformity—such as material success—become a matter of pull or luck, thus decreasing still further the stature of those who stand on the side of the law-abiding. The validity of this jaundiced viewpoint is not so important as its function in turning back or deflecting the negative sanctions attached to violations of the norms. The delinquent, in effect, has changed the subject of the conversation in the dia-

[18] Gresham M. Sykes and David Matza, "Techniques of Neutralization: A Theory of Delinquency," *American Sociological Review*, Vol. 22, December, 1957, pp. 664–670.

logue between his own deviant impulses and the reactions of others; and by attacking others, the wrongfulness of his own behavior is more easily repressed or lost to view.

Resort to these rationalizations—as well as use of alcohol and group-encouraged delinquency—indicates that guilt reactions must be dealt with even when they are not sufficient to *prevent* deviant behavior.

Shame: Sensitivity to Social Disapproval. Socialization is an effective defense against deviance to the extent that deviant impulses arouse in advance sufficient guilt to prevent their overt expression. But guilt is not the only internal control. Reinforcing whatever guilt feelings the individual may have are the pressures exerted upon him by others. In addition to his feeling that certain actions are *wrong* is the individual's awareness that they may arouse disapproval in his family, among his peers, in his school, or at his place of employment. To the extent that he anticipates general disapproval and wishes to avoid it, **shame** reinforces guilt in the control of deviance.

A survey of 5422 college students from 99 American colleges contained questions dealing with the following 10 forms of deviant behavior on the campus:[19]

1. Destroying school property.
2. Taking articles from the school store without paying for them.
3. Disorderly conduct in the local community.
4. Taking books from the library without properly checking them out.
5. Underlining or marking up library books.
6. Becoming friendly with a teacher in hopes of getting a better grade.
7. Getting drunk.
8. Drinking alcoholic beverages on campus in violation of campus regulations.
9. Gambling on campus.
10. Overcutting class.

The questionnaires were analyzed in such a way so that each college was classified according to the proportion of respondents from that college who said that they disapproved of each deviant act. Then the student who reported engaging in one of the acts was classified in terms of the college disapproval level for that act. Figure 13.3 shows the relationship between the context of disapproval and the tendency for an individual student to engage in the disapproved behavior. The greater the disapproval, the less likely was deviant behavior.

In contemporary society, the large variety of subgroups and subcultures makes shame as problematic as guilt. For example, if all parents disapproved emphatically of stealing and brawling, children sensitive to their parents' reactions—girls and preadolescents especially—would be less likely to steal and

[19] William J. Bowers, "Normative Constraints on Deviant Behavior in the College Context," *Sociometry*, Vol. 31, December 1968, pp. 370-385.

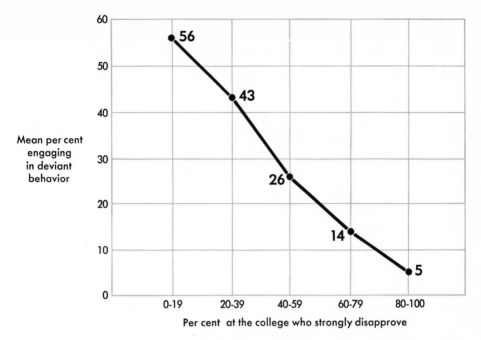

FIGURE 13.3 **Mean level of deviant behavior (excluding item nine) for varying contexts of disapproval.** Source: William J. Bowers, "Normative Constraints on Deviant Behavior in the College Context," *Sociometry,* Vol. 31, December 1968, p. 377.

to fight. But family units differ not only in cohesiveness, that is, in the extent to which children are sensitive to parental disapproval, but also in the *strength* of parental disapproval of delinquency. Thus in one family a boy who brings home a stolen item will be forced to return it to its owner with apologies; in another he will be lectured but allowed to keep it; in some families there will be no questions asked; and in a few he may gain approval for his contribution to the family's possessions.[20] It is too much to expect that millions of family units in a complex and highly differentiated society will react to violations of normative consensus in precisely the same way.

To complicate the problem of shame further, relatives by no means exhaust the circle of significant others. Even in the preadolescent years, peers are important to youngsters. By adolescence, however, approval and disapproval from peers is of greater concern to many youngsters than the reactions of their parents.[21] There are, of course, youth groups with conventional values: church groups, 4-H clubs, YMCA groups, and such. But adolescent peer groups in industrial societies are more likely than families to condone nonconformity because their members are struggling to emancipate themselves from family

[20] The same point can be made about the expression of aggression. See Albert Bandura and Richard H. Walters, *Adolescent Aggression: A Study of the Influence of Child-Training Practices and Family Interrelations,* New York: McGraw-Hill, 1959.

[21] Talcott Parsons, "Age and Sex in the Social Structure of the United States," *American Sociological Review,* Vol. 7, October 1942, pp. 604-616.

controls, and in the process they may also repudiate *values* espoused by their parents.[22] Thus it is possible to find delinquent and quasi-delinquent groups in suburban communities where parental disapproval of such activities is unequivocal.[23] Such groups derive support from adolescent rebelliousness against parental authority.

The adolescent peer group is not necessarily rebellious, but it is usually structurally unstable. Its members grow older, and, unless younger adolescents are admitted to membership, the group disintegrates. Groups which enjoy adult sponsorship or support—boys' clubs, settlement house youth groups, Scouts, church youth clubs—do not disintegrate in this way. They recruit younger adolescents to take the place of the older adolescents who lose interest. Hence these adult-sponsored youth groups are permanent. Although the membership is constantly changing, the basic structure of the group remains intact. Youth groups that develop spontaneously on street corners are less likely to be age-graded and thus less capable of preserving group identity beyond the current membership. Millions of these spontaneous groups come into being, exist for several years as vehicles for expressing the interests and the solidarity of a particular group of adolescents, and then disintegrate. This flux is conducive to nonconformity because such autonomous groups are structurally isolated from adults whose responsibilities in the larger society are likely to make them sympathetic interpreters of conventional values.[24]

Some peer groups are actively organized to promote delinquent activities: fighting gangs, drug-using cliques, car thieves. But much adolescent nonconformity is tolerated rather than required by peers. In the *raggare* clubs of Stockholm (the Road Devils, the Car Angels, the Car Comets, and the Teddy Boys were the names of the main groups in 1960) it was prestigeful to have an American car in which to cruise around the city looking for girls. A boy who stole a squirrel tail to hang on the aerial of his car would probably not be disapproved of by his friends. And he would be able to signal to boys in other cars, by raising or lowering the squirrel tail, indicating how he was making out in his quest.

In short, peer groups vary considerably in their response to delinquent behavior. Among those that *require* stealing or fighting, shame operates in favor of delinquency instead of against it. The more common situation, however, is a peer group that will *tolerate* stealing, drunkenness, or assaultive behavior, often because these are ways of expressing daring or toughness—but not the only ways.

The Differential Stake in Conformity. The deterrent value of shame depends on the sensitivity of the individual to disapproval from other people. But just as it cannot be assumed that everyone in a person's milieu will approve or

[22] Herbert A. Bloch and Arthur Niederhoffer, *The Gang: A Study in Adolescent Behavior,* New York: Philosophical Library, 1958.

[23] Seymour Freedgood, "Life in Bloomfield Hills," *Fortune,* July 1961, pp. 234-236.

[24] Sophia M. Robison, "Autonomous Groups: An Unsolved Problem in Group Loyalties and Conflicts," *Journal of Educational Sociology,* Vol. 20, October 1946, pp. 154-162.

Bob Combs — Rapho Guillumette

disapprove of the same acts, neither can it be assumed that disapproval is equally threatening, no matter who expresses it. The individual is far more sensitive to pressures emanating from small face-to-face groups in which he interacts extensively than to pressures from larger, more inclusive groups like the neighborhood or "society."[25] Disapproval from people one cares about is more threatening than disapproval from strangers. Nevertheless, human beings do feel shame in relationship to strangers they have never seen before or expect

[25] Edward A. Shils, "The Study of the Primary Group," in Daniel Lerner and Harold D. Lasswell, Eds., *The Policy Sciences,* Stanford, Calif.: Stanford University Press, 1951, pp. 44-69.

Hanns Kohl—PIX

to see again. Even in contemporary cities where neighbors are a blurred streak of constantly changing faces, people ask themselves, "What will the neighbors think?" But, of course, the sting of neighbor disapproval is greatly reduced if population mobility and density creates an anonymous atmosphere—as in a rooming-house district. Another factor reducing the effectiveness of neighborhood controls in industrial societies is the extent to which the individual's reference groups are physically separated from the area in which he lives. That is to say, one's home may be the place where one sleeps and little else. One's place of work, one's school, or one's friends may be separated from one's home by a 15-minute (or more) drive in an automobile.

The sting of social disapproval is greater the more approval the individual previously enjoyed. This proposition has implications for the understanding of shame. Disapproval costs the high-status individual more than the person already disesteemed by his community. The captain of the high-school football team or the president of the Student Council has more to lose by being caught cheating on a test than a below-average student taking the general course and intending to quit school as soon as he reaches 16. More generally, anything that affects the individual's prestige—his occupational prospects or achievements, the social position of his family, the color of his skin, his athletic exploits, even a neighborhood reputation as a "good fellow"—provides a stake in conformity.[26] This is one reason why unskilled workers and Negroes are dis-

[26] Jackson Toby, "Social Disorganization and Stake in Conformity: Complementary Factors in the Predatory Behavior of Young Hoodlums," *Journal of Criminal Law, Criminology, and Police Science*, Vol. 48, May-June, 1957, pp. 12-17.

proportionately represented in the criminal statistics; they have little to lose. Jail is not so threatening to those at the bottom of the social hierarchy.

Disapproval has greater deterrent value—even in the anonymous urban community—for those held in high esteem by respectable members of society than for those regarded as of no particular consequence. This statistical prediction rests on the principle that the individual's self-respect fluctuates with the respect he is accorded by others.[27] Individual personalities vary in the extent to which they can tolerate adverse judgments from others without unfavorable modifications of their self-conceptions; but the overall correlation between reputation and self-respect is quite high. There is a combination of guilt and shame at work. At a particular moment, an individual's self-conception may permit him to feel no guilt despite intense disapproval from the people around him. But the norms incorporated in his personality took root in the context of interaction with persons who expressed approval and disapproval—and whose point of view he adopted.

Although high-status people have a greater stake in conformity than low-status people, they also have greater resources for resisting definitions of themselves as nonconformists. Criminologists have shown that white-collar crimes are less likely than ordinary crimes to result in conviction in a criminal court.[28] Indeed, the criminal violations of business and professional people, such as fraudulent advertising, income-tax evasion, or collusive bidding on government contracts, are not usually regarded with the same repugnance by the general public as burglary or assault. And even when the offense charged is one like shoplifting, which clearly violates community norms, high-status people have a better chance than low-status people to escape condemnation. Their protests of innocence, put forward by skillful lawyers, are more readily believed than the monosyllabic denials of the shabby and uncouth. When they plead "kleptomania" and offer to submit to psychiatric treatment, their superior financial resources are regarded as evidence that they are ill and not antisocial.[29]

SOCIAL DISORGANIZATION: THE BREAKDOWN OF COMMUNITY CONTROL

Deviance exists in every community because situations arise where the temptation to violate a rule is more powerful than the deterrent capacity of the individual's guilt feelings and his fear of social disapproval. In some communities, *rates* of deviant behavior are unusually high. The term **social disorganization** has been applied to such communities by sociologists on the assump-

---

[27] Hans L. Zetterberg, "Complaint Actions," *Acta Sociologica,* Vol. 2, 1957, pp. 179-201.

[28] Edwin H. Sutherland, *White Collar Crime,* New York: Holt, Rinehart and Winston, 1949.

[29] Donald R. Cressey, "The Differential Association Theory and Compulsive Crimes," *Journal of Criminal Law, Criminology and Police Science,* Vol. 45, May-June 1954, pp. 35-38.

tion that high rates of deviant behavior are best accounted for in terms of peculiarities of the social structure. The term "social disorganization" calls attention to basic characteristics of industrial societies: their heterogeneity and fluidity. As compared with preindustrial societies, industrial societies are, because of their heterogeneity and fluidity, far less successful in using guilt and shame to control deviance. Slum neighborhoods manifest this failure to a greater degree than middle-class neighborhoods, largely because slum residents participate marginally in the institutions of urban industrial society. The marginality of adults—sometimes because they are recent migrants, sometimes because of personal disabilities—weakens traditional adult control over adolescents, as the following comments of Henry D. McKay show.[30]

> The European immigrant came largely from backgrounds which were stable and well integrated. But many of the institutions which they brought did not fit the situation in the new world, or if they served the adults well they were often unacceptable to the children.
>
> When one considers the more recent immigrants to the city the problem is even more serious. These groups have the same disabilities as the immigrants in that they represent largely rural backgrounds without much experience in city life but they have others as well. In many instances they lack the stabilizing influence of long-established and well-integrated cultural institutions which European immigrants had as part of their backgrounds, and some of the migrants have had the additional disadvantage of limited freedom and lack of opportunity to participate in some of the basic activities of social life.
>
> Another element in the situation in the inner-city areas where most of the immigrants must make their adaptation to city life is the fact that there are kinds of problems with which they are totally unfamiliar but which must be dealt with in the American city. Foremost among these are problems of employment and participation in the political process, but others almost equally disturbing are those arising out of the fact that adolescent males are not part of the labor force, that child rearing presents new kinds of hazards, or that luxury items can be secured with a small downpayment.
>
> Thus life in the inner-city area lacks integration either because the institutions are weak, or because there are no institutions through which the new problems can be dealt with. Of course, the situation is not the same in all of the inner-city areas. Areas in which there has been some stability have tended to become more integrated because old institutions have been readapted to new problems and have thus brought some order into the community. In others where there has not been time for such an integrative development, persons are largely free from institutional ties and at liberty to operate with relatively little control.
>
> In extreme form this absence of stabilizing influence is seen among the adolescent males who do not only have the freedom which comes from weak institutional structure, but tend also to be detached from whatever basic institutions

---

[30] Henry D. McKay, "Basic Considerations in Delinquency Prevention," testimony at *Hearings before the Subcommittee to Investigate Juvenile Delinquency of the Committee on the Judiciary,* United States Senate, May 28 and 29, 1959, pp. 164-173.

there are. For this group, ties with family and church tend to be weak and only the school represents the thread which ties them to respectability.

When the boy finishes school, or leaves school because he cannot get along there, this last thread is broken. Ties with church and family are often reestablished when the boy reaches maturity and marries. Then family responsibility tends to bring him back into the economic order and into other conventional activities. But during this period between leaving school and the assumption of adult roles, young men in the inner-city areas of Chicago today are free in a sense seldom known in social life.

These boys without institutional ties tend, in the inner-city areas, to become identified with one another in groupings often called gangs, but for the purpose of this report designated as corner groups. These groups are functional for their members; that is, they take the place of and perform many of the functions performed by conventional institutions in other areas. Sometimes these groups have names or other symbols of identification, and within them the members have status, win approbation, and achieve a sense of belonging.

These corner groups and the social-athletic clubs into which some of them develop, may be regarded as natural institutions which came into existence to meet the needs of the detached adolescent males. They would represent positive contributions to the stability of the community were it not for the fact that oftentimes they are organized in opposition to middle-class values and conventionality. It is for this reason that it can be said that corner groups represent the center of the organized attack on conventional values such as life and property.

The corner group is not alone in this activity. In the absence of control through conventional institutions, many other forms of illegal, quasi-illegal, or marginal activities become organized as part of the social life of these inner-city areas. Often these activities are known as the rackets, or collectively as the activities of the syndicate. For the task at hand this development is highly significant. It means that children growing up in these areas have intimate and personal knowledge of two moral worlds, each of which offers a livelihood and a path for upward mobility. To the child, each seems to have its advantages and disadvantages, and each recruits some members. This conflict of values is one of the striking characteristics of inner-city areas.

The Nashville study referred to earlier demonstrated the ecological basis of delinquent subcultures.[31] In this survey of 9238 white boys, 12 years of age and older, attending school in the Nashville metropolitan area, researchers found that the *neighborhood* in which a boy lived affected his chances of becoming a delinquent apart from *personal* characteristics conducive to delinquency. For instance, sons of laborers or men in service occupations had a higher delinquency rate in slum areas with a delinquency tradition than in predominantly middle-class neighborhoods. This study was a survey rather than a controlled experiment, so other variables may have been involved. But

---

[31] Albert J. Reiss, Jr., and Albert Lewis Rhodes, "The Distribution of Juvenile Delinquency in the Social Class Structure," *American Sociological Review*, Vol. 26, October 1961, pp. 720-732.

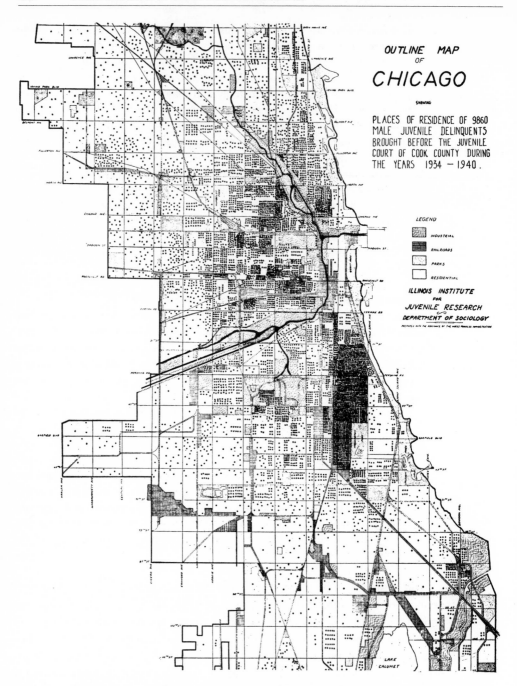

FIGURE 13.4   **Distribution of male juvenile delinquents, Chicago, 1934–1940.**

ecological researchers have generally agreed that social disorganization is more likely to be found in slum areas (Fig. 13.4).

One reason social disorganization is concentrated in slum neighborhoods is that the unsuccessful members of urban communities cannot pay the rentals in more desirable neighborhoods. Different types of slums exist, however, and they collect different assortments of the casualties of a competitive society:

1. Rooming-house districts are characterized by extreme anonymity. The weakness of interpersonal relations constitutes a serious obstacle to the effective mobilization of shame against potential offenders. On the other hand, rooming-house districts cater to unattached adults, often elderly adults. As a result of these demographic factors, mental illness, alcoholism, and suicide are more typical problems in rooming-house districts than delinquency.[32]

2. Decaying tenement districts are *family* slums and are sometimes ethnically homogeneous (Italian, Negro, Puerto Rican). Autonomous peer groups are likely to transmit delinquent values. Unless parental controls are unusually strong, *normal* socialization into "street-corner society" makes for delinquency. But parental controls are likely to be *weak* in urban slums because of the concentration in such neighborhoods of families with serious health and welfare problems. Adolescent gangs fill the vacuum.[33]

3. Public-housing projects for low-income families in the United States frequently combine the anonymity of the rooming-house district with the child socialization and control inadequacies of the family slum. The reason is that public housing is usually preceded by complete demolition of existing structures and the dispersal of site residents. Tenants are then recruited on the basis of financial need. They start as strangers to one another, and they are likely to remain so, for the existence of income limits and the high turnover of tenants give an air of impermanency to project living. These powerful delinquency-producing tendencies are partially offset by the age structure of the child population: many preadolescents and few adolescents, at least in the early years of the housing project.[34]

By what interpersonal mechanism does the disorganization of a neighborhood result in deviant behavior on the part of its inhabitants? This question was investigated in a comparative study of two working-class neighborhoods in Cambridge, Massachusetts, one with a high delinquency rate and one with a low rate.[35] Interviewers were sent to dwelling units (selected by probability sampling) with instructions to interview 50 per cent of the adults in the des-

[32] Harvey W. Zorbaugh, "The Dweller in Furnished Rooms: An Urban Type," in Ernest W. Burgess, Ed., *The Urban Community,* Chicago: University of Chicago Press, 1929, pp. 98-105.

[33] Frederic M. Thrasher, *The Gang,* Chicago: University of Chicago Press, 1927; Clifford R. Shaw and Henry D. McKay, *Juvenile Delinquency and Urban Areas,* rev. ed., Chicago: University of Chicago Press, 1969.

[34] Harrison F. Salisbury, "Problem Youngsters Spring from Housing Jungles," *The New York Times,* March 28, 1958; Lee Rainwater, "A World of Trouble: The Pruit-Igoe Housing Project," in Robert E. Will and Harold G. Vatter, Eds., *Poverty in Affluence,* 2nd ed., New York: Harcourt, Brace & World, 1970, pp. 147-155.

[35] Eleanor E. Maccoby, Joseph P. Johnson, and Russell M. Church, "Community Integration and the Social Control of Juvenile Delinquency," *Journal of Social Issues,* Vol. 14, No. 3, 1958, pp. 38-51.

ignated household. The interview schedule concerned juvenile misbehavior witnessed in the neighborhood, the relationship of the respondent to the deviating children, "and the nature of the control action (if any) taken by the respondent or other individuals in the neighborhood." In the high-delinquency neighborhood, the interviewers surveyed 129 adults, in the low-delinquency neighborhood, 107. Respondents from the two neighborhoods did not differ appreciably in their negative evaluations of juvenile misbehavior. In the high-delinquency neighborhood, 36 per cent judged minor thefts from stores "serious" compared with 49 per cent in the low-delinquency neighborhood; 57 per cent of the respondents from the high-delinquency neighborhood judged abusive remarks "serious" compared with 47 per cent in the low-delinquency neighborhood; and so forth. There *was* a difference between the neighborhoods in the readiness of adults to intervene—either directly or by informing the police or the child's parents. Thus the child in the high-delinquency neighborhood had a better chance than the child in the low-delinquency neighborhood to deviate without adult criticism or punishment. Disorganization means (in practice) fewer adult controls.

Just as *neighborhood* disorganization means reduced controls, so *family* disorganization implies a lack of intervention by adults. Some youngsters do not have to account to parents for their comings and goings. Their parents do not supervise their recreational activities, enforce a regular bedtime, or inquire about their homework. There is food in the refrigerator for them to take when they are hungry, but the family does not sit down to eat a meal together. They do not watch television with their parents, go to the weddings of relatives or on family outings. They have no regular responsibilities in the home, partly because their parents do not consistently require such contributions. It is a life free of constraint, but it is also a life without guidance; there is no adult to depend on. Émile Durkheim's theory of *anomie* is relevant to the situation of such youngsters.[36] Durkheim considered the absence of normative constraint unpleasant for the individual because it gave him no standards for judging his situation and therefore no stability of expectations. Durkheim believed that for his own happiness the individual needs to place limits on his desires and that society is the ultimate source of these limits. Social restrictions begin the process of self-regulation. Thus Durkheim might have expected a child from a disorganized household to be more resentful of adult authority than a child from a strict home. His anomic situation prevents him from recognizing *any* adult supervision as legitimate. Similarly, Durkheim would have expected a philandering university student to be more frustrated sexually than a celibate priest. The priest's vows constitute a moral commitment regulating his sexual drive, whereas this student has no social or personal basis for curbing his sexual appetite. If freedom is the opportunity for self-discipline, self-discipline is nevertheless learned from society.

PUNISHMENT: SYMBOLIC DEFINITION OF THE DEVIANT AS UNENVIABLE

Nonconformity occurs despite the socialization process, despite *informal* sanctions, and despite the anticipation of *formal* sanctions such as arrest and imprisonment—although it must be pointed out that mechanisms for social control prevent nonconformity most of the time. When nonconformity *does* occur, it forces conformists to reevaluate the normative situation. For example, a student who studies hard and gets a lower grade on a quiz than students who cheat may become cynical about the principle of honest effort on examinations. One socially significant consequence of punishing nonconformists is that

[36] Talcott Parsons, "Émile Durkheim," *International Encyclopedia of the Social Sciences,* New York: Macmillan, 1968, Vol. 4, pp. 311-320.

punishment may reduce the potentially disruptive effect of their noncon- formity. Punishing the deviant may convince conformists that he has not "gotten away with it," as the following analysis shows:[37]

> Punishment is the purposive imposition of unpleasant experiences like im- prisonment on the deviant. From the point of view of social functioning, however, punishment is a means of containing the demoralizing consequences of the crimes that cannot be prevented. Punishment is not mere vindictiveness. With- out punishment "upright people" might be demoralized by defiance of the col- lective conscience. If unpunished deviance tends to demoralize the conformist, punishment is a means of repairing "the wounds made upon collective senti- ments."[38] As Durkheim put it, the deviant is punished to promote the solidarity of conformists.
>
> One who resists the temptation to do what the group prohibits would like to feel that these self-imposed abnegations have some meaning. When he sees others defy rules without untoward consequences, he needs some reassurance that his sacrifices were made in a good cause. If "the good die young and the wicked flourish as the green bay tree," the moral scruples which enable conform- ists to restrain their own deviant inclinations lack social validation. The social significance of punishing offenders is that deviance is thereby defined as unsuc- cessful in the eyes of conformists. Thus, conformists are satisfied that the in- hibition or repression of their own deviant impulses is worthwhile. The law- abiding person who unconsciously resents restraining his desire to steal and murder has an opportunity, by identifying with the police and the courts, to af- fect the precarious balance within his own personality between internal controls and the temptation to deviate. A bizarre example of this psychological mech- anism is the man who seeks out homosexuals and beats them up mercilessly. Such pathological hostility toward homosexuals is due to the sadist's anxiety over his own sex-role identification. By "punishing" the homosexual, he denies the latent homosexuality in his own psyche. No doubt, some of the persons in- volved in the administration of punishment are sadistically motivated. But Durkheim hypothesized that the psychic equilibrium of the *ordinary* member of the group may be threatened by violation of norms.

Punishment can be discussed on three distinct levels: (1) in terms of the motivations of the societal agents administering it; (2) in terms of the definition of the situation on the part of the person being punished; and (3) in terms of its impact on conformists. At this point let us consider the third level, the impact on conformists. Note that punishment of offenders sustains the morale of con- formists only under certain conditions. The first has already been discussed— conformists unconsciously wish to violate the rules themselves. The second is that conformists implicitly assume that the nonconformity is a result of *delib- erate defiance* of society's norms. For some conformists, this second condition is not met. Under the guidance of psychiatric thinking, some conformists as-

---

[37] Reprinted by permission. Adapted from Jackson Toby, "Is Punishment Necessary?," *Journal of Criminal Law, Criminology, and Police Science.*

[38] Émile Durkheim, *The Division of Labor in Society*, Glencoe, Ill.: Free Press, 1947, p. 108.

sume that violation of norms is the result of illness rather than wickedness.[39] Punishment of the offender does not contribute to the morale of such conformists. Since they assume that the nonconformity is an involuntary symptom of a disordered personality, the offender is automatically unenviable because illness is (by definition) undesirable. Of course, one does not really know the relative proportions of the conforming members of society who make the "wicked" or the "sick" assumption about the motivation of the offender, but this can be discovered by investigation.

In Western industrial societies, there is an increasing tendency to call contemporary methods of dealing with offenders "treatment" rather than "punishment." Perhaps this means that increasing proportions of the population are willing to accept the "sick" theory of nonconformity. Note, however, that the emphasis on **treatment** may be more a matter of symbolism than of substance. Although the definition of the situation as treatment rather than punishment tends to be humanizing — both to the offender and to the persons who must deal with him — there are still kind guards and cruel nurses. Furthermore, it would be an error to suppose that punishment is invariably experienced as painful by the criminal, whereas treatment is always experienced as pleasant by the psychopathological offender. Some gang delinquents consider a reformatory sentence an opportunity to renew old acquaintances and to learn new delinquent skills; they resist fiercely the degrading suggestion that they need the services of what they call the "nut doctor." Some psychiatric patients are terrified by shock treatment and embarrassed by group therapy.

What then is the significance of the increasing emphasis on "treatment"? Why call an institution for the criminally insane a "hospital" although it bears a closer resemblance to a prison than to a hospital for the physically ill? Perhaps the increased emphasis on treatment in penological thinking and practice reflects the existence of a large group of conformists who are undecided as between the "wicked" and the "sick" theories of nonconformity. When they observe that the offender is placed in "treatment," their provisional diagnosis of illness is confirmed. Therefore they do not feel that he has "gotten away with it." Note that "treatment" has the capacity to make the offender unenviable to conformists whether or not it is effective in rehabilitating him and whether or not he experiences it as pleasant. Those old-fashioned conformists who are not persuaded by official diagnoses of illness will not be satisfied by "treatment"; they will prefer to see an attempt made to visit physical suffering or mental anguish on the offender. For them, punishment is necessary to prevent demoralization.

Is Punishment Compatible with Resocialization? Most of the arguments against imprisonment and other forms of punishment boil down to the assertion that punishment is incompatible with **resocialization.** The high rate of re-

---

[39] Talcott Parsons has repeatedly suggested the analogy between illness and criminality. See also Vilhelm Aubert and Sheldon L. Messinger, "The Criminal and the Sick," *Inquiry,* Vol. 1, No. 3, 1958, pp. 137-160; and Barbara Wootton, *Social Science and Social Pathology,* New York: Macmillan, 1959, pp. 203-267.

peaters for prisons and reformatories (the technical term is "recidivism") is cited as evidence of the irrationality of punishment in general and imprisonment in particular. If rehabilitative programs are designed to help the offender cope with frustrations in his life situation, which presumably were responsible for his nonconformity, imprisoning him hardly seems a good way to begin. To generalize the argument, the loss of social standing inherent in punishment makes it more difficult to induce the offender to play a legitimate role instead of a nonconforming one. Whatever the offender's original motivations for nonconformity, punishment adds to them by neutralizing his fear of losing the respect of the community; he has already lost it.

Punishment may be compatible with **rehabilitation** if one precedes the other. Perhaps some types of deviants become willing to change only if the bankruptcy of their way of life is conclusively demonstrated to them. On this assumption, punishment may be a necessary preliminary to a resocialization program in much the same way that shock treatment makes certain psychotics accessible to psychotherapy.

The compatibility of punishment and rehabilitation could be clarified (although not settled) if it were considered from the point of view of the meaning of punishment to the offender. Those offenders who regard punishment as a deserved deprivation resulting from their own misbehavior are qualitatively different from offenders who regard punishment as a misfortune bearing no relationship to morality. A child who is spanked by his father and the gang member who is jailed for carrying concealed weapons are both "punished." The child may accept the deprivation as legitimate, and the gang member may bow before superior force. Punishment has rehabilitative significance only for the former. If this is so, society must convince the deviant that his punishment is just before he can be motivated to change. This is never simple, and it is especially difficult in prisons for three reasons:

1. It is obvious to convicted offenders that some so-called "criminals" are being punished disproportionately for trifling offenses, whereas some predatory business men and politicians enjoy prosperity and freedom. To deny that injustices occur confirms the cynical in their belief that "legitimate" people are not only as predatory as criminals but hypocritical to boot.

2. The more cases of injustice known to offenders, the harder it is to argue that the contemporary approximation of justice is the best that can be managed. Negro inmates will not think that their incarceration has moral significance if their life experiences have demonstrated to them that the police and the courts are less scrupulous of their rights than of the rights of white persons. An indigent inmate will not think that his imprisonment has moral significance if his poverty resulted in inadequate legal representation.

3. Finally, the major form of punishment for serious offenders (imprisonment) tends to generate a contraculture which denies that justice has anything to do with legal penalties. It is too costly to confine large numbers of people in isolation from one another, yet congregate confinement results in the mutual reinforcement of self-justifications. Even those who enter prison

feeling contrite are influenced by the self-righteous inmate climate; this may be part of the reason recidivism rates rise with each successive commitment.[40] The sting of community rejection is neutralized by the acceptance of fellow inmates.[41] In other words, an unintended consequence of group punishment is to create solidarity among offenders, and this primary group support becomes an additional obstacle to the abandonment of the deviant role. Many a reformatory inmate is proud of his criminal record because this record gives him status in the delinquent subculture. He would be ashamed to be a "square" college boy. Some illegitimate roles, though stigmatized, are not punished in a congregate fashion—for example, the alcoholic. Partly as a consequence of this circumstance, most alcoholics do not have the support of a primary group encouraging continued drinking. The individual alcoholic is a less difficult problem of rehabilitation than the ex-inmate.

In view of the preceding considerations, punishment—as it is now practiced in Western societies—is usually an obstacle to resocialization. Some exceptions to this generalization should be noted. A few small treatment institutions have not only prevented the development of a self-righteous contraculture but have managed to establish an inmate climate supportive of changed values. In such institutions punishment has rehabilitative significance for the same reason it has educational significance in the normal family: it is perceived as legitimate.

CONCLUSION

The socialization process generates enough guilt and shame to prevent deviance most of the time—even in highly differentiated industrial societies. However, guilt and shame are not completely successful in preventing deviance because child socialization is not uniform in millions of families and peer groups. Social heterogeneity works against the universal rules laid down in the criminal code. In addition, status differentiation means that there is inequality with respect to the stake in conforming behavior. Adolescents and others whose interpersonal ties with conventional adults are weak are insensitive to disapproval of their antisocial activities. So are the residents of slum neighborhoods. Being at the bottom of the hierarchy of prestige and other rewards, they are used to lack of approval. What they do not have cannot be taken away. In short, the diversity and the differentiation of an industrial society

---

[40] Thorsten Sellin, "Recidivism and Maturation," *National Probation and Parole Association Journal,* Vol. 4, 1958, pp. 241-250.

[41] Lloyd E. Ohlin and William C. Lawrence, "Social Interaction among Clients as a Treatment Problem," *Social Work,* Vol. 4, April 1959, pp. 3-13.

guarantee that some people some of the time will defy the institutionalized rules.

Formal agencies of social control—the police, the courts, the prisons—attempt to deal with those whom guilt and shame do not deter. In one sense, these formal agencies are fighting a losing battle. It is not possible under contemporary urban conditions for the police to arrest and the courts to convict more than a fraction of the persons who violate criminal statutes. From the point of view of preventing the breakdown of the rules and the demoralization of conformists, however, formal agencies are useful. In punishing the luckless deviants who are caught, formal agencies of control help to define deviance as dangerous as well as immoral. Thus conformists are reinforced in their self-imposed tendencies to conform.

Deviant *acts* violate the social rules, but the problem of societal control is more serious when such acts are not occasional lapses from an essentially conformist style of life but are organized into deviant *roles*. A deviant role is not mere nonconformity. It is nonconformity supported by the individual's self-conception and by the attitudes or behavior of others. Thus the usual internal controls of shame and guilt do not operate.

Why should nonconformity sometimes occur in the context of deviant roles and sometimes not? For two reasons:

1. Some individuals develop feelings of inadequacy during socialization which impair their capacity to play one or more legitimate roles, as Chapter 5 showed.
2. Deviant roles enjoy overt or covert support from outwardly conforming members of society; a deviant subculture is quasi-institutionalized.

These two circumstances mutually reinforce one another in industrial societies. Individuals who feel, rightly or wrongly, that they cannot play legitimate roles are attracted to illegitimate roles when they perceive that the disapproval of these roles is far from unanimous.

How can deviance be controlled more effectively? One strategy is to destroy the social support which the deviant role enjoys. The difficulties that this strategy face are great. Gambling, for example, is deeply rooted in American society. Whether it is possible to reorganize American social structure sufficiently so that bookies have no place in it is an intriguing question. Another strategy is to reduce deviant motivation by giving present and potential incumbents of deviant roles hope that they can succeed in playing *legitimate* roles. Peer-group support, natural or contrived, helps to give the individual the self-confidence to attempt this transformation. Even with peer-group support, however, reintegration into legitimate society is difficult. It is impeded not only by the objective disabilities of the individual for playing legitimate roles and by his lack of self-confidence. It is also impeded by the understandably suspicious—and sometimes hostile—attitudes of conventional society.

The existence of deviant subcultures and the obstacles preventing some people from playing legitimate roles lead to the same consequence: a constant flow of recruits into illegitimate roles. This poses a problem of social control for industrial societies, which is coped with partly by situationally oriented deterrence (an efficient police force), partly by punishing offenders, and partly by attempting to induce deviants to switch to legitimate roles. Unfortunately, the last two social responses often work at cross-purposes. However necessary the punishment of deviants may be for sustaining the morale of conformists, most forms of punishment tend to reinforce commitment to the illegitimate role. *Formal* punishment through arrest, trial, conviction, and imprisonment is clearly stigmatizing. Furthermore, it brings the offender into contact with other persons being dramatically extruded from the ranks of respectable citizens. A society of outcasts develops with a subculture supportive of deviant roles.[42] *Informal* punishment through social disapproval, including disapproval from the family and the neighborhood, may also isolate the deviant and make return to legitimate society more difficult. For example, an alcoholic or a parolee believes that his chances of obtaining employment are reduced if the prospective employer learns of his deviant history. This belief is an obstacle to motivation to secure legitimate employment. The informal stigma that accompanies a deviant history poses an identity problem for the individual.[43] However, the identity problem is not uniform through society because different ethnic groups and social classes respond differently to former deviants. A Chicago study of parolees of Italian and Polish extraction shows that the Italian community is more accepting of the former-inmate than the Polish community and that this acceptance influences parolee adjustment after release from prison.[44]

Punishment of deviance is not the only obstacle to rehabilitation. Playing an illegitimate role incapacitates the individual to some extent for playing legitimate roles. This principle is equally relevant to the alcoholic and the criminal. The alcoholic eventually becomes unemployable. When this happens, his unemployability adds to his original motivation for drinking and creates a further obstacle to rehabilitation. Similarly, it is an unusual gang delinquent who does well in school or has a steady job. That is to say, inadequacies in playing legitimate roles which preceded the adoption of the illegitimate role become accentuated. Playing one role requires time and energy that is not available for learning and practicing another.

In a pluralistic society, value consensus is precarious in two senses. It does not pervade every subgroup within the larger society at any given time. And it is subject to change from one year to the next. Therefore, even though the legal system must define criminal behavior unequivocally at any given time, sociologists recognize that the nonconformist of today may be the forerunner of to-

---

[42] Gresham M. Sykes, *Society of Captives: A Study of a Maximum Security Prison*, Princeton, N.J.: Princeton University Press, 1958.

[43] Erving Goffman, *Stigma: Notes on the Management of Spoiled Identity*, Englewood Cliffs, N.J.: Prentice-Hall, 1963.

[44] Harold Finestone, "Reformation and Recidivism among Italian and Polish Criminal Offenders," *American Journal of Sociology*, Vol. 72, May 1967, pp. 575-588.

morrow's consensus. The history of medicine is filled with accounts of men of genius vilified in their lifetime and ultimately vindicated—for example, Semmelweiss, the Viennese physician who realized that his colleagues carried childbed fever to their patients on unwashed hands, was considered a crank. This uncertainty of the ultimate value of nonconformity does not mean that societies can ignore deviance. Without social control of deviance, not only order but orderly change is impossible. Still, it is appropriate that this chapter on deviance and its control should be followed by the next on social change; one often leads to the other.

SOME SIGNIFICANT LITERATURE ON DEVIANCE AND SOCIAL CONTROL

Joseph Bensman and Israel Gerver, "Crime and Punishment in the Factory: The Function of Deviancy in Maintaining the Social System" *American Sociological Review,* Vol. 28, August 1963, pp. 588-598. In a large aircraft factory working on United States Air Force contracts, use of a tap to align bolts in recessed nuts is so serious a violation of work rules that a worker possessing a tap, even though he is not caught using it, can be summarily fired. Nevertheless, mass violation of the rule occurs because without the use of taps this factory cannot attain a high enough level of productivity. The authors therefore regard the use of taps not as deviant behavior but as "a permanent unofficial aspect of the organization." What is considered a crime in this factory is not so much using a tap, regarded as necessary under some circumstances, but failing to observe the rituals of concealment in its use or of penitence when reprimanded for using one. Informal controls are brought to bear on workers who violate the rules regulating tapping, thus tending to limit the use of the tap to what are considered "necessary" situations. This article deals with a crime defined by a private organization rather than by the state, but it throws light on an important problem: the redefinition of legitimacy by persons other than the law makers. Tapping is thus a second cousin of traffic violations, public drunkenness, and other folk crimes.

Donald J. Black and Albert J. Reiss, Jr., "Police Control of Juveniles," *American Sociological Review,* Vol. 35, February 1970, pp. 63-77. Police encounters with juveniles were studied in Boston, Chicago, and Washington, D.C., during the summer of 1966 by 36 observers who accompanied officers in their squad cars or, less frequently, walked with them on patrol. Most of the 281 encounters arose in response to citizen-initiated complaints to police. In a sense, then, the citizenry rather than the police determines the recorded rate of delinquency in a community. The authors distinguish between deviant behavior, defined as any act negatively sanctioned on detection, and deviant behavior with varying probabilities of detection. Thus marijuana smoking may have a low probability of detection but a high probability of severe official sanctions if it is detected. The authors use arrest as a criterion of official negative sanction by the police and point out that only 15 per cent of police-juvenile encounters produce arrests. This selectivity reflects (1) the trivial nature of most offenses from a legal point of view, (2) the discretion of police, and (3) the effect of a defiant or deferential attitude by the subject on the likelihood of official action.

Albert K. Cohen, "The Study of Social Disorganization and Deviant Behavior," in Robert K. Merton, Leonard Broom, and Leonard S. Cottrell, Jr., Eds., *Sociology Today: Problems and Prospects,* New York: Basic Books, 1959, pp. 461-484. The prospective deviant has several courses in a situation in which conformity is unsatisfactory, yet nonconformity will result in sanctions from persons with whom he interacts. "One [course] is for our hypothetical subject to continue to conform, despite continued frustration, because conformity is the only alternative that is morally and symbolically validated by his reference groups. . . . A second [course] is for him to break with the reference groups and acknowledge other reference groups, whose norms legitimize deviant solutions and attribute favorable role symbolism to them. . . . A third [course] is for the individual to 'go it alone,' violating the institutionalized expectations without the legitimation and validation that come from consensus." Cohen calls attention in this theoretical article to the deviant act as a "cumulative and collective product." By this he means that the deviant act should be examined as the outcome of a social process consisting of: (1) the motivations for nonconformity on the part of its ultimate author, (2) his exploratory moves in the direction of deviance, and (3) the responses of persons in his milieu to these tendencies. For an application of this theory to gang delinquency, see Albert K. Cohen, *Delinquent Boys: The Culture of the Gang*, New York: Free Press, 1955.

Kingsley Davis, "Sexual Behavior," in Robert K. Merton and Robert A. Nisbet, Eds., *Contemporary Social Problems,* 2nd ed., New York: Harcourt, Brace and World, 1966, pp. 322-372. Davis distinguishes five related, although separable, issues in the understanding of prostitution as a universal phenomenon: (1) the causes of the *existence* of prostitution, (2) the causes of *different forms* of prostitution, (3) the causes of *differing* rates of prostitution from one society to another, (4) the factors inducing some women to enter the "profession," and (5) the factors inducing some men to patronize prostitutes. As part of his discussion of reasons for the existence of prostitution, Professor Davis compares it with the black market in a controlled economy. When the demand for sexual thrills cannot be satisfied within the framework of marriage or other socially approved practices, some women are tempted to violate the norms by establishing a black market in sex. This is extremely difficult to control in an anonymous commercial society.

Jack P. Gibbs, "Suicide," in Robert K. Merton and Robert A. Nisbet, Eds., *Contemporary Social Problems,* 2nd ed., New York: Harcourt, Brace and World, 1966, pp. 281–321. Suicide is a form of deviance for which the perpetrator cannot be punished—at least in this world. This makes for difficulties in the control of suicide and thus explains its existence: when individuals get into situations that they define as intolerable, suicide provides escape. Sociologists are particularly interested in explaining variations in the resort to suicide from one society to another and from one social category to another within the same society. For example, why is Denmark's suicide rate three times Norway's? Why does the urban suicide rate exceed the rural rate in virtually all countries? Why does the suicide rate of males exceed the rate for females? Why does the suicide rate of old people exceed the rate for young adults in most industrial countries? Why are divorced persons more prone to suicide than married persons? As contrasted with these sociological interests, psychologists and psychiatrists are more interested in the related question of explaining why one individual in a given society or social category rather than another takes his life. For this purpose, they may interview persons who attempt unsuccessfully to commit suicide.

David Matza, *Delinquency and Drift,* New York: Wiley, 1964. Matza's central insight is to call attention to the pluralism of urban industrial societies and to deduce from this pluralism a lack of radical opposition between conventional culture and the culture of delinquency. He infers from this lack of radical opposition that the subcultural delinquent is not passively stamped out by his slum milieu. The delinquent chooses his role from elements supplied by idiosyncratic and social experiences just as sociologists and artists choose theirs. The principle of freedom of choice is embodied in contemporary society, and it is by reference to this principle that the delinquent can best be understood. Matza's denial of a radical opposition between the values of delinquents and the values of conforming adolescents was called into question in a recent study by one of his students. A sample of middle-class high school boys reported on their participation in 26 delinquent acts on an anonymous questionnaire—and also on their approval or disapproval of each act. In general, boys who reported engaging in an act were more likely to express approval of that act. See Michael J. Hindelang, "The Commitments of Delinquents to Their Misdeeds: Do Delinquents Drift?" *Social Problems,* Vol. 17, Spring 1970, pp. 502-509. On the other hand, it has been found that the differences between the delinquency rates of adolescents who attend church regularly and those who do not are negligible because church attenders are no more committed to ethical principles than nonattenders and only slightly more respectful toward conventional authority. See Travis Hirschi and Rodney Stark, "Hellfire and Delinquency," *Social Problems,* Vol. 17, Fall 1969, pp. 202-213.

Lyle W. Shannon, "Types and Patterns of Delinquency Referral in a Middle-Sized City," *British Journal of Criminology,* Vol. 4, July 1963, pp. 24-36. Although juvenile and criminal court cases show a definite concentration in the lower socioeconomic neighborhoods of large cities, some criminologists suspect that the police are more lenient to middle-class suspects, thus exaggerating the socioeconomic differences in crime and delinquency rates. In the course of analyzing police contacts with juvenile suspects in Madison, Wisconsin, from 1950 to 1955, Shannon throws light on this issue. The rate of police contacts with juveniles in the Central zone (low socioeconomic status) is about three times the rate in the East zone (highest socioeconomic status). Although the Madison police are less likely to make an official referral of a juvenile contact in the East zone, this is almost entirely because of the less serious offenses in those neighborhoods. ". . . [J]uveniles engaging in comparable types of delinquent behavior receive pretty much the same treatment from Madison police." Nondiscriminatory handling of referrals is characteristic of *first* contacts with the police as well as of subsequent contacts. Unless it is assumed that the police discriminate in their contacts but not in their referrals, which is rather unlikely, this study is evidence of class differences in actual delinquent behavior, not merely in recorded delinquency. An independent study conducted in Ypsilanti, Michigan, sought to determine whether the higher arrest rate for Negroes as compared with whites was due to racial bias. The conclusion of the study was that occupational and nativity characteristics of the two groups adequately accounted for the variation in arrest rates. See Edward Green, "Race, Social Status, and Criminal Arrest," *American Sociological Review,* Vol. 35, June 1970, pp. 476-490. However, a third study suggested that white police officers are more prone to refer black than white youngsters who came to their attention for misbehavior to the juvenile court—even though the black youngsters had comparable attitudes and behavior to the white. See Theodore N. Ferdinand and Elmer G. Luchterhand, "Inner-City Youth, the Police, the Juvenile Court, and Justice," *Social Problems,* Vol. 17, Spring 1970, pp. 510-527.

James F. Short, Jr., Ray A. Tennyson, and Kenneth I. Howard, "Behavior Dimensions of Gang Delinquency," *American Sociological Review,* Vol. 28, June 1963, pp. 411–428. The activities, both delinquent and nondelinquent, of 598 members of 16 Chicago gangs were check rated by detached workers who had been in contact with them for at least six months. Sixty-nine activities were rated including basketball, skating, arson, carrying concealed weapons, rape, and attempted suicide. The gangs ranged in size from 16 to 68 members; 11 gangs were Negro and five white. Statistical analysis of the ratings show considerable overlap of delinquent behavior among all the gangs rather than stealing in one type of gang, violence in another, and alcohol or drug use in a third. The authors suggest that an undifferentiated "parent delinquent subculture" may exist out of which more specialized delinquent groups emerge.

Rita Volkman and Donald R. Cressey, "Differential Association and the Rehabilitation of Drug Addicts," *American Journal of Sociology,* Vol. 69, September 1963, pp. 129–142. Synanon is a self-help organization of former drug addicts with a culture that is strongly opposed to drug use. The authors analyze the five rehabilitative principles implicitly embodied in the Synanon program to account for its success with confirmed heroin addicts: (1) Admissions to the program are restricted to addicts who demonstrate by personal sacrifices a willingness to accept the guidance of the group. (2) Indoctrination makes clear that the central purpose of Synanon is not recreation or vocational therapy but keeping addicts away from drugs. (3) Partly as a result of members living and working together voluntarily, the group achieves great cohesiveness and *esprit de corps.* (4) Synanon House "has an explicit program for distributing status symbols to members in return for staying off the drug and, later, for actually displaying antidrug attitudes." Furthermore, status in the outside community is also gained as the individual develops a deeper commitment to the organization. (5) The group sessions (synanons) at which each member of the group is encouraged to evaluate the progress of his fellows provides members an opportunity to be "moral policemen." The identification with the legitimate community implicit in the role of critical evaluator helps members to change.

Lewis Yablonsky, *The Violent Gang,* New York: Macmillan, 1962. Yablonsky presents a detailed case study of a fighting gang in New York City (including excerpts from tape-recorded interviews) which fails to fit the conception of the fighting gang as a tightly integrated group of a hundred boys or more. He argues that most fighting gangs are loose aggregates of youths around a handful of dedicated warriors. On occasion the phantom membership can be mobilized, but a gang fight bears more resemblance to a riot than to the disciplined maneuvers of a modern army. Yablonsky has been criticized strongly by sociological reviewers for failing to link his research to theories of collective behavior, which seek to explain riots, lynchings, and other forms of spontaneous crowd phenomena. See the review by Solomon Kobrin, *American Sociological Review,* Vol. 28, April 1963, pp. 316–317, and the article by Harold W. Pfautz, "Near-group Theory and Collective Behavior: A Critical Reformulation," *Social Problems,* Vol. 9, Fall 1961, pp. 167–174.

SOCIAL CHANGE

In contemporary industrial societies, technological development and the growth in scientific knowledge are so much a part of everyday life that they serve in the public mind as the prototype of change. However, technological and scientific development has a cumulative character different from all other kinds of cultural and **social change.** On the reasonable assumptions that knowledge is superior to ignorance and that greater resources for carrying out objectives, whatever they are, are more desirable than fewer resources, the cumulative nature of technological and scientific development generates **progress** (in the sense of improvement over the past). There is no inherent reason why other types of sociocultural change constitute analogous improvements.

During optimistic periods of world history, such as the late nineteenth century, intellectuals argued that evolutionary progress was not limited to science and technology but was the principle behind all sociocultural change.[1] One hundred years ago, the belief was widespread that poverty and war were on the verge of elimination and that human beings would soon reach new plateaus of happiness and morality. Marxism, though it condemned captalist society, shared an essentially optimistic prognosis for the future.[2]

> The Marxist theory, too, is basically a theory of progress, although not of linear progress. The advance toward the classless society proceeds through "dialectical" conflicts, in each of which one subordinate class overthrows its ruling class (e.g., the bourgeoisie overthrows the aristocracy), only to establish a new society in which a new subordinate class rises to overthrow it. But these cycles are neither endless nor meaningless. As Marx saw it, the wheel has now reached its last turn; with the proletarian revolution, the story is about to come to an end. The proletariat's victory will give rise to a classless society, one which knows no major conflict and hence no revolutions.

Even during the nineteenth century, pessimistic voices were heard. A German social philosopher maintained that societies, like organisms, are born, grow to maturity, reach a period of decline, and ultimately disintegrate.[3] But not until the twentieth century did doubt spread about the validity of the idea of *general* progress. The First World War, the Second World War, and the period of international tension following the Second World War demonstrated that peace is no easier to attain today than it was 1000 years ago. The brutalities perpetrated by the Nazi regime in Germany—including concentration camps and gas chambers where millions of men, women, and children were put to death because they belonged to supposedly inferior "races"— showed that industrial development was not necessarily accompanied by moral development. German atrocities were more disillusioning for believers

[1] J. B. Bury, *The Idea of Progress,* New York: Macmillan, 1932; Herbert Spencer, *Sociology,* New York: Appleton, 1892, Vol. 1.

[2] Amitai Etzioni and Eva Etzioni, *Social Change: Sources, Patterns, Consequences,* New York: Basic Books, 1964, p. 4.

[3] Oswald Spengler, *The Decline of the West,* New York: Knopf, 1926.

in "progress" than the rape of nuns in the Congo or ritual murders in Haiti because Germany was an advanced industrial society with impressive cultural achievements behind it. This modern society invented a technique for manufacturing soap out of the fatty tissues of corpses removed from gas chambers and used this technique on a large scale. In the face of genocide, contemporary intellectuals are reluctant to assume that change means improvement. To be sure, change sometimes is improvement; the abolition of slavery can be so regarded. But progress is no longer considered synonymous with change.

With the assumption of automatic progress abandoned, it becomes more difficult to explain why some patterns of interaction change and others do not. Why, for example, was the automobile permitted to transform American life whereas the Mormon practice of polygamy was short-lived, even in Utah?[4] The automobile is not a self-evident blessing. About 50,000 Americans are killed every year in highway accidents, and hundreds of thousands are injured.[5] Between the cost of vehicles and the cost of the highways that carry them, automotive transportation is almost as expensive as litter bearers. Furthermore, the speed and convenience of automobile transportation is declining as traffic jams and parking problems grow.[6] On the other hand, the Mormon attempt to re-establish the polygamous households described in the Hebrew Bible could be justified by the American tradition of religious freedom. The Mormons did not insist that every man have several wives. They merely wished to *permit* a man to have more than one wife if he could induce more than one woman to marry him. If the popularity of the automobile and the repression of polygamy cannot be explained as instances of "progress," perhaps a general theory of change in interactive systems can account for such phenomena.

One theory of social change assumes the evolutionary tendency of cultures and societies to become more differentiated.[7] For instance, medieval Catholicism contained within its relatively undifferentiated culture the roots of secular philosophy, science, the performing arts, the graphic arts, and creative writing; these gradually evolved into separate subcultures. Societal differentiation resulted in a similar separation of what had previously been a diffuse whole. Thus the Industrial Revolution transformed British society from one in which the family was both a producing and consuming unit to one in which the family became a specialized socializing agency while production was transferred to another specialized agency, the factory.[8] How can this evolutionary theory

[4] Kimball Young, *Isn't One Wife Enough?*, New York: Holt, 1954.

[5] Department of Health, Education, and Welfare, *Vital Statistics of the United States*, annual report; National Safety Council, *Accident Facts*, annual report.

[6] For a thoughtful discussion of the traffic problems of large cities, see Scott Greer, "Traffic, Transportation, and Problems of the Metropolis," in Merton and Nisbet, Eds., *Contemporary Social Problems*, New York: Harcourt, Brace and World, 1961, pp. 605-650.

[7] Talcott Parsons, *Societies: Evolutionary and Comparative Perspectives*, Englewood Cliffs, N.J.: Prentice-Hall, 1966.

[8] Neil J. Smelser, *Social Change in the Industrial Revolution: An Application of Theory to the British Cotton Industry*, Chicago: University of Chicago Press, 1959.

of social change explain one of the most dramatic changes in contemporary American society, the Negro Revolution? Probably in terms of the differentiation of American society into a more complex community than it used to be. Before the Second World War, Negro Americans belonged overwhelmingly to the working class in terms of occupational and educational criteria. These economic and educational disadvantages reinforced the symbolic association remaining from the slavery era between black pigmentation and social inferiority. Over the past generation black Americans have moved into the middle class in sufficient numbers to challenge the white stereotype that a black skin meant inferior educational and occupational status. Skin color was becoming a less and less accurate clue to the class position of Negro Americans. But American social institutions generally (and white thought patterns in particular) did not recognize rapidly enough that the Negro community was now more differentiated than it was before. Most whites continued to behave as though a black skin was a good indication of illiteracy, low occupational status, and possible criminality. The evolutionary theory of social change sees the upheaval in American race relations as the adjustments whites and blacks are making to a Negro community that now includes a substantial proportion of middle-class families, many of which insist on being treated as white middle-class persons are treated, rather than as black ex-slaves.

Does the theory of societal differentiation adequately explain the Negro Revolution? As with any sociological theory, the critical questions are its success in interpreting known facts and its ability to forecast future developments. Let us attempt to describe in sociological terms what has happened to race relations in the United States as a test of the interpretive adequacy of one theory of social change.

AN EXAMPLE OF SOCIETAL CHANGE: THE NEGRO REVOLUTION

When Eli Whitney invented the cotton gin in 1794, the demand for cheap labor in the cotton fields spurred the slave trade, which had been declining, and thousands of Negroes were brought from Africa to serve white plantation owners.[9] Their consequent degradation by plantation owners is undeniable, even though it contravenes the Western tradition of the brotherhood of man. Human dignity has long been a concern of philosophers. Greek philosophers speculated about the essential rights of human beings more than 2000 years ago. These speculations were not taken sufficiently seriously to challenge the

---

[9] Gunnar Myrdal, *An American Dilemma: The Negro Problem and Modern Democracy*, New York: Harper, 1944, pp. 86, 118.

institution of slavery in Greece or Rome, perhaps because slavery provided the margin of leisure and comfort upon which civilization then depended. Later, the Roman emperor Marcus Aurelius was intrigued by the idea that all human beings have intrinsic dignity, and many thinkers in less prominent positions were stimulated by this noble but impractical notion. Christianity gave the ideal new vitality. The early Christians expected the Second Coming of the Messiah imminently; hence they were not concerned with the contribution of slavery to the maintenance of civilization. They took over the Platonic doctrine of the freedom of the human soul and applied it to everyone, slaves included. But the world did not end; and a dominant Christianity accepted for many centuries human degradation in this life if not in the next.

In the eighteenth century, the belief in human dignity won new and eloquent adherents. The French Declaration of the Rights of Man and the American Declaration of Independence expressed the same humanitarianism. Yet slavery continued. Jefferson, who wrote in the Declaration of Independence "that all men are created equal; that they are endowed by their Creator with certain unalienable rights; that among these are life, liberty, and the pursuit of happiness . . .," himself owned slaves. Perhaps the Founding Fathers had troubled consciences. The American Constitution never used the word "slave," although it provided that only "three fifths of all other persons" would be counted in determining a State's delegation in the House of Representatives and that "the migration or importation of such persons as any of the States now existing shall think proper to admit, shall not be prohibited by the Congress prior to the year 1808 . . . ." Congress passed a law outlawing the slave trade as soon as the Constitution permitted it to do so (1808), but this prohibition was not effectively enforced. About half a million slaves were smuggled into the United States between 1808 and 1860.[10]

Pushed by the Methodist movement, Great Britain abolished the slave trade in 1808 and purchased and freed all slaves in British dominions in 1833. Pushed by religious and by secular abolitionists, the United States fought the Civil War over slavery. After the South had been defeated, the thirteenth amendment to the Constitution was adopted. "Neither slavery nor involuntary servitude, except as a punishment for crime whereof the party shall have been duly convicted, shall exist within the United States, or any place subject to their jurisdiction." The thirteenth amendment could not, of course, erase decades of social, educational, and economic disadvantages. A great change had occurred in the *legal* status of Negroes. But this did not mean that blacks were in a position to compete with whites on equal terms. Even if there were no prejudice against them, Negroes would have had great difficulty breaking out of the underprivileged status which was their legacy from slavery. Discriminatory treatment reinforced their existing socioeconomic disadvantages and served to perpetuate them. Still, as the Swedish economist and sociologist Gunnar Myrdal pointed out, white Americans are torn between equalitarian

---

[10] Myrdal, *An American Dilemma*, p. 119.

ideals and discriminatory practices.[11] Most whites cannot deny equality of opportunity to blacks with a clear conscience. Writing in October 1942, Myrdal predicted that white Americans, pressed to choose between their ideals and their prejudices, would prefer to change their behavior: ''. . . not since Reconstruction has there been more reason to anticipate fundamental changes in American race relations, changes which will involve a development toward the American ideals.''[12]

Events since 1942 have partially justified Myrdal's optimism. American Negroes have improved their educational, economic, and social status.[13] The ideological dilemma, upon which Myrdal laid so much stress, is only one among several factors responsible for the change. Another factor is the migration of millions of Negroes from the rural South to cities of New York, New Jersey, Pennsylvania, Ohio, Michigan, Illinois, Missouri, and California. This migration, a consequence of the shrinking manpower requirements of Southern agriculture, was accelerated by industrial expansion during the Second World War and the postwar years in Northern cities. The massive redistribution of the Negro population—from one-party states in the South to big industrial states in the North—gave Negro voters ''potentially irresistible political power.''[14] In the presidential election of 1960, the margin by which John F. Kennedy won the crucial industrial states was much smaller than the Negro electorate of those states. Post-election surveys have in fact shown that a substantial majority of Negro voters preferred Kennedy to Nixon and that these votes provided the margin of victory. Certainly the political leverage of American Negroes has improved as a result of population redistribution. On the other hand, black support might not help a candidate if the bulk of white voters were unenthusiastic about racial integration. Under such circumstances, a call for greater opportunities for Negroes would lose a candidate more *white* votes than it would gain him *Negro* votes. This may have happened in the presidential election of 1968. Hubert Humphrey received about 97 per cent of the Negro vote, according to post-election surveys, but Richard Nixon received enough white votes to win the election. [15]

As Negroes moved out of the rural South and into Northern and Southern cities, they obtained access to better educational opportunities for their children. The predominantly black schools in the ghettoes of large cities did not provide as good an education as suburban schools, but they educated more

[11] Myrdal, *An American Dilemma*. The dilemma referred to in the title of the book is this problem of squaring discrimination with American ideals.

[12] Myrdal, *An American Dilemma*, p. xix.

[13] Bureau of the Census, *Recent Trends in Social and Economic Conditions of Negroes in the United States,* Washington, D.C.: Government Printing Office, 1968.

[14] Samuel A. Stouffer, *Social Research to Test Ideas,* New York: Free Press of Glencoe, 1962, p. 232.

[15] For a breakdown of the vote in the 1968 presidential election by race, see Philip E. Converse et al., ''Continuity and Change in American Politics: Parties and Issues in the 1968 Election,'' *American Political Science Review,* Vol. 63, December 1969, p. 1085.

effectively than the underfinanced schools of the rural South. Ever since the First World War, psychologists have been aware of the fact that Northern Negroes test higher, on the average, than Southern Negroes on standard intelligence tests. At first it was thought that more intelligent Negroes were more likely to migrate. Then Otto Klineberg of Columbia University conducted a series of studies which demonstrated that the average I.Q. scores for Southern-born Negro children rose proportionately to the length of time they were residents in the North. "Selective migration" could not explain the intellectual superiority of Northern Negroes; better educational opportunities made the difference.[16]

Professor Klineberg's studies demonstrate how changes in the cultural climate can contribute to social change. As evidence accumulated relating poor performance on intelligence tests to insufficient and inadequate schooling, the belief in inherent Negro inferiority grew less respectable, especially among better-educated segments of the white population.[17] The cumulative impact of anthropological, psychological, and sociological opinion denied intellectual support to the old belief in the inherent inferiority of darkly pigmented people. The Supreme Court decision on May 17, 1954, outlawing racial segregation in public schools, showed the effect of social science opinion on white decision makers. In holding that "separate educational facilities are inherently unequal," the Court considered explicitly the psychological consequences of segregated education, not merely the usual superiority of white schools in physical facilities and budget. Implementation of the 1954 Supreme Court decision is equalizing Negro and white education further. The gradual elimination of segregation will improve the quality as well as increase the quantity of Negro education. Hopeful expectations aroused by the decision help to explain the accelerated upgrading shown in Table 14.1.[18] The years 1920 to 1960 witnessed a substantial increase in the proportion of *nonwhite* youngsters who completed at least four years of high school, but the rate of increase between 1960 and 1968 showed a dramatic spurt.

The increase in the proportion of *white* youngsters completing at least four years of high school has also increased. Even today, whites as a group complete more years of school than blacks, but the gap narrowed appreciably between 1960 and 1968. There is a good chance that it will narrow further — and that qualitative improvements will consolidate the quantitative changes that have already occurred. As Table 14.2 shows, élite colleges are now accepting

[16] Otto Klineberg, *Negro Intelligence and Selective Migration,* New York: Columbia University Press, 1935.

[17] A recent article suggesting that there may be a genetic basis for the inferior average performance of Negro school children created a furor among social scientists. See Arthur R. Jensen, "How Much Can We Boost IQ and Scholastic Achievement?" *Harvard Educational Review,* Vol. 39, Winter 1969, pp. 1-123.

[18] This upgrading is also a consequence of the redistribution of Negro population, of the rising aspirations of Negro parents for their children, and of the trend toward educational upgrading of urban industrial populations throughout the world.

TABLE 14.1

White and Nonwhite Americans, 25 to 29 Years of Age, with Four Years of High School Education or Beyond, by Sex, 1920-1968

Year	Percentage of Nonwhites 25 to 29 Years Old with 4 Years of High School or Beyond		Percentage of Whites 25 to 29 Years Old with 4 Years of High School or Beyond	
	Male	Female	Male	Female
1920	6	7	21	24
1940	11	14	39	43
1960	36	41	63	65
1968	60	56	75	75

Source: John K. Folger and Charles B. Nam, "Educational Trends from Census Data," *Demography,* Vol. 1, 1964, p. 254; Bureau of the Census, *Recent Trends in Social and Economic Conditions of Negroes in the United States,* Washington, D.C.: Government Printing Office, 1968, p. 18.

black applicants almost in proportion to the 11 per cent proportion of blacks in the American population.

What are the consequences of this closing educational gap? In view of the relationship between educational attainment and social allocation analyzed in Chapters 11 and 12, increased numbers of black high school and college graduates make possible a proportionate increase in the black middle class. But if white employers discriminate in their hiring practices against black job applicants, educational achievement will not be translated into middle-class occupations and incomes. However, the rising concern about black unemployment, the rate of which has been twice the rate for whites for two decades, has produced federally sponsored job upgrading and retraining programs as well as the mobilization of business leaders (for example, in the Urban Coalition) to provide new jobs for the hard-core unemployed.[19] Although the actual accomplishments of such programs are modest, they are evidence that the American conscience is not dead. These compensatory programs offer special consideration to lower-class blacks lacking educational qualifications or job skills — as well as active recruitment in ghetto communities and the simplification or elimination of written applications. Moreover, discrimination against qualified black applicants for middle-class jobs is less likely today because the bureaucratization of personnel work in large corporations (described in Chapter 10) favors rational hiring procedures. Selecting on the basis of race or any characteristic of the applicant irrelevant to job performance is unprofessional.

[19] National Advisory Commission on Civil Disorders, *Report,* New York: Bantam, 1968, pp. 413-424.

TABLE 14.2

Number of Black Applicants Admitted to Some Leading Colleges

	Accepted	Freshman Places	Black Accept- ances	Percentage of Blacks Accepted
Brown	1,350	800	140	10
Columbia	1,200	700	115	10
Cornell[a]	1,725	750	145	8
Dartmouth	1,300	820	130	10
Harvard	1,400	1,200	109	8
Pennsylvania	2,900	1,725	230	8
Princeton	1,346	820	111	8
Yale	1,708	1,265	155	9
Totals	12,929	8,080	1135	
Barnard	870	425	81	9
Bryn Mawr	379	220	30	8
Mount Holyoke	1,050	535	61	6
Radcliffe	380	320	40	11
Smith	1,269	713	86	6
Vassar	760	470	43	6
Wellesley	722	500	87	12
Totals	5,430	3,183	428	

[a] College of Arts and Sciences

Source: *The New York Times,* April 20, 1969.

Thus, insofar as the American economy is bureaucratically organized, and it *is* substantially organized in this way, existing prejudices of white personnel officers are opposed by professional considerations as well as by the new national emphasis on equal opportunity.

It is too soon for the potentialities of Table 14.1 to be fully translated into an occupational redistribution of Negro Americans. However, some dispersion has already occurred; Table 14.3 shows sharp increases in professional and clerical workers between 1960 and 1967 as well as in higher-level working-class jobs (craftsmen and foremen). The growth of the black middle class seems to be a continuing trend. [20] As the black middle class grows, there will be more contact between middle-class blacks and whites; whites will respond to blacks who are like them in education, income, and occupation rather than thinking of Negroes as a homogenous lower-class group. If this does take place, it will

[20] Eli Ginzberg and Dale L. Hiestand, *Mobility in the Negro Community: Guidelines for Research on Social and Economic Progress,* Washington, D.C.: United States Commission on Civil Rights, 1968.

TABLE 14.3

Changes in American Employment of Whites and Nonwhites, by Occupation, 1960–1967

Major Occupational Group	Number (in thousands)		Percentage	
	Nonwhites	Whites	Nonwhites	Whites
Professional and technical	+263	+2,141	+80	+30
Managers, Officials, etc.	+31	+396	+17	+6
Clerical	+391	+2,158	+77	+23
Sales	+25	+99	+22	+2
Craftsmen and Foremen	+203	+1,083	+49	+13
Operatives	+465	+1,434	+33	+14
Service workers, except private household	+287	+1,136	+23	+23
Private household workers	−169	−278	−17	−23
Nonfarm laborers	−70	−61	−7	−2
Farmers and farm workers	−453	−1,389	−52	−31
Total	+970	+6,721	+14	+11

Source: Bureau of the Census, *Recent Trends in Social and Economic Conditions Of Negroes in the United States,* Washington, D.C.: Government Printing Office, 1968, p. 16.

duplicate the process of inclusion of previous immigrant groups into American society.[21] Irish, Italian, and Polish immigrants constituted a working class differentiated from the Anglo-Saxon élite by adherence to the Catholic religion, which was suspect by a Protestant society. As these groups became acculturated to American society through education, they became part of the middle class. Eventually the cultural definition of these groups changed from working class to heterogeneous American. One reason that John Kennedy won the presidency in 1960 and Al Smith, also a Catholic, lost by a landslide in 1928 was that few Catholics were middle class in 1928; Kennedy could draw support from all social levels because Irish Catholics had achieved middle-class status in substantial numbers. When sufficient numbers of Negroes are middle class, a Negro president will become possible because he will not be symbolically working class. Religious prejudice against Catholics and color prejudice against Negroes are both reinforced by class homogeneity. The dispersion of Negroes throughout the class system is just beginning, whereas the class dispersion of Catholics is far advanced, but the Catholic experience provides a basis for anticipating full inclusion for the Negro in American society. Class dispersion of blacks, however, is not proceeding evenly: the poorest fifth of the Negro population has not shared proportionally in the

[21] Talcott Parsons, "Full Citizenship for the American Negro? A Sociological Problem," *Daedalus,* Vol. 94, Fall 1965, pp. 1009-1054.

occupational upgrading that increased the average income of Negro families.[22] The poorest fifth is deprived not only in comparison with whites but also in comparison with blacks moving out of poverty and into the middle class. One million nonwhites escaped from poverty between 1967 and 1968, but they left behind 35 per cent of the nonwhite population; the lowest 20 per cent were very poor indeed.[23]

The median family income of Negroes is lower in the South than in other regions; it is also a smaller percentage of the median family income of whites.[24] Yet in the South the improved status of the Negro is *visible* for those whose memories extend back ten years or more. Even the poorest Southern blacks can see that Negroes utilize motion picture theaters, gasoline stations, restaurants, sports arenas, and hotels where local custom had barred them before. Even though they personally may not have the opportunity to use integrated places of public accommodation, for those who remember "white only" signs on bus terminal rest rooms and drinking fountains, the new right is precious. Similarly, for those who recall when few Negroes were permitted to vote, the increase in voter registrations in the eleven Southern states (Ala-

[22] Andrew F. Brimmer, "The Negro in the National Economy," in John P. Davis, *The American Negro Reference Book,* Englewood Cliffs, N.J.: Prentice-Hall, 1966, pp. 251-336.

[23] Bureau of the Census, *Recent Trends in Social and Economic Conditions of Negroes in the United States,* Washington, D.C.: Government Printing Office, 1968, p. 10.

[24] Bureau of the Census, *Recent Trends,* p. 7.

bama, Arkansas, Florida, Georgia, Louisiana, Mississippi, North Carolina, South Carolina, Tennessee, Texas, and Virginia) from thousands in 1940 to two million in 1964 to three million in 1968 is cause for satisfaction.[25] On the other hand, for *Northern* Negroes, who have enjoyed legal equality with whites in voting rights and the use of public accommodations for decades, improvement in their social status has been less dramatic. For example, due to the in-migration of blacks to the central cities of metropolitan areas and the out-migration of whites to the suburbs, desegregation efforts were able to achieve only small decreases in the pattern of racially segregated housing between 1950 and 1960.[26] However, as surveys conducted by the National Opinion Research Center have shown, integrated housing is not so rare as many Americans think (see Table 14.4). Still, **de facto segregation** in housing is the usual pattern, and segregated neighborhoods limit the possibilities of massive school desegregation in large cities despite programs for producing integration by boards of education.[27]

Although factors making for racial equality have been discussed one at a time, the joint effect of all of them together may be considerably greater than the additive effect of each separate one. (Statisticians call this phenomenon "interaction" and can measure it precisely with analysis of variance techniques.) The changing status of Negroes in American society is not due to any factor, however important, acting alone: to ideological dilemmas, to social-science research, to the redistribution of Negro population, to rising Negro demands, or to governmental sponsorship of **racial integration.** These factors exist in a dynamic equilibrium; a change in one makes a change in another easier to achieve.[28] Government-sponsored change, like the 1954 Supreme Court decision declaring segregated education unconstitutional, rested on ideological and social scientific as well as constitutional foundations. But it also depended on the existence of a Negro protest movement, one arm of which (the National Association for the Advancement of Colored People) paid the legal expenses enabling four test cases to be appealed to the Supreme Court.

Another arm of that protest movement sponsored sit-ins, freedom rides, and other challenges to segregation. A generation ago, Bayard Rustin, currently Executive Director of the A. Philip Randolph Foundation, and James Farmer, currently Assistant Secretary of Health, Education, and Welfare, began to mobilize the moral resources of Christian pacifism on behalf of civil rights for Negroes:[29]

---

[25] Bureau of the Census, *Recent Trends,* p. 29.

[26] Karl E. Taeuber and Alma F. Taeuber, *Negroes in Cities: Residential Segregation and Neighborhood Change,* Chicago: Aldine, 1965.

[27] Raymond W. Mack, Ed., *Our Children's Burden: Studies of Desegregation in Nine American Communities,* New York: Vintage, 1968.

[28] See Myrdal, *An American Dilemma,* pp. 1065-1070, for a discussion of vicious circles and benevolent circles.

[29] Reprinted by permission. From Carleton Mabee, "Evolution of Nonviolence," *The Nation, Vol. 193, Aug. 12, 1961, pp. 78-81.*

TABLE 14.4

Estimated Number of Integrated Neighborhoods and Households, by Region

Region and Type of Neighborhood	Estimated Number of:			Percentage of Total Households
	Neighborhoods		Households	
Northeast:				
Total integrated	2,480		4,592,440	31.8
Open		1,158	2,272,800	15.7
Integrating		773	1,543,360	10.7
Substantially integrated		357	419,280	2.9
Integrated in localities with very few Negroes		192	357,000	2.5
Total segregated	8,720		9,854,560	68.2
Total	11,200		14,447,000	100.0
North Central:				
Total integrated	1,271		2,064,360	12.6
Open		124	462,400	2.8
Integrating		208	319,040	2.0
Substantially integrated		372	427,920	2.6
Integrated in localities with very few Negroes		567	855,000	5.2
Total segregated	11,429		14,346,640	87.4
Total	12,700		16,411,000	100.0
South:				
Total integrated	3,765		2,050,720	11.3
Open		42	120,000	0.7
Integrating		220	141,600	0.8
Substantially integrated		980	725,120	4.0
Integrated rural areas		2,523	1,064,000	5.8
Total segregated	10,435		16,183,280	88.7
Total	14,200		18,234,000	100.0
West:				
Total integrated	1,200		2,490,880	25.6
Open		170	370,000	3.8
Integrating		292	447,200	4.6
Substantially integrated		121	215,680	2.2
Integrated in localities with very few Negroes		617	1,458,000	15.0
Total segregated	6,300		7,217,120	74.4
Total	7,500		9,708,000	100.0

Source: Seymour Sudman, Norman M. Bradburn, and Galen Gockel, "The Extent and Characteristics of Racially Integrated Housing in the United States," *Journal of Business,* Vol. 42, January 1969, p. 57.

As early as April, 1942, the pacifist Fellowship of Reconciliation's Youth Secretary, Bayard Rustin, a young Negro of compelling charm, was trying one-man sit-ins. He believed that American Negroes were peculiarly fitted to experiment with non-violent action, he said, because they not only had a history of enduring suffering without bitterness, but also a rich religious heritage of which non-violence was a part.

When Rustin went into a restaurant in a small Midwestern town, the manager refused to serve him, because, she explained, if she did "everybody would walk out." Rustin proposed that they try an experiment: he would sit at a table with a hamburger in front of him, and they both would watch for ten minutes to see if anyone walked out because he was there. If anyone did, Rustin would also walk out. After some hesitation, the manager agreed to try the experiment. Rustin waited the ten minutes without anyone's walking out, and then the manager served him a hot hamburger. Thereafter the restaurant continued to serve Negroes.

Rustin found other opportunities to refuse to cooperate with segregation. On a bus near Nashville, he sat up front with whites, was dragged out of the bus and kicked, but did not retaliate. Attending a Quaker conference at Cape May, N.J., he appeared with white friends one afternoon at a "whites only" section of a beach. When guards asked him to go elsewhere, he expressed concern for the difficult position of the guards. He explained that it was against his principles to acquiesce in segregation and therefore he could not willingly leave, but suggested various humorous ways by which they could remove him. The guards were so taken aback that they left him alone; during the rest of the conference, Rustin and his friends continued to use the beach. When he arrived late one rainy night by train in Baltimore, Rustin found that the taxi drivers at the station refused to pick him up because of his color. He walked into the middle of the narrow taxi driveway alongside the station, and stood there, blocking all taxi traffic for ninety minutes, until he got a taxi.

During 1942 Rustin described his one-man sit-ins, ride-ins, swim-ins and stand-ins to many audiences, and thus prepared the way for the organized non-violent movement.

In February, 1942, James Farmer, the young Race Relations Secretary of the Fellowship of Reconciliation, proposed to the Fellowship that it attempt to create an organization, composed of both pacifists and non-pacifists, committed to non-violent action against racial discrimination. It was hoped that, after a period of five to ten years of education and experiment, the organization would be ready to use on a large scale "relentless non-cooperation, economic boycott, [and] civil disobedience." In April, 1942, the Fellowship's National Council decided to endorse such a campaign, and authorized Farmer to work on it. The decision was soon to bear fruit.

Meanwhile, among the several Fellowship of Reconciliation "cell" groups in Chicago, one, composed largely of University of Chicago students, was devoted to race relations. One evening two members of this group—Farmer, who is colored, and James Robinson, white—went into Jack Spratt's, a restaurant in their neighborhood. They were served reluctantly. Later, a larger interracial party from the same "cell" also went into the restaurant. They were also served reluctantly; and after they had eaten, their waiter refused to give them a bill. They left money in payment, but the waiter followed them into the street to throw the money after them.

By this time the group working on Jack Spratt's had grown to include several non-students and non-pacifists. The enlarged group deliberately planned a non-violent demonstration, patterned on a combination of Gandhian methods and the methods of the 1936-7 "sit-down strikes" in auto factories (the sitters first called their demonstrations "sit-down strikes"), in an attempt to change the restaurant's policy.

One day in May, 1942, the group sent an all-white party into Jack Spratt's, and it was served; then a mixed party went in, and was seated; finally, an all-Negro party entered. The hostess told the all-Negro group it would not be seated except in the basement, but the group refused to leave. The hostess called the police who, upon finding only a quiet group of people waiting to be served, refused to arrest anyone. Patrons in the restaurant who were not part of the sit-in became curious about it and stayed on, occupying seats, thus in effect helping the cause. After two hours in which business in the restaurant was almost at a standstill, the management decided to change its policy, and the hostess personally served the waiting Negroes.

Deciding that they had found a technique that worked, the sitters led in forming, in June, 1942, the Chicago Committee on Racial Equality to experiment further with non-violent direct action. The following year the committee, with the help of the Fellowship of Reconciliation, led in creating a national federation of groups devoted to non-violent, direct action, called the Congress of Racial Equality (CORE) which chose Farmer as its chairman. The major vehicle of the non-violent movement of the 1940s had been created.

CORE was an interracial, urban movement, centered in the North, with only a few member groups south of the Mason-Dixon Line at any time during the 1940s, and these all in the upper South — in Baltimore, Washington, St. Louis and Bartlesville, Oklahoma (where, under pressure from "patriotic" societies, the leader of the CORE group was eventually forced from the library post which she had held for thirty-five years). The number of local groups affiliated with CORE was ten in 1945, thirteen in 1947, fifteen in 1949 and twenty in 1950; and there was usually a number of cooperating non-affiliated groups.

Not all of the activities of CORE and CORE-related groups were carried out along strictly non-violent, direct-action lines. Some activities followed conventional patterns, and in these CORE was often able to work with other organizations. CORE encouraged letter-writing campaigns to government officials or owners of businesses; petitions (as in Washington, D.C., to protest segregation in the public parks); and publicity by press releases. (In Denver, after a Negro was refused a room at a YMCA on Christmas Day with the explanation that there was no room available, a CORE press release drew a parallel with what happened, a long time ago, at another inn at Christmas time.)

Some activities were less conventional, and in these it was harder to find cooperating organizations. When the "Freedom Train" was circulating the country to exhibit copies of the Constitution and the Declaration of Independence, CORE groups picketed it with signs saying, "There is no freedom till all are free."

CORE groups conducted opinion surveys to find out if department store patrons objected to being served by Negro sales clerks (in Cleveland, where department stores employed only white sales clerks, 68 per cent of patrons were willing to be served by Negroes); listed restaurants, outside of Negro sections, which had no racial bars (in Washington, sitters could recall when there were only four such restaurants; by 1950, there were still only seventeen they could list); printed cards for CORE friends to leave on the tables of desegregated restaurants expressing appreciation of their policy; solicited business for newly desegregated enterprises; bought stock in companies which practiced segregation — like the Greyhound bus company — and then appeared at stockholders' meetings to protest company policy; distributed leaflets at Pennsylvania Station in New York and the interstate bus terminal in Washington, informing passengers that in interstate travel, despite custom, the Supreme Court had ruled in the

Morgan case in 1946 that segregation was unconstitutional; and promoted a song that urged interstate travelers to sit where they liked:

> "And if the driver-man says 'Move,'
> And if the driver-man says 'Move,'
> And if the driver-man says 'Move,'
> Speak up polite,
> But sit there tight,
> You're in the right,
> You don't have to ride Jim Crow."

But it was in the more clearly non-violent, direct-action projects that the CORE and CORE-related groups found their real métier. They adapted Gandhian methods imaginatively to the American scene, developing the techniques which sitters and freedom riders have made well known. . . .

Sitters in the 1940s . . . found eating places their most convenient target. As early as 1944, the CORE group in Washington, D.C., decided that dime-store lunch counters were excellent places to hold "sit-down strikes" . . . "Because there is a good deal of Negro trade in these stores," they explained, and "also because colored people are served at the present time standing up at the [lunch] counter." But they did not at that time discover that the dime stores were also a good choice because sympathy boycotts might spread against chain dime stores all over the nation; that idea would not catch hold while the non-violent movement remained small.

In the 1940s, CORE groups also held sit-ins at fancy restaurants, like the "plush and hush" restaurant in Los Angeles where a hundred persons at a time "sat-in." Sit-ins were held in a Negro-owned restaurant in Washington which discriminated against whites; at drug-store lunch counters and in department-store restaurants.

In addition to eating places, there were also sit-ins in churches, as in Frankfort, Kentucky, and Bartlesville; in theatres, as in Yellow Springs, Ohio, and Baltimore; in swimming pools, as in Palisades Park, N.J., and Cleveland; in roller-skating rinks, as in Chicago; and in the religious services of prisons, as by the conscientious-objector inmates of the federal prison in Ashland, Kentucky.

Other planned forms of non-violent, direct action included stand-ins to buy tickets at discriminatory theatres, as in Washington, D.C., or at discriminatory swimming pools, as in Los Angeles, or to buy food at discriminatory cafeterias, as in Detroit; the picketing of segregated YMCAs, as in New York, and offices which promoted restrictive covenants for real estate, as in Chicago; small-scale boycotts, as of a tavern in Yellow Springs (it lost 60 per cent of its business), or metropolitan-wide boycotts protesting discrimination against Negro employment, as of Carnation milk in San Francisco and Los Angeles, and of Wonder bread in Chicago (both these actions were successful in changing company policy); testing for hotel discrimination in Boston; hunger or work strikes against segregated dining in prisons, as by conscientious-objector inmates of the federal prisons at Lewisburg, Pennsylvania, and Danbury, Connecticut; sitting desegregated on buses and trains, as on a long "Journey of Reconciliation" through Virginia, North Carolina, Kentucky and Tennessee in 1947, for which Rustin and three others were sentenced to thirty days in a North Carolina road gang on the charge of disobeying state segregation laws.

Neither these early sit-ins nor the 1947 Journey of Reconciliation attracted national attention. In 1960, however, when black students at Southern colleges sat in at lunch counters in Greensboro, North Carolina; Tallahassee, Florida; Atlanta, Georgia; Portsmouth, Virginia; Nashville, Tennessee; and Baton Rouge, Louisiana, they won widespread approval and sympathy.[30] Photographs of clean-cut Negro college students being attacked by hoodlums as they sat waiting for service helped their cause. So did their failure to respond in kind to the violence of their tormentors. Middle-class white readers of the newspapers and magazines in which these photographs appeared had to choose between identifying with white thugs or with black college students struggling nonviolently in a cause in which they believed. The hoodlums were not appealing role models despite their white skins.

On May 4, 1961, the "freedom rides" began. A group of 13 Negroes and whites recruited by CORE left Washington in a Greyhound bus to challenge segregation in interstate buses and bus terminals.[31] The timing of the freedom ride was significant. In December 1960, the United States Supreme Court had extended its 1946 ruling in the Morgan case, which had prohibited segregation of interstate passengers only in the vehicles in which they traveled. The Boynton case added the prohibition against segregation in facilities used by passengers *outside* the vehicles: waiting rooms, rest rooms, terminal restaurants. What the freedom riders wanted to do was to follow up the legal right with a demonstration of its actual implementation. The first bus was scheduled to end a tour of the coastal states in New Orleans; on May 14 it was set upon by an angry mob near Anniston, Alabama, and burned. Some of the occupants were beaten badly enough to require hospitalization. A second bus of freedom riders reached Birmingham, where they were attacked by another angry mob. Although some of the hoodlums smashed the camera of a photographer for the Birmingham *Post Herald,* he had already removed the film showing one of the freedom riders being beaten. (The victim required 53 stitches in his face and head.) This photograph appeared the next morning in the *Post-Herald* and shortly thereafter in newspapers throughout the United States and other countries. American public opinion was on the side of the nonviolent integrationists and against not only the hoodlums but Southern police officials who had failed to protect the freedom riders. CORE had no difficulty recruiting additional volunteers from every section of the United States for further freedom rides.

Attorney General Robert Kennedy filed a petition on May 29, 1961, with the Interstate Commerce Commission suggesting procedures to enforce the integration of terminal facilities. On September 22 the Commission forbade interstate bus companies to segregate bus seating on the basis of race, color, creed, or national origin and to use bus terminals where facilities were segre-

---

[30] James Peck, *Freedom Ride,* New York: Simon and Schuster, 1962, Chap. 6, "Sit-Ins– the Students Report."

[31] Peck, *Freedom Ride,* Chap. 8; Tuskeegee Institute, *Race Relations in the South–1961,* Tuskeegee, Ala.: Department of Records and Research, 1962, p. 15.

gated. Signs showing this nondiscriminatory policy were ordered posted in all interstate buses and eventually on all tickets sold. On October 16 three major railroads serving the South announced an end of segregation in both trains and terminals.[32] Freedom rides continued because segregation continued in some bus terminals, especially in small communities, but it was a lost cause. American public opinion and the federal government stood behind the freedom riders; they had won.

Self-sacrificing nonviolent efforts in behalf of racial equality antedated the ghetto riots and campus disruptions in the more militant 1960s. But without such nonviolent resistance as freedom rides and sit-ins the later militance might have produced violent repression. Nonviolence assured a sympathetic hearing of Negro grievances by the white middle class—and a growing moral consensus that racial discrimination is wrong. When President Lyndon Johnson incorporated in his 1965 speech before a joint session of Congress the words of the civil rights movement hymn, "We Shall Overcome," he was doing more than calling for a voting rights bill (which he got). He was expressing the indignation of middle-class Americans against violence directed at respectable citizens, both black and white, who wished to protest denial of voting rights to blacks. Like most Americans, he was shocked by the death of white Unitarian minister Reverend James Reeb, on March 11. Reeb had come to Selma, Alabama, from Boston to march the 54 miles to Montgomery, the state capital, with Martin Luther King and the civil rights protesters. Clergymen from all parts of the country as well as private citizens flocked to Selma to take his place. Ultimately, 25,000 marchers entered the state capital under the protection of federal troops. The March 26, 1965 cover of *Life* magazine showed Martin Luther King holding in his hands a floral wreath "to the martyred Reverend James Reeb" while Archbishop Lakovos stood to his left, Reverend Abernathy to his right, and United Auto Workers president Walter Reuther stood behind him. The headline on the cover read, "HISTORIC TURNING POINT FOR THE NEGRO'S CAUSE." The savage repression of non-violent civil disobedience had helped to establish a moral consensus on behalf of racial equality. A genteel intransigence on the part of Southern whites might have prevented the crystalization of this consensus without which the federal government could not have acted effectively against segregation.[33] The Civil Rights Acts of 1964 and 1965 symbolized the commitment of the white middle class to racial equality.

Thus the desegregation of public facilities and the securing of voting rights for Southern blacks should be credited to the civil rights movement—and particularly to its adoption of nonviolent resistance, an idea set forth in Henry David Thoreau's essay on civil disobedience. In the case of educational desegregation, however, the federal government did not merely support

---

[32] Peck, *Freedom Ride,* p. 159.

[33] Kenneth B. Clark, "The Civil Rights Movement: Momentum and Organization," *Daedalus,* Vol. 95, Winter 1966, pp. 256-257.

Paul Conklin—PIX

private initiatives; it led the way. On January 4, 1954, the Secretary of Defense announced a new regulation directing "that the operation of all school facilities located on military installations shall be conducted without segregation on the basis of race or color" regardless of other considerations.[34] This meant that dual schools operated by local school boards on military bases (to teach the children of military personnel) were no longer permitted.

The desegregation of schools on American military installations was part of a broader policy transforming the American military establishment, which had been completely segregated until after the Second World War, into the most fully integrated sector of American society.[35] This was government-sponsored change on a massive scale, affecting millions of young adults every year. It occurred because American Negroes were sufficiently educated to be aware that segregation violated equalitarian ideals and sufficiently powerful politically not to be ignored and because most white Americans were ideologically prepared to make concessions. When President Truman signed the executive order of July 26, 1948, leading to sweeping changes, this was official sponsorship of a reform which had to come. Once desegregation of the Armed Services was carried out, segregation in civilian life became less practicable. It seemed anomalous that soldiers and sailors stationed in southern

[34] James C. Evans and David A. Lane, Jr., "Integration in the Armed Services," *Annals of the American Academy of Political and Social Science,* Vol. 304, March 1956, p. 82.

[35] Charles C. Moskos, Jr., "Racial Integration in the Armed Forces," *American Journal of Sociology,* Vol. 72, September 1966, pp. 132-148.

bases were integrated on the base and segregated while off duty. With schools on military installations desegregated, a precedent for integrated civilian schools existed. When the Supreme Court declared racially segregated schools inherently unequal in May, 1954, its words seemed radical to many Southerners. But its decision occurred four months after the Secretary of Defense had acted to eliminate segregation in schools located on military bases but operated by local school boards.

The pace of the Negro Revolution accelerated after the 1954 Supreme Court decision, and its character shifted from nonviolent demands for faster integration to militant action on behalf of a variety of goals: more jobs, greater political influence, better schools, unsegregated housing and, perhaps most important, greater respect from white Americans. One of the first clues to the new mood was the Montgomery, Alabama, bus boycott. On December 1, 1955, seamstress Rosa Parks refused to move to the back of the bus (in accordance with the white supremacy tradition) and was arrested; the black community supported her.[36] Reverend Ralph Abernathy and Dr. Martin Luther King, Jr., helped organize the Montgomery Improvement Association; car pools and a willingness to walk miles to work when necessary enabled Montgomery's 40,000 blacks to maintain a boycott of the public bus system.

[36] *Ebony,* Vol. 24, August 1969, p. 32; Peck, *op. cit.,* Chapter 4.

After 12 months of economic pressure, the bus company capitulated. Not only did blacks achieve the right to sit where they pleased in public buses, but they accomplished this victory through civil disobedience on a mass scale. Futhermore, they catapulted Martin Luther King into the national role of activist leader: [37]

> Unlike the old accommodating leaders, even unlike the militant but elite leadership of the earlier NAACP, the new Negro leader could no longer retain his position by doing things *for* his people; he had to do things *with* them. He had to march!

Before his assassination in 1968, Martin Luther King marched many times, most successfully in 1963 when he led the March on Washington. A quarter of a million persons (about a fifth of them white) thronged the Lincoln Memorial, listened to his "I have a dream . . ." speech, and joined in singing "We Shall Overcome." Dr. King consistently worked for racial reconciliation; his speech at the Lincoln Memorial stressed the integration theme:[38]

> I have a dream that one day on the red hills of Georgia the sons of former slaves and the sons of former slave owners will be able to sit down together at the table of brotherhood. I have a dream that one day even the state of Mississippi, a state sweltering with people's injustices, sweltering with the heat of oppression, will be transformed into an oasis of freedom and justice.
> I have a dream that my four little children one day will live in a nation where they will not be judged by the color of their skin but by the content of their character.

Two developments give Dr. King's words an archaic ring: the destructive riots in black ghettoes from 1965 to 1970 and the increasing incidence of violence. When Watts erupted in August, 1965, in riot, burning, and looting (34 persons lost their lives and 35 million dollars of damage occurred), a black lower-class mob joined the Negro Revolution "on their own terms".[39]

> The negative, almost aimless behavior of the crowd, and the substitution of "Burn, Baby, Burn" for the specific, negotiable demands with which the civil rights organizations justify their demonstrations, both signify that the riots marked a turning point in the revolution.

Martin Luther King was jeered in Watts when he pleaded with the mob to disperse. To the mob he symbolized the Establishment. The lesson was not lost on black activists. By 1966 Stokely Carmichael of the Student Nonviolent Coordinating Committee was calling for "black power" — and other voices

---

[37] Lewis M. Killian, *The Impossible Revolution: Black Power and the American Dream,* New York: Random House, p. 55.

[38] Coretta Scott King, *My Life With Martin Luther King,* New York: Holt, Rinehart, and Winston, 1969, p. 239.

[39] Killian, *The Impossible Revolution,* p. 101.

Charles Harbutt—Magnum

joined him. CORE moved from a militant integrationist organization under the directorship of James Farmer to black-power separatism under Floyd McKissick and later Roy Innis. The Black Panthers, who explicitly advocated the stockpiling of weapons and their defensive use, obtained a following in big-city ghettoes across the country. Black-power advocates exercised influence out of proportion to their numbers because no one could be sure how many alienated blacks would follow them. Established white and black leaders were fearful of riot-torn cities and indeed of a black revolution. Many believed that such a revolution, if it occurred, would stiffen white resistance to racial equality and defer, perhaps indefinitely, Martin Luther King's dream of justice.

What is the meaning of "black power"? Black servicemen are using the black power symbol of the clenched fist as greeting and insisting on the right to wear natural hairstyles.[40] Two winners of medals at the 1968 Olympic games in Mexico raised their fists in the black power salute during the playing of the Star Spangled Banner in the victory ceremony. Black athletes on college campuses across the nation are protesting against alleged racism by boycotting practice, wearing black armbands, and refusing to play in some games.[41] As one University of Wyoming football player put it, explaining the protest

[40] Paul Good, "A Proud Esprit Soiled by Racial Hate," *Life,* September 26, 1969.

[41] Anthony Ripley, "Irate Black Athletes Stir Campus Tension," *The New York Times,* November 16, 1969, p. 1.

against Brigham Young University that led to 14 black players being dropped from the team, "It was a question of our eligibility—our education—or our manhood." Even more dramatic and militant than the behavior of black athletes has been the occupation of campus buildings by black students and their community supporters. In numerous colleges black students have demanded courses in black studies and separate living and eating facilities, demands for segregation that whites find hard to understand.

It is possible that these angry young blacks no longer want to be integrated into American society; they wish to create (by armed revolution if necessary) a separate black society. But it is also possible that their actions reflect role strain rather than rational effort to realize their objectives. Black college students today are under greater strain than were the smaller numbers of black college students before the Negro Revolution. Segregation was unjust, but it protected the ego of the minority group member from the impact of failure. If he did not measure up to the performance standards of the larger society, he could claim to be the victim of prejudice, as he may well have been. He could also retreat to less demanding competition in the black community. A ghetto school alumnus who never read a book to completion before entering college now receives the same reading lists in his courses as a prep school graduate who has read 300 books. Is it surprising if he feels inadequate? In crying out for "relevance" and demanding a black studies curriculum, is he expressing such fears? He may also feel insecure in the unfamiliar milieu. Despite greater acceptance of blacks today than formerly, there remain prejudiced individuals; the black student never knows from what quarter a slight will arise: a campus security guard, a fraternity man, a professor, an obscene scrawl on the wall of a toilet.

If this interpretation of the attractiveness of black power is correct, the same emphasis on black pride ought to manifest itself in the larger black community, although perhaps not so strongly because role strain is less great. A number of observers have pointed out that the growing militance in black communities, including but not limited to political lobbying, is less a matter of getting a traffic light or a new school than of getting it *for themselves*:[42]

> In the last analysis, the rejection by Negroes of the conventional offers of help —the resentment they show—springs less from injustice per se than from their sense of inadequacy and impotence. White philanthropy, white liberalism, white sympathy and support, no less than white bigotry and discrimination, have had the effect of preventing Negroes from standing on their own feet, from "exercising their full manhood rights," to use W. E. B. DuBois's phrase. What Negroes need more than anything else is to be treated like men—and to believe in their hearts that they *are* men, men who can stand on their own feet and control their own destinies. Consequently, Negroes will not be able to climb out of their slums *en masse* until they can act in their own behalf—until they are in a position

[42] Charles E. Silberman, "Up from Apathy—The Woodlawn Experiment," *Commentary*, Vol. 37, May 1964, p. 52.

United Press International

to make or to influence the decisions that affect them—until, in a word, they acquire power.

In short, the position of the Negro in American society is especially frustrating in this era of transition from subordination to equality. Some Negro behavior, both individual and group, may be a response to this frustration: a symbolic affirmation of power to control their own fate. The natural hair styles, the dashikis, the soul food, and the interest in Swahili are symbolically important from the point of view of black pride. From the point of view of gaining full inclusion in American society, however, the increasing numbers of black college students and the efforts to open opportunities for blacks in skilled trades mean more. They foretell a distribution of blacks between the middle and the working class more like that of whites. One effect of the growth in the relative size of the black bourgeoisie has already been noted: class cleavages will not continue to reinforce color cleavages; whites will be increasingly aware of similarities to blacks. This will not solve the problem of poverty or the problem of urban blight, but it can achieve racial justice and thereby racial reconciliation.

Such an outcome is not inevitable. If blacks settle for the *symbols* of power, the cheap victories that come, for example, from intimidating deans and college presidents, instead of for the *substance* of participation—educational, occupational, and political achievements—it is still possible for the Negro Revolution to fail. Another obstacle to racial reconciliation are the extremists, both black and white, whose predictions of race warfare might feed on themselves and produce an unnecessary battleground: predictions of racial conflict

can be self-fulfilling. But the likelihood is the continuing differentiation of the black community into middle and working classes and a concomitant recognition on the part of whites that skin color is increasingly irrelevant.

This evolutionary description of developments in race relations in the United States suggests that the differentiation of middle-class blacks from a more homogenous black community underlies much of what is going on in race relations in the contemporary United States. The awakening on the part of middle-class *whites* to the fact that blacks are not necessarily uneducated, surly laborers lies behind the increased willingness of whites to accept desegregation. Recognition on the part of middle-class *blacks* that they possess political, economic, intellectual, and moral power feeds the increased militance of the black community and especially of black college students. The realization of working-class *whites* that some blacks are moving past them into the middle class arouses white backlash. Finally, a dim awareness of ghetto *blacks* that they lack the opportunities of the middle-class blacks to escape from an underprivileged status underlies the urban riots that express their frustration. It also explains why Martin Luther King was booed in Watts when he attempted to "cool" the mob violence.

A SYSTEMATIC APPROACH TO SOCIAL CHANGE

How can we tell whether or not a theory of social differentiation explains the Negro Revolution as satisfactorily as, say, a theory of class conflict? After all, the foregoing account necessarily selected from an enormous number of developments in race relations. Perhaps the selection was biased in favor of a differentiation theory of social change. We need more systematic criteria of relevance. Let us reanalyze the Negro Revolution in terms of the four problems of interactive systems: socialization of members, adaptation to the environment, policy making, and integration of role players. If these four functional problems are basic to social order, they should also be relevant to social change. A sociologist should not be able to explain change in a society—including a change in black-white relations in the United States—without demonstrating (1) cultural developments affecting child or adult socialization, (2) environmental influences impinging on the society, (3) political reorganization within the system, (4) integrative tendencies, or some combination of these.

Cultural Development. The socialization of role players, one of the four functional problems of interactive systems, assumes for any point in time a stable culture. Socialization is the process of internalizing the culture into new members of the system. But time moves on, and the culture changes, often in response to the logic of its own development. **Cultural change** refers to any change in the stock of ideas of the society: an advance in scientific knowledge, a new religion, a new political ideology, a change in fashion, an addition to the poetry, music, or literature of the society, or a new technique for adapting to the environment. Technological and scientific change is only one type of cultural change, but it is the most prominent type of change in industrial societies. Technological innovations and scientific discoveries are frequent; they produce modifications in economic organization and social life; and their cumulative character makes them appear so automatic as to obscure the human element behind them.

One reason for the quasi-automatic character of technological and scientific progress is the sheer size of the culture base. Knowledge breeds new knowledge, for the larger the stock of ideas, the more possibilities for combining them in a novel way. As Sir Isaac Newton put it, "If I have accomplished anything, it is because I stood on the shoulders of giants." He stated a principle applicable to any scientist, engineer, or inventor. The capacity of one generation to make innovations depends on what preceding generations have transmitted to them. What could Albert Einstein have accomplished if he had been born in a preliterate society—for example, among the Murngin?

Technological and scientific development is a major factor in social change in industrial societies. This observation is at the heart of the theory of **cultural lag,** which holds that patterns of interaction change *in response* to maladjustments brought on by technological progress, but social changes lag behind the technological ones.[43] For instance, the automobile not only made outlying suburban areas more accessible; it also influenced the ways Americans commute to work, shop in shopping centers, travel during vacations (stopping in motels), attend drive-in movies, and carry on courtships.[44] Technology influences interaction in other ways: for example, the facilitation of communication. With television supplementing other mass media, all segments of the population are increasingly exposed to one another.[45] Rural populations are aware of urban life; the obscure share the experiences of the famous; and the poor can observe the pleasures of the rich. One consequence of this is the breakdown of social insulation. Negroes became less willing to accept *second*-class citizenship in the South when they observed blacks on their television screen enjoying a closer approximation to *first*-class citizenship in other parts of the country. The discrepancies and contradictions within the culture are pitilessly illuminated. Resentment grows; some of this resentment motivates individuals to work to make social organization more consistent. Even in industrial societies, however, not all social change can be adequately accounted for by the effects of technology. Changes in ideas are equally dynamic. Our brief history of race relations in America traced some of the religious, philosophical, and scientific *ideas* that bore on the American conception of the Negro. The basis of equal rights for Negroes was rooted in the Greek notion of human dignity, the Christian notion of the worth of every soul, and the French notion of the rights of man—as well as in the scientific finding of biologists, anthropologists, psychologists, and sociologists. The mingling of these intellectual strands in the civil rights movement of the 1950s and 1960s was partly accident; but their persistence through the cen-

[43] William F. Ogburn, *Social Change,* New York: Huebsch, 1922; William F. Ogburn, *The Social Effects of Aviation,* Boston: Houghton Mifflin, 1946.

[44] In 1920, 63.7 per cent of the population in United States standard metropolitan areas lived in central cities, but each decennial census thereafter showed declining percentages in central cities and increasing percentages in suburban areas. See Amos H. Hawley, *The Changing Shape of Metropolitan America: Deconcentration Since 1920,* Glencoe, Ill.: Free Press, 1956.

[45] Ninety-eight percent of American homes possessed one or more television sets in 1968. Bureau of the Census, *Statistical Abstract of the United States,* Washington, D.C.: Government Printing Office, 1968, p. 710.

turies resulted from the momentum of ideas.[46] In short, cultures are influenced by technology and by noncultural forces, but they also change as *ideas* are successively passed from mind to mind, slowly developing an inherent logic that assumes jurisdiction over new sectors of society. The incompatability of old and new ideas can stimulate social change. Changes in race relations in America were influenced by the incompatibility of equalitarian ideals and the doctrine of white supremacy, as Myrdal predicted. The United States, an urban society with some faith in rationality, is uncomfortable with such contradictions and is relatively willing to permit social changes that might resolve them.

Had the United States been a peasant society, the strength of the white-supremacy tradition would have resisted change more strongly despite the intellectual contradictions it produced. Rural populations cling to tradition, retarding change even in the urban areas of advanced societies like France. The United States, being so urbanized, fosters rationality not only in cities but in a usually conservative rural population. Thus American farmers are receptive to new techniques for raising productivity. This same rationality made it difficult to maintain Negro subordination in the face of religious, scientific, and philosophic ideas incompatible with the white-supremacy tradition.

The ubiquity of television and other mass media has helped to expose the inconsistency between American ideals and American practice and between race relations in the South and in the rest of the country. This has been an important cultural development in American society. The inconsistencies shown through the mass media are not easily explained away in an urbanized society that values rational behavior. This is one cultural development that clearly stimulated demands for public and private *action* on behalf of "equal opportunity."

Influences from the Biological, Physical, or Sociocultural Environment. A society, though it can be analyzed as a self-contained phenomenon, has an environment. In addition to cultural influences impinging on it from other societies, climatic disturbances, epidemics, crop failures, and genetic changes in the population can induce changes in social organization. Chapter 6 dealt with the major societal response to the environment, its economic organization. The impetus for social change frequently arises within the economy as it copes with the physical and biological environment. Economic factors play a major role in the changing status of Negroes in American society. The industrialization of Southern agriculture displaced millions of rural Negroes, funneling them into cities of the North and West as well as the South. Mechanization and a more scientific approach to farming made small-scale farming unprofitable. Farmers without the educational background to approach agriculture as a business or the capital to invest in increased acreage and in power machinery gave up farming, as Fig. 14.1 shows. More than two million persons

---

[46] Crane Brinton, *Ideas and Men,* New York: Prentice-Hall, 1950; Alfred North Whitehead, *Adventures of Ideas,* New York: Macmillan, 1933.

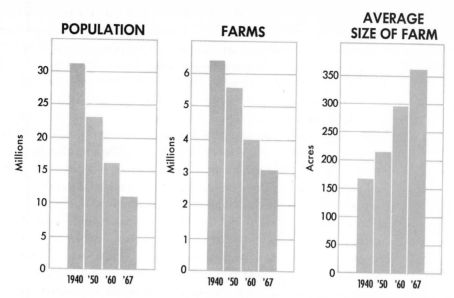

FIGURE 14.1 **The decrease in the American farm population and the number of farms and the increase in farm size, 1940–1967.** Source: Bureau of the Census, *Statistical Abstract of the United States: 1968*, Washington, D.C.: Government Printing Office, 1968, p. 590.

moved off farms in 1953, the high point of the rural to urban population shift.[47] Not all of these were Negroes; Appalachian-Mountain whites were well represented among newcomers to the cities. Nonetheless, the impact of the *black* population shift on race relations was the decisive one.

The positive impact on the Negro Revolution was the educational and economic opportunities that blacks found in the cities and their increased political power. The negative impact was the personal and family disorganization that resulted from the influx of hundreds of thousands of rural blacks into central cities, producing housing, welfare, crime, health, and educational problems. The urban crisis of the 1950s and 1960s has been largely the result of inadequate socialization of black migrants into city life. A historical parallel is the large-scale immigration from southern and eastern Europe in the first two decades of the twentieth century; if this parallel is valid, rural blacks will eventually become part of the urban economic mainstream.

The industrialization of American agriculture is virtually complete. Except for the tobacco country of eastern North Carolina, mechanization has proceeded far enough that the present farm population will not shrink further.[48] Of the 22 million Negroes in the United States in 1968, only one million were on farms. There is now very little black in-migration to central cities. In the past,

[47] Bureau of the Census, *Statistical Abstract of the United States: 1968*, Washington, D.C.: Government Printing Office, 1968, p. 594.

[48] Statement by Calvin L. Beale, chief demographer of the U.S. Department of Agriculture, quoted in *The New York Times*, March 23, 1969, pp. 1, 66.

the piling up of rural migrants in the slum neighborhoods of central cities was the most visible aspect of black migration. Urban problems (including crime and riots) are more conspicuous than rural poverty, disease, malnutrition, and illiteracy; thus even though conditions in the North were better, they did not seem so. In the 1970s and 1980s, however, more and more of the children of rural migrants will rise into the middle class, providing clearer proof of this improved situation.

Modern societies are probably less responsive to changes in their environments than primitive societies. However, the **diffusion** of culture traits from neighboring societies sometimes stimulates change. For example, the transformation of Japan from a feudal to an urban industrial society began following the unwelcome visit of Commodore Perry and his warships in 1853. The humiliation stemming from the military inferiority of Japanese society to western nations helped make Japan receptive to western industrial methods. More recently, a less drastic change was introduced into Norway from the United States. During the Second World War a courier from Britain was dropped by parachute in a remote rural area to join a guerrilla band operating against the German occupation forces. Unfortunately, his parachute failed to open, and he died. In his knapsack was some chocolate, which the partisans proceeded to eat, and a sociology textbook by George Lundberg. Since there was very little to do, all of the young men who could read English read it. Furthermore, they passed it along to other partisan groups. When the war ended, some of Lundberg's "students" established the Institute for Social Research at the University of Oslo, and sociology took root in the Norwegian academic community.

In what ways have the biological, physical, and sociocultural environments of American society influenced the course of the Negro Revolution? Unlike Britain, where in-migration of colored people has substantially increased the proportion of blacks in the population, race relations in the United States have not been appreciably affected by changes in the population composition. True, the greater rate of natural increase of the Negro population has raised the Negro proportion of the American people from 9.9 per cent in 1950 to 11.1 in 1967.[49] However, this change was less significant than the massive shift of Negro population from the rural South to large metropolitan areas. Only in a symbolic sense did the population composition change in response to outside influences. The emergence of new nations in Africa gave Negro Americans an identity as members of an important group on the world scene rather than merely as a downtrodden minority in the United States. The presence of delegates from these countries at the United Nations reinforced this identity, as is shown by the following excerpt from a speech by the Permanent Representative of Nigeria to the American Negro Leadership Conference:[50]

[49]Bureau of the Census, *Statistical Abstract of the United States: 1968,* Washington, D.C.: Government Printing Office, 1968, p. 23.

[50] Rupert Emerson and Martin Kilson, "The American Dilemma in a Changing World: The Rise of Africa and the Negro American," *Daedalus,* Vol. 94, Fall 1965, p. 1080.

A great many of the things that happened to you here, which you thought happened to you because you were a minority people, happened to us in Nigeria. . . . I no longer think simply as a Nigerian; I no longer think simply as an African. I think more as a person of color. And the objective of all of us is to restore to the man of color, wherever he may be, whether in Nigeria, or in the United States, or in Moscow, or in Brazil, the dignity of a human being. That is why we are involved in the same struggle in Africa, here, and elsewhere.

In August, 1961, Secretary of State Dean Rusk said that "the biggest single burden that we carry on our backs in our foreign relations in the 1960s is the problem of racial discrimination here at home."[51] White Americans did not consistently accord respectful treatment to nonwhite emissaries from Asian and African countries in hotels, restaurants, and places of entertainment because such treatment was not generally available for black Americans. Some Negro Americans took to wearing turbans or African costumes as an inside joke on American prejudice. They were often treated better, but this discrimination in favor of foreign nonwhites satisfied neither the increasing numbers of African envoys and students nor Negro Americans. In short, contact with the new nations of Asia and Africa stimulated increased American determination to accord dignified treatment to all black persons.

Political Reorganization. Policy-making responsibility tends to be dispersed among groups or individuals in all interactive systems. However, the policy voice of different classes of members is subject to change. A shift in political power means that members who have hitherto had little voice in collective decisions assume a larger role. Turmoil in universities and colleges has resulted in part because students are increasingly unwilling to allow their elders to make policy decisions that control their lives. The 1968 disruption on the campus of Columbia University, precipitated by student resentment of what some considered racist attitudes and of military research being conducted on the Columbia campus, reflected also the desire of students to participate in policy making. A survey of student and faculty attitudes showed that a large student majority supported greater student power.[52] In reply to the question, "How much decision-making power should students, faculty, administration, and trustees have in making major University policies?," 23 per cent of the students wanted "equal power" and 48 per cent wanted "some power."[53] Both at the 1964 Berkeley disruption[54] and at Columbia a majority of the students approved the goals of the militants but disapproved of their tactics, namely, the occupation of buildings and the interruption of the educational process. But at both universities the use of police to remove the rebels brought a

[51]Emerson and Kilson, "The American Dilemma, p. 1063.

[52] Questionnaires were mailed to the entire faculty mailing list (2000 persons) and to a random 20 per cent of the students registered in Columbia College and in the graduate and professional schools on the Morningside campus. Allen H. Barton, "The Columbia Crisis: Campus, Vietnam, and the Ghetto," *Public Opinion Quarterly*, Vol. 1968, pp. 333-351.

[53] Barton, "The Columbia Crisis," p. 338.

[54] Seymour Martin Lipset and Sheldon S. Wolin, Eds., *The Berkeley Student Revolt: Facts and Interpretations*, Garden City, N.Y.: Anchor, 1965, pp. 548-553.

shift of sentiment *against* the administration. A possible explanation of this re-action is that students perceived a call for the police as a refusal to redistribute power and a reversion to a policy of *in loco parentis.*

The redistribution of power within colleges and universities occurring in the wake of student disruptions may prevent future confrontations. The redistribu-tion of power within American society between blacks and whites began, as our descriptive account pointed out, with the migration of hundreds of thou-sands of Negroes into industrial states where their votes counted. "Black power" became a slogan of the activist branch of the civil rights movement in 1966, but black political power has been a reality for at least two decades.[55] Black power is growing (1) because more Negroes live in key industrial states and (2) because the educational attainment of the black population has climbed steeply in the last decade. Education leads to power for an ethnic group most immediately because voting registration and actual voting increase with educational attainment. More fundamentally, education leads to political power because it helps the leadership group understand the nature of the so-ciety in which it operates, thereby helping to sustain a political movement. The Negro leadership class traditionally has consisted of the better educated—min-isters, lawyers, teachers, and physicians—in addition to businessmen and labor leaders with economic power,[56] and their numbers are growing.

Educational upgrading in the black community also helped to desegregate the Negro middle class (who are the members of the black community most able to take advantage of desegregated educational facilities, occupations, and public accommodations). When the "black bourgeoisie" was an insignificant fraction of the Negro population, the prospects for exercising political power seemed remote. Even the economic strength of the Negro middle class de-pended on protection from white competition in segregated institutions—in medicine, law, insurance, the hotel business, and retail stores.[57] The black bourgeoisie had "status without substance" and in some large cities concen-trated on conspicuous consumption in an unconscious caricature of the white social élite.[58] The increase in educational and occupational opportunities offered substance to the status of the Negro middle class. Opportunities opened up in universities, business corporations, and government agencies that had previously been staffed overwhelmingly by whites. This placed the new Negro middle class in direct competition with whites. Thus many Negro professional and white-collar workers earn more than they could have earned under segre-gated conditions, but they have the less secure status characteristic of a com-

[55] Stokely Carmichael and Charles V. Hamilton, *Black Power: The Politics of Liberation,* New York: Random House, 1967.

[56] Daniel C. Thompson, *The Negro Leadership Class,* Englewood Cliffs, N.J.: Prentice-Hall, 1963.

[57] Andrew F. Brimmer, "Desegregation and Negro Leadership," in Eli Ginzberg, Ed., *Business Leadership and the Negro Crisis,* New York: McGraw-Hill, 1968, pp. 33-49.

[58] E. Franklin Frazier, *Black Bourgeoisie,* Glencoe, Ill.: Free Press, 1955.

petitive situation.[59] This hidden cost of desegregation may be an unconscious source of separatist fantasies to those whose feelings of security and adequacy are threatened by the increased possibility of rejection and failure. These feelings may also lead to an emphasis on "blackness," rejection of the term "Negro," and denunciation of acquiescent "Uncle Tom" leadership of the past.

Some black leaders recognize that full economic participation in American life means that incompetence will be grounds for firing or nonpromotion; all failures are not due to white prejudice:[60]

> Negroes must be given a chance to fail. People have to grow up by trying and failing as well as by trying and succeeding.

A distinguished Negro economist (a member of the Board of Governors of the Federal Reserve System) made this remark in the context of a plea for greater business and professional opportunities for blacks. Unless American society provides such opportunities, Brimmer argued, responsible leaders will not emerge in the Negro community to take the places of the old-style leaders developed in the sheltered environment of segregation.

Unlike the old middle class, which had *one* constituency, the new middle class has two: the white occupational and political world and the black community. The shrill attacks on "Mr. Charlie" or "the white power structure" affirm a black identity. For those who have left the slum to attend college, who are employed by white-oriented corporations, and who may live in a predominantly white community, this affirmation is necessary. It quiets guilt feelings about possible disloyalty to one's "black brothers" as well as affording respite from the pressures of the larger society. The existence of two constituencies helps to explain why the new middle class is more radical in word and deed than accommodating leaders were; the earlier black middle class had an undivided allegiance. Furthermore, middle-class blacks have discovered that militancy does not necessarily spoil their chances of "making it" in the larger society. Many whites are trying to compensate for the prejudiced and discriminatory treatment of previous generations; such feelings make them more responsive to a militant black than to one they consider an "Uncle Tom." The radicalism of the new generation of middle-class blacks makes them push harder for redistributing power and rewards between whites and blacks.[61] Thus increasing militancy in the civil rights movement tends to accelerate the Negro Revolution.

So far, however, few economic benefits of black power have trickled down to the most deprived fifth of the black community. Employment opportunities

---

[59] Brimmer, "Desegregation," p. 48.

[60] Brimmer, "Desegregation," p. 49.

[61] Research has demonstrated that militant advocacy of civil rights is most likely on the part of young, well-educated, upper-income blacks. See Gary T. Marx, *Protest and Prejudice: A Study of Belief in the Black Community*, rev. ed., New York: Harper & Row, 1969, pp. 49-79.

opened up rapidly for social workers in the poverty program, for teachers in schools and colleges, and for executives and white-collar workers in industry and government. Jobs for the hard-core unemployed—those with no skills and little education—gave a new start to only a small proportion of the slum dwellers.[62] The charge of "tokenism" hurled by militants at racial moderates, perhaps false in terms of white intentions, makes sense from the standpoint of ghetto blacks still dependent on welfare allowances. Since black leadership must be validated by its constituency and since the majority of Negro Americans are not middle class, the prognosis for moderate leadership is in doubt. Will the majority of blacks continue to support organizations like the National Association for the Advancement of Colored People (N.A.A.C.P.) and the Urban League, which work for Negro betterment within the established political system? Or will they turn to separatist groups like the Black Muslims, the Black Panthers, and the Revolutionary Action Movement?

Within the past decade a shift has occurred away from leaders regarded as timid. In Tallahassee, Florida, for example, a bus boycott provided the issue over which nonviolent activist leaders won out over leaders who believed that progress resulted from behind-the-scenes maneuvering with white politicians.[63] Other boycotts, as well as sit-ins and freedom marches and rides, demonstrated the effectiveness of nonviolent confrontations in producing change. The 1965 Voting Rights Act, a tangible outcome of a 54-mile freedom march from Selma to Montgomery, Alabama, on behalf of Negro voting rights, suspended literacy tests in states and counties where a presumption of discrimination could be made from the fact that less than half of the voting-age population voted in the 1964 presidential election; it also empowered the Attorney General to send federal examiners to register voters in counties where such action seemed necessary to prevent discrimination against black voters.

Whether there will be shifts in black leadership away from nonviolence toward greater militancy is not yet clear. Poorly educated segments of the Negro community associate nonviolence with acquiescence. G. Franklin Edwards of Howard University demonstrated this communications gap in an experiment sponsored by the Youth Development Program of the Ford Foundation. Professor Edwards conducted a seminar in race relations with five Howard University students who had participated in sit-ins (four Negro students and one white) and five inmates of the federal reformatory at Lorton, Virginia (four Negro inmates and one white). The reformatory inmates understood what the students were trying to accomplish and respected them for it. What they could not understand was nonviolent methods: letting their enemies slug them with-

---

[62] The Urban Coalition and the National Alliance of Businessmen have created training programs and tens of thousands of new jobs for the hard-core unemployed, but the problem is too vast to improve quickly. See Allan T. Demaree, "Business Picks Up the Urban Challenge," *Fortune*, Vol. 79, April 1969, pp. 103-184.

[63] Lewis M. Killian and Charles U. Smith, "Negro Protest Leaders in a Southern Community," *Social Forces*, Vol. 38, March 1960, pp. 253-257.

out defending themselves. Apparently the reformatory inmates converted at least some of the students. One of them, Stokely Carmichael, led the Student Nonviolent Coordinating Committee into direct confrontations with white communities. Disagreement over methods of protest also exists in the larger Negro community between law-abiding leaders of organizations like the National Association for the Advancement of Colored People and the more impatient members of the Black Muslims and the Black Panthers.

Before Malcolm X left the Black Muslims to establish his own version of black nationalism, he gave an interview explaining that his original surname, "Little," belonged to the white man who owned one of his ancestors. He considered it degrading to use this name; he chose "X" to indicate that his real name was unknown:[64]

> "The X means that I dont' know who I am," he said. "No one knows who these Negroes are—their identity was destroyed during slavery. All of the Muslims take X—the unknown. Sixty-seven brothers in our mosque alone have the name James X with the number of their sequence—James X-11, James X-12, etc. We have done this deliberately.
>
> "I feel more intelligent saying my name is X," he added, icily, "than I would saying my name was Little—or Bunche or Powell or King. They don't know that they don't know what their name is."

In opposing cooperation with white liberals, the Muslims refuse to distinguish between white Ku Klux Klan members and the Reverend James Reeb, the white minister who went to Selma to participate in the civil-rights march and was beaten to death. This promiscuous hatred of "whitey" is retribution for the promiscuous contempt of white supremacists for *all* Negroes. It also reflects hopelessness about achieving an integrated society. Unlike Gunnar Myrdal, who wrote that white ideals, as well as Negro protests, would lead to an unsegregated America, black supremacists consider white liberals hypocrites and Negroes who cooperate with them "suckers." Malcolm X himself came to believe that he could work with atypical whites to improve black conditions; he repudiated Elijah Muhammad and left the Black Muslims, some members of which later assassinated him.[65]

Roy Wilkins, Executive Director of the N.A.A.C.P., decried black extremism in a speech to the 1966 national convention of his 400,000-member organization, and called for a continuation of nonviolent defense of Negro rights:[66]

> Though it be clarified and clarified again, "black power" in the quick, uncritical and highly emotional adoption it has received from some segments of a beleaguered people can mean in the end only black death. Even if, through

---

[64] Quoted in Gertrude Samuels, "Two Ways: Black Muslim and N.A.A.C.P." *The New York Times Magazine,* May 6, 1963, p. 86.

[65] *The Autobiography of Malcolm X,* New York: Grove Press, 1966, pp. 364-382.

[66] *The New York Times,* July 6, 1966, p. 1.

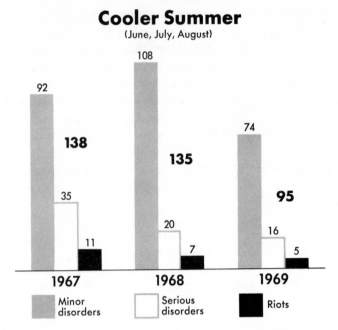

Cooler Summer
(June, July, August)

FIGURE 14.2 **The incidence of civil rights disorders in the United States, 1967–1969.** Source: *Time,* September 12, 1969, p. 16.

some miracle, it should be enthroned briefly, the human spirit, which knows no color or geography or time, would die a little, leaving for wiser and stronger and more compassionate men the painful beating back to the upper trail.

We of the N.A.A.C.P. will have none of this. We have fought it too long. It is the ranging of race against race on the irrelevant basis of skin color. It is the father of hatred and the mother of violence.

It is the wicked fanaticism which has swelled our tears, broken our bodies, squeezed our hearts and taken the blood of our black and white loved ones. It shall not now poison our forward march.

We seek therefore, as we have sought these many years, for the inclusion of Negro Americans in the nation's life, not their exclusion. This is our land, as much as it is any American's—every square foot of every city and town and village. The task of winning our share is not the easy one of disengagement and flight, but the hard one of work, of short as well as long jumps, of disappointments and of sweet success.

If the level of black educational attainment rises, if increasing numbers of Negroes compete successfully in business and the professions, if the Negro vote becomes increasingly important in all sections of the country, extremism will be less appealing to the average black. The status of Negroes is improving, but the improvement falls short of rising expectations. This anomic situation provides an opportunity for black and white extremists to polarize the country and generate divisive conflicts, perhaps even another Civil War. But Fig. 14.2 shows that the level of interracial violence *decreased* from 1967 to 1969.

Nevertheless, black separatists increased their influence during this same period—partly because confrontations seemed to "pay off" in white concessions, especially in the public school system and in the colleges. On the other hand, the same tactics did not achieve comparable *occupational* gains. For instance, in the skilled crafts in 1967, blacks were 1.6 per cent of American union carpenters, 0.6 per cent of electrical workers, 3.7 per cent of painters, 0.2 per cent of union plumbers, and 0.2 per cent of sheet metal workers.[67] And despite confrontations on construction sites, the situation was about the same in 1969.

In short, it is not yet clear who speaks for American blacks and who will speak for them in the years ahead. The heightened visibility of extremist black leaders may reflect a temporary shift rather than a permanent trend. The fact that black mayors have been elected in Fayette, Mississippi, and Chapel Hill, North Carolina, as well as in Cleveland, Ohio, Newark, New Jersey, and Gary, Indiana, suggests that Negroes willing to work for change within the system can win the support of both the black and the white communities. Charles Evers, the mayor of Fayette, Mississippi, offered a strong argument for reconciliation:[68]

> We know that whatever happens in Mississippi affects the people in New York, and that whatever happens in New York affects the people in Mississippi. We're all God's children. He brought us all here. And those of us who are more affluent have something special to do. . . . But He equipped us to go out and help our brothers. We're going to show the whites down there—the whites who have done so much to hurt us—that it's so easy to do good. We're going to say to all the blacks: Don't get mad, get smart. Don't shoot your brother, and don't bomb him. Just vote him out of office. Because the right will prevail.

Whether racial reconciliation comes soon or is delayed indefinitely by turbulent conflict depends partly on the current struggle for leadership within the Negro community. Whether moderate Negro leaders like Charles Evers direct the Negro Revolution hinges on their ability to demonstrate to their constituency that "whitey" does not have to be burned out before he makes concessions—and on the response of "whitey" himself.

Integrative Forces. No interactive system is perfectly integrated: value commitments work at cross-purposes, particularly in large, heterogeneous, evolving societies. In the United States, for example, the values of an urban industrial society are displacing older, incompatible values as urbanism spreads and the economy becomes more fully industrialized. The notion of white supremacy (a legacy of slavery) is an example of a historical accretion incompatible with the individualistic achievement values of modern society. In particular, the development of a market economy (described in Chapter 6) ties a large proportion of the population to these values through their roles of employees or consumers or both. The industrial economy is individualistic in two senses:

---

[67] Data from the United States Equal Opportunity Commission. Quoted in *Ebony*, Vol. 25, December 1969, p. 34.

[68] *The New Yorker*, June 14, 1969, p. 29.

1. It requires the individual rather than the family to assume a productive role in the economy and judges his performance in that role independently of his social characteristics.
2. It gives the individual the right to consume — and through consumption to satisfy his needs and fulfill his desires — by virtue of possession of that symbol of productive achievement, money.

Some categories of persons, such as children or the aged, are not expected to live in accordance with individualistic achievement values. Such categories create an integrative problem for the society. Exceptions have to be made; insulating mechanisms must be called into play. American society makes exceptions for children fairly easily by institutionalizing the solidarity of the conjugal family; treatment of the aged creates greater difficulty.[69] But the ascribed inferior status of Negroes and other ethnic minorities is impossible to reconcile with the evaluation of individual worth in accordance with productive contribution, especially in a society where high-achievement Negroes are likely to receive extensive coverage in the mass media.

The civil rights movement can be interpreted as an integrative force in American society. Recent legislation, judicial decisions, and administrative orders have brought blacks — and to a lesser extent other disadvantaged minorities — under the canopy of the individual achievement values of the society. Other integrative forces contributing to the same result are the market mechanism and increasing role differentiation. The freedom to sell goods and services in the open market should be conducive to changing the American pattern of race relations in almost the same way that the market mechanism changed American transportation by allowing the adoption of the automobile. A free market meant that Henry Ford did not need authorization from federal, state, or local governments in order to manufacture and sell his early cars. Nor did he have to win the approval of a majority of American people. A minority interest has representation in the marketplace, and eventually it may win over the majority. At first, only the farsighted and the eccentric bought cars. Eventually the automobile became crucial to the American way of life, and Henry Ford became a billionaire. In short, the market system facilitated the change from horse to automotive transport. The promoters were more interested in selling cars than the general public was in clinging to an old habit. Moreover, interests opposed to the "horseless carriage" — blacksmiths, livery stable keepers, horse breeders, and carriage makers — gradually lost their power to obstruct as support for the automobile grew.[70]

Private enterprise promotes technological innovations only when they are made in the form of products or services that consumers wish to buy. Not all

---

[69] Matilda White Riley and Anne Foner, *Aging and Society,* Vol. 1, New York: Russel Sage Foundation, 1968.

[70] Talcott Parsons discusses the role of vested interests in social change in Chapter 11 of *The Social System,* Glencoe, Ill.: Free Press, 1951.

technological innovations, even in the automotive field, are attractive to consumers. For example, American car manufacturers were reluctant to incorporate safety features in automobiles because experience had convinced them that the car market was more responsive to horsepower, chromium strips, and sleek lines than it was to interior design capable of reducing injuries to passengers in the event of accidents.[71] Thus, when the Ford Motor Company introduced new safety features voluntarily during the first half of 1956, Ford car sales fell markedly compared with Chevrolets. Where the market works *against* a technological innovation, as appeared to be the case in the field of automotive safety, political decisions (laws and administrative regulations) were necessary to force change on an apathetic public.

The movement of Negro Americans into the mainstream of the economy bears a resemblance to the process by which the automobile supplanted the horse. Discrimination against blacks in hiring runs counter to the logic of the industrial economy. In accordance with the criterion of competence, a person should be employed regardless of sex, age, color, religion, or family background *provided he is qualified to perform the job.* Color discrimination, like discrimination against women or Jews, is an ascriptive intrusion into an achievement-oriented society. The market mechanism makes it possible to overcome gradually these ascriptive exclusions when well-qualified Negroes or women or Jews apply for jobs. At the same time that the logic of performance works against irrelevant *exclusion,* it also works against irrelevant *inclusion,* especially the selection of the social élite for top-level jobs.[72]

> There is a story in Boston that in the palmy days of the twenties a Chicago banking house asked the Boston investment firm of Lee, Higginson & Co. for a letter of recommendation about a young Bostonian they were considering employing. Lee, Higginson could not say enough for the young man. His father, they wrote, was a Cabot, his mother a Lowell; farther back his background was a happy blend of Saltonstalls, Appletons, Peabodys, and others of Boston's First Families. The recommendation was given without hesitation.
> Several days later came a curt acknowledgment from Chicago. Lee, Higginson was thanked for its trouble. Unfortunately, however, the material supplied on the young man was not exactly of the type the Chicago firm was seeking. "We were not," their letter declared, "contemplating using Mr. — —for breeding purposes."

The market mechanism swept the automobile into popular favor, whereas it has produced so far only a token representation of Negroes in high-level jobs. The vested interests opposing the automobile were weaker than those opposing full integration of Negroes into the economy. Nonetheless, legal and political obstacles do not exist in the United States (as they do in South Africa) that might

---

[71] Daniel P. Moynihan, "Epidemic on the Highways," *The Reporter,* Vol. 20, April 30, 1959, pp. 16-23; Ralph Nader, "The *Safe* Car You Can't Buy," *The Nation,* Vol. 188, April 11, 1959, pp. 310-313.

[72] Cleveland Amory, *The Proper Bostonians,* New York: Dutton, 1947, p. 11.

TABLE 14.5

Patents Issued for Inventions by the United States Patent Office, 1790–1890

Year	Number of Inventions Patented
1790	3
1800	41
1810	223
1820	155
1830	544
1840	458
1850	883
1860	4,357
1870	12,137
1880	12,903
1890	25,313

Source: Bureau of the Census, *Historical Statistics of the United States: Colonial Times to 1957,* Washington, D.C.: Government Printing Office, 1960, pp. 607-608.

interfere with Negro inclusion. The logic of the market permits employers to select able Negroes for business and professional positions just as it permitted consumers to buy cars instead of horses. This logic is more consistently applied in large organizations with rational personnel policies, and large organizations dominate the urban industrial economy. It is also more consistently applied when qualified employees are scarce. Ascriptive irrelevancies do not impair economic efficiency if large numbers of qualified job seekers are available.[73] The tight labor market associated with war explains why Negro Americans made great economic gains during wartime.

However, the market mechanism may not be capable of *equalizing* the economic achievements of blacks and whites (or at least of producing equalization quickly) any more than it was of marketing as safe a car as engineers could design. One obstacle to equalization is the differential advantage of middle-class over working-class children in school and the greater occupational opportunities this advantage makes possible. Class differences were discussed in Chapters 11 and 12, although the discussion did not specifically address the issue of racial inequality. The fact is, though, that the majority of black Americans are still working class while the majority of whites are middle class. This unfavorable starting point handicaps Negroes in competing against whites for high-status positions in the economy. If public policy determines that Negroes should be distributed more evenly throughout the economy, a political mech-

[73] Leon Mayhew, "Ascription in Modern Societies," *Sociological Inquiry,* Vol. 38, Spring 1968, p. 113.

anism will be invoked just as a political mechanism was invoked (federal legislation) to provide safer automobiles.

Like the market mechanism, the increasing differentiation of occupational roles helps to integrate Negroes into American society. Again the effect is indirect and is easier to see in a technical-scientific speciality. Consider the differentiation of the role of inventor. The Constitution of the United States gives Congress the power "to promote the progress of science and useful arts, by securing for limited times to authors and inventors the exclusive right to their respective writings and discoveries." Table 14.5 shows the growth of inventions (patents) in the United States from 1790 to 1890, a period of rapid industrialization. The patent system was designed to encourage invention by holding out hope of considerable financial reward to the technological innovator. Thomas A. Edison became a rich man as a result of his development of the electric light, the phonograph, and other useful gadgets. The patent system also legitimizes the role of the inventor. During the eighteenth and nineteenth centuries, the inventor was mainly an amateur; very few persons were full-time inventors. The twentieth century has witnessed the bureaucratization of invention. Private industry, government agencies, and universities have established laboratories with full-time jobs for technological and scientific innovators.[74] One result was that corporations started patenting more inventions than private individuals in 1932, and the trend to corporate and governmental patents has continued.[75]

However dedicated the scientist may be, he is also filling a role that demands innovation. Perhaps he would rather watch television, play with his children, or go on a picnic instead of working in his laboratory or writing articles for scholarly journals. He knows, however, that his chances for promotion and perhaps his job itself depends on his "productivity" — on the impact of his research on the existing state of knowledge. Even without this pressure, he might wish to do research out of distinterested curiosity and to publish the results for the benefit of humanity. But bureaucratization means that scientific and technological discoveries do not depend on curiosity and humanitarianism alone. Once a man has become a scientist, he cannot escape the pressure to do research. Granted that he had curiosity and creativity to begin with, or he would not have chosen a scientific career. Once in the role, he had better mobilize all his curiosity and creativity in a search for innovations. Contrast this situation with that of a preliterate inventor, who, if he builds a better canoe than his neighbor, may be suspected of witchcraft. In preliterate societies, the balance of rewards and punishments frequently operate to stifle creativity; in con-

---

[74] William Kornhauser, *Scientists in Industry: Conflict and Accommodation,* Berkeley: University of California Press, 1962; for a parallel development in the social sciences, see Paul F. Lazarsfeld, "The Sociology of Empirical Social Research," *American Sociological Review,* Vol. 27, December 1962, pp. 757-767.

[75] Bureau of the Census, *Historical Statistics of the United States: Colonial Times to 1957,* Washington, D.C.: Government Printing Office, 1960, p. 607.

temporary societies, patent systems, laboratory organizations, and professional specialization encourage the maximum expression of creativity.

Although the institutionalization of inventiveness is most obvious in the technological and scientific fields, the differentiation of specialized roles also favors change in other fields. For example, the prospect of professional recognition encourages the social worker to discover more efficient ways of alleviating human distress, the surgeon to reduce postoperative mortality, and the teacher to communicate his subject matter more efficiently. Even when innovations arouse the opposition of the general public, the professional has an incentive to make them to impress his reference group, his colleagues. The existence of specialized roles dedicated to innovation means that self-interest is mobilized in behalf of cultural change.

In the course of increasing occupational differentiation, specialties have emerged that made middle-class blacks more visible and therefore made ascribed inferior status more anomalous. To treat a black chemist or physician or lawyer as the social inferior of a white laborer raises questions about American commitment to the value of occupational achievement. Occupational specialization also favors the Negro Revolution by creating occupations in the larger society concerned with the Negro community or with its relation to whites. Examples of this are professionals in the field of intergroup relations (often employed by municipal governments), specialists in Negro history (employed by universities), and specialists in the Negro market (employed by advertising agencies). Similarly, "soul" music, as part of the American entertainment industry, helps to establish the dignity of blacks as a constituent group of American society.

CONCLUSION

Early sociologists were impressed with the cumulative character of technological and scientific development and with the impact of technological change on social life. They tended to assume that evolutionary improvements would automatically occur in family organization, intergroup relations, and social ethics. Contemporary sociologists, like contemporary historians and philosophers, are less confident that social change is synonymous with social progress. They are sensitive to a wider range of factors capable of changing patterns of interaction than were the nineteenth-century evolutionists. Contemporary sociologists are again becoming interested in social evolution but as social differentiation rather than as inevitable improvement.[76] Whereas nineteenth-century sociologists spoke as though human agency had nothing to do

---

[76] Talcott Parsons, *Societies: Evolutionary and Comparative Perspectives.*

with social change, twentieth-century sociologists, along with other social scientists, credit purposive human action more generously:[77]

> We must base our hopes, not on a progress that is to be achieved for us by the inexorable movement of historical law, but on ourselves and our children and our children's children, who will make the world better or worse according to the good will, the courage, and the skill with which they face the tasks of the present and the future. In place of the belief in a progress guaranteed by the order of nature we need to put a faith in our collective power to make the good prevail, if we try hard enough—but not otherwise.

The theory of cultural lag, though not explicitly evolutionary, also placed too little emphasis on the purposive factors in change. While a large cultural base makes technological innovations easier to *devise,* the *acceptance* of innovations depends on social values and institutions. The more rationally oriented the society, the more acceptable will be technological innovations; and when the innovator occupies a differentiated role in the context of which innovation is rewarded, the likelihood is increased that inventiveness will result in inventions.

Once innovations are made, social values and institutions do not cease being important. Even technological and scientific development do not produce social change automatically. The ideals and ideas of a society provide a basis for evaluating current patterns of interaction. Demographic and educational processes disturb the balance of power supporting the status quo. Social movements organize the proponents of change so as to influence the general public or specific decision makers. Political authorities support changes opposed to a greater or lesser degree by vested interests within the society. In short, technological and scientific development is a catalytic factor in social change in industrial societies, perhaps the most important single factor, but it is by no means the only one.

Changes in race relations in the United States can best be understood in terms of a theory broader than "progress" or "cultural lag," broad enough to encompass the increasing self-awareness of agents of change in modern societies. An adequate explanation of the Negro Revolution, like an adequate theory of social change generally, should systematically consider the four basic problems of interactive systems: socialization of members, adaptation to the environment, policy making, and integration of role players. Therefore, we considered the relevance of each of these problems to an example of change in American society, the rising status of Negroes:

1. *Cultural development* refers to changes in the stock of ideas of a society transmitted to individuals in the course of socialization. For example, the consensus among biologists, psychologists, anthropologists, and sociolo-

---

[77] G. D. H. Cole, "The Idea of Progress," *British Journal of Sociology,* Vol. 4, September 1953, pp. 282-283.

gists over the past half century that belief in Negro inferiority is scientifically invalid undermined the respectability of this belief, especially among population segments with commitments to rationality and to science.

2. *Influences from the biological, physical, or sociocultural environment* refer to the forces impinging on an interactive system from outside. For example, the rise of new nations in Africa and the presence in the United States of black envoys and students from these countries called attention to the foreign-policy implications of American race relations.

3. *Political reorganization* refers to shifts of responsibility within an interactive system for policy determination. For example, the civil-rights movement has given substance to the leadership status of the Negro middle class. The stronger voice of Negro leaders in American policy making means that they are not restricted to leading the black community; they have become justices of the Supreme Court, cabinet members, and senators.

4. *Integrative forces* refer to the tendency within an interactive system for incompatible principles of social organization either to become reconciled or to lead to reorganization of the system. For example, the civil-rights movement dramatized the incompatibility of ascribed subordination for Negro Americans with the principle of evaluation according to individual achievement in economic, political, and educational affairs. The emerging victory of achievement over ascription has broader implications than the inclusion of blacks as full citizens in American society, but this is perhaps its most notable result. One index of this victory is the results of a poll conducted in March, 1969, by the Gallup organization in more than 300 American communities throughout the United States.[78] The following question was asked, as it was in previous surveys dating back to 1958:

> There's always much discussion about the qualifications of Presidential candidates — their education, age, race, religion and the like. If your party nominated a generally well-qualified man for President and he happened to be a Negro, would you vote for him?

The trend in the replies to the question was as follows:

	Yes	No	No Opinion
1958	38%	53%	9%
1963	47	45	8
1965	59	34	7
1967	54	40	6
1969	67	23	10

[78] *The New York Times,* April 3, 1969, p. 16.

Like social change in the field of race relations, social change in other areas is initiated by altered responses to the four basic problems of interactive systems: through cultural developments affecting socialization, through the effect of the biological, physical, or sociological environment, through political reorganization, or through integrative reorganization. In the United States political reorganization has been especially prominent in processes of change. Within universities, students and faculty have obtained a larger voice than previously in university decision making. Within the society as a whole, the young, ethnic minorities, and intellectuals have grown relatively more influential. Recent concern over pollution of the natural environment has contributed to the influence of conservationists and reduced the influence of business enterprises that had casually polluted the air and waterways. Many of these shifts in influence are indirect responses to the educational upgrading of contemporary society; such upgrading has made it possible to question in the name of rational considerations the legitimacy of traditional practices and traditional authorities. For instance, more voters perceive opposition to contraceptive information as ill-advised in view of the population explosion, and more perceive strict anti-abortion laws as antiquated. In short, alongside the turmoil of protest, a shift in political power is occurring that will not necessarily destroy contemporary society but will certainly change it.

SOME SIGNIFICANT LITERATURE ON SOCIAL AND CULTURAL CHANGE

H. M. Blalock, Jr., "Urbanization and Discrimination in the South," *Social Problems,* Vol. 7, Fall 1959 pp. 146-152. In 150 counties selected at random from a universe of all Southern counties reporting at least 250 nonwhite households in the 1950 census, the following data were obtained for whites and nonwhites: (1) percentages of homeowners, (2) percentages of dwelling units not overcrowded, (3) percentages of families having incomes of $1500 or more, and (4) percentages of males 25 and over who completed more than six years of schooling. Blalock uses the difference between the white and the nonwhite percentages for each of these four indices as a measure of discrimination. Although both whites and nonwhites enjoyed higher living standards in the more urbanized counties, the *differences* between whites and nonwhites were equally great in urban and rural counties. Bear in mind that the survey is limited to *Southern* counties. In a study of school desegregation in Kentucky and Missouri, it was found that the more prosperous and urbanized counties of these border states were much more likely to desegregate than the poorer rural counties. See Thomas F. Pettigrew, "Demographic Correlates of Border-State Desegregation," *American Sociological Review,* Vol. 22, December 1957, pp. 683-689. For case studies of desegregation in communities of varying size, see Raymond W. Mack, Ed., *Our Children's Burden: Studies of Desegregation in Nine American Communities,* New York: Vintage, 1965.

G. D. H. Cole, "The Idea of Progress," *British Journal of Sociology,* Vol. 4, September 1953, pp. 266-285. Cole takes his point of departure from a book by the distinguished social theorist

Morris Ginsberg, *The Idea of Progress: A Revaluation.* The notion of social progress was originally linked to a belief in a benevolent deity who was the force behind it. When skepticism arose about the existence of God, confidence in progress could continue only under special assumptions. For example, Karl Marx and his followers assumed that the class struggle was the force that would impel mankind "toward a classless society in which social co-operation would find its complete expression, and a return would be made . . . to the Communism that was supposed to have prevailed in primitive societies." A second course was to develop an optimistic conception of human nature, such as that of Condorcet, who equated moral failure with ignorance. Condorcet assumed that the advance of knowledge was an impetus to higher moral achievement, and therefore he insisted on the importance of universal education. A third possibility was to assume that social institutions were generating moral advance even though individual weaknesses remained unchanged. Although Cole criticizes all three of these assumptions, he shares some of the sociological optimism of the third view. He points out that social life requires ". . . rules of behavior, assignment of things to be done, and means of deciding disputed points." This results in laws and means of enforcing them, and these tend to generate a demand for fairness (justice). Cole refers to T. H. Marshall's book, *Citizenship and Social Class,* for a concept of developmental stages of increasing justice in Western civilization: stage 1, the right to equality before the law and the concomitant abolition of slavery; stage 2, the extension of political rights, particularly the right to vote for political leaders; stage 3, the claim to economic rights and social security.

A. J. Jaffee, Walter Adams, and Sandra G. Meyers, *Negro Higher Education in the 1960's,* New York: Praeger, 1968. This careful analysis of trends in applications, admissions, and enrollments at Negro colleges reveals the limitations of segregated higher education. Although some of these colleges are capable of preparing graduates to take their places in middle-class jobs, many are not. A complementary approach (from the occupational side) argues that job and income upgrading efforts will not be fully successful until black education and training prepare more effectively for white-collar and technical jobs. See Charles C. Killingsworth, *Jobs and Income for Negroes,* Washington, D.C.: National Manpower Policy Taskforce, 1968.

Elihu Katz, Martin L. Levin, and Herbert Hamilton, "Traditions of Research on the Diffusion of Innovation," *American Sociological Review,* Vol. 28, April 1963, pp. 237-252. The authors of this article compare approaches to the study of diffusion of innovation in cultural anthropology, rural sociology, education, public health, marketing, and other fields. Although the basic idea of diffusion as a source of change is the same, different aspects of the process have been emphasized in different traditions. Combining these approaches gives a more adequate conceptualization of diffusion and a better basis for further research. "Viewed sociologically, the process of diffusion may be characterized as the (1) *acceptance,* (2) over *time,* (3) of some specific *item*—an idea or practice, (4) by individuals, groups, or other *adopting units,* linked (5) to specific *channels* of communication, (6) to a *social structure,* and (7) to a given system of values, or *culture.*"

Lewis M. Killian, *The Impossible Revolution? Black Power and the American Dream,* New York: Random House, 1968. According to the author, a white sociologist, the prospects for racial reconciliation in the United States are bleak. He is pessimistic because he observes the Negro community growing increasingly impatient with the slow progress toward racial equality. The old civil rights leadership, symbolized by the N.A.A.C.P. and the Urban League, helps small numbers of blacks join the middle class but does not materially improve the situation of the mass of blacks. And even those blacks who "make it" in American society are subject to occasional humiliations because of their color. Furthermore, the tactics of protest, at first nonviolent and then increasingly violent, prove more effective in securing equal treatment than old-style legal actions. This combination of circumstances shifts the leadership within the black community toward increased militance and escalating demands. Because Killian does not believe that the white community will meet these demands — or be perceived as meeting them — he expects increasingly violent confrontations between blacks and whites. Since blacks constitute only 11 per cent of the American population, he anticipates that the United States will move toward repression of its black minority instead of toward continuing reconciliation. For a seeming confirmation of the validity of Killian's analysis, see the journalistic account of the Washington, D.C., riot following the assassination of Martin Luther King, Jr.: Ben W. Gilbert, *Ten Blocks from the White House: Anatomy of the Washington Riots of 1968,* New York: Praeger, 1968.

C. Eric Lincoln, *The Black Muslims in America,* Boston: Beacon Press, 1961. This book contains a scholarly account of the origin and growth of the Black Muslim movement and its relationship to non-Muslim Negroes. "Information on the movement's recruitment practices is presented, particularly those revolving around its proficiency in stealing ministers and religious 'bigwigs' from Baptist and other Negro congregations." This quotation is from a review by Nathan Hare, *American Sociological Review,* Vol. 27, June 1962, p. 423. For an account of the Black Muslim movement from the point of view of one of its most brilliant, bitter, and eloquent members, see Alex Haley, Ed., *The Autobiography of Malcolm X,* New York: Grove, 1964. For the perspective of a man who later became the Black Panther Minister of Information, see Eldridge Cleaver, *Soul on Ice,* New York: Dell, 1968.

Margaret Mead, *New Lives for Old: Cultural Transformation — Manus, 1928 — 1953,* New York: Morrow, 1956. In 1928 Margaret Mead studied the Manus, a New Guinea tribe only casually exposed to Western technology, religion, and law. *Growing Up in New Guinea,* published in 1930, was her report of the Manus culture. During the Second World War, the Australian administration of New Guinea was interrupted, first by Japanese invasion and occupation and then by the use of Manus Island by American troops as a staging area. The American reliance on machine technology and American equalitarianism impressed the 14,000 Manus who had led essentially a Stone Age existence. Led by middle-aged men who had observed Western ways as youths employed by plantation owners and the police, the Manus changed their society radically. This summary is based on a review by Leonard Mason, *American Sociological Review,* Vol. 22, February 1957, pp. 125-126.

Louis Ruchames, *Race, Jobs and Politics: The Story of FEPC,* New York: Columbia University Press, 1953. The main emphasis in this book is the history of origins and achievements of the President's Committee on Fair Employment Practice — created in 1941 by Executive Order 8802 of President Franklin D. Roosevelt. This Order prohibited discrimination in defense employment and in government agencies; the Committee was established to secure compliance with the Order. For material on the Negro protest movement that preceded the issuance of the Order, see Herbert Garfinkel, *When Negroes March: The March on Washington Movement in the Organizational Politics for FEPC,* Glencoe, Ill.: Free Press, 1959. Although a march on Washington to demand racial equality was proposed by Negro labor leader A. Philip Randolph in January 1941, it was abandoned during the Second World War at the request of President Roosevelt. Not until the summer of 1963 was it actually held. For more recent studies of the civil rights movement, see Inge Powell Bell, *CORE and the Strategy of Non-Violence,* New York: Random House, 1968; Leon H. Mayhew, *Law and Equal Opportunity: A Study of the Massachusetts Commission Against Discrimination,* Cambridge, Mass.: Harvard University Press, 1968; and Charles J. Levy, *Voluntary Servitude: Whites in the Negro Movement,* New York: Appleton-Century-Crofts, 1968.

Gunnar Myrdal, *An American Dilemma: The Negro Problem and Modern Democracy,* New York: Harper, 1944. In the summer of 1937 the president of the Carnegie Corporation of New York, Frederick P. Keppel, invited Professor Myrdal of the University of Stockholm to take charge of "a comprehensive study of the Negro in the United States, to be undertaken in a wholly objective and dispassionate way as a social phenomenon." This 1500-page book is the end-product of that research project. At least one hundred social scientists worked on Myrdal's staff, producing dozens of research memoranda and several books, which Myrdal integrated in his monumental assessment of the changing place of Negroes in American society. The unpublished memoranda were deposited in the Schomburg Collection of the New York Public Library for scientific reference. One of the important books to be published out of material gathered for the Myrdal study was E. Franklin Frazier's analysis of ". . . the emergence of the Negro as a minority group and his gradual integration into American life." See Frazier, *The Negro in the United States,* New York: Macmillan, 1949. For a more recent approach, see Thomas F. Pettigrew, *A Profile of the Negro American,* Princeton, N.J.: Van Nostrand, 1964.

Wilson Record, *The Negro and the Communist Party,* Chapel Hill: University of North Carolina Press, 1951. This book is concerned with the unsuccessful efforts of the American Communist Party to woo the Negro since the First World War. One reason for the failure was the ignorance of American Communists of the Negro community, which was reflected in inept tactics. Record estimates that Negro Communists never numbered more than 8000 at any one time. This summary is based on a review by Maurice R. Davie, *American Sociological Review,* Vol. 16, October 1951, pp. 740-741.

SOCIAL INTEGRATION
AND DISINTEGRATION

Julio Mitchel

All interactive systems must integrate their constituent parts into a functioning unity. The more differentiated the parts of the interactive system, the greater the integrative problem. That is why a complex society has more serious integrative problems than a small group. Consider New York City as an illustration of an interactive system with integrative problems. The Police Department and the Traffic Commissioner of New York City spend much time, effort, and money to keep motor vehicles moving on the hundreds of miles of streets and highways within the city limits. The Port of New York Authority, which owns and operates the bridges and tunnels leading into New York City (as well as the airports and bus terminals), charges motor vehicles tolls for using the bridges or tunnels. The more passenger cars, buses, and trucks using the bridge and tunnel facilities of the Authority, the more money the Authority takes in and the more additional bridges and tunnels it can build. The officials of the Authority are not responsible for traffic congestion on the streets of New York City, and the Traffic Commissioner of New York City cannot stop the Port of New York Authority from building an additional tunnel or from triple-decking the George Washington Bridge. There may be conflict here between officials of the City of New York and officials of the Port of New York Authority; this is not role conflict. No person is torn apart by incompatible loyalties to different social structures. The trouble is rather that social structures have not been coordinated adequately.

It is obvious why societies have integrative problems. Groups, organizations, and institutions develop to deal with particular functions. Roles are established to mobilize individual effort in the discharge of these functions. Often, however, there are unanticipated consequences for other social structures dealing with other functions.[1] As an example of this phenomenon, consider the rapid introduction of automated processes in American industry. Corporation officials decide on self-regulating machines to reduce costs or to improve quality, or both. They are conscientiously playing their roles. But the cumulative impact of large numbers of companies simultaneously introducing such equipment is to create massive retraining and relocation problems for workers. And, since workers are usually members of families, the ultimate impact of automation may be far indeed from the economic area in which it originates. Similarly, the substitution of diesel for steam locomotives destroyed the economic basis of small towns that served as watering stations. From the point of view of railroad management, fewer stops meant cheaper and better service. The residents' point of view was quite different.

In a California desert town, Caliente, Professor W. F. Cottrell found that residents . . .[2]

---

[1] Robert K. Merton, "The Unanticipated Consequences of Purposive Social Action," *American Sociological Review,* Vol. 1, December 1936, pp. 894-904.

[2] W. F. Cottrell, "Death by Dieselization: A Case Study in the Reaction to Technological Change," *American Sociological Review,* Vol. 16, June 1951, pp. 358-365.

who have raised children see friendships broken and neighborhoods disintegrated. The childless more freely shake the dust of Caliente from their feet. Those who built their personalities into the structure of the community see their work destroyed.

Cottrell contrasted the economic advantages to the railroad with the effects on other segments of American society. Railroad officials did not consider all of the social costs of switching to diesels.[3] Even if they had been aware of the economic and social losses to the residents of Caliente, their occupational roles required them to consider only costs appearing in the balance sheet of the railroad. But in society's balance sheet, the economic advantage to the railroad might have been offset by the economic and personal losses of the families and other interactive systems of Caliente.

A society must achieve some minimum level of integration if it is to continue functioning, just as an individual must achieve some unity of purpose. John's right hand cannot decide to drop heavy weights on John's right foot; similarly, groups and institutions cannot work at cross-purposes in contemporary societies. The responsibility for coordinating an interactive system ultimately rests with those having legitimate political power. Differential responsibility for policy making—that is, the existence of political roles—implies that some role players are expected to keep the rest from working at cross-purposes. Sometimes this responsibility does not produce direct intervention because impersonal mechanisms *prevent* conflict from arising. This is what Adam Smith called the "invisible hand" in a free-enterprise society.[4] But in a free-enterprise society, the degree of tolerable malintegration varies. Government intervention in economic processes occurs whenever automatic mechanisms fail to integrate economic activities sufficiently well. Governments do not chronically intervene in the economy and a small interactive system like a family also may function without grievance procedures. Nevertheless, when divisive differences emerge between husband and wife or between parents and children, they jeopardize the unity of the family and call for a political settlement. Such a settlement involves both consensus and power, as Chapter 9 pointed out. That is, family conflict can be resolved by a person who has the right to make an authoritative decision. In some societies the *father* has this right, legitimated by tradition. In other societies the right to decide for the family as a whole depends on consensus of the members; the family leadership is informally elected.

Social integration has at least two aspects. One aspect is coordination of the activities of role players and collectivities of role players—what has been called **functional integration.**[5] Another aspect, solidarity, is related to the normative

[3] Karl William Kapp, *The Social Costs of Private Enterprise,* Cambridge, Mass.: Harvard University Press, 1950.

[4] Adam Smith, *The Wealth of Nations,* London: Dent, 1910.

[5] Werner S. Landecker, "Types of Integration and Their Measurement," *American Journal of Sociology,* Vol. 56, Jan. 1951, pp. 332-340.

regulation of behavior (discussed in Chapter 1) because people whose values are similar are more likely to develop solidary relationships.[6] In the remainder of this chapter, functional integration and solidarity will be considered at some length.

SOLIDARITY

Socialization for Value Consensus. A large part of the population of affluent societies consists of people who live in poverty—they exist within industrial societies but are not *of* them (see Chapter 6). "Working class" refers to those persons on the lower rungs of the system of social stratification who feel part of the society; "lower class," on the other hand, refers to people marginally integrated into the society. The most obvious difference between working-class and lower-class people is that working-class families are usually self-sufficient economically, whereas lower-class families are more often dependent on welfare assistance. But a more fundamental difference is that lower-class families are not fully included in the **societal community** because they do not learn the values and skills they need to participate effectively in the highly symbolic culture of urban industrial societies. Sometimes this deficit in values and skills is due to a history of exclusion of certain ethnic groups from the mainstream, as with the *burakumin* in Japan or the Negro in the United States. Whatever the genesis of the deficit, however, its existence is an obstacle to full membership in an urban industrial society, and thus to the solidarity of the entire society.

Mass education is potentially able to inculcate verbal and arithmetical skills in everyone. But, as Chapter 11 showed, the system of formal schooling differentiates the population by level of educational attainment. Dropouts inhabit a different culture from college graduates and participate only marginally in a society for which symbolic facility is increasingly necessary. But in addition to providing necessary skills, involvement in the school program has consequences for the student's values and, indirectly, for his relationships with other members of his society. For example, a relatively uneducated person does not know as much about the pleasures an affluent society can offer as does a university student. The university student may obtain pleasure out of reading a book, attending a concert or ballet, visiting a museum, appreciating natural beauty, fighting for social justice—as well as out of driving a powerful car, getting "high," and wearing fashionable clothes. The poorly educated in affluent societies may desire material pleasures intensely—some are willing to risk going to prison for them—but they are aware of only a part of the opportunities

[6] Theodore M. Newcomb, "The Study of Consensus," in Robert K. Merton, Leonard Broom, and Leonard S. Cottrell, Jr., Eds., *Sociology Today: Problems and Prospects,* New York: Basic Books, 1959, pp. 277-292.

for gratification that their societies offer. Opportunities they are unaware of are those that are awakened or cultivated by the educational system. Educational socialization broadens the desires of young people and stimulates the emergence of some values that bear little relation to money income.

Orientation to market consumption is characteristic of industrial societies and contributes to ostentatious expenditures for food, clothing, travel, housing. The appeal of commercial pleasures is greater for lower-class adolescents than for middle-class youth because the socializing impact on them of the educational system is less. If they leave school as soon as they legally may, they have less opportunity to experience art, literature, serious music, science, religion, and meaningful work, than they have of being attracted to the gadgets and entertainments available in the marketplace. Isolation of school-leaving youths from what are generally conceded to be the accomplishments of industrial civilization may partially account for the statistical association between low educational attainment and criminality. As Nelson Algren put it in his paraphrase of Richard Wright, ". . . when a crime is committed by a man who has been excluded from civilization, civilization is an accomplice of the crime."[7] Selective exposure to industrial society is not merely an internal problem. Anthropologists have called attention to the selective diffusion of culture traits to underdeveloped societies. Trinkets, tools, hard liquor, and Coca-Cola are easier to export than arts and sciences or even religion.

In contrast to the well educated, the poorly educated are not only economic underdogs but socially and psychologically deprived as well. They write fewer letters and read fewer books; they vote less in elections; they have fewer friends; they are members of fewer organizations; they are less interested in the world around them; they express fewer opinions; they have lower levels of aspiration; they are less well informed about current events, job opportunities, and comparative values in the marketplace. They participate marginally in their society mainly because they are ignorant and timid. They are also economically deprived, but the economic deprivation is as much effect of psychological withdrawal as it is cause. The author of the study of "underdog" psychology in contemporary society summarized her findings as follows:[8]

> [C]losely linked with economic underprivilege is psychological underprivilege: habits of submission, little access to sources of information, lack of verbal facility. These things appear to produce a lack of self-confidence which increases the unwillingness of the low status person to participate in many phases of our predominantly middle-class culture even beyond what would be a realistic withdrawal adapted to his reduced chances of being effective.
>
> Our theme is summed up by P. F. Lazarsfeld in his conclusion from a study of youth in Austria: "The underprivileged youth has seen less, read less, heard about

---

[7] Nelson Algren, "Remembering Richard Wright," *The Nation,* Vol. 192, January 28, 1961, p. 85.

[8] Genevieve Knupfer, "Portrait of the Underdog," *Public Opinion Quarterly,* Vol. 11, Spring 1947, p. 114.

less, has in his whole environment experienced fewer changes than the socially privileged, and he simply knows of fewer possibilities."

The phrase "the culture of poverty" captures the phenomenon of a restricted mental world though it is not clear about the reason for the restriction. The major reason is that those dragged down by the culture of poverty cannot use, as effectively as those in the mainstream, the techniques of communication of an urban industrial society. On the plane of *face-to-face* communication, ineffectiveness is due to limited vocabularies and lack of facility in conversation. On the plane of *secondary* communication, ineffectiveness refers to unfamiliarity with the more impersonal techniques for linking together people who are not spatially adjacent. The telephone, for instance, may not appear to require sophistication for its use, but it is a more abstract form of communication than face-to-face conversation; it does not permit visual cues. Those segments of the population who have difficulty communicating with others cannot afford to risk the loss of information required in telephonic communication. They take the time and effort to *see* the person they wish to communicate with. The price they pay is a reduction in the frequency and extent of their relations with other people. Similarly, they do not readily exchange letters with friends or relatives because it is difficult for them to transmit meaningful communications through this medium. Perhaps the most serious restriction is their reduced capacity to utilize the mass media as a means to knit themselves into the web of membership with other readers, listeners, and viewers.

Of course, in all societies, including urban industrial ones, face-to-face communication is the most important type of communication. Electronic devices and the printing press have not supplanted face-to-face exchange. They have added a new technique for transmitting information through the intervention of nonhuman media. Although a human agency is the ultimate source of mass media messages, the relationship between sender and receiver is no longer symmetrical as in ordinary face-to-face communication. The recipient of information from newspapers or television is necessarily more passive than the participant in a conversation. Interaction still occurs between the initiator of the communication and its recipients, but response requires more initiative and more training than in the face-to-face situation. Thus readers of a newspaper can interact with the editorial staff through letters to the editor if they have enough education and patience to compose a coherent note. Similarly, television viewers can exert considerable influence on sponsors and network officials by expressing reactions in letters or by telephone. Yet it takes a certain level of self-confidence (or indignation) to attempt to interact with something as impersonal as a television station.

Living in an urban industrial society without responding to some extent to mass communications is impossible. Poorly educated segments of the population respond minimally: to comic strips, soap operas, news of sports.[9] Better

---

[9] For a classic study of the psychology of the listener to radio soap operas, see Herta Herzog, "What Do We Really Know about Daytime Serial Listeners?," in Paul F. Lazarsfeld and Frank N. Stanton, Eds., *Radio Research, 1942–1943,* New York: Duell, Sloan, and Pearce, 1944, pp. 3-33.

educated persons use the mass media more extensively: to keep abreast of public affairs, new books, comparative values in consumer goods. Members of the industrially oriented in-group have incorporated the mass media into their lives. They depend on the newspaper not only for current events but also for the radio and television logs, information about the movies at neighborhood theaters, sales in retail stores, stock-market prices, and other activities and events. The following article reports a piece of research which took advantage of a newspaper strike to gauge the place of the newspaper in the lives of New Yorkers:[10]

In the late afternoon of Saturday, June 30, 1945, the deliverymen of eight major New York City newspapers went on strike. They remained on strike for over two weeks, and during that period most New Yorkers were effectively deprived of their regular newspaper reading. They were able to buy the newspaper *PM* and a few minor and specialized papers at newsstands, and they could buy copies over the counter at central offices of some newspapers. But the favorite papers of most readers were simply inaccessible to them for seventeen days.

These unusual circumstances presented a good opportunity for various interested parties — advertisers, newspaper publishers, radio executives, social scientists — to gauge public attitudes toward the newspaper, and at least three general polls of opinion were independently conducted during the strike. Some if not all findings of two polls have been made public, one by the Elmo Roper agency and the other by Fact Finders Associates, Inc. This article is a report on the third, an exploratory survey conducted for the Bureau of Applied Social Research, Columbia University. . . . Respondents were asked directly, "What news stories or events which happened last week (i.e., before the strike) did you particularly miss not being able to follow up?" Almost half the respondents were unable to name any such story or event whereas others named such non-"serious" news stories as the then-current Stevens murder case. About a third of the respondents did cite a "serious" news event, most of them the Far Eastern war. Furthermore, directly following this question, the respondents were asked which of a list of six front-page stories of the week before they had missed "not being able to follow up in your regular paper." Here, too, only a little more than a third of the respondents said that they had missed reading about the average serious event in this list. Thus, although almost all the respondents speak highly of the newspaper's value as a channel of "serious" information, only about a third of them seemed to miss it for that purpose.

In brief, there seems to be an important difference between the respondents' *general* protestations of interest in the newspaper's "serious" purposes and their *specific* desires and practices in newspaper reading. The respondents' feeling that the newspaper "keeps me informed about the world" seems to be rather diffuse and amorphous, and not often attached to concrete news events of a "serious" nature. Again, for example, take the answer to our question, "Now that you don't read your regular newspaper, do you feel you know what's going on in the world?" Fully two-thirds of the respondents felt that they did not know what

[10] Reprinted by permission. From Bernard Berelson, "What 'Missing the Newspaper' Means," in Paul F. Lazarsfeld and Frank N. Stanton, Eds., *Communications Research, 1948–1949*, New York: Harper, 1949, pp. 111-129.

was going on although, as we have seen, only about half that many had any notion of what in the world they wanted more information about. To miss the newspaper for its "serious" news value seems to be the accepted if not the automatic thing to say.

But this does not mean that the newspapers were not genuinely missed by their readers. There were many spontaneous mentions of the intensity with which the respondents missed their papers, and several of those who missed them a good deal at the beginning of the strike felt even more strongly about it as the week wore on. The question is, *why* did people miss the newspaper so keenly. However, let us first review the several uses to which readers typically put the newspaper. This is the next step in our effort to put content into a check mark on a poll questionnaire by suggesting what "missing the newspaper" really means.

The modern newspaper plays several roles for its readers. From the analysis of our intensive interviews, we have attempted to construct a typology of such roles, or functions, of the newspaper. Obviously the types enumerated here, while discrete, are not necessarily mutually exclusive for any one newspaper reader. Undoubtedly, different people read different parts of the newspaper for different reasons at different times. The major problem is to determine the conditions under which the newspaper fulfills such functions as those developed here—and perhaps others—for different kinds of people. In this connection, the special value of a small group of detailed interviews lies in the identification of hypotheses which can then be tested, one way or the other, by less intensive methods. In other words, such "qualitative" interviews suggest the proper questions which can then be asked, in lesser detail, for "quantitative" verification.

In this section we shall mention briefly several immediate uses of the newspaper which we found in the interviews. The illustrative quotations are typical of those appearing in the interviews. Some of these uses correspond to acknowledged purposes of the newspaper, others do not.

FOR INFORMATION ABOUT AND INTERPRETATION OF PUBLIC AFFAIRS

There is a core of readers who find the newspaper indispensable as a source of information about and interpretation of the "serious" world of public affairs. It is important to stress, in this connection, that this interest is not limited simply to the provision of full information about news events. Many people are also concerned with commentaries on current events from both editorials and columnists, which they use as a touchstone for their own opinions. For example:

"I don't have the details now, I just have the result. It's almost like reading the headlines of the newspaper without following up the story. I miss the detail and the explanation of events leading up to the news. I like to get the story behind and the development leading up to—it's more penetrating . . . I like to analyze for myself why things do happen and after getting the writers' opinions of it from the various newspapers, in which each one portrays the story in a different manner, I have a broader view and a more detailed view when I formulate my own opinion."

AS A TOOL FOR DAILY LIVING

For some people the newspaper was missed because it was used as direct aid in everyday life. The respondents were asked, "Since you haven't been able to get your regular newspaper, have you found some things that you can't do as well without it?'' Fully half of them indicated that they had been handicapped in some way. Many people found it difficult if not impossible to follow radio programs without the radio log published in the newspaper. Others who might have gone to a motion picture did not like the bother of phoning or walking around to find out what was on. A few business people missed such merchandising comments as the arrival of buyers; others were concerned about financial and stock exchange information. Several women interested in shopping were handicapped by the lack of advertisements. A few close relatives of returning soldiers were afraid they would miss details of embarkation news. A couple of women who regularly followed the obituary notices were afraid that acquaintances might die without their knowing it. Finally, there were scattered mentions of recipes and fashion notes and even the daily weather forecast in this connection. In short, there are many ways in which many people use the newspaper as a daily instrument or guide and it was missed accordingly.

FOR RESPITE

Reading has respite value whenever it provides a vacation from personal care by transporting the reader outside his own immediate world. There is no question but that many newspaper stories with which people readily identify supply this ''escape'' function satisfactorily for large numbers of people. Exhibit A in this connection is the comics, which people report liking for their story and suspense value. Beyond this, however, the newspaper is able to refresh readers in other ways, by supplying them with appropriate psychological relaxation. The newspaper is particularly effective in fulfilling this need for relief from the boredom and dullness of everyday life not only because of the variety and richness of its ''human interest'' content or because of its inexpensive accessibility. In addition, the newspaper is a good vehicle for this purpose because it satisfies this need without much cost to the reader's conscience; the prestige value of the newspaper as an institution for ''enlightening the citizenry'' carries over to buttress this and other uses of the newspapers.

''When you read, it takes your mind off other things.''

''It [the strike] gave me nothing to do in between my work except to crochet, which does not take my mind off myself as much as reading.''

''I didn't know what to do with myself. I was depressed. There was nothing to read and pass the time. I got a paper on Wednesday and felt a whole lot better.''

FOR SOCIAL PRESTIGE

Another group of readers seem to use the newspaper because it enables them to appear informed in social gatherings. Thus the newspaper has conversational value. Readers not only can learn what has happened and then report it to their associates but can also find opinions and interpretations for use in discussions on public affairs. It is obvious how this use of the newspaper serves to increase the reader's prestige among his fellows. It is not that the newspapers' content is good in itself but rather that it is good *for* something—and that something is putting up an impressive front to one's associates.

''You have to read in order to keep up a conversation with other people. It is embarrassing not to know if you are in company who discuss the news.''

TABLE 15.1

Hours Spent Voluntarily Exposed to "Culture" Among American Adults, According to Source of "Culture"

Source	Thousands of Hours Spent Per Month	Percentage of Total (N = 447,000,000)
Commercial television	96,285	22
Magazines	89,310	20
Books (all sources)	76,172	17
Radio	38,192	8
Records	36,960	8
Musical, artistic, and theatrical performing (amateur)	27,500	6
Motion pictures	22,252	5
Educational television	21,800	5
Adult education	12,750	3
Newspapers	12,000	3
Museums	5,600	1
Concerts	4,250	1
Theater	3,950	1

Source: Bernard Berelson, "In the Presence of Culture," *Public Opinion Quarterly*, vol. 28, Spring, 1964, pp. 1-12.

"Not that I am uneasy about what's happening but I like to know about the country so when people ask you questions you don't feel dumb and silly."

"It makes me furious, absolutely furious, because I don't know what's going on and all my friends who are getting the papers do know."

The foregoing article reported a natural experiment. Researchers inferred the dependence of urban industrial man on his newspapers from observing him when they were temporarily unavailable. But the newspaper is not the only instrument of mass communication in industrial societies. Glossy magazines are sold in kiosks and newsstands all over the world. In 1968 the United States had 74 million television sets in use, Japan and the Soviet Union each had 19 million, Great Britain had 14 million, West Germany 13 million, Italy 7 million, Canada 6 million, France 4 million, and Australia and Brazil had 3 million each.[11] Radio receivers are even more common than television receivers. The motion picture industry has a world market. Mass communications carry so much information that a British or American family without a radio, television set, newspapers, or magazines would be almost as isolated as the shipwrecked household in *Swiss Family Robinson*. Table 15.1 sets forth the total exposure of Americans to highly symbolic culture: 447 million hours per month.

[11] Bureau of the Census, *Statistical Abstract of the United States: 1968*, Washington, D.C.: Government Printing Office, 1968, pp. 862-863.

Participation within a highly symbolic culture leads to consensus about some of the values embodied in that culture and, through shared sentiments, to solidarity. Thus members of urban industrial societies tend to believe that maximal exposure to formal education is desirable, that museums are superior to taverns, and that small families enable parents to provide better opportunities for their children. Among these opportunities is a home in a suburban community with a good school system.[12] One sociologist concluded from a study of movement into suburbs in the Chicago metropolitan area in the 1950s that a major motive was the desire "to find a location in which to conduct family life . . . more suitable than that offered by central cities."[13] Suburbs, which mushroomed in the United States following the Second World War, have varied compositions. A few contain only middle-class families; some have a working-class flavor. For example, a suburban tract in Milpitas, California, is inhabited by Ford auto workers who relocated along with their plant.[14] Yet in a sense suburbs are homogeneous: their inhabitants tend to share the values of a highly symbolic culture and most function comfortably within that culture. Even within a wealthy suburb like Westfield, New Jersey, families differ in their economic resources, religious affiliations, and recreational interests. The white Protestant business executive living in a costly mansion and the Catholic carpenter living with his larger family in a modest Cape Cod cottage have different outlooks. Beneath these differences, however, is a common value commitment to the industrial way of life, perhaps reflected in similar educational and occupational aspirations for their children. This value commitment is to *individual achievement,* especially achievement that increases the material wealth of the society. The business executive is admired (by those who admire him) not only because he is rich but because he is accomplishing what many people think is important.

Census data, though helpful in describing the social and economic characteristics of the population, do not reveal value similarities underlying manifest differences. Because American data on family composition of the population include families that share urban industrial values and those who do not, the contribution of these shared values to family stability is obscured. Nevertheless, these aggregative data suggest that family life is viable in American society — and the data for the more value-homogeneous suburban communities show it more clearly. Suburban Westfield had proportionally fewer divorced persons in 1960 than the United States as a whole and much fewer than central cities like Newark or Pittsburgh. In the country as a whole, family breakdown also is the

---

[12] James B. Conant, *Slums and Suburbs: A Commentary on Schools in Metropolitan Areas,* New York: McGraw-Hill, 1961.

[13] Wendell Bell, "Familism and Suburbanization: One Test of the Social Choice Hypothesis," *Rural Sociology,* Vol. 21, September-December 1956, pp. 276-283.

[14] Bennett M. Berger, *Working Class Suburb: A Study of Auto Workers in Suburbia,* Berkeley: University of California Press, 1960.

exception rather than the rule.[15] Of the 99 million Americans recorded in the 1960 census as having *ever* been married, 81 million were living with their spouses at the time of census; 10 million were widows or widowers; 5 million persons were living apart from their spouses due to marital discord, institutionalization, or other reasons; and only 3 million were divorced (and not remarried).[16] These statistics do not fully reflect family breakup in the United States because some of the 81 million persons living with their spouses in 1960 had been *previously* married. Fourteen per cent of the 99 million Americans reported as "ever married" had been married more than once. Usually, though, divorces occurred after a relatively brief period of marriage and did not discourage the individuals involved from establishing more stable marriages.[17]

The increase in the birth rate is another indication that some of the resources of affluent societies are devoted to family life. The American birth rate rose from 77.2 live births per 1000 females aged 15-44 in 1935 to 119.0 in 1960.[18] The rise in the birth rate after the Second World War is not restricted to the United States. All industrial countries have enjoyed a baby boom along with the prosperity that encouraged married couples to undertake larger families. In the United States the baby boom has been accompanied by an expansion of home ownership. In 1940 only 41.1 per cent of nonfarm homes were occupied by their owners; in 1960 61.0 per cent of nonfarm homes were owner occupied.[19] Higher birth rate and increased home ownership suggest that family life is not deteriorating.

Can value consensus contribute to the social integration of American society when approximately one-eighth of the American population moves to a different residence each year, and about one-fifteenth go far enough to change counties?[20] Can value consensus persist when families are not firmly rooted in the community? Transiency as a way of life seems more compatible with rugged individualism than with group solidarity, but family organization in urban industrial societies (Chapter 4) has adapted to a dynamic occupational system that makes mobility advantageous.

Business and professional men accept "transfers" as the price of occupational success.[21] Business and professional families move from one part of the

[15] The argument in this paragraph and the one following leans on Talcott Parsons, "The American Family: Its Relations to Personality and to Social Structure," in Talcott Parsons and Robert F. Bales, *Family, Socialization and Interaction Process,* Glencoe, Ill.: Free Press, 1955, Chap. 1.

[16] Bureau of the Census, *United States Census of Population: 1960, United States Summary, Detailed Characteristics,* Washington, D.C.: Government Printing Office, 1963, pp. xxi-xxii.

[17] Bureau of the Census, *United States Census: 1960, Summary,* 1963, p. xxii.

[18] Department of Health, Education and Welfare, *Health, Education, and Welfare Trends: 1961,* Washington, D.C.: Government Printing Office, 1961, p. 6.

[19] Bureau of the Census, *Statistical Abstract of the United States: 1962,* Washington, D.C.: Government Printing Office, 1962, p. 758.

[20] Bureau of the Census, *Statistical Abstract of the United States: 1968,* Washington, D.C.: Government Printing Office, 1968, p. 33.

[21] William H. Whyte, Jr., *The Organization Man,* New York: Simon & Schuster, 1956, pp. 269-275.

United States to another. Homes are sold and new ones bought. New friendships are developed; children are enrolled in different schools; charge accounts are opened in other stores. Yet the impact on family life and community organization does not seem appreciable. The moving about takes place with so little disruption partly because of the value homogeneity of American communities. Westfield, New Jersey, may be 3000 miles from Palo Alto, California, but each is an affluent suburb on the periphery of a metropolis; this sociocultural similarity means that a Westfielder understands the way of life in Palo Alto even before he moves there. The organization man moves from one urban community to another very much like it; hence he feels "transferred," but not uprooted. Moreover, in a society in which moving around is so common, geographic mobility is the normal expectation. Only 6.3 per cent of the Americans enumerated in the 1960 census (including infants!) were living in the houses they occupied at birth.[22] People who feel justified in moving to a new community out of boredom or a desire for adventure are psychologically prepared for the adjustments that moves entail.

These considerations are most relevant for the interurban moves of *white-collar* persons. For poorly educated, rural Negroes, migration to urban areas *is* a threatening experience. Migration has an entirely different meaning to a Mississippi farm laborer who moves to Chicago and an electronics engineer who is transferred from New York to San Francisco. An industrial society is never wholly industrialized. Preindustrial population elements persist, often in rural areas. In the United States, the preindustrial minority consists of those who have not learned the values necessary for effective participation in a highly symbolic culture.

Law: The Implementation of a Value Consensus. Law is a system of formal procedures courts and lawyers are concerned with. It is also the embodiment of impersonal principles members of an interactive system use to protect their interests. They turn to principles like "due process" or "free speech" or "equality before the law" because they have been socialized to believe that following such principles results in justice. All societies provide at least minimum order; some societies legitimize order by establishing a legal system embodying principles to which the bulk of the population is committed. A legal system helps perpetuate the faith that the values of the society are fair to everybody, that justice is possible, that the political system does more than minister to self-interest. In such a society, a legal system explicates the logic of its value consensus.

A legal system can exist in a society whose values are poorly integrated. This means that values either are not implemented consistently or are not subscribed to by the bulk of the population. Thus South Africa has a legal system; judges and lawyers seem to apply rational procedures; and white Afrikaners are reasonably satisfied with its operation. But the Bantu population, the majority

---

[22] Bureau of the Census, *United States Census of Population: 1960, United States Summary,* Washington: Government Printing Office, 1962, p. 205.

of its citizenry, does not have the same legal rights as whites; and many of them feel unjustly treated.[23] In American society, not all elements of the population are equally confident that the legal system serves their interests. Until the Office of Economic Opportunity established a legal services program to help the poor, the civil courts were far from equally useful to the well-to-do and the poor; in 1968 this program supported 1800 full-time lawyers in 850 community law offices throughout the country.[24] In the criminal courts, legal aid and public defender services are becoming increasingly available for indigent defendants and experimental bail projects are reducing the likelihood of the poor languishing in jail awaiting trial; however, studies have shown that economic resources make a difference at many stages of law enforcement. For example, a seasoned criminal lawyer is more likely than a public defender to make a deal with the prosecuting attorney, often exchanging a guilty plea for a reduced charge.[25]

Since the jurisdiction of the legal system is universal, it is officially oblivious of the ethnic and class distinctions within a society—indeed, the goddess of justice is traditionally shown blindfolded. In practice, however, consistent implementation of values is difficult. Chapter 14 dealt with the gradual extension to Negro Americans of the opportunity to achieve middle-class status. Supreme Court interpretations of the Constitution formed part of the process by which American society recognized that it had implemented achievement and equality values differently for blacks and whites. In short, the judicial process—and especially judicial review in the light of constitutional principles—tends to extend the logic of the value commitments of a society.

Law unifies a society by implicitly defining class, status, and power differentials as subordinate to the binding rules of an overarching value consensus. Even though some cleavages remain, shared commitment to a rule of law minimizes their divisive or polarizing effect. For example, the differences in economic rewards within a society are divisive partly because they make possible different styles of life on different economic levels and partly because those in the disadvantaged strata may subscribe to belief systems (ideologies) holding themselves exploited. But legal systems are designed to be independent of the class system. If legal decisions are not biased in favor of the affluent, they generate an attitude of moral respect in poor as well as rich, which is necessary for social solidarity.[26] As long as the government can lose criminal and civil cases in the courts, the legal system cannot be considered a tool of government of-

[23] Colin Legum, "Color and Power in the South African Situation," *Daedalus,* Vol. 96, Spring 1967, pp. 483-495.

[24] Jerome E. Carlin, Jan Howard, and Sheldon L. Messinger, *Civil Justice and the Poor,* New York: Russell Sage Foundation, 1968; Herbert Mitgang, "The Storefront Lawyer Helps the Poor," The New York Times Magazine, November 10, 1968, pp. 34-130.

[25] Donald J. Newman, "Pleading Guilty for Considerations: A Study of Bargain Justice," *Journal of Criminal Law, Criminology and Police Science,* Vol. 46, March-April 1956, pp. 780-790.

[26] Émile Durkeim observed that religious integration also produced solidarity by generating a common feeling of moral respect for society. See *The Elementary Forms of the Religious Life,* Glencoe, Ill.: Free Press, 1947.

ficials. The outcomes of litigation are perceived as the implementation of principles rather than the rationalization of power.

The legal system depends on the state for enforcement of its decisions. Courts can tame the naked power at the disposal of the executive branch of government, scrutinizing it in the light of principles embodied in constitutions and in legislative authorizations. Only when executive power has been legitimated in these terms is it permitted to operate in democratic societies. Talcott Parsons has pointed out that the legal system is especially important to the integration of urban industrial societies; diverse interest groups would surely be in perpetual conflict without an institution capable of enforcing authoritative compromises:[27]

> Law has special importance in a pluralistic society where there are many different kinds of interests that must be balanced against each other. In the totalitarian type of society, which is in a great hurry to settle some fundamental general social conflict or policy, law tends to lack independent authority. Both individually and collectively, law imposes restraints on precipitate and violent action. It is to these restraints that the president of Harvard alludes when he greets the recipients of law degrees at every Commencement with the words, "You are now qualified to help administer those wise restraints which make men free."

Pluralism and Cross-Cutting Solidarities. Shared values are a basis for the solidarity of a society. However, when the population is large and the social structure differentiated (the situation in modern societies), value sharing is problematical. Interpersonal communication promotes value sharing, but small group research demonstrates what logic suggests: the larger the group, the less opportunity for individual communications and the less consensus.[28] In modern societies, mass communication supplements interpersonal communication in linking people together in a web of solidarity, but the mass media provide no assurance that value consensus will in fact emerge. Members of urban industrial societies are differentially receptive to mass media messages. Integration is also promoted by cross-cutting solidarities, which result from pluralistic social organization; they promote societal solidarity by mutually undermining more parochial loyalties.

Cross-cutting solidarities are one contribution of religious diversity to American social integration (Chapter 8). Cross-cutting solidarities also reduce the fervor of political partisanship and thereby help stabilize a democratic political system (Chapter 9). Pluralism in any institutional realm works *against*

---

[27] Adapted from Talcott Parsons, "Law and Social Control," in William M. Evan, Ed., *Law and Sociology,* New York: Free Press of Glencoe, 1962, p. 72.

[28] A. Paul Hare, "Study of Interaction and Consensus in Different Sized Groups, *American Sociological Review,* Vol. 17, June 1952, pp. 261-267; Theodore M. Newcomb, "The Study of Consensus," in Robert K. Merton, Leonard Broom, and Leonard S. Cottrell, Jr., Eds., *Sociology Today: Problems and Prospects,* New York: Basic Books, 1959, pp. 277-292.

polarization of the society. Of course, pluralistic social organization is a more effective integrating mechanism when the pluralism is recognized by members of the interactive system. If, on the other hand, members of a society think society is *polarized* economically, politically, or religiously, a polarized definition of the situation works *against* societal solidarity. The Marxian focus on the privately owned firm and on the distinction within the firm between owners and propertyless wage earners worked this way. Marx inferred the inevitability of class conflict in capitalist society by generalizing from conflict of interest within the firm to exploitation within the occupational system as a whole.[29] Marx held that this class solidarity was an international force because the community of wage earners against capitalist employers was more powerful than, say, national or ethnic solidarities. Worker solidarity in the face of exploitation would polarize industrialized countries along economic lines even though other cleavages existed and could be similarly emphasized ideologically. The patriotic fervor of French and German workers during the First World War surprised many Marxists; they had exaggerated the strength of worker solidarity and underestimated nationalism. But twentieth-century developments clearly demonstrated the pluralism of the industrial economy:[30]

1. The expansion of the professions obliterated the distinction between propertyless workers and owner-exploiters. Great occupational growth occurred in professional and other white-collar categories. The commitment of teachers, lawyers, engineers, and research scientists to their professions transcends the distinction between self-employment and salaried employment. That is, a lawyer working for a large corporation tends to have the same occupational identity as a solo practitioner.
2. The emergence of large, bureaucratic organizations, corporate as well as governmental, introduced a managerial-executive category into the occupational system. Technically, business executives and government officials are employees, responsible to stockholders or to the citizenry collectively. In practice, though, these managerial employees are relatively autonomous of their nominal bosses.
3. The requirements of industrial development led to occupational differentiation, including professionalization and the emergence of a managerial élite, in communist as well as capitalist societies. This convergence of economic organization cast doubt on the Marxian assumption of class conflict on one side of the Revolution and a classless society on the other.
4. Programs to promote the health, education, and welfare of all segments of the population are prominent in capitalist as well as communist societies.

[29] Talcott Parsons, "Social Classes and Class Conflict in the Light of Recent Sociological Theory." Papers and Proceedings, *American Economic Review,* Vol. 39, May 1949, pp. 16-26.

[30] The specific illustrations as well as the general argument are drawn from Talcott Parsons, "The Problem of Polarization on the Axis of Color," in John Hope Franklin, Ed., *Color and Race,* Boston: Houghton Mifflin, 1968, pp. 349-369.

The term "welfare state" was coined in Great Britain but applies to all affluent industrial societies (with the possible exception of Japan). In the welfare state, the polarity between rich and poor is blurred by governmental provision of basic services.

These developments reveal the complexity of the occupational structure of industrial societies and cast doubt on Marxist predictions of economic polarization. An intellectual recognition of this complexity underlies the declining enthusiasm for Marxist ideology.[31]

Cross-cutting solidarities are almost inevitable in fluid urban societies where the voluntary association rather than the ascribed relationship is typical. The principle of *voluntary choice* now works in the formation of families of procreation in nontraditional societies like the United States although the solidarity of the family of *orientation* is as necessary for urban industrial societies as it was for preliterate societies. In modern societies ascriptive restraints are at a minimum; "love" is extolled as the basis for marriage.[32] Since love is a principle of mutual choice, western marriage is the prototype of voluntary associations — in the same category with peer groups, bowling teams, residential neighborhoods, political parties, religious denominations, and labor unions. This freedom to choose relational commitments has often led to concern that solidarities are weak in contemporary society. Yet voluntarily assumed commitments are not necessarily weaker than ascribed commitments. A man may love his wife as much or more than he does his parents. Moreover, he may consider the marital tie as permanent as that of blood. Some empirical data, however, such as the high divorce rates of industrial societies, are interpreted as evidence for the weakness of voluntary commitments.

Although associational pluralism may be responsible for some individual maladjustment, it also ties together people who might otherwise remain in parochial enclaves. Religious intermarriage in the United States increases somewhat the probability of divorce, but it also links Catholics to Protestants and Christians to Jews, thereby promoting the normative integration of American society (Chapter 5). In a sense, all marriages are intermarriages because the bride and groom come from different families of orientation.[33] The social significance of the incest taboo is that it compels the individual to make emotional as well as sexual commitments *outside* of his family of orientation.[34] Associational pluralism is thus an elaboration of the logic of the incest taboo.

[31] Daniel Bell, *The End of Ideology: On the Exhaustion of Political Ideas in the Fifties,* New York: Collier Books, 1961.

[32] William J. Goode, "The Theoretical Importance of Love," *American Sociological Review,* Vol. 34, February 1959, pp. 38-47.

[33] Hyman Rodman, *Marriage, Family, and Society: A Reader,* New York: Random House, 1965, p. 54.

[34] Talcott Parsons, "The Incest Taboo in Relation to Social Structure and the Socialization of the Child," *British Journal of Sociology,* Vol. 5, June 1954, pp. 101-117.

FUNCTIONAL INTEGRATION

Only for analytical purposes is it useful to discuss solidarity apart from functional integration. Solidarity means that members of an interactive system *feel* included in the system, and such a feeling is difficult to sustain unless they actually *are* included. Conversely, when members of an interactive system are included in its adaptive, socializing, and decision-making roles, they develop loyalty to the system; they regard it as theirs. For purposes of sociological analysis, however, the coordinated activities of role players can be distinguished from their normative commitments and feelings of solidarity. The problem of functional integration implies reciprocal relations between role players. In complex societies where institutions are fully differentiated from one another, functional integration implies a special kind of reciprocity: exchange between representatives of different institutional realms. For example, the family supplies a labor force to industry in exchange for monetary claims on industry's current production.[35]

Mere existence is not participation in the societal community. One reason why census enumerators sometimes fail to record the presence of infants in a household is that infants do not participate as family members; they have not yet learned to interact as role players. All societies contain persons who are only peripherally included in its role structure. In American society, for instance, aged persons frequently experience a reduction in the number of roles they play; subjectively they tend to feel useless.[36] From the societal point of view, the disengagement of the aged is an integrative failure. The aged are a responsibility but not full-fledged role players. Other categories of persons are marginal members of society in varying degrees: women, adolescents, physically handicapped persons, ethnic minorities, the unemployed. Still other persons are forced into marginality by social rejection when their behavior is interpreted as criminal or as symptomatic of mental illness.[37] A major integrating process in modern societies is the extension of societal membership to these various marginal participants, sometimes purposively, sometimes unwittingly.

The Extension of Societal Membership. Membership in the societal community encompasses three levels of citizenship: the legal, the political, and the

[35] Talcott Parsons emphasizes the importance of symbolic media of exchange—money, power, influence, and commitments—in the integration of complex societies. See "On the Concept of Political Power," *Proceedings of the American Philosophical Society*, Vol. 107, June 1963, p. 260.

[36] Matilda White Riley and Anne Foner, *Aging and Society: An Inventory of Research Findings*, New York: Russell Sage Foundation, 1968, especially Part 4.

[37] Some recent literature on social control insists that deviance is as much in the eye of the beholder as in the behavior of the "criminal" or the "crazy" person, for example, Thomas J. Scheff, *Being Mentally Ill: A Sociological Theory*, Chicago: Aldine, 1966. But the social rejection is similar whatever the basis for the interpretation.

Dan Budnick—Woodfin Camp Inc.

social.[38] Legal citizenship is the most elementary and involves rights to own property, to freedom of expression, to freedom of association, to sue and be sued. The extension of legal citizenship to the entire adult population was achieved in France in the revolution of 1789. By contrast, the American Revolution failed to extend legal citizenship to all adults; Negro slaves had no legal standing. Political citizenship refers to participation, directly or indirectly, in the setting of societal policy. Those who have the right to vote enjoy political citizenship—unless voting has no effect on government leadership. Although women possessed *legal* citizenship in eighteenth-century America, they did not achieve *political* citizenship until the twentieth century. The exclusion of women and those without property from political citizenship rested on the assumption that legal rights were one thing and capacity to choose society's leaders another. Social citizenship refers to the individual's ability to take advantage of the opportunities offered by his society. In practice, this ability hinges on his financial resources, education, and health. Thus social citizenship has to do with the welfare activities of a society rather than its legal and political institutions.

Talcott Parsons points out that modern societies have gradually extended citizenship on all three levels to large proportions of their populations.[39] The broadening of legal and political citizenship was largely achieved by the end of the nineteenth century, and the broadening of social citizenship is a twentieth-

[38] With a slight change in nomenclature, this argument follows T. H. Marshall, *Class, Citizenship, and Social Development,* Garden City, N.Y.: Anchor, 1965, Chap. 4.

[39] Talcott Parsons, "Full Citizenship for the Negro American? A Sociological Problem," *Daedalus,* Vol. 94, Fall 1965, pp. 1009-1054.

century phenomenon. The war against poverty in the United States can be thought of as an attempt to extend social citizenship by increasing educational, occupational, residential, and health opportunities for the poor. This has already occurred in Sweden, where income differentials exist but do not carry with them implications of social exclusion. Thus less affluent Swedes live in modest apartments, but there are no slums. The Negro Revolution in the United States is another major attempt at social inclusion. As Americans make available more educational, religious, political, and other associational opportunities, Negroes will become full members of pluralistic America.

The effort to extend social citizenship to the physically handicapped is proceeding more slowly than the Negro Revolution or the War on Poverty. Nevertheless, efforts are being made to eliminate architectural barriers that reduce the access to buildings of 250,000 persons in wheelchairs, 200,000 persons with heavy leg braces, 140,000 with artificial limbs, and 5,000,000 with heart conditions.[40] For example, Philharmonic Hall at New York's Lincoln Center is fully accessible to disabled persons. On the other hand, Dr. Howard A. Rusk cited the case of a young lawyer, a polio victim, who was forced to turn down a faculty appointment to a large Eastern university because he could not climb the flight of steps to the classroom area. Similarly, the traffic control system in general use — red, green, and amber lights — prevents color-blind persons from obtaining a driver's license. If concern about social inclusion proceeds far enough, a traffic control system may be devised that does not depend on color vision.

Coercive Coordination. As we have seen, the extension of membership in the societal community promotes functional integration. But a society may be organized so that some people are superfluous in the sense that no vacant roles exist for them to play. The unpleasant alternative may then be to give them jobs or political offices that are already filled or to treat them as dependents of society. One of the obstacles to the successful integration of the poor in American society is that the poor are not genuinely *needed* to play important roles:[41]

> Poverty in an affluent society is the condition of not being important enough to other people to induce them to supply one with whatever level of goods and services is defined as the level of "minimum subsistence," or "minimum adequacy" or "minimum comfort" in the historical period one is concerned with. The poor are poor because they have no labor services, no goods or property, no talents, no beauty, no information, no anything that the nonpoor value.

The same argument can be applied to the problem of integrating the Negro into American society. If Negroes are needed to fill roles presently unfilled or

---

[40] Howard A. Rusk, "Lack of Access to Buildings Thwarts a Cripple's Efforts to Lead a Normal Life," *The New York Times,* June 19, 1966.

[41] From Harry C. Bredemeier, "The Politics of the Poverty Cold War," *Urban Affairs Quarterly,* Vol. 3, June 1968, p. 4.

not played very well, it is comparatively easy to develop public support for their inclusion.[42] When they seek a larger share of roles that are already filled or for which there are eager candidates—for example, election to public office—rationalizations are found to justify a more gradual approach to their full participation.

It is in these situations that coercive coordination is necessary: the political process is used to redistribute people to roles. The poor may be poor because they lack talents that the nonpoor value, or they may possess qualities that the nonpoor regard as morally reprehensible. Can a society afford to permit them to remain outside of the community? In the preface to his play *Major Barbara*, George Bernard Shaw denounced the social cost of poverty:[43]

> If a man is indolent, let him be poor. If he is drunken, let him be poor. If he is not a gentleman, let him be poor. If he is addicted to the fine arts or to pure science instead of to trade and finance, let him be poor. If he chooses to spend his wages on his beer and his family instead of saving it up for his old age, let him be poor. Let nothing be done for the "undeserving": let him be poor. Serves him right! Also—somewhat inconsistently—blessed are the poor!
>
> Now what does this Let Him Be Poor mean? It means let him be weak. Let him be ignorant. Let him become a nucleus of disease. Let him be a standing exhibition and example of ugliness and dirt. Let him have rickety children. Let him be cheap, and drag his fellows down to his own price by selling himself to do their work. Let his habitations turn our cities into poisonous congeries of slums. Let his daughters infect our young men with the diseases of the streets, and his sons revenge him by turning the nation's manhood into scrofula, cowardice, cruelty, hypocrisy, political imbecility, and all the other fruits of oppression and malnutrition. Let the undeserving become still less deserving; and let the deserving lay up for himself, not treasures in heaven, but horrors in hell upon earth. This being so, is it really wise to let him be poor? Would he not do ten times less harm as a prosperous burglar, incendiary, ravisher or murderer, to the utmost limits of humanity's comparatively negligible impulses in these directions? Suppose we were to abolish all penalties for such activities, and decide that poverty is the one thing we will not tolerate—that every adult with less than a thousand a year shall be painlessly but inexorably killed, and every hungry half naked child forcibly fattened and clothed, would not that be an enormous improvement on our existing system, which has already destroyed so many civilizations, and is visibly destroying ours? surely the sensible course would be to give every man enough to live well on, so as to guarantee the community against the possibility of a case of the malignant disease of poverty, and then (necessarily) to see that he earned it.

Shaw was arguing for the social inclusion of the poor, and implicitly, for political action to secure this objective. Western societies have attempted to

---

[42] Sidney M. Wilhelm and Edwin H. Powell, "Who Needs the Negro?", *Trans-action*, Vol. 1, Sept./Oct. 1964, pp. 3-6.

[43] Reprinted by permission. From Bernard Shaw, *Major Barbara*, New York: Penguin, pp. 2-3.

functionally integrate the poor through such efforts as the community action programs of the War on Poverty, and they have come far closer to doing so than any previous society. A seventeenth-century gentlewoman might be "passionately attached to her children, always ready to sympathize in the sorrows of her friends, and notably indulgent to servants and retainers,"[44] but she also might contemplate hangings without a quiver of sympathy because, as Alexis de Tocqueville pointed out, she possessed "no clear notion of suffering in anyone who was not a person of quality." "The gradual widening and institutionalization of compassion"[45] has now become so widespread that urban industrial societies are not only willing to provide for the welfare of the poor, but they also make efforts to incorporate the poor into the role structure. For the most part, efforts at incorporation require not only a consensus that even the "underserving" poor are ultimately deserving of membership but also the coercive coordination of the political process so that room is made for them in the role structure.

These efforts produce strains in the society, particularly among those population elements that will suffer economic and social losses. The efforts to train the hard-core unemployed for jobs in the auto industry and the construction trades may increase unemployment among those who have long worked in these industries. Similarly, the efforts to give blacks opportunities to live in less congested communities, including the suburbs, may appear to threaten real estate values of working-class whites. But the political process in democratic societies works by developing a coalition of self-interested and disinterested supporters of collective policies (Chapter 9). The most feasible way to establish a base of political support for the inclusion of the poor and of nonwhite minorities is to enlist the help of groups that have little to lose from such a policy. Thus middle-class liberal groups are accused by working-class whites of demanding integration at no cost to themselves. Indeed, the only way to mobilize the political power of the state is by uniting those who are not directly involved with those who are involved to form a majority on an issue.

THE DISINTEGRATION OF VALUE CONSENSUS

We have assumed that a society, if it is to continue in operation, must maintain its value consensus. This does not mean that it is necessarily a placid, undynamic society. Agreement on basic values does not imply agreement on the allocation of the facilities and rewards of the society. The economic, political, and stratification systems provide frameworks within which these allocative

[44] Robert K. Merton and Robert A. Nisbet, Eds., *Contemporary Social Problems,* 2nd ed., New York: Harcourt, Brace, & World, 1966, p. 9.

[45] Merton and Nisbet, *Contemporary Social Problems,* p. 8.

conflicts can be resolved. Deviant behavior is also likely despite a prevailing value consensus. Members of a society violate its values and norms, sometimes because the particular individuals violating them are exceptions to the general consensus, more often because no individual's behavior is perfectly coordinated with his normative standards (Chapter 13).[46] Social change occurs— sometimes profound change like the Negro Revolution—through more consistent implementation of established values and fuller differentiation of social structures. Confrontations and protests can be mounted against perceived injustice, and ameliorative steps can be taken without abandoning the ultimate values of the society:[47]

> [P]rotestors—even when they resort occasionally to desperate means—need not reject the values of those to whom they protest. They may share the same values and seek only their share of what others already have. Therefore, the belief in widespread protest calls into question the mechanics of society's operation, but not necessarily the value consensus.

On the other hand, widespread deviant behavior and social conflict *may* be a symptom of the disintegration of value consensus, a prelude to the "war of all against all" about which Hobbes wrote. The classicist Gilbert Murray called the collapse of Greek civilization 2000 years ago "a failure of nerve."[48] Does the turmoil of contemporary industrial societies reflect a similar "failure of nerve," a loss of faith in individual achievement and social progress? Disaffection with current governmental policy and policy makers is not necessarily abandonment of a commitment to the basic values underlying the political, economic, and stratification systems. Many disaffected people affirmed their commitment to American values by working for change within the political system during the 1968 presidential campaign.

Some members of society, however, do revoke their value commitments. One group widely publicized during the 1960s were the hippies, who repudiated the struggle for personal accomplishment and material rewards.[49] But there have been value alternatives for disaffected individuals in every society.[50] In a pluralistic society like the United States, the coexistence of a dominant cultural tradition and semilegitimate subcultures provide opportunities for such individuals to express their alienation from the dominant tradition

---

[46] Some sociologists call societal discrepancies between values and behavior a failure of normative integration. Robert C. Angell, "Social Integration," *International Encyclopedia of the Social Sciences,* Vol. 7, New York: Macmillan, 1968, p. 382.

[47] Ralph Turner, "The Public Perception of Protest," *American Sociological Review,* Vol. 34, December 1969, p. 820.

[48] Gilbert Murray, *Five Stages of Greek Religion,* Garden City, N.Y.: Anchor, 1955, pp. 119-165.

[49] Jesse R. Pitts, "The Hippies as Contrameritocracy," *Dissent,* Vol. 16, July–August 1969, pp. 326-327.

[50] Florence Kluckhohn, "Dominant and Substitute Profiles of Cultural Orientations: Their Significance for the Analysis of Stratification," *Social Forces,* Vol. 28, May 1950, pp. 376-393.

more easily. Thus one student of hippie values concluded that hippie morality was an expression of the established bohemian tradition:[51]

> More than 30 years ago (a "generation," as Karl Mannheim reckoned social time, two generations as Jose Ortega y Gasset reckoned it, and three, four, or more as contemporary journalists and other grabbers of the main literary chance reckon it), the literary critic Malcolm Cowley wrote *Exile's Return,* a book about the experience of American literary expatriates in Europe in the 1920s. In it he treats to some extent the history of bohemianism, starting back in the middle of the 19th century with that important document of bohemian history, Henry Murger's *Scenes of Bohemian Life.* By 1920, Cowley says, bohemia had a relatively formal doctrine, "a system of ideas that could be roughly summarized as follows" (and as I go through these eight basic ideas, please keep in mind the hippies — and the fact that these ideas were formulated 33 years ago about phenomena that were then more than a hundred years old):

> •The first point in the bohemian doctrine is what Cowley calls "The idea of salvation by the child. — Each of us at birth has special potentialities which are slowly crushed and destroyed by a standardized society and mechanical modes of teaching. If a new educational system can be introduced, one by which children are encouraged to develop their own personalities, to [listen!] blossom freely like flowers, then the world will be saved by this new, free generation." The analogues here are hippie innocence (more on this later), flower power, and the educational revolution.

> • "The idea of self-expression. — Each man's, each woman's, purpose in life is to express himself, to realize his full individuality through creative work and beautiful living in beautiful surroundings." This, I believe, is identical with the hippies' moral injunction to "do your thing."

> • "The idea of paganism. — The body is a temple in which there is nothing unclean, a shrine to be adorned for the ritual of love." Contemporary paganism, by no means limited to the hippies but especially prevalent among them, is manifest in the overpowering eroticism that their scene exudes: the prevalence of female flesh (toe, ankle, belly, breast, and thigh) and male symbols of strength (beards, boots, denim, buckles, motorcycles), or the gentler and more restrained versions of these, or the by-now hardly controversial assumption that fucking will help set you free.

> • "The idea of living for the moment. — It is stupid to pile up treasures that we can enjoy only in old age. . . . Better to seize the moment as it comes. . . . Better to live extravagantly . . . 'burn [your] candle at both ends. . . .'" Today, this might be formulated as something like being super WOW where the action is in the NOW generation, who, like, know what's happening and where it's at. (It was a gentle English cleric who said many years ago that the man who marries the spirit of his own age is likely to be a widower in the next. Prophets of rapid social change, please take notice.)

---

[51] Reprinted by permission. From Bennett M. Berger, "Hippie Morality — More Old Than New," *Trans-action,* Vol. 5, December 1967, pp. 19-20.

• "The idea of liberty. — Every law . . . that prevents self-expression or the full enjoyment of the moment should be shattered and abolished. Puritanism is the great enemy." Today, this is manifest in the movement to legalize marihuana, to render ecstasy respectable (dancing in the park, orgiastic sex, turning everybody on, etc.), and to demonstrate the absurdity of laws against acts that harm no one and the hypocrisy of those who insist on the enforcement of these laws.

• "The idea of female equality. — Women should be the economic and moral equals of men . . . same pay . . . same working conditions, the same opportunity for drinking, smoking, taking or dismissing lovers." For the hippies, insistence on equality in smoking and the taking and dismissing of lovers is already quaint, and drinking is increasingly irrelevant. But the theme of sexual equality is still important with respect to cultural differences between the sexes, and evident in the insistence that men may be gentle and women aggressive, and in the merging of sexually related symbols of adornment (long hair, beads, bells, colorful clothes, and so on).

• Hippies often tell me that it is really quite difficult, if not impossible, to understand their scene without appreciating the importance of psychedelic drugs in it. Although I am inclined to believe this, the importance of mind-expansion in the bohemian doctrine was plain to Cowley 33 years ago. The references are dated but the main point of his seventh basic idea is unmistakable: "The idea of psychological adjustment. — We are unhappy because . . . we are repressed." To Cowley, the then-contemporary version of the doctrine prescribed that repression could and should be overcome by Freudian analysis, or by the mystic qualities of George Ivanovich Gurdjieff's psycho-physical disciplining, or by *a daily dose of thyroid.* Today, repression may be uptightness or "game reality," and it is not Freud but Reich, not thyroid but LSD, not Gurdjieff but yoga, I Ching, *The Book of the Dead,* or some other meditational means of transcending the realities that hang one up.

• Cowley's final point in the bohemian doctrine is the old romantic love of the exotic. "The idea of changing place. — 'They do things better in . . .'" (you name it). At some times the wisdom of old cultures has been affirmed, at other times, wild and primitive places — anything that will break the puritan shackles. Paris, Mexico, Tahiti, Tangier, Big Sur. The contemporary hippie fascination with American Indians has a triple attraction: They were oppressed, they were nobly savage, and by a symbolic act of identification they became a part of one's American collective unconscious, reachable under the influence of drugs.

The bohemian subculture has remained a *subculture* for many years, and it is likely to remain so. The hippie communes that appeared during the 1960s have largely disappeared due to lack of organization. In San Francisco, the hippie community disintegrated when organizational problems ended the free food distribution program.[52] Thus the hippie subculture provides support for individuals who oppose the existing value consensus, but it seems incapable of organizing the roles and institutions necessary for modern society.

[52] John Robert Howard, "The Flowering of the Hippie Movement," *Annals of the American Academy of Political and Social Science,* Vol. 382, March 1969, pp. 45-48.

CONCLUSION

If they are to continue functioning, societies must coordinate their constituent parts, both individual role players and collectivities. An obvious aspect of this coordination is the structuring of activities so that role players do not work at cross-purposes. If ten times as many plumbers are being trained as American society can employ, 90 per cent of them will be unhappy. If half as many bridges and tunnels exist as are needed to accommodate commuters to New York City, frustrated people will fume and curse during mammoth traffic jams. This meshing of roles and institutions is called functional integration. The inclusion of all members of the society in its role structure is equally crucial to functional integration. No society is wholly successful in giving all persons living within it, the young and the old, males and females, the handicapped as well as the able-bodied, "a piece of the action." But modern societies are especially sensitive to the problem and are probably more successful at solving it than their forerunners were.

Another aspect of societal integration is solidarity, the *feeling* of members of an interactive system that they belong together. Many sociologists assume that similar socialization experiences create a value consensus necessary for solidarity. Through a process of interpersonal communication and common exposure to mass media, members of the society become aware of this consensus (consciously or unconsciously). Mutual identification develops. In addition, the value consensus is explicitly implemented by the legal system *in democratic societies.* Law makes a reality of the abstract principles to which the bulk of the population is committed. The power of the state is placed at the disposal of the legal system, thus subordinating political and economic power differentials within the population to considerations of justice. In despotic societies, on the other hand, law cannot serve this integrative function because the legal system does not enjoy autonomy; it is the servant of the state.

Social pluralism also helps to maintain the overall value consensus. It does this through the mutual cross-cutting of the parochial solidarities of the constituent subgroups within the society. Thus political, economic, and religious partisanship cannot polarize the society into hostile camps. The centrifugal forces of limited loyalties tend to cancel one another out. Until recently, ethnic loyalties did not threaten to polarize contemporary societies either, even in such ethnically heterogeneous societies as the United States and the Soviet Union. Color has, however, proved a far more divisive cleavage than previous ethnic loyalties. The United States is currently undergoing a natural experiment testing whether religion, economic interests, political commitments, and other ties unrelated to color can neutralize the polarizing force of race. The present turmoil might lead to a pessimistic conclusion, but it is much too soon to write off the integrating capabilities of cross-cutting solidarities.

Integration of societies is no foregone conclusion. The value consensus necessary for solidarity is chronically threatened by competing values hawked by dissident social movements. Although this has always been so, current attacks on the values of contemporary society—by the hippies, for example— seem unusually strong, perhaps because they resonate in the echo chamber of the mass media. The prophets of societal disintegration may well be correct. On the other hand, social systems, like biological systems, resist destruction; they have capacities to adapt, to change, to cope with threats to their integrity. Before we conclude that this is indeed a lost generation, recall that generations have been getting lost for countless centuries. The following rebuke of a way- ward son was inscribed on stone tablets some 3700 years ago in Sumeria:[53]

> "Where did you go?"
>
> "I didn't go anywhere."
>
> "If you didn't go anywhere, why do you idle about? Go to school! Stand before your school father, recite your assignment, and after you have finished your assignment, report it to your monitor; then come to me, and do not wander about in the street! Come now, do you know what I said? Come now, be a man! Don't stand about in the public squares and wander about the boulevards! And when you walk in the street, don't look around! Be humble! You wander about the public square! You want to achieve success? Then look at the first generation and learn from your elders! Others like you support their parents by working. If you spoke to your kind and appreciated them, you would emulate them. They multiply barley for their father, maintain him in barley, oil and wool. But *you,* you're a man when it comes to perversity, but compared to them you are not a man at all! You certainly don't labor like them. They are the sons of fathers who make their sons labor . . . but me, I didn't make you work enough. Night and day I'm tortured because of you. Night and day you waste yourself in pleasures."

So what else is new?

SOME SIGNIFICANT LITERATURE ON INTEGRATIVE PROCESSES

John A. Clausen, "Drug Addiction," in Robert K. Merton and Robert A. Nisbet, Eds., *Contemporary Social Problems,* 2nd ed., New York: Harcourt, Brace and World, 1966, pp. 193-235. The social characteristics of known American drug addicts supports Clausen's observation that addiction is "primarily a symptom of a deeper pathology that derives from our failure to integrate into the social fabric the more deprived migrants to our metropolitan centers, especially those disadvan- taged by minority group status." "Nearly three-fourths of the 'active addicts' recorded by the Bu- reau of Narcotics are Negro, Puerto Rican, or Mexican-American in extraction" (page 206).

---

[53] Marvin E. Wolfgang, "Crime in Urban America," in *The Threat of Crime in America,* New- ark: University of Delaware, 1969, p. 24.

Marshall B. Clinard and B. Chatterjee, "Urban Community Development in India: The Delhi Pilot Project," in Roy Turner, Ed., *India's Urban Future,* Berkeley: University of California Press, 1962, pp. 71-93. The slums of Indian cities are incredibly congested. It is not unusual for people to sleep six to twelve to a room, shack, or mud hut. Open drains spread disease, and infant mortality rates are high. Bazaars add to the dirt and congestion; their drains are often choked with garbage and filth. Beggars make the rounds in the bazaars; some of these are lepers. The slum dwellers are so demoralized that they take no initiative to improve conditions. Moreover, they are often antagonistic to local authorities and apathetic toward programs of neighborhood improvement: "manhole covers are stolen, and streets and public places are dirtied in numerous ways." With a grant from the Ford Foundation, an experimental project was started in Delhi to learn how to promote self-help and civic pride in slum or near-slum populations. Six neighborhoods, each containing 250 to 400 families, were organized into Vikas Mandals (citizens' development councils) to discuss neighborhood problems and develop self-help action projects. The community organization effort was fairly successful, largely because the *women* of the neighborhood "are not satisfied with either the conditions under which they live or their subordination to men." Furthermore, the poor transportation of the Indian city ties the population to the neighborhood more closely than in Western countries. Thus residents have a greater stake in neighborhood improvement.

Herbert J. Gans, *The Urban Villagers: Group and Class in the Life of Italian-Americans,* New York: Free Press of Glencoe, 1962. Gans lived in the West End section of Boston between October 1957 and May 1958 in connection with a study of the relocation of people displaced by urban redevelopment. According to standards of physical dilapidation, the West End was a slum, but this was not the evaluation of the local residents. Gans thinks of the West End — torn down between 1958 and 1960 to make way for a luxury apartment-house complex — as possessing a different way of life from middle-class Americans but an equally viable one. Gans considers his book a contribution to ". . . the continuing conversation between the upper and the lower levels of our culture. Actually, most of the talking has usually been done by the upper level; the people of the lower one sit by quietly, and even sullenly, often without listening. . . . I have tried to describe the way of life of lower level people as they might describe it themselves if they were sociologists. In a sense, then, I am reporting to the upper level for them and urging that they be given more consideration when policy decisions are made." For another approach to the integration of the diverse segments of a complex society, see Robert Gutman, "Population Mobility in the American Middle Class," in Leonard J. Duhl, *The Urban Condition,* New York: Basic Books, 1963, pp. 172-183. Suburban developments do not integrate all newcomers smoothly and quickly. "Working-class wives, or wives with only high school or less than high school education had more distant relationships with neighbors . . . than did wives of middle-class husbands and wives with some college experience." And if residents of the developments studied are divided into those who regard the community as their permanent home and those who regard it as a temporary stopping place on the way to better things, the transients are more likely than the permanents to report extensive social contact with their neighbors. In established suburbs — as contrasted with developments — newcomers sink roots into the community by joining established organizations rather than by informal neighboring. Again it is the middle-class newcomer who is more likely to accomplish this, partly because the voluntary association in the suburb is likely to be oriented to middle-class interests, partly because middle-class newcomers are more likely than working-class newcomers to assume initiative for meeting other people and to devote time and energy to community activities.

Morris Janowitz, *The Community Press in an Urban Setting: The Social Elements of Urbanism,* 2nd ed., Chicago: University of Chicago Press, 1967. The mass media in contemporary urban societies perform important functions in knitting together national communities. Television, national magazines, and metropolitan newspapers provide information for significant proportions of the American population. But the mass media, by definition, are not oriented to *local* communities and to their internal needs for communication. Janowitz studied in 1950 the 82 community newspapers within the political boundaries of the city of Chicago to explore their role in the integration of local communities. They had a combined circulation of 983,000 in 1950. In 1966 the number of community newspapers in Chicago had grown to 94 with a combined circulation of 1,200,000. Janowitz found that the community press has become a sound business venture because it promotes social cohesion on the neighborhood level. As Scott Greer put it in his postscript to the book, "Janowitz rediscovered community within the metropolis, and did so through the study of communications" (page 245). A sociological classic in the University of Chicago tradition out of which the Janowitz study emerged is Ralph H. Turner, Ed., *Robert E. Park on Social Control and Collective Behavior,* Chicago: University of Chicago Press, 1967.

Solomon Kobrin, "The Chicago Area Project—A 25-Year Assessment," *Annals of the American Academy of Political and Social Science,* Vol. 322, March 1959, pp. 19-25. Assuming as it does that adolescent delinquency in the large city is principally the result of a breakdown in *spontaneous* social controls, the Chicago Area Project attempts to *organize* adult controls over adolescents in high-delinquency neighborhoods. To accomplish this objective, the Project seeks to induce indigenous residents of these neighborhoods to work together on youth problems as the local community perceives them. Through the use of street workers hired by neighborhood committees, the committees reduce somewhat the isolation of the male adolescent peer group from adult controls. (The Area Project apparently invented the technique of sending young adults to work with adolescent gangs on street corners.) The committees also interpret the impersonal operation of police departments, courts, probation and parole systems, and schools to many youngsters so as to make bureaucratic decisions and procedures more acceptable. The Area Project does not claim to have effected permanent reduction of delinquency rates—even in neighborhoods where years of effort have been made—because the social forces working to isolate adolescents from adult controls in the large city have so far proven stronger than the manufactured controls of the committees.

Leon Mayhew and Albert J. Reiss, Jr., "The Social Organization of Legal Contacts," *American Sociological Review,* Vol. 34, June 1969, pp. 309-318. A sample survey of the legal problems and legal experiences of 780 residents of the Detroit Metropolitan area, 604 white and 176 Negro, shows that contact with lawyers varies with social status. For example, whereas 84 per cent of white males with an income of $15,000 per year or more sought advice from a lawyer, only 40 per cent of Negro females with an income of less than $7000 sought legal advice. The reason for this relationship is mainly that the legal profession is heavily oriented to property problems; therefore when problems involving property arise (even among low-income persons) the probability is high that an attorney will be consulted. Thus one-third of the Negro sample consulted a lawyer about buying a house—the same proportion as in the white sample (despite the smaller percentage of home ownership in the Negro sample). "But the introduction of Negroes to the property complex through home ownership has not yet become sufficiently institutionalized to incorporate Negroes fully into the organized system for the transmission of property" (page 314). A smaller proportion of Negroes than of whites consult lawyers about making a will. Nevertheless, "property as an institution is socially organized so as to bring its participants into contact with attorneys" (page 312). Hence, as blacks move into the middle class and acquire substantial property, they will be increasingly exposed to the socializing influence of the lawyers with whom they are thrown into contact. They tend to be integrated into the society not only by the similarity of the resources they and whites possess but by the similarity of the attitudes toward property encouraged by common exposure to the legal profession.

Talcott Parsons, "Youth in the Context of American Society," *Daedalus,* Vol, 91, Winter 1962, pp. 97-123. One of the features of industrial societies and particularly of American society is the increasing differentiation of institutions. Thus longer schooling means sharper segregation of youngsters from adult society, and this makes for autonomous youth cultures. Furthermore, the differentiation of institutions gives youngsters more choices. "[T]ypes of interest motivation and evaluation that were embedded in a less differentiated complex come to be separated out to become more autonomous and more visible. . . ." As an example of increased choices, Parsons points to greater freedom for the expression of erotic interests, not only in the private life of the individual but also on the stage, in movies and television, and in books and magazines. Sex is less confined to the family context. Parsons suggests that new patterns should be expected as a result of increased differentiation and are not necessarily signs of breakdown. Unfortunately, whether they constitute a new, fairly stable way of organizing social life or are temporary maladjustments can be assessed only after the passage of time. Parsons' interpretation is that contemporary society is going through transitional maladjustments as the differentiated parts of a pluralistic society become integrated more loosely than before. Thus the significance of more explicit sexuality in films and the theater is not that American society is entering a period of moral decline but rather that the arts are being given greater autonomy vis-à-vis political authorities.

Matilda White Riley and Anne Foner, *Aging and Society,* Vol. 1. *An Inventory of Research Findings,* New York: Russell Sage Foundation, 1968. Much of this monumental compilation of research studies on the place of older persons in contemporary society is relevant to the question of the social integration of older persons. In particular, Part 4 is concerned with the social roles linking the older person to society: occupational roles, political roles, religious roles, memberships in voluntary associations, leisure roles, family roles, informal friendship and neighborhood roles, and, finally, roles in the hospitals, nursing homes, and homes for the aged.

Edward A. Shils, "Daydreams and Nightmares: Reflections on the Criticism of Mass Culture," *Sewanee Review,* Vol. 65, Autumn 1957, pp. 597-608. This article is concerned with the charge that popular culture has vulgarized the taste of the average man by exposing him to comic books, sensational newspapers, and magazines that concentrate on illicit sexual activity and crimes of violence. Shils replies that preindustrial societies have at least as impoverished an esthetic life as contemporary societies. "Hunger and the imminence of death, work such as we in the West would now regard as too burdensome even for beasts, over very long hours, [prevent] the development of individuality, of sensitivity or refinement in any except those very few in the lower classes who [are] either extremely strong personalities or extremely talented or extremely fortunate in forming a connection with the aristocratic or mercantile classes, or all three together." In short, Shils does not defend the level of mass culture in industrial societies, but he deplores the romantization of preindustrial societies. And if mass culture is not synonymous with mass elevation of taste, at least it provides a common experience for the bulk of the population and thereby a focus of cohesion.

William H. Whyte, Jr., *Is Anybody Listening?* New York: Simon and Shuster, 1952. Taking his point of departure from the preoccupation with "communication skills" in American corporations

William Whyte, a former editor at *Fortune,* examines not only advertising but the internal communications in memoranda, through the office grapevine, in conferences, and in executive speeches. He concludes that American business is making a basic mistake by regarding communications skills as a tool by means of which customers and employees can be manipulated — provided that the right techniques are used. People cannot be fooled for long with the *trappings* of participation. If they are not themselves being listened to in meaningful ways, they will stop listening. Potential customers will disregard advertising "propaganda" and employees will resent being treated like clay to be molded into the appropriate shape. In short, Whyte suggests that communication has the potentiality of integrating the business organization (or the larger society) but only if communication is a two-way street. The way to get people to listen is not to package the messages more cleverly but to establish an atmosphere of mutual trust based on the mutual willingness to listen and respond.

GLOSSARY

activism A philosophy of mastery over physical or social obstacles as opposed to passive acceptance or mystical escape.

adaptive requirement The necessity for a functioning interactive system to cope with its physical, biological, cultural, and social environments. (Talcott Parsons*)

age cohort See **cohort, age.**

alienation A feeling of estrangement from the values and norms of one's society, sometimes accompanied by a denial of the legitimacy of those values and norms. Alienation has also been defined as a sense of powerlessness. (Melvin Seeman)

analysis, content Quantitative analysis of the meanings of symbolic communications.

anarchy, philosophical The ideology which holds that political authority inevitably produces injustice and that social organization can function without political authority.

anomie A breakdown in the power of social norms to regulate and discipline men's actions. (Albert K. Cohen)

area, natural See **natural area.**

ascription Assignment to roles because of biological or relational *qualities* (age, sex, community of residence) rather than *performance* or performance capacity.

assimilation A process in which persons of diverse ethnic and racial backgrounds come to interact, free of these constraints, in the life of the larger community. (G. E. Simpson)

association, voluntary See **voluntary association.**

authority A recognized right to make a binding decision on behalf of an interactive system.

authority figure A person who elicits reactions based on previous experiences with other persons in power positions.

*Names in parentheses refer to sociologists whose definitions have been closely adapted here.

593

basic research   Research oriented to the development of scientific theory in a discipline rather than for the purpose of solving a practical problem.

bureaucracy   An organization whose functions are performed by persons in occupational roles arranged in a hierarchy of executive authority and specialized in terms of technical competence. Duties are performed in premises separated from the households of the workers, and selection for roles in the organization often involves assessment of competence. (Talcott Parsons)

career   An orderly sequence of occupational roles in government, business, or the professions.

caste   An endogamous and hereditary subdivision of an ethnic group occupying a position of superior or inferior social esteem in comparison with other such subdivisions. (A. L. Kroeber)

census   A complete enumeration of the population of a society, usually undertaken at regular intervals.

charisma   The quality imputed to persons, actions, roles, institutions, symbols, and material objects because of their presumed connection with "ultimate," "fundamental," "vital," order-determining powers. (Edward Shils)

church   A religious organization that accepts the secular society in which it is imbedded as legitimate. See **sect.**

class, social   An aggregate of kinship units having approximately equal prestige in the stratification system of an industrial society. (Talcott Parsons)

class consciousness   A feeling of solidarity with persons occupying a similar position in the economic system. Marx developed the concept to evaluate the presence or absence of mutual identification among propertyless workers.

class crystallization   The coinciding of various criteria of social rank so that persons with a high rank on one criterion tend to be high on others. This makes for fairly distinct social classes. In a pluralistic society, class crystallization is low and class boundaries blurred.

coding   A research procedure by which data are classified into distinct categories to facilitate tabulation and analysis.

cohort, age   All persons in a population born in the same year.

collective conscience   The normative consensus defining the limits of acceptable behavior within an interactive system.

community   A feeling of mutual belongingness within a concentrated settlement of people in a demarcated territorial area.

consensus General agreement on beliefs or values among members of an interactive system.

contraculture A subculture oppositional to the dominant culture and sustained by the personality needs of its members.

control, social Institutionalized arrangements (1) that prevent the building up of motivation to deviance or (2) that reduce the individual's opportunities to translate his deviant motivation into action. Psychotherapy illustrates the first type of arrangement and imprisonment the second.

control, statistical The process of manipulating data so that the effect of a particular factor is the same in the experimental and the control groups—even though the actual effect in the real world is *not* the same.

cosmopolitans People whose identification is primarily with the institutions of the larger society which transcend the loyalties of their local community. See **locals.**

courtship Interaction between an unmarried man and an unmarried woman, leading through progressively deeper mutual involvement toward marriage.

crime An act defined through the political process as punishable by the state. In a sense then, all prison inmates are political prisoners. See **deviance.**

crime, white-collar See **white-collar crime.**

cult, cargo A millenarian religion that developed in New Guinea and surrounding islands based on the expectation that ancestral spirits would soon bring a large ship containing Western machines and consumer goods for the native population. With the help of the cargo and the spirits, the European rulers would be killed or driven out.

cultural artifacts, evaluation of A method of allocating members of a community to different social ranks by observing whether or not they possess or use objects symbolically associated with those ranks.

cultural change Change in the stock of ideas available to the role players of an interactive system.

cultural lag The theory that technological-scientific change occurs faster than change in nonmaterial culture in modern societies causing temporary maladaptations until changes in social organization "catch up."

cultural norm See **norm, cultural.**

culture The distinctive symbols for communicating shared meanings within an interactive system. These intellectual, expressive, and evaluative symbols provide a shared vo-

culture *(continued)* cabulary for members of the system, thus making common interpretations of human experience possible.

demeanor That element of the individual's ceremonial behavior typically conveyed through deportment, dress, and bearing, which serves to express to those in his immediate presence that he is a person of certain desirable or undesirable qualities. (Erving Goffman)

demographic transition A society's passage from a high birth rate-high death rate population to a low birth rate-low death rate balance in the course of industrialization and urbanization.

denomination One of a plurality of organizations each of which is widely regarded as a legitimate vehicle for the expression of religious interests.

dependent variable A factor that changes in response to changes in a correlated variable believed to be its cause.

deprivation, cultural Inadequate participation in the cultural mainstream of a modern industrial society — one consequence of which is reduced aptitude for formal education. See **poverty, culture of.**

deprivation, relative The *feeling* of disadvantage arising from implicit or explicit comparison with those in superior circumstances. Since it is a subjective experience, this feeling may arise among persons not disadvantaged by objective criteria.

deterrent A threat of punishment intended to discourage potential violators of societal rules.

deviance The purposive evasion or defiance of a normative consensus.

deviant role What a person is expected to do in a forbidden interactive relationship.

differential association, theory of An explanation of socialization into criminal roles in terms of a preponderance of criminal over noncriminal associations which facilitates the learning of criminal skills.

differentiation The process by which a structural unit of a society evolves into two or more units, each more specialized than the unit out of which it emerged. Thus the modern factory and the modern family are outcomes of a process of differentiation that transformed a feudal unit in which family life and economic activity were inseparable.

diffuse role A relationship which involves broad aspects of the personalities of the participants rather than narrowly defined aspects.

diffusion The imitative process by which one interactive system adopts the culture traits of another.

disorganization, social	See **social disorganization.**
dissensus	Disagreement on beliefs or values among members of an interactive system.
domestic system	A preindustrial economic system in which handicraft production took place in the home. The worker was paid for his work by the piece rather than by time, but he worked on raw materials supplied by merchant entrepreneurs as in the later factory system. See **factory.**
ecology, human	The study of the spatial distribution of persons, groups, and activities within a community or society.
economy	A relatively autonomous complex of roles concerned with the production and distribution of goods and services in industrial societies. In preindustrial societies (where economic activities are usually fused to the rest of the social structure) a distinct economy does not exist.
effect, contextual	The enhanced effect of variable A on variable B due to social circumstances in which both variables are imbedded. For example, intelligent high school students are more likely to aspire to attend college in high schools where a large proportion of students attend college.
empathy	The self-conscious effort to share and accurately comprehend the presumed consciousness of another person, including his thoughts, feelings, perceptions, and muscular tensions, as well as their causes. (Lauren G. Wispé)
empirical	Concerned with data obtainable through observation.
error, response	Incorrect survey data due to some failure of communication between the interviewer and the respondent.
error, sampling	The difference between the true population statistic (e.g., the mean or the standard deviation) and the estimated value of that statistic in the sample.
ethnic group	A people with a common cultural tradition and sense of identity.
etiquette	The symbolic expression of moral judgments—especially of who is important and who unimportant. (Erving Goffman)
experiment, contrived	A carefully observed comparison between two groups (the experimental group and the control group) each of which was designed in advance to be as similar as possible before the introduction of a test factor.
experiment, natural	A carefully observed comparison between two groups (the experimental and the control group) not initially comparable before the introduction of a test factor but made comparable by the statistical elimination of the effects of other variables.

expressive action Action intended to communicate an emotion, as contrasted with action calculated to attain an ultimate objective (instrumental action).

facilities Possessions significant as the means to some more ultimate goal rather than rewarding in themselves. (Talcott Parsons) Thus a factory is a facility for a manufacturer, but his home is a reward. See **reward.**

factory A place in which workers gather under the discipline of the employer for the purpose of production. By this criterion, an airplane pilot and a stewardess work in a factory as do high school teachers. See **differentiation.**

family, conjugal A husband and wife and their unmarried children.

family, extended A unit including three or more generations, for example, grandparents, their unmarried children, and some of their married children with spouses and grandchildren.

family, matrilineal A family system in which descent is traced through females, that is, a woman, all of her children, and the children of her daughters (but not of her sons).

family, multiproblem A family having a variety of problems requiring the intervention of outside agencies (the police, welfare services, family counseling) in order to enable it to function.

family, patrilineal A family system in which descent is traced through males, that is, a man, all of his children, and the children of his sons (but not of his daughters).

family of orientation The conjugal family into which the individual is born.

family of procreation The conjugal family the individual creates by marriage and parenthood.

fertility The rate of reproduction of a population as measured by the number of births.

folk crime Violations of law tolerated by the general public. (H. Laurence Ross)

folk society A small, isolated, preliterate community with intense solidarity, minimal division of labor, and a predominant influence of kinship in social organization. (Robert Redfield)

frequency distribution A classification of data showing the number of occurrences in each subcategory of a variable. In the case of a quantitative variable, a frequency distribution shows not only the central tendency of the data but the variability around the central tendency (median, mode, or mean).

generalized other The internalized perspectives and expectations of other people toward oneself as a result of multiple socialization experiences.

group   A plurality of interacting individuals with some sense of solidarity. (Members of a *social category*, e.g., the physically handicapped, are a group only in a classificatory and not an interactive sense.)

group, natural   An interactive system that develops spontaneously as contrasted with one that is artificially assembled for a specific purpose. See **group, contrived.**

group, contrived   An interactive system artificially assembled for a specific purpose, often an experiment, and therefore having minimal solidarity among its members.

group, control   An aggregate of research subjects used to evaluate the effect of the test variable on the experimental group.

group, primary   A collectivity characterized by intimate association among members.

group, secondary   A collectivity characterized by purposive, specialized, segmental associations among members.

guilt   Self-condemnation resulting from a sense that one has violated internalized norms or values.

heterogamy   Marriage between persons of different backgrounds. See **homogamy.**

homogamy   Marriage between persons of the same social class, racial and religious background, or educational experience. See **heterogamy.**

hypothesis, null   The hypothesis that no difference exists between the two (or more) groups under consideration.

identification   The process of establishing a solidary relationship with a socializing agent, for example, a parent, in the course of which the values of the socializing agent are adopted as one's own. See **internalization.** Parsons has pointed out that the role learned by the socializee is usually complementary rather than identical to that played by the socializing agent despite underlying common values.

identification, morbid   A feeling of solidarity with a deceased person so strong that it interferes with the individual's will to live.

identity   The meaning placed on one's self by the individual.

identity crisis   The uncertainty on the part of adolescents in urban industrial societies about the ultimate meaning of their lives. This questioning comes at adolescence because it marks a point in the life cycle where crucial educational, occupational, and marital choices have to be made.

ideology   The belief system, true or untrue, shared by members of a society or of a collectivity within a society. (Talcott Parsons) The sharing is not a coincidence because sub-

ideology *(continued)*   scribing to the belief system is an obligation of membership.

incest taboo   A requirement that young adults choose sexual and marital partners outside their families of orientation.

independent variable   A factor whose change leads in a correlated variable. See **dependent variable.**

individualism   The belief that an individual possesses some fundamental rights that arise from his inherent worth and are not derived from his membership in kinship or other social groups. This belief is supported by a form of social organization in which individuals participate as individuals rather than as representatives of groups.

in-group   Persons linked to one another by feelings of solidarity — in contrast to persons not included. See **out-group.**

institution   A cluster of roles that are of strategic significance to a society.

institutions, political   A cluster of roles concerned with making binding decisions on behalf of the society. In a democracy, the incumbents of these roles are selected, directly or indirectly, by most of the persons bound by the decision.

interaction   Behavior based on the reciprocal taking into account of the potential actions and reactions of other role players.

interactive system   A plurality of goal-directed persons mutually responding in an environment defined by shared symbols. (Talcott Parsons)

integration, functional   Coordination of the activities of role players and collectivities of role players so that their specialized contributions complement one another.

integration, racial   An interactive system in which racial origins are irrelevant for social participation. Thus integration goes beyond the absence of segregation.

integrative requirement   The necessity for a functioning interactive system to induce, persuade, influence, or coerce its constituent role players (1) to coordinate their contributions and (2) to commit themselves psychologically to the system as a whole. (Talcott Parsons)

internalization   The incorporations within the psyche of the socializee of the values or norms of his socializer. See **identification.**

intervening variable   A factor regarded as a connecting link between two correlated variables and therefore part of the explanation of the mechanism whereby one leads to the other. See **independent variable** and **dependent variable.**

invasion   A process by which one type of population or land use moves into an area already occupied by another population or utilized in a different way.

justice Consensus in a population that the legal order operates to apply societal values *fairly* instead of merely serving the interests of the rich and powerful. Note that this definition sidesteps the *philosophical* problems involved in the concept and treats it as a social psychological problem.

line organization The hierarchical organization of the right and responsibility to organize the work of subordinates within a bureaucracy. See **staff.**

locals People whose loyalties are primarily to their local community rather than to the institutions of the larger society. See **cosmopolitan.**

mass communication Any message that reaches the diverse elements of a society rather than special segments of it.

mass society A conception of the population of modern urban industrial societies that emphasizes its atomistic character rather than the organized relations among subgroups.

matrilineal family See **family, matrilineal.**

median That value which divides a frequency distribution into two equal parts—one-half of the cases falling below this value and one-half exceeding it.

metropolitan area One or more central cities containing at least 50,000 population and the surrounding built-up areas in close economic and social communication with the central city (or cities).

metropolitan dominance The tendency for a large territory outside the central city to be directly under the influence of the central city for trade and employment.

millenarian An expectation of a sudden transformation of society through supernatural intervention. See **cargo cult.**

mobility, gross The proportion of persons in a society who have been *either* upwardly or downwardly mobile. See **mobility, net.**

mobility, horizontal A change in social location within the society without appreciable change in one's status in the hierarchy of prestige, wealth, or power.

mobility, intergenerational An upward or downward change in social status from one generation to the next.

mobility, intragenerational An upward or downward change in social status within the life cycle of the same individual.

mobility, net The difference between the proportion of persons who have been upwardly and the proportion downwardly mobile compared with the parental generation. In modern societies net mobility is positive—that is, more persons rise than fall in social status.

mobility, vertical Upward and downward changes of status.

moral determinism A belief that social rewards should be proportionate to the individual's conformity to the moral norms of his society. (Kingsley Davis)

mortality The death rate of a population.

natural area A territorial area with some common land use arising from unplanned competition among alternative uses.

norm, cultural A prescriptive suggestion, arising from the tradition of an interactive system, for dealing with the nonhuman environment, with other persons, or with the expression of feelings.

norm, social A specification of value commitments so that they apply differentially to different members of an interactive system. Thus achievement is a value of American society, but educational norms specify what kinds of achievements the school system can expect from American children.

objectivity A data-gathering situation where an observation does not depend on the peculiarities of the observer.

observer, participant A method of observation in which the investigator has a role in the community or organization he studies; it is from this vantage point he observes other role players facing everyday situations.

occupational prestige The differential ranking of occupations of industrial societies in accordance with the prestige accorded them by members of the society.

occupational role An instrumentally oriented and remunerated economic activity that is relatively independent of the private life of the incumbent in terms of premises, kinship relations, and property. (Talcott Parsons)

opportunities, illegitimate Access to socialization into deviant roles.

organization, formal A structural group having explicit objectives, explicit rules and regulations, and specifically defined roles, each with designated rights and duties. (George A. Theodorson and Achilles G. Theodorson)

out-group Those persons not included in an in-group. See **in-group.** Sometimes members of an out-group are united by solidarity as well as common exclusion, sometimes not.

particularism A relationship defined in terms of common group membership, for example, kinship, rather than in terms of common qualities. See **universalism.**

patrilineal family See **family, patrilineal.**

peer group An equal status group, usually of agemates.

pluralism, cultural Peaceful coexistence of ethnic subcultures within modern societies.

pluralism, social The existence of multiple centers of power and influence in a society instead of a single power base.

pluralism, denominational A religious system in which a number of religious organizations recognize one another's legitimacy. See **denomination.**

polarization A deep social cleavage within a society in which individuals are forced to choose between extremes because compromise positions are not regarded as tenable.

policy-making requirement The necessity for a functioning interactive system to organize action for the attainment of collective goals — as contrasted with the personal goals of individual members. (Talcott Parsons) This involves a solution to the problem of differing proposals for collective action on the part of different members of the system, for example, by majority vote. See **political process.**

political apathy The absence of intense concern about issues or candidates.

political machine A voluntary association which treats the political process like a market in which votes and other forms of support for candidates are traded for jobs and other benefits obtainable from government.

political process The policy-making mechanism of interactive systems.

poverty, culture of A climate of hopelessness in a population arising from generations of deprivation or from personal experiences suggesting that the future holds no further promise.

power The socially recognized right to mobilize punitive sanctions on behalf of the collectivity if expected compliance is not forthcoming.

prestige The amount of deference an individual is entitled to receive and from whom according to an approximate consensus prevailing in a society.

primary group See **group, primary.**

privatism A tendency to be concerned with private concerns like family life and hobbies rather than with societal issues like the political process.

probability theory The mathematical theory of chance occurrences. It provides a basis for deciding that certain results are improbable and therefore unlikely to have occurred by chance.

product image The identity which a given product, for example, a brand of automobile, perfume, or cigarette, helps the

product image *(continued)* user to communicate to other members of his society. See **identity.**

progress The notion that improvement over the past is an inevitable evolutionary trend in societal development.

Protestant Ethic The achievement values and attitudes of the ascetic Protestant sects (such as the Calvinists), values and attitudes favorable to the development of capitalism in Western Europe.

psychopathy A personality disorder whose major symptom is an absence of internalized feelings of right and wrong usually found in socialized adults.

punishment The purposive imposition of unpleasant experiences on persons who have transgressed the rules of an interactive system.

quota-control sample See **sample, quota-control.**

rank system The hierarchical ordering of statuses within a social field, for example, in terms of wealth, education, or ethnic prestige.

reference group An interactive group or social category used by the individual to provide standards for himself. One's reference group consists of the most significant others in one's milieu.

regressive behavior A psychological retreat to an earlier and less adequate means of coping with a frustrating environment—for example, a temper tantrum on the part of an adolescent.

rehabilitation The process of developing conventional attitudes in those who formerly lacked such attitudes. See **resocialization.**

relative deprivation See **deprivation, relative.**

reliability The consistency with which trained observers can agree on a rating by a measuring instrument. A special instance of reliability is test-retest reliability, namely, the correlation between the scores of research subjects on successive administrations of a standardized test.

reputation Status in a community.

resocialization Socialization of a person in a deviant role so that he is willing and able to play conventional roles.

revolution of rising expectations Originally this meant the rising economic and political aspirations of people in underdeveloped countries but it now also refers to the general tendency for social improvement to generate an expectation for further improvement, thus leading to the paradoxical result that objective benefits may *increase* subjective dissatisfaction. See **anomie.** See **deprivation, relative.**

role   What a person is expected to do in a prescribed inter-active relationship.

role, achieved   A social status filled by competition among potential candidates for it on the basis of their supposed capacities to play it, for example, an occupational role.

role, ascribed   See **ascription.**

role, diffuse   See **diffuse role.**

role, occupational   See **occupational role.**

role allocation   The process by which the members of an interactive system are assigned obligations that must be fulfilled if the system is to function.

role conflict   A situation presented by competing obligations to two or more interactive systems each expecting conformity to its norms.

role structure   See **social structure.**

sample, area   A random sample of dwelling units whose occupants then constitute the sample. If the population under study is associated with dwelling units on a one-to-one basis—that is, everyone lives somewhere and few people have several homes—an area sample is essentially a random sample of the population.

sample, quota-control   A sample chosen by the fulfillment of preestablished members of cases in various categories (quotas). The fulfillment of such quotas is usually done by non-random procedures. See **sample, random.**

sample, random   A sample selected in such a way that each member of the population has the same chance of appearing in the sample. The advantage of a random sample is that the laws of mathematical probability provide precise estimates of the likely discrepancies between the sample and the population from which it is drawn.

sample, stratified   A sample containing homogeneous segments of the universe under investigation each of which is treated as a separate random sample. This procedure is more economical than simple random sampling because it gives a more accurate estimate of the true population values of the universe for a sample of given size.

sanction   An interpersonal reward (or punishment) intended to encourage (or discourage) certain behavior.

secondary group   See **group, secondary.**

sect   A religious group, recruited through voluntary affiliation, that rejects its secular environment.

segregation, de facto   The unplanned separation of races or ethnic groups within a society due to customary land use p
especially residential ghettoes. De facto segreg

segregation, de facto often contasted with de jure segregation, which is le-
(continued)   gally enforced separation, as, for instance, in the system
of dual school systems once the rule in the South.

self-conception   What a person judges himself to be like. See **identity.**

self-fulfilling prophecy   A cultural definition, initially untrue, which affects interaction in such a way as to generate its own confirm-
ing evidence. (Robert K. Merton)

self-placement   A subjective conception of social class membership in
which the researcher accepts the respondent's judgment
of where he belongs in the prestige hierarchy.

self-selection   The tendency for members of the experimental and
control groups in natural experiments to select themselves for exposure to the factor in which the researcher
is interested (as well as a variety of other intercor-
related factors). For example, children who watch violent television programs may have different personality tendencies from those who do not watch such programs, thus confusing *effects* of viewing with causes of
viewing.

serendipity   The quality of making accidental discoveries that are
only possible because painstaking preliminary work
gave the perspective necessary to appreciate their significance.

shame   Self-condemnation resulting from a sense that significant others disapprove of one's behavior.

sibling   A general term for a brother or sister.

significant other   A person with great influence on the individual's attitudes and on his evaluation of himself.

slum   A residential neighborhood, usually densely populated,
inhabited by families and individuals whose lack of economic resources prevent them from obtaining more desirable housing.

social change   Altered patterns of interaction in a society or subsystem of society.

social class   See **class, social.**

social disorganization   The failure of a community to function well due to institutional malintegration or lack of solidarity or both.
See **integration.**

social sanction   See **sanction.**

social stratification   The relatively permanent organization of deference in an
interactive system.

social structure   The framework of order of a society provided by meshing role expectations and shared values.

socialization	The process whereby the individual is taught to conform to role expectations and to internalize cultural norms in a particular interactive system. By extension, therefore, socialization is a fundamental process in every interactive system.
socialization, anticipatory	The learning of the values and expectations appropriate to a social role preparatory to assuming it.
socialization, inadequate	The failure of the socializee to internalize the values and norms being taught by the socializing agent because one or more of the conditions for successful internalization are absent. (Harry C. Bredemeier and Richard M. Stephenson) This failure is in contrast to "inappropriate socialization" where *deviant* values or norms are successfully taught by the socializing agent.
socialization, inappropriate	The failure of the socializee to internalize institutionalized values or norms because he has been socialized by a socializing agent committed to *deviant* definitions of the situation.
socialization, mutual	A socialization situation where the roles of socializee and socializing agent shift back and forth because each has an equal voice in establishing the norms of the interactive system, for example, an equalitarian marriage or a small delinquent clique.
socializing requirement	The necessity for a functioning interactive system to maintain the stability of its institutionalized culture by insulating and reinforcing the motivational commitment of individuals to its role structure. (Talcott Parsons)
societal community	The patterned normative order (including both general values and specific norms) through which the life of a community is normatively organized. (Talcott Parsons)
society	An interactive system (1) that is self-subsistent, (2) that transcends the life span of the ordinary human individual, and (3) that recruits by biological reproduction. (Talcott Parsons)
society, folk	See **folk society.**
society, mass	See **mass society.**
solidarity	The feeling of mutual loyalty on the part of members of an interactive system.
staff organization	The organization of specialists and technicians in an advisory capacity to executives within a bureaucracy.
standard metropolitan area	See **metropolitan area.**
status	The social evaluation of a role. By extension, a person's composite social evaluation on the basis of his various roles is also referred to as "status."

status consciousness An awareness of prestige distinctions within a community. Unlike "class consciousness," status consciousness does not imply solidarity with other persons of equivalent prestige. More usually the status-conscious person is oriented to social mobility.

strain Psychological distress arising (1) from expectations from significant others that the individual does not feel he can fulfill or (2) from the failure of significant others to live up to what the individual feels are legitimate expectations.

stratification, social See **social stratification.**

stratified sample See **sample, stratified.**

streaming The allocation of children in the system of formal education to separate tracks depending on their presumed intellectual capacities and their vocational objectives.

style of life The standard of living which an individual (or group) uses to express a status in the prestige hierarchy.

subcultural differentiation The tendency for subsystems of complex societies to develop distinct ways of life.

subculture A normative system of groups smaller than a society, which, because of isolation or other inadequacies of communication, have a different tradition from the larger society of which they are a part, for example, the subculture of American Indians. (J. Milton Yinger)

succession An ecological process in which one type of land use (or of population) replaces another. See **invasion.**

survey A systematic investigation of one or more characteristics of a large population through standardized interviews or questionnaires.

symbolic act A gesture whose significance lies not in its objective effect but in its expressive symbolism. See **expressive action.**

system, domestic See **domestic system.**

test of significance A statistical test, based on mathematical probability, indicating whether differences observed between data samples are likely to be chance variations between samples drawn from a single population or, on the other hand, are likely to have come from distinct populations.

total institution A service organization whose clients interact mainly within its context, for example, prisons, hospitals, boarding schools, military organizations. (Erving Goffman)

treatment An effort applied to a person not conforming to social expectations based on the assumption that his nonconformity is due to illness or disability rather than to willful defiance or evasion.

underenumeration	A failure to count some members of the population in the course of a census.
universalism	A relationship defined by the possession of an attribute—for example, all students in a class who get high grades—rather than one defined in terms of common group membership. See **particularism.**
urban place	According to the United States Census Bureau, any place that has a population of 2500 or more and is incorporated. In addition, densely populated communities on the fringe of large cities are also considered urban. See **metropolitan area.**
value	A criterion of choice between alternative principles of personal or social organization. For a more specific commitment to action, see **norm.**
variance	A statistical measure of the dispersion of the values of a frequency distribution around its central tendency.
veto group	A bloc within a pluralistic society possessing enough influence to prevent other blocs from acting without its consent but not enough power to establish societal policies without the acquiescence of other blocs.
voluntary association	An organized group of persons (1) that is formed in order to further some common interest of its members, (2) in which membership is voluntary in the sense that it is neither mandatory nor acquired through birth, and (3) that exists independently of the state. (David L. Sills)
white-collar crime	Offenses committed by business and professional people against laws regulating their activities, for example, patent infringement. (Edwin H. Sutherland)
zone in transition	The area immediately surrounding the central business district of a growing city. According to the five-zone theory of urban growth developed by University of Chicago ecologists, this second zone is a residential area being invaded by commercial and industrial uses. During a transitional period residential structures deteriorate because the land has become too valuable for residential use.

NAME INDEX

Entries in bold face indicate definition in the glossary.

SUBJECT INDEX

Entries in bold face indicate definition in
the glossary.